INTERACTIONS
COLLABORATION SKILLS FOR SCHOOL PROFESSIONALS

EIGHTH EDITION

Marilyn Friend
The University of North Carolina at Greensboro (Emerita)

Lynne Cook
California State University, Dominguez Hills, Professor
(1947–2015)

Boston Columbus Indianapolis New York San Francisco Upper Saddle River Amsterdam
Cape Town Dubai London Madrid Milan Munich Paris Montréal Toronto Delhi
Mexico City São Paulo Sydney Hong Kong Seoul Singapore Taipei Tokyo

Vice President and Editorial Director:
    Jeffery W. Johnston
Executive Editor: Ann Castel Davis
Development Editor: Alicia Santamaria
Editorial Assistant: Anne McAlpine
Executive Field Marketing Manager:
    Krista Clark
Senior Product Marketing Manager:
    Christopher Barry
Project Manager: Kerry Rubadue
Program Manager: Joe Sweeney
Operations Specialist: Carol Melville
Text Designer: Lumina
Cover Design Director: Diane Ernsberger
Cover Art: Illustration Source
Media Producer: Autumn Benson
Media Project Manager: Kerry Rubadue
Full-Service Project Management: Lumina
Composition: Lumina
Printer/Binder: RR Donnelley/Harrisonburg South
Cover Printer: Phoenix Color/Hagerstown
Text Font: ITC Berkeley OldstylePro 10/12

Copyright © 2017, 2013, 2010 by Pearson Education, Inc. or its affiliates. All Rights Reserved. Printed in the United States of America. This publication is protected by copyright, and permission should be obtained from the publisher prior to any prohibited reproduction, storage in a retrieval system, or transmission in any form or by any means, electronic, mechanical, photocopying, recording, or otherwise. For information regarding permissions, request forms and the appropriate contacts within the Pearson Education Global Rights & Permissions department, please visit http://www.pearsoned.com/permissions/.

Acknowledgements of third party content appear on pages within text, which constitute an extension of this copyright page.

Unless otherwise indicated herein, any third-party trademarks that may appear in this work are the property of their respective owners and any references to third-party trademarks, logos or other trade dress are for demonstrative or descriptive purposes only. Such references are not intended to imply any sponsorship, endorsement, authorization, or promotion of Pearson's products by the owners of such marks, or any relationship between the owner and Pearson Education, Inc. or its affiliates, authors, licensees or distributors.

LOC data is available upon request from Library of Congress

9 2020

Package
ISBN 10:   0-13-416854-2
ISBN 13: 978-0-13-416854-8

E-text
ISBN 10:   0-13-425680-8
ISBN 13: 978-0-13-425680-1

Loose Leaf Version
ISBN 10:   0-13-425679-4
ISBN 13: 978-0-13-425679-5

In fond memory of Fred Weintraub (1942–2014) and Lynne Cook (1947–2015),
who loved each other and life; who both fought illness but couldn't win; and
who, separately and together, changed in an immeasurably positive way
the lives of children with disabilities and their teachers.

PREFACE

Collaboration has become a defining characteristic of modern society. As the world becomes increasingly complex but at the same time ever smaller because of instant worldwide communication, professionals in virtually every discipline have realized that there is simply too much to know and understand, too much to complete and accomplish for individuals to succeed in isolation. And this assertion is confirmed by a quick look at best-selling books and top results in a web search. Collaboration is everywhere, and it is presented as the most effective strategy for reaching meaningful goals.

Schools are a reflection of our larger society. Diversity has grown exponentially. Evidence-based information about instructional practices that can improve student outcomes is ubiquitous, and educators are scrambling to respond to the federal mandates that require increasingly high standards and a clear trajectory of improving student academic performance, including that of learners with disabilities and other special needs. It is in this complex, sometimes raucous but mostly exhilarating, context that we prepared this eighth edition of *Interactions: Collaboration Skills for School Professionals*.

New to This Edition

Whenever our book is revised, our goal is to make it better by updating critical information, eliminating information deemed less important, and addressing questions and concerns that have been raised by those teaching from it and those reading it. For this eighth edition, these are several of the most significant revisions:

- One major change in textbooks over the past several years has been the increasing addition of technology. In this edition of *Interactions*, technology has become integral to demonstrating concepts and skills and fostering critical analysis of them. For example, each chapter has several examples of a feature called Learn More About, which include hyperlinks to videos and other materials related to the topic being discussed.
- A second example of technology use in *Interactions* is the inclusion, for the first time, of brief quizzes throughout each chapter. Called Apply Your Knowledge, these exercises permit readers to immediately practice what they are learning and, often, to apply the knowledge and skills to situations that may occur in their work settings.
- A third technology feature is the end of chapter quiz. These summative assessments bring together the information from throughout each chapter. The quizzes may serve as the assessments for a course, or they may be used as another strategy for checking understanding of the chapter's content.
- Some material in this eighth edition of *Interactions* has been changed in order to reflect contemporary approaches. For example, instead of devoting a section of one chapter to electronic collaboration, that topic is now embedded in every chapter in the same way that technology is becoming integral to all aspects of education. Similarly, interactions with parents and families and with professionals such as speech/language therapists are reflected in nearly every chapter. However, because readers often note the importance of family collaboration for student success, that topic also has additional coverage in Chapter 11.
- Another change in this edition is the topic of paraprofessionals. Most special educators, many general educators, and other professionals interact with these essential school personnel, and usually the resulting working relationships are positive. However, complications can also occur, and Chapter 10 carefully explores the management of such situations.

- Other chapters have been updated. It is sometimes surprising to realize how much change has occurred in just a few short years. For example, Chapter 7 on co-teaching now reflects the increased emphasis on the quality of instruction for students with disabilities occurring as part of co-teaching. Chapter 6 on teaming was adjusted to more clearly emphasize the real-world work of teams, whether it is related to response to intervention, special education, or other school collaborative activities.
- Yet other chapters have been streamlined. Those using *Interactions* noted that there was some redundancy in the concepts presented in the communication chapters: Chapters 2, 3, and 4. Those chapters were revised to minimize repetition, and that created a place for more examples and applications.
- In the seventh edition, an entire chapter was devoted to interagency collaboration and another to the many issues related to collaboration. In this eighth edition and based on feedback from those who use the book, those topics have been blended into a new chapter called "Special Considerations." We hope that this revision will provide enough information about key topics while assisting instructors in being able to complete all the chapters within a single semester course format.
- One additional element of *Interactions* that had been dropped has been brought back. Each chapter's introductory case study is now revisited at the end of the chapter through a feature called Back to the Case. Included are questions that help readers to synthesize what they have learned and apply it to the case. It is not only a way to foster comprehension but also critical thinking and application.

These are not the only changes made to enhance the quality and timeliness of *Interactions*. New examples have been added that reflect the realities of today's schools. Research that informs collaborative practice has been updated, with over 250 new references to ensure that the material is current. In addition, our emphasis on recognizing, respecting, and responding to all types of diversity has been strengthened by expanding discussions of how culture may affect interactions and by ensuring that examples represent multiple points of view. We sincerely hope you will find the entire package of revisions helpful.

Overview of the Book

Each edition of *Interactions* has been carefully written to include a balanced amount of theory and related conceptual principles as well as practical examples, cases, and applied activities. The same is true for the eighth edition. It is written specifically to enable readers to quickly use in their professional settings the knowledge and skills they acquire. We intend for the book to be a useful tool for preservice educators and practitioners in improving their skills and deepening their understanding, whether they are engaged in formal instructional settings, study groups, or independent study. Our examples are not intended to be comprehensive. Instead, they were prepared so that readers could use the concepts they illustrate and apply them to their own interactions. Moreover, because many situations are complex with numerous variations and outcomes, we have tried to avoid being prescriptive and instead present possibilities, while still allowing the reader to think critically about alternatives.

We have had the good fortune of working and learning with talented teachers, administrators, parents, paraprofessionals, and providers of related services as they developed collaboration skills and specific applications of collaboration. We have benefited immensely from our interactions with these diverse educators who are implementing collaborative practices, and we believe that much of what we have learned is reflected in the pages of this eighth edition of *Interactions*. Specifically, we have maintained our core information about collaboration concepts and applications, significantly revised some material from the seventh edition (as noted previously), omitted a few topics that have dropped in priority in today's schools, combined information from the final two chapters of the previous edition based on instructor and student recommendation, and augmented the practical applications of the textbook's ideas.

Chapter 1 presents a conceptual foundation for understanding collaborative interactions and activities as well as the settings and structures that support them. In this chapter, we define collaboration and highlight its benefits and risks. In addition, we distinguish *collaboration* from other terms that are sometimes used interchangeably, and we explore the development of collaboration as it relates to special education, including the current trend to educate students with disabilities and other special needs in general education classrooms. Also included is the twenty-first century context of collaboration as it pertains to fields beyond education.

Chapters 2, 3, and 4 introduce the communication skills on which effective collaboration rests. Chapter 4 provides an integrated structure for learning and applying communication skills by focusing on the topic of interviewing. These chapters have been streamlined to eliminate redundancy and to allow additional examples and applications.

Chapter 5 builds from the communication skills by introducing the key interaction process in which those skills are used and the most central process in professional collaboration: group problem solving. It draws on but is differentiated from professional skills for individual problem solving. Most educational collaborative applications involve some type of problem-solving process; therefore, the information in this chapter is integral to all the chapters that follow.

The next three chapters of *Interactions* explore school services and applications in which success relies heavily on collaboration. Chapter 6 addresses the topic of teaming, including ideas for establishing and maintaining teams and problem solving to help teams work efficiently. Teaming is addressed in a pragmatic manner that emphasizes the nature of teams and how to make them function effectively as well as what to do when problems arise. Chapter 7 explores the topic of co-teaching, the service delivery option in which two educators share instructional responsibility in a single classroom. Among this group of chapters, this one signals more than any other the evolution of and increased interest in professional collaboration, and it has been updated to reflect the most recent trends related to this instructional arrangement. Suggestions for setting up co-teaching programs, specific information about how such arrangements should function, and the role of specially designed instruction in shared classrooms are provided, as are ideas for the universal co-teaching issue: the need for common planning time. Chapter 8 presents indirect service models, including consultation, coaching, and mentoring. Emphasis is placed not only on guidelines for providing these services but also on strategies to effectively receive them.

Chapter 9 deals with awkward and adversarial interactions by focusing on both conflict and resistance. Strategies such as negotiation and persuasion are emphasized. These require the use of many of the interactive processes and communication skills addressed in the previous interpersonal communication and problem-solving sections of the text. Further, as professionals begin implementing the collaborative approaches from the preceding three chapters, the value of the information in this chapter quickly becomes apparent.

Chapter 10 represents a shift to a different dimension of collaboration: the unique circumstances of role-specific collaboration. It focuses on the use of paraeducators in providing services to students with special needs. This chapter directly addresses appropriate and inappropriate roles for paraeducators, professionals' responsibilities for supervising the work of paraeducators, and issues that may arise when paraeducators are part of an educational team. Practical ideas for interactions with this valuable group of educators is a central theme for this chapter.

Chapter 11 considers in detail the nature of professional interactions with parents and families. The chapter reminds educators of the history as well as the current roles of families in the education of students with disabilities and other special needs, and it provides an overview of family systems theory. It stresses strategies for effectively interacting with family members, and with particular emphasis on families from diverse cultural groups. More than anything, this chapter focuses on how to ensure that family members are truly partners in educational decision making for their children.

Chapter 12 has been completely rewritten and blended with Chapter 13. Titled "Special Circumstances," it addresses four topics that often need explicit attention: (a) interagency collaboration; (b) the impact of professionals' roles and responsibilities on collaboration; (c) systemic barriers to collaboration in education; and (d) ethical issues that sometimes arise as part of collaboration. We believe this chapter provides an opportunity for additional reflection on significant topics that are briefly touched upon in earlier chapters.

The features in the eighth edition include most of those from previous editions of *Interactions*, and others have been added or revised. The features include the following:

- *Collaboration framework graphic.* At the opening of each chapter is a graphic that depicts five components of collaboration and their relationship to one another. The components consist of personal commitment, communication skills, interaction processes, programs or services, and context. These are components of the framework described in Chapter 1. The components most relevant to the content of each chapter are highlighted in the icons at its opening.
- *Connections.* Each chapter begins with a section entitled Connections, which is designed to assist the reader in understanding how the specific chapter content relates to material in other chapters and to the overall goals and organization of the book.
- *Learner Objectives.* Each Connections section is followed by Learner Objectives, which inform the reader about the main purposes of the chapter, generally the objective is written for each major section of a chapter. The objectives also help the reader set expectations for what he or she will be able to do after studying the chapter.
- *A Case for Collaboration.* Instructors have shared with us that realistic cases, in which professional candidates can apply what they are learning, are particularly effective learning tools. Thus, each chapter includes a case designed to encourage this application. The case is introduced at the beginning of the chapter, and it is referred to several times as relevant concepts are introduced. This strategy provides a mechanism for ongoing class discussion of the material.
- *Back to the Case.* Based on instructor feedback, we have brought back a feature that had been dropped. At the conclusion of each chapter, readers are directed back to the introductory case and asked several questions that enable them to apply the knowledge and skills they have acquired. This feature brings full circle the learning of chapter content.
- *Photographs.* In this eighth edition, photographs are inserted to illustrate collaboration in action.
- *Case materials.* Brief case descriptions and vignettes occur throughout the text to illustrate relevant concepts and principles. These often include descriptions of specific school situations and extended dialog between professionals or parents. The goal is to bring the concepts and skills to life for professional candidates.
- *Learn More About.* Each chapter includes an array of video clips, web sites, and other linked material that supports the topics being addressed. Items in this feature often include questions or explanations to extend readers' thinking about a topic.
- *Apply Your Knowledge.* At least two (and usually three) linked quizzes are part of each chapter. Located at the conclusion of major chapter sections, these brief assessments enable readers to apply what they have just studied. The assessments are another means of encouraging readers to reflect on what they are learning and to incorporate information into their own collaboration.
- *Putting Ideas into Practice.* In each chapter, additional elaboration of concepts or skills practice is offered in Putting Ideas into Practice. These features are another means of making written ideas come to life for application in real school settings.
- *A Basis in Research.* A research base is developing in the area of collaboration, and research-based practices are increasingly necessary. A Basis in Research, with many updated studies presented in this eighth edition, highlights pertinent research findings related to the topics addressed in each chapter.

- ***E-Partnerships.*** Given the rapidly growing use of technology across disciplines and across topics, electronic collaboration must receive considerable attention in this book. In every chapter, you will find a feature that addresses a technology application. Some are familiar to most; others may stretch readers' experience in the world of electronic collaboration.
- ***Summary.*** Each chapter concludes with a bullet-point summary in which the major points addressed in the chapter are recapped; the points are based on the major chapter sections. The summaries are intended to assist readers in reviewing their understanding of the chapter's primary concepts.
- ***Collaborative Activities.*** Application items are found at the end of each chapter. Consideration has been given to the very real need for candidates to be able to address the activities during a class session without accessing outside resources, and most can be completed within that constraint. Many of these exercises may also be used as out-of-class or independent assignments.
- ***End of Chapter Quiz.*** The final item in each chapter is a quiz accessed through a hyperlink. These quizzes span all the topics addressed in the chapter and are intended as an overall check on reader understanding.

Our text is accompanied by an **Online Instructor's Manual** and **Online PowerPoint Presentation**, both accessible to you at the Instructor's Resource Center at http://www.pearsonhighered.com. To access the manual and online PowerPoint slides, go to http://www.pearsonhighered.com and click on the Instructor's Resource button. Here you will be able to log in or complete a one-time registration for a username and password. The manual includes chapter outlines, additional activities and cases, and a test bank. It provides many more resources for teaching about collaboration than can be placed within the pages of the book itself.

We hope this eighth edition of *Interactions: Collaboration Skills for School Professionals* is useful to you and that you enjoy reading it. We continue to hold to our belief that collaboration is the foundation on which successful contemporary public schools are based, as well as the most effective means to provide services to students with disabilities and other special needs. If you are reading this material as a teacher, teacher candidate, or other preprofessional, we hope this edition of *Interactions* helps you further understand collaboration as it occurs in your workplace and enables you to refine your skills as a collaborative educator. If you are an instructor, we hope you find the revisions we have made useful as you prepare professionals for the high-pressure, complex world of today's schools.

Acknowledgments

The material in this book is a deliberate mix of the technical and scholarly literature on collaboration from a variety of disciplines as well as the real-world stories that we hear from teachers, administrators, family members, related services personnel, and teacher candidates. Although the former information is essential and establishes the validity of the topics presented, it is the latter that breathes life into this book. And so, a sincere thanks to all the school professionals and family members who explained, with satisfaction or dismay, their experiences in working with others in school and related settings. It is their wisdom and insights about what it takes to make collaboration a reality that enables us to offer practical examples and exercises in *Interactions*. Thank you for all you have taught us.

We are also indebted to our colleagues who teach coursework on collaboration and who engage us in fascinating discussions on topics related to contemporary education, whether in panel presentations at conference sessions or over cocktails after the day's professional work is concluded. As we write and edit, we are frequently using your thoughts to guide our own. Even though we cannot name all of you, we hope you see your perspectives reflected in this edition and know of our appreciation.

We would also like to thank the following colleagues who provided professional reviews of the seventh edition of *Interactions* to make suggestions for the eighth edition: Jane Bogan, Miami University; Gabrielle N. DiLorenzo, Pace University; Dorothy Fulton, Fort Hays State University; and Tracey Sulak, Baylor University. We appreciate the amount of time you took to complete a thorough review, and we are appreciative of the detailed analysis you provided. Although we cannot make every change suggested by every reviewer, we carefully combed through your reviews, looking for themes, and genuinely tried to be responsive. We sincerely hope that you can see your influence.

The process of revising a book seems to become more complicated with each edition, and we rely heavily on the expertise of the professionals at Pearson to ensure *Interactions* is completed in a timely manner and with all essential components, and we would like to thank them for their guidance, encouragement, patience, and advice. Ann Davis, our editor, has an uncanny ability to find solutions to what sometimes seem like insurmountable problems, and she has an unfailingly positive approach toward the work that she does. She was truly instrumental in shaping the eighth edition. We also want to profusely thank Alicia Reilly. We have worked with Alicia for many years, and she often goes far beyond her specific responsibilities of working with the interactive elements of the books. She combines careful attention to detail, gentle reminders about deadlines, direct communication when something is amiss (like overdue chapters), and all the positive support and patience that any authors could hope for. We would also like to thank Kerry Rubadue for her leadership in the actual production process, as well as the team at Lumina Datamatics for their careful attention to all the details that take a book from text manuscript to final product, from editing for clarity and checking references to correcting typos and ensuring that all the features and links are in place.

Finally, we could not write acknowledgments without including our family and friends. Marilyn's husband Bruce and Lynne's daughters Marya Long and Heather Moore offer us a support network that is as strong as steel but has the flexibility that is part of writing a book. Thanks for your patience, your encouragement, your understanding of our quirky schedules and occasional writing angst. And then our friends ... they are too many to name, but we cannot understate the importance of their direct and indirect input, whether it is listening to a passage to offer an opinion on how it sounds or being available to take a walk or go out for dinner as a break from the work at hand. Thank you so much for all you do for us.

Marilyn Friend
Lynne Cook

BRIEF CONTENTS

1. Foundations and Perspectives xxii
2. Interpersonal Communication 24
3. Listening, Responding, and Giving Feedback 50
4. Integrating Skills in Formal and Informal Interviews 78
5. Group Problem Solving 102
6. Teams 130
7. Co-Teaching 156
8. Consultation, Coaching, and Mentoring 184
9. Difficult Interactions 208
10. Paraeducators 238
11. Families 262
12. Special Considerations 288

References 318
Name Index 341
Subject Index 356

CONTENTS

Preface iv
Features at a Glance xviii

1 Foundations and Perspectives xxii
- Connections 1
- Learning Outcomes 1
- A Case for Collaboration 2

Introduction 3

Collaboration Concepts 4
  Definition 5
  Defining Characteristics of Collaboration 6
  Emergent Characteristics 10

Collaboration in a Societal Context 11
  Societal Trends 11
  Collaboration Across Professions 12

School Collaboration 12
  Response to Intervention 12
  Additional Examples of School-Wide Collaboration 13
  Special Education Collaboration 14

The Challenges of Collaboration 16
  School Culture 16
  Professional Socialization 17
  Power in the Relationship 18
  Pragmatic Issues 19

A Framework for Learning About Collaboration 21

Summary 22
Back to the Case 23
Collaborative Activities 23

2 Interpersonal Communication 24
- Connections 25
- Learning Outcomes 25
- A Case for Collaboration 26

Introduction 26

Understanding Communication 26
  Views of Communication 27

Defining Interpersonal Communication 30
  Concepts Reflected in the Interpersonal Communication Process 31
  Principles of Interpersonal Communication 33

Interpersonal Competence 35
Perspective 35
Perception 35
Competent Communication 43
Suggestions for Improving Your Communication Skills 45

Summary 48
Back to the Case 48
Collaborative Activities 49

3 Listening, Responding, and Giving Feedback 50

- Connections 51
- Learning Outcomes 51
- A Case for Collaboration 52

Introduction 52

Nonverbal Communication 53
The Value of Nonverbal Communication 53
Types of Nonverbal Communication 54

Listening and Communication 57
Rationale for Listening 58
Listening As a Process 59
Factors That Interfere with Effective Listening 60
Suggestions for Improving Listening Skills 61

Responding 63
Prompting 64
Paraphrasing 65
Reflecting 66
Questioning 68

Principles for Effective Verbal and Nonverbal Communication 69
Congruence 70
Individuality 70
Concreteness 71

Giving Verbal Feedback 72
Characteristics of Effective Interpersonal Feedback 72
Guidelines for Giving Effective Feedback 74

Summary 76
Back to the Case 76
Collaborative Activities 76

4 Integrating Skills in Formal and Informal Interviews 78

- Connections 79
- Learning Outcomes 79
- A Case for Collaboration 80

Introduction 80

Seeking Information 82
Question Format 82
Focused Inquiry 87

Providing Information 93
    Descriptive Statements 93
    Guiding Statements 96

Suggestions for Effective Interviews 98
    Use Pauses Effectively 98
    Monitor Information-Seeking Interactions 99
    Attend to the Cultural Context 99
    Final Thoughts on Interviewing 100

Summary 100
Back to the Case 100
Collaborative Activities 101

5 Group Problem Solving 102

- Connections 103
- Learning Outcomes 103
- A Case for Collaboration 104

Introduction 104

Group Problem Solving as a Professional Responsibility 105
    Reactive and Proactive Problem Solving 107
    Problem Solving and Diversity 107
    Deciding Whether to Problem Solve 108
    Response to Intervention: A Special Type of Problem Solving 111

Steps in Group Problem Solving 112
    Identifying the Problem 112
    Generating Potential Solutions 117
    Evaluating Potential Solutions 121
    Selecting the Solution 122
    Implementing the Solution 122
    Evaluating the Outcome 125

Putting the Problem-Solving Pieces Together 126

Summary 128
Back to the Case 128
Collaborative Activities 128

6 Teams 130

- Connections 131
- Learning Outcomes 131
- A Case for Collaboration 132

Introduction 132

Team Concepts 133
    Characteristics of Teams 134
    Developmental Stages for Teams 136
    Rationale for and Benefits of Teams 139
    Drawbacks of Teams 139

Disciplinary Relationships on Teams   140
   Multidisciplinary Teams   140
   Interdisciplinary Teams   142
   Transdisciplinary Teams   142

Student-Centered Teams   144
   Instructional Teams   144
   Student-Centered Problem-Solving Teams   146
   Special Education Teams   149

Effectiveness of Teams   151
   The Team's Goals Are Clear   152
   Members' Needs Are Met   152
   Members Have Individual Accountability   153
   Group Processes Maintain the Team   153
   Team Members Have Leadership Skills   153
   Collaboration and Teams   153

Summary   154
Back to the Case   154
Collaborative Activities   154

7 Co-Teaching   156

- Connections   157
- Learning Outcomes   157
- A Case for Collaboration   158

Introduction   158

Co-Teaching Concepts   158
   Co-Teaching Definition   159
   Characteristics of Co-Teaching   160

Rationale for Co-Teaching   163

Co-Teaching Approaches   165
   One Teaching, One Observing   165
   Station Teaching   167
   Parallel Teaching   168
   Alternative Teaching   169
   Teaming   170
   One Teaching, One Assisting   170

Co-Teaching and Collaboration   172
   Understanding the Co-Teaching Relationship   173
   Maintaining Collaborative Relationships in Co-Teaching   174

Administrative Matters Related to Co-Teaching   176

Time for Planning   177
   Options for Creating Shared Planning Time   179

Summary   182
Back to the Case   182
Collaborative Activities   182

8 Consultation, Coaching, and Mentoring 184

- Connections 185
- Learning Outcomes 185
- A Case for Collaboration 186

Introduction 186

Consultation 187
    Characteristics of Consultation 187
    Rationale for and Benefits of Consultation 190
    Consultation Models 192
    Consultation Models in Practice 195
    Consultation and Collaboration 195

Coaching 197
    Rationale for and Benefits of Coaching 198
    Coaching Models 198
    Coaching in Practice 201

Mentoring 201
    The Impact of Mentoring 203

Issues Related to Indirect Services 204
    Understanding of the Professional Relationships 204
    Time Allocation for Professional Collaboration 204
    Cultural Differences 205
    Confidentiality 205

Summary 206
Back to the Case 206
Collaborative Activities 206

9 Difficult Interactions 208

- Connections 209
- Learning Outcomes 209
- A Case for Collaboration 210

Introduction 210

Understanding Conflict 211
    Causes of Conflict 213
    The Influence of Organizational Variables 215
    Conflict Response Styles 216
    Resolving Conflict Through Negotiation 219
    Resolving Conflict Through Mediation 221
    Conflict and Diversity 223

Understanding Resistance 224
    Causes of Resistance 225
    Indicators of Resistance 227
    Assessing Whether to Address Resistance 227
    Persuasion as a Strategy for Responding to Resistance 229

Putting the Pieces Together 231
Summary 232
Back to the Case 233
Collaborative Activities 233
Appendix 9.1 234

10 Paraeducators 238

- Connections 239
- Learning Outcomes 239
- A Case for Collaboration 240

Introduction 240

Understanding Paraeducators 241
    Paraeducator Qualifications 241
    Paraeducators as Key Personnel in Today's Schools 243

Paraeducator Roles and Responsibilities 243
    Instructional Responsibilities 244
    Noninstructional Responsibilities 245

Ethical Considerations 247
    Paraeducators Supplement Rather than Supplant Instruction 248
    Paraeducators Complete Only Routine Parent Communication 249
    Paraeducators Balance the Need for Support with the Goal of Independence 250

Working with Paraeducators 251
    Teaching Paraeducators About Their Roles and Responsibilities 251
    Planning with Paraeducators 254
    Assigning Responsibilities to Paraeducators 254
    Communicating with Paraeducators 255
    Supervising Paraeducators 256

Paraeducators and Collaboration 259
Summary 260
Back to the Case 260
Collaborative Activities 260

11 Families 262

- Connections 263
- Learning Outcomes 263
- A Case for Collaboration 264

Introduction 264

Understanding Families 265
    Family Systems Theory 266

Family Life Cycles 268
    Birth and Early Childhood 269
    Childhood 271
    Adolescence 272
    Adulthood 273

Factors Affecting Professionals' Interactions with Families 274
    Cultural Influences 274
    Factors Related to Having a Child with a Disability 277
    Factors Related to Life Conditions 278

Family Participation in Decision Making 279
    Providing Information to Families 279
    Assisting Families to Participate in Student-Centered Meetings 285

Summary 287
Back to the Case 287
Collaborative Activities 287

12 Special Considerations 288

- Connections 289
- Learning Outcomes 289
- A Case for Collaboration 290

Introduction 290

Community and Interagency Collaboration 291
    Community Outreach 291
    School–Community Partnerships 292
    Community Liaisons 293
    Interagency Contexts 294
    Early Intervention and Preschool Programs 295
    Vocational and Community-Based Services 296

Collaboration Influenced by Roles and Responsibilities 300
    Working with Administrators 300
    Working with Specialists 302
    Working with Other Teachers 304
    Student–Professional Collaboration 306

Systemic Barriers to Collaboration 307
    Scheduling for Collaboration 307
    Coordinating Services for Collaboration 311

Ethics in Collaborative Practice 312
    Common Ethical Issues 312
    Responding to Ethical Issues 313

Final Thoughts About Professional Collaboration 314

Summary 316
Back to the Case 316
Collaborative Activities 317

References 318
Name Index 341
Subject Index 356

FEATURES AT A GLANCE

E-PARTNERSHIPS

Chapter 1
Collaborating on the Internet   19

Chapter 2
Using Old-Fashioned Technology to Your Advantage   34

Chapter 3
Using E-Mail Effectively   58

Chapter 4
Asking Questions Electronically … Options and Cautions   89

Chapter 5
Special Circumstances: Virtual Group Problem Solving   110

Chapter 6
Teaming in the Cloud   145

Chapter 7
Electronic Planning for Co-Teachers   179

Chapter 8
Virtual Coaching   200
Electronic Mentoring   203

Chapter 9
Skills for Difficult Interactions   217

Chapter 10
Paraeducators on the Web   253

Chapter 11
Families on the Web   284

Chapter 12
RSS: Sorting Through the Avalanche of Internet Information   299
Collaboration 2.0? Twitter!   315

PUTTING IDEAS INTO PRACTICE

Chapter 1
Working with Diverse Families   4
The Many Faces of School Collaboration   14
Internet Resources for Collaboration   17
Managing Stress   20

Chapter 2
Coming to Terms with Communication Terms   29
What Channel?   32
Perception Is a Selective Process   37

Managing Perceptions   38
Developing Cultural Self-Awareness   40
Planning for and Evaluating a Communication Event   47

Chapter 3
Body Language Communicates Powerful Messages   55
Strategies for Successful Listening   64
Avoiding Pitfalls in Practicing Empathic Listening   67
Watch Out for Insincere Questions   69

Chapter 4
Details for Conducting Interviews   81
Questioning Yourself   83
Seeking Information in Nonthreatening Ways   88
Generalities Require Closer Examination   89
Funnel Approaches to Sequencing Questions   92
Tips for Sharing Information   96
Handling Uncooperative Communications   98

Chapter 5
When Problem Solving Is Not the Best Approach   109
Response to Intervention: Technical Problem Solving   111
Problem-Solving Practice   123

Chapter 6
A Checklist for Effective Teamwork   135
Managing Relationships During the Stages of Team Development   138
Three Models of Team Interaction   141
IDEA Guidelines for IEP Team Composition   150

Chapter 7
Co-Teaching Versus Student Teaching   159
Beginning Co-Teaching on a Positive Note   164
Co-Teaching Dilemmas   171
Finding Common Planning Time   180
Making the Most of Common Planning Time   181

Chapter 8
Fidelity of Implementation: A Key to Consultation Effectiveness   190
Response to Intervention Through Consultation   191
Being a Consumer of Consultation, Coaching, or Mentoring   199

Chapter 9
Effective Negotiation   221
Addressing Difficult Interactions in Diverse Groups   223
Using Communication Skills During Difficult Interactions   232

Chapter 10
Delegating Responsibilities to Paraeducators   251
Communicating with Your Paraeducator When There Is No Time to Meet   256
At Odds … When Professionals and Paraeducators Disagree   258
Collaborating with Paraeducators   259

Chapter 11
Tasks and Functions at Four Family Life Stages 269
Some Parental Concerns About Inclusion 271
Enhancing Successful Transitions 274
Cultural Continua 276

Chapter 12
Getting the Most from the Pros 292
Ten Key Strategies for Effective Partnerships 293
Enhancing Collaboration with Vocational Rehabilitation Counselors 300
Strategies for Developing Administrative Support 303

A BASIS IN RESEARCH

Chapter 1
Does Collaboration Improve Student Achievement? 9

Chapter 2
Competent Communication and School Principals 44

Chapter 3
Smile, If You Want the Full Scoop! 59
Teaching Communication Skills 62

Chapter 4
Some Evidence-Based Information About Questions 84

Chapter 5
Understanding How Bias May Occur in Group Problem Solving 108

Chapter 6
Successful Teamwork: Facilitators and Barriers 143
General Education Teachers and Pre-Referral Teaming 149

Chapter 7
Co-Teaching: Promise Versus Evidence 160

Chapter 8
Demonstrating the Effectiveness of Direct Behavioral Consultation 193

Chapter 9
Conflict in Special Education: Advocates and Due Process 214
Constructive Conflict and Psychological Safety 219

Chapter 10
Paraeducators Supporting Students from Diverse Backgrounds 247

Chapter 11
Family Involvement in and Satisfaction with Special Education Processes 280

Chapter 12
Roles and Responsibilities of Novice General and Special Educators 305

1 Foundations and Perspectives

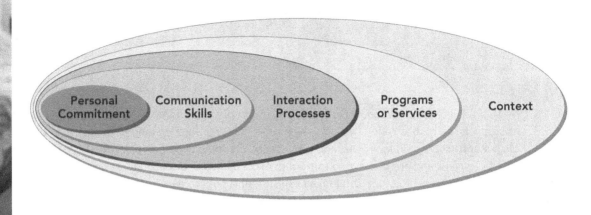

CONNECTIONS

Collaboration has become a distinguishing characteristic of effective educators and the culture of successful schools. Chapter 1 begins your journey of the study of collaboration and lays the groundwork for all the information covered in subsequent chapters; in fact, you may find as you read those chapters that it is helpful to refer back to the concepts outlined in this chapter. Specifically, in the pages that follow you will learn what collaboration is (and is not) and how it fits into a broader societal context. You will also find out about the increasing attention collaboration is receiving throughout education as well as some of the challenges educators face as their collaborative responsibilities increase and become more complex. Finally, you will be introduced to a framework for studying collaboration that serves as the organizational structure for this textbook.

LEARNING OUTCOMES

After reading this chapter you will be able to:

1. Define *collaboration* and describe its critical characteristics, distinguishing it from related but distinctly different concepts.
2. Outline the importance of collaboration from a broad societal perspective, including its place in disciplines such as business, health, and human services.
3. Analyze the place of collaboration within contemporary schools in the context of current legislation and reform initiatives, including formal and informal collaborative practices and those specific to special education.
4. Discuss challenges that may arise as educators increase their collaborative activities.
5. Describe a framework for studying collaboration.

A CASE FOR COLLABORATION

A Day in the Life . . .

The Madison Independent School District is in the midst of many efforts to improve academic outcomes for its students. All of those efforts include an emphasis on collaboration among its staff members, between district and school staff members, and parents and community members. At the district level, administrators meet regularly, and any committee formed to make curricular or program decisions includes representatives from special education, gifted/talented services, and English as a Second Language (ESL) programs. Administrators are participating in ongoing leadership professional development to increase their knowledge and skills for fostering leadership among teachers and building a strong sense of community in schools. At the school level, principals are held accountable for fostering a collaborative culture in their schools. Here are examples of professionals' typical days and their collaborative roles in their schools.

Ms. Williams is a middle school social studies teacher. In addition to her daily teaching responsibilities, she is a member of her school's leadership team, and so today she attends a team meeting from 7:30 to 8:15 a.m. to discuss several issues, including the staff development plan for the next school year. At lunch, Ms. Williams arranges to meet with Mr. Newby, the school psychologist, to discuss the needs of a student who recently arrived unaccompanied from Guatemala and who is demonstrating many acting-out behaviors. Ms. Williams knows the upcoming field trip will be the primary topic for discussion during her team preparation period, and during her individual preparation period she needs to call two parents. After school, she plans to meet with her assistant principal, Mr. Robinson, to discuss the peer tutoring program the university interns would like to establish.

Mr. Garcia is a second-year student support teacher (SST) at Hawthorne High School. He begins each day touching base with his colleagues in the math department and working on paperwork. Once classes begin at 7:50 a.m., he spends the morning co-teaching two sections of Algebra I and teaching one section of a study skills class that has a math emphasis. During his preparation period, he meets with two students and the counselor about problems the students are experiencing in their classes. He also prepares directions for the paraprofessional assigned to support Matt, a student with significant physical disabilities. In the afternoon, Mr. Garcia facilitates an annual review and transition planning meeting for one of the students on his caseload. After school, he meets briefly with Ms. Young, the social studies teacher with whom he co-chairs the school's response to intervention (RTI) team. Mr. Garcia considers himself an advocate for students, and he finds that he must pay close attention to the personalities of the teachers with whom he works; if he establishes a strong working relationship with them, students are the beneficiaries.

Mrs. Lee is an instructional coach at Fairview Elementary School. Her primary responsibility is to assist teachers, especially those in the first two years of their teaching careers, to refine their instructional practices so as to increase student achievement. Her job usually does not include directly teaching students unless it is to model a technique or demonstrate a strategy. Thus, Mrs. Lee spends her time observing in classrooms, meeting with teachers individually and in small groups, advising the principal about needs she identifies related to instruction, conducting staff development on specific strategies and approaches, and analyzing and sharing data with school staff members. She also works closely with the school's parent advisory group to help families foster student learning at home.

Introduction

Of all the complex tasks facing educators today, none is as demanding or as critical as creating a school culture of collaboration because it is a foundation of collaboration that enables all the other work of educators to be successful. To accomplish this goal, each person who works in schools must have the disposition, knowledge, and skills to collaborate. For example, each of the professionals described in A Case for Collaboration has adult–adult interactions as a significant job responsibility. Ms. Williams, whose primary responsibility is instruction, is also expected to work with colleagues and parents. Half of Mr. Garcia's teaching occurs in partnership with general education teachers in that setting. Mrs. Lee's job illustrates today's emphasis on improving student outcomes. School leaders have realized that teachers need support in their classrooms in order to ensure that all students access the general curriculum and reach high standards. Taken together, these professional interactions illustrate three critical points for understanding the premise of this text.

First, collaboration has become an integral part of today's schools (e.g., Barth, 2006; Butera & Martinez, 2014; Henning, 2013). In the past, educators who were not very effective in working with other adults were often excused with a comment such as, "But she's really good with students." Although working effectively with students obviously is still the most important aspect of educators' jobs, it is not enough. Everyone in schools—including special and general education teachers, paraprofessionals, administrators, related services providers, and other specialists—needs the knowledge and skills to work with one another and parents (Stearns, Banerjee, Mickelson, & Moller, 2014). This is true in early childhood programs, in elementary schools, and in middle and high schools. It is true in schools that are still regarded as traditional in terms of programs and services as well as in those leading the way in educational innovation. Part of the reason for the importance of collaboration is the general trend of expanding and increasingly complex responsibilities, which are more realistically addressed when professionals pool their talents (e.g., DuFour & Mattos, 2013; Martinez, 2010; Sparks, 2013). Part of it is legislation setting high standards for academic achievement and clear accountability systems for all students (e.g., Eslinger, 2014; U.S. Department of Education, 2010), and part of it is the continued trend toward inclusive practices (Lalvani, 2013; Thew, 2014).

Second, examples of professionals' collaborative activities demonstrate that such interactions occur both formally and informally. School leadership teams, middle school teams, co-teaching teams, teams that meet to discuss students who are struggling to learn, and consultative meetings are representative of the growth of formal structures and activities in schools that rely on collaboration for success. Models emphasizing collaboration such as these are described in detail later in this text. Meetings between teachers to respond to immediate student needs and phone calls to parents are examples of informal collaboration. Both types of collaboration are important. However, informal collaboration often occurs whether or not a context for collaboration has been fostered and whether or not any formal structures for collaboration are in place. Formal collaboration typically requires that strong leadership has ensured that a collaborative school culture—one that values collegial interactions—has been created.

Third, this text is based on the belief that collaboration is the common thread in many current initiatives for school reform (Dulaney, 2013; McCoach et al., 2010; Weiss & Friesen, 2014). Collaboration is crucial as educators move to implement RTI practices, differentiate instruction, meet standards of accountability for student achievement as measured through high-stakes testing, and design and implement local professional development strategies (Richardson, 2011; Sun, Penuel, Frank, Gallagher, & Youngs, 2013). Likewise, collaboration is crucial as professionals work with the parents and families of their increasingly diverse student groups (Miller, Arthur-Stanley, & Lines, 2012). An initial illustration of this point is captured in Putting Ideas into Practice, which explores challenges that families may face and ways educators may effectively interact with them. Collaboration is also part of special education through initial referral and assessment procedures, individualized education program (IEP) development, service delivery approaches, conflict resolution, and parent participation.

> **Learn More About**
> This compelling video clip will give you a sense of how critical collaboration is in today's world. How do these concepts apply to teachers and schools?
> (https://www.youtube.com/watch?v=y_m9nReouVY)

PUTTING IDEAS INTO PRACTICE

Working with Diverse Families

Collaborating with the parents and family members of your students is one of your first responsibilities as a professional educator, and doing this requires an understanding of the diversity and needs they represent. Ray (2005) offers some examples of family characteristics or circumstances and challenges that may arise.

- *Single-parent families* may experience a great deal of stress and isolation, and the children from these families are more likely than other children to live in poverty.
- *Blended families*, in which parents have children from former relationships, may need time to bond and to resolve issues related to child rearing (e.g., discipline). Sibling rivalry may also occur.
- *Multigenerational families*, in which grandparents, great-grandparents, or other relatives care for children, may face economic challenges, and the energy required to raise children may be daunting for the caregiver.
- *Foster families* are typically temporary, and so the bonds may be a bit different from those in other families; children in foster families may experience stress because of not knowing exactly what the next steps in their lives may be.
- *Same-sex families* often face societal discrimination, and some teachers may feel uncomfortable interacting with these parents. Legal issues related to topics such as access to school records may also arise.

As a professional educator, you can enhance your interactions with diverse families by using strategies such as the following:

1. Be sure to know the correct last name of every parent, regardless of the family structure.
2. Avoid language that implies that "family" refers only to traditional family structure.
3. Regardless of family structure, offer information to parents or caregivers on their children's strengths and abilities.
4. Avoid making requests that may place parents in an uncomfortable position related to time or money. Some families cannot afford to contribute materials for classrooms, and some parents cannot come to conferences during typical school hours or on a specific day; therefore, options and alternatives should be offered.
5. Remember that projects and activities that presume students are part of a traditional family may not be appropriate. For example, alternatives should be found to creating a family tree and making Mother's Day gifts.
6. In some cases—for example, when grandparents or great-grandparents are raising children—you may need to explain school procedures if these caregivers are unfamiliar with them.

Most important, all educators should reflect on their own beliefs about nontraditional families and set aside any assumptions they may have about them. Being positive with students and families and being alert to and stopping teasing or bullying of students from these families are your responsibilities as a professional educator.

This book, then, is about effective interactions. It presents the universal concepts, principles, skills, and strategies that all school professionals—regardless of their roles and responsibilities—can use to enhance their shared efforts to educate their students. Although slight variations in practice may occur related to one's specific area of expertise (general education teacher, special educator, speech/language therapist, or administrator), learning about collaboration generally is an area that truly brings educators together.

Collaboration Concepts

The term *collaboration* is something of an educational buzzword. One can easily get the sense that collaboration is viewed as the preferred approach in nearly any school situation. It is touted as the mechanism through which school reform can be accomplished (Anderson-Butcher et al., 2010; Ash & D'Auria, 2013) and the instrument through which diverse student needs can be met (Honigsfeld & Dove, 2012b; Olivos, 2009; Lopez, 2013). Principals are admonished to use a collaborative leadership style

FIGURE 1.1 Some of the many misunderstandings about collaboration in schools.

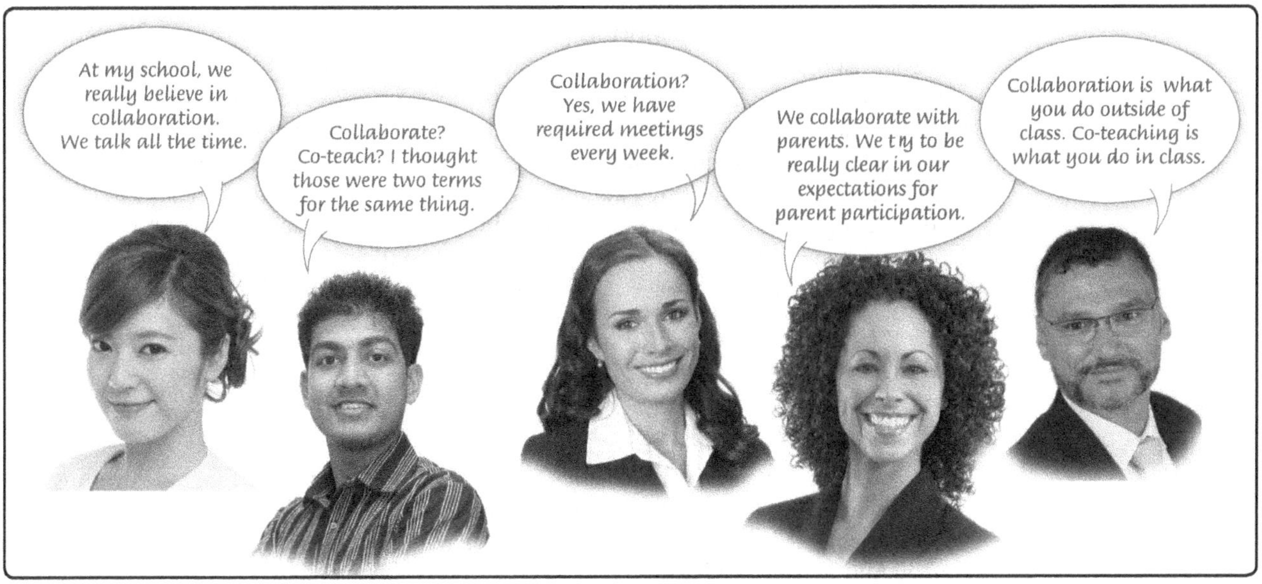
At my school, we really believe in collaboration. We talk all the time.
Collaborate? Co-teach? I thought those were two terms for the same thing.
Collaboration? Yes, we have required meetings every week.
We collaborate with parents. We try to be really clear in our expectations for parent participation.
Collaboration is what you do outside of class. Co-teaching is what you do in class.

From left: 41/Shutterstock, Ashwin/Shutterstock, kurhan/Shutterstock, vgstudio/Shutterstock, Christian Schwier/Fotolia.com

(e.g., DuFour & Mattos, 2013), and teachers are encouraged to use collaboration to improve student outcomes (e.g., Ertesvåg, 2014; Huberman, Navo, & Parrish, 2012). Unfortunately, the term *collaboration* often is carelessly used and occasionally misapplied, as suggested in Figure 1.1.

Despite all the current discussion about collaboration, definitions of the term have remained unclear, which has contributed to confusion about its character and implementation. In fact, some dictionary definitions of *collaboration* include reference to treason or working together for sinister purposes! In education literature and practice, you may find that *collaboration* either is used as a synonym for related but distinctly different concepts addressed elsewhere in this book—including teaming, consultation, co-teaching, and inclusion—or is not defined at all beyond a sense of working together (e.g., Kampwirth & Powers, 2015; Pugach, Johnson, Drame, & Williamson, 2012). Because we firmly believe that a precise understanding of the term *collaboration* is far more than semantics, we begin by carefully defining it. Knowing what collaboration is and is not and how it applies to school initiatives and other applications can help you articulate your practices, set appropriate expectations for yourself, and positively influence others to interact collaboratively.

Definition

The term *collaboration* is used frequently in casual conversation, but it also has a technical definition that establishes it as a specific professional concept:

> Interpersonal collaboration is a style for direct interaction between at least two coequal parties voluntarily engaged in shared decision making as they work toward a common goal.

Notice that we call collaboration a *style*. In the same way that writers use various styles to convey information to readers so, too, do individuals use interpersonal styles or approaches in their interactions with one another. Some professionals may choose to be directive when they interact; others may choose to be accommodative or facilitative; still others may choose to be collaborative. At first glance, referring to collaboration as a style may appear to detract from its significance by equating it with something ephemeral and seemingly lacking in substance. However, using this definition enables you to distinguish the nature of the interpersonal relationship occurring during shared interactions—that is, collaboration—from the activities themselves, such as teaming, problem solving, or co-teaching.

As just implied, because collaboration is a style of interaction, it cannot exist in isolation. It can occur only when it is used by people who are engaged in a specific process, task, or activity. To clarify this point, consider the following: If colleagues mentioned to you that they were collaborating, would you know what they were doing? Probably not. They could be collaboratively discussing strategies for supporting a student who has just enrolled at the school, sharing the responsibilities for an academic lesson in a co-teaching arrangement, or planning an interdisciplinary unit. What the term *collaboration* conveys is *how* the activity is occurring—that is, the nature of the interpersonal relationship occurring during the interaction and the ways in which individuals are communicating with one another. Think about this in relation to Ms. Williams, Mr. Garcia, and Mrs. Lee. In what activities are they engaged? Are these activities likely candidates for collaboration?

Defining Characteristics of Collaboration

Considered alone, the definition we have presented only hints at the subtleties of collaboration. Through our writing (e.g., Cook & Friend, 2010; Friend, Cook, Hurley-Chamberlain, & Shamberger, 2010; Friend & Barron, 2015), our own ongoing collaboration, and our experience facilitating the collaboration of others, we have identified several elements of collaboration that we refer to as defining characteristics, as they more fully explain the basic definition.

Collaboration Is Voluntary It is not possible to force people to use a particular style in their interactions with others. States may pass legislation, school districts may adopt policy, and principals may implement programs; but unless school professionals and their colleagues choose to collaborate they will not do so. Perhaps the best illustration of this notion is the increasingly common mandate that professionals collaborate in designing and implementing programs for students with special needs in general education classes. If you are familiar with a school where this expectation is in place, you probably are also aware that some teachers are unwilling to collaborate, regardless of the mandate. For example, a teacher may spend a significant amount of time complaining about the demands of teaching certain students, apparently unaware that this is time that otherwise could be spent collaboratively designing instruction to foster these students' success. If that individual attends meetings as required but undermines the reading specialist's, ESL teacher's, or special educator's efforts to support students, he or she is not collaborating in the sense outlined in this chapter. The professional relationship is constrained, the students are still in the classroom, and the specialist or special educator bears most of the responsibility for making accommodations. Similarly, a specialist or special educator may repeatedly express doubts that student needs can be addressed in a general education setting. If this time were spent designing and carefully implementing strategies for supporting students, the concern could be addressed with data that would support or refute it.

Alternatively, a professional unsure about inclusive practices—whether a special educator, a general educator, a bilingual educator or ESL teacher, or another professional—can express anxiety and uncertainty, but that person may also work closely and constructively with others to support students with special needs. In essence, schools and other education agencies can mandate administrative arrangements that require staff to work in close proximity, but only the individuals involved can decide whether a collaborative style will be used in their interactions. In our work in schools, we sometimes find ourselves emphasizing that there is no such thing as collaboration by coercion.

Does this mean that people cannot collaborate if programs are mandated? Not at all. Consider the situation at Jefferson High School, where general education teachers have been notified that each department will have collaborative planning time for the upcoming school year and will be expected to develop common assessments, implement consistent grading practices, and gather data to guide instructional practices. Mr. Turner might say, "I understand the need for us to be consistent in our work with students, but I'm not sure about this. I'm worried that this is going to take away my creativity and autonomy as a teacher. But if we all work together, perhaps we can improve our students' achievement." The mandate is present, but so is the teacher's voluntariness to carry out the mandate, even though he and others may be voicing objections to it or ignoring it.

As with the other characteristics of collaboration described in this section, voluntariness should be viewed through a lens of cultural diversity. For example, you may interact with parents from a culture in which school and learning is the business of teachers and administrators, not parents. The typical notion of collaboration may be invalid, in part because the parents do not adopt the style because it would never occur to them that this would be appropriate. What are other interactions in which the characteristic of voluntariness could be affected by cultural differences? How might this influence your efforts at collaboration with colleagues? With paraprofessionals? With others?

Collaboration Requires Parity Among Participants Parity is a relationship status in which each person's contribution to an interaction is equally valued, and each person has equal power in decision making; it is fundamental to collaboration. If one or several individuals are perceived by others as having significantly greater decision-making power or more valuable knowledge or information, collaboration cannot occur. To illustrate, think about a principal's participation on a multidisciplinary team. If the principal is considered to have equal, not disproportionately greater, power in the decision-making process, other team members may disagree with the principal's position, and the team's ultimate decision may be one the principal did not support. Without parity, it is likely that some team members will acquiesce to the principal's preferences because of concern about repercussions for disagreeing. Another example can provide further illustration: In an interdisciplinary teaching team, when one content-area (e.g., biology) teacher believes that another (e.g., English) does not have expertise to contribute to the instructional planning, parity is unlikely to develop. Look back at the case at the beginning of this chapter. How could the concept of parity affect each depicted educator's roles and responsibilities?

As with the notion of voluntariness, a discussion of parity must include consideration of diversity. For example, several young female special educators once shared privately that they were concerned about their roles when co-teaching. In their culture, younger people are expected to defer to those who are older. They found that even in their professional environment, their colleagues expected them to take without question all directions and to function more as helpers than partners, and they were very discouraged about changing this, given the strong cultural basis for the situation. In another example, gender may sometimes be a factor in establishing parity, with either a male or a female educator perceiving imbalance in the value attributed to the other's contribution. Think, too, about parity when professionals interact with parents from a culture different than theirs. Who might be perceived as having the power to control the interaction? How might parents communicate based on their perception of whether their contribution is valued?

Keep in mind that individuals may have parity as they work together on a specific collaborative activity even though they do not have parity in other situations. For example, you may have parity in interactions with a paraprofessional to plan a community-based activity, but you may interact directively and with appropriately greater authority and decision-making power when giving instructions to the same paraprofessional about working with students. Similarly, administrators and staff on a curriculum committee may have parity; outside of the committee, though, the relationship among the members may be markedly different.

Collaboration Is Based on Mutual Goals Individuals who collaborate must share at least one goal. Imagine a meeting at which a decision must be reached about the special education and related services a student should receive and the setting in which they should be delivered. In one sense, the mutual goal of designing an appropriate education program seems to be obvious. In reality, however, at least two goals may be under consideration. The parents, social worker, and principal might think that the student should be in a general education setting for most of the day; whereas the special education teacher, general education teacher, and psychologist might believe—because of professional literature they have read and their interactions with the student—that great care needs to be taken before there is any discussion of placement in a general education setting. In this case, a collaborative group will look at the greater goal of designing a program in the best interests of the student and will resolve their differences. In a group without a strong commitment to collaboration, the focus is likely to remain on the apparently disparate goals, and the matter may become contentious.

Professionals do not have to share many or all goals in order to collaborate, just one that is specific and important enough to maintain their shared commitment. They may differ in their opinions about a new student's achievement potential but share the goal of ensuring that the student participate in the remedial reading program. Their differences can be set aside as not being essential to the immediate issue. They may agree that a student with multiple needs coming to the school should spend most of the school day with typical peers but disagree about who should have primary teaching responsibility for the student, how appropriate supports should be put in place, and what arrangement should be made for assessing student progress.

Collaboration Depends on Shared Responsibility for Participation and Decision Making If you collaborate with a colleague, you are assuming the responsibility of actively engaging in the activity and the decision making it involves. We have found it useful to distinguish between responsibility for completing tasks associated with the collaborative activity and responsibility for the decision making involved in that activity. Shared participation in task completion does not imply that the individuals involved must divide tasks equally or participate fully in each task required to achieve their goal. In fact, participation in the activity often involves a convenient division of labor. For instance, as a speech/language therapist, you might collaborate with a kindergarten teacher to plan a series of language lessons for the entire class. You volunteer to outline the concepts that should be addressed and to prepare several activities related to each. The teacher agrees to locate needed materials and to plan student groupings and instructional schedules for the lessons. In this case, you and the teacher are both actively participating in accomplishing the task, even though the division of labor may not be equal.

The second component of responsibility concerns equal participation in the critical decision making involved in the activity. In the example just described, you and the teacher had different responsibilities for the task, but to be collaborative you must participate equally in deciding the appropriateness of, and possible needed adjustments in, the material you prepare; and you are equally responsible for deciding whether the grouping and proposed schedule are workable.

Individuals Who Collaborate Share Resources Each individual engaged in a collaborative activity has resources to contribute that are valuable for reaching the shared goal. The type of resources professionals have depends on their roles and the specific activity. Time and availability to carry out essential tasks may be the critical contribution that one person offers. Knowledge of a specialized technique may be another's resource. Access to other individuals or agencies that could assist in the collaborative activity may be a third person's contribution. If professionals cannot contribute a specific resource, they may be perceived as less committed to the collaborative goal, and they may encounter difficulty establishing parity. If you were collaborating with the professionals introduced in the case at the beginning of this chapter, what resources would you expect them to contribute? What resources would you contribute if you were one of the depicted colleagues?

For a different type of situation in which resources are shared, think about working with parents. For example, sharing resources often occurs when parents and school professionals collaboratively plan home reward programs for students. The parent is likely to have access to rewards to which the student responds (e.g., video games, computer access, special meals, access to a bicycle or car). The special services providers may be able to recommend the number of positive behaviors the student should display, the frequency of rewards, and the plan for systematically phasing out the rewards once success has been achieved. The program would not be possible without the contributions that everyone makes.

You may have found that sharing resources is sometimes the key motivator for individuals to collaborate. In fact, pooling the available—but too often scarce—resources in schools can lead to tremendously satisfying efforts on behalf of students; at the same time, it enhances the sense of ownership among professionals. Unfortunately, the reverse may also occur: A scarcity of resources sometimes causes people to hoard the ones they control. Collaboration becomes unlikely when that happens. Ultimately, when resources are limited, the choice becomes this: Come together through collaboration and make the best of what is available, or fall apart as individuals compete to obtain resources that may even be inconsequential in terms of value. Or, as Benjamin Franklin is reported to have said at the signing of the Declaration of Independence, "We must, indeed, all hang together, or assuredly we shall all hang separately!"

Individuals Who Collaborate Share Accountability for Outcomes Whether the results of collaboration are positive or negative, all the participating individuals are accountable for the outcome. Suppose you and several colleagues plan a parent information meeting. One person arranges for a room, another makes arrangements to provide coffee, and a third reserves a media projector for the presentation. Shortly before the meeting is to begin, you realize that no one has remembered to pick up the media projector. In a collaborative effort, all the professionals share the resulting need to change the program at the last minute or to arrange to have someone dash to retrieve the projector. Similarly, if a school leadership team is meeting to discuss the results of the monthly student progress data collected, but one member has not finished compiling his or her part of the results, the team is accountable for rescheduling the meeting date or for assisting the member aggregating the information.

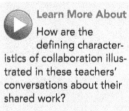

Learn More About How are the defining characteristics of collaboration illustrated in these teachers' conversations about their shared work?

(https://www.youtube.com/watch?v=Vpitq8I3YhA)

The examples just given relate to the outcomes of the shared work. However, in today's schools a second type of discussion of outcomes is equally important—that is, outcomes related to students. One question sometimes asked is whether collaboration makes a difference for students. The studies described in A Basis in Research address that question.

A BASIS IN RESEARCH

Does Collaboration Improve Student Achievement?

Collaboration has intuitive appeal. That is, it seems to make sense that when school professionals work together, student outcomes will improve and teachers will gain increased knowledge and skills. But is there any evidence to support such ideas? A number of studies do indicate that collaboration makes a difference. Here are some examples.

Huberman, Navo, and Parrish (2012) studied the characteristics of four California school districts that had higher than expected academic outcomes for students with disabilities. The districts share several common characteristics, but one found in all of them was an emphasis on collaboration. One particularly interesting finding was that in some of the schools co-teaching was part of these partnerships, but in others collaboration consisted primarily of shared work outside the classroom.

A study commissioned by the Center for School Improvement in cooperation with the Office for Exceptional Children, Ohio Department of Education, examined 30 Ohio school districts that had made significant improvement in students' reading and math proficiency (Silverman, Hazelwood, & Cronin, 2009). The researchers found that these districts emphasized strong leadership that included shared leadership among professionals and principals, a strong collaborative culture and structures to support collaboration (e.g., common planning), co-teaching, and a priority on many types of teaming.

Over the past 15 years, collaboration has emerged as integral to effective schools (e.g., Caron & McLaughlin, 2002). However, additional research is needed to address topics such as the differences in collaborative activities between exemplary and struggling schools, ways to build a collaborative culture when it does not exist, and strategies for sustaining such a culture.

Emergent Characteristics

Several characteristics of collaboration can have multiple functions—they are mentioned both as prerequisites for as well as outcomes of collaboration. We refer to these as emergent characteristics. These characteristics must be present to some discernible degree at the outset of collaborative activity, but they typically grow and flourish from successful experience with collaboration.

Individuals Who Collaborate Value This Interpersonal Style Collaboration is challenging but rewarding. Professionals who anticipate collaborating must believe that the results of their collaboration are likely to be more powerful and significant than the results of their individual efforts or else they are unlikely to persevere. Typically, success in collaboration leads to increased commitment to future collaboration, and so beliefs and attitudes become increasingly positive. Two examples from former students illustrate this point. One student reported, "I used to work in a school where there was no collaboration. I worked very hard, but it was like beating my head against a wall. Now I work in a place where collaboration is the norm. I work even harder than I used to, but now it's fun." Another former student commented, "I used to think that collaborating meant that I had to have answers and get others to agree to my ideas. What I've learned is that by talking less and listening more and being more open to others' thoughts and ideas, we get better results—and that makes collaboration really worth the effort." Individuals who collaborate truly believe that two (or even more) heads are better than one.

Professionals Who Collaborate Trust One Another Even if you firmly believe in the beneficial outcomes of collaboration, you cannot suddenly introduce it, fully developed, into your professional interactions. If you already have worked in a school, you probably recall your experiences as a new employee, a phase in which you learned about your colleagues, the norms of the school setting, and the manner in which to approach the other professionals with whom you worked most closely. And even though you interacted with other professionals during that time, the extent to which you could collaborate was limited. Only after a period of time in which trust and, subsequently, respect are established can school professionals feel relatively secure in fully exploring collaborative relationships. Once begun, however, those relationships may be strengthened until trust of colleagues becomes one of the most important benefits of collaboration. This scenario describes the emergence of trust: At the outset, enough trust must be present for professionals to be willing to begin the activity, but with successful experiences the trust grows and the relationship becomes better able to withstand problems or disagreements.

Conversely, trust is most fragile when a collaborative relationship is relatively new, as may be the case for Mr. Garcia, the SST you met at the beginning of this chapter. If he violates a shared confidence, fails to contribute to planning for instruction, or communicates inaccurately, trust is likely to be damaged, and such damage can take a long time to repair. How long trust takes to develop can depend on many factors, including the overall support and administrative expectations for collaboration in the school; the similarity or dissimilarity among participants in terms of professional preparation, culture, and life experiences; the number and quality of the opportunities for interacting; and the commitment each person makes to the shared work.

A Sense of Community Evolves from Collaboration In collaboration, participants know that their strengths can be maximized, their weaknesses can be minimized, and the result will be better for all. The concept of community is receiving significant attention in contemporary professional literature (e.g., National Association of Secondary School Principals, 2013; City, 2013; Hord, 2009). What is increasingly recognized is that the development of a sense of professional community leads to better outcomes for students and satisfaction and support for educators (Conoley & Conoley, 2010; Katz & Sugden, 2013; Knox & Anfara, 2013). Perhaps you have experienced the sense of community in a faith-based, social, or student group. The willingness to work toward a common goal is accompanied by a decrease in concern about individual differences. This is the goal of the Madison Independent School District, as described at the beginning of this chapter.

Taken together, these emergent characteristics highlight the opportunities you have and the risks you take when you begin to collaborate. You may attempt to establish trust and either succeed or are rebuffed; you may attempt to communicate an attitude supportive of collaboration and find that some but not others share your beliefs. Collaboration certainly is not easily accomplished, nor is it appropriate for every situation. More than anything, the emergent characteristics capture the powerful benefits of accepting the risks of collaboration. When collaborative efforts result in higher levels of trust and respect among colleagues and between professionals and parents/families, and working together results in more positive outcomes for students, the risks seem minor compared to the rewards.

Collaboration in a Societal Context

How has collaboration come to be so important in education that it is the subject of entire books and courses in professional preparation programs? What is fostering the development of so many collaborative structures in schools? Why is so much attention now devoted to the quality of the working relationships among professionals, paraprofessionals, and parents/families? What is occurring for students, including those with disabilities or other special needs, is simply a reflection of the direction of many endeavors in society and their application in education (Fidelman, 2013; Reardon, 2011; Williams & Williams, 2014). By examining the larger context for collaboration, you can better understand its pervasiveness in today's world and its necessity for today's schools.

Societal Trends

Consider the world in which you now live. A valuable starting point is the arena of work: The vast majority of jobs currently available are in service industries in which individuals interact with clients or customers to meet their needs (e.g., sales, customer support, telecommunications). This situation is in sharp contrast to preceding eras in which many workers toiled in isolation on assembly lines. Contemporary life is also characterized by an accelerated flow of information: People are inundated with it, whether through the resources of the Internet, social media, the seemingly endless array of television talk shows, or the stacks of print materials that pile up—often unread— in many homes, offices, and classrooms (e.g., Frenkel, 2014). Mass participation (e.g., Facebook, Instagram, Wikipedia) is also commonplace. With the enormous amounts of information constantly available, few individuals can hope to keep up with even the most crucial events occurring in their communities and their professions much less throughout the world.

One response to the pressures of contemporary society's changing labor needs and its information explosion is an increasing reliance on collaboration (Gobillot, 2011; Goold & Barber, 2014; Harvard Business Review, 2013). For example, business managers, much more so now than in the past, are involving employees in decision making as a strategy for improving organizational effectiveness. Further, employees report that they find their jobs more satisfying if they participate in reaching decisions. A sense of ownership and commitment appears to evolve through participation in such activity, and cutting-edge employers target team approaches that foster shared decision making and clear communication as a major training topic for employees at many levels (e.g., Kuehner-Hebert, 2014). All of these ideas, not coming from education but from business and industry, are directly related to collaboration.

> **Learn More About**
> This video about the power of collaboration suggests its potential for creating new solutions to student problems and enabling students to truly reach their potential.
> (https://www.youtube.com/watch?v=7KMM387HNQk)

Collaboration Across Professions

Business is not the only domain in which collaboration is essential. In fact, collaboration seems to have become a standard for much that is worthwhile in contemporary professional culture. For example, Bennis and Biederman (1997), in their examination of the most significant innovations of the twentieth century—including the personal computer, aviation technology, and feature-length animated films—concluded that none of them would have been possible had it not been for a high degree of collaboration among very talented people. That is, the ability to bring people together to form professional relationships is a fundamental skill that enables contemporary leaders to help people develop commitment and tackle the exceedingly complex problems facing many disciplines, whether business management, industry, education, or computer or biological sciences (e.g., Goman, 2014).

Collaboration has also become increasingly important in the area of human services. For example, it is viewed as a means through which welfare, medical, mental health, and other services can be more effectively provided to children and their families (e.g., Garland & Brookman-Frazee, 2015; Savina, Simon, & Lester, 2014). In health care, collaboration is a means of bringing together medical and healthcare providers to integrate the delivery of services, a means of increasing the community's health, a means of improving public health agency performance, and a means of improving other community health services (e.g., Johannessen & Steihaug, 2014; McComb & Simpson, 2014; Stichler, 2014).

School Collaboration

Beginning with the premise that schools are a reflection of the larger society, the current trend toward collaboration in the United States and around the world makes it quickly apparent why collaboration is such a significant trend in schools. Many examples of this trend are evident, and this section outlines just a few.

Response to Intervention

Perhaps one of the most important types of collaboration emerging in twenty-first-century schools is one that originated in special education legislation but is implemented in general education: response to intervention (RTI). As you may have learned already, RTI is an alternative procedure for identifying students with learning disabilities, a move away from what has been called a "wait to fail" model that required a discrepancy between expected and actual achievement (Bradley, Danielson, & Doolittle, 2007; Nellis, Sickman, Newman, & Harman, 2014). It is also evolving as a data-driven vehicle for proactively responding to many students' learning difficulties. In RTI, students who are falling behind despite being taught through high-quality, research-based instructional approaches are placed in successively intensive interventions (e.g., Tier 2, Tier 3) for specific periods of time (e.g., 16 weeks), most often because of concerns about reading skills, although this procedure is also being applied in some locales when concerns arise about students' math achievement or behavior (e.g., Harlacher & Siler, 2011). Detailed data are gathered to determine whether the interventions being implemented are resulting in accelerated student learning, a process referred to as progress monitoring. If the interventions are effective they are continued, or if determined inappropriate they are discontinued. If, after a series of such increasingly focused interventions, a student is not making enough progress to eventually reach the same level of achievement as peers, a team may decide that a learning disability may exist and determine that the student is eligible for special education services. In a few states, just the series of interventions is a basis for that decision; in many states, additional assessment procedures are also used.

Collaboration characterizes many twenty-first-century professions, including those in business, science, and medicine.

RTI calls for a high degree of collaboration (e.g., Brown-Chidsey & Steege, 2010; Dulaney, 2013). Consider the experience of Ms. Jackson, a third-grade teacher, who is very concerned about her student Cecil's reading skills. As she has reviewed his progress and taught him for the first part of the school year, she has found that he still has tremendous difficulty with many basic phonics skills affecting his ability to master the third-grade curriculum. She asks her school's RTI team to problem solve with her for Cecil. After reviewing Cecil's school records and assessment data, the team agrees that he is significantly behind his peers and is unlikely to make adequate progress without more intensive intervention. The reading specialist, speech/language therapist, assistant principal, and Ms. Jackson decide that Cecil should participate in a daily 30-minute specialized supplemental reading program that focuses on systematic development of phonics skills. After 10 weeks of this intervention, the same team reconvenes and reviews the weekly data on Cecil's progress. Although he has not caught up with his peers, the team decides that the intervention is resulting in significant progress and should be continued.

It is beyond the scope of this book to provide detailed information about the many dimensions of effective RTI procedures. What is important for you to remember is that these procedures are based on collaboration. When a team of professionals come together to analyze student needs and design instruction that will accelerate learning, the results are better ideas, an increase in learning, and less need for the more structured and regulated services of special education.

> **Learn More About**
> This high school meeting is an example of collaboration in action.
> (https://www.youtube.com/watch?v=cveEkYba7CY)

Additional Examples of School-Wide Collaboration

RTI is an important model emphasizing collaboration among school professionals, but there are many others. For example, teachers are being asked to team with each other and with other school professionals, including media specialists, science consultants, literacy coaches, counselors, and speech/language therapists to improve student learning (e.g., D'Agostino, 2013; Canter, Voytecki, Zambone, & Jones, 2011; Nellis et al., 2014; Watson & Bellon-Harn, 2014). In all these efforts, the goal is to provide enhanced instruction to improve student learning.

Middle school approaches are an especially interesting application of teacher–teacher collaboration because they are premised on strong collaboration among teaching teams in core academic areas (J. Noonan, 2014). Teachers in middle schools have regularly scheduled shared planning time so that they can integrate curricula, coordinate assignments and other major activities such as field trips, and discuss issues related to their instructional work. They also share data about their shared students and collectively find strategies to effectively meet their students' special learning needs.

Another type of collaboration emphasized in the school literature concerns school–university partnerships, often under the guise of school reform (e.g., Officer, Grim, Medina, Bringle, & Foreman, 2013). One example of partnership for preprofessional preparation is a residency program (Solomon, 2009), in which university faculty members collaborate in school settings, especially urban settings, with school professionals to recruit, prepare, induct, and mentor new teachers. Another example is blended teacher preparation, in which general and special

"In an increasingly complex world, sometimes old questions require new answers."

education preservice teachers learn together and sometimes receive dual licensure when they complete their professional training (e.g., Fullerton, Ruben, McBride, & Bert, 2011).

Yet another type of school collaboration receiving renewed attention is peer collaboration (e.g., Henry, Castek, O'Byrne, & Zawilinski, 2012). When students work with partners on various instructional tasks, they generally learn more than if they had worked alone. Further, professionals have come to value peer interactions as a means of preparing students for their likely roles in the world of work.

Finally, collaboration has not been ignored by school administrators. Principals are forming school leadership teams and collegial work groups to share decision making on critical school issues (Nappi, 2014). They are also working collaboratively with teachers to nurture their skills as leaders, help them set professional goals for each year, and make judgments about their schools' reform efforts (e.g., Mangin & Stoelinga, 2010). Principals are emphasizing that teachers should work with each other to solve problems about students experiencing difficulty, to establish and assess academic standards, and to create positive working relationships with parents and family members (e.g., Geller, Doykos, Craven, Bess, & Nation, 2014). The school as a collaborative community of learners is now a central theme for effective administrators.

Keep in mind that even these examples represent only a small fraction of the collaborative activities in today's schools. Some additional examples are included in Putting Ideas into Practice.

Special Education Collaboration

Special education collaboration is a subset of school collaboration, but it has such a rich history and has become so much a part of policy and practice that it merits separate attention (Ludlow, 2011). For example, even before the passage of the first federal special education law in 1975, special educators were providing indirect services to students with disabilities

PUTTING IDEAS INTO PRACTICE

The Many Faces of School Collaboration

Throughout this book, you will read about many school applications of collaboration. But there are so many ways professionals collaborate that not all can be adequately addressed between these covers. Here are just a few examples of formal and informal collaborative activities occurring in contemporary schools:

- *Professional learning communities* (PLCs) are a structured approach for professional development. In PLCs, educators come together based on a shared need (e.g., all seventh-grade math teachers learning about the new curriculum; all teachers interested in learning more about co-teaching; all teachers teaching U.S. history and who are expected to incorporate writing and literature into the course). The teachers meet regularly, share readings, and take turns leading the group with the goal of jointly increasing their knowledge and skills.
- *Apprentice teaching programs* are being used in some universities that are partnering with schools to create student teaching and internship experiences that are highly collaborative. In this model, novice educators work in partnership with a veteran teacher so that students receive more intensive instruction than might otherwise occur. The professionals have a rich opportunity to learn from one another.
- *School reform teams* often are formed when school professionals are faced with an urgent challenge to raise student achievement. There may be a leadership team that includes representative teachers, support staff, and parents. There may also be grade-level or department teams that meet regularly to create common assessments, review student data, discuss changes to instruction dictated by the data, and evaluate the effectiveness of the changes made.
- *School–community collaboration* usually has a goal of improving outcomes through a unified effort. Collaboration among school professionals, community members, and agency representatives may focus on preventing dropouts, raising achievement, reducing gang activities, and enlisting parents and families in educational efforts.

Are you aware of other collaborative school programs and practices? To what extent do they include the defining and emergent characteristics as outlined in this chapter?

by working with their general education teachers in a model called consulting teaching (McKenzie, 1972). Likewise, school psychologists have long been urged to multiply their impact by helping teachers, who could then better address the learning and behavior problems of all their students (Tharp & Wetzel, 1969). When P.L. 94–142 became law, collaboration was firmly integrated into special education with the provisions of parent participation and the mandate for the least restrictive environment. With each revision of special education law the place of collaboration has been strengthened. The law has, in essence, made collaboration a required part of special education services. As shown in Figure 1.2, collaboration is either mandated specifically or strongly implied in the entire process of identifying students who receive special services, delivering their instruction, and interacting with parents.

A discussion of special education collaboration would not be complete without mention of early childhood programs, for which collaboration generally is integral (e.g., Fulton & Myers, 2014; Vuorinen, Sandberg, Sheridan, & Williams, 2014). For example, early intervention services are based on the belief that parents or other caregivers are the primary teachers of young children and that professionals can foster their participation through collaboration. Further, early intervention programs are mandated to coordinate services among all providers (e.g., educators, social service agencies, medical professionals), and this mandate exists within a context of collaboration. Although you will learn more about collaboration in early childhood special education in Chapter 12, for now you should

FIGURE 1.2 Direct and indirect expectations of collaboration in the Individuals with Disabilities Education Act (IDEA).

- *IEP teams.* Each student's educational program must be designed by an IEP team that generally includes special education and general education professionals as well as parents. This team also includes speech/language therapists, occupational and physical therapists, administrators, and any other needed personnel.
- *Least restrictive environment.* The law requires justification for any placement not for general education. This presumption strongly suggests that general education teachers, special educators, related services personnel, administrators, and others should work together on behalf of students.
- *Highly qualified teacher requirement.* Special educators who teach core academic content in a separate setting (e.g., math, social studies, science, English) to students not taking alternate assessments must be highly qualified in those areas. However, if a highly qualified general education teacher and a special educator share teaching responsibilities, in most states the special educator does not have to be highly qualified in the content area. That is, the special educator's highly qualified status in these situations relates to the learning process, whereas the general educator's relates to the core academic content. This requirement of the law can foster collaborative service delivery.
- *Assessment process.* Parents must give permission for their children to be assessed, and they must also have a voice in the decision making that occurs as a result of assessment. Even more communication responsibility occurs when students are reevaluated. Because a decision may be made in some cases to omit standardized testing, parent involvement in decision making is even more critical (although if parent input cannot be obtained, the process continues).
- *Transition.* Transition relies on strong collaboration among educators as well as students and parents. Further, transition plans often require the involvement of professionals from other agencies, and so interprofessional collaboration may be required.
- *Discipline and behavior support plans.* For any student with behavior problems, a functional assessment and behavior support plan is required. The process of gathering data, identifying the problem, designing alternative interventions, implementing them, and evaluating the outcomes typically will include participation by several professionals, paraprofessionals, and parents/family members.
- *Paraprofessionals.* Paraprofessionals, teaching assistants, and other individuals in similar roles should receive appropriate training for their jobs and supervision of their work. Although not all interactions with paraprofessionals are collaborative, the specific expectation for teacher–paraprofessional interactions can foster collaboration.
- *Mediation and dispute resolution.* Unless declined by parents, states must make no-cost mediation available to parents as a strategy for resolving disagreements concerning their children with special needs. Further, prior to a due process hearing, the district must convene the IEP team members and parents in an attempt to informally resolve the dispute. The implication is that a strong bias exists for all parties, working together on behalf of students, to design the most appropriate education rather than escalating conflicts.

> **Learn More About**
> Collaboration in special education is essential but can be complex, especially when many professionals are involved, a point clearly illustrated in this brief interview.

realize that many professionals point to this area when seeking exemplary practices in school collaboration.

Another dimension of collaboration for special educators concerns the partnerships formed among the professionals who provide special education and related services. For example, special educators often work closely with speech/language therapists to create effective language interventions that can be implemented across the special education and general education settings. Likewise, they may collaborate with an assistive technology specialist to help a student with a communication disability become proficient using a new communication device. They may also interact on a regular basis with the school nurse, a counselor, and a consultant who advises the teacher on working with students with visual impairments. That is, collaboration within the field of special education is as crucial as collaboration between special educators and those outside the field.

The Challenges of Collaboration

Despite collaboration's clear importance and increasing emphasis in education, a number of challenges may arise when school professionals attempt to establish collaborative relationships. These issues pertain to overall school culture, professional socialization, power and status among participants in a relationship, and pragmatic issues. You can explore other issues related to collaboration and possible solutions for addressing them by visiting web sites such as those described in Putting Ideas into Practice.

School Culture

A strong collaborative culture has been associated with improved student outcomes (e.g., Walsh, 2012; Huberman et al., 2012). That might lead you to conclude that school leaders consistently work to create and sustain such a culture; unfortunately, that is not always the case. In too many schools, collaboration is serendipitous, informal, and sporadic rather than deliberately fostered.

One example of a cultural challenge to collaboration concerns professional participation and integration. In some schools, decisions about curricula adoption, teacher and student schedules, and professional development priorities may be made with input from few or only certain staff groups. When the perspectives of ESL teachers, special educators, and related arts teachers are not considered, not only is participation incomplete, but students' education may be negatively affected. The math curriculum adopted may have serious weaknesses in terms of techniques for ensuring that students with disabilities or those learning English can access it. Schedules may preclude art, music, drama, or physical education teachers from having opportunities to meet with the professional who could help them better understand how to reach their students with special needs. Collaboration has value because the diversity of participants leads to better decisions; when diversity is limited poor decisions result, which is detrimental and frustrating to students and professionals.

A second example of a challenge related to school culture concerns the expectations that are set and structures put in place. In some schools, professionals volunteer to work together, and if a teacher wishes to decline it is permitted. This means that some teachers work closely to educate students with extraordinary needs while others simply do not. The impact can be that the school's culture has two distinct parts; one focusing on doing whatever it takes to maximize student potential and the other expecting students to meet certain baseline requirements prior to instruction. An example of school structure that can interfere with a collaborative culture is the design of programs and services. In some schools, special education services may be delivered, at least in part, within the general education setting, while ESL, speech/language, and other services are provided only in separate settings. Such an arrangement is based on decisions about service options, not necessarily on student needs. Another structure may concern scheduled collaboration time

PUTTING IDEAS INTO PRACTICE
Internet Resources for Collaboration

The Internet is a tremendous source of information about almost any topic. Although only a few sites specifically address the professional collaboration that occurs among school staff members, the following sites include information on collaboration and pertinent related topics.

The Beach Center
www.beachcenter.org

The goal of the Beach Center on Disability at the University of Kansas is working with all stakeholders to enhance the quality of life for individuals with disabilities and their families. This family-focused site contains many articles of interest and links to other sites emphasizing family collaboration.

Pinterest
www.pinterest.com

As you probably already know, Pinterest is a web site on which individuals collect a wide array of favorite information on topics of interest. If you type the term *teacher collaboration* into its search bar, you will find many collaboration hints and tips as well as more detailed information on common collaborative school practices (e.g., teaming, co-teaching, mentoring).

All Things PLC
www.allthingsplc.info

At All Things PLC, you can learn about this increasingly common form of school collaboration, blog with others about PLC, and look at data related to the impact of PLC on student achievement and other outcomes. Recent articles on the site addressed the use of technology and the implementation of behavior interventions.

Teach Thought
http://www.teachthought.com/

The goal of TeachThought is to improve learning; it includes schools but also extends to communities. Typing in the term *collaboration* on its search bar will take you to a set of articles about collaboration among teachers, student collaboration, and the positive impact of collaboration on learning.

Middle Web
www.middleweb.com

As you might guess, Middle Web is a web site devoted to topics of interest to middle school educators. However, because collaboration is so integral to middle school models, you will find many helpful resources on this site. Some recent discussions included collaborating about grades and considerations related to working on a team instead of as an individual.

One other suggestion: As you seek information related to collaboration and related topics, don't forget to check your own state department of education's web site. Many have practical information that is directly related to state policies as well as links to other valuable local and national sites.

(Dever & Lash, 2013): Some professionals report that each time the grade level, team, or department meets the agenda is already set (e.g., discussion of student data, administrative announcements, test preparation). Professionals do not have the opportunity to determine key decisions that should be addressed, and they often find these so-called collaborative meetings are anything but collaborative.

The list of school culture components that may positively or negatively affect collaboration is lengthy, and you can easily add to the examples just given. In fact, several of the items in the sections that follow may also influence a school's collaborative culture. As you read about them, think about the influence they could have on the sense of community and the "we're all in this together" mindset that characterizes collaborative schools.

Professional Socialization

Another factor that may be a challenge to collaboration is professional socialization. First, in some teacher and other professional preparation programs, you may discover that as you are successfully completing your student teaching, practicum, or internship experiences your supervisor must leave you alone to work with students. In other words, your professional training itself may encourage a belief that working in isolation is the role of the professional. Even if you entered the teaching profession through an alternative route to licensure or in a program that encourages collaboration during student teaching or internships, you might have found that your proficiency was directly or indirectly judged based on how well you handle instruction, student matters, and planning on your own...but not on your work with others. When we work with professionals in the field, we often ask general educators to raise their hands if they have had a course on working with other adults in schools; at most, only a handful of them respond positively. It should not be surprising that an orientation toward working alone, especially in the classroom, is still fairly common among teachers.

Second, this socialization of isolation may continue as you enter your profession and gain experience. Even for some teachers who participated in collaborative preparation programs, school cultures of independence or self-reliance are so strong that what evolves is a belief that you should handle your professional responsibilities and problems yourself. If you seek help, it is often only after you have decided that whatever is occurring is no longer your problem; your goal becomes seeking another to take ownership of it.

This discussion of school culture and professional socialization may leave the impression that collaboration is unlikely in school settings. That certainly is not the case, as was illustrated by Ms. Williams, introduced at the beginning of this chapter. In fact, attention to collaboration has gained significant momentum over the past several years (e.g., Taylor, Hallam, Charlton, & Wall, 2014). We mention such challenges only to raise your awareness of the difficulties in collaborating and to stress that, even if you have learned about the importance of collaboration and embrace its value, you may work with colleagues who have not and who may resist participating in collaborative work. We want to also convey—realistically—some of the resulting challenges that you will undoubtedly experience as you attempt to collaborate. These challenges are not unique to your specific school setting or professional role; they result from many factors that are part of all school professionals' experiences. Ultimately, these dilemmas provide the rationale for exploring the skills described later in this text because it is those skills that can empower school professionals to complement their other professional skills with collaborative ones.

Keep in mind that if you are in a school setting where isolation is more common than collaboration, possibilities for forming positive working relationships still exist. You might find one colleague with whom you can forge a partnership. It may be that teachers in your field from other schools in your district are eager to collaborate. A third way to seek collaboration opportunities is through the use of technology. E-Partnerships offers a few suggestions for using the Internet to reach out to, and learn from, colleagues.

Collaboration is based on parity, and so when there is a power imbalance between colleagues, collaboration is undermined.

Power in the Relationship

Whenever there are interactions among people, the topic of power should be mentioned because the entire character of interactions is based in large part on each participant's power or perceived power (e.g., Bangou & Austin, 2011; Raven, 2008; Ylimaki & Brunner, 2011). For example, Robin is a fourth-grade teacher who has worked in her school district for many years. She is well respected and has a specialist's degree in reading. When she takes the role of reading coach, her colleagues are happy to follow her advice because she has expert power; that is, she is viewed by others as knowing more than they do on the topic of reading instruction. She may also have what is called referent power; that is, the likelihood that others will follow her suggestions because they admire her and value her input. Another type of power generally held by principals or other supervisors is called legitimate power; that is, educators follow the directions of administrators because those leaders have the right to require compliance. Other types of power include reward power (the perception that the other person controls valuable resources), coercive power (the perception that the other person may punish an individual for ignoring direction), and informational power (the perception that the other person's knowledge of the details of an explained change demonstrates a reason to implement it).

E-PARTNERSHIPS
Collaborating on the Internet

The array of e-options for collaboration seems to grow daily. Although it sometimes takes a bit of work to find the best tools for any particular collaboration goal, the result is usually worth the effort. In today's schools you can collaborate with colleagues across town, across your state, across the country, and around the world to address concerns about students, find new teaching ideas, and ask questions about effectively working with students with special needs. Here are a few examples of options you may wish to explore:

Teacher Lingo
(http://teacherlingo.com/blogs/default.aspx)

The Teacher Lingo web site is dedicated to providing teachers with a platform for collaboration. The web page provided opens to the teacher blogs. A wide variety of topics are under discussion at any point in time and may include the following: assistive technology, instructional dilemmas and possible solutions, teaching ideas, responses to conflict at school, and general information about working in schools, including not only working with students but also working with other professionals and parents. You can access blogs about particular student groups (e.g., English language learners), grade levels, or areas of specialty (e.g., technology, world languages).

Tumblr (https://www.tumblr.com)

Tumblr is another blog site that is highly popular. With a free account, you can access many blogs about working with students with special needs and follow others' comments as well as make your own contributions. The range of topics is as diverse as those posting, everything from teaching tips to ideas for addressing behavior problems and concerns about working with colleagues.

CEC and Other Professional Association Communities and Discussion Groups
(www.cec.sped.org)

Have you joined a professional association? If so, most have communities of members with ongoing discussion on a wide range of topics and participants ready to assist colleagues with their questions and concerns. For example, topics being discussed recently on one of many communities offered by the Council for Exceptional Children (CEC) included student behavior assessments, accommodations for students with disabilities in a music class, and distinctions between students learning language and those with language-related disabilities. CEC also has a blog dedicated to early career educators written by first-year teachers.

These suggestions for making e-connections are just a beginning. You may already have favorite social media sites that include professional sharing, and your school district may make such options available. There is no need for any twenty-first-century teacher to believe that he or she is isolated without access to the support and inspiration of others.

Think about the implications of power for collaboration. For example, if you are a preservice teacher, what will be your power base for collaboration as you begin your career? You may find that you have to work diligently to cultivate informational and reward power. If you are an experienced educator, you may already have referent power as well as expert power, and you may need to be aware that you are somewhat intimidating to novice educators because of your power. Consider other interactions in which power may be unbalanced: For example, an early career special educator co-teaching in an advanced high school class may perceive that the general educator holds nearly all the power. When educators interact with parents, especially those who live in poverty or who have recently come to the United States from another country, they should understand that they may be perceived as holding power. A similar situation might exist in working with paraprofessionals.

What is important to remember is that collaboration is based on parity; that is, a balance of power based on the valued contributions made by each participant. As perceived differences in power increase, the likelihood for true collaboration decreases. Further, if an expectation for collaboration exists and there is not a balance in power, stress—the topic of Putting Ideas into Practice—is likely to increase.

Pragmatic Issues

When we described the defining characteristics of collaboration, we noted that resource sharing is essential and mentioned items such as time, space, and materials. Collaboration

PUTTING IDEAS INTO PRACTICE

Managing Stress

Collaboration not only offers support to educators but may also lead to stress. Here are sources of stress related to collaboration and ideas for how to deal with the inevitable stress of being a professional educator in a collaborative school.

Sources of Stress

- *Role responsibilities.* The evolving nature of the educators' jobs, including the increased expectation of working with many colleagues and managing student learning across settings, is a significant source of stress.
- *Assignment to collaborative tasks.* Teachers who are told they will co-teach, educators assigned to RTI teams, and professionals directed to contribute to professional development may find such assignments stressful.
- *Work conditions.* When educators must attend frequent meetings, participate in professional development activities, serve on committees, and still find time for their own planning, stress is likely to be high.
- *Support.* Educators who perceive that their administrators do not support their work experience a high degree of stress.
- *Collegiality.* In addition to administrative support, teachers need support from colleagues. If they believe their contributions are not valued stress is likely to occur.
- *Cultural differences.* When professionals interacting with each other and with parents are from different cultures, stress may increase as special care is needed to avoid misunderstandings and miscommunication.

Dealing with Stress

- *Set realistic and flexible goals.* Some educators create a set of expectations that are so difficult to achieve that failure is inevitable, and guilt—and stress—may follow. For example, a dedicated special educator recently said, "I know what co-teaching should be, and we are nowhere near implanting it the way it should be. And so I come to school every single day feeling like a failure." A more constructive approach would be to set small goals related to co-teaching and feel positive about achieving them.
- *Focus on student learning.* Teachers can directly affect student learning. Stress can be reduced when educators keep track of, and can point to, student gains in learning and appropriate behavior that they have directly influenced.
- *Establish priorities.* When there are so many tasks to complete that the list seems endless, it is very easy to tackle them from a crisis perspective; that is, giving attention to whichever item is most pressing or obvious. Instead, step back and set priorities. If you encounter difficulty in setting priorities, a more experienced educator or your principal may be able to assist you.
- *Take care of yourself.* Working nonstop sounds admirable, but it is not a healthy habit and can lead to burnout. Some educators try to keep up with their many job responsibilities by seeing students during their lunch period and working before and after school. Each night they may take home a large tote filled with work, and try to work for a couple of hours after their own children go to bed. Educators should follow the same general advice for stress reduction that could be offered to any busy professional:
  1. Take breaks (and teachers have precious few of those, lunch being one).
  2. Develop healthy eating habits.
  3. Exercise regularly.
  4. Make sure to keep a boundary between your work life and your personal life.
- *Celebrate your accomplishments and your profession.* Don't lose sight of all you are accomplishing. If you have led a committee that provided professional development to teachers, that is a reason to celebrate. If your students have made significant growth—even if it was not reflected in scores on high-stakes tests—that is a reason to be proud.
- *Access outside support.* Elsewhere in this chapter is information about accessing social media and other teacher collaboration sites. Asking your questions of others, participating in discussions, and offering insights as you learn can be great ways to reduce stress.

in schools often is constrained when these items and other logistics are not adequately considered. For example, some professionals have regularly scheduled time to collaborate, whether as a school team or co-teachers, but other educators can find only a few moments to touch base before or after school or during a hurried lunch (e.g., Carter, Prater, Jackson, & Marchant, 2009; Murawski, 2012). Similarly, some school administrators ensure that team members can attend meetings by providing coverage for their classes; others schedule all such meetings after school. Some special education co-teachers spend a significant amount of time or the entire class period with their teaching partner, but in other cases special educators or specialists are expected to provide services in two or even more classes during a single instructional period.

You will find that a number of these pragmatic issues are discussed in more detail in later chapters (e.g., time for collaborative planning is included in Chapter 7 on co-teaching). We mention the topic here just to acknowledge that logistics and other details of arranging for high-quality collaboration sometimes comprise the greatest obstacle facing those who collaborate.

This discussion of the challenges that school structure, professional socialization, power, and pragmatic issues present for collaboration could have a somewhat sobering effect on your enthusiasm for it. In part, we hope this is so. Collaboration can be a powerful vehicle for accomplishing professionals' goals of educating students, but it can also be overused and misused. Collaborative efforts should be implemented only with a deep understanding of its complexities and difficulties, because such understanding will lead to careful consideration of the extent to which these efforts are feasible and recommended.

APPLY YOUR KNOWLEDGE 1.3

A Framework for Learning About Collaboration

The importance of collaboration in society and schools, and recognition of the challenges of collaboration, form a rationale for studying it and for understanding that it is a technical field of study. That is, the fact that you interact well with others does not mean that you understand all the dimensions of collaboration. The complexity and subtlety of collaboration (e.g., Cook & Friend, 2010) suggest that in order to learn to form effective partnerships with others, you should strive for as complete an understanding of it as possible. To accomplish this purpose, we offer a framework in Figure 1.3 for learning about collaboration; it presents the components of collaboration and their relationships to one another:

- Personal commitment
- Communication skills
- Interaction processes
- Programs or services
- Context

This framework shapes the material presented in this textbook as well as its organization, and you will find that each chapter opens with a graphic to remind you which part of the framework is addressed in that chapter.

FIGURE 1.3 **Components of collaboration.**

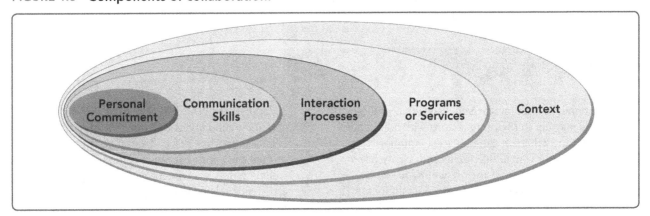

> **Learn More About**
> How do these components of successful collaboration align with the key concepts presented through this chapter?

The first component of the study of collaboration concerns your *personal commitment* to collaboration as a tool for carrying out the responsibilities of your job, including your beliefs about the benefits of working closely with colleagues and parents/families and the added value of learning from others' perspectives. Although it is difficult to offer specific skill training related to this commitment and no chapter is devoted solely to this component of collaboration, you will find that throughout this textbook you are asked to reflect on the importance of, and merit in, collaborating with others. For example, the professionals introduced at the beginning of this chapter demonstrated through their actions that they are committed to their collaborative efforts.

The second component of collaboration is *communication skills*, the basic building blocks of collaborative interactions. Although most educators have relatively strong communication skills in order to be in their professions, the skills needed for collaboration are somewhat more technical and are best learned with focused practice. In addition, most educators need to consider their communication skills in the context of working with colleagues and parents from diverse cultures (e.g., Dibble & Gibson, 2013). For this reason, Chapters 2, 3, and 4 outline those skills, provide many examples of their uses (and misuses), and offer opportunities to practice them. The assumption is that you will use these skills to implement services you learn about in other chapters.

The third component of collaboration includes *interaction processes*—that is, the steps that take an interaction from beginning to end. The most common interaction process is problem solving. Because many educators' collaborative activities are actually specialized forms of problem solving, that topic is addressed in Chapter 5 and referred to later in the chapters on teaming and indirect services. Other processes include responding to conflict and resistance—topics addressed in Chapter 9. For all interaction processes, strong communication skills are essential.

The fourth component of collaboration is the set of *programs or services* in which collaborative activities occur. In this textbook, the services emphasized include teams (Chapter 6), co-teaching (Chapter 7), and consultation and related programs such as mentoring and coaching (Chapter 8). It is within these services that interaction processes to design and deliver strong educational programs and services occur.

The final component of collaboration is *context*, which refers to the overall environment in which collaboration occurs. Because people so often are critical in determining the climate for collaboration, special attention is given in this book to paraprofessionals, parents, and others (e.g., related services personnel, representatives of community agencies) in Chapters 10, 11, and 12. Pragmatic issues, such as time for collaboration (Chapter 7), and issues related to collaboration, such as ethics (Chapter 12), complete this part of the framework.

As with any textbook, some topics cannot be adequately addressed. For example, although mention already has been made of student–student collaboration and of such collaboration being an important part of creating schools supportive of all students and improving outcomes, the emphasis here is on adult–adult interactions; and so student partnerships are briefly mentioned but are not prioritized. Likewise, even though professionals often collaborate around designing and implementing academic and behavior interventions for students, those topics merit separate attention; we believe that attempting to address collaboration as well as instructional and behavioral strategies in one textbook does a disservice to both topics.

SUMMARY

- Collaboration is an interpersonal style that professionals may use in their interactions with colleagues, parents, and others. It can only exist voluntarily in situations in which individuals with parity have identified a mutual goal and are willing to share responsibility for key decisions, accountability for outcomes, and resources. Several characteristics of collaboration both contribute to its development and are potentially its outcomes: attitudes and beliefs supportive of a collaborative approach, mutual trust, and a sense of community.
- Collaboration is a reflection of contemporary societal trends related to changes in business and other professions, and the continued rapid increase in

FOUNDATIONS AND PERSPECTIVES 23

- information flow and exchange, especially through electronic channels.
- Collaboration in schools is mandated or implied in legislation and related reform efforts, including various forms of teaming (e.g., response to intervention programs) and practices that provide curriculum access to all learners. Collaboration is particularly central to special education services, from early childhood partnerships with parents, to the teams that makes decisions about student services, to the collegial efforts of professionals delivering students' education.
- Individuals who collaborate may find that challenges occur related to the structural and professional isolation of schools, professional socialization, power in relationships, stress related to managing interactions with others, and practical matters concerning resources such as time.
- Studying collaboration includes understanding your personal commitment, learning communication skills and interaction processes, creating programs and services in which collaborative approaches can be used, and recognizing context factors that foster or constrain collaboration.

BACK TO THE CASE

1. Select one of the professionals whose typical days were profiled in this chapter's opening case. Use this professional's profile as the basis for analyzing the extent to which the defining characteristics of collaboration are present or could be established.
    - Which characteristics can most easily be met?
    - Which may pose significant barriers to developing effective collaborative relationships?
    - If you were the professional profiled, what are two challenges to collaboration that you might face? What could you do to address these challenges?

2. Now think about the educators profiled in the opening case study in terms of power. What types of power does each of these educators have? What could be the impact of their power (or lack thereof) on their interactions with colleagues?
3. Consider the framework for collaboration presented in this chapter. Which elements of it can you identify as being present for the professionals in the cases? What evidence can you provide to support your opinion?

COLLABORATIVE ACTIVITIES

1. Discuss the issue of parity with your classmates. To what extent do they perceive that special educators, general educators, bilingual or ESL educators, administrators, paraprofessionals, parents, and related services providers have equal status in schools? Should they? In what situations? If parity does not appropriately exist, how could issues related to it be addressed?
2. Suppose you are a new teacher in a school in which collaboration occurs informally among some teachers but is not a highly valued part of the school's culture. Further, imagine that the school has received a mandate to move strongly toward inclusive practices. What do you believe your role is in accomplishing the dual goals of collaboration and inclusive practices? How might you use Figure 1.3 to analyze the steps that should be taken and to discuss them with your administrator?
3. If you have worked in a setting in which collaboration was valued and encouraged, write a summary of your experience. Use this as the basis for a discussion with others to generate specific examples of the characteristics of school collaboration.
4. What is your responsibility if collaboration is needed but is not occurring? For example, what if you are on a grade-level or department team, and some members spend meeting time grading papers, or they seldom complete the tasks they agreed to do? What if you are a co-teacher, and your partner does not want to plan together or does not want to share classroom instruction?
5. Peruse recent issues of popular news magazines. What examples of societal collaboration are addressed? What universal themes related to the advantages and disadvantages of collaboration can you identify from these materials? How might current trends in collaboration in business, health services, social services, and other disciplines affect school collaboration in the future?

 CHECK YOUR UNDERSTANDING

Click here to gauge your understanding
of this chapter's essential concepts.

2 Interpersonal Communication

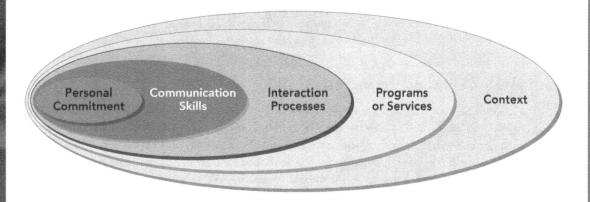

CONNECTIONS

The foundational understandings of collaboration presented in Chapter 1 provide a basis for beginning an exploration of the specific communication skills that contribute to its effectiveness and is the focus for this chapter as well as the two that follow. In this chapter, you will learn about the nature of interpersonal communication and how it occurs, topics that appear to have a commonsense origin but that have technical meaning for collaboration and profoundly affect its outcomes. You will also explore how perspective influences communication, consider factors that affect listening, examine the impact of nonverbal communication, and outline principles to guide your interpersonal communication success. The information in this set of three chapters should be applied in the collaborative endeavors that are described in later chapters, including teaming, co-teaching, and consultation.

LEARNING OUTCOMES

After reading this chapter you will be able to:

1. Apply your understanding of differing views of communication and their common elements to communication situations you have encountered or will encounter as an education professional.
2. Define the term *interpersonal communication* and its critical elements, describing the process by which meaning is communicated through it and illustrating your understanding with examples from your professional or related experiences.
3. Analyze interpersonal competence, including perspective and perception and the influence of culture on them, and outline strategies for attaining it.
4. Explain how the perceptual process creates misunderstandings, and generate ways to improve your perceptual accuracy.

A CASE FOR COLLABORATION

A Matter of Misunderstanding

Kim and Lena, two of the grade-level team leaders in Kirby Middle School, have worked together for a year and have come to view themselves as friends and good teammates. As Lena entered the cafeteria to get coffee before school, she greeted Kim enthusiastically and exclaimed, "How about Sparks last night? He's something else with those dunks. I'm so stoked for the next game!" She pretended to shoot a basketball to punctuate her comments as she almost squealed, "We're going to Bloomington!" Lena was talking excitedly about their alma mater's basketball game the night before. Without waiting for a reply, she plunged into more details, describing several of the plays as well as the team's certain chances for sweeping the conference and the championship. Lena soon realized that Kim was looking at her with a seemingly disinterested, possibly irritated, expression. She couldn't determine whether Kim was unhappy, angry at her, or, for that matter, whether Kim's response had anything to do with her at all. Lena's sports commentary trailed off and she asked Kim what was wrong. Kim flatly said, "Nothing." She looked away and shook her head, got up from her chair, took her coffee, and as she left the cafeteria with what Lena now determined to be a disapproving look, Kim remarked, "Not everyone had the luxury of watching the game. Some of us had to work." Lena called after her saying she was sorry Kim had missed the game and suggested they could make up for it with a girls' night out on Friday. As Kim was leaving, Lena thought, "It's too bad that she had work to do, but I don't know why that has anything to do with me."

Introduction

Does the preceding story sound familiar? How you communicate is critical to both your personal and professional success. In this chapter, we focus on how communication influences your professional interactions and their effectiveness. Your knowledge of the nuances of communication and your communication skills are essential in the performance of your instructional, administrative, planning, or other educational responsibilities, as well as in your collaboration with colleagues and parents. Because of this, many professional preparation programs and school-based performance reviews include an evaluation of communication skills, and increasingly, certification and licensure in education and related professions require similar evidence of strong communication abilities.

But this emphasis on communication also creates a problem: Many professionals argue that they understand communication and do not need to review information such as that presented in this chapter. However, knowing about communication is vastly different from grasping its nuances and deliberately using it as a tool for fostering effective interactions with others. It is the more specialized and technical view of communication skills that is the focus of the information that follows.

Understanding Communication

To become adept at professional interpersonal communication, you must first become familiar with the general and universal aspects involved in all human communication, which shares a set of characteristics and elements, a set of root principles. By mastering these features, you will become a student of interpersonal communication practices and skills, applying them to support your collaborative endeavors.

Human communication is considered a rich and complex field of study, explored by scholars and theorists who describe it in diverse ways. That diversity represents the many disciplines from which this relatively new area of inquiry has evolved—including psychology, sociology, social psychology, and philosophy. Consequently, the definitions of communication found in scholarly sources vary tremendously: A recently conducted extensive review identified 15 different conceptual components associated with over 126 different definitions (Lustig & Koester, 2013). Some scholars view communication as a process of transmitting information from one person to another or to groups. Others are more concerned with the processes by which people express meaning and exchange understandings through communication. To avoid these sometimes confusing alternatives, for this text the following definition is utilized:

> Communication is the management of messages with the objective of creating meaning.

Using such a definition, it can be clarified that communication occurs within and across various contexts, cultures, channels, and media and includes both verbal and nonverbal messages as well as technology-mediated messages (Beebe & Masterson, 2015; Floyd, 2014). In addition, the definition provides the basis for examining traditional and contemporary views of communication as they exist in today's schools.

> **Learn More About**
> What does this brief video clip about teachers collaborating in the classroom suggest to you about the importance of interpersonal communication for establishing parity?

Views of Communication

Advances in educational thinking and instructional practice encourage teachers to interact collaboratively with learners and extend learner interactions with others, both locally and globally (Council for Chief State School Officers, 2011; Ladd et al., 2014). What view of communication do such models encourage? On the other hand, in too many settings the primary instructional mode continues to rely on teacher presentation. In fact, despite extensive conversations in the profession about student engagement and participation (e.g., Cooper, 2014), the majority of communication in schools involves the presentation of information by one person to others. This is often the case when leaders provide information school-wide as well as when teachers provide instruction. What perspective of communication does this suggest? As you reflect on the following three views of communication, think about how they are manifested in schools, how common each is, and how you have experienced each of them. Figure 2.1 provides an overview of these perspectives.

Linear View In the linear view or model, communication is seen as a one-way "information transfer" event in which a sender encodes, or constructs, a message and delivers it to a relatively passive receiver who decodes or interprets it. A message is not limited to words; it is the totality of what is communicated—the words, noises, facial expressions, and stance of the communicator. Verbal messages are composed of printed or spoken words; nonverbal messages are conveyed by behaviors other than words (e.g., facial expressions, vocal noises, and gestures). Everything a communicator says or does, as well as the richness of the expression, is potentially part of the message. The communication occurs within an environment—that is, the surroundings or a physical location—but the environment is influenced by personal experiences. Naturally, that relationship goes both ways because the environment can also affect interpretation. Varying kinds of noise can interfere with the accurate transmission of a message. Noise may be physical (e.g., an alarm or siren), psychological (e.g., thoughts, biases), semantic (e.g., language differences), or physiological (biological influences). The nature of the message, the channel selected, the noise, and the environment may all influence the success of the communication. The terms used to label features in this communication view apply to the other views as well, and they are highlighted in Putting Ideas into Practice.

The linear model is quite common among professionals in school settings; it is the unilateral communication that is used to transmit information through such differing channels as memos, podcasts, online modules, web postings, and announcements over

FIGURE 2.1 **Views of communication.**

Understanding of the communication process have advanced over the years. In each of the three views outlined here, the roles of the individuals involved and the understanding of the message being communicated vary according to the interactivity available to both the sender and the receiver.

Linear View. Communication is a one-way process in which a sender constructs and transmits a message to a relatively passive receiver who decodes it. It is generally not face-to-face, often technology mediated, and asynchronous. Feedback, if any, is delayed. The sender's message is to be understood as delivered.

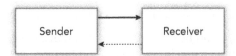

Interactional View. In this two-way process, a sender and a receiver alternately exchange information. The sender transmits a message; the receiver decodes it and responds with feedback. If feedback indicates misunderstanding, the sender is likely to revise the message. Communication is complete when the receiver's feedback indicates understanding of the message.

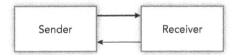

Transactional View. As a communicator sends a message, he or she simultaneously receives information from the message itself and from the person with whom he or she is communicating. The communicators are interdependent in that they co-construct shared meanings by continuously exchanging messages.

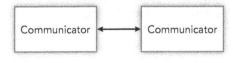

the school's public address system. When this type of communication occurs, it is often technology mediated and usually does not occur in person. Feedback is not expected, and if it does occur, it is delayed. The sender's initial message contains the meaning of the communication, and others are expected to understand it as it was transmitted. Of course, those who receive the message may understand the message in a manner not intended by the sender. An illustration of such misunderstood communication occurred in Lena's experience in the opening case, which is continued here.

> Later that day as Lena was leaving the lunchroom, another team leader, Jill, asked rather pointedly where she had been the afternoon before. Lena was surprised at her directness, but explained she had left right after school to shop for drinks and snacks because she had invited college friends over to watch the playoff game that evening. Jill was again direct as she told Lena that their team leader meeting had lasted until 7:30 p.m. because there was no one there to represent Lena's area, and the other team leaders had to research the databases to gather the information she was to have collected earlier. Lena looked shocked and asked, "What team meeting?" Jill was hurrying to get to her class but quickly told Lena it was the meeting described in the e-mail she had received two days earlier.
>
> Lena was confused and went directly to check her e-mail after she finished lunch. She had been happy to get the principal's message early the other morning. It described the ways the principal wanted some data to be managed and stated, "Team leaders may defer their meeting until after school is out to aggregate the data sets." Lena had been relieved that the meeting was

PUTTING IDEAS INTO PRACTICE

Coming to Terms with Communication Terms

Communicator: one who simultaneously performs the *sender* functions (formulates and sends messages) and the *receiver* functions (perceives and comprehends messages) in communication.

Encoding: the process of putting thoughts and feelings into verbal and/or nonverbal messages.

Decoding: the reverse of encoding; involves developing a thought or meaning based on hearing and/or seeing messages, whether verbal and/or nonverbal.

Message: spoken, written, or unspoken information sent from one communicator to another.

Feedback: a verbal or nonverbal response to a message that provides information about how the message was received. Feedback may be internal (how we assess our own communication) or external (feedback from others).

Channel: vehicle or pathway through which a message is sent (e.g., face-to-face, podcast, paper memo).

Noise: anything that interferes with the accurate transmission or reception of a message. It may be physical (e.g., siren, pop-up ad), physiological (e.g., biological, hearing loss), psychological (e.g., biases, emotions), or semantic (e.g., language, jargon).

Environment: physical location, surroundings, or context that can affect how individuals understand others' behaviors.

---

deferred until next week after the school year ended. Now she realized, based on reactions from Kim and Jill, that there was more than one definition of "after school is out" operating. Apparently, it had meant "after school is out" on the day of the regularly scheduled team leader meeting.

This illustrates a misunderstanding caused by linear, or unilateral, communication. Without feedback or opportunities to seek clarification of the message, Lena gave it her own, albeit incorrect, meaning.

Precisely because of the lack of feedback, linear view communication of all kinds runs the risk of being misunderstood. Ensuring accurate understanding is difficult in the absence of reactions or responses indicating whether the receivers understand the message. Straightforward reports of facts, events, or previously debated policy are the types of information that have the least potential for troubling misunderstanding, for example, in e-mail communication.

Interactional View The interactional view extends the linear model to recognize communication as occurring through an interactive and two-way process in which information is exchanged alternately between a sender and a receiver who take turns speaking and listening. In this view, speaking and listening are considered sequential and separate acts that occur at different times and one after another. The sender encodes a message in a way that can be understood by the receiver and then delivers it to the receiver. The receiver perceives the message, decodes it, and responds. The receiver's response, or feedback, lets the sender know how the message was received and whether it was understood. This real-time, two-way communication is highly dependent on feedback. Feedback may be external, coming from the receiver, or internal, insofar as the sender assesses and reflects on his or her own communication. Communication is considered complete when the receiver's feedback lets the sender know or conclude that the information has been understood.

In schools, interactional communication occurs as someone describes, directs, explains, or lectures, and others read, listen, understand, and respond. Those interactions are routine as teachers present information or give directions to their students and students provide feedback in the form of questions, comments, or performances. Similarly, leaders deliver information or give directions in staff meetings, lectures, and professional development activities and receive feedback from those involved. Based on feedback, a teacher may decide to reteach or explain material differently, and a

E-mail, social media, and other electronic communication options are useful, but they also include a significant risk for confusion and misunderstanding.

leader may see the need to rephrase a concept or describe something in a different manner. Had the information about rescheduling the team leader meeting to "after school is out" been given in face-to-face interaction, Lena may well have commented to the group or to Kim about how glad she was to have the extra time to prepare for her guests that evening. That statement would have served as feedback that she did not understand the meaning as others did, and it could have been corrected.

Transactional View A transactional view is regarded as a more contemporary and sophisticated framework that better represents the complexity and subtlety of the communication process (Beebe & Masterson, 2015; Harris & Sherblom, 2011; Wood, 2013).

In the transactional model, the concepts and roles of sender and receiver are extended and blended as both participants are in both roles simultaneously; both of them participate as communicators. At the same time that Communicator A is sending a message, she is also receiving information from Communicator B. At the same time Communicator B is receiving a message, he is also sending information to Communicator A. The communicators are interdependent in that they co-construct meaning through their continuous, simultaneous communications. In a transactional view, both communicators share responsibility for developing and understanding the meaning of the message.

The concepts of channel, noise, and environment mentioned in association with the other views of communication are also seen in this model, though they manifest in different ways. Their influence on the transactional communication process is significant because transactional interactions are seen in familiar dyadic or small group relationships in which you participate, in educational and community settings, in meetings you may have with individuals or small groups of students; and even when you jointly plan a project or facilitate student efforts on an assignment. Team meetings, interactions in the staff room or cafeteria, co-teacher planning and debriefing sessions, and parent conferences are all examples. In those and similar exchanges, you interact with others with whom you have or are building relationships. You are likely to be working toward a shared goal. In such cases, you often share some background and common context with the people you are working alongside. Through verbal and nonverbal means, you exchange information with them, and the process takes you closer to or further from your goals. Through your interactions, you influence your relationships with varying degrees of interpersonal communication skills.

Generally speaking, transactional communication requires that both participants are equals in communicating meaning, because meaning in an interaction is truly a co-constructed product. What does this imply for professionals' communication in schools?

Defining Interpersonal Communication

Communication scholars have embraced the transactional communication model as the best representation of how interpersonal communication occurs, and this model serves as the foundation for the interaction skills and processes presented in this text. Building on the already-presented definition of basic communication, interpersonal communication can be understood as an extension of it that incorporates transactional aspects:

> Interpersonal communication is a complex, transactional process through which people create shared meanings through continuously and simultaneously exchanging messages.

This definition and the introductory description of the transactional model provide a basis for thinking about effective interpersonal communication. Your skills in applying this information in your own interactions can significantly enhance your effectiveness in the full range of your professional and personal collaborative responsibilities.

Concepts Reflected in the Interpersonal Communication Process

As you might suspect, the interpersonal communication process includes a number of critical components. Useful insights regarding this process identified by scholars such as Adler, Rosenfeld, and Proctor (2015), DeVito (2013), and Steinfatt (2009), are discussed next.

Interpersonal Communication Is Transactional Identifying interpersonal communication as transactional underscores that both communicators are simultaneously sending and receiving information, making it impossible to distinguish between a sender and a receiver. To illustrate that concept, try to discern who is sending and who is receiving information in the following instances:

- One teacher is telling another about a graphic organizer she thinks would be useful for a student in his class. The second teacher is shaking his head and scowling.
- The after-school program leader is asking a parent about her son's study space and homework schedule at home. The parent is looking sheepish and uncomfortable.
- In a staff meeting, the principal is describing a new school-wide behavior support program she observed. Most teachers are sitting quietly, but two are whispering about an earlier disruption, another is filling out a field trip request, and three others are correcting papers.

It is tempting to see the teacher, after-school program leader, and principal as senders of messages and the other teacher, parent, and group of teachers as receivers. But the teacher being told about the graphic organizer is registering a negative response; the parent is communicating that she is uncomfortable either with the question or with her child's homework situation; and the teachers at the staff meeting are displaying a lack of interest while grading papers and whispering to one another. In those examples, the receivers are sending verbal and nonverbal messages to the speakers even as the latter are speaking.

Now imagine yourself in such a situation. If at the same time you are speaking the person you are addressing responds by nodding and showing you a piece of student work that illustrates exactly the point you are making, this person is letting you know your message is being received and understood. A confused look, a frown, or a question may cause you to restate your message, whereas a smile, a nod, or an interested look may encourage you to continue speaking or to go on to your next point. It is not just others' messages that may change your communication. Consider this: When you speak, you can hear yourself and judge whether you are saying what you intended. If you think that you are being unclear, you may elaborate on or restate your message to clarify it. You may also perceive that you are talking very quickly and decide to slow your rate of speech. In fact, messages are being sent constantly by everyone involved in the communication including your messages to yourself.

Communication Through Multiple Channels *Channel* refers to the medium through which messages are transmitted. Messages are typically either seen or heard; they are transmitted through visual and vocal-auditory channels. However, all human senses may be involved in sending and receiving messages. A firm handshake or a literal pat on the

Communication occurs simultaneously through multiple channels (e.g., verbal, nonverbal), and when the messages are contradictory, others may be uncertain about the communicator's true meaning.

back transmits messages through tactile channels. Similarly, the cologne one wears or other odors one emits communicate through chemical channels.

At any given point during interpersonal communication, several messages are probably being transmitted simultaneously over different channels. Logically, sending a single message over multiple channels can strengthen or emphasize the message. You do this when you smile, nod, and touch someone's shoulder while giving that person a compliment. Alternatively, the simultaneous sending of discrepant messages through different channels complicates the communication. A person who says, "Oh, it's fine; I can make some modifications later," while crumpling a report and tossing it into the trash is sending contradictory messages over different channels. This causes confusion and misunderstandings.

It would, of course, be upsetting to a parent to learn that his or her child was injured at school. It would be far easier for you to be supportive if you could tell the parent in person rather than through another medium. But the urgency of the situation may require that you communicate it as quickly as possible by telephone, text message, or e-mail. Other disturbing or complex information that is not urgent may best be held for a day or two until you can meet directly with the individual. Putting Ideas into Practice highlights some factors to consider when you are selecting the primary channel to use in a communication.

People Create Meanings When a colleague interrupts you and says, "I hate to bother you, but..." after having interrupted several times earlier, several meanings could be inferred: a serious apology for another disturbance, an insincere effort to diffuse your irritation, or even a sarcastic dig because he thinks you should be helping him rather than

PUTTING IDEAS INTO PRACTICE

What Channel?

The channel you use as the primary one for your communication will affect the way an individual receives, understands, and responds to your message. It is likely that you use different means of transmitting messages if you are sharing daily assignments and progress reports with parents or colleagues versus sharing potentially upsetting information with those individuals. In the latter situation, for example, consider the level of support you can give when communicating face-to-face, via e-mail, or through a voice mail message. Many writers recommend considering the following factors when deciding which channel to use in communications with colleagues, friends, or parents (Adler & Elmhorst, 2013; Brantley & Miller, 2008):

- The confidentiality of the message
- How promptly you desire feedback
- The amount and complexity of the information to be conveyed
- Your control over how the message is composed
- Your control over the receiver's attention
- Your ability to assess the other's understanding
- The channel's effectiveness in conveying detailed messages

The words and nonverbal signals are given meaning by those who use and those who interpret them. Whenever individuals interact, they must observe and interpret the symbols (e.g., words, nonverbal cues) of others. They must assign some significance to the behaviors in order to make meaning of others' actions. That is, meanings are created both in and among people who express and interpret them. Together, by exchanging multiple messages, the communicators develop shared meanings.

being otherwise engaged. In fact, "I hate to bother you" seems to have almost no meaning in and of itself; it is merely a string of sounds that serves as an introduction to other communication. To have any of the meanings mentioned, then, the sentence itself—and all sentences, realistically—relies on the subtle exchanges and contexts inherent in interpreting meaning.

But the interpreting that occurs in communication often confronts barriers, and because there are many possible points of view, it is necessary to negotiate shared meanings. That negotiation creates tremendous possibilities for misinterpretation of messages, so the importance of the communicators working to establish shared meanings should not be underestimated. In order to grasp the principles at work, then, it is vital that you deeply understand some of the barriers that can interfere with clear meaning.

Environment and Noise in Communication Communicators exist in different environments, or contexts, and the extent to which their environments differ can constitute a significant problem for interpretation because those fields of experience help communicators derive meaning from each other's messages. Thus, the environments for two communicators often can be viewed as a simple two-part Venn diagram. The section of the diagram that overlaps demonstrates that the communicators share some common backgrounds or experiences that facilitate their ability to derive shared meaning from their communication. However, those areas of background or context where they differ—they do not overlap—may interfere with, or cause misunderstanding in, their communication. Significant differences in age, political orientation, or cultural or ethnic background are examples of these areas. Noise is another important element in understanding communication. *Noise* is anything that interferes with or distorts the ability of communicators to exchange and make meaning of messages, and three main types of noise generally are identified:

Learn More About
In this video clip you will hear a straightforward explanation of how "noise" in our communication affects its clarity and can lead to conflict and misinterpretation.
(https://www.youtube.com/watch?v=iNoyhOab2jc)

- *Physical* noise comprises sounds and visual distractions that are external to the communicators and may interfere with the exchange, such as public address system announcements, others' unique physical characteristics, visual gestures, or loud talking.
- *Physiological* noise is created by conditions internal to the communicators, such as physical discomfort or hearing loss.
- *Psychological* noise is a prejudicial or emotional barrier that allows biases, preconceived ideas, and the like to distort communication. An inappropriate choice of words, a person's tendency to frown, and a person's physical appearance are stimuli that may create psychological noise and interfere with the transmission of a message.

Recently a teacher observed that the appearance of a scantily dressed mother at a parent conference created so much "noise" that he was not able to concentrate fully on the mother's spoken concerns. In this case, the woman's appearance was jarring to such an extent as to disturb or interfere with the verbal communication. How might this noise have a negative effect on the conference? What other examples of "noise" can you identify from your recent professional interactions?

Principles of Interpersonal Communication

To better understand the concepts of interpersonal communication, here are a number of principles that may help you to appreciate how interpersonal communication develops and the effects it has on its participants.

Interpersonal Communication Is Unavoidable By understanding that messages are continuously exchanged through multiple channels, you will also understand that "it is impossible *not* to communicate" (Watzlawick & Beavin, 1967, p. 5). That is, whether intentionally or unintentionally, you are always communicating. It might be through a prepared statement, a slip of the tongue, a welcoming gesture, or a disinterested expression.

When you speak or remain quiet, act reserved or animated, laugh or maintain a straight face, you communicate feelings and thoughts. These may not be intended communications, but others observe and interpret them nevertheless.

Interpersonal Communication Is Irreversible What a luxury it would be to be able to edit some past conversations as we can do to word-processed documents! Everyone has seen television shows in which a calculating attorney asks a condemning question or makes a slanderous remark only to have the opposing attorney call to "Strike that remark from the record!" as it becomes indelibly imprinted on the minds of the jury. Most people can recall, often with regret, occasions when they have spoken out of turn, in frustration, or under circumstances when their better judgment or self-monitoring strategies failed them. What we say or transmit to others electronically cannot be taken back. Apologies and regrets may alleviate some of the consequences, but everyone knows all too well that they do not reverse the message. Increased mindfulness and self-monitoring can help to reduce the number of such occurrences. Strategies to avoid issues related to irreversibility when conversing on the telephone are the topic of E-Partnerships.

Learn More About
This animated professional interaction highlights several key communication principles, including the inevitability of communication and its irreversibility.

(https://www.youtube.com/watch?v=401Y_U5GpH4)

Interpersonal Communication Has Both Content and Relational Dimensions Nearly every message exchange operates on two levels: The content level involves the explicit information being discussed, and the relational level expresses how the people involved feel about each other. This may be whether they like or dislike each other, or feel anxious or comfortable, angry, grateful, in control, subordinate, and so on. Content and relationship levels work simultaneously in a message, but their relative levels of importance vary in different circumstances (Beebe, Beebe, & Redmond, 2014; Knapp & Vangelisti, 2014). Depending on the situation, the content dimension of a message may be paramount. For example, a department head may not care much about whether the customer service

E-PARTNERSHIPS

Using Old-Fashioned Technology to Your Advantage

Many new technologies are used to support communications, but we still rely on telephones for many interactions. Many professionals conference in the evening by telephone, and much communication with families takes place the same way. Throughout this text, we stress the importance of facial expressions, stance, gestures, and other behaviors in shaping others' perceptions of you and what you are communicating. Yet on the telephone, these parts of the message are missing. Instead, you are communicating feelings as well as meaning just as you are in face-to-face communications. Thus, it is just as important that you try to communicate the concern and attention you would in person.

- Use your body position and smile. If you are feeling anxious or angry and want to convey a calmer tone, try putting your feet on the desk or sitting in a comfortable armchair. It is also helpful to smile and nod as if you were speaking face-to-face. A smile often changes the tone of your voice. It is said that many successful salespeople have mirrors on their desks or near their telephones.
- If you take notes, tell the other person that you are doing so. Note-taking is helpful for your memory and your records, but it may also lead to periods of silence as you try to keep up with the conversation. It is wise to tell the person in advance that you will be jotting down notes. This will help diminish the impact of the short periods of silence. It is also helpful to backtrack and ask for clarification of a previous point to demonstrate that you are indeed listening.
- When using the telephone, avoid using your computer to play games, take notes, or type e-mail messages. Computer activity is distracting, and you will miss points the other is making. Worse than that, the other person may hear your keyboard and may conclude that you are not fully attending to the conversation.
- Signal that you are listening. Your nods and smiles may help the tone of your voice, but you will need to have more than a calm tone to indicate that you are listening. Small utterances such as "Uh, huh," "Really?" "Oh, how frustrating that must be!" and "I can imagine" let the person on the other end of the line know you are tuned in.

representative likes her as long she gets a technician scheduled to repair the Data Director program. But the relational dimension is more important than the content when she communicates with her colleague who manages the data at the school site.

Interpersonal Communication Effectiveness Is Learned Interestingly, biology affects individuals' communication styles to some extent (Horvath, 1995; McCroskey & Beatty, 2000). Based on studies of fraternal and identical twins, sociability, anger, and relaxation seem to be partly a function of genetics. Fortunately, biology is not the only factor that determines how people communicate. Effective communication, called *communication competence*, is largely a set of skills that can be learned and continually refined. In fact, a core premise of this text is that your learned communication skills facilitate or impede the array of collaborative processes and activities in which you engage as a professional.

Interpersonal Competence

How do you become better at collaboration? How do you enhance your relationships with other professionals, your students, and your students' parents? Successful collaborative relationships require much more than just initiating interactions and hoping that the characteristics described in Chapter 1 fall into place. They require interpersonal competence. As with any area of competence, interpersonal competence includes behavioral or skill dimensions, including communication competence, as well as cognitive ability dimensions. The cognitive dimension, called *perspective*, involves understanding how we and those with whom we interact perceive and understand the world—in other words, how we think and feel about issues, others, and ourselves. The behavioral dimensions are seen in the development, adaptation, and skillful use of communication strategies. So, how do you maximize your collaborative effectiveness? It begins with the cognitive dimension, that is, understanding the components and power of personal perspective. This domain includes perception, cultural influences on perspective, and the subsequent impact these have on interpersonal interactions.

Perspective

Each individual brings a unique perspective to every life experience. Your past experiences, attitudes, values and beliefs, personal qualities, professional preparation, and expectations of others are among the things that affect what and how you observe and perceive, and ultimately how you behave. Your perspective is a personal lens through which you filter information; it affects how you view and interpret the messages you receive or make meaning from the information others provide you. Perception and perspective are intricately entwined, and both are affected by cultural influences.

Perception

How often do you discuss a shared experience with a friend or colleague only to find later that you have quite different opinions about what transpired? Your understandings of what occurred may be so different that you even question whether you were actually at the same meeting or whether you participated in the same interaction. This is not uncommon. People are constantly bombarded with more information than their sensory systems can handle. It is impossible for people to attend to and understand everything that occurs around them. Every experience has an infinite number of sounds, sights, smells, feelings, and tastes that compete for your attention; and it is not possible to process all of these stimuli. Here is an example:

> Abbie and Travis attended an after-school professional development session concerning inclusive practices and likely upcoming changes in their school's programs and services.

The speaker mentioned the importance of insisting that students with learning and behavior problems reach the highest standards but cautioned that some services in a separate setting are likely to still be appropriate and must be offered. The next day, Abbie, who finds that many students with disabilities are "too low" to succeed in her class, mentioned to Travis that she was in disbelief that she was going to be expected to have even more students—"lower" students—in her class, and without any assistance. Travis, currently enrolled in a master's degree program emphasizing inclusive practices, disagreed. He thought the speaker was urging the teachers to rethink their assumptions about students and to become even more creative in addressing their needs. Even after a lengthy discussion, Abbie and Travis each left the conversation convinced of their own accurate understanding and of the other's misunderstanding.

Perception, then, is the process of selecting, organizing, interpreting, and negotiating meaning from all of the information available in a given situation (McKay, Davis, & Fanning, 2009; Ventura, Salanova, & Llorens, 2015; Wood, 2013). Everyone uses that selective process. When individuals *select*, they choose, either consciously or unconsciously, to focus on certain pieces of information while largely ignoring others. This selective process is essential for coping with the tremendous amounts of both internal and external data that are part of everyday life experiences. This is often necessary in professional interactions because such communication is quite complex (Lustig & Koester, 2013). When you receive more information than you can assimilate, you ignore or filter out some information and focus your attention on other information. Generally, you pay attention to those things that capture your interests, address the purpose of the experience, or fit within a preconceived notion. After selecting and attending to specific information, you *organize* it, usually by assigning it to a category based on a schema that carries meaning for you, such as welcoming–rejecting, engaged–aloof, competitive–cooperative, hardworking–lazy, and so on. This categorization process is sometimes referred to as stereotyping and given a negative connotation. It is worth remembering that stereotypes can be negative or positive. They are the products of categorizing in the perceptual process.

> **Learn More About**
> After you watch this video on selective perception, discuss with classmates what you learned and how it applies to your professional responsibilities.
>
> (https://www.youtube.com/watch?v=-sdCN7JcJrk)

Perception does not necessarily follow a sequential process. You may categorize information and then consider and interpret it. Or as you categorize, you may *interpret* immediately, or assign meaning to the information without first considering what was imparted. When someone repeatedly says, "Let's get together for lunch sometime" but is never able to schedule the meal, you are likely, based on your past experiences, to quickly interpret the message. A final step, described by Adler and his colleagues (Adler & Elmhorst, 2013; Adler & Proctor, 2011; Adler, Rodman, & du Pré, 2014), is *negotiating*. This requires that the communicators use transactional communication to negotiate or create a shared meaning for the information being exchanged. It requires open-mindedness, suspension of judgment, and commitment to developing mutual understanding.

The steps of perception are summarized in the next Putting Ideas into Practice. They illustrate that perception is a selective and, thus, an incomplete process because it does not necessarily grasp the totality of what is being communicated. Consequently, understanding perception helps us to recognize how we form impressions of people with whom we interact, how those impressions influence our encounters, and how we then interpret our interactions and their meaning. Consider the following exchange during a district-wide meeting of the math department chairs.

> Theresa, a recently appointed department chair, has been an active union member since she began teaching four years ago. In the last department chair meeting, she strongly supported district-wide adoption of a new instructional program for the math departments but advised against doing anything that might be perceived as violating the teachers' contract, especially regarding uncompensated time. She was asked to give a report and propose a solution at the next meeting.
>
> Today she distributed a memo detailing five points and commented, "This proposal will honor the contract and teachers while requiring no additional costs. The program calls for 10 hours of uncompensated staff development time beyond the

PUTTING IDEAS INTO PRACTICE

Perception Is a Selective Process

Perception is an active process of becoming aware of objects, events, and people through sight, sound, smell, hearing, and taste. It is a necessary process for managing the enormous amount of internal and external data accompanying every life event.

- *Attending and selecting* involve sorting out stimuli—paying attention to some and ignoring others. With selective perception, attention is given to the things that are of most interest, are most pronounced, or seem most likely to meet one's needs.
- *Organizing* is arranging selected information in some meaningful way. Typically this requires categorizing information using schema based on similarities (e.g., age, gender, profession). This is also a selective process; choosing one category ignores another.
- *Interpreting* occurs when meaning is assigned to what has been perceived. This is influenced by such factors as involvement and past experience with a person, general assumptions about human behavior, expectations for the situation, and knowledge of a similar experience.
- *Negotiating* clearly reflects the transactional nature of communication. This is the process through which communicators influence each other's perceptions during communication and create shared meanings.

---

eight hours provided for in our contract, but we can't make teachers do more than the contract requires. I've reviewed the contract carefully and discussed it with the chapter president. We agree that using some of the pooled collaboration times we've created for team planning would not violate the contract, and so it wouldn't be the basis of a successful grievance either."

Theresa was a bit self-conscious. This seemed so simple and the information hardly warranted a memo and presentation. "Everyone must think I'm trying to be in charge—or they think I don't think they know anything! I need to avoid making this a bigger deal than it is." She looked at the group and saw that Vanessa was frowning, shaking her head, and whispering to David. Sino and Elaine were also whispering, but smiling and pointing to a section of the memo. Jasmine and Andrea were quietly reading the memo. Theresa thought, "Vanessa is always so negative about everything. She seems to take joy in making others look bad. Let's see what she has in store for me before I sit down." She asked, "So, Vanessa, do you have a problem with this?" Vanessa said she had no questions. Theresa asked the others, and no one else had questions or comments. Theresa was satisfied that her introductory statement and memo were clear, and rather than continue with the details, she smiled and ended her report.

Before reading further, reflect on this vignette, and test your perspective-taking skills. Using just the information provided, what meanings could be attributed to each person's behavior in the scenario? How would you analyze Theresa's perceptions of this experience? Did she believe others understood and accepted her proposal? What about the perceptions of the others? In this case, there were several different perceptions operating, including these possibilities:

- Vanessa and David were talking about how difficult implementing any change would be in their departments. They did not listen to much of what Theresa had to offer.
  - They attended to the notion of change and its meaning to them.
  - Theresa perceived Vanessa's behavior according to past experience.
- Sino thought, "Oh, of course! It's Theresa, and here she goes with another collective bargaining lecture and why we should all be active in the union." He looked at the memo and marked a few less-than-critical points.
  - His bias focused his attention only on union references in her memo and presentation.
- Andrea thought, "This really made it worth coming to this meeting! It's a real advantage to have Theresa's sensitivity to the contract in this group."

- Jasmine wanted more details, but Theresa hadn't welcomed even a questioning look from Vanessa. Jasmine didn't want a similar response.
  - Her focus went to Theresa's affect with Vanessa. She interpreted it as aloof and off-putting. Jasmine's need to avoid such a response kept her from asking for information.

Throughout the day, different group members queried Theresa about details and thanked her for her insight and creative solution. Jasmine talked with her individually and was surprised at how friendly and patient she was. Theresa provided Jasmine with the details she needed to understand the proposal. As Theresa welcomed her questions, Jasmine revised her initial perception of Theresa as aloof and off-putting, and Theresa revised her initial perception that her proposal had been simple and fully understood.

Following the exchange just described, group members gathered more information during the day, fleshed out the plan, and then adopted it. The scenario illustrates ways in which members of the group picked up on information she presented, but attended to different aspects of it based on their prejudgments and individual needs. You can understand the thoughts of the various members when you consider their different biases and interests. The group members identified and selectively perceived something in Theresa's statements that corresponded with elements in their own perspectives. Theresa also responded to the messages she perceived were being communicated, and in this example she inaccurately assumed that the group did not need to discuss details to understand the proposal.

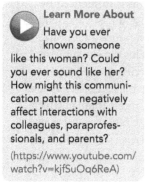

Learn More About Have you ever known someone like this woman? Could you ever sound like her? How might this communication pattern negatively affect interactions with colleagues, paraprofessionals, and parents?

(https://www.youtube.com/watch?v=kjfSuOq6ReA)

The take-away message for professionals who engage in collaborative activities is clear: Your perceptions and prejudgments strongly influence your understanding of others and their communication with you. You can become more aware of how you perceive others and learn to consider multiple perspectives of others by constantly challenging yourself to develop alternative explanations for others' statements. Other approaches to improving the accuracy of your perceptions are suggested in Putting Ideas into Practice.

Professional Perspective Your general professional socialization contributes to your perspective and merits separate attention. For example, the traditional professional preparation experiences of many teachers and other school personnel have focused on solo professional or isolated practice, and that approach is only slowly shifting to collaborative models. Thus, student teaching or practicum often is considered successful when these

PUTTING IDEAS INTO PRACTICE

Managing Perceptions

Understand Your Personal Views

Each person enters interpersonal encounters with a unique perspective or worldview. This is an individual or personalized frame for viewing life and its events. You need to be aware of your own biases and monitor to ensure that they do not unduly influence how you regard and interact with others.

Analyze Your Personal State

Recognize how your emotional or physiological state influences your perceptions. An event may seem pleasant or enjoyable if you are in a good mood and well-rested and unpleasant if you are not.

Avoid Early Conclusions

Recall that one of the purposes of the perceptual process is to select what gets your attention. Therefore, you ignore other information. You should seek additional cues before making judgments.

Seek Clarification

Ask others for explanations or clarification about your perceptions. It promotes dialogue and communicates that you truly wish to gain an accurate understanding.

Watch for Confirmation or Disconfirmation Biases

People have a tendency to look for and believe that which supports their biases and to avoid or discount anything that challenges or disconfirms their position. Your task is to stay alert and avoid the effects of either of those types of bias.

novice educators can manage their assignments independently. Despite this similarity in professional preparation, the specific discipline into which you were socialized (e.g., school psychology, literacy, library science, special education) and through which you prepared for a particular professional role (e.g., English teacher, administrator, counselor, speech/language therapist) also contributes elements to your frame of reference. This latter component may be considerably different from that of colleagues in other disciplines.

For example, general education teachers and special services providers may have pronounced differences in how they perceive their responsibility for facilitating the learning of individual students. Consistent with their disciplinary preparation in general education, general education teachers are likely to view their primary responsibilities as facilitating the progress of a *group* of students through a prescribed curriculum to meet established grade-level standards. Their professional studies emphasized curriculum scope and sequence, instructional methodology, pacing, techniques for group management, and strategies for delivering specific subject-matter content. Group instructional strategies, curriculum coverage, and assessment of performance based on established standards are central—appropriately so—in the ways in which they think about their responsibilities.

On the other hand, the professional preparation and socialization of special services providers probably placed more emphasis on individual variations in human development and learning, assessment of individual differences and learning needs, learning models stressing mastery, and intervention strategies to respond to unique needs of individual students. Not surprisingly, these professionals typically believe their primary responsibilities are to identify a student's current level of functioning, learning needs, and preferred learning mode and then to design and deliver services tailored to meet those needs. Their professional background, a major influence on their perspective, leads them to focus on the unique needs of *individual* students. These differences in teachers' and special services providers' professional perspectives may have a profound impact on how they interact with one another. For you to collaborate successfully, you will no doubt find that awareness of these variations and sensitivity to their influences are essential.

Although the various disciplines that provide specialized services may share many similarities, substantial differences can also characterize their perspectives. Some of these differences reflect the diverse philosophical and theoretical orientations within these fields (e.g., a preference for developmental versus behavioral approaches), some reflect variations in the nature of the special services provided (e.g., specialized instruction, clinically based therapy, or diagnostic evaluation), and still others relate to the specific knowledge bases of the disciplines. It is easy to understand how a speech/language therapist with responsibility for a student's articulation therapy may have a very different frame of reference from the adaptive physical educator. The former may work individually with students, diagnosing the speech disability, designing interventions to remediate it, and perhaps delivering services in a one-to-one situation. However, the adaptive physical education specialist may focus on assessing a student's general physical status and then designing a program to maximize the strengths and reduce the deficits of the student. This specialist often will deliver individualized services for the particular student within the group of students served. Similarly, reading specialists are likely to have perspectives that differ in significant ways from those of occupational and physical therapists, administrators will differ from special education teachers, and so on.

Culture and Perspective A wealth of engaging literature on cultural competency and cultural responsiveness offers extensive guidance to education and related professions that is, unfortunately, beyond the scope of this book to address. In order to address this dimension of communication, though, the critical topic of cultural perspective—the connection between culture and interpersonal communication—can be explored, starting with Lustig and Koester's (2013) definition of culture:

> Culture is a learned set of shared interpretations about beliefs, values, norms, and social practices, which affect the behaviors of a relatively large group of people. (p. 25)

Your cultural perspective is composed of your cultural background, your awareness of it, and how you have internalized it. It also includes your awareness, understanding, and views of others' cultures. In terms of the previous discussions, it can be conceptualized as

PUTTING IDEAS INTO PRACTICE

Developing Cultural Self-Awareness

Awareness of your cultural roots is helpful as you strive to develop sensitivity and knowledge of others. Here are some topics you could address with classmates to get started exploring your cultural roots. Think of and describe the following:

- A country (or countries) other than the United States that your family considers its "home" or country of origin
- Holidays or other celebrations your family may celebrate that derive from another country
- Family members who speak the language of their country of origin
- Languages other than English you heard at home while growing up
- A special piece of advice or perhaps a cultural adage that you recall from childhood
- A time growing up when something a parent or grandparent did seemed "old country," out of place, or embarrassing in school or in front of other children who didn't share your culture

For a more reflective interaction, discuss the following:

- An observation you made about yourself or others when involved with people from a different culture that shocked or upset you. Describe how you felt and reacted. Upon reflection, do you view it differently now?
- An occasion when you interacted with others from a different culture and did something particularly insensitive and thoughtless that you would now do differently. Describe the situation and your behavior. How do you understand the situation now? Describe how you would respond now.

---

part of the environment in the transactional model. It is also easily understood as one of the factors that influence what and how you perceive an interaction or another person.

The component in understanding and expanding your cultural perspective of others is achieving cultural self-awareness (Tuleja, 2014). This begins with learning about your own cultural heritage and the values, beliefs, and customs that are identified with it. Scholars have observed that many Anglo-European Americans have less awareness of their cultural influences than do people from other groups, perhaps because the "melting pot" aspirations of early immigrants took a toll on their diversity awareness (Hammond & Morrison, 1996; Lustig & Koester, 2013). Gathering family narratives, reviewing documents, listening with greater interest to family stories, and researching countries of origin enhances knowledge of family backgrounds. Further, it can be instructive to compare your own beliefs with those attributed to your cultural group. In addition, as part of your quest for cultural self-awareness it may be useful to take a few minutes to consider the discussion points in Putting Ideas into Practice.

Learn More About What is the message for you as a professional educator in this video snapshot that illustrates communication, perspective, and cultural differences?
(https://www.youtube.com/watch?v=eeee9zY1-3U)

The second component of cultural perspective is awareness and understanding of others' cultural perspectives. Whether or not we are immediately aware of it, our cultural backgrounds inform our decisions and provide contexts to our actions that may not be completely visible to others' perspectives. How we behave during our day-to-day activities reflects, in some ways, composites of many ideologies that construct our identities. Though not the focus of this chapter, a brief overview of some of the cultural patterns that underlie different cultures can provide a strong basis for self-reflection of how we perceive each other.

Of the many taxonomies and continua used to describe cultural values, beliefs, norms, and practices, these three seem especially applicable to educators:

- high-ambiguity-tolerant and low-ambiguity-tolerant cultures
- high- and low-context cultures
- individualist and collectivist orientations

However, any discussion of cultural similarities and differences must be preceded with a strong admonition: *There is no validity in adhering to culture-specific descriptions of cultures.* It is well established that significant variations exist within cultural groups, often based on such factors as gender, age, marital status, and socioeconomic status. Individual members of a group should not be assumed to possess the characteristics attributed to the group, nor should any group be considered to exemplify all of the characteristics associated with a continuum.

High-Ambiguity-Tolerant and Low-Ambiguity-Tolerant Cultures Uncertainty is responded to differently in different cultures. In some, it is a normal part of life and people take it in stride. Those are cultures with high ambiguity tolerance. Because the people in those cultures are comfortable with ambiguity and unknown situations, they are tolerant of those who do not follow the rules of the majority culture and may even encourage differences in perspectives (Hofstede, 1997; Kim, Seo, Yu, & Neuendorf, 2014). Examples of high-ambiguity-tolerant cultures are those of Singapore, Denmark, Ireland, India, Malaysia, and the United States.

At the other end of the continuum, people from cultures with low ambiguity tolerance exert great effort to avoid uncertainty. They experience much anxiety in the face of the unknown; not knowing what will happen next is threatening and must be counteracted. Examples of such cultures are those of Guatemala, Greece, Japan, Chile, Spain, and Costa Rica (DeVito, 2015). People from low-ambiguity-tolerant cultures prefer very concrete, specific rules for communication that are not to be violated. They prefer highly structured experiences, detailed instructions, and clear timetables.

High- and Low-Context Cultures In high-context cultures, people prefer to use high-context messages in which most or all of the meaning is implied by the physical setting or assumed to be something already internalized by the individual (Brantley & Miller, 2008). For example, there is a strong emphasis on verbal shorthand or nonverbal codes in communicating information that is known by the communicators but is not explicitly stated in the verbal message; it may be something that was in a previous communication or shared experience. The cultures of Japan, Mexico, and Thailand are considered high-context cultures, whereas Germany, Sweden, Norway, and the United States are viewed as having low-context cultures (DeVito, 2015). In low-context cultures, the information would be explicitly and precisely in the words people use as they communicate.

The case that opened this chapter includes an example of high-context messages. Lena and Kim shared a background of supporting their college basketball team. Lena referred to a key player by name and signaled that she was certain the team would make it to national playoffs when she said, "We're going to Bloomington!" where the championship games would be held. She emphasized the excitement of the basketball shots nonverbally by pretending to make one herself. Lena's communication served to illustrate the types of nonverbal cues and verbal codes common in high-context cultures.

Individualist and Collectivist Orientations This continuum represents the emphasis a culture places on individual goals, achievement, and fulfillment versus interdependence and emphasis on the well-being of the group as a whole (Lynch, 2011b; van Hoorn, 2015). In these cultures, an individual's autonomy, uniqueness, self-realization, and self-expression are highly valued, and people are supposed to take care of only their immediate families and themselves. Key words are I, self, independence, and privacy. Communication styles within the categories of context, talk, directness, and turn-taking and associated with both extremes of the continuum (Watkins & Eatman, 2001) and are outlined in Figure 2.2. Generally, the dominant cultures of Austria, Belgium, the Netherlands, and the United States are thought to reflect an individualistic orientation. However, about 70 percent of the world's cultures can be viewed as collectivistic (Rothstein-Fisch, Trumbull, & Garcia, 2009; Trumbull & Rothstein-Fisch, 2008). In collectivist cultures—such as those in Guatemala, Indonesia, most U.S. immigrant groups, as well as African American, Native American, and Alaskan Native cultures—the groups to which people belong are the most important social units. Those cultures require loyalty to the group and place value on meeting the needs of the group. In these cultures, the relevant group is likely to extend beyond the nuclear family and be oriented toward the extended family and kinship-help patterns.

Granted, no ethnic or other cultural group is only individualistic or collectivistic in its orientation, and not all members of a cultural group share the same values. Those orientations are used to describe a continuum of values that may help distinguish key beliefs and

FIGURE 2.2 **Individualistic and collectivistic influences in intercultural communication.**

Individualistic	**Collectivistic**
Low-context: Explicit and direct communication gets "right to the point."	**High-context:** The context, past experiences, and indirect cues are the basis for communication. Parties talk about what they know and have experienced.
Talk: One asserts oneself through talk and talk is used to create a sense of comfort in interactions and especially in groups.	**Silence:** Silence is golden. It is valued and may be used to communicate respect and provide comfort.
Directness: Communication with individuality and uniqueness; the intent of opinions is to oppose, disagree, persuade, and make explicit.	**Indirectness:** Ambiguity is often present. It reveals and is thought of as a means of maintaining harmony. Subtle cues and suggestions are used to maintain harmony.
Uneven turn-taking: One person may dominate, but both parties are likely to introduce subjects and talk at length about them. There is no apparent sense of parity or equity in turn-taking.	**Balanced turn-taking:** Parties take turns in an evenly distributed manner. Turns are short and relinquished so that others may speak. Parties do not shift topics; instead, they are likely to respond to what the other said.

patterns of groups and individuals. Such a continuum serves as a framework for considering characteristics of cultural styles and patterns that are evident in intercultural communication.

Just as the many aspects of a single culture cannot all be classified as fitting the same place on a given continuum, one continuum cannot be used to describe the central patterns of a culture. Any culture can be found to have a place on each of the three illustrative continua discussed here and on the many others not addressed here.

Now consider a personal application of these orientations: How do your views align with each of the three continua? How do they align with the orientations of others in your professional setting? You will likely find you are more aligned with certain individuals than others—this is one indication of cultural similarities and differences. Those individuals are probably those with whom you believe you can most easily work collaboratively. However, your efforts to achieve cultural self-awareness can help you begin to expand the range of people to whom you can relate effectively and with whom you can develop culturally competent communication skills that will enhance your collaborative interactions.

In today's culturally pluralistic and self-conscious society, a temptation exists to try to avert the complexity of cultural differences by ascribing specific cultural values to groups of people who are of the same ethnicity, gender, or age. We hope that the examples of variation in perspective summarized here help you focus on how your perspective—unique because of your personal, professional, and cultural history—is both similar to and different from those of others with whom you may want to collaborate. What is most important to understand is that no two people experience a single interaction in exactly the same way. Your responsibility is to

Professionals are more effective in their communication with family members from diverse backgrounds when they are aware of their own cultures and biases and work diligently to understand others' cultures.

simultaneously be aware of how you are influenced by your own and others' perspectives and how others may dynamically react to yours.

Ethics in Intercultural Communication As you contemplate your cultural roots and their influences, you may also wish to consider some of the ethical considerations that have been identified and how they relate to helping people improve the success of their intercultural communications with those from other backgrounds. Samovar, Porter, McDaniel, and Roy (2013) include these:

1. Respect for others' culture is nonnegotiable, as most would readily agree. However, it is important to realize that a comment you consider innocuous could be disrespectful to a person from another culture. Offhand jokes, even when hastily explained as not meaning anything negative, can significantly reduce your communication competence.

2. Look for areas of commonality that you share with those from other cultures. This is not an effort to minimize differences in cultures nor to diminish the value of each culture's uniqueness. Instead, the goal is to build a foundation for effective communication by looking for ways that we share the human experience.

3. Even as you look for similarities, respect cultural differences. The point is that people are in many ways alike, and in many other ways they are different. This is simply the way it is, and communication is facilitated when each person understands and is comfortable with this status.

4. Accept responsibility for your communication behavior. Whether words or actions, your communication has both intended and unintended consequences, an especially important element in intercultural communication. If you inadvertently offend another person, an apology rather than an explanation that "you didn't mean it" is appropriate.

Each of these ethical components can serve to guide all your communication, not just that occurring in an intercultural context. And one of the best sources to illustrate why these principles are so essential is to simply watch the media for examples of how celebrities and those who experience momentary, sometimes unanticipated, celebrity status frequently violate these ethics, often with unfortunate consequences.

Competent Communication

Having considered perspective, the cognitive dimension of interpersonal competence, and how perception and culture influence perspective, the concept of competent communication now can be directly considered. This is the second major component of interpersonal competence. It is the behavioral dimension that includes the development, adaptation, and adept use of communication skills.

Most definitions of communication competence include two criteria: It is both effective and appropriate (Martin & Nakayama, 2015; Spitzberg, 2000). *Effective* communication is that which achieves the intended outcome or the goals of the specific situation in which it is used. Communication is considered *appropriate* when it is adapted to be proper and suitable to particular situations and people. Noted interpersonal and intercultural communication scholars offer the following definition (Adler et al., 2014; Trenholm, 2014):

> Competent communication is effective and appropriate communication that achieves its intended outcomes in ways that maintain or enhance the relationship in which it occurs.

Although you will learn about many aspects of communication and interaction skills throughout the remainder of this book and in the course you are taking, the following four factors are overviewed as central to the development of communication competence. The discrete skills and the skills embedded within interaction processes are explored in depth in other chapters. In A Basis in Research you can see how communication competence is studied and how it affects the outcomes of professional interactions.

Learn More About
Each of these humorous vignettes has a serious meaning about fostering effective communication and avoiding ineffective communication behaviors.

(https://www.youtube.com/watch?v=ypquQYbilyU)

A BASIS IN RESEARCH

Competent Communication and School Principals

Although school professionals may strongly believe that they have exemplary communication skills, research suggests that this may not be the case, especially in the context of challenging interactions. For example, Le Fevre and Robinson (2015) asked principals to meet with an actor portraying a teacher about whom a parent had made a complaint (the parent claimed the teacher was picking on a fictional child and threatened to go to the school board). The interactions were video recorded, and the principals were rated using a validated instrument on the extent to which they demonstrated six critical communication skills:

1. Presenting a point of view based on some type of specific evidence
2. Being able to explore the other person's reasoning about, and interpretation of, the problem
3. Checking understanding of the other's point of view
4. Assisting the other person to consider alternative meanings or explanations for the problem
5. Demonstrating a willingness to self-reflect, to question his or her own assumptions and beliefs
6. Working to plan the next steps for addressing the problem

The authors found that the principals, overall, demonstrated skills that were low to moderate across the six skill areas. They were particularly prone to describing their own points of view, but without providing evidence to support those views. They generally did not work to better understand the perspective of the teacher who had been accused of treating a student unfairly, nor did they consistently check the accuracy of their understanding of the teacher's perspective. Perhaps most notably, the principals were not skilled in challenging statements made by the teacher in order to help the teacher understand the parent's point of view. These results were consistent despite the fact that the principals were at the elementary, middle school, and high school levels and had a wide range of educational experiences.

Principals generally are more experienced, have education specific to their roles as school leaders, and are charged with a wide range of communication responsibilities. If they have difficulties with effective communication, what does it suggest about teachers, paraprofessionals, related services providers, and others? What steps could you take as a professional educator to continue to refine your own communication skills?

Develop a Skills Repertoire Effective communicators must develop and be able to use a large range of communication skills. No single style of communication is effective in pursuing all goals or for interacting with all people in all situations. They must also be able to perform the skills. Simply reading about communication skills or even insisting that you already know them, will not be of much help unless you can put them to work. This is the reason for the end-of-chapter activities throughout this text; they are intended to assist you to explore your communication skills repertoire and to expand it. As a starting point, completing the self-assessments in this chapter and in Chapter 3 can help you to know whether your skills are as broad and well developed as you would like.

Choose and Adapt Behavior Having a variety of communication skills is a necessary but not a sufficient requirement for successful communication. Knowing what to do in specific instances is also important because a response that works well in one setting could be less successful in another. For example, knowing whether being deferential, direct, or humorous is likely to have a positive or negative influence in a given situation or when pursuing a particular goal. Appropriately adapted communication is sensitive to context (situation, time, and place), goals, and uniqueness of communicators (e.g., your audience is elderly, youthful, family, community).

Watch Yourself! You learn to understand others better with increased perspective-taking skills, but competent communicators focus on better understanding themselves as well. They employ self-monitoring to pay close attention to their own behavior and use these observations to change their behaviors. Monitoring occurs both before and during an interaction. Before talking with someone who recently expressed much unwarranted anger toward you and complained to the principal, you remind yourself not to get defensive and to avoid getting pulled into an argument. During the interaction, you stay alert and catch yourself if the person says something hurtful and you want to snap back with something equally so. In short, people who are aware of their behavior and the impression it makes are more skillful communicators than people who do not exercise self-monitoring.

Communicate Ethically with Others as Unique Individuals   Competent communicators are committed to interacting effectively and ethically. They demonstrate this commitment in two ways. First, their commitment to the other person is evident. It is seen in their interest in the person's thoughts, ideas, and feelings; their desire is to spend time together; and their willingness to listen rather than talk all the time. All of this reveals their investment in the other person. The second way competent communicators demonstrate their commitment to effective and ethical communication is in their concern that the message is accurate, understandable, and understood. Their ethical commitment is reflected in their steadfast understanding of others as unique human beings, not simply as members of a particular category or a particular type of person.

Suggestions for Improving Your Communication Skills

Now that you have focused your methods and intentions to communicate competently with others, the next step requires that you mindfully seek to improve and refine your skills. Naturally, you may be wondering how to best begin honing them. It is a journey and one that takes practice. Some basic steps to help you refine your verbal and nonverbal communication skills include the following.

Become a Student of Communication   Because communication is the smallest unit of concern in interactions and comprises the most basic set of skills needed in collaborative activities, you should study and become a highly skillful communicator. A note of caution is warranted, however. Like most people, you may conclude that you already have a high degree of communication skill, because you communicate regularly in your professional and personal life. "Practice makes perfect," right? As you read about the skills in this and the following chapters, you may believe you have "had that course" or acquired the skills elsewhere. Keep these two points in mind: First, understanding or being aware of communication skills alone does not improve your communication. Only through self-reflection and continuing practice does improvement occur. Our students repeatedly share with us that focusing on and rehearsing the skills is somewhat humbling; implementing the skills is much more difficult than simply recognizing them. Second, regardless of your knowledge or proficiency level after much practice, you will never fully master communication, because each new person, interaction, and situation will require you to practice and refine your skills further. As all professionals teach and learn from one another, interactions are enhanced by being open to opportunities to acquire new knowledge and skills. Communication competence is truly an example of lifelong learning.

Nurture and Communicate Openness   Perhaps the most pronounced theme that runs throughout the discipline of collaboration is an absolutely essential requirement for openness. Openness refers to a person's ability to suspend or eliminate judgment and evaluation of information and situations until he or she has explored adequately the various potential meanings and explanations. For example, when emergent characteristics of collaboration were discussed in Chapter 1, it was noted that in order to collaborate, individuals should value joint decision making or at least be willing to experiment with it. In the perspective-taking exercises at the end of this chapter, you can practice and expand your openness to alternative meanings. In Chapter 5, the importance of exploring problems to avoid formulating hasty and inaccurate problem statements is stressed.

Hopefully, the importance of an attitude of openness has become very clear to you. Openness, in the context of verbal communication, is similar to the earlier caution to avoid drawing conclusions early, but the focus in that discussion was on eliminating judgments about people rather than deferring judgments about situations. In this context, the point is for you to set aside your biases and explore various aspects of a situation before attempting to decipher the message. As you think of examples when this application of openness could facilitate or impede your interactions? With a colleague? A paraprofessional? A parent?

Keep Communication Meaningful People will invest more in communication when they believe the information shared will be meaningful to them. Conversely, you (and others) are unlikely to invest significantly in communication pertaining to topics or information in which you are not interested or that you do not see as important. If you do not share a friend's interest in knitting, you probably will not make a significant effort to engage in discussion about it.

The amount of information being communicated influences perceptions of the meaningfulness of communication. Too much or too little information is not meaningful. Have you had the experience of asking a colleague or coworker a simple question, such as, "How is the new student adjusting?" and getting a diatribe with more information than you ever wanted to know about the situation? You may have asked the question in passing or out of general interest and started a verbal landslide. You probably know a number of people who tend to give such lengthy responses. Do you try to avoid giving them an opening to speak? This, or simply "tuning out," is a common response to such highly talkative people. Conversely, have you ever found yourself providing too much information to others? As you observe your own communication, you may find that you sometimes obscure the meaning of what you are trying to communicate by doing this.

Alternatively, everyone experiences exchanges in which too little information is shared. You may have had experiences trying to communicate with someone who seems to expect you to be a mind reader. If so, you know how difficult it can be to ensure clear understanding when others withhold needed information and how easily such interaction can become difficult, as this example illustrates:

> Zoe, a first-year special educator, is touching base with Mary Jo, the 15-year veteran paraprofessional providing support for Jake in his 7th-grade general education classes. She asks, "Did you implement all the steps in the note-taking procedure that Jake has been learning?" Mary Jo responds, "Yes, I did that." Zoe continues, "How accurately did he complete each step?" to which Mary Jo replies, "He's doing fine." Slightly frustrated, Zoe says, "I really need more information so I can decide if it's time to begin helping Jake to complete note-taking without so much support." Mary Jo, speaking a bit louder now and staring at Zoe, states, "Don't you trust me to do my job?"

As you reflect on this unfortunate interaction, what could Zoe and Mary Jo have done differently to improve their communication by sharing the appropriate amount of information?

As you work toward effective interpersonal communication, you should ensure that communication is meaningful by judging what and how much information the people with whom you are interacting want to have. When you want information from others, you may find that they give you too little or too much information. Your task then is either to work to obtain more information or to focus and narrow the information they are supplying. Putting Ideas into Practice summarizes additional information to assist you in keeping communication meaningful.

Use Silence Effectively Silence and pauses are important nonverbal behaviors that are related to speech flow and pace, and they may be used as minimal encouragers. However, beyond these uses, silence is an extremely powerful communication tool in its own right. You are undoubtedly familiar with the "deadly silence" used by parents and teachers to communicate disapproval to children. You may have even used it or experienced it yourself in adult relationships. Surely, silence can be awkward or seem punishing in conversations, but few people seem to understand how powerful it is in communicating interest, concern, empathy, and respect to others. It also has another advantage as a very helpful communication strategy because it allows others to pause and think through their communication, thus enhancing the quality and meaning of their messages.

The definition of *silence* in communication is the absence of verbal noise or talk. But how long must there be no talk before a space in the talk can be considered silence?

PUTTING IDEAS INTO PRACTICE

Planning for and Evaluating a Communication Event

Becoming a proficient communicator requires awareness of and attention to the factors that influence communication. As a student of communication, you should give advance thought to factors that will make your task easier or more difficult. In addition to the suggestions offered throughout this chapter, try to also include the following:

- *Establish your communication goal.* Identify ahead of time what information you want to share, obtain, or explore in this interaction.
- *Identify the most appropriate setting in which to accomplish this goal.* Think about such things as privacy, convenience of location, and access to materials or resources that may be needed.
- *Consider the potential message-to-noise ratio.* It is impossible to eliminate all noise or communication interference, but you can and should work to minimize its effects on your interaction.
- *Evaluate the message and think about how the channel(s) to be used might affect the communication.* Assess the amount of information to be conveyed, your desired control over how the message is composed, your desired control over the receiver's attention, your ability to assess the other's understanding, and how quickly you need feedback. These elements should help you determine the most appropriate channel(s) for meeting your communication goal.

After the interaction, assess your success in attaining your communication goal. Write a summary of your colleague's primary points and concerns. Summarize your listening behaviors, and decide which were most and least useful in accomplishing your listening goal.

Goodman (1978, 1984) offers several concepts that help to clarify this. He suggests that the length of time between two speakers' verbal expressions varies within each conversation, and the amount of silent time that qualifies as a "silence response" is dependent on each conversation's tempo and patterns of speech. For example, if two people exchange several comments and pause for about one and a half seconds after each speaker completes a thought and before another starts, then a pause of two or three seconds may be required for a silence response. On the other hand, if two people are talking but only allowing about a quarter of a second of verbal space between taking turns to talk, one second may constitute a silence response.

Silence and its contributions to communication are more easily understood when you consider the alternatives: interruptions, overtalk, and reduced verbal spacing. Interruptions occur when one speaker disrupts another's message in order to deliver his or her own. When someone is speaking and another interrupts, there is a period of overtalk in which both speakers are talking at the same time until one relinquishes the conversation to the other. The final alternative, reduced verbal spacing, is related to, but distinct from, silence and pauses. It refers to the pace of the turn-taking in verbal interaction. It occurs when a new speaker begins talking during what is meant to be a brief pause in someone else's speech. In its most exaggerated form, one speaker appears to clip off the last word or two of the previous speaker's talk.

Several similarities characterize interruptions, overtalk, and reduced verbal spacing. Perhaps they occur because the person using them has a need to control the situation, to demonstrate knowledge, to try to reduce the speaker's rambling talk, or simply to be the center of attention. Whatever the reason, these responses are likely to have a negative impact on the conversation and relationship. They seem to say, "Listen to me," "It's my turn," or "What I have to say has more value than what you're saying." Those responses certainly suggest to the other person that he or she is less competent, less important, or less interesting than the person attempting to take control of the conversation. They are likely to produce frustration and sometimes anger as the person who is verbally "crowded" feels less and less understood and valued.

In your interactions, try to develop a habit of protecting verbal space. It will give the other person the opportunity to finish talking and give you the opportunity to consider what the other has said and how you want to respond. In addition to avoiding verbal crowding, the silence response or verbal space conveys that you are interested in the other's comments and are taking the time to comprehend the message before responding.

A final point to consider is that the amount of silent space that creates the positive impact you desire varies with each conversational pair. Analogous to inadequate silence, unnaturally long periods of silence can convey disinterest or other negative messages. There are no precise rules about verbal spacing. Sometimes, in a fast-paced discussion, three seconds is a significant silence. At other times, particularly if the topic is emotional and one or more speakers are describing personal feelings, silences of several seconds or more than a minute may be appropriate nonverbal cues. Through experimentation you can learn to determine the desirable amounts of silence in each relationship and conversation within that relationship.

Adapt Your Communication to Match the Task and the Relationship Ultimately, effective communicators tend to adapt their communication according to the task, the relationship, and the characteristics of the individuals involved. They choose clear and efficient language, identify the information that is needed, and use verbal communication strategies that will best elicit their preferred responses. The nature of the desired responses and relationships and their levels of development should influence your choice of communication style. Simply, if you think about the individuals with whom you interact, you will probably include colleagues, administrators, parents, paraeducators, and professionals from other agencies. And you may further differentiate ongoing and regular relationships from more temporary and infrequent interactions, such as those in annual review meetings. The nature of your relationship and its level of development should influence your choice of the communication style. As you collaborate in established or developing relationships, one of your responsibilities is to use communication strategies that will best facilitate the collaborative activity. Because there are no simple rules or strategies for adapting your verbal communication, your ability to understand the principles and learn to use many of the skills included in this book can help you do this.

SUMMARY

- Competent interpersonal communication is the basis for successful collaboration. Of the three primary models of communication, transactional, which includes simultaneous and ongoing communication, is considered most applicable to professional interactions, more so than linear or interactional models.
- Interpersonal communication is a transactional process by which communicators continuously and simultaneously exchange messages through multiple channels in order to create shared meanings. It is premised on the understanding that communication is unavoidable, irreversible, comprised of both content and relational dimensions, and learned.
- Interpersonally competent individuals have sophisticated perspective-taking skills. They continually work toward accurate perception and increased intercultural awareness, grounded in understanding their own and others' perspectives and how these have been shaped by past experiences, professional preparation, and cultural identity. These individuals also use appropriate communication skills suitable to the persons and situations involved and are effective in achieving communication goals.

BACK TO THE CASE

1. Think about the initial exchange between Kim and Lena. What channels were being used in their cafeteria communication? Which were most effective? Least effective? Why?
2. How does Kim and Lena's interaction illustrate transactional communication? One way to do this is to imagine they had communicated through e-mail, an interactional approach, and with a classmate, to construct their e-mail exchange. How might an e-mail interaction have been better or worse? Relate your answers to the type of communication approach employed.

3. Apply the communication concept of perspective to this interaction. With a classmate, take on the roles of Kim and Lena. Using *your* perspective as a basis, write at least three or four paragraphs about what you're thinking before, during, and immediately after the interaction. Then attribute your comments to an element of your perspective (e.g., your parents' messages to you as a child, other childhood or school experiences, your professional preparation, your culture, your professional experiences). In what ways is your perspective similar to/different from that of your partner? Which elements most strongly shaped your perspective? What does this tell you about your communication with colleagues and parents in an educational setting?

COLLABORATIVE ACTIVITIES

1. As a way to practice considering alternative meanings and differing points of view, try to generate four distinctly different possible meanings for each of the following statements. Get additional practice by doing the same for statements made by others in the course of conversations during the next few days.

    Teacher: I'm all for accountability. Let's start with the school board and their accountability for our working conditions! Then the administration—shouldn't they be accountable for us having books, supplies, and building maintenance? And then the *Times*—is it accountable for reporting about conditions as well as our individual value-added scores?

    Parent: We do everything we can to protect Bobby. I bring him to school and pick him up as soon as school is out. He is in safe after-school clubs. But when he's with you, he can't even go to the restroom without getting bullied or beaten up or threatened!

    Speech Therapist: I haven't had any teaching courses or professorial development about group instruction. How am I going to be able to provide Jill's speech services in her general education classroom?

2. No doubt you communicate with colleagues and/or parents using notes and e-mail, or forms that you have created or that have been created by colleagues or the school district. Collect a sample of teacher- or district-developed forms and share them with colleagues from other settings. Work together to identify ways in which the forms could be made more teacher or parent friendly, and modify the forms accordingly. Note that when you do this with classmates from other districts or settings, you are likely to get many more new ideas and time-saving strategies than if you simply exchange with colleagues who share your setting.

3. "It is well known that people don't always 'speak their minds,' and it is suspected that people don't always 'know their minds.' " Harvard University's Project Implicit (https://implicit.harvard.edu/implicit/demo), the source of this quote, presents a method that demonstrates the conscious–unconscious divergences much more convincingly than has been possible with previous methods. Learn about the method, and take a short confidential assessment by visiting the web site. Consider taking two different assessments and comparing results.

4. Because culture affects communication, begin a search for your cultural roots. For example, ask the oldest family members for their recollections. Perhaps they have journals, photo albums, notes of important events, old letters, or any number of things that provide information about your family traditions. When this information is not available, with a bit of effort you can use document searches in courthouses to uncover marriage records, deeds, and birth certificates. As genealogy has become increasingly popular, online services have made such information accessible as well. What have you found that is surprising? What is there in your cultural roots that could affect your communication with others?

5. Identify a classmate or colleague with whom you seemingly have many differences and do the following:
   - Individually, compile a short list of three or four differences that you believe both of you might consider as the primary distinctions between you. These differences might be your philosophies, ideologies, most valued relationships (e.g., friends, family, spouse, or significant other), views of success, and so on.
   - In order to reflect on how we all ascribe certain meanings to the differences we perceive in others, compare your lists to see which items, if any, you agreed were your areas of greatest difference.
   - Then, take turns speculating about why your greatest differences exist. The more you clarify these differences and the possible reasons for them, the more you will be drawn to reconsider the impressions that you have of each other and, perhaps more importantly, why you formed those impressions.

 CHECK YOUR UNDERSTANDING

Click here to gauge your understanding of this chapter's essential concepts.

3 Listening, Responding, and Giving Feedback

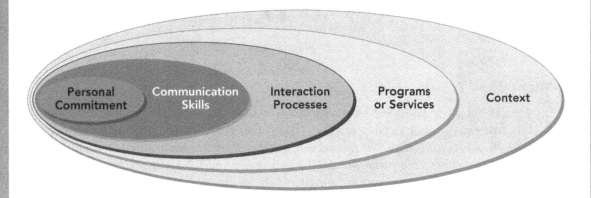

CONNECTIONS

In Chapters 1 and 2, you developed an awareness of the frameworks for understanding collaboration and the communication that it requires. These broad topics provided the basis for exploring specific skills essential for successful interpersonal communication. This chapter examines several of those skills, ones often considered the core of proficient professional interactions, including nonverbal communication, listening, and strategies for effectively providing feedback to collaboration partners.

LEARNING OUTCOMES

After reading this chapter you will be able to:

1. Identify and give examples of four types of nonverbal cues and describe how they affect communication.
2. Define listening and describe its process, analyzing challenges to it and applying strategies to enhance listening skills.
3. Use prompting, paraphrasing, reflecting, questioning, and checking to respond to speakers and confirm information they communicate.
4. Describe and apply to your professional responsibilities three principles that characterize effective verbal and nonverbal communication.
5. Give others feedback that meets the criteria for effectiveness and describe guidelines for verbal feedback.

A CASE FOR COLLABORATION

More Than Words

Jake Meyer talked quietly with several parents while others freshened their coffee. When everyone returned to the seating area, he smiled and said, "If we're ready to continue, I'd like to describe the role of the Community Liaison Office." He paused and, smiling, looked around the room as people took their seats in the semicircle of chairs. "We are here to talk things over with you. Whenever you have questions or want more information about your child's program, we will be here to discuss your concerns and try to answer your questions." He paused, smiled slightly, and looked slowly around the room again. When he made eye contact with a group member, he maintained it long enough to give the member the opportunity to raise a question or offer a comment.

Lisa Correa quickly looked down when Jake looked at her. Jake knew that Lisa's husband had been very forceful and somewhat disruptive with questions at the last school meeting. Her husband was not here tonight, and Lisa did not say anything.

"As parents, we all have concerns," he continued, moving a chair into the semicircle facing Lisa and sitting between Diane Long and Jerome Jackson. Putting his hand on the arm of Diane's chair and looking at her, he interrupted himself. "Diane, do you remember last year when my son started talking about getting a job and I ran background checks on the business through the employee relations department at your office?"

Smiling shyly and laughing, Diane said, "I sure do! That was one long week in our neighborhood."

Jake laughed while still looking at Diane and then glancing briefly at Lisa, who was watching him. He leaned forward in his chair, put his elbows on his knees, and let his clasped hands fall between them. He glanced down for a silent second. Then, looking up, he said slowly, "Yes, I was a bit excessive in those background checks and perhaps I focused on the wrong things. I thank you again for understanding and supporting me through my transition! As parents, we all have concerns about the decisions our children make and the challenges they must face. We know that we have to let go if we want our kids to grow into independent, productive adults. But it's hard—especially because we know their special vulnerabilities." Quickening his tempo slightly, he looked directly at Lisa and then at each group member and back at Lisa again and said amiably, "That's where the Community Liaison Office comes in. We have information about community opportunities, hazards, and supports; and we know your sons and daughters. Maybe most important," he continued while sitting up and smiling broadly, "is that we understand what you're experiencing. We've been there! We want to listen to you. We want to help get answers to your questions."

Introduction

As discussed in Chapter 2, competent communication is needed for success in nearly every life activity. It is even more essential in your professional life, where others hold high expectations for your communication competence (Hybels & Weaver, 2012). In fact, the various professions that are central to the education of P–12 students have promulgated codes of ethics and standards of professional practice that establish expectations for professional conduct including how professionals communicate with one another and with their students and their families. Review of such professional standards of practice (e.g., American School Counselor Association, Council for Exceptional Children, National Association of School Psychologists) reveals a consistent emphasis on honest, culturally relevant, respectful, and open communication. These and related expected practices, such as confidentiality, informed consent, and commitment to social justice, constitute the underpinning of professional and ethical communication competence for educators.

FIGURE 3.1 **Communication foundation for interaction skills.**

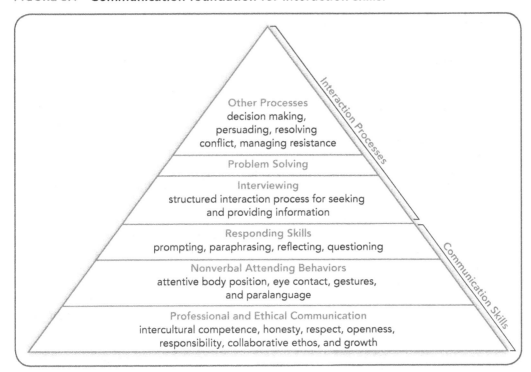

Figure 3.1 illustrates how communication skills and interaction processes relate to each other. You can see that the first level—ethical and professional communication—has already been addressed. In this chapter, nonverbal attending behaviors and responding skills are added. Nonverbal attending behaviors include attentive body position, eye contact, gestures, and paralanguage, as well as others. Responding skills include prompting, paraphrasing, reflecting, and questioning skills. Together these are used to demonstrate interest in the speaker and to create a trusting and safe environment that encourages the speaker to share thoughts and information. Collectively, the first three levels prepare you for interviewing, problem solving, and the other interaction processes that follow and are addressed in subsequent chapters.

Nonverbal Communication

We stressed in Chapter 2 that you "cannot *not* communicate" as you continuously exchange messages with others through multiple channels. That is relatively easy to believe: Everyone generally accepts that body language and voice can influence communication. Realistically, though, the impact of nonverbal behaviors is greater than you may have suspected. In fact, the words used in your verbal communication may convey far less information than do the nonverbal components. If you think back to the examples provided in Chapter 2 to illustrate transactional communication, you will recognize that most included nonverbal cues to demonstrate the nonspeaking ways in which we communicate. Much, if not most, of the meaning of a message is communicated nonverbally.

The Value of Nonverbal Communication

Does nonverbal communication really matter? Yes! The ability to skillfully use and understand others' use of nonverbal behaviors is essential in communicating the attitudes necessary for establishing and maintaining positive relationships (e.g., interest, acceptance, warmth) and powerful as a tool in clarifying, emphasizing, or obfuscating the meaning of verbal messages (Egan, 2014; Johnson, 2013). Logically, you communicate most effectively and positively if you understand the nonverbal communications that you both send and receive.

Nonverbal messages are the central mechanism for communicating emotion and attitudes. This was established through research more than three decades ago, and contemporary studies continue to demonstrate that the nonverbal elements are the most significant means of expressing emotion to others (e.g., Buck & Miller, 2015; Elkins & Derrick, 2013). That significance arises from a core feature of nonverbal communication: Nonverbal messages are generally more credible than verbal ones. Researchers have also demonstrated that nonverbal communication is more difficult to feign than is verbal communication. For example, longer time lags in responding to a question, lessened eye contact, increasing shifts in posture, prolonged pauses, less smiling, and a slower rate of speech are some of the most significant cues that someone is not being truthful (Burgoon, Proudfoot, Schuetzler, & Wilson, 2014; Pozzato, 2010).

Meaning, then, is created by a combination of verbal and nonverbal messages (Stukenbrock, 2014). Nonverbal cues help manage verbal messages. They can substitute for verbal messages, contradict them, or reinforce them. Holding up five fingers as you announce, "We have five minutes to finish our discussion before the bell rings," reinforces or repeats your verbal message. If someone laughs and writes a new idea on the board while saying, "That's a terrible idea! That kind of talk can shut down the entire brainstorming session," her laughter and continued contributions to the brainstorming contradict her words. If someone says, "You know. It's time to…" and then pulls a finger across his throat as if cutting it, you may determine that he is using substitution and indicating it is time to end this discussion.

Whether responding to nonverbal substitutions, contradictions, or reinforcements, people react and adapt to the nonverbal messages of others. Often we "read" others' nonverbal communication and adjust our interactions with them accordingly. You probably have used the strategy of lowering your speaking volume as a classroom of students gets too noisy. They then lower their voices to match yours. The same is true with other nonverbal behaviors. For instance, when a friend leans forward to tell you something, you are likely to also lean forward to listen. It is not uncommon for people consciously or unconsciously to mirror each other's posture, gestures, eye contact, movements, rate of speech, or other nonverbal behaviors during interactions (Spunt, 2013). When this is done naturally and not at a level that appears to be purposeful imitation, it is perceived as mutual interest and positive regard for the speaker; and it strengthens their relationship (Egan, 2014).

Nonverbal communication, including facial expressions, gestures, and physical distance between people, may convey more information about participants' feelings and opinions than their words.

Types of Nonverbal Communication

In order to understand the collection of nonverbal cues that all people use to communicate, it is useful to categorize nonverbal behaviors into three primary classes. For the purposes of this discussion, these comprise body language (e.g., movement, facial expression, eye contact, body orientation, and gestures); vocal cues (e.g., quality of voice and the pacing or flow of speech); and spatial relations (e.g., the physical distance between the participants). Each of these categories of cues affects the nature of interpersonal communication by creating nuanced meanings.

Body Language When Martha Graham, the renowned American choreographer and dancer, said, "The body says what words cannot," she revealed the insight she used to transform dance as an art form (Public Broadcasting System, 2005). That same insight can transform how people interact. Understanding how body language communicates and using it to influence your interactions can have a profound impact on your collaborative success (e.g., Koppensteiner, Stephan, & Jäschke, 2015; Mara & Appel, 2015).

Learn More About
How could you apply the information about gestures in communication from this video of Charlie Rose and Bill Gates to your interactions with colleagues and parents?
(https://www.youtube.com/watch?v=VfE7aVa_mSo)

The category of body language includes body movement, posture, facial expression, and gestures. Hand movements, a raised eyebrow, a frightened stare, rounded shoulders, and a kindly smile are all part of this category. The numbers of cues and the seemingly innumerable meanings they carry are formidable (e.g., Kostić & Chadee, 2015). Nonverbal behavior carries the largest proportion of a message's meaning, and body language carries the largest proportion of the nonverbal message. More specifically, the face is the most powerful element in the nonverbal communication system. An illustrative list of three key elements of body language with some of the more common possible interpretations is provided in Putting Ideas into Practice.

Cultural influences can be seen in the expression or interpretation of any of the body language elements, but none more dramatically than eye contact (Jones, 2010). In

PUTTING IDEAS INTO PRACTICE

Body Language Communicates Powerful Messages

Although body language conveys much information during communication, there are no universal interpretations of these nonverbal cues. However, some behaviors tend to be associated with certain messages, as the following examples illustrate.

Facial Expression

This is the most powerful of the body language cues.

Eyebrows and Forehead

- Raised eyebrow—often conveys surprise or fear (duration is longer with fear)
- Furrowed brow—may indicate worry, stress, or concentration
- Sweaty brow—suggests nervousness, fear, or physical exertion

Eyes ("the mirror of the soul")

- Downcast eyes—suggests shame, shyness, guilt, or "don't call on me"
- Wide eyes—may indicate surprise, wonder, or fear
- Tears—may signal sadness, nostalgia, or joy
- Eye contact—length and directness of gaze can indicate liking, interest, likability, openness, and many other characteristics. Making and interpreting eye contact is so heavily influenced by culture that it defies generalization

Mouth

- Smiles—convey friendliness
- A relaxed face—may naturally have a neutral expression, a slight smile, or a frown

Posture and Orientation

- Slumped, rounded shoulders—suggest one is overburdened with the weight of the world
- Open body position (uncrossed arms and legs)—indicates liking the other person
- Tense and rigid body—often conveys hostility, anger, or fear
- Forward lean, tilt of upper body—generally indicates interest

Gestures

- Wink of an eye—indicates attraction or that one is joking
- "OK" sign (circle with thumb and forefinger)—signals a positive situation in the United States; refers to money in Japan; and says, "you're worth zero," in Belgium
- Index finger to pursed lips—signals others to be quiet

Anglo-European American culture and conversation, people are expected to make eye contact with short glances in a different direction throughout the interaction. Research summarized by Lynch (2011a) shows that among Anglo-European Americans such eye contact communicates trustworthiness and sincerity. Among many African Americans, making eye contact with those in authority is considered disrespectful. In Asian American groups, eye contact with strangers may be thought to be shameful; in Japanese and Latino cultures, if eye contact is prolonged, it may be a sign of disrespect. Lynch cautions that a nonverbal behavior, gesture, or expression that is positive in one culture may be viewed as negative or even obscene in another.

Vocal Cues   Vocal cues, often called paralanguage, constitute the vocal, rather than verbal, component of language. It also communicates a great deal of information separate from the verbal content of the message. Paralanguage includes voice tone, pitch, volume, speech rhythm, and pacing or tempo, as well as the use and timing of silence.

Many of the elements of paralanguage may reach extremes when the speaker is experiencing strong emotions. For example, pitch results from the tightness of one's vocal cords. When you are calm, depressed, or tired, your vocal cords are relaxed and your pitch is lower, whereas excitement or anxiety tends to make your pitch higher. The pace or flow of speech may also indicate emotion; rapid speech can signal excitement and enthusiasm or nervousness and insecurity. Thus, you may observe that someone who is anxious or uncertain about a situation may speak very rapidly at a high pitch, whereas someone more confident and relaxed is likely to speak slowly at a lower pitch. Most importantly, research has demonstrated that people listening to a speaker will attribute weakness/uncertainty or power/strength based on this voice characteristic (Claeys & Cauberghe, 2014).

Spatial Relations   Spatial relations refers to the physical distance you keep between yourself and another in an interaction (Buck & Miller, 2015). Contemporary scholars continue to subscribe to Edward Hall's (1966) description of four spatial zones that people generally use in their interactions with others: (1) intimate distance, (2) personal distance, (3) social distance, and (4) public distance. These spatial zones are illustrated in Figure 3.2. Typically, the greater the distance between people during an interaction the less their intimacy. Perhaps you have had experiences where you felt uncomfortable because the person with whom you were speaking stood too close to you. During interactions between colleagues who do not know each other well, the amount of space between them should be great enough to avoid such discomfort. Professional colleagues are likely to belong in both

FIGURE 3.2   **Relationships and proxemic distances.**

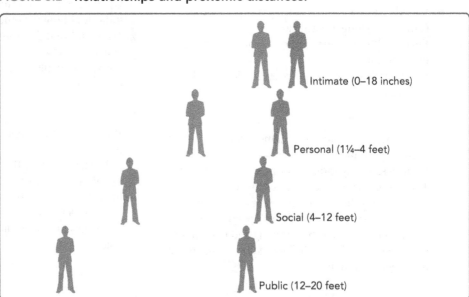

the personal and the social zones because most professionals have closer relationships with some colleagues than others based on the nature of their interactions, their individual characteristics, and interpersonal preferences.

Another way of making judgments about appropriate personal space during interactions is to consider the topic of conversation. Generally, when two people discuss a problem that is disturbing to one of them, the listener should be near enough to the speaker to indicate concern but not so close as to seem threatening or intrusive. If the speaker is distressed or sad, physical closeness and a touch on the shoulder might be exactly what he or she needs. Obviously, that varies with individuals, and all professionals are well advised to watch for verbal and nonverbal cues that help us to know whether others wish greater or less distance and closeness.

Interpreting nonverbal communication is highly subjective. In the previous Putting Ideas into Practice, you learned that downcast eyes may indicate shame, shyness, guilt, or a hope that one will not be called on to speak or respond to a question. Similarly, rapid speech may indicate enthusiasm or anxiety, but the varying interpretations of the downward glance and the rapid speech are distinctly different emotions. The physical distance between two individuals should be "near enough to" but "not so close to;" what is appropriate for any particular interaction may be inappropriate for another. There simply are no universal gestures or body language cues and no specific prescriptions for "correct" body language. Instead, you should engage in mindful observation and reflection to better understand the meaning of your own nonverbal communication and that of others.

How aware are you of nonverbal communication in your interactions—body language, vocal cues, and spatial relations? To develop effective nonverbal skills, first you need to identify your own patterns of nonverbal behavior that affect communication positively or negatively and learn to anticipate individual differences in how others react to your nonverbal behaviors. One strategy is to observe nonverbal behaviors and, when appropriate, discuss them with others to gain deeper understanding of their meanings. Similarly, you may wish to ask others about your nonverbal communication and what it conveys to them. Most people are surprised when they learn that they unintentionally use nonverbal cues resulting in untended communication.

Although technology-mediated communication is not a focus in this text, it should at least be mentioned as a specialized aspect of nonverbal communication. People are increasingly using e-mail, chats, videoconferencing, instant messaging, and similar technology applications for their communication. E-mail is becoming the most frequently used technology-based medium for teacher exchanges with colleagues and parents. The asynchronous nature of e-mail holds much appeal for many people, yet the lack of nonverbal cues and transaction between communicators are limitations to this medium. In E-Partnerships several strategies for the effective use of e-mail are presented.

Learn More About
Although teachers increasingly use a variety of social media to communicate with parents, this video reviews a teacher's use of e-mail, still the most commonly used communication tool.

Listening and Communication

Listening involves the simultaneous use of multiple skills, both verbal and nonverbal, many of which are introductory to the development of other skills. It is a multidimensional, difficult-to-measure process of selecting, attending to, understanding, recalling, and responding to verbal and nonverbal messages, and little research directly addresses this complexity (Adler, Rodman, & du Pré, 2014; Spunt, 2013; Wood, 2013). At the core of listening skills is being able to accurately comprehend what another person is saying and then demonstrate that this has occurred (Beebe, Beebe, & Redman, 2014; Egan, 2014; Goulston, 2010). It is the primary means for gaining information, but it is also a means of conveying interest in the messages of others. In A Basis in Research, you can explore the complexity of listening as it relates to listening styles and context.

Whatever its intended purpose, listening is essential to every part of life. People listen for pleasure at concerts and movies, for learning in courses and meetings, and for understanding in day-to-day interactions with families and friends. For professionals, accurate and effective listening can make the difference between strong partnerships or unfortunate misunderstandings.

E-PARTNERSHIPS
Using E-Mail Effectively

E-mail has become a significant mode of communication, especially among those with schedule challenges who value its asynchronous elements. The dilemma is that many people receive an unreasonable number of e-mails each day and can miss or inadvertently delete an important message when it is buried among many others. Another obvious downside to e-mail is that you lose the nonverbal cues in the interaction that could clarify your messages.

Here are some recommendations that will set your e-mails apart from the multitude of others your colleagues and students' parents receive. These suggestions may also help ensure that your messages convey what you intend and are taken seriously by others.

- *Get a response to your message.* Use your colleague's name or another signal such as "important" or "please respond today" in the subject line. This calls attention to your message when it is buried in a long list of messages.
- *Be professional.* Use a professional e-mail address. For correspondence about school matters, you should avoid using that cute or irreverent e-mail address that you have for personal communication. You should also avoid other options that could be considered unprofessional, such as embedded animated characters.
- *Keep it short and easy to read.* Short, to-the-point messages are the best for e-mail. If you have a large amount of information to share, add it as an attachment. People generally do not want to read detailed e-mail messages, especially not on hand-held devices with small screens.
- *Avoid controversy.* E-mail is best for routine or information purposes (e.g., to remind participants of a meeting, to announce upcoming events). It is not appropriate for contentious issues and detailed problem solving.
- *Take time to think.* Often a hasty reply conveys an unintended tone and produces undesired consequences. Review your message before sending. When you are upset, vent all you want (before you enter the recipient's address) and e-mail the message to yourself to review again before sending. You probably will delete that message or edit it significantly.
- *Develop an off-limits response.* Create, save, and routinely use a standard response to messages that address a topic requiring face-to-face interaction.
- *Restate the topic.* If you are responding to a message from someone else, either leave that message attached or cut and paste the particular items from that message into yours. Messages such as, "Great. I'll meet you there but let's make it half an hour later" or "Interesting, send a copy" with no reference to the previous message may be irritating and meaningless.
- *Use e-mail judiciously.* Ask yourself if this information is worth sharing. Guard against having your messages becoming "inbox clutter."
- *Treat your e-mail as nonconfidential.* You should think of anything you write in an e-mail as something that might be seen on a billboard along the highway. That won't happen, but similar results may occur as others may forward or broadcast it across their networks without permission. Moreover, your e-mail could be subpoenaed as part of a legal proceeding, and a careless remark in an e-mail message may cause harm to you or others.
- *Treat others' e-mail as confidential.* You should guard against indiscriminate forwarding of others' messages. This is recommended in order to preserve others' trust of your communication as well as to avoid conveying that you are not reflective in sharing information.

E-mail is a remarkable tool if used properly and thoughtfully. Talk with your colleagues about other pet peeves or preferences and ensure that you maximize the value of this technology in your work.

Rationale for Listening

You may best understand the importance of listening if you recall experiences of not being listened to—whether at a party, in a work setting, or at home. In all these settings, you may have participated in parallel conversations, much like the parallel play of children, in which individuals, either simultaneously or alternately, talk about the topic that most interests them without much regard for others. The speakers appear to have agreed to take turns speaking and acting as an audience for each other without responding in any meaningful way to what the other person communicates. If you have been part of such

A BASIS IN RESEARCH

Smile, If You Want the Full Scoop!

A listener's nonverbal responses have great impact on the nature of the information speakers provide. In a recent study, undergraduates in the Netherlands watched an eight-minute film and were then asked to describe it as fully as possible to other participants (Beukeboom, 2008). The other participants were confederate research assistants trained to give positive or negative responses when listening. Half of the group described the film to a confederate who adopted a positive expression by smiling, nodding, returning smiles of the participant, and maintaining an open body position. The other half spoke with a confederate who adopted a negative affective expression by not returning smiles of the participant and displaying a serious, frowning facial expression and a closed body position. When describing the film to a positive listener, participants used more abstractions and interpretations and included more of their own opinions when they described elements of the film that could not be viewed, such as a character's thoughts and emotions. Participants talking to frowning listeners stayed with the concrete and descriptive facts. The researcher suggests that people have a tendency to interpret the smiles and nods of a positive listener as a sign of agreement and understanding, encouraging them to provide a more interpretative account. Negative listeners, by contrast, provoke a more cautious and descriptive thinking style.

adult parallel play, you surely recognize that dissatisfaction and feelings of being dismissed result.

To avoid instilling those feelings in others, remember that listening is essential in establishing camaraderie and building relationships (Goulston, 2010; Seeley, 2005). When you listen, you show concern and a desire to understand the other person and the situation, that is, you establish rapport. By listening, you communicate both concern for the speaker as an individual and the intent to understand what that person has to say, two elements attributed to communication competence. In addition, accurate understanding enables you to build and maintain a sense of affiliation. Ultimately, when you listen carefully you are perceived as being both competent and worthy of trust (Bawany, 2014; DeVito, 2013; Ivey & Ivey, 2014). These perceptions of others contribute to their willingness to collaborate with you.

Another major benefit of effective listening is that you obtain sufficient and accurate information necessary for participating in a collaborative activity. Too frequently, professionals assume they understand an inadequately articulated comment and begin acting on it as they perceive it. This is a dangerous practice for several reasons. First, it is unlikely that anyone can accurately understand a situation that is not clearly described. Without accurate understanding, appropriate actions are rare. Second, a rapid-fire response may give others the impression that their concerns are trivial or that they are not competent. Perhaps you have had the following happen: People listened haphazardly as you described a problem, responded too quickly, and left you thinking, "If it was so simple, why couldn't I think of an answer? I'm embarrassed to have thought it was such a problem!" Or, more likely, you thought something like this: "That person didn't hear anything I was saying. How could she give such a superficial response?" That kind of situation does nothing to establish parity or rapport.

Finally, and perhaps most threatening to the collaborative relationship, a rapid and inaccurate response to a person's comments suggests little concern for his or her perception of the issue and, thus, little regard for the person as a significant individual.

Listening As a Process

Fully understanding the mechanics of listening requires an understanding of the listening process, which consists of hearing, attending, understanding, responding, and

> **Learn More About**
> Are you truly a skillful listener? Find out in this listening quiz.
>
> (https://www.youtube.com/watch?v=848MrvcOnfk)

remembering. Those elements are operational in the listening process, although the sequence of their occurrence varies in different models (Adler et al., 2014; Gamble & Gamble, 2013).

- *Hearing* involves receiving sound waves transmitted at a certain frequency and loudness. It is an involuntary physiological process that is influenced by the hearing capacity of the listener. Hearing capacity can be influenced by sustained exposure to sounds of the same frequency or loudness, background sounds similar to what you are trying to hear, and other factors. Many people have hearing deficits due to genetics or acquired hearing loss, and communicators need to adjust strategies accordingly. "Hearing," therefore, is not always dependent upon sound as people who rely on sign language demonstrate.
- *Attending* is a psychological process and part of the selection processes described in Chapter 2. Because individuals cannot attend to all the sounds and information that bombard them each day, they filter out some messages and focus on others. Attending is closely allied with perception, and you are similarly likely to attend to those messages that have personal meaning for you, meet your needs, or otherwise capture your interest.
- *Understanding* is the sense-making element in the listening process. We may not understand or we may misunderstand any given message. *Listening fidelity* is a term used to describe the congruence between what a sender intended to communicate and what a listener understands. Understanding unfolds in the same way as organizing and interpreting did in our earlier discussion of perception. As you select and attend to information from speakers, you categorize it in a way that is meaningful to you, oftentimes by virtue of how mindfully you listen to what is being said.
- *Responding* is the provision of verbal and nonverbal feedback to the speaker. This demonstrates the transactional nature of listening through which communicators collaborate to develop shared meanings. How one responds also influences the feelings the communicators have about each other and the relationships they develop.
- *Remembering* is the ability to recall the information in the message. Research shows that listeners typically remember up to 50 percent of what they hear immediately after hearing it. That percentage falls rapidly over time with about 25 percent of the information being accessible to memory after two months.

Factors That Interfere with Effective Listening

Though different in some ways, all three dangers of quick responses point to several key causes that can act as obstacles to effective listening, thus inhibiting professional collaboration. To illustrate the interfering factors, consider the following example: Have you ever found that despite good intentions to listen carefully to a colleague, by the time the person finished giving a clear and precise description, you were not at all sure what had been said? This experience is common, and it illustrates how difficult it is to listen. In fact, although people spend about 50 percent of their communication time "listening" to others, their listening effectiveness is only about 25 percent (Boyd, 2001). Think back to times when you recognized that you were not listening to someone else. Can you identify which, if any, of the following interfered with your listening?

Faulty Assumptions The discussion of perspective in Chapter 2 pointed to the many assumptions we make when interacting with others. When a topic is familiar, we may assume we have heard it all before, or a related topic arises and we assume the speaker's thoughts are too simple to deserve careful attention. Often, school professionals are so busy that they respond to their first impression of what an issue is—or what it may be—without having explored it with an open mind. People who recognize that they do this will note that they tend to interpret what others are saying whether they have said it or not. Responding to assumptions—especially inaccurate ones—often communicates a lack of investment in, or concern for, the other person.

Insufficient Time for Communication School professionals are asked to do many things simultaneously and often in too little time. One of the most frequent barriers to listening and detriments to effective relationships is the especially unproductive "Okay, I'll take care of it" response. That reply may piggyback on the tendency to rely on assumptions and occur when you have not spent the time to fully understand what "it" is; thus, you may "take care of" the wrong thing. Regardless of your level of understanding, this response to limited listening time adds another task to an already overcommitted schedule, making future communication equally as hurried.

Daydreaming Listening, although important, is an inefficient process. People usually speak at a rate of about 125 to 150 words per minute but can think at a rate of as many as 500 words per minute. Thus, even if a speaker talks at an unusually high rate, that speech–thought differential results in some spare time to think even while you listen. Unfortunately, you may use this time for a thinking excursion, that is, to prepare a shopping list, plan a week's vacation, or think about a new instructional unit. You may find yourself suddenly daydreaming and discover that you have lost track of the conversation.

Rehearsing a Response Perhaps while your colleague is talking, you catch the drift of what is being said and proceed to work on framing what you will say when you have the opportunity to speak. Similarly, perhaps you anticipate that it will soon be your turn to report at a team meeting, and so you review your notes to prepare your comments and miss what someone else is saying. Rehearsing may seem attractive because of the goal of speaking in an articulate manner, but it has the serious risk of resulting in you missing essential information.

Filtering Messages Occasionally, you may have little interest in, or simply not want to listen to, a particular message. Think about a time when you may have "tuned out" at a meeting. In these cases, your perceptual process will cause you to selectively attend to specific parts of a message and ignore others, thereby causing you to perceive the message incompletely or inaccurately.

Being Distracted by Noise Stumbling on "hot words," being distracted by uncomfortable room temperature, or attending to extraneous details such as a colleague's unfortunate new haircut are examples of responding to semantic, physical, and psychological noise. You can understand these, and many other interfering factors discussed by communication experts, without further elaboration based on your understanding of the transactional model of communication.

Lack of Training Although you have been listening since childhood and are probably certain that you need no instruction or practice with this skill, you should recognize that lack of training hampers most listeners. Listening is not a naturally occurring function like breathing. It is the communication that is learned first by infants, used most throughout life, but taught least. Research has shown consistently that listening can be improved through instruction and practice (Ivey, Ivey, Zapaquett, & Quirk, 2016). A Basis in Research describes research findings regarding successful teaching and learning of communication skills including listening.

Suggestions for Improving Listening Skills

With the right attitude, instruction, and effort, you can undoubtedly improve your listening. Refining those skills, however, requires addressing your ability to sustain attention and monitor message comprehension. The following are some straightforward practices that are powerful guidelines to help you do this.

Establish Listening Goals One of the simplest and most overlooked strategies for effective listening is to know why you are listening and what you are listening for. Be clear about what you want to accomplish by listening, and then remind yourself of the purpose

A BASIS IN RESEARCH

Teaching Communication Skills

Communication skills are essential tools for collaboration. And that is based on more than intuitive logic—research supports it as well.

Hundreds of studies have demonstrated that providing educational professionals with direct instruction and related practice in communication skills results in increased skill. Bulach (2003) examined direct instruction and practice of such communication skills and their effects on the sense of openness and trust among preservice administrators. These administrators grew in all but one aspect of openness and trust as measured on a valid and reliable survey. McNaughton, Hamlin, McCarthy, Head-Reeves, and Schreiner (2007) demonstrated that instruction in listening skills for preservice preschool teachers resulted in statistically significant improvement for targeted skills. Kuntze, Molen, and Born (2009) examined the impact of counseling skills training on seven basic (microskills) and five advanced communication skills on preservice counselors, and they found that students made significant growth in basic skills during a semester program, but advanced skills required a longer training period.

Extensive research on teaching microskills, or single skills as presented in this text, has been conducted with preservice educators and counselors since 1966. Ivey and Ivey (2014) report implications from more than 450 studies that show the following:

- Microtraining produces results; specifically, it improves skills.
- Specific skills are more likely to reliably produce certain responses.
- Practice is essential for skill development and maintenance.
- Cultural differences are real, and effective communicators adapt skills to ensure their cultural appropriateness.

Skills in this text are presented in a manner that extensive research has shown to be most efficacious. A skill is first presented as an example with the goal that it will then be modeled by the instructor, in a role play, or through a video. The text discussion that follows the introduction of each skill is designed to help you understand the rationale for and definition of it. Practicing the skill is the third critical component. Finally, assessment and self-assessment are needed if you are to master the skill.

---

should your attention stray. You will listen and respond differently if your goal is to support an upset parent whose child has performed very poorly on a significant assessment as opposed to listening to a very upset parent whose reason for distress is unknown, or listening to the parent in order to make sure the parent hears your point of view.

Eliminate Distractions Before you begin interacting with someone, do what you can to get rid of internal distractions (e.g., thirst, need to call home) and external ones (e.g., hallway noise, music, cell phone beeping that text messages are arriving) that interfere with listening. Clear your mind and deliberately shut out competing thoughts.

Talk Less This seems almost too obvious to mention, but it is also one of the greatest challenges to overcome on your journey toward improved listening. Most school professionals spend much of their time interacting with students and parents about their concerns, behaviors, or programs, and in these interactions they tend to talk a great deal. When afforded the opportunity to interact with another professional, it is very common for them to continue this pattern, talking more than listening, even if the topic is really about the other's concern. This tendency sometimes is viewed as "hogging the stage" or "one-upmanship." You probably have experienced it yourself when describing a frustrating situation you had with a student, and rather than empathizing or supporting you, a colleague says, "I know! I had a worse situation last week when Jerome...." And then the topic of conversation turns to the colleague's story.

Avoid Prejudgments Despite the psychological need to select and organize tremendous amounts of incoming information, good listeners recognize that a given listening situation is not the occasion for such filtering, and they hold their prejudgments in abeyance. As we have noted, people are most apt to judge prematurely if the subject is very familiar or seems simplistic, but it is also common if the speaker's ideas conflict with their own beliefs. Good listeners guard against prejudgments and listen for understanding.

Avoid Interruptions Many interruptions are avoidable. In order to reduce your own interruptions, we recommend that you take some time to identify how the speaker approaches message sharing. Some people begin with a clear and direct statement of their main point and then give supporting details. Others give background explanations and then reveal their main idea. And still others give many details with varying levels of relevance but never state a clear topic or central point because they assume the listener has inferred it. You should avoid interruptions by waiting until the message seems relatively complete before speaking. If you have a question, you may find that the speaker's next comment will supply the answer. There are obvious exceptions to this guideline, such as when speakers lose focus and their talk does not contribute to the goal of the interaction. This is relatively infrequent, and its occurrence does not justify the prevalence of interruptions typically occurring in discussions.

Learn More About This video clip, showing inappropriate and then appropriate listening skills, has direct applicability to school professionals. How can you avoid being a participant in the first scenario?
(https://www.youtube.com/watch?v=bO-a-Yz4xA8)

Focus on the Content of the Spoken Message Seek to understand the main content of the message while avoiding trivial details. Identify themes or key words in the message. Use the time derived from the speech–thought differential to mentally summarize and repeat those themes; add others as the speaker presents them. Differentiate and make connections between inferences and facts, and identify where the speaker has omitted important facts. Ask yourself whether you have adequate information to understand the message.

Focus on the Context of the Message Sometimes this strategy is referred to as "listening with a third ear" or "listening with your heart." How something is said often is as important to understanding a message as what was said. For example, in the opening case, just before Jake shared with the others a time when he felt he had overreacted and misplaced his energies, he "leaned forward in his chair, put his elbows on his knees, and let his clasped hands fall between them. He glanced down for a silent second." When Jake looked up, he spoke slowly to describe his reaction and thank Diane for her support. Jake's body position, silence, and slower rate of speech all conveyed a depth of feeling and sincerity, nonverbal messages that reinforced and strengthened his message. These strategies and others presented in Putting Ideas into Practice will help you improve your listening skills.

Keep in mind that your effectiveness as a listener does not require additional money, additional time, or other resources; it is up to you. And the most significant key to improving your success in listening lies in deliberately monitoring and reflecting on your listening behavior and then systematically using such strategies. Committing to becoming a student of communication is a useful step to accomplish this.

Responding

When listening, you respond in two stages: first, while the person is talking and, second, after he or she stops talking. Responses while the other is speaking should be supportive and let the speaker know that you are listening: head nods, smiles, and eye contact are examples (e.g., Balconi & Pagani, 2015; Ruben, Hall, & Mast, 2015). After the person stops talking, you should respond verbally and nonverbally using different response styles and different levels of complexity, depending on the purpose of the communication.

If the speaker has said something that requires little discussion, you are likely to respond directly without needing any clarification. For example, if someone says, "Everyone who is staying after school for the parent meeting, let me know," you may simply say, "Count me in," or "I'll be there." Alternatively, if a speaker says, "Are you volunteering to work on the committee?" you may want to ask questions about the

Learn More About Although a bit of an exaggeration, this video clip demonstrates why professionals should hone their responding skills in order to be viewed as effective listeners.
(https://www.youtube.com/watch?v=Qg8PIK74KO4)

PUTTING IDEAS INTO PRACTICE
Strategies for Successful Listening

Start with an open mind. Acknowledge your biases and set them aside, even if only temporarily, so that you can listen openly. Adopt a positive attitude and do not assume you will be bored.

Use appropriate nonverbal cues. You communicate openness, attention, and interest when you face the speaker and maintain eye contact. A forward lean, a head nod, an "uh-huh" utterance, uncrossed arms, and a slightly tilted head are among the types of cues that also convey attention and interest. These and similar cues are likely to be appropriate in most situations.

Note details. If a large amount of information is being shared, ask permission to jot down important details or concepts if you feel you might lose track of them. This action eliminates another potential reason for interrupting the speaker.

Concentrate. Listening is an intense mental process, and it requires you to deliberately direct your attention to the speaker and refrain from distractions, such as looking at messages on your cell phone or papers on a desk. Monitor your attention, and when it wanders, refocus it on the speaker.

Focus on the message content. Identify themes or keywords in the message, and avoid trivial details. Mentally repeat those themes and add others as the speaker presents them. Notice also what is *not* being said, and identify important facts or sequences the speaker omits. Also, because *how* something is said is often as important as *what* is said, you should attend to relevant contextual and nonverbal cues.

Check your perceptions. During the exchange, check your perceptions for accuracy. This indicates your interest in the speaker and your intent and effort to understand, while it also helps you to establish shared understandings.

Respond effectively. There are many types of responses that may be appropriate for a given communication situation, depending upon the nature of your relationship with the speaker, the speaker's apparent need, and the context for the communication.

---

committee. If a friend tells you about an ailing parent, her stress over upcoming exams, or her anxiety about a performance review, you will probably show empathy and try to discover more information so that you can support her. These differing response styles are addressed through various combinations of verbal and nonverbal strategies. Several critical verbal responses—prompting, paraphrasing, reflecting, and questioning—are addressed here.

Prompting

A category of responding that involves nonverbal and very limited verbal communication is prompting. Also referred to as minimal encouragers, these responses include words, phrases, silence, and other nonverbal cues designed to meet two purposes—first, to encourage the speaker to continue communicating and, second, to indicate that you are listening and understand what the speaker is expressing. Common prompts include silence, head nods, quizzical facial expressions, hand gestures, and spoken cues such as "uh-huh," "hmmm," "and," "so," and "okay."

Prompts invite the person with whom you are interacting to continue sharing information with you. One of the most effective, but seriously underused, prompts is silence. Many people have difficulty waiting in silence for another to respond. Terms such as *pregnant pause*, *lull in the conversation*, and even *deadly silence* convey awareness of, and possible discomfort with, silence in a conversation. It is not unlike the difficulty many teachers have in providing enough wait time for a student response to an academic question. You should try to use a short period of silence—a brief pause—as a supportive prompt. As you become comfortable with allowing a few seconds of silence, you will likely find that it gives others time to gather their thoughts and then continue to convey them to you. When you use silence, or when you nod or use one of the other encouragers, you also allow yourself time to phrase your next question or statement; you will find this to be a real asset for effective communication.

"WOOF, WOOF, WOOF — BUT I'M PARAPHRASING."

Paraphrasing

In paraphrasing, you restate in your own words what you think another person has said. Paraphrasing focuses on relatively small units of information and involves little or no inference. Consider the following example of a teacher and principal discussing a problematic situation that involves a student's parents.

> **Teacher:** I'm not sure I should meet alone with his parents. We seem to be in conflict all the time.
> **Principal:** You have ongoing conflict with these parents....
> **Teacher:** Well, not "ongoing." Actually, it was just once—at our meeting last month. They were furious at me when I told them what his grades were. The father got red in the face, hit the table a couple of times, and left really angry. He won't return any of my phone calls.
> **Principal:** So, it was only one event, but it's still unresolved and you think they—especially the father—are still angry with you.
> **Teacher:** Yes, but I did talk to the mother on the phone. She apologized and explained that her husband has been working two shifts, is really tired, and has been getting angry easily. He also feels guilty because he can't help with homework because he works so much. The mother says he wants to meet with me to see how we can help their son—I'm just not sure.
> **Principal:** Even though the parents seem to have gotten over their anger and say they want to respond constructively, you're still not certain you should meet with them.
> **Teacher:** Yes. It may be calm now, but I've given two tests since our last meeting. He failed both of them. And his father's having problems with his temper.
> **Principal:** His father may get angry again if you tell him about the test grades.

This example demonstrates directly the ways in which paraphrasing may influence relationships. By accurately restating the main points in the teacher's statements, the principal demonstrated attention to, and accurate understanding of, what the teacher was relating and thus conveyed interest in the teacher as well as in the problem.

The principal's paraphrasing actually served a dual purpose, because it also helped to clarify the information provided. When the principal incorrectly restated that the teacher and parent had ongoing conflict, the teacher was able to rephrase the message so that they both understood it in the same way. Because the principal's paraphrases were succinct and captured the essence of the teacher's comments, they also helped to focus the discussion and encourage the teacher to examine the situation more closely. This strategy maintained the teacher as the central figure and helped the principal and the teacher establish a shared understanding of the situation. If you were the teacher, how do you think you would feel about your principal at the conclusion of this interaction?

The aforementioned effects on the relationship may become clearer if you contrast that example with the following alternative:

> **Teacher:** I'm not sure I should meet alone with his parents. We had a falling-out last month.
> **Principal:** I agree. We don't need conflict between parents and staff. Let's have the counselor meet with them instead.

Here, the principal may appear to be supporting the teacher, but such a quick response reveals the principal's tendency to solve problems independently and suggests both lack of concern for the teacher and her perception of the problem as well as lack of respect for the teacher's own resources. Perhaps more important, by contrasting the two examples and their resolutions, you can see how the principal's quick solution or advice in the second example neither solved the problem nor demonstrated respect for the teacher as an independent professional capable of solving a problem with some support.

These examples illustrate how paraphrasing can establish communication and shared vocabulary, and how it compares to a faster, independent problem-solving response from the principal. What was your response to the question about how the teacher might feel? Did you sense that the teacher might be less than satisfied with either of the interactions? Although the first example demonstrated paraphrasing responses and communicated support, it did not end with any sense of resolution. As with the other skills, we are presenting this one out of context. For the teacher to have a satisfactory resolution in this situation, paraphrasing would need to be combined with a wide range of other communication skills as well as the interpersonal problem-solving process described in Chapter 5.

Reflecting

Learn More About
How effective might this "magic phrase" be in your interactions with colleagues and parents? What additional communication skills should be partnered with use of this phrase?
(https://www.youtube.com/watch?v=JgBS337b5UY)

Reflection is similar to paraphrasing but more complex and involving inference. When reflecting, you not only describe what another person has said but try to also capture the affective meaning of the speaker's message. Because you cannot directly observe another's feelings, you examine the verbal and nonverbal aspects of the communication and infer what this information communicates about the speaker's emotional meaning. Reflection is a way of making explicit the inferences you make from the information that is being conveyed implicitly during interaction. It demonstrates that you understand another's feelings, as the following conversation illustrates.

Imagine that the previous example of the teacher and principal discussing an angry father ends like this.

> **Teacher:** Yes. It may be calm now, but I've given two tests since our last meeting. (*Heavy sigh.*) He failed both of them. (*Laughs and looks away.*) His father's having problems with his temper.
> **Principal:** His father may get angry again if you tell him about the test grades. From your laughter I get the sense that you're anxious about this.
> **Teacher:** Yes. I met with another angry father alone last year. He was really a bully, and he actually pushed me. I know he was trying to scare me, and he was successful. I'm afraid to meet alone with people like that. Can you meet with us?

Principal: His father may get angry again and possibly even pose a physical threat. It sounds as though you'd feel safer if someone could meet with you and the parents. I'm quite sure I'm available, but if not, can we reschedule the meeting or ask someone else—perhaps our counselor—to attend?

In this example, the principal restated in her own words the teacher's messages and reflected the teacher's feelings, thus conveying her understanding of the situation from the teacher's point of view. This response is often integral in building relationships and in promoting a sense of trust because it conveys that the speaker's ideas and feelings are understood and valued. In this way, the principal has validated, not diminished, the teacher's experience.

These illustrations of reflection are presented out of context and can only suggest how reflection functions. In fact, the examples may unintentionally suggest that reflection is a simple type of verbal statement. Quite the contrary—although the wording of a reflective comment may be simple, accurately perceiving and reflecting someone's verbal and nonverbal messages is an extremely complex endeavor.

When you reflect accurately, you convey understanding of another person's thoughts, feelings, and experiences; in other words, you *empathize*. Understanding accompanied by congruent nonverbal behavior that conveys intent to help someone deal with a problem is referred to as *empathic listening* (Stains, 2012; Trenholm, 2014). When you convey empathy through reflection and supportive nonverbal behaviors, you help establish trust in your relationship with others. Reflection has other advantages as well. When people hear their messages reflected, it gives them the opportunity to consider complex thoughts a little longer and may allow them to better understand their experiences. Despite these benefits of reflection, there are cautions to observe when using reflection and empathic listening. Some of these are described in Putting Ideas into Practice.

Keep in mind that reflection is a means of expressing understanding of what is said and felt; it is not intended to explain anything new to the speaker. Reflection is thus

PUTTING IDEAS INTO PRACTICE

Avoiding Pitfalls in Practicing Empathic Listening

Empathy is an important element in developing trust in a relationship. By listening carefully and reflecting accurately the other's words, feelings, thoughts, and situations, you express empathy and encourage an authentic exploration of the problem or situation. Yet people often undermine their own efforts at expressing empathy, even though they have the best of intentions. Communicators may invalidate another's experience through misguided efforts to provide encouragement and lessen the person's distress. Mancillas (2005) suggests that responses such as the following invalidate the speaker's experience and should be avoided.

1. *Finding the silver lining*. Statements such as "At least you've still got a job" and "At least the child wasn't seriously hurt" rarely allow the speaker to feel truly understood. Such a statement detracts from understanding how the speaker experienced the situation.
2. *Being overly optimistic*. Although seemingly supportive, some statements may interfere with the speaker's willingness to reveal his or her true concerns by trivializing the situation through identification of a relatively small positive aspect. "How fantastic for you! Now you have extra time for collaborating with the English teachers" is less likely to console a speaker than to invalidate his disappointment in not being selected to sponsor the yearbook.
3. *Offering blind reassurance*. It is appropriate to offer the speaker hope that a situation may be improved, but to offer assurances that "everything will improve" is dangerous because it cannot be guaranteed.
4. *Engaging in mind reading*. Although motivated by the desire to encourage or support the speaker, "mind-reading" comments invalidate the speaker's experience and interfere with efforts at deeper understanding. Such comments include "I know just how you feel," "Your strength is inspiring," and "I completely understand what you're going through."

distinguished from *interpretation*, which attempts to explain the speaker's experience in terms of a theory or a level of understanding beyond what the speaker knows. As Goodman (1978) pointed out, interpretation is usually an attempt to show an understanding of the speaker that is deeper than the speaker's self-understanding. Consider this alternative response to the teacher's concern about meeting with an angry parent:

> **Principal:** You're afraid the father will be angry and violent. This is a lot like your discomfort with many of the male teachers. You seem to be easily threatened by them.

This example is exaggerated to emphasize the potentially intrusive nature of this type of response and to support the view that interpretation should be used sparingly, if at all, between school professionals in work settings. Interpretation may be very appropriate in help-oriented or therapist–client relationships, but interpretation as described here goes beyond the scope of what is generally appropriate among colleagues or with parents.

Questioning

One of the most common and seriously overused responding behaviors is asking questions. Questions have been referred to as "the most popular piece of language" (Ryan, Giles, & Sebastian, 1982). Despite the overuse of questions, they can be helpful in several ways. Clearly, questions facilitate gathering information that refines your understanding of a situation (e.g., "What happened just before that?" "What were the results?"). They can also help you to learn about how someone feels (e.g., "How does that make you feel?" "What is your reaction to that?") or what someone prefers as an action (e.g., "What do you think we should do?").

Well-crafted questions may benefit you by helping you to understand a situation better, and they also benefit the person being queried. "What do you see as your options?" or "What would you like to do about that?" may prompt the person to think of alternative solutions to a situation. When a speaker is sharing a litany of woes, questions such as "What would you like to see happen?" or "What would be your preferred outcome?" may prompt the person to think of solutions, but it is also a very useful way to refocus the discussion and to determine what the person wants to happen or be different. This strategy is particularly valuable when the speaker's emotion or confusion about a situation leads to unfocused descriptions that obscure his main points.

Asking questions does have drawbacks: These and their potential solutions are discussed in greater depth in Chapter 4. Here we call attention to problems that reside in the question's intent and general phrasing. Sometimes the problem lies in the purpose of the questions, especially when they are not questions at all but a means of sending messages to others. Such pseudo-questions, illustrated in Putting Ideas into Practice, are insincere and should be guarded against.

Sometimes the way in which questions are phrased interferes with communication. Some questions are too narrow and truncate the speaker's effort to communicate. This is often the case when a listener asks direct and closed questions calling for a limited range of responses. For example, imagine a teacher telling the coach about a student who was oppositional today and refused to complete his work because he wanted to leave early for football practice instead. If the coach asks, "Did he finish his work?" or "What time did he try to leave?" before the teacher finishes describing the situation, he may push her to answer inconsequential questions and stop her from communicating more important information. The questions the coach asked had very few potential responses, refocused the discussion away from what needed to be communicated, and required him to ask more questions because the initial ones did not lead to adequate information. His subsequent questions, "Was the work too much for him?" "Has he refused to do his assignments before?" and "What are the consequences?" simply continued the nonproductive pattern. Consider that the teacher wanted to explain that when she reminded the student of the consequences, he had an outburst and revealed that one of the school bullies would hurt him unless he made sure his team lost the football game today. None of the coach's

PUTTING IDEAS INTO PRACTICE
Watch Out for Insincere Questions

Questions that seek to clarify a message sometimes are necessary and often are helpful in interpersonal communication. Unfortunately, questions may also be used to send a message rather than seeking to understand one. Such insincere questions hinder relationships and should be avoided. Some examples are offered here.

Advising questions. "Have you tried graphic organizers?" may be a sincere question, but more often is advisory; the question is a vehicle for making a suggestion. A more extreme form such as "Haven't you tried graphic organizers?" is evaluative. It suggests a preferred behavior and implies failure for not having done something.

Questions that make statements. "Are you *finally* going to call her mother?" By using and emphasizing the word *finally*, the question communicates the speaker's opinion (e.g., it's high time you made that call!).

Questions based on unconfirmed assumptions. "Why can't I get your attention?" assumes that another person is not paying attention.

Questions that look for agreement. "Don't you agree?" or "Isn't that right?" almost coerce agreement. Instead of "don't you," try starting the question with "do you."

Questions that seek a predetermined response. "Who do you think should present this at the meeting?" may be a sincere question or a setup for someone's already decided preference. These insincere questions are not always easy to recognize until they elicit an "incorrect" answer that is rejected by the speaker.

---

questions would have uncovered the entire situation in this example, yet they probably functioned to interfere with the teacher's effort to describe it fully.

One special type of question merits attention in this section on responding; *checking*, sometimes also referred to as *perception checking* or *checking for accuracy*. Checking functions to clarify and confirm information and also conveys an intent to understand. This function frequently is addressed through combining a statement and a question, such as when you share an observation and inference followed by an honest request for clarification: "When you didn't respond to me or answer my question, I thought you weren't listening. Was that an accurate perception?"

Checking the accuracy of what you have heard or perceived is another way that questions improve communication. In fact, if paraphrasing and reflecting are to be maximally effective, they need to be checked, or followed up with a question to ensure agreement and correctness. After paraphrasing or reflecting, you might ask, "Is that a fair description?" "Have I described the situation as you see it?" or "Is that an accurate understanding?"

Prompting, paraphrasing, reflecting, and questioning are very useful listening responses. They facilitate the interaction by clarifying or confirming information, and they are also strong indicators of the intent to understand, a powerful force in building solid relationships needed to collaborate. And, although there are no simple solutions for becoming a more effective listener, you can improve your skills by remaining aware of the listening process, recognizing common barriers to good listening, and honing your skills in using appropriate listening responses.

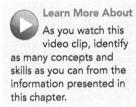

Learn More About
As you watch this video clip, identify as many concepts and skills as you can from the information presented in this chapter.
(https://www.youtube.com/watch?v=IL0sDXCzRu0)

Principles for Effective Verbal and Nonverbal Communication

In addition to the concepts and specific practices already addressed for verbal and nonverbal communication, understanding three critical concepts—congruence, individuality, and concreteness—can help you develop a better understanding of when and how to apply your knowledge as well as other communication suggestions offered throughout the text.

Congruence

As should now be clear to you, communication consists of clusters of simultaneously occurring verbal and nonverbal behaviors. When talking, an individual is also communicating through gestures, movements, facial expressions, posture, and paralanguage (e.g., Kang, Tversky, & Black, 2015; Mehu & van der Maaten, 2014). As Rogers (1951) noted more than 60 years ago, believable behavior generally occurs in congruent clusters; that is, several behaviors that have the same or highly similar meanings occur simultaneously. Rogers attributed the characteristics of genuineness to congruence. Incongruence may unintentionally reveal feelings or attitudes one is hoping to conceal (e.g., the principal who chuckles while telling a staff member, "This is serious!"). Consider these descriptions:

- "I'm really interested in what's going on with Kim and Amir," the counselor said as she set her papers aside and sat down facing the teacher. She looked at the teacher, leaned forward slightly in her chair, and asked, "Do you have any insights that would help me understand their situation? Please let me know what you think about their progress." She then sat quietly, looking at the teacher and waiting for a response.
- "I'm really interested in what's going on with Kim and Amir," the counselor said as she entered the room. She glanced first at the teacher and then at the papers she was carrying, sat down at her computer, and said, "Do you have any insights that would help me understand their situation?" She looked at her watch, then at the teacher, and began reading and responding to e-mail as she said, "Please let me know what you think about their progress."

How congruent were the counselor's verbal and nonverbal behaviors in each example? What did the counselor's body language communicate to you? In the first example, it probably suggested that she was interested in the other person's information and ideas. In the second example, her nonverbal message clearly contradicted her verbal message. In the actual situation, one would observe many more nonverbal cues and the message would have been even stronger. Yet even with this limited information, you can understand the likely impact of her incongruous verbal and nonverbal communication on the teacher. The counselor's contradictory behaviors were unlikely to convey anything genuine.

Now consider in the chapter's opening case examples of Jake's nonverbal cues that were congruent with and strengthened his verbal message. You are likely to tag his body movements or gestures (e.g., eye contact, touching Diane's chair, and smiling) and his vocal cues (e.g., speaking softly or decidedly, laughing, and changing verbal pace) as consistent with his verbal message. Together, his verbal and nonverbal strategies communicated sincere understanding and genuine interest in parents' concerns. His use of space was also congruent with his verbal message. By physically joining the group and sitting among its members, he strengthened his verbal message that he was one of them. By leaning into the group while sharing his feelings, he suggested that the group is a safe place to express personal feelings.

Individuality

The meaning of a single word or nonverbal cue depends not only on the context in which it occurs but also on its specific meaning to the individual using the word or demonstrating the behavior *and* to the individual observing and interpreting it. You already understand that no universal body language exists and that culture has a significant influence on the meaning of verbal and nonverbal cues. So, too, do the individual perspectives of those involved, and those perspectives may diverge from a few, many, or all cultural or professional expectations. For example, you may nod your head frequently, say "uh-huh" and "interesting" to encourage a colleague to continue talking, but she may feel you are expressing agreement in order to hurry her along so that you may speak. Or you may consciously maintain the accepted form of eye contact with a colleague to demonstrate your interest and attention. Your colleague, on the other hand, may be uncomfortable with your "interested" eye contact and see it as a penetrating stare that makes her feel exposed, overly scrutinized, or generally uncomfortable. Effective communicators should avoid making premature assumptions about the meaning of others' word choice or nonverbal cues. This is just as important as avoiding assumptions that the intended meanings of your communications are clear to others.

Concreteness

You are more likely to understand verbal interactions if they involve the exchange of concrete, specific information. Vague language may so obscure the message that it may not be possible to determine what the speaker intended. For example, if a teacher says he "handled" the problem, is it possible to determine what the teacher's actions were? If a colleague asks you for assistance with a student's disruptive behavior, do you know whether the colleague wants you to suggest strategies to use in class, or whether he wants you to intervene with the student? Do you even know the nature and extent of the student's "disruptive behavior"? The answer to each of these questions is "Of course not." In each of these interactions, the language was far too vague to reveal the speaker's true intent. The following examples illustrate how a vague statement or question may be made more concrete. Although these are simple illustrations taken out of context, the very different meanings conveyed in them underscore the level and range of misunderstanding that is invited by vague communication.

> *Statement*: I was concerned about her reaction.
> *Alternative A*: I felt angry and rejected when she asked to change her son's class.
> *Alternative B*: I feared that she might turn her anger on her son.
>
> *Question*: Has Coretta improved in your class?
> *Alternative A*: Has Coretta's off-task behavior decreased in your science class?
> *Alternative B*: Has Coretta's participation in literature improved since we provided her with books on tape to listen to before the class discussions?

As you review these examples using the information included in Figure 3.3 you can easily see how important concrete language is. Yet, listen to yourself and to your colleagues as you discuss students and school-related issues, and see how routinely conversations proceed around vaguely described topics. As you listen, you probably will recognize that

FIGURE 3.3 **A sample feedback continuum: Abstract to concrete.**

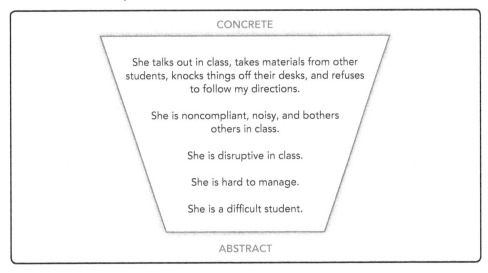

concreteness exists on a continuum from completely abstract to very specific. As you practice and develop proficiency in communicating clearly, you will learn to judge the amount of concreteness needed for successful communication in any given situation.

Giving Verbal Feedback

In the strictest sense, all transactional communication, as discussed in Chapter 2—whether verbal statements, questions, or nonverbal messages—includes feedback. Such feedback is often not intentional, but it provides important information and may lead to changes in behaviors of the participants. In this section, the focus is on intentional verbal feedback as a skill that should be purposefully developed and used by school professionals.

Most simply, feedback is providing others with information about your observations of their behaviors. It can be given for many different purposes, including providing others with objective information about observed behaviors or observed conditions, providing information about the impressions or feelings that these behaviors or conditions cause, and clarifying what the observed behaviors or conditions might mean or signify.

Characteristics of Effective Interpersonal Feedback

To collaborate successfully, you need to be adept at giving effective feedback. In this context, by *effective* we mean feedback that others can and do use to evaluate their own situations or behavior. In addition to giving useful feedback, you should also develop a habit of soliciting and accepting feedback from others as a means of securing valuable information about your own behaviors, situations, and collaborative relationships. This is true whether your collaboration is aimed at helping each other develop and refine the skills presented in this text or targeted at other work-related activities.

Effective feedback statements have a clear set of characteristics. They should be (1) descriptive, (2) specific, (3) directed toward changeable behaviors and situations, (4) concise, and (5) checked for clarity. For feedback statements to be accepted with comfort and to be useful to those who receive them, they should include all of these characteristics.

Descriptive Rather than Evaluative or Advisory Feedback An individual is more likely to listen to potentially useful information when someone simply describes what has occurred and what he or she has observed. Descriptive feedback is nonthreatening and nonjudgmental. Descriptive feedback is contrasted with evaluation and advice as depicted in the following example.

Say: "You said James didn't follow directions when you gave the two options."
Rather than: "You shouldn't give two alternative directions at the same time."
Or: "Have you tried giving one direction at a time?"

When you describe a personal observation, you communicate information without suggesting what action one should take. The other individual is free to use or ignore the information. On the other hand, when you offer evaluative or advisory feedback, you convey that the other person should take action or make a change, often one implied or directly stated in your statement. This has the potential to cause the person to feel defensive and criticized rather than interested in making a change. The following statements are evaluative and are likely to be seen as critical or threatening to the person hearing them: "Your activity sequence doesn't seem to work," and "You should try the outlining strategy with Jennifer."

Evaluative comments are not always negative. It is important to recognize that positive comments also convey a judgment, such as "You do such a good job with James," or "That was a great lesson." As you may have surmised, avoiding judgmental statements requires the elimination of both negative and positive comments. Individuals who make positive judgments are likely to also make negative ones. The person receiving the feedback is justified in assuming that those who give praise also make critical evaluations, whether they are stated openly or not. The alternative is to instead describe the behavior that was effective or successful. For example, "when you used visuals for the three directions given, every student began to work promptly—no one asked questions or seemed to be off task."

Specific Rather than General Feedback Descriptions of specific behaviors are more easily understood than are general comments. "You lost it when he got out of his seat again" communicates much less than "When he got out of his seat that last time, you responded very quickly and raised your voice as you told him to sit down." This specific and concrete language makes communication clearer.

Feedback Directed Toward Changeable Behaviors and Situations If feedback is to be useful, it needs to be directed at something over which the receiver has control. Feedback directed toward an attribute or situation the receiver cannot control generally is pointless and likely to interfere with effective communication. Physical traits, such as height, age, and gender, and situational factors, such as the size of the room and the administrator's leadership style, are not behaviors that an individual can change. Telling someone that his age and physical appearance make it hard to talk to him could be more detrimental than helpful. On the other hand, information such as "You were busy filing papers when I was talking to you" or "I notice that you usually look at the desk when I'm talking" is information that may be acted on if one chooses. Reminding others of things they cannot change is likely to increase their frustration.

Concise Feedback Concise feedback is easier to understand than feedback that contains extraneous detail or information. When first learning to give feedback, you may feel obligated to offer very detailed information or to make many statements. Keep in mind that too much information or too much irrelevant information and redundancy detract from the main message. For example, compare the following two feedback statements. Which is more likely to help a teacher understand the colleague's confusion?

- "In terms of your language, I mean the words you used, you kept using complex and technical words. The vocabulary was too specialized. I didn't know what your words meant so I missed your point. Everything has to be explained well, or I get really frustrated and close out what you say. Then I can't help the kids in their work."
- "I got lost when you used technical terms. It would help me if you would clarify the terms and make your point again."

Feedback Checked to Ensure Clear Communication Perceptions of any event usually vary among individuals. That is, several people may participate in the same situation yet experience it differently. Similarly, when you give feedback, the receiver may not receive the information the way you intended it. To check others' understanding of the feedback you give, you might ask them to paraphrase your feedback to see whether it corresponds to what you intended. You might say, "I'm concerned whether I'm communicating clearly. Could you summarize what you've understood me to say?"

Frequently when receiving feedback, someone will spontaneously confirm or appear to understand the feedback with a general comment, such as "Yes, I did do that," or "That's right." Even so, it is still advisable to check for understanding by rephrasing or questioning, as shown here:

Rephrasing: "So, you were giving different directions to James and Juanita?"
Questioning: "You said, 'That's right.' Which comments were correct?"

> **Learn More About**
> How can you avoid being a perpetrator or victim of the "Cap'n Crunch" phenomenon? How is this issue seen in schools in a way similar to business environments?
> (https://www.youtube.com/watch?v=CbUh8yht1vg&list=PL631E9A96CD0E3602)

You also may want to check the accuracy of your observations that are the subject of your feedback, particularly if you are uncertain about what you observed. In checking for accuracy, you might ask whether the receiver agrees with your observation. Two examples follow:

> "It seemed that you asked James more questions than the others. Do you agree?"
> "Does it seem accurate to you that you asked James more questions than you asked the others?"

Guidelines for Giving Effective Feedback

Regardless of how well worded feedback is, it will have little value if it is not delivered under the right conditions or in the proper context. Four guidelines for providing feedback are extremely important and increase the likelihood that the information will be useful. Feedback should be (1) solicited, (2) direct, (3) culturally sensitive, and (4) well timed.

Solicited Rather than Imposed Feedback Feedback is most effective when someone has requested it. An individual who requests feedback is more likely to use it than one on whom feedback is imposed. Unsolicited feedback may make the receiver feel defensive and assume a "And-you're-telling-me-this-because?" attitude. When you first begin to work collaboratively with a colleague, you should not assume that person actually wants feedback. One way to avoid ineffective interactions is to wait for your colleague to provide an opportunity for you to share observations. Then you merely need to confirm the request with a question, such as:

> "Are you asking for my feedback?"
> "Is that something you want to know more about?"
> "Would it be helpful if I shared my observations on that?"

Even if a speaker asked for judgment and advice, the responder is much safer resisting the temptation and staying focused on feedback, especially initially.

Frequently your colleague will not ask for feedback, and you will need to find a way to be invited to provide it. Depending on the openness and attitude of the person, you may emphasize different aspects of the situation and use different communication skills to set the stage for giving feedback. Modeling the desired behavior is also useful. Many school professionals are so accustomed to working in isolation that they feel vulnerable when being observed and discussing their own behaviors. When you ask someone for feedback and accept and explore it, you demonstrate to him or her that this mutual sharing can be safe and helpful.

When feedback is unsolicited it is unlikely to be welcomed or effective.

Direct Rather than Indirect Feedback Feedback is most effective when it is given directly to the person who can use it by the person who has made the observation. For example, instead of asking the principal to tell your co-teacher about your concerns regarding the co-taught classroom, generally you should discuss it with your co-teacher directly. Similarly, notes also may decrease the effectiveness of feedback. Indirect feedback is more easily misinterpreted than is feedback given directly to the person involved. This is due in part to the lack of transactional communication in notes or in other mediated forms of information exchange. The giver cannot check the feedback for accuracy, and the receiver cannot adequately clarify it. Thus, even if it seems challenging or uncomfortable, feedback should be given directly in face-to-face communication.

Culturally Sensitive Feedback In Chapter 2, collectivistic and individualistic cultures, high- and low-context cultures, and cultures with high and low tolerance for ambiguity were described. It is not that any culture exactly "fits" those textbook descriptions, and individuals vary in these characteristics regardless of their cultures. Nevertheless, some strategies recommended for all feedback situations have particular benefits for making the giving and receiving of feedback more comfortable in intercultural situations.

One suggestion is to begin a session or conversation by creating a welcoming environment with salutations and inquiries about the individual's well-being. Demonstrations of interest in, and respect for, the other are important elements of any relationship. Ensure that this is a comfortable time for the other person to participate in discussing and responding to the feedback.

In presenting the observations you have made, include contextual examples and descriptions. Use the same communication skills you would in any feedback meeting, but deliberately insert pauses and short periods of silence to allow the other person to speak, clarify, or question. You also should consider incorporating exploratory reflection to provide the other with feedback about subtle cues and behaviors you observed. This might include tentative statements such as "I notice that you look away when we talk about what you contribute to the classroom instruction. Sometimes that suggests discomfort. Is this an awkward topic for you?" Exploratory measures such as these will help minimize misperceptions or impressions based on cultural components.

Well-Timed Feedback The immediacy of feedback is a subject of considerable attention in the research on learning. Corrective feedback is most beneficial to learners when it is given immediately following the relevant event or behavior (e.g., Houmanfar, 2013). This is not always possible or appropriate for interpersonal feedback, partly because it is not necessarily meant to be corrective or instructional in nature. But several guidelines can help you determine the appropriate timing for feedback.

You should always ask yourself, "Is now the best time to give feedback to this person?" If your colleague is extremely busy or rushed, the feedback may seem like an irritating intrusion. Or if some event has left your colleague upset and confused, immediate feedback may be seen as unduly demanding or even critical. Our recommendation is to provide feedback as soon as appropriate, not only so that it is timely but so that it also demonstrates your sensitivity to the other's receptiveness.

Whenever you offer feedback, you should include recent examples in your statements. The receiver is more likely to understand and benefit from recent examples than from those that are more distant and possibly forgotten. The more time that passes between the event and the feedback, the less vivid the event will be in the person's memory.

In general, when giving feedback to others, ask yourself these questions:

- Will this person understand me?
- Will this person be able to accept my feedback?
- Will this person be able to use the information?

The most significant consideration is that feedback be constructive for, and appreciated by, the recipient. These considerations, along with the other strategies we have presented, should maximize the effectiveness of your feedback.

Having read about nonverbal communication, listening, responding, and verbal feedback, are you beginning to see how important skills in these domains can be for collaboration? One suggestion is to practice these skills when they are not particularly critical, for example, when interacting with a sales associate as you make a purchase, as you converse with the mechanic working on your car, or when you are in a general social situation. Such low-risk practice can prepare you for situations in which having and using the skills may be crucial to a successful outcome.

SUMMARY

- Nonverbal cues are powerful communication mechanisms that include body language, vocal cues, spatial relations, and minimal encouragers.
- Listening is a complex process of selecting, attending to, understanding, recalling, and responding to verbal and nonverbal messages, but its effective use includes many challenges that can be addressed by using specific listening improvement strategies.
- Prompting, paraphrasing, reflecting, and questioning are verbal response skills that convey an interest in and intent to understand the speaker while enhancing relationships.
- Three significant concepts for understanding effective verbal and nonverbal communication are congruence, individuality, and concreteness; and these principles should guide your communications in the entire range of your professional responsibilities.
- Effective verbal feedback is descriptive, specific, directed toward changeable behaviors and situations, concise, and checked for accuracy; it also is solicited rather than imposed, direct, culturally sensitive, and well timed.

BACK TO THE CASE

1. What did Jake say and do that functioned as an invitation for Lisa to speak? What is a professional situation you might encounter in which you could use similar skills?
2. What messages was Lisa sending to Jake? What evidence from the case support your response?
3. Jake displayed several nonverbal messages as he explained his approach to the background checks. For each behavior mentioned and for the behaviors collectively, discuss with classmates what the behaviors communicate. If there are disagreements, consider how your culture or background experiences could be influencing your perspective.

COLLABORATIVE ACTIVITIES

1. Select and observe two different interpersonal interactions, and identify examples of each type of nonverbal cue (body language, vocal cues, use of distance zones, and minimal encouragers).
    - Describe the ways in which nonverbal cues strengthened or detracted from the messages being conveyed.
    - Identify the degree of congruence between the verbal and nonverbal messages. How did it affect the communication?
    - Select some specific behaviors you observed. Consider what these behaviors might be communicating. Are they consistent with the words being used? Do they suggest a stronger or weaker interest than the words convey?
2. Advice and feedback are not likely to have much impact unless the person receiving this information has requested it or is at least open to receiving it. Meet with a colleague or classmate, and discuss ways to assess someone's openness to hearing feedback or advice. Then reflect on ways in which you might get an individual to "invite" your feedback.
3. The power of silence or pauses in interactions can improve communication. Yet nearly everyone has to learn to allow and use silence in interactions. Challenge yourself to allow increasingly greater verbal space (pauses) in conversations. Lengthen, ever so slightly, the verbal space that follows someone else's statements before you begin speaking. As you do this in different interactions, observe how it affects the pace and comfort of the conversation. When did it work well? When did it seem particularly awkward or ineffective?
4. Review the factors that interfere with listening and the suggestions for improving listening. As you consider how these elements affect your listening, think, too, about the ways in which they influence how others listen to you. Describe ways in which you can use this information to improve how others listen to, understand, evaluate, and remember your messages.

5. Critique each of the following examples to determine whether they demonstrate the characteristics of effective feedback. Revise statements as necessary to include all characteristics.

"After you smiled and said, 'Okay,' Juan looked very relieved. Then when you nodded for him to join the group, a big smile covered his face. Is that what you observed, too?"

"You dealt with James better today. He's advanced a lot in math, and you seem to be tolerating his antics better."

"You've really managed to get Sandy to behave in class. You should be very proud of yourself for what you've accomplished!"

 CHECK YOUR UNDERSTANDING

Click here to gauge your understanding of this chapter's essential concepts.

4 Integrating Skills in Formal and Informal Interviews

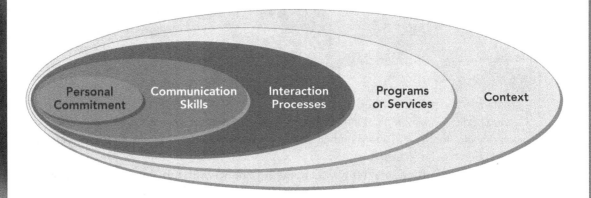

CONNECTIONS

In Chapters 2 and 3 you learned discrete skills of professional and ethical communication: listening, prompting and nonverbal attending, and responding through paraphrasing and reflection. In this chapter, interviewing is explored as a central interaction process in which those and other basic communication skills are integrated in order to accomplish a goal. Interviewing, whether formal or informal, is often particularly helpful during the early stages of an interaction as a means for understanding the other person's perspective. Further, through interviewing you collect and share information needed for problem solving (Chapter 5), co-teaching planning (Chapter 7), and resolving conflict and responding to resistance (Chapter 9).

LEARNING OUTCOMES

After reading this chapter you will be able to:

1. Seek information during interviews by asking questions and making statements deliberately crafted for that purpose, using specific formats (e.g., open/closed; direct/indirect) and content (e.g., presupposition) and employing strategies of focused inquiry.

2. Provide information during interviews by making statements that are descriptive, relying on guiding statements when the specific purpose of the interaction is to provide an explanation or advice.

3. Enhance the effectiveness of the interviews you complete with colleagues, other professionals, parents, and others by applying recommended practices such as using pauses, carefully monitoring the interaction and adjusting your communication strategies as needed, and attending to the cultural context in which the interview is occurring.

A CASE FOR COLLABORATION

Think Before Asking

Jerome and Wyatt met for a cup of coffee during their conference period and were talking casually about having had to work more than they had wanted to over the last weekend. Jerome was sensing some tension coming from Wyatt, a tension that Jerome could understand as he was also disappointed in having had to give up part of his weekend.

"So, they say it gets easier after we get some experience with this standards-based system," Jerome commented, trying to discern Wyatt's mood.

Wyatt rubbed his forehead and replied uneasily, "I don't know. This stuff is so tedious. I hope it's not more work than it's worth. Do we really have to go to another meeting on it?"

Jerome asked with concern, "Well, yeah. Why? Do the meetings bother you or something?"

Wyatt replied, "I don't know. I mean, it's always the same thing, but 'with just a small twist.' And it just creates more work for us."

Surprised by Wyatt's sullen attitude, Jerome remarked, "You really don't know? It sounds like you do. Is something going on? Did something happen? Why don't you like the meetings?"

Wyatt protested mildly after realizing his tone had raised concern for Jerome. "No, no. It's nothing. I thought we were going to have a speaker. Now it just looks like more of the same." He added hurriedly, "But I don't know. I guess we have to go? I don't know.... And now Ms. Hackner is running the meeting."

Jerome doggedly pushed to ascertain what Wyatt's concerns were. "Why don't you like Ms. Hackner?"

"Oh, no, no, she's okay," Wyatt said without regard for clarity. "She's so organized—she is literally color coded—and really eager to talk about next steps. She always has next steps. You know what? Let's just forget about it. Forget I said anything about it. Everything's fine."

Wyatt is in for another confusing meeting. He resents that Ms. Hackner adds something new to the standards-based system at each meeting, making it more complex and different—and more work. He can't imagine why she has to change it all the time. If Wyatt had been more willing to share his feelings and more able to express himself clearly, Jerome might have understood the problem and done something to support or help. If Jerome had put more thought into his questions rather than blurting them out, he might have been able to elicit useful information from Wyatt. Had the situation been clarified, Jerome could have reminded Wyatt of the yearlong plan they had all developed when planning to implement the standards-based grading. The plan included four incremental steps in installing the system. Each "new twist" wasn't a change but rather a new accomplishment, and this week's addition was the last one. If remembering the plan did not help Wyatt, Jerome might have suggested that they talk to Ms. Hackner about possibly getting more comfortable with the accomplishments for a couple more weeks before adding new challenges. But this discussion left Jerome confused—not knowing what Wyatt was disturbed about and, thus, not knowing how he might help his friend.

Introduction

In Chapter 2 we presented a model for skill development that places professional and ethical communications as the foundation of effective interactions and builds the other basic communication skills—nonverbal attending and responding—upon that base. But these skills have limited utility in isolation. They are only helpful to the extent that they can be applied in your day-to-day professional exchanges, that is (if you refer back to the figure in Chapter 2), in the interaction processes common in schools.

The first interaction process to consider, and the focus for this chapter, is interviewing. Although an interview traditionally has been regarded as a process in which one person elicits information from another, the current trend is to view it as an interactive process through which participants both gather information and provide information to each other. An interview may be formal, such as may occur at a parent–teacher conference or during an individualized education program (IEP) team meeting. But an interview may also be an exchange of information, such as may occur when co-teachers meet to learn about each other's ideas for designing lessons to ensure all their students master the curriculum competencies at hand. Generally, interviews have a structure, whether articulated or not, and they typically are essential as a first step in other interaction processes, such as problem solving and resolving conflict, addressed in later chapters.

Like all interaction processes, interviews can be thought of as occurring in steps or stages (Gamble & Gamble, 2013; Ivey, Ivey, Zalaquett, & Quirk, 2016). These steps happen whether the interview is formal or informal, although they often are more carefully planned for the former type of interaction. First, you prepare for an interview by identifying your information needs, generating and sequencing appropriate questions, letting others know ahead of time about the intent of the interview, and arranging the setting so that it is comfortable. Second, you initiate the discussion with general comments to welcome others and create a comfortable situation for them. Next, you introduce the interview by stating its purpose and ensuring the others understand the intent. You then enter into a process of seeking, providing, and clarifying information about the substantive questions of concern, and you eventually close the interview by reviewing the information discussed, checking its accuracy, and stating the actions, if any, to be taken later. Finally, after the interview, you carry out those responsibilities you agreed to during the interview. The steps of the actual interaction process are summarized in Putting Ideas into Practice.

PUTTING IDEAS INTO PRACTICE

Details for Conducting Interviews

Interviews, whether they are formal or informal, occur in steps or stages, and specific actions should be taken at each stage to maximize its effectiveness.

The Introduction

The introduction should establish ground rules and put both the interviewee and yourself at ease. The introduction includes several tasks:

- Spend a short period of time chatting to establish a relaxed atmosphere.
- State the purpose of the interview and clarify any confidentiality issues. For example, is the information to be shared with anyone else? Under what conditions?
- Indicate how much time should be needed for the interview.
- If you plan to take notes, explain that and how the record will be used.

The Body

Two important tasks are accomplished in the body of the interview: (1) Agree on mutual goals for the interview and its outcomes, and (2) gather information about the topic. The following interviewing suggestions (Brinkley, 1989; Ivey et al., 2016) may be helpful:

- Carefully order your questions and statements.
- Cluster your questions and statements by topic. This assists the logical flow of information.
- Use silence and minimal encouragers. The more you as interviewer talk during an interview, the less likely it is that you will achieve the interview purpose.
- Monitor your time. Once time limits have been established, try to adhere to them even if it means scheduling an additional session.

The Close

Before you conclude an interview, summarize what has occurred, create a sense of closure, and review any plans. Here are some suggestions for closing your interviews:

- Review the major topics and summarize all perspectives discussed.
- Outline plans and clarify who has agreed to what actions.
- Set a time to follow up on any actions you have planned.
- Ask whether any additional topics should be addressed. If a new topic is introduced and time is short, you may decide to schedule an additional interview.
- Indicate again what you will do with the information you have gathered. This should be a repetition and clarification of introductory comments on confidentiality.
- Express appreciation for the person's time and participation.

What you say in interviews generally can be dichotomized as having the purpose of seeking or providing information. The success of an interview requires knowledge about the context and process of such interactions and deliberate use of specific types of statements and questions to foster a productive exchange of information (McKenzie, 2014). That is, how you phrase questions and statements can have a significant impact on the immediate outcome of your interaction. But the impact often is even greater: How others receive your communication has significant influence on your relationships with them and on the nature of the information exchanged in the future (Patterson, Grenny, McMillan, & Switzler, 2002). In this chapter, the focus is on how statements and questions are used most effectively in seeking and providing information and supporting productive interactions.

Seeking Information

> **Learn More About**
> Although Katie Couric's tips on interviewing are focused on interactions with celebrities or people otherwise newsworthy, many of them are applicable to professionals seeking information from colleagues and parents.
>
> (https://www.youtube.com/watch?v=4eOynrI2eTM)

After introductory statements, interviews typically focus on gathering information in order to better understand the situation, concern, or task to be addressed. And as you think of how you would obtain information from a colleague or family member, you no doubt think of asking questions. This is certainly the most commonly used means for seeking information from others. Yet, because questions are often overused or poorly constructed, they may make your information-seeking efforts ineffective (e.g., Powell, Hughes-Scholes, & Sharman, 2012). In this section, you will explore ways to formulate, sequence, and ask questions to facilitate the interview process and secure desired information. However, you will also learn about using statements, rather than questions or a part of a question, to enhance interviews and enrich information gathering.

A starting point for seeking information is to think about questions, the most straightforward way to obtain information during interactions (e.g., Schein, 2013). You ask questions when you do not have sufficient experience or knowledge of a key topic, and you must obtain that information in order for the interaction to be productive. You might ask whether a student's program is effective, what steps need to be taken to arrange a new service for a student, or when the next team meeting will be. All of those questions have information seeking as their foundation, as do these examples:

- "What are your instructional goals for your English learners this school year?"
- "Which behavioral interventions have you used with him?"
- "What led the parents to ask for another evaluation?"
- "How do you think her feelings about the team will influence her decision?"

Question-asking may be the central behavior in many of your efforts to gather information from others, and you may consider yourself adept in this communication skill, but have you ever had the experience of not obtaining the information that you want? It would be expected that some of your efforts to gain specific information through questioning may be unsuccessful or frustrating for a variety of reasons. Sometimes questions are less effective than intended because the interviewer's perspective influences how the question is asked, and the question conveys an unintended message. Putting Ideas into Practice poses some questions intended to help you understand how your personal frame of reference may influence your interaction with others. It also includes questions to help identify your information needs before you begin an interview so that you can design appropriate questions. Other causes of unintended messages being communicated in questions are discussed in the following sections.

Question Format

One strategy for ensuring that your questions efficiently lead to the information that you need is to recognize and strategically differentiate question formats and their degree of focus (Stewart & Cash, 2014). Varying those question attributes will help you phrase your

PUTTING IDEAS INTO PRACTICE

Questioning Yourself

Reflection and introspection are essential for the effective communicator. Understanding your own motivations and opinions and how they influence your communication is important to your success. Try questioning yourself to assess whether your personal perspective or frame of reference may interfere with the success of your communication. Consider the following questions:

- What is my emotional response to the situation?
- What is my opinion—of the situation, of the others involved, or the possible outcomes?
- What assumptions am I making about the person or situation?

Questioning yourself is also critical for planning for effective interviewing:

- What is the goal of this interaction?
- How much do I really understand about the situation?
- What information do I need?
- How will the person respond to different approaches I could use to get the information we need?
- Which approaches are best for gathering information?
- What will I do with this information?

---

questions more effectively, because format is essential to the value of every question. The ways in which the words are arranged and sequenced not only form the question but also provide much of the tone of the communication.

Although format is not a particularly critical dimension of the statements someone makes during interactions, format is critical in crafting questions to seek information. You are likely to receive widely varying responses to questions based simply on how you word them (Brammer & MacDonald, 2003; Johnson, 2013). With that in mind, consider these three specific question format elements: direct/indirect, open/closed, and single/multiple.

Direct/Indirect Questions Most questions use a direct format. That is, the question is phrased as an interrogative and, if written, would end with a question mark. All of the examples in the previous section were direct questions. They are specific and focused on a particular issue. You typically use direct questions when you are asking for particular information from a person presumed to have the information or know the answer and who is comfortable in sharing that material. Asking direct questions is a skill that most professionals have practiced and are confident in applying in their interactions.

However, an alternative question-asking format—one that may not be as familiar to you—is the indirect question. In this format, it is not completely clear that anyone is being queried, as the question is phrased as a statement (Corey, 2013; Hackett & Martin, 1993). Perhaps you have used indirect questions similar to these. Compare them to the direct questions that follow them.

Indirect: "I wonder what would happen if we included Manny in the community-based training program."
Direct: "Why shouldn't we include Manny in the community-based training program?"
Indirect: "I would like to know what might happen if we asked Brittany's parents to talk to the other parents about accessing support groups."
Direct: "Shouldn't we ask Brittany's parents to talk to the other parents about joining a support group?"

Direct questions may be perceived as offensive, inappropriate, or intrusive, especially when they are asked of people whose cultures value more indirect interactions or if the topic being addressed is one that might be considered sensitive or awkward. For these reasons, they sometimes may be less desirable than indirect questions for gathering information in an interview.

Asking indirect questions is useful when you are unsure whether a direct question would offend another person. Notice that by using the first-person singular pronoun ("I wonder"; "I would like to know"), the implied responsibility for the idea contained in the question stays with the question asker; the person answering the question need not assume ownership for the idea expressed. In contrast, when you ask direct questions, you assign responsibility for the response to the other person. Thus, in uncomfortable situations, or in other cases in which you want to be certain you are not imposing a potentially unwanted idea, an indirect format may be preferable. Some indirect question starters include the following:

- "I'm wondering how you responded to..."
- "I can't remember how..."
- "It might be helpful if we knew..."
- "I hope you will say a bit more about..."
- "I'd be interested in knowing..."
- "I don't understand what..."
- "I'm getting the feeling that..."
- "I wonder whether..."

Indirect questions are not without drawbacks. For example, your question could be perceived as rhetorical; if this occurs, you might not receive any response at all. You should then rephrase the question to be direct if you judge that a response is required. Another risk is that indirect questions, if carelessly worded, may come across as commands ("Tell me..." or "Describe..."). Nevertheless, indirect questions are generally nonthreatening, and they facilitate efforts to obtain important information. A Basis in Research examines different reactions to questions.

Indirect questions offer a viable alternative to a series of direct questions, but they cannot substitute entirely for them. Indirect questions and inflection express one's interest and invite others to continue talking, but they can be vague and may not adequately communicate that your query relates to particular information. Thus, open, information-seeking statements tend to be most effective in initiating discussions, the earliest part of an interview. As discussions progress and require greater focus, you typically would use more focused information-seeking statements, such as commands (e.g., "Tell me which of the students was late") to obtain specific information. However, a

A BASIS IN RESEARCH

Some Evidence-Based Information About Questions

Open questions prompt longer, more detailed answers than closed questions (Daniels & Ivey, 2006; Sternberg et al., 1996). Appropriate open questions can help avoid leading respondents to false statements, which has been seen to be a problem in forensic research, especially that involving children.

- When assessing qualities of good relationships, adults are more likely to form good connections with one another when their interpersonal communication is characterized by balanced attentive listening, questioning, and commenting (Littauer, Sexton, & Wolf, 2005).

- In many non-Western cultures, questions may be viewed as offensive or overly intrusive and, thus, should be used judiciously (Ivey & Ivey, 2014).

Richardson (2002) described the advantages of open questions as contributing to the development of trust, being perceived as less threatening than their closed-question counterparts, and allowing free, unrestrained responses. When you want to encourage others to continue speaking or to obtain their perception of an event or situation without imposing any limits on their responses, an open question is the best choice.

caution is warranted: Commands may be perceived by others as highly directive and non-collaborative, especially if overused. Your skill as an interviewer includes selecting a direct question, a general indirect question, or a focused indirect question, such as a command based on the context and the nonverbal communication you observe from other participants.

Open/Closed Questions Another format for questions concerns openness: An *open question* is defined as one for which an infinite range of responses is possible (Brantley & Miller, 2008; Johnson & Johnson, 2013). For example, "How did things go today?" or "What was Sharroky's behavior like in the cafeteria today?" You cannot predict the nature of the response you will receive with such questions that ask the respondent to think and reflect. They give control of the conversation to the person being interviewed, because he or she has the option of what information to share. Other examples of open questions include the following:

"What kinds of behaviors are you considering to be disruptive?"
"How could I assist you with Mary?"
"What would be most helpful to you now?"

> **Learn More About**
> This simple animated video illustrates the power of asking open versus closed questions when seeking information.
> (https://www.youtube.com/watch?v=RoB--jhPIus)

In contrast, a *closed question* is one in which the range of responses is limited either explicitly or implicitly (Gamble & Gamble, 2013; Ivey & Ivey, 2014; Johnson & Johnson, 2013). Such questions often solicit circumscribed responses and are easier and quicker to answer than open questions. By using closed questions, you retain more control of the discussion because you specify the parameters for the response you seek. The downside of closed questions are many: They are often perceived as too limiting and as interrogating. They can be seen as leading and may result in inaccurate conclusions being made about the needed information. Perhaps the greatest disadvantage occurs when an interviewer narrows the responses in an interview in which he or she does not have adequate understanding of the context or situation. When this happens, poorly informed closed questions may steer the interaction in the wrong direction based on the interviewer's restricted understanding. The result is likely to be disappointing or frustrating to all participants.

You should guard against these potential difficulties with closed questions, but you need to develop skills in constructing and using closed questions that will enable you to appropriately secure the specific information needed in your interactions. Several suggestions can be made to assist you in this regard.

First, you may explicitly limit the range of response options by specifying them in the questions, as in the following examples:

"Would you prefer to have me observe during math, reading, or science?"
"Is Robert older or younger than the others in his group?"
"Does Jennifer have no friends, just one friend, or several friends as playmates?"

A second way in which you may limit response options is by making them implicit in the wording of the question. Analyze these examples:

"May I observe during the reading period today?"
"How old is Robert?"
"How many friends does Jennifer have on the team?"

In the first example, the implicit limit on the response is yes or no. In the second, the limit is set because there is only one correct answer. In the third, the limit is established by the assumption that there is a finite number of students on the team with whom Jennifer may have friendships.

As already noted, both open and closed questions have advantages and disadvantages, so how do you choose which type to use? One basis for deciding should be whether you are seeking an elaborated response or a narrower one. Closed questions are used to limit the scope of the conversation or confirm information. However, sometimes when you ask a carefully constructed closed question in order to focus a response, you will receive an

An interview that is poorly planned and implemented may seem more like an interrogation than a conversation, typically resulting in limited information being shared and disappointing outcomes.

elaborated response. For example, the question "How much has William's time on task increased?" may launch a five-minute description of the student's latest spate of time off task, missed classes, and incomplete work. Conversely, even an open question such as "Oh, Susan, I can see how upset you are! What's the matter?" may elicit only the very narrow, yet paradoxically open to all forms of interpretation, "Nothing." Your choice of open or closed question format nevertheless establishes general parameters for the type of response you hope to receive, and you should intentionally develop facility in designing such questions.

Another consideration in choosing between open and closed question formats is the nature of your relationship with the person from whom you are seeking information. Sometimes your concern about building a relationship will be as great as, or greater than, your need for specific information. In those cases, you may decide to ask open questions that allow your colleague to freely offer any information he or she wishes to share. When you use open questions, the person being queried is less likely to infer that you are seeking certain correct answers or precise responses. Questioning only with closed questions may cause the person being queried to feel that he or she is being tested, as the range of appropriate responses is limited. Such a situation may cause the person to become defensive and less forthcoming, and it may negatively influence relationships. Balancing the use of open and closed questions generally results in comfortable interactions and allows you to obtain rich and useful information.

Note, too, that you can combine the open/closed characteristic of questions with the direct/indirect dimension in order to create even more options for asking questions. This idea is illustrated in Figure 4.1.

Single/Multiple Questions Another element of how you format your questions concerns the number of questions you ask at one time (Hargie, Saunders, & Dickson, 1994; Ivey et al., 2016). In general, single questions are preferable to multiple questions. To illustrate, consider which of these examples you think is likely to result in the most constructive interchange:

> "When you think about the changes we've been making for Erminia over the past couple of weeks, which ones seem most responsible for the improvement in her behavior?"

FIGURE 4.1 Examples of open/closed and direct/indirect questions.

	Open	Closed
Direct	What is your opinion of Fred's performance in math?	What was Fred's score on the math section of the test?
Indirect	I'm interested in knowing more about Fred's performance in math.	It would be helpful to know Fred's score on the math section of the test.

"What do you think of the changes we've made for Erminia over the past couple of weeks? Do you agree that they're really improving her behavior? Which ones do you think have been most effective? Are there any you think are not effective?"

In the first example, one well-phrased question is asked, and the other person has the opportunity to share ideas and perceptions. In the second example, four questions are asked, and the respondent is likely left wondering which one to answer. This is similar to the opening case when Jerome asked Wyatt, "You really don't know? It sounds like you do. Is something going on? Did something happen? Why don't you like the meetings?" Jerome's multiple questions did nothing to help Wyatt clarify his concerns.

Most people sometimes ask multiple questions. There are several reasons for this. First, perhaps you begin to talk while you are still mentally constructing your question. This could cause you to need several tries to finally arrive at the question you intended. Another cause of multiple questions relates to specificity. You may first ask a vague question, then realize that it will not elicit the specific information you intended, and so you make the question more specific and try again, and perhaps again. A third reason multiple questions occur is that individuals may conversationally rush past the person with whom they are speaking. That is, they ask at one time an entire series of questions they wish to have answered. Examples of these types of multiple questions follow:

- *Thinking and talking at the same time.* "Is Heather mastering her math facts? How about her problem solving? Is she turning in her math homework? Overall, how successful is Heather in her math class?"
- *Moving from vague to focused questions.* "How is Michael doing? How has he adjusted to his vocational program? What issues are still coming up in having Michael work with his job coach?"
- *Asking a series of related questions at one time.* "What are the greatest needs the parents listed on the community services questionnaire? What resources do we have available for meeting their needs? When can we meet to begin planning the partnership program for next year?"

Regardless of the reason for multiple questions, when you use them you leave your interaction partner unsure of how to respond. That person may wonder which question you really meant to have addressed. Or the person may simply answer the single question that was best remembered, often the first or last one asked. Alternatively, you may put him or her in the position of being suspicious or defensive, as multiple questions sometimes convey the impression that you are "fishing" for information. Putting Ideas into Practice offers effective alternatives for seeking information.

Generally, your goal should be to develop strategies that allow you to avoid asking multiple questions. If you have several questions, carefully phrase each one, ask the questions in a logical sequence, and permit the other person time to respond after each one. If you find that you often ask multiple questions, first analyze why this occurs and think about strategies to avoid this ineffective communication practice. Then monitor this behavior, and learn to pause for a few seconds before asking a question in order to phrase it in a way that is clear and likely to elicit the response you are intending. Another advantage of increasing your use of pauses is that it provides space for the other person to process the information, reflect, and better answer the question.

Focused Inquiry

In Chapter 3, we discussed the importance of using concrete language in your communication. Both statements and questions can be phrased with varying levels of specificity or concreteness. At times, you should intentionally pose very general questions, such as when you are initiating relationships or just beginning to explore situations.

PUTTING IDEAS INTO PRACTICE

Seeking Information in Nonthreatening Ways

Whether in team meetings, parent conferences, or meetings with one colleague, seeking information through asking questions can cause those being questioned to become uncomfortable or feel threatened. You can probably recall times when you were asked questions for which you may not have felt prepared or for which you did not have a ready answer. Perhaps an instructor, a parent, or an administrator asked you an unanticipated question that you did not know how to answer. Such experiences likely caused you surprise, anxiety, or embarrassment, and they probably led you to be a less active participant in the interaction. Here are some actions you can take when asking questions, especially in small groups, to avoid creating that situation for others and to promote participation.

1. *Begin by asking a question without directing it to a particular person.* When meeting with parents, for example, ask a question openly so that either may answer, rather than asking, "Mrs. Sumner, how many times each week does Sabine fail to complete her homework?"
2. *Pause and wait for one of the participants to develop and offer an answer.* Like many others, you may become anxious when there is not an immediate answer to a question you ask. Although it may seem like a painfully long wait, pausing and allowing participants time to think about how they wish to answer goes a long way toward getting useful information and setting a supportive climate.
3. *If no one responds after the pause, look for cues that someone may want to be involved and direct the question to him or her. It may also help to rephrase the question.* You might say, for example, "Mrs. Sumner, it looks as though you have some thoughts on this. I'd welcome any comments you might like to offer about Sabine not finishing her homework."
4. *Construct questions that incorporate the characteristics most likely to elicit the desired response while being viewed as inviting participation. Single, direct, and open questions are most appropriate for this purpose.* Depending on your assessment of the relationship and the others' readiness for direct questions, you might ask a direct question that is a bit more focused than the preceding indirect question, such as "Mrs. Sumner, what activities compete with Sabine's efforts to get her homework done?"

These strategies may not result immediately in the specific information you want, but they are examples of techniques that can help you create a nonthreatening climate necessary for effective communication.

As you gain general information about the topic at hand, you may begin to use questions and statements that elicit more specific and concrete information. You also may need to seek more concrete information when your conversation partner uses general, nonspecific words or overly precise words. Examples of generalities that are likely to require questioning to clarify the speaker's meaning are included in the Putting Ideas into Practice. Asking questions designed to address an appropriate level of concreteness is referred to as *focused inquiry*.

Focused inquiry delimits the topic sufficiently so that the respondent can clearly identify the specific type of information requested. With few exceptions, once you have established a relationship and gathered contextual information, you should be able to increase your use of focused inquiry in your interviews and more advanced interaction processes (DeVito, 2013; Gamble & Gamble, 2013). Possibly the most convincing evidence of this comes from one of the experiences most special services providers have had. Remember a time when you sought information with a nonspecific comment, such as "Tell me how Katie is doing," when you specifically wanted to know about Katie's response to the intervention you had recently designed. If so, you may have found that your vague or unfocused inquiry resulted in an accounting of Katie's overall progress, her upcoming surgery, the progress she was making in other areas, and so on. A more focused inquiry, such as "How is Katie progressing in the language program we designed?" would have been more likely to elicit the specific information you wanted. See E-Partnerships for how technology can help with this and similar information seeking with groups.

> **Learn More About**
> How do the questions suggested for parents to ask teachers at parent conferences illustrate the concept of focused inquiry?
> (https://www.youtube.com/watch?v=TBHYEqv1eMk)

PUTTING IDEAS INTO PRACTICE

Generalities Require Closer Examination

Sometimes questions elicit very general responses rather than the specifics that are needed. Generalities communicate little. "I really value that" or "He's doing absolutely great work" may suggest that someone is pleased, but it is unclear what aspects of the event are valued, great, or otherwise pleasing. Sometimes overly precise words (e.g., *always, every time*) are used carelessly and have the effect of a generality. To understand the message, it is necessary to examine the situation further with such responses as "What elements do you most value?" or "What aspects of the work do you think he did well?" The following words and phrases are a few of those that signal the need for further clarification:

all	every	more	all the time	usually
never	always	soon	worse	rarely
more or less	nearly	once in a while	they say	sometimes
almost	about	better	a bit	everyone knows
could be	sort of	like	nice	generally

E-PARTNERSHIPS

Asking Questions Electronically...Options and Cautions

Have you thought about how you could use a variety of forms of electronic communication to seek information from parents and families? Many parents will follow quick communication options more often than a class web page. Here are a few ideas:

Twitter

Twitter can be set up so that only approved individuals can be followers. This enables you to use Twitter as a communication tool for simple, direct queries. For example, if it is flu season and you would be helped by donations of hand sanitizer, your request could be tweeted. You can also tweet individual parents with simple requests, such as whether a student's permission form for a field trip made it home yesterday afternoon. Twitter is also used by many teachers for daily updates of class activities.

E-Mail

If parents are using e-mail, it is most effective as one-to-one communication for questions about just their child that are not so sensitive that they require live communication. For example, if you know that a parent works long hours and is difficult to reach by phone, you could send the parent a message outlining an upcoming after-school event and asking if the child would participate in it. If a serious matter is at hand, e-mail could be used to invite the parent to a phone meeting. When you use e-mail for such purposes, it is wise to include a read receipt so that you know the parent has seen your message. You may also want to send yourself a blind cc: to ensure your own record. If you do not hear back from a parent, follow-up communication would, of course, be necessary.

Facebook Group

In Facebook Group you can invite parents of your students to join; information you provide and questions you ask are seen only by those you invited (and who responded). This is a safe, professional way to use Facebook with parents and can eliminate issues related to friending students and posting information on your broader Facebook account.

Remember, research suggests that parents using electronic communication prefer e-mail and newsletters over Facebook and Twitter (National School Public Relations Association, 2011), but patterns in the use of electronic communication are changing rapidly, and this information may be less true than just a few years ago. Also, keep in mind that if you are in a community where some parents do not routinely use electronic options for interacting, you are obligated to ensure that they are not inadvertently excluded from your communication. Finally, electronic communication can be an effective supplement to face-to-face or phone communication, but it cannot replace it. No matter what type of precautions you take, electronic communications should be considered available to the public. If you wish to seek information from a parent and confidentiality is needed, a phone call or face-to-face meeting probably is preferred.

As you can easily surmise, focused inquiry plays a critical role in clear communication. When questions or statements are too vague, they encourage respondents to provide abstract, nonspecific answers. In those cases, you may have to interpret someone's abstract response or, at the very least, seek additional data in order to refocus attention on the information you need. Too often, a vague inquiry may lead the respondent in a direction that pulls the entire interaction off a constructive course. Focused inquiry, on the other hand, helps guide the course of the interaction and directs attention to specific, concrete information that is requested.

You can focus inquiries in two primary ways in order to obtain the desired information you are seeking. First, when you carefully consider the purpose of your inquiry, determine the type of information you wish to access, and then select the most appropriate format. This, in turn, increases the likelihood of question-asking success. Second, particular wording or phrasing considerations can also help you further focus your inquiries. Presupposition and prefatory statements are focusing techniques, described next, that can be used whether the question is open, closed, single, direct, or indirect.

Presupposition *Presupposition* refers to specific question content that conveys to respondents an expectation of what they already know or believe and thus helps focus their responses. Presupposition can vary from little to great, depending on question construction. In the opening case Jerome presupposed that Wyatt had negative feelings about Ms. Hackner when he asked, "Why don't you like Ms. Hackner?" Notice that this question has an embedded assumption about Wyatt's feelings toward Ms. Hackner.

The following questions also contain a high level of presupposition:

"What is your greatest concern about having Erin in your classroom?"
"What behavior management system are you using with April?"

In the first question, the presupposition is that the respondent has concerns about having Erin in her classroom and that the concerns are prioritized. In the second, the presupposition is that the respondent is using a behavior management system with the student and can describe it. In contrast, the following questions have little presupposition.

"How is Erin doing in your classroom?"
"What do you do about April's behavior?"

The first question includes a general assumption about the person monitoring Erin's progress or participation in the class. The second hints that the person is addressing April's behavior, but this question, too, is quite vague. Presupposition is a potent tool for focusing interactions. When used with an open question, it is a means of embedding in the question a particular topic that you want targeted in the elicited response. It enables you to query in a way that maximizes the likelihood you will receive elaborated, accurate, and specific information. For example, consider the following versions of the same basic question that you might ask parents about their satisfaction with their child's current educational program:

"Are you satisfied with your child's program this year?"
"Are you satisfied with the progress your child has made in her program this year?"
"With what aspects of your child's program have you been most satisfied this year?"
    (*After parents' response*) "What aspects have caused you the most concern?"

Little presupposition is contained in the first version of the question. If you use that question format, the parents probably will give a yes or no answer, and they might not explain their specific reactions to the program. The second variation includes a greater degree of presupposition by acknowledging that the student has made progress; but because the question is closed, you may receive a response similar to what you received with the first example. The third set of questions contains a high level of presupposition. Those questions assume that the parents have identified program strengths and weaknesses and that some of these are more important than others. Be aware that you should consider what and how much information can be presupposed. The third set of questions is valuable only if you have reason to believe that the parents are satisfied with some aspects and concerned with other aspects of the child's program. Because they are focused, those highly presuppositional questions are likely to elicit the requested information. And because they use an open format, they encourage the parents to share the information that is of most importance to them. Finally, another benefit to presupposition is that it often conveys that you value another person's perception of and interest in a situation. Communicating such valuing may help strengthen your relationship.

Prefatory Statements You can also focus your inquiry by providing information about the context in which the inquiry is made. One technique for doing this is the use of *prefatory statements*. To do so, you precede your question with a carefully structured statement to establish the context and expectations for the desired response (Wolf, 1979). With this technique, you use a statement when you want to ask a question but must first "set it up." In this way you establish parameters for the question and the response, sometimes by raising possible answers, sometimes by reminding the other person of previously discussed issues, and sometimes by cuing your interaction partner that you are going to change the subject.

Interviewing may be formal or informal, but the usefulness of both types depends on your clarity in establishing the purpose and your skill in crafting deliberately worded questions and statements.

The following questions are preceded by prefatory statements. What purpose does each statement accomplish?

- "We've considered two options for James. One is to make an immediate program change for him, and the other involves implementing several interventions that might eliminate the need for the change. At this point, which strategy do you think would be best for him?"
- "Yesterday, you mentioned that the modification to Maria's communication board was not working. I wanted to get back to you about that. What seems to be the problem with it?"
- "We've been talking about finding ways for teachers to be released to attend team meetings. I am also concerned about the scheduling difficulties of arranging for the occupational therapist [OT] to be here. What are our options for adjusting the OT's schedule to match the rest of the team's?"

In the first two examples, the prefatory statement focuses the respondent's attention on specific aspects of the topic the interviewer wants addressed. In the final example, the prefatory statement signals the person about a change in topic ("I am also concerned"). All these examples better prepare the respondent to participate in the interaction.

In addition to the general prefatory statements just illustrated, two specific types may sometimes be appropriate during your interactions: the exemplar and the continuum. In an *exemplar*, you phrase a prefatory statement that provides examples of the types of answers that you might be seeking. For example, in the following segment of the interaction, an administrator sets up some options in her prefatory statement.

> "We've agreed that we'd like to have a series of meetings with the special education teachers to clarify the ways in which they might work more closely together while also examining how the general education setting could be more supportive of students with special needs. There are quite a few options for doing this. We could use the upcoming staff development day or ask the superintendent for an extra day at the beginning of the next school year. Another option would be to

Learn More About
Electronic communication is one tool for seeking information, but this video illustrates its shortcomings by focusing on nonverbal signals only available when face-to-face.

(https://www.youtube.com/watch?v=OvEci5Bjgd4)

discuss this at the staff meeting. I'm sure there are others. What ways do you think would be best for holding these meetings?"

The examples of alternatives for conducting the meetings help the others think about options. And yet, the phrasing of the question conveys that the administrator has not already selected a specific option.

The other type of prefatory statement, the *continuum*, is similar to the exemplar but is used when feasible responses tend to fall along a range. For example, you might use a continuum prefatory statement to raise options for reward or punishment systems to employ with a student, to describe potential levels of staff involvement in decision making on a special services team, or to suggest programming options that are progressively more restrictive. The following example illustrates a continuum prefatory statement:

> "Through the years, Juan's teachers have used a wide variety of behavior management techniques with him. Some have preferred to rely almost totally on a system of rewards, others have used a combination of rewards and consequences, and still others have found that consequences alone are most effective. What type of behavior management system have you found most appropriate for Jorge?"

In general, the statements with which you preface your questions become integral to them, informing them and providing context. You can use prefatory statements to raise issues you believe should be noted but that are not being discussed. You also may implicitly give the person you are interviewing permission to address a sensitive or awkward topic by mentioning it.

The skillful use of well-phrased questions results in productive interactions and positive relationships. One additional strategy for accomplishing this goal, the sequencing of questions, is addressed in Putting Ideas into Practice.

PUTTING IDEAS INTO PRACTICE

Funnel Approaches to Sequencing Questions

The sequence of the questions one asks may be as important to the quality of the communication as the specific question format. If you are trying to decide between using closed or open questions to obtain information from a colleague or parent, you will no doubt weigh the advantages and disadvantages of each. But consider, too, the advantages of two different approaches to how you sequence questions.

As the name suggests, the *funnel* approach to questioning begins with broad, open questions and proceeds to the narrower and limiting closed questions. Use this technique when

- the topic is sensitive
- the person being questioned is uneasy or insecure about the questions
- the person is highly invested in the topic and has much to share before focusing on specifics
- the interaction has been initiated by another person who is seeking your assistance

Generally, the funnel approach helps when the problem—or the person's perception of it—is so complex that it should be explored broadly before it can be accurately focused and identified.

An *inverted funnel* approach begins with closed questions and proceeds to more open ones. The objective is to use very focused questions in the beginning to get the respondent to recall issues and facts about the topic of concern. Use the inverted funnel:

- when the respondent possibly should think about elements of the situation that he or she might not otherwise consider, and your goal is to raise his or her consciousness of them
- when the person, situation, or topic indicates guardedness; this approach offers a gradual process for addressing sensitive issues

Both ways of sequencing questions are useful. You will learn the advantages of each as you practice implementing them in a variety of situations.

APPLY YOUR KNOWLEDGE 4.2

Providing Information

The purpose of formal or informal interviewing is to exchange information and gain an understanding of a situation or concern. Thus far, only the information-seeking aspects of the interview have been discussed—the strategies used to obtain information from others. Interviews also require that participants provide each other with information. Statements are the most commonly used verbal means for providing information to others. They are utilized to express observations, facts, thoughts, feelings, or judgments and to offer advice.

You use statements when your primary purpose is to tell others something you think they want or need to know, or to tell them what you want them to know. You may tell someone about a newly developed intervention strategy; you may explain how the changing composition of an interagency council will influence your program; or you may describe direct observations you made of instruction in a classroom or of a particular student's performance. You may also tell others about a situation or experience you have had, how you feel about an event or a person, or you may give them advice about situations they face. Whatever the reason, two types of statements have as their overall purpose providing information: descriptive statements that outline events or experiences without giving advice or making an evaluation, and guiding statements that subtly or explicitly direct others' actions by evaluating or advising them.

Descriptive Statements

Often, statements are used to provide a verbal account of a situation, behavior, opinion, or feeling. When such a verbal account is offered without any accompanying evaluation or advice, it is *descriptive*. Descriptive statements can be used to relate both overt and covert information.

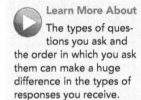

Learn More About The types of questions you ask and the order in which you ask them can make a huge difference in the types of responses you receive.
(https://www.youtube.com/watch?v=cvsMOw6D1M0)

Describing Overt Information The most straightforward form of descriptive statement is that which addresses overt content by providing a verbal account of an observable event, situation, or behavior. Such descriptive statements focus on facts. DeVito (2013) characterizes a factual statement as one that is made by an observer following an observation and is limited to what is observed. Facts can be directly verified because they are something that one can see, hear, or feel. Thus, making descriptive statements of this sort requires identifying observable behaviors or permanent products, such as students' written work, and describing them without making judgments about them. You probably already have skill in this area because providing precise and objective descriptions of behavior and work products is a basic component in the professional preparation of most education and related professionals, even though practice in this skill is usually aimed at describing student behavior.

Examples of descriptive statements appear throughout this section. Because the definition of descriptive statements specifically excludes evaluating or advising, after each descriptive statement, examples of evaluative statements and advice are given as nonexamples: They illustrate what descriptive statements are *not*. Keep in mind that these examples are provided solely to help you discriminate among descriptive, evaluative, and advisory statements. They are not meant to model effective means of delivering advice or evaluation, two topics addressed later in this chapter. Contrast the different ways three observers might describe a single event:

Descriptive: When Maryanne left the room during the discussion, several team members looked at each other. You stopped speaking and asked the group, "Should I wait for Maryanne to return?"
Evaluative: "You shouldn't have let Maryanne leave like that. It's rude for one of us to leave while we are trying to make a group decision."
Advisory: "You need to get everyone's agreement on ground rules for participation before you have that team try to work together on problem solving again."

The first of the examples meets the criteria for descriptive statements and addresses overt events—the observable behaviors of Maryanne, the group leader (in this case, you), and the other group members. Those behaviors are described without evaluation or advice in the first example. The next statements do not meet those criteria. The second is evaluative: "You shouldn't have" conveys judgment about another's behavior. The third statement is advisory: "You need to" generally precedes specific advice.

Describing Covert Information Descriptive statements are also used in detailing covert events or conditions that are not observable, such as attitudes, perceptions, and feelings. When you discuss concerns and problems with colleagues or parents, they may describe their feelings about a situation as well as the details of it. This often is termed *self-disclosure*, a communication about the self that is shared with another person (Beebe, Beebe, & Redmond, 2014; Johnson, 2013; Knapp & Vangelisti, 2014). This is information that is not directly observable and is sometimes referred to as part of one's private self (Adler, Rosenfeld, & Proctor, 2015; McKay, Davis, & Fanning, 2009). The nature of the self-disclosure and its usefulness in your collaborative problem solving are dependent on the speaker's depth of self-awareness as well as his or her openness and willingness to share that information with another. In the opening case, Wyatt was ill prepared to describe covert information, specifically his feelings about Ms. Hackner's adding to his workload. To avoid relegating others to Wyatt's fate of awkward nondisclosure, you may decide to express empathy and encourage self-disclosure by using responding skills, as described in Chapter 3.

Because others' covert experiences cannot be observed directly, your perceptions of their internal experiences will necessarily involve some inference (e.g., Roulston, 2014). An *inference* is a statement about the unknown that is based on something known or assumed. Because they are sometimes based on assumptions, naturally, inferences are not strictly limited to what is observed. Instead, they are more assumptions derived from reasoning about known evidence. This is precisely what was described in Chapter 3 as reflecting. For example, you might infer that someone is angry after observing him throw a book across the room, raise his voice, and slam the door. That is a reasonable conclusion to draw based on your consideration of the behaviors displayed. Describing that conclusion is reflecting.

There is nothing wrong with making inferential statements. In fact, they generally are very important when talking about things that are most relevant to those involved. But keep in mind that they are just that: They are inferences, not facts. To illustrate the importance of this distinction, consider the inferences to be made if you were walking down the hall and glanced into a colleague's classroom to see that person sitting at her desk, head in hands, shoulders sagging, and rocking slightly. Would you infer that your colleague is upset about something? That might be a reasonable inference. But it is also possible that this teacher's young child is ill, and so she was up for much of the night tending to her. Unless supported with a highly congruent set of nonverbal indicators and knowledge of context, inferences often include a significant risk of being inaccurate.

We caution against using inferential statements before assessing known evidence carefully because fact–inference confusion can be problematic and most certainly interferes with clear communication. To avoid that confusion, be sure you explicitly express tentativeness when you make inferential statements. That communicates that you know you are making an assumption, even though it is based on your perception of facts. It also indicates that you are aware that the inference you drew may be wrong and you

Giving unsolicited advice is rarely welcomed or effective.

are open to considering other explanations. Openness is equally important in listening, as discussed in Chapter 3. The tentativeness recommended here can also be likened to the responses discussed in Chapter 3 and mentioned later in this chapter for confirming information (e.g., paraphrasing, reflecting, and questioning).

As was the case with describing overt information, statements expressing covert information can be classified as descriptive, evaluative, and advisory, as is illustrated in the following examples.

Descriptive: "I was absolutely terrified when Lindsey's mother came to my class. I'd heard so much about her and none of it good. I was really anxious and actually found that my hands, and the papers in them, shook. My voice cracked, and I thought the floor would fall out from under me."

Evaluative: "I'm such a coward! I'm really worthless with these kids—well, at least with their litigious parents. I get nervous, and I'm not at all clear with them."

Advisory: "I have to get out of situations where I have to teach students with difficult parents. It is too stressful for me. Or I have to learn how to handle these parents and their advocates. This just isn't working."

Those examples manifest the covertness of the teacher's feelings and reaction to a parent who may come across as litigious. The descriptive statement includes neither evaluation nor advice, as it describes feelings ("terrified," "anxious"). The statement also includes descriptions of behavioral indicators (e.g., "hands shook," "voice cracked"). The second statement is not descriptive because it contains evaluation ("I'm such a coward"; "I'm really worthless"). Similarly, the third statement is not descriptive because it offers self-reflective advice ("I have to") rather than description.

Those statements were artificially designed to illustrate the descriptive, evaluative, and advisory concepts. However, you are not likely to find such clear-cut examples in your day-to-day interactions. Instead, you generally will encounter statements similar to the next two examples. They combine both descriptive and nondescriptive components. Consider each of these carefully, and see whether you can identify their descriptive, evaluative, and advisory elements. Consider, too, the levels of inference they incorporate.

- "I watched Jordan in her power play group, and I was amazed! She was so devastated when she skipped a block that she knocked the equipment over and kicked it. Then she threw a rock at the hopscotch squares. Her behavior really showed how angry she was at herself."
- "I observed your group, and you shouldn't feel so bad about your session. You're a really good therapist, and you do a great job with some very challenging students. Your presentation took only one minute, and you demonstrated all of the three movements we talked about."

The first example contains some descriptive phrases ("I watched," "knocked the equipment over," "kicked it," and "threw a rock"). It also contains an implied evaluative phrase (behavior was outrageous) and a highly inferential reference ("so devastated"). It does not contain any advisory phrases. Similarly, the second example also includes descriptive and nondescriptive elements ("I observed," "your presentation," "the three movements we talked about"). An evaluative phrase ("you're a really good therapist") and an advisory one ("you shouldn't feel so bad") also are present. The statement does not include inferences, but it contains nonspecific terms and would be improved by more concrete language.

As you begin to attend more closely to the statements you and others make during your interactions, you undoubtedly will find that purely descriptive statements are rare. Despite it being difficult to describe something without evaluating or advising, you can still improve your skills in that area by monitoring your own statements. By conveying information without judging or advising, purely descriptive statements minimize the likelihood of offending the receiver. Such statements promote clear and honest communication without causing listeners to become defensive. Some additional tips for providing information effectively are highlighted in Putting Ideas into Practice.

PUTTING IDEAS INTO PRACTICE

Tips for Sharing Information

Knowledge is power. Information is power. When you provide others with accurate, objective, and useful information, you are empowering them. Once empowered with information, and the knowledge and skills to use it, people are increasingly able to take control over their professional and personal lives and to take action to get what they want and need to succeed (DeVito, 2013; Turnbull, Turnbull, Erwin, Soodak, & Shogren 2015). As teacher and service provider (and a busy professional who spends many hours communicating information to students), you may explain regularly and provide copious information that may not be perceived as useful or relevant to colleagues or parents. Here are some tips for sharing information:

- Determine what information is needed or requested.
- Offer objective, accurate descriptions or explanations that communicate intended information.
- Identify and focus on main points. ("Keep the main thing the main thing.")
- Check that the information is relevant to the person receiving it.
- Avoid the use of jargon, and clarify those terms that cannot be avoided.
- Minimize the use of evaluation and advice unless it is requested.
- Do not offer interpretations of behaviors or try to assign meaning without adequate information.

> **Learn More About**
> What types of questions could you use at the beginning of a parent conference to address concerns, such as those addressed in this video, and truly put parents at ease?
> (https://www.youtube.com/watch?v=zWPwC-HboiU)

Guiding Statements

As you have learned, descriptive statements take on various forms and permutations. Understand, though, that those kinds of statements are purely for the sake of reporting information. Whether factual or inferential, descriptive statements still do only what their label suggests: describe. On the other hand, some statements provide information to guide action. Guiding statements, the other primary category by which communicators provide information, urge others to act, feel, or think in a certain way. Guiding statements are themselves split into two categories: those that explain and those that advise.

Explanations are statements that explain information in an instructive way and rely on reasoning, understanding cause-and-effect relationships, or logic. They translate ideas and interpret information. Use of these statements nearly always conveys that the person offering the explanation has greater expertise or knowledge than the one receiving it. Explanations can be appreciated, particularly when someone requests them—such as when you ask a colleague to explain a new policy to you or when you ask a colleague to help you interpret student performance data. Statements of this type are particularly valuable when you are asked to share your knowledge to clarify a point, elaborate an idea, or answer a question. Explanations also can effectively help others to understand your position if you are discussing options in problem solving, weighing program alternatives for a student, or interacting in similar situations. And they can be helpful in clarifying perceptions and developing the shared meanings that are so important in effective communication.

Although the ability to give clear explanations is considered an essential competency for teachers, it traditionally has been addressed for them as an instructional rather than interpersonal skill (Cavanagh, Bower, Moloney, & Sweller, 2014; Johnson & Roellke, 1999). As an instructional skill, explaining typically involves clearly presenting material and using examples. Some explanation frameworks also include use of advance organizers, demonstrations, paraphrasing, or review of salient points. The skills of defining concepts, answering questions, and giving corrective feedback also are considered part of explaining in instruction, but the focus in all of these domains is on communication with students rather than colleagues.

As a school professional, then, you are familiar with explanations and aware of their value in your instructional interactions. The caution here, however, is that because you are likely to be proficient in giving explanations in instruction, you may tend to overuse them. In your professional interactions, explanations should be employed infrequently. They are most appropriate when someone explicitly requests that you or others provide them with information. When uninvited, explanations may have all of the undesirable effects of unsolicited advice. One additional point can be made: This discussion of explanation also is a reminder that, although some overlap exists between the communication skills that contribute to effective teaching and those for interactions with other adults, the domains also have distinct differences.

The other type of guiding statement, *advice*, is a category of information-providing statements intended to imply a recommended action by suggesting, hinting, or even commanding that someone take specific steps or accept certain beliefs. *Suggestions* are statements of "gentle advice" offered as possibilities for consideration; they communicate clearly that they are tentative and subject to the evaluation of their recipient. For example, when a colleague suggests to you, "One option might be to consider some of the new materials we just received," he or she is giving you a hint or a tip. Your colleague is simply offering one piece of potentially many sets of information for your evaluation and is acknowledging that in your role as decision maker you may accept or reject it.

Advice also may be offered as a direct *command* that directly or indirectly insists on compliance or cooperation. In many interactions, commands may seem overly directive, such as when someone says, "You will definitely have to change that," or "You can't do that until you get some hands-on training." Commands are likely to be received badly by the person to whom they are directed. They may remind recipients of someone's previous inappropriate exercise of authority over them or of years of parental directives. They often imply that the speaker has greater power than those to whom the command is issued. When any of these perceptions exist, commands are likely to cause resistance and become less effective than other efforts to guide behavior.

However, commands are not always negative, and they do not necessarily imply that the recipient is less powerful than, or inferior to, the speaker. Sometimes they are time-savers, such as when the participants agree that one party has greater expertise than the others in a given area. When such agreement is present, it can eliminate the air of pretentious superiority that some people associate with commands. The following example illustrates this point: A physical education teacher is telling another teacher how to adapt a classroom game so a particular student can participate. In this example, a series of commands may well be the most efficient approach to guiding the action of a colleague.

> "First, point to the target and say, 'Throw it there.' Then wait 10 seconds to see whether Victor responds. If not, physically prompt him to throw the ball."

Like explanations, whether offered as a suggestion or a command, advice is unlikely to be helpful and may well be detrimental to relationships if given to someone who has not requested or otherwise demonstrated an openness to it. Unfortunately, advice is a frequently overused response when people are trying to assist others in problem solving and often even in casual interactions. That should not be difficult to understand in the context of the professional socialization factors discussed in Chapter 2. School professionals are likely to be competent, independent problem solvers who are used to working alone. They may quickly take on the role of designing and presenting solutions as advice when they begin working with others. However, unsolicited advice is often perceived as intrusive and even arrogant. As this adage, attributed to Mason Cooley (a professor and aphorist from the early twentieth century), so aptly notes, "Advice is more agreeable in the mouth than in the ear." Although advice may seem appropriate and helpful when you are formulating it, and your intentions in offering it may be completely understandable, your comment may backfire, with the recipients feeling defensive and misunderstood. For these reasons, we encourage professionals in collaborative situations to wait until asked before giving advice to other adults. See Putting Ideas into Practice for dealing with uncooperative communicators, when such skills are essential.

PUTTING IDEAS INTO PRACTICE

Handling Uncooperative Communications

Regardless of how well developed your communication skills are, you will encounter colleagues and parents whose communication styles challenge you and require extraordinary effort. Here are a few examples of uncooperative communicators and some suggestions for responding to them.

1. The *passive communicator* seems to participate not at all, reveals no expression, and does not contribute to the interaction.

   Pause and use brief silent spaces to allow time for her to process what is being discussed and say something. Ask her questions. Use facial expressions to indicate that you are waiting for a response or seeking agreement.

2. The *overly expressive communicator* has an excited or enthusiastic response to everything. Even when what you are saying seems inconsequential, this person has extremely intense reactions.

   This individual may make you feel like a skilled communicator, especially if some people do not respond at all. You might also find the quantity and intensity of the responses disconcerting; they may interfere with your intended communication. If this is the case, try slowing the pace of your speech and speaking more quietly. Often a communication partner will modify his speech to more closely match yours. Alternatively, say to him, "You seem animated in discussing this. Help me understand the two items you are most enthusiastic about."

3. The *overly talkative communicator* seems to talk incessantly and often about things quite unrelated to your intended topic.

   Listen with the goal of determining why the person is so talkative. Reasons may include nervousness, other emotional states, feeling rushed, being typically talkative, or characteristically lacking clear focus. Emotional states may require you to listen and reflect. Being rushed may lead to rescheduling. With the simply unfocused and talkative communicator, you typically should summarize relevant elements and use redirection statements such as, "Getting back to your concerns about Mike's reading, what else could you tell me about...."

4. The *pseudo-communicator* seems to be interacting, but his responses are inconsequential—they never vary and always seem to be noncommittal restatements of what you have said, providing you with no real sense of his perspectives.

   Ask for a response. For example, you might say, "What elements of what I've mentioned do you agree with?" or "What part of what I said seems most plausible to you? Least plausible?"

5. The *preoccupied communicator* may claim to be a multitasker; she is doing other things while you are talking.

   If you feel that the person is not attending and what you are saying requires her concentration, ask for it. You could say, "This is really important. I need your attention and input." Or if the person is unable to give full attention at this time, you might offer to reschedule, and say, "This topic really needs both of us to concentrate on it. When could we reschedule for a time when you have fewer competing responsibilities?"

6. The *distracted communicator* looks all around the room, at others, but rarely at you.

   As you think about past interactions with this person, is this a common behavior? Is he easily distractible? If so, consider changing your position in the room so that you are facing the others and he is facing you and the wall behind you. This way he will have fewer visual distractions. If he still is not making eye contact, try to maintain a direct gaze at him while varying your communication style to ask more questions that will engage him. This distraction could have any of several reasons, including resistance (discussed in Chapter 9), competing priorities, or disinterest in the conversation.

 APPLY YOUR KNOWLEDGE 4.3

Suggestions for Effective Interviews

In addition to the principles and examples for constructing effective queries that are given throughout this chapter, these specific suggestions may help you further refine your information-seeking skills.

Use Pauses Effectively

A key to being a skilled interviewer is pausing (Adler & Elmhorst, 2013; Jacobs, Masson, & Harvill, 2009; Liao, 2006). Two particular uses of pauses can improve the effectiveness of your information-seeking interactions. The first involves pausing for a moment before you ask for information. This type of pause ensures that you have a moment to think about your questions so that your request is phrased to convey exactly the message you intend. Second, you should pause after asking for information or inviting elaboration to allow the person you are interviewing time to formulate and deliver a reply.

Many school professionals find that pausing is an initially frustrating technique; but once they master it, they find it very powerful. Perhaps you know that you have a tendency to keep talking if someone does not respond immediately to your request for information. Do you follow it with another question? Do you propose a response for the person? Both habits seriously interfere with your primary purposes of obtaining information from the respondent. Adding pauses to your repertoire of communication skills can only increase your effectiveness. This is a direct application of the skill of responding with silence that was introduced in Chapter 3.

> **Learn More About**
> One of the most simple but effective communication strategies that professionals can use when seeking information from others is to allow a brief pause between the other person's comments and your next communication.
>
> (https://www.youtube.com/watch?v=8k39oKz19gA)

Monitor Information-Seeking Interactions

Another strategy for becoming a successful interviewer is to monitor your understanding of the relationship between how you seek information and the type of response you receive (Moore, 2014). If you consciously observe others seeking information, you will increase your own skill in discriminating appropriate from inappropriate strategies. Another variation of this effort, of course, is monitoring your own question-asking skills. How often do you use a closed question when your intent is to obtain an open response? In what situations do you tend to resort to vague instead of focused questions? How aware are you of the effect your approach has on others?

No one would disagree with you if you are thinking that sometimes you have successful interactions in your collaborative activities even though the quality of your information-seeking efforts is mediocre. However, that serendipitous outcome should not lead you to assume that how you phrase questions and statements is not important. For example, some people simply want to interact and tend to respond in great detail, relevant or not, even to closed questions, and thus the elaborated response may not be providing you with the information you need. Thus, in some situations you may need to be especially careful that your queries are accurate, well phrased, and designed to elicit the type of information you seek. Otherwise, the information you receive may be simply a reflection of what you unintentionally conveyed that you wished to hear.

Attend to the Cultural Context

The individualist/collectivist continuum introduced in Chapter 2 can serve as a useful framework for observing and responding to communication patterns in intercultural contexts. By the very nature of their work, busy educational professionals who operate on tight schedules are likely to adopt communication patterns that are characteristic of individualistic cultures. This may result in communication challenges with families or colleagues who hold more collectivistic orientations. You can work to bridge these cultural differences by using high-context strategies when seeking information. The suggestions that follow are appropriate for any interaction, as they tend to make the person comfortable and thus are apt to enhance your relationship. However, they are mentioned here because they are especially responsive to people with collectivistic orientations.

Using high-context strategies would suggest that you employ a general conversational tone and style when appropriate. When you are ready to ask a question, ask permission by saying, "May I ask you a question?" It is best to rely more on indirect questions initially and accept the ambiguity in responses likely to result. This encourages the person to talk more openly about past and current experiences. When you are ready to increase the focus in your questions, use prefatory statements and presupposition. Be patient and attend to the relationship at least as carefully as your need for information (Turnbull et al., 2015). The Putting Ideas into Practice on seeking information in nonthreatening ways presents some additional ideas to make questioning nonthreatening and to promote participation.

> **Learn More About**
> How could you apply the suggestions made by this social worker to interactions you may have with parents who challenge you or who are hostile?
>
> (https://www.youtube.com/watch?v=wgQEoB9UbmY)

Final Thoughts on Interviewing

This overview of steps for interviewing, whether formal or informal, describes the process as it should occur in ideal conditions. Realistically, you may find that you have to interview parents or colleagues when insufficient time is allocated, no private space is available, or your respondent is uncooperative or uncommunicative. In such situations, our advice is to assess the situation and adjust your expectations for what you will be able to accomplish during the interaction. Once you have recognized the challenges of this interview and revised your goals, you should consider the extent to which you attempt to follow all the recommendations offered.

Other unexpected events may also cause you to alter your plan. For example, if you are interviewing a parent who becomes angry, it may be nonproductive to summarize points and propose follow-up strategies. Instead, you should quickly adjust the goal to be one of listening and demonstrating understanding of the parent's feelings and perceptions. An alternative would be to spend time listening carefully to the parent and use your skills in paraphrasing, reflecting, and questioning. You can telephone the parent at a later time and propose a follow-up to the meeting. Similarly, if only 10 minutes are available to seek information, you probably should make the judgment to dispense with introductory visiting and conversation (except purpose). Being able to assess the appropriateness of situations for interactions such as interviews and to adapt your goals, skills, and techniques indicates a high degree of interactive competence.

Most educators know well that the quality of the questions they ask their students can significantly influence student learning (e.g., Heritage & Heritage, 2013). Fewer professionals understand that the same is true for interactions with colleagues, paraprofessionals, parents, and the other adults who may participate in the education of students with disabilities or other special needs (Dixon, 2013). Giving the adult–adult question-asking skills the same attention that you give to your skills for asking strong questions of students can foster strong collaborative relationships and effective and efficient collaboration.

SUMMARY

- An interview, formal or informal, is an interactive process, often embedded in other processes such as problem solving and conflict resolution, through which individuals gather information and also provide information to each other by implementing well-developed basic communication skills. Question-asking skills, including the use of open questions, indirect questions phrased as statements, and focusing questions are central to interviewing.
- Interviews generally also incorporate the effective use of statements, including those that are descriptive or, when the purpose is to explain or offer direction, those that are guiding.
- Interviewing outcomes generally are more successful when you effectively use pauses to gather your thoughts and to provide others with time to offer their responses, adjust your communication strategies to account for opportunities or challenges in the situation at hand, and use strategies that are responsive to the culture of the person(s) with whom you are interacting.

BACK TO THE CASE

1. Analyze the case that opened this chapter. As you think about the interaction between Wayne and Jerome, what do you think was the over-arching problem that cause the communication to be less than satisfactory? Include in your consideration information about each teacher's perspective and factors that might exist outside what was shared in the case description.
2. If you were Jerome, what are some alternative questions that you could have used during the interaction? What is your rationale for the potential value of your questions in improving the outcome of the interaction? That is, why are your questions better than Jerome's?
3. Given that Jerome senses that Wayne is frustrated at having to attend another meeting, what questions could Jerome ask at the outset of the meeting that might lead to Wayne hearing information that would alleviate his concerns?

COLLABORATIVE ACTIVITIES

1. Many professionals report that they have confidence in their interviewing skills and that they already possess the skills outlined in this chapter. Nevertheless, our experience in working with thousands of educators suggests that the skills are more challenging than they appear. Review the examples and question formats embedded in this chapter, and try to write additional examples of each type of question. Practice is critical, and this first practice might best be done as a paper-and-pencil exercise in response to the practice suggestions in this chapter.

2. Think of a colleague who has mentioned a concern he or she has about a student. Imagine that you are going to interact with your colleague to better understand these concerns. Write down a list of information you will need from your colleague in order to understand the situation. Review the list and develop six questions, including those that incorporate statements, you will use to obtain the needed information. Pair with a classmate and compare responses. Discuss whether you use certain types of questions more than others and whether there are improvements you can make to your questions. If you find you are not using an appropriate range of strategies, review your written responses to this situation and construct different types of questions and statements.

3. Attending to all the elements of sophisticated question-asking while you are interacting with someone can cause frustration and make it difficult for you to carry on the conversation. To build your skills, select one or two of the characteristics of questions, and practice asking questions that focus on those characteristics. Once you master those, select another, and then another, until attending to the way in which you phrase questions becomes an automatic part of your communication. Ask a classmate to assist you in assessing your question-asking skill.

4. People often have patterns they use in interviewing. However, it is important to use queries with different formats to achieve different communication goals. This activity is designed to ensure that you have practice with two information-gathering patterns, including the one you would be least likely to select on your own. Pair up with a classmate and practice interviewing, with each of you taking two turns as interviewer. Use the funnel approach in one interview and the inverted funnel in the other. After both of you have interviewed the other two times, discuss the experience. Was one format more comfortable for the interviewer? How did the interviewee feel about each format? Which format provided the most useful information? Which format would likely enhance your relationship and willingness to talk again later?

5. Explain to a colleague or a parent that you are trying to improve your interview skills. Obtain permission and audio-record an interview with him or her. Review your recording and classify each utterance according to its format. Consider which statements or questions could be improved, and write improved versions. Discuss your recording and written responses with a classmate or colleague. A variation of this activity is to ask the other participants to listen to the recording with you and then discuss your questions and explain why they elicited particular responses. Afterward, exchange recordings with a classmate and repeat the analysis. Compare your results and resolve any discrepancies.

6. Observe a colleague or one of your instructors to listen for the use of yes–no questions, such as "Does that make sense?" or "Do you understand?" Every time the individual asks such a question, construct a question of your own that would better assess understanding. Compile a list of the closed, dichotomous questions and the alternatives that you constructed, and analyze the list with a classmate.

 CHECK YOUR UNDERSTANDING

Click here to gauge your understanding of this chapter's essential concepts.

5 Group Problem Solving

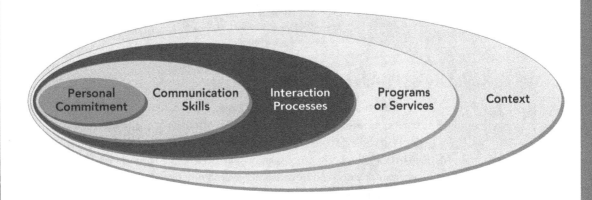

CONNECTIONS

Chapter 5 presents group problem solving as the most commonly used interaction process through which professionals in education as well as other disciplines collaborate, a process that relies on the communication skills you learned in Chapters 2, 3, and 4. Shared problem solving is the gateway to the chapters that follow. For example, it is at the heart of programs and services such as teaming (Chapter 6), co-teaching (Chapter 7), and consultation, coaching, and other indirect services (Chapter 8). And, of course, it is essential during challenging or awkward interactions, the focus of Chapter 9.

LEARNING OUTCOMES

After reading this chapter you will be able to:

1. Analyze group problem solving as an integral part of professional educators' roles, including three types of problems you may encounter, the importance of distinguishing proactive from reactive problem solving, and the conditions under which problem solving is worth the effort it requires.

2. State and carry out with colleagues, other professionals, and parents or family members the steps in a systematic group problem-solving process, using appropriate strategies to facilitate the process.

3. Identify situational, individual, and administrative factors that may affect the effectiveness of group problem solving.

A CASE FOR COLLABORATION

The Complexity of Problem Solving

Ms. Perez (kindergarten teacher) and Ms. Turner (special educator) are meeting about Willie, a student identified as having a developmental disability and attention deficit/hyperactivity disorder (ADHD). Ms. Lewis (school psychologist) and Mr. Ennis (principal) are also present, along with Willie's guardian, his grandmother, Ms. Richardson. The professionals know that Willie came to kindergarten without any preschool experience and that he was quickly noticed because his overall functioning level was at least two years below that of his classmates. Even with the services he now receives through special education and the medication that has been prescribed for him, Ms. Perez thinks that he is overwhelmed, her evidence being his increasingly disruptive behavior, especially during instructional activities that are particularly difficult for him, including reading and writing. She also expresses concern for the other students and notes the pressures of the highly academic kindergarten curriculum. Ms. Turner echoes Ms. Perez's concerns; she spends approximately 45 minutes each day in the kindergarten classroom, and her assistant spends an additional 45 minutes there, supporting Willie.

Ms. Richardson states how pleased she is with Willie's progress and how sure she is that Willie will soon catch up with his peers. During the sudden pause in the conversation caused by this comment, both teachers turned to Ms. Lewis for support of their point of view: They have concluded that Willie should spend more time in a special education classroom, and they are expecting her to support their perspective.

Introduction

Whatever your role as a professional educator, your day is spent solving problems. You do this when you decide which materials, activities, interventions, therapeutic techniques, or equipment would be best used with particular students. You also problem solve when you plan an interdisciplinary unit with a colleague, create a schedule for individualized education program (IEP) annual reviews, and/or set priorities for supplies you need for the next school year. You problem solve as you decide how to ask your administrator for a schedule change or reassignment and how to approach parents who sometimes do not respond well to conversations focused on concerns related to their children.

Each of the examples of problem solving just noted shares the feature that it is carried out in isolation. You have the responsibility to address each problem, and you do so, assuming responsibility and holding sole accountability for the outcome (Clark & Flynn, 2011). Increasingly in school settings, however, responsibility for problem solving is shared with others. This type of activity is referred to as interpersonal or group problem solving. For example, the team meetings you attend to determine appropriate interventions and placement for students are group problem-solving activities originating in special education legislation, as are your planning sessions with colleagues to discuss how to provide instructional accommodations and modifications to meet students' needs (e.g., Cho & Kingston, 2013; Weiss & Friesen, 2014). Group problem solving also is the operational basis for elementary grade-level and middle school teams, high school departments, and school leadership teams. Some group problem solving is fairly broad and involves many people, but other problem solving is quite specific and involves only two people (Tidikis & Ash, 2013). Even the other common activities in which you are likely to engage with colleagues or parents (e.g., meeting as a committee, interviewing, conferencing) often are specialized applications of group problem solving (e.g., Cheatham & Jimenez-Silva, 2012; Newman, Salmon, Cavanaugh, & Schneider, 2014). A single set of principles applies to the entire range of problem-solving activities you undertake with others, and that set of principles is the focus of this chapter.

Group problem solving is perhaps the most fundamental component of successful interactions (e.g., Sio & Ormerod, 2015). In fact, we are convinced that it is virtually impossible to collaborate with colleagues and parents without systematically and effectively employing a group problem-solving process; and the centrality of problem solving to contemporary society is illustrated by the attention it receives in a wide variety of professions, including business, health, medical, psychology, technology, engineering, and economics (e.g., Castledine, 2010; Emelo, 2014; Fiore, Wiltshire, Oglesby, O'Keefe, & Salas, 2014). However, a dilemma often occurs when educators problem solve: School professionals spend so much time problem solving by themselves that they sometimes presume that they naturally have the skills for problem solving with others. What is essential to realize is that group problem solving requires all the skills of problem solving alone as well as additional skills for going through this process with others (Chiu, 2000).

Group Problem Solving as a Professional Responsibility

Before turning to the steps in the group problem-solving process, it is important to explore problem solving as you are likely to encounter it. Analyze these three interactions.

> **Principal:** At our last meeting, we discussed the priorities for this year's school improvement plan. Today we need to be sure that someone is leading the work related to each element, who else will be on these teams, and the type of data we'll gather to document our progress.
> **Teacher 1:** Let's get ourselves assigned first and then decide who to place on each team. It seems the teams could then identify the data needed.
> **Teacher 2:** I agree—I'll volunteer to lead the team working on a before-school homework program.
> **Teacher 1:** And I'm fine leading the group working on setting up interdepartmental professional learning communities (PLCs).
>
> **Principal:** Thanks for making the time to work on the schedule. The more innovative things we do for kids, the tougher it seems to be to fit everything into the master schedule. I wanted to be sure that we touched base about your schedules for co-teaching and consultation as well as resource services and schedules for the paraprofessionals. We also have to be sure that all our related services fit well into the schedule, too.
> **Teacher 1:** I don't know how I'm going to get a schedule that I can live with this year. Based on students' IEPs, I'm supposed to get to three different classrooms for co-teaching, and I just don't see how to do it and still see the students as necessary in the resource room.
> **Teacher 2:** I know what you mean. I have four classes to co-teach, need to have a time to meet with two other teachers at least once per week, and I have six students who need a resource period for study skills and reading instruction.
> **Teacher 1:** Let's start with the "givens." One of us has to be available to cover English classes during first and second hour because so many students with IEPs are in those classes.
> **Teacher 2:** And we promised that at least one of us would be free to meet with teachers during fourth-hour lunch.
> **Principal:** Let's start blocking these "givens" on the master schedule, and perhaps we'll begin to see some ways to make the schedule fit student needs and keep it feasible for both of you. Once we see where both of you need to spend time, we can talk about roles for the paraprofessionals. We also might want to start this today and follow up later this week; it seems that when we have time to think for a bit we generate better ideas to address our scheduling challenges.

Principal: We've taken many positive steps toward ensuring that our students with disabilities are educated with their peers in general education classes whenever possible, but we've actually created another set of dilemmas. We're offering all of our services for our students who are English language learners in separate classrooms, and we're doing the same for services for students who are gifted. It seems that being inclusive should lead us to a single integrated set of programs and services, all operating on the same basis, rather than each type of program operating as though it is the only one in our school.

ELL teacher: I see your point, but I wonder if we're ready to make more changes. I was just reading about co-teaching for ELL [English Language Learners] teachers, and it makes sense for some students, but I'm not convinced it's the best option for all our English learners.

General education teacher: Moving in this direction does seem to be complicated, but what comes immediately to mind for me is how great it would be to have all my students in class more of the time. Right now, there is barely an hour of the day when all of my students are in my class.

Principal: This conversation is making me think that we need to spend some time at our upcoming faculty meeting hearing from everyone. That will give us valuable information about the positives and negatives of moving in this direction. Then we'll need to figure out how we can create a more unified system for supporting our students while minimizing the issues that might arise.

Although we will address in detail the topic of problem identification in the next section, it is clear that the situation addressed in the first interaction illustrates a straightforward, *well-defined problem*: identifying specific actions to implement the school improvement plan. The primary task is to assign leadership responsibilities and then create teams to implement the plan and gather needed data. Well-defined problems usually are fairly easily identified and understood. Difficulties in solving them often are the result of overlooking necessary elements of the solutions or encountering obstacles in implementing the solutions (e.g., budget constraints prevent the establishment of a homework program). This type of problem generally can be readily understood by all involved and adequately addressed. In some cases, one person may be able to manage the change on behalf of the group and just confirm decisions with other members.

In the second interaction, the problem is somewhat more complex. The principal and teachers have identified the problem as arranging their schedules, but no clear-cut, single solution is apparent. Instead, they are working within a set of factors that have to be accommodated (e.g., the need to "cover" English classes, arrange for resource services, and have someone available during lunch). This is a *partially defined problem*, in which the goal is clear and some guidelines exist for addressing it, but the specific means for reaching it are varied. The problem could have multiple solutions, but the range is constrained by external factors. Partially defined problems typically are not difficult to identify. Resolving them depends on the potential for successfully implementing any of several possible solutions.

Learn More About
This video captures a positive approach when addressing ill-defined problems, a situation you will find common as a professional educator.
(https://www.youtube.com/watch?v=z1jrnMnO-dY)

The third interaction is the most complex. The problem is identified as a need to expand inclusive practices to all the programs and services in the school. What types of changes are necessary to redesign services for students who are gifted and those who are English learners? What are reasonable expectations for teachers and other staff related to these changes? What resources are necessary to take the programs and services to the next level? How should decisions be made regarding the distribution of resources? The options for specifying and accomplishing the broad goal of increased inclusiveness are nearly infinite. This is an illustration of an *ill-defined problem*. It does not have clear parameters, nor is it easily resolved. Further, it is quite possible that whatever solutions are implemented, at least some of those affected by the solutions will disagree that they are appropriate.

You will undoubtedly address all three types of problems in your role as a professional educator, but ill-defined problems probably will occupy a significant portion of your time. Much of the complexity of collaborating to provide services to students is related to the number of ill-defined problems that must be addressed. The steps for problem solving outlined in the next section are valid for the first two types of problems, but they are especially critical for successfully addressing ill-defined ones (Laughlin, 2011). It is such problems you are likely to face almost daily that provide the justification for becoming an expert in problem solving in a collaborative way (Martinez, 2010/2011).

Reactive and Proactive Problem Solving

Another aspect of problem solving that may vary is the urgency of the problem-solving activity. In *reactive problem solving*, you are faced with responding to a crisis or dilemma that requires attention and action in a relatively brief time frame. A specific event focuses your attention on a matter to be resolved. Examples of this type of situation might include the following: the interactions you have with a parent concerning an incident in the classroom or the cafeteria, a meeting between an ELL teacher and a general educator to find resource materials at the proper reading level so a student can participate in a report-writing assignment, and a consultation with an occupational therapist about the student's difficulty in grasping pencils and other small items. Much group problem solving in schools is reactive, as is the problem solving needed in the case of Willie, introduced at the beginning of this chapter.

Conversely, in *proactive problem solving*, an anticipated situation focuses your attention and triggers the problem-solving process before a crisis occurs. For example, in the interaction described earlier in this section proactive problem solving is illustrated: The principal and teachers are working to create effective teacher schedules so that all services can be delivered. Other illustrations of proactive problem solving include creating a school-wide system of positive behavior supports prior to the start of the school year, arranging strategies for helping a student with autism transition from homeroom to his first-period class because of concerns he may not be able to navigate the rather noisy hallways without assistance, and deciding how best to use staff time (e.g., number of sections of co-teaching, number of sections of a study skills class) for the next school year given anticipated student enrollment and students' special needs.

Using a systematic approach for problem solving is beneficial in addressing both proactive and reactive problems. In fact, one benefit of following specific steps in problem solving is that less time may eventually be required for resolving reactive problems, so more proactive problem solving is possible.

Problem Solving and Diversity

The topic of group problem solving would not be complete without attention to the impact that cultural diversity may have on the process. This may occur in several ways. First, bias may occur among team members when the student who is the focus of problem solving is from a different background, a point illustrated by the long-term problem of certain groups of students being overidentified as having learning or emotional disabilities (Artiles, Kozleski, Trent, Osher, & Ortiz, 2010; Bal, Sullivan, & Harper, 2014). A similar issue has been identified related to students who are English learners when the problem solving occurs as part of the consideration to refer a student for special education services (e.g., Sullivan, 2011). The topic of bias in group problem solving is addressed in A Basis in Research.

A second example of the impact of diversity concerns team members themselves (Aramovich, 2014; Lopez-Fresno & Savolainen, 2014). When participants in problem solving hold strong beliefs, group problem solving may be particularly complex. For example, one teacher may believe, based on culture, that students have the obligation to behave in class, regardless of special needs. Another teacher may perceive that classroom expectations for behavior are not realistic for the student. Similarly, one educator may believe that parents should accept teacher recommendations without question, whereas others believe that parent acceptance depends on negotiation. At the same time, diversity in a problem-solving group often has a positive impact. For example, a group's varied backgrounds, experiences, and understandings may lead to better quality and more solutions, a fact supported in problem-solving research (e.g., Aramovich, 2014).

Keep in mind that most collaboration is based on problem solving, and so reflection on your own culturally determined views should accompany your consideration of the information

A BASIS IN RESEARCH

Understanding How Bias May Occur in Group Problem Solving

Just because professionals engage in group problem solving does not mean they are unbiased. These two research studies demonstrate how a process that appears objective on the surface can still reflect biases.

- Knotek (2003) observed elementary school teams. He found that when professionals' discussions of students began with negative comments or focused on misbehavior, students were likely to be referred for special education assessment. When students lived in poverty, their academic or behavioral difficulties often were attributed to their backgrounds—other explanations were not explored. Knotek discussed these findings in terms of the social processes occurring during problem solving, noting that teachers may support a colleague's perceptions because of their interpersonal relationship. He also noted that group problem solving can be significantly influenced by participants perceived as having the most power, for example, principals and school psychologists.

- Newell (2010) studied how school psychologists address cultural and racial diversity when conceptualizing acting-out behavior of boys in elementary schools. Using a case study approach and consultation with teachers, she found that the school psychologists did not consider the impact of race or culture on the students' behavior, nor did they adjust their problem-solving process because of potential cultural differences between the students and teachers. Some psychologists held a negative, within-student focus concerning the students identified as African American, but they did not do this for the students identified as European American. Newell concluded that professionals should be taught how to engage in constructive dialogue about race. Her findings are particularly sobering based on the conclusion drawn by Knotek (2003) about the influence of these professionals on decision making in group problem solving.

in this chapter. In addition, as you read about implementing collaborative options (e.g., teaming, co-teaching), working with families, and managing difficult interactions, keep in mind that your own culture is likely to strongly influence your beliefs and interaction styles with others.

Deciding Whether to Problem Solve

In addition to understanding the type of problem to be solved collaboratively and knowing whether the process will be reactive or proactive, you and your colleagues are faced with a crucial question prior to beginning problem solving: Is this a problem we should solve? Your immediate answer to this question might be "Of course—it's our job!" But that thinking is why professionals sometimes repeatedly discuss the same problem without progress. The belief that any ill-defined problem, proactive or reactive, *must* be solved once it is recognized undoubtedly arises out of the professional socialization factors discussed in Chapter 1. Although laudable, it should be balanced by an analysis of the realities of the immediate situation.

Before even considering whether you should undertake problem solving with a colleague or group of colleagues, you should first consider the circumstances from the point of view of your own involvement. For example, you can reflect on whether the problem is one that you should even be involved in solving. If a student's parent is dissatisfied with the remedial reading services delivered by the reading specialist, whether your time should be spent in interactions about the issue is questionable (unless you are the reading specialist, of course). Another consideration is whether a *collaborative* approach to problem solving is indicated. If you are an occupational therapist meeting with a group of teachers to develop fine-motor activities for students in inclusive classrooms, you are likely to provide technical assistance and use a somewhat directive style. Because you have the expertise that others need to access, this may be more efficient and effective than collaboratively problem solving.

After you consider your own role in the problem-solving situation, you can turn your attention to factors that affect problem solving with colleagues. The following are questions to ask yourself as you encounter a problem that you and others are being asked to resolve.

1. Are the persons who have responsibility and resources for addressing the problem committed to resolving it?
2. What might happen if nothing was done to resolve the problem?
3. Are adequate time and resources available to resolve the problem?
4. Does the problem merit the effort and resources required to make significant change?

Combined, the answers to these questions can help you decide whether undertaking collaborative problem solving is warranted. In some cases, the information will lead you to an affirmative decision: Perhaps you are not familiar enough with the situation to make judgments about the impact of not addressing the problem. Or perhaps the individuals involved have expressed a strong commitment to tackling the problem. On the other hand, sometimes the answers to these questions lead you to a negative decision. Perhaps the people who would be key in addressing the problem do not have adequate time to devote to it. Or perhaps the problem—although affecting a student, a program, or some other aspect of the school setting—is beyond the control of the people interested in addressing it and therefore not a constructive use of staff time. For example, a student problem may be the direct result of a family issue, and the best strategy might be referring the family to the appropriate social agency.

The problem-solving situation described at the beginning of this chapter is one that meets the criteria for shared problem solving: The participants seem committed to addressing the matter, not addressing Willie's behavior is likely to lead to further discipline issues, time and resources apparently are available, and overall, the problem seems to merit an intervention. If Willie's behavior difficulties had been ascribed to a change in medication, the need for group problem solving would have been diminished—a referral to his pediatrician would have been an immediate step to take. In Putting Ideas into Practice, other suggestions are outlined for what to do when group problem solving does not seem justified.

PUTTING IDEAS INTO PRACTICE

When Problem Solving Is Not the Best Approach

What should you do if a problem is not appropriate for you and your colleagues to address? The following are options you might consider:

- In some cases, group members should try to reconceptualize the problem so that it becomes appropriate for them to address. For example, instead of focusing on the difficulty of implementing inclusive practices without additional staff members, a group might examine how to prioritize in-class services given the current resources.
- Changing some of the members of the problem-solving group might be helpful. Perhaps the reason the problem was not considered appropriate was because of specific member perceptions. Often, it can be helpful to bring in someone who can view the situation with a "fresh eye"—that is, without the extensive background knowledge that might be shaping others' opinions.
- If an issue is significant, but not worth the time of a problem-solving team, one member might take responsibility for following up on the situation. For example, if Willie, mentioned at the beginning of this chapter, received a change in medication, the case might be an example of this type of situation. By having one person keep in touch with his guardian as the medication is adjusted, time is saved but important information is available if needed by the team.
- If a problem is not appropriate for a team, it might be because directive or supervisory action is needed as opposed to a collaborative process. When this occurs, the problem should be referred to the principal or another administrator. Examples of problems in this arena include scheduling, teachers' reluctance to work together in a classroom, and strong concerns expressed by a parent about a particular teacher.
- If problem-solving team members table a problem situation, a group member should keep a record of the action. That individual can then prompt the group to review the situation periodically. This might occur when a group of teachers meets as a grade-level or middle school team if formal record keeping is not typical for those interactions.
- Occasionally, a problem situation needs to be brought to the attention of a professional or group outside the problem-solving team. For example, if a student does not get adequate clothing at home, a social services group might be able to help.

In addition to enabling you to assess the feasibility of problem solving, these preliminary questions also help you judge the possibility of collaborating to problem solve. The questions can alert you to participants' beliefs that there are probably many "right" solutions for this or any problem and that group problem solving and decision making are the preferred approaches for this situation. These are applications of the emergent characteristics of collaboration described in Chapter 1.

Because your judgment about whether to problem solve is based on preliminary information, throughout problem solving you should continually reassess the appropriateness of your decision. At any point in the process, you may find that a key participant has lost commitment to solving the problem, that the problem is no longer within the control of the persons addressing it, or that the problem is no longer significant. If any of these situations occurs, you may want to reconsider your initial decision to address it, or at least realistically assess the potential for meaningfully resolving the problem. One way to be sure that you have the information necessary to make such decisions is to use technology throughout problem solving, the topic of E-Partnerships, so that you have documentation of what has been accomplished that can be shared by team members to inform their next steps.

E-PARTNERSHIPS

Special Circumstances: Virtual Group Problem Solving

Already common in business and other disciplines, virtual group problem solving is also emerging in education. For example, you might be asked to work on a committee of members from a large high school (or several schools across a district) to set priorities for professional development for the upcoming school year. Your interactions with colleagues may occur on a social learning platform such as GROU.PS or Yammer, or you may be expected to participate using tools from the Google suite of apps (e.g., Docs, Chat, Groups). But keep in mind that virtual group problem solving encompasses all the complexities of face-to-face problem solving, as well as a few others (e.g., Engelmann, Kolodziej, & Hesse, 2014; Janssen & Bodemer, 2013). The following chart provides several examples of challenges that may occur and suggestions for addressing them.

Challenge	Suggestions for Effective Problem Solving
Lack of familiarity with others' knowledge and skills	■ Members post brief biographical information ■ Members post three to five types of knowledge or skills they have that are directly related to the group assignment
Fewer communication channels	■ Because neither facial expressions nor voice tone can help explain the nuances of communications, members explain their thoughts and ideas in more detail ■ If in doubt, members delay posting information until it can be read after a period of time to check for communication clarity
Low levels of trust	■ Members communicate often because ongoing contact can increase trust ■ Members carry out assigned tasks in a timely manner to demonstrate trustworthiness ■ Members set operating rules about sharing information with others
Uneven or limited member participation	■ Members create operating rules that include expectations for participation ■ If a member is not participating, other members directly request that person's input
Need for coordination	■ Members address content coordination (i.e., the task at hand) by establishing a virtual space or procedure for capturing resources, discussions, and decisions ■ Members address relational coordination (i.e., the tone of the group) making constructive comments, praising others' contributions, avoiding pejorative remarks, and encouraging participation by all

Have you problem solved in a virtual group (e.g., for a course)? If so, how do these challenges apply to your experience?

Response to Intervention: A Special Type of Problem Solving

You might be wondering why, among the examples already presented in this chapter, response to intervention (RTI) has not been mentioned. That is because RTI is a special type of problem solving. Specifically, RTI is a type of problem solving that is called *technical*; and although some of the information contained in this chapter applies to it, some of the ideas do not. For example, all the complexities of problem solving in a group versus in isolation are valid for RTI as is the influence of your own cultural background on the beliefs you bring to the RTI process. However, asking questions such as those just described about whether persons are committed to addressing the problem simply is not valid: If a student's data indicate she is not succeeding, problem solving must occur. In addition, RTI systems typically have a prescribed set of solutions (e.g., a particular remedial reading program

PUTTING IDEAS INTO PRACTICE

Response to Intervention: Technical Problem Solving

Response to intervention (RTI) is an example of a very specialized type of problem solving that occurs in schools. This chart demonstrates how it is in some ways similar to, but in many ways different from, the broader creative problem-solving process presented in this chapter.

Problem-Solving Element	RTI	General Group Problem Solving
Problem target	Student	Student, programs, practices, professionals, or other areas of concern
Approach	Reactive—Begins when evidence of a gap in achievement or behavior is identified	Proactive or reactive, depending on target
Domains of intervention	Generally, reading, math, and/or behavior	Unspecified; determined by the participants
Data utilized	Predetermined (e.g., DIBELS, quarterly formative assessments) and generally quantitative	Quantitative and/or qualitative, including perceptions, depending on the problem being addressed
Solutions available	Interventions often specified in school district procedures (e.g., Reading Mastery)	Any idea generated by participants and not excluded as preposterous or unrealistic
Decision-making process	Primarily formulaic and established; analysis of target student data, data from typical peers, and assessment of the existing gap	Any procedure selected by participants (e.g., analysis of success criteria; plus/minus/implications analysis)
Implementation timeline	Established in district or school policy, often 12 to 20 weeks	Determined by participants based on problem and solution
Evaluation of solution effectiveness	Decreasing gap between student achievement/behavior and that of peers	Effectiveness defined by participants in the process prior to implementation
Strategy if solution is effective	Implement a less intensive, prescribed intervention	Conclude problem-solving process or maintain implementation
Strategy if solution is not effective	Implement more intensive, prescribed intervention and/or refer for special education services	Review each step of the problem-solving process to determine the point at which a breakdown might have occurred; begin process again from that point

APPLY YOUR KNOWLEDGE 5.1

offered four days per week for 40 minutes for 16 weeks), and so aspects of problem solving (discussed later in this chapter), including brainstorming, might not be applicable. The chart in Putting Ideas into Practice highlights these and other similarities and differences between general group problem solving and the technical problem-solving approach of RTI.

Steps in Group Problem Solving

> **Learn More About**
> If you prefer a visual representation of the problem-solving process, this flowchart is a summary of all the steps.

Once you and your colleagues have determined that you can and should address a given problem and that necessary conditions are in place for successful collaborative problem solving, you are ready to begin the problem-solving process. The steps for group problem solving have been described by many authors (e.g., Kampwirth & Powers, 2015; Laughlin, 2011), and although the steps seem straightforward, their complexity lies in skillful implementation (Arslan, 2010; Monroe, 2014).

The steps of group problem solving are outlined in Figure 5.1. Although in real life they rarely occur in the neat and linear fashion implied, if you are thoroughly familiar with the model and can easily and flexibly follow the process, you will be well prepared to make a significant contribution in all the different types of group problem-solving situations that are part of your role. Each problem-solving step is explained in greater detail in the following sections.

Identifying the Problem

When professionals are asked to list the steps for group problem solving, they nearly always correctly specify at least the first one: identifying the problem. However, in working with educators, we have learned that this step is far more easily recognized than implemented. Problem identification is difficult to accomplish, and often it is made even more so when the problem is ill defined or the number of participants in group problem solving increases in number or diversity (Wheelan, 2009).

Not surprisingly, research supports the fact that problem identification is the most critical step in problem solving (Carey & Jasgur, 2014; Newell, 2010) and that the rest of the process can be successful only if the problem is accurately delineated (Brightman, 2002; Laughlin, 2011). We find that phrasing problems as questions is a successful means of encouraging constructive problem identification. Phrasing problems as questions conveys to participants that answers are possible and lends a constructive tone to collaborative problem solving. Problems worded as statements are more likely to be seen as insurmountable. Here are some examples to illustrate this point:

- *Statement:* Roger does not turn in his homework assignments.
- *Question:* How can we increase the rate at which Roger turns in his homework?
- *Statement:* We don't have enough common planning time to effectively plan for our students.
- *Question:* How could we use available time more effectively and efficiently or find some additional time to better plan for our students?

Using questions creates a climate that fosters group problem solving. This question-wording approach to stating problems is followed throughout this chapter.

Characteristics of Well-Identified Problems When you identify problems, the issue may be as specific as addressing a student behavior problem (e.g., What strategies could be implemented to increase Jeff's appropriate play with other students on the playground?) or as broad as designing approaches for integrating students with disabilities (e.g., In what ways could we make our high school more inclusive for all students—those with disabilities and English learners, as well as those with other special needs?). Regardless of the scope of the problem, it should have the following characteristics.

An Identifiable Discrepancy Exists Between Current and Desired Situations In group problem solving, you should state the problem clearly enough so that the discrepancy

FIGURE 5.1 **A model for group problem solving.**

ANALYZE THE PROBLEM-SOLVING CONTEXT
- Assess factors related to the likelihood of problem-solving process success.
  - Are participants committed to engaging in group problem solving?
  - What might happen if the problem is not addressed?
  - Does the group have the necessary resources to address the problem, or can they obtain them?
  - Is the problem worth the time and other resources of interpersonal problem solving?
- Decide with others whether interpersonal problem solving is the appropriate approach.

IDENTIFY THE PROBLEM
- Share data and other information from multiple sources to describe the problem, keeping participants' points of view in mind.
- Using concrete and specific language, state the problem, preferably as a question.
- Check to be sure that all participants agree with the description of the identified problem.

GENERATE SOLUTIONS
- Use a specific strategy to propose as many solutions as possible for the problem.
- Follow widely accepted rules for encouraging divergent thinking, including these: avoid evaluating solutions, include unusual and unlikely solutions, create a written record of ideas.

EVALUATE POTENTIAL SOLUTIONS
- Eliminate creative solutions unlikely to be implemented or inappropriate for the problem at hand.
- For student problems, eliminate ideas that are not evidence-based.
- For the remaining solutions, use a specific strategy to consider the advantages and disadvantages of each.
- Select one (or more) of the potential solutions for detailed consideration.
- Make a comprehensive plan for the solution(s) to be implemented.
- Set a time for reviewing the effectiveness of the solution.

SELECT THE SOLUTION(S)
- Make final selection based on low instrusiveness, feasibility, or preference.

IMPLEMENT THE SOLUTION(S)
- Carry out the solution(s) as planned.
- Monitor for consistency of implementation.

EVALUATE OUTCOMES
- Using data, determine whether the implemented solution has had the desired effect.
- Make a decision to (a) continue implementation; (b) discontinue the solution because the problem is resolved; (c) revise the solution to improve its impact on outcomes; or (d) discontinue the solution because of its ineffectiveness.
- If the solution was not effective, determine the reason and re-enter the problem-solving process at that point (e.g., generating more solutions).

Having an Internet connection available during problem solving can be very helpful. For example, if a student record indicates an unfamiliar material the student has used, someone can look up details about that material.

---

between the current situation and the desired situation is apparent. For example, in a situation concerning a student's inappropriate classroom behavior, a description of the current conditions might focus on how often, for how long, and at what intensity the behavior is occurring. The desired situation might be the specification of appropriate behavior expectations for the classroom, using the same types of detail. In problem solving concerning a team's intent to plan a staff development program, the current situation might include information regarding the staff's knowledge about a topic of concern, and the desired situation might be a description of the knowledge required for proficiency to be demonstrated.

Participants Share the Perception That the Problem Exists For group problem solving to occur, all participants need to share recognition of a specific problem (Lyons et al., 2012). This is directly related to the concept of a mutual goal, which was presented as a defining characteristic of collaboration in Chapter 1. If a teacher is satisfied with the progress a student is making, but the parent believes the progress is inadequate, the shared recognition of a discrepancy between the actual and the ideal is missing. This is the situation in the case presented at the beginning of this chapter. Likewise, if a school social worker expresses concern about a student's self-concept, but the teacher does not perceive a problem, the teacher and social worker are unlikely to engage in group problem solving. Note that, in both examples, a different problem might be mutually identified if the participants discuss further their initial perceptions. But unless this occurs, the problem-solving process is not likely to be successful.

Participants Agree on the Factors That Indicate the Discrepancy Efforts to clarify the factors that define the gap between what is and what should be facilitate clear communication in problem solving. For example, analyze the problem of successfully including a student with a physical disability in a general education class. What is success? Without specifying how to define the current status of the student and the status after some intervention selected on the basis of group problem solving, there is no way to determine whether successful integration has been accomplished. In this example, success could be indicated by the student's improved attitude toward school, parents' and teachers' perceptions of student attitude, the extent to which other students interact with the student with a disability, the extent to which the student accesses the same general curriculum standards as other students, the student's performance on achievement tests, or any number of additional measures. (You will read about the importance of specifically measuring the factors defining the gap in a later section, "Finalizing Implementation Plans.")

Problem Statements Suggest Many Kinds of Solutions The objective of problem identification is to describe in the clearest terms possible the discrepancy between the current and the ideal situations so participants can look for alternative strategies to move from the former to the latter. Therefore, you should avoid unnecessarily narrowing the problem statement. To clarify this point, analyze this initial problem statement: How can we assist this student who is an English learner to succeed in his math class? Although the problem is as yet incomplete because the gap has not been specified and the factors defining the gap have not been outlined, it is appropriate because it does not attempt to suggest a single strategy that is needed to ensure success. But the problem could have been stated in this way: How can we assist this student to learn his basic multiplication facts? The latter problem statement includes the assumption that success in math will occur if math facts are learned. If the goal of problem solving is to help a student succeed, it might be appropriate to provide a calculator and work on real-life problem-solving applications. The second problem statement might preclude this possibility from being discussed. The first problem statement is more likely to leave this option available, along with many other strategies that include the student, his peers, his teacher, other professionals, his family, and so on. The range of potential solutions is broadened because the problem statement is free of preferred strategies. In essence, the second problem statement transforms an appropriately ill-defined problem and artificially turns it into a partially defined one.

Suggestions for Identifying the Problem The following strategies can help you and your colleagues identify problems in ways that foster creative and effective thinking during your group problem-solving efforts.

Think of Problem Identification as Having Both Divergent and Convergent Elements Too often in schools, problem identification is thought of as primarily a convergent process—that is, one that focuses on rapidly narrowing the problem description. Although this may appear

---

Learn More About
When a problem is particularly complex, a process called concept mapping, explained in this video, can assist participants in building a shared understanding of the situation.
(https://www.youtube.com/watch?v=A625Yh6v6uQ)

expedient, it is usually neither efficient nor constructive. Instead, we encourage you to think of the early phase of problem identification as a divergent process—that is, as a phase in which the goal is to explore all possible problem definitions so that none is overlooked.

One means of keeping early problem identification divergent is to challenge the assumptions that underlie initial problem statements. For example, this is a problem statement that you might encounter:

- How can we get Josh's parents, Mr. and Mrs. Keller, to participate in the behavior management program that Josh needs?

It has a number of assumptions, including the fact that Josh's parents should be involved in a behavior management program, that Josh truly needs the program, and that "we" should take responsibility for involving Mr. and Mrs. Keller. What would happen if you negated one or several of these assumptions? Perhaps the problem would be reconceptualized as one of these:

1. How can we get Josh's behavior management program to work at school?
2. How can we improve Josh's behavior at school?
3. How could Josh learn to be more involved in controlling his behavior?

Once underlying assumptions have been challenged and alternative conceptualizations of the problem have been explored, participants in problem solving are more likely to be able to identify the problem's most essential characteristics and use them to formulate a revised problem statement. This reformulation of the problem is convergent. It emphasizes that all participants need to reach agreement on the problem prior to generating solutions for it. However, it is also important to recognize that challenging assumptions may or may not lead to a redefinition of a problem; the point is that it is a strategy for making problem identification deliberate for all participants in the problem-solving process.

Describe the Problem Precisely The need for using concrete and specific language in verbal communication was addressed in detail in Chapters 2, 3, and 4 when you learned about communication skills (Nardon, Steers, & Sanchez-Runde, 2011). Its importance in problem solving, especially during problem identification, cannot be overstated (e.g., Arslan, 2010; Shelly & Shelly, 2009). For example, in problem solving about a student, you should strive to describe the observable behaviors or performance indicators that characterize the student's academic or social performance. Some teachers might describe a student as "unmotivated." Your task during problem identification is to clarify what is meant by that descriptor. Does it mean that the student is absent? Does it mean that the student does not complete assigned work? Does it imply that the student sleeps during lectures? Only by specifying the exact behaviors or performance indicators that comprise the meaning of "unmotivated" can the problem be identified clearly.

In addition to using concrete and specific language, when identifying a problem you should confirm that all participants share the same understanding of the particular words used. An example of a term whose definition often is perceived differently by professionals is *inclusion*. For some special services providers, inclusion refers to integrating students with disabilities into general education classes, primarily for social purposes. For others, it means having students attend classes in which they can complete the academic work. For yet others, inclusion means integrating students physically, instructionally, and socially, regardless of the disability. And for yet others, *inclusion* and *co-teaching* are used as synonyms. Imagine the difficulties that might result if a group of individuals were problem solving on this topic without establishing a shared meaning for the word! What other words might cause confusion in the schools where you work or will work?

Learn More About
You can use a technique called *The Five Whys*, presented in this video, to ensure that your problem solving group has identified the real problem needing attention and not just a symptom of it.
(https://www.youtube.com/watch?v=EOIW8j8MH10)

Confirm Problems with Multiple Sources of Information One of the dangers in group problem solving is that participants may rely on a single source of information to identify a problem (Anderson & Lennox, 2009). An important strategy for ensuring successful problem identification is the use of multiple sources. In problems related to students, this might entail completing an observation of the target student in several different school

"I need more time. Unlimited minutes aren't enough!"

settings; reviewing student data regarding academic achievement, behavior, social skills, or physical needs; and interviewing parents and teachers. In problems related to programs, teams, or services, this might include confirming district policies, reviewing available data (e.g., needs assessment, a staff development activity evaluation), and interviewing key people to ascertain their perceptions.

Problems can be confirmed in many ways. Sometimes data already exist in the form of student records, district surveys, or state guidelines. In other cases, some type of data collection may be needed, whether formal or informal, quantitative or qualitative. The important point is to be certain that the problem identified is an accurate description of what is actually occurring.

Allow Adequate Time for Problem Identification All of the strategies for accurately identifying problems require time. Successful problem identification relies on high-quality interactions among the participants in group problem solving and opportunities for reflection and analysis. Unfortunately, in many school settings there seems to exist an implicit assumption that the problem identification step should be completed as quickly as possible so that the more important task of resolving the problem can begin. Such thinking overlooks one key point: Without adequate time, accurate problem identification is unlikely and valid problem resolution is improbable. In Chapter 7, you will learn more about prioritizing time use and making the best possible use of time for collaboration; the suggestions in that chapter apply directly to group problem solving as well.

Our recommendation is to begin to systematically increase the amount of time spent on identifying problems. In some situations, multiple sessions are preferred for this, especially when additional data need to be gathered or the problem is particularly complex. Although this approach may seem awkward and time consuming at first, the long-term benefit is far more efficient problem solving. For example, at an initial meeting, a problem experienced by a student could be outlined and team members asked to consider the situation and gather information for the next week's meeting. At the follow-up meeting, the student's problem would be discussed in detail and the problem-solving process implemented.

One strategy for ensuring that adequate time is allowed for problem identification is to use a checklist for exploring various aspects of a problem. For problems related to students, the checklist could include medical factors, instructional items, social areas, family or community factors, and so on. For problems related to programs or services, the checklist might address scheduling, personnel/staffing, district policies, school priorities, professional development needs, and others.

Monitor the Problem-Solving Context At the beginning of this chapter, we noted the importance of monitoring the problem-solving situation. This is particularly critical during problem identification. Participants may not have had enough information initially to determine whether group problem solving was appropriate for a given situation; such information may emerge during this problem-solving step and lead to a different decision about the appropriateness of problem solving. Likewise, you should monitor to ensure that other participants remain committed to solving the problem once its parameters are set.

Generating Potential Solutions

After you have clearly identified the problem, you are faced with the sometimes daunting task of proposing alternative means for resolving it. The purpose of the second major step of problem solving is to stimulate the creation of the maximum number of potential solutions by the widest range of participants (Gobble, 2014b; VanGundy, 2005). This problem-solving step relies heavily on divergent thinking (Liu, 2014).

Suggestions for Generating Potential Solutions Studies of both creative processes and critical problem solving have contributed greatly to knowledge about how to generate potential solutions in group problem solving (Honig, Lampel, & Drori, 2014; Paulus, Kohn, & Arditti, 2011). The following are some solution-generating techniques designed to encourage divergent thinking.

Brainstorming The most familiar strategy for generating potential solutions is *brainstorming* (Castellano, 2013; Gobble, 2014a). In brainstorming, the participants in the problem-solving process call out solutions as they think of them, facilitating their own thinking by listening to the ideas generated by others. The rules typically given for brainstorming during group problem solving include the following:

1. Accept all ideas that are offered without evaluating them.
2. Propose solutions freely, even if they seem impractical.
3. Have someone write down the ideas being generated.
4. "Play" with the ideas to generate even more ideas.

In addition, you may find it helpful to set a time limit for generating solutions; this not only focuses attention on the process but also acknowledges the time constraints of school-based problem solving.

The following example is an illustration of brainstorming in order to resolve a student problem:

> A teacher described this situation to colleagues at a problem-solving meeting. He was responsible for Jorge, a student with ADHD who demonstrated significant challenges related to peer and adult social interactions. The student's behaviors included pushing other students, teasing and bullying, refusing to respond to requests by teachers and others, and often saying that any problem was someone else's fault. The teacher was particularly concerned because other students were beginning to say they didn't like Jorge and they didn't want him in their groups. After the problem was identified as how to improve Jorge's social interactions in the classroom, professionals generated these potential solutions:
>
> 1. Begin a formal social skills training program.
> 2. Enlist the assistance of the counselor to meet with Jorge.
> 3. Teach the other students tolerance.
> 4. Involve the family in designing an intervention.
> 5. Video record Jorge so he can see his behaviors.
> 6. Video record the teacher to see whether her responses to the behaviors might be maintaining them.
> 7. Video record the entire class to observe students' interactions.
> 8. Transfer Jorge to another class so he can get a "fresh start."
> 9. Transfer the teacher so Jorge can get a "fresh start."
> 10. Ask the counselor to schedule several sessions with the class on respectful interactions and understanding diversity.
> 11. Ask the principal to visit the class to convey to students the seriousness of the matter.
> 12. Check the media center for a video on social interactions to use with the class.
> 13. Set up a class-wide system that rewards respectful interactions.

14. Give bonuses to Jorge for appropriate social interactions.
15. Design some nonthreatening activities and arrange small student groups that include Jorge in order to help him practice social skills.
16. Have a class meeting to discuss the problem.
17. Hire a paraprofessional for the classroom.
18. Ask the district to provide an external consultant to observe the student and classroom and make recommendations.
19. Ask the school psychologist to observe the class and offer input on the seriousness of the problem.
20. Ask the principal to teach the class for several days while the teachers work on a solution.
21. Look for a pattern based on the observations: Is Jorge experiencing more problems after weekends or holidays? Late in the day? During particular subjects (e.g., math) or activities (e.g., independent work time)?
22. Do an Internet search for web sites on addressing social interaction problems and generate additional ideas from that search.

> **Learn More About**
> This video clip provides a quick and straightforward summary of the dos and dont's of brainstorming.
> (https://www.youtube.com/watch?v=9K8W4ooygUU)

This example demonstrates why brainstorming can be such a powerful technique in problem solving. First, notice that playfulness was an integral part of the brainstorming. For example, no one seriously expects the student or the teacher to transfer for a "fresh start," and yet letting those ideas surface led to the idea of asking the counselor to come to the class to work with students—in essence, a fresh start for the entire class.

Another brainstorming concept illustrated in this example is *chaining*, which is linking a series of ideas through a concept or other stimulus. Ideas 5, 6, and 7 form a chain about using video recording to understand teacher–student and student–student dynamics in the classroom. Ideas 18, 19, and 21 comprise a chain about classroom observation. In fact, the value of chaining in generating potential solutions is a primary reason why all ideas are accepted without evaluation: Each time you stop brainstorming to evaluate an idea, you decrease the likelihood that any participant will chain with the idea just presented.

Brainstorming is the preferred strategy for generating potential solutions in many problem-solving situations. It is best used when you and other participants

- Know each other reasonably well
- Have comparable knowledge about the problem context
- Comprise a relatively small problem-solving group
- Perceive the problem is not particularly emotion laden

When these conditions are not present, for example, when the group is large, members do not know one another, or the problem is particularly complex or sensitive, brainstorming is generally not recommended.

Brainwriting Another strategy for generating potential solutions is brainwriting (Liu, 2014; Michinov, 2012). In brainwriting, participants individually write three or four potential solutions on a blank sheet of paper. They then place their lists in a pile on the table, from which they select someone else's list. The ideas on that list are the stimuli for them to generate additional solutions. This exchange of ideas continues until no new ideas are forthcoming. The complete set of ideas is then presented to the group with duplications eliminated. Figure 5.2 is an example of how brainwriting sheets might look.

Brainwriting is a productive option when open discussion of ideas may not be fruitful. For example, if you are problem solving about an emotionally charged issue, more ideas may be generated through this written process than through one involving verbal exchange. The same principle holds for topics that might be considered sensitive—for example, if teachers are uncertain about their responsibilities for helping students who are English learners. Another reason for choosing brainwriting is simply to change the procedure for generating alternative solutions to encourage a fresh perspective. Finally,

FIGURE 5.2 **Example of brainwriting activity.**

Problem addressed by the school staff: In what ways might we increase the involvement of parents and family members as instructional partners in our school?

ROUND ONE

Anna	Jennifer	Travis
1. Create a parent task force with lots of fanfare.	1. Talk to J. Montgomery in Columbus Schools, where there is a high level of parent involvement.	1. Search Internet for ideas on parent involvement.
2. Set up a strong parent volunteer program with T-shirts, rewards, publicity.		2. Search Internet for formal programs or successful examples of parent involvement.

ROUND TWO

Travis (read Anna's list)	Anna (read Jennifer's list)	Jennifer (read Travis's list)
3. Get materials from the state department of education on parent involvement.	2. Send a group of our staff to visit the Columbus program.	3. Ask parents how they could partner with us electronically.
4. Use our parent organization as a basis. Meet with them?	3. Pay a parent to lead this effort and contact other parents.	4. Explore options such as volunteer-staffed homework hotlines or homework e-mail.
5. Ask students how they would like their parents to be involved at school.	4. Survey parents to ask how they want to be instructional partners.	5. Open school so parents can access technology.
6. Be careful to work on ideas that will let lots of parents be involved, not just those who can come to school during the day.		6. Hold parent invitational coffees to solicit input.
		7. Find an off-site location to hold parent meetings (place of worship, community center).

brainwriting sometimes is preferred when the problem-solving group is so large that not everyone may have ample opportunity to speak if brainstorming is used.

Nominal Group Technique A third strategy to generate potential solutions combines aspects of brainstorming and brainwriting. In *nominal group technique* (NGT; McMillan et al., 2014), participants are assigned to groups of four to five individuals, and they first individually generate and write down as many potential solutions as they can.

Then the ideas are shared by having one person in the group state one idea, writing it so that all can see the idea. Then the next individual shares one idea. This process of persons sharing single ideas from their lists continues until all alternatives are presented. Individuals may "pass" at any time they are asked to share an idea and they do not have a new option to offer. The total list of ideas is then discussed by participants to identify the most important potential solutions and to begin the process of data reduction or idea combination. Each participant writes each prioritized solution on a separate card (as many as 10 ideas) and then rates each on a scale from very important (a ranking of 5) to unimportant (1). The facilitator gathers these cards from each group and records all participants' votes for ideas. If a clear pattern of preference for particular ideas emerges, the procedure is complete; if not, additional discussion is held and a second vote is taken.

NGT is valuable when many people need to participate in generating potential solutions and some means is necessary to ensure their equal opportunity for participation. This might occur when the number of participants is particularly large, when the participants traditionally have had unequal status, or when some individuals tend to dominate the group. Although you might not use this technique in day-to-day group problem solving or even when a team meets to discuss options for students struggling to learn, it is a helpful option for generating solutions with a long history of successful application that you might be able to suggest when, for example, the entire school staff needs to problem solve about an important issue.

Whether you choose to use brainstorming, brainwriting, NGT, or other approaches for generating potential solutions, you should adhere to the rules outlined as part of brainstorming. Sometimes it is tempting to stop to evaluate each idea as it is expressed. But this derails the entire purpose of generating potential solutions; we have seen many problem-solving sessions in which participants never returned to this critical step once they began prematurely discussing an idea that had been offered. Worse, participants often seem to be unaware of the fact that they have strayed from the problem-solving process and of how this is limiting their effectiveness.

When individuals from diverse cultures engage in problem solving, care must be taken that communication is clear, various perspectives are respected, and solutions are appropriate for the cultural context.

Remember, generating as many solutions as possible is the point of this problem-solving step (Kaye, 2013).

Evaluating Potential Solutions

The list of potential solutions you generate serves as the raw material for making the specific decision about which solution to implement. In order to make an informed decision, each of the potential solutions should be evaluated. This involves two problem-solving steps: (1) delineating the positives and negatives of each potential solution and (2) outlining the tasks required to implement each.

Delineating the Positives and Negatives of Each Potential Solution In this evaluative step, your task is to examine each potential solution from a balanced perspective. This entails listing the positive and negative aspects of each intervention or strategy. For example, in the brainstormed list of options for Jorge, the student experiencing social interaction problems, one idea was to video record the student. Positive aspects of that solution might include the following:

1. The very presence of the video camera might improve Jorge's interactions because of his concern about being captured on video acting in an inappropriate manner.
2. A video recording would provide objective evidence of the seriousness of the problem.
3. A video recording would allow teachers and others to demonstrate to Jorge's parents the nature of the problem, hopefully enlisting their support for a planned intervention.

Negative aspects of that solution might include the following:

1. Jorge, as well as other students, might be distracted from their schoolwork by the video equipment.
2. Jorge's behavior might be artificially positive because of his awareness of the video recording.
3. Jorge's behavior might deteriorate as he "performs" for the camera.
4. District policies might prohibit the video recording of any student without explicit parental permission. Obtaining permission for all the students might make the entire project too difficult to implement.

On the basis of these positive and negative aspects of video recording, would you retain it as a potential solution? If your response is no, then you would eliminate it from the list. If your response is yes, then you would leave it on your list of options for further discussion.

This step of weighing advantages and disadvantages should be completed for all the items on the list of potential solutions, although for some the task will be brief. For example, another idea for addressing Jorge's behaviors was for a consultant to teach the class for several days. This was a preposterous idea that emerged from the playful part of brainstorming and then led to the generation of other possible solutions. This cost-prohibitive and unrealistic potential solution and others similar to it should be quickly discarded.

One way of formalizing this process of considering the opportunities and constraints of potential solutions is called *Plus/Minus/Implications*, or PMI. In a simple chart, each alternative is listed and three columns are used for the PMI. For example, idea 10, asking the counselor to intervene with the class, might include these points:

- *Plus (positive results)*. Removes the teacher from the immediate situation, permitting someone with a fresh perspective to get involved.
- *Minus (negative effects)*. Counselor has many responsibilities and may have to miss sessions if a crisis occurs.

- *Implications (possible positive or negative outcomes of the action).* Potential increased class understanding of Jorge's behavior, so fewer complaints about it; possibility that Jorge would not gain any understanding from this indirect intervention.

Outlining the Tasks for the Potential Solutions By eliminating some of the potential solutions on the basis of their positive and negative aspects, you shorten considerably the list of potential interventions or strategies. But you probably still have several options, all of which seem possible. The second evaluation step, outlining the tasks that would be required to implement each of the remaining potential solutions, is the means through which these possibilities are further analyzed and narrowed.

Consider another idea from the brainstormed list. One of the potential solutions is to set up a class-wide reward system for appropriate social interactions. What are the tasks that would have to be completed for this option to be implemented? You and your colleagues would have to discuss with Jorge's teacher what type of system might be consistent with classroom expectations already in place. You would need to specify what "appropriate social interactions" are and how they would be observed. Additionally, you would identify what the rewards would be and when they would be given. You might decide to discuss alerting parents/families that a system was being implemented, so a letter of explanation might have to be generated. What other tasks would be required?

After considering the tasks associated with each of the possible solutions, you should decide whether each option still seems feasible. If not, you would discard the idea. If so, you would retain it as a likely solution, and you might select it for implementation.

Selecting the Solution

Following all of the steps described thus far should have led you to a list of several clearly articulated, carefully outlined potential solutions, all appropriate for resolving the problem. Now the task is to select one of these.

This selection can be based on several factors. One consideration may be intrusiveness. If an intervention or strategy will disrupt classroom routines or require changes in staff assignments, it may become the second choice after one that fits into existing routines and staff responsibilities.

Feasibility is another factor that influences selection of solutions. A simple solution that requires no new resources typically is preferable to one that involves separate budget items or inordinate amounts of time. Similarly, a solution that necessitates coordinating multiple activities and people may be less feasible in a busy school setting than one that minimizes the number of implementers.

A third—and admittedly not very systematic—means for selecting among the potential solutions is individual preference. Although all the solutions may be feasible and none particularly intrusive, the people who have the most responsibility for implementing them may simply be more comfortable with one over the others. This consideration should not be ignored; the likelihood of a successful outcome is dependent to some extent on the commitment and attitude of those directly involved in implementation. That is, some teachers might prefer a behavior contract written specifically for a student such as Jorge, whereas others might prefer a class-wide intervention strategy.

As you and your colleagues select a solution, try to identify the basis on which this decision will be made. There are no "correct" criteria for making this judgment, but the criteria used should be clear to all participants. The decision is one that should be made carefully, with a balance between caution and reliance on the collective careful judgment of the group (Ray & Romano, 2013).

Implementing the Solution

Now you have selected the solution to be implemented, and you have addressed challenges such as those outlined in Putting Ideas into Practice. Because you have done a great deal of planning throughout the problem-solving process, many details for

> **Learn More About**
> Decision-making skills are integral to group problem solving. How does this problem-solving story relate to your professional responsibilities?
> (https://www.youtube.com/watch?v=rlfolkJzlxU)

PUTTING IDEAS INTO PRACTICE

Problem-Solving Practice

Problem solving in groups often is more easily discussed than implemented. Here are a few situations that might occur and some suggestions for addressing them. If you have time, you could set up each of these situations as a role-play.

- At the very beginning of a problem-solving meeting, one teacher says, "We know what the problem is. Let's spend our time finding a way to solve it."

Among harried educators, this type of comment is not unusual. However, it can undermine problem-solving success. You might respond using strong communication skills, stating that you are not completely clear on everyone's perspective and that you would prefer that the group clarify the problem first.

- As ideas are being generated, one participant makes a negative comment about each idea, pulling the conversation into arguments about the merit of each potential solution.

Creativity and chaining are unlikely to occur when brainstorming is interrupted by such discussion. If the problem is chronic, the problem-solving group might want to review its operating rules prior to the start of a meeting. Brainwriting could also be used as an alternative. A last-resort strategy is to say to the individual, "When we discuss each idea, instead of getting a lot of ideas out together, it interferes with my thinking. I'd like to get a long list of ideas and then discuss whether each has value for this situation."

- It is time to stop the meeting, but no one has agreed to take on responsibility for implementing the planned student intervention. People are packing up their belongings and moving toward the door.

Time problems can be especially acute for group problem solving. If a situation is complex, participants could plan to devote two sessions to the conversation. They might also use e-mail to complete the assignment of responsibilities after the meeting. However, if the issue is that everyone seemed reluctant to take on the responsibility of the selected intervention, participants might need to assess why that is occurring. If the solution is too time consuming to be realistic or too complex to be easily put into place, perhaps another idea should be selected.

---

implementing the plans have already been identified. However, one more planning phase is required before actual implementation of the intervention or strategy.

Finalizing Implementation Plans In preparation for implementation, your responsibility is to review with other participants the plans that were made during the evaluation step of problem solving. Finalizing these plans typically includes

1. Reviewing and refining detailed plans for implementing the solutions
2. Determining the criteria by which success will be determined
3. Scheduling a time to evaluate the outcome(s) of the applied solution

Detailed Arrangements The selected solution is more likely to be successful if you and your colleagues specify all necessary arrangements and assign all responsibilities. Some professionals find that listing responsibilities is helpful in accomplishing this. In the sample chart in Figure 5.3, the first column includes the task to be done, the second shows the person responsible, the third includes the target completion date, the fourth addresses the outcomes expected, the fifth includes the outcomes achieved, and the final column contains space for writing comments.

Criteria for Success Yet another issue to clarify in the final planning for implementation is the selection of specific variables and criteria that will be used to determine whether the intervention or strategy has been successful. This is consonant with the definition of the desired situation discussed as part of problem identification. In interventions related to students, this could include specific levels of achievement on designated assessment instruments or a quantifiable improvement in attendance. In strategies that address

FIGURE 5.3 **Example of a problem-solving responsibility chart.**

Student: _____ Date: _____

Summary of problem: _____

Solution to be attempted: _____ Evaluation Date: _____

Criteria for success: _____

Results: _____

Action/Task	Person(s) Responsible	Target Completion Date	Expected Outcomes	Outcomes Achieved	Other Comments

problems about programs or services, this may require the development of a needs assessment questionnaire or survey and clarification of what outcomes will signal success. The form presented in Figure 5.3 includes space for specifying criteria.

Scheduled Time for Evaluation of Outcomes A final topic to address prior to implementation is a specific time for assessing the success of the solution (or the outcomes). Inattention to this issue is a mistake we repeatedly observe in group problem solving in schools. Well-intentioned interventions or strategies sometimes are abandoned because of failure to assess systematically whether they are having the desired impact, and the first step of assessment is arranging for a time to jointly discuss the solution and its effectiveness. This discussion should be heavily based on data, not only professionals' perceptions, and it should be intended to make a decision about continuing, revising, or discontinuing the solution.

Carrying Out the Solution After completing all of these steps, you are ready to implement the intervention or strategy. Quite simply, you *do* whatever it is you have planned—whether it is a student intervention concerning academic or social behavior, a new structure for school-wide professional development, a parent involvement project, a beginning Spanish course for teachers who wish to learn the language many of their students use, a co-teaching unit, or a schedule change for the following school year so that collaborative planning time can be arranged. The "what" of implementation is as varied as the problem situations you encounter. During implementation, you rely on the commitment and expertise of those in your problem-solving setting.

The more complex the problem, the more important a formal group problem-solving process becomes.

Evaluating the Outcome

The evaluation time scheduled during final planning functions as "no-fault insurance" for group problem solving. During this step of the process, you should determine whether the established goal has been reached. You also determine whether those involved in the problem-solving process are satisfied with the impact of the intervention or strategy.

Depending on what you learn during this problem-solving step, you will plan different courses of action. If the intervention or strategy (i.e., the selected solution) is meeting with success, it becomes an opportunity for congratulating each other on that success. In such a case, the decision to be made is whether to continue the intervention or strategy for another defined period of time or, if the problem has been resolved, to terminate it. A school-wide positive behavior management system is an example of a "solution" that might be continued over a long period of time; a student reward system for completing assignments is one that you might choose to phase out.

If the implemented solution is only partially successful, your decisions focus on continuing the intervention for more time to see whether effectiveness will improve, or somehow revising the strategy to make it more successful. You and other participants in the problem-solving process would analyze whether elements of the solution are unsatisfactory and should be modified or whether a longer implementation might make a difference. In either of these situations, another date for feedback would be scheduled so that you can continue to monitor progress.

An unsuccessful outcome is a third possibility in group problem solving. Although this is much less likely if the steps in the process have been systematically followed, you still may need a set of strategies for addressing this type of frustrating situation.

The first action you and your colleagues should take when faced with an unsuccessful outcome is to analyze the reasons for the lack of success. You might examine the intervention or strategy itself to ascertain whether it was flawed and consider whether the solution was implemented with fidelity or consistency, a topic addressed in more detail in

Chapter 9. You also might consider whether other ideas might have been more effective in solving the problem, whether the problem was accurately identified, and whether the problem-solving context was inappropriate. For example, perhaps you lacked certain information that was important for the success of the solution, or perhaps new information emerged during the problem-solving process that affected implementation. Additional possibilities might also account for the lack of success. In fact, your analysis may include a reexamination of each phase of the problem-solving process in a search for information that would explain what prevented the intervention or strategy from being successful. This procedure of tracking back through problem solving helps all participants to reflect on decisions made and to consider alternatives to them. Some of the following questions might guide this process:

- Was the solution implemented consistently? If not, what prevented consistency? Could these factors be successfully addressed?
- Might another solution from those considered by the problem-solving group be implemented instead?
- Should the group generate several new possible solutions and evaluate those as alternatives?
- Has the problem been accurately identified? Is there a common understanding of the problem among all the participants in the process?
- Is this a problem that this group should be attempting to resolve?

After you and your colleagues have identified the source of the breakdown, the next task is to return to the point of the group problem-solving process at which the difficulty occurred and complete the steps again, correcting it. As implied in the questions presented earlier, this may be as simple as selecting another solution that was previously proposed and evaluated, or it may be as complex as returning to the very beginning of the problem-solving process to reanalyze the context and the presenting problem.

Putting the Problem-Solving Pieces Together

As you review the information you have learned about group problem solving, you may be thinking that the process seems cumbersome, that in your own experiences in schools no one seems to take such care in implementing each of the problem-solving steps. That often may be true, but here are some points to consider as you work to incorporate this technical information about problem solving into your own professional practice.

- The care with which problem-solving steps are implemented depends to a certain extent on the seriousness of the problem at hand. If a student with complex needs is being discussed, more explicit attention to each step may be warranted. If the problem at hand is well defined or partially defined, or if the matter is not particularly serious—perhaps how to revise an instructional unit to incorporate a specific evidence-based practice prioritized for implementation school-wide—a somewhat less formal approach may be successful. It should follow the same steps, but they may occur quickly and without each one being explicitly discussed, even though you may be internally following the problem-solving model. One example of a situation in which this may occur is a conversation with a colleague about a student with an attentional problem.
- Even if your colleagues are not accustomed to using a clear problem-solving procedure, you can use your knowledge to guide the process. For example, during problem identification you might comment, "We're assuming that Matthew does not want to come to school on time, and I'm not convinced that's a valid assumption." You are using the strategy of questioning assumptions, but doing so in a way that fits into the conversation in a natural manner. Can you generate ideas for how to work other

problem-solving strategies into conversations as they often occur during school problem-solving meetings? Think about the case of Willie that opened this chapter. What questions could you ask to help clarify the problem-solving process that has just started?

- Group problem solving relies on collaboration, and as noted at the beginning of this chapter, it can be enhanced or constrained when participants are from different cultures. For instance, differences among participants may lead to some tensions. These can result in spirited discussions and the need to clarify terms being used and strategies being suggested. For example, one teacher strongly believes that the student should either be expected to behave or be sent to the office for classroom infractions. Another sees that the behavior is the result of being overwhelmed by classroom demands and that providing structure and clarity is the true problem. In another example, a teacher focuses on helping get a student ready for post-school employment, focusing on self-advocacy and independence; while the parent anticipates that her child will live at home and be supported by the family and is puzzled by the discussions about independence. Similarly, individuals with diverse backgrounds may think very differently about how to solve a problem. The result can be a longer list of potential solutions and a greater variety of ideas. Some individuals might believe that family involvement is essential for success, but others may stress focusing on what can be accomplished at school with or without parent involvement.

- Participants' individual styles, depth of expertise, as well as the level of trust in the group may affect the process and outcomes of group problem solving (Aramovich & Larson, 2013; Rijnbout & McKimmie, 2014; Trouche, Sander, & Mercier, 2014). For example, if one group member is dominant, the solutions reached are most likely to reflect that individual's preferences rather than the group's collective decision. If members do not trust one another, they are likely to withhold information that could be crucial or to feel less accountability for the work of the group. But if the trust level is high, individuals are more likely to share, actively participate in the problem-solving process, and feel responsible for the outcome. Principals or other administrators who are participants in problem-solving sessions can play a key role in facilitating the process (Carmeli, Sheaffer, Binyamin, Reiter-Palmon, & Shimoni, 2014). However, each person engaged in the process has a responsibility to help move the problem-solving process effectively through each step. All participants can slow down a discussion when a problem is being identified too quickly or add ideas during brainstorming. Likewise, they can help realistically analyze solutions with the most potential and offer to play a part in implementing them.

- Be especially aware of the tendency in some school situations for meetings or conversations to be described as "problem solving" when in fact they are primarily interactions in which one person is trying to convince another person that a particular predetermined solution is the right one. For instance, early in a meeting, someone says, "We all agree that we don't like the way department meetings are scheduled, so don't you think we should approach administration about changing how often they are required?" This type of comment suggests that one person has decided what the problem is without adequate discussion, that same person has a favored way to address the problem, and an expectation is being set that others will agree with the intervention. This example illustrates the point just made about the importance of all problem-solving participants contributing to the process. As a professional who understands problem solving, your role should be to speak up, to slow down the process, and to ensure that all participants have the opportunity to participate in all phases of this essential collaborative process.

Your knowledge about group problem solving and your skill in implementing its steps are applicable across countless professional situations, and you probably will find that they are also useful in other interactions. Your goal should be to practice following the steps of problem solving so that when they are most needed—especially in challenging meetings or contentious professional situations—they are at your fingertips.

APPLY YOUR KNOWLEDGE 5.3

SUMMARY

- Interpersonal or group problem solving is the central process used in collaborative activities, whether you are addressing well-defined, partially defined, or ill-defined problems and whether the process is proactive or reactive; however, such problem solving is appropriate only when the situation suggests it will be effective.
- These are the steps for group problem solving: Identify the problem; generate potential solutions; evaluate the potential solutions—by outlining the pros and cons of each solution and then specifying the tasks that would have to be completed to accomplish each one; select a solution from those preferred and finalize the implementation plan; implement the solution; and evaluate the outcome of the intervention or strategy.
- On the basis of the outcome, you may decide to continue with the implementation, make adaptations to it, or, if the outcome is unsuccessful, assess at which point the process may have broken down and return to that step in the group problem-solving process.
- The process and outcomes of group problem solving may be affected by situational (e.g., seriousness of the problem), individual (e.g., cultural differences, interpersonal styles, expertise), and administrative (e.g., principal support) factors.

BACK TO THE CASE

Use the case of Willie from the beginning of this chapter to practice group problem solving:

- Assign classmates to take on each of the roles.
- Have the remaining class members take notes during the role play for discussion at its conclusion.
- Try following the problem-solving steps to clarify the problem, generate solutions, and analyze them.
- Consider adding a twist to the case: Change Willie's age and school level, assign him to a particular cultural group, or add other professionals to the interaction, depending on the interests of your group or class.
- After this exercise and using the notes taken by observers, analyze what occurred. Was each step implemented? How well? What could have been said (using communication skills learned in Chapters 2, 3, and 4) to improve the interaction? Which problem-solving step is the most difficult to implement? Why? The easiest? Why? What questions do you and your classmates have after completing the exercise?
- What does this role-play exercise teach you about implementing the group problem-solving process?

COLLABORATIVE ACTIVITIES

1. Across nearly all disciplines—whether education, business, health and medicine, or technology—one of the most common pieces of advice concerning problem solving is to slow down at the beginning of the process to be absolutely certain that identification of the problem is accomplished with accuracy and agreement from all participants. Why is this advice so often needed? How important is this advice for educators? What difficulties arise when problems are not identified with accuracy and through consensus?

2. Describe a problem you are addressing in your school or field placement. After generating a list of potential solutions, use the PMI strategy to analyze them. Which ideas generate more plus comments than minus comments? Do any of the implications you list influence your thinking on the solutions' feasibility? Once you have identified three solutions that seem workable, create a chart that specifies all the tasks that would have to be completed to implement each of these options.

3. With a small group of classmates, generate a list of school situations in which group problem solving should be implemented. Then, analyze each using the set of factors summarized in the final section of this chapter. What might be the influence of each factor on the problem-solving process? On its outcomes? For each situation, how could your skilled participation lead to a positive result?
4. Consider the concepts that characterize collaboration that you learned in Chapter 1. Then think about the principles of group problem solving. How does the style of collaboration contribute to the process of group problem solving? Take each problem-solving step and analyze it using the defining and emergent characteristics of collaboration. How does this help you understand how these essential dimensions of school practice intersect?
5. Think about your responsibilities as a novice educator. What is your role if, during problem solving with a colleague or on a team, you notice that the process is not being followed—perhaps the first problem noted was too quickly accepted as the "correct" problem, or just one or two ideas for addressing the problem were generated, or details for implementation were not discussed? How would you respond in such a situation? Why?

 CHECK YOUR UNDERSTANDING

Click here to gauge your understanding of this chapter's essential concepts.

6 Teams

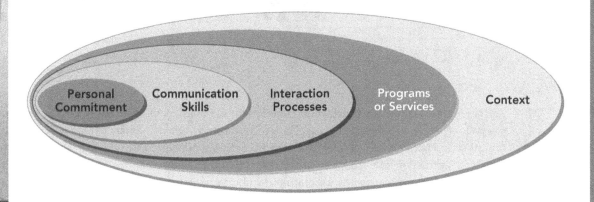

CONNECTIONS

In Chapters 1 through 5 you learned many of the critical skills that contribute to effective professional collaboration. However, those skills do not exist in a vacuum. They are used as you work with colleagues and as you participate in designing services and delivering them to your students. The topic of Chapter 6—teams—represents the first and perhaps broadest application of education-based collaboration. To be an effective team member, you must appropriately use the communication skills you have been perfecting and embed those skills within a problem-solving process. In Chapters 7 and 8, other collaborative school structures and service delivery options are explored, including consultation, mentoring, and coaching as well as co-teaching.

LEARNING OUTCOMES

After reading this chapter you will be able to:

1. Define the term *team*, outline essential characteristics and stages of teams, and examine both the advantages and drawbacks of teaming in school settings.
2. Compare and contrast how multidisciplinary, interdisciplinary, or transdisciplinary relationships among the professionals on a team directly affect its priorities and function.
3. Apply knowledge of three distinct purposes for student-centered teams to determine when each is appropriately used in educating students with disabilities or other special needs.
4. Analyze components that contribute to effective teaming, identifying ways that you contribute to ensuring those components are in place.

A CASE FOR COLLABORATION

A Team Decision?

Ms. Liberatore has organized everything needed for the team meeting about to begin—an annual review for Nathan, a student on her caseload who is moving from elementary to middle school. Nathan's mother and father have indicated that they do not want Nathan to be placed in separate classes for his core academic instruction, but other team members doubt that Nathan can succeed in the general education setting. As the meeting begins, Ms. Liberatore distributes an agenda and makes sure that everyone has been introduced: Mr. Wayte, the principal; Ms. Stokes, the school's new social worker; Mr. Sebastian, Nathan's fifth-grade teacher; Ms. Springer, the middle school special education teacher who will be responsible for implementing Nathan's individualized education program (IEP); Nathan's parents; and Ms. Esposito, the family's legal advocate. Mr. Wayte and the others use recent achievement data to stress the strides in achievement that Nathan has made, and they comment on how they will miss him. Nathan's IEP goals are based on the sixth-grade curriculum, and when a special education setting is recommended for English and math instruction and Nathan's parents decline, each team member is asked to address this topic. The key points offered by each person are listed in the electronic minutes being projected on the wall. Ms. Liberatore is serving as the note-taker, but she does not offer her opinion. By the conclusion of the meeting, the team agrees that Nathan should begin the year in all general education core academic classes but that a meeting will be held after the first month of school to evaluate this placement decision. The team finishes its work shortly thereafter and all members sign the IEP. With best wishes, the team adjourns. Ms. Liberatore reflects on the meeting and feels a sense of loss at the conclusion of the team's work for this student. She knows that middle school is more challenging for students like Nathan; departmentalized classes and new groupings of students for each period seem to her to be complexities that he may not be able to manage. She wonders if she should have spoken up more forcefully about the possible need for more instructional time in a special education setting; a month of struggling in general education classes before the scheduled reconsideration meeting could negatively affect Nathan's entire sixth-grade experience. Most of all she feels conflicted about the perceptions of her colleagues, the parents' insistence on general education classes, and about how a different team would have addressed this issue.

Introduction

You were born into a social group—your family—and you have become increasingly involved in a wider and wider range of groups and affiliations as you have become an adult and a professional. For example, you still are a member of a family group; and you may belong to a neighborhood or community group, sports group, faith-based community, recreational or fitness club, professional association, electronic social network, political party, or civic group. If you were to conduct an inventory of the groups to which you belong, you might be surprised to discover that your participation in these groups accounts for nearly all of your social activities. Although social scientists describe many different types of groups, they identify the three most important types relative to daily interaction as family, friendship, and work groups (Ephross & Vassil, 2005; Lustig & Koester, 2013). The focus of this chapter is on just one of these social groups: work groups or teams.

Team approaches have become increasingly popular structures for addressing a wide range of school matters (e.g., Rhodes, Stevens, & Hemmings, 2011; Taylor, Hallam, Charlton, & Wall, 2014). Teaming is the most frequently advocated structure for implementing school reform initiatives, as illustrated by continuing attention to site-based leadership teams, interdisciplinary and grade-level teaching teams, project-based teams, professional development teams, school improvement teams, and so on. Such teams engage in wide-ranging activities, and they make decisions in highly varied areas. For example, they address school improvement planning, curriculum redesign, student achievement review and goal-setting, school-wide behavioral interventions, professional development, and resource management. The work of these teams has resulted in changes in such areas as school schedules, curriculum structures, budgeting priorities, school organization, and personnel roles and responsibilities (e.g., Kaufman & Ring, 2011; McIntosh et al., 2014; Sawchuk, 2011; Schwanenberger & Ahearn, 2013). The topics addressed throughout this text are appropriate for the full range of school teams, but in this chapter the focus is primarily on teams that directly benefit students.

Being a leader or a member of a team requires much more than a passing knowledge that teams are common in schools and that most educators will regularly participate in various types of teaming. The extent to which both special educators and general educators are prepared for their responsibilities on teams can have a profound influence on the productivity of the team. This chapter, then, is designed to clarify key concepts related to teams and to emphasize their collaborative nature so that you are equipped to be a highly effective team member.

> **Learn More About**
> This set of three brief animated vignettes illustrates that teams are integral to twenty-first-century society.
> (https://www.youtube.com/watch?v=w9j3-ghRjBs)

Team Concepts

The importance of team structures has been emphasized in nearly every area of today's society. Teams have been touted as the unit that accomplishes extraordinary things in all conceivable disciplines including sports, science, emergency response, health and medicine, business, art, schooling, psychology, and counseling (Galloway, 2015; Jehn & Techakesari, 2014; Polsky, 2015; Qiu, Qualls, Bohlmann, & Rupp, 2009). In discussing the wide impact of teams in today's world, broad consensus exists that teams generally can accomplish and produce more innovative ideas than individuals (e.g., DuBois, Koch, Hanlon, Nyatuga, & Kerr, 2015; Gustavson & Liff, 2014; Marks, 2006).

This understanding of the importance of teams has existed in special education and related services for many years, even before teams were mentioned in federal and state laws. Teams of mental health specialists served the needs of students with emotional disorders long before schools were obligated to educate them (Elliott & Sheridan, 1992; Menninger, 1950; Walker & Schutte, 2005). Similarly, a rich tradition exists of professional teams meeting to discuss and plan for students with mild to moderate disabilities (Armer & Thomas, 1978) and for students with moderate to severe disabilities (Gallivan-Fenlon, 1994; Orelove & Sobsey, 1987). A team approach to assessment and decision making for students with disabilities has been mandated by federal law since the 1975 passage of P.L. 94-142, the Education for All Handicapped Children Act, and this continues today in the Individuals with Disabilities Education Act (IDEA).

Countless definitions of the term *team* have been offered by authors in various disciplines. These definitions generally emphasize individuals from a variety of specialties and experiences with unique expertise collaborating to reach specific goals through shared problem solving. They also stress the importance of clear

Teams, whether they are in sports or in education, must develop and commit to common goals.

and direct communication, interdependence, coordination, and clear procedures as essential team features.

Additional conceptualizations of teams that emphasize service delivery have emerged in the literature on education and services for students with disabilities and other diverse learning needs. For example, interactive teaming is described by Correa, Jones, Thomas, and Morsink (2005) as a mutual or reciprocal effort made by groups to provide a student with the best educational program possible. One strength of interactive teaming is its emphasis on effective, comprehensive, and cohesive services derived from the collaborative work, rather than individual efforts, of team members. Other authors have stressed the importance of strong interpersonal relationships and a sense of team cohesion, clarity of team goals, and clearly defined outcomes as being essential to teams (e.g., Beebe & Masterson, 2015; Kozlowski, 2008). Certain definitions specify that the purpose of special services teams is to make decisions about programs for children (Torres-Rodriguez, Beyard, & Goldstein, 2010); others not only have decision making as their purpose but also include the direct delivery of services (Brandel & Loeb, 2011; Silverman, Hong, & Trepanier-Street, 2010). If all these definitions of teams—from outside the field of education as well as from within—are considered, the following working definition can be extracted to serve as a framework for this chapter:

> An educational team is a set of interdependent individuals with unique skills and perspectives who interact directly to achieve their mutual goal of providing students with effective educational programs and services.

Characteristics of Teams

This definition and the preceding discussion provide a starting point for understanding teams. This foundation can be clarified further by examining the five characteristics integral to teams:

1. Teams have clearly articulated goals; an educational team's goal is effective service delivery leading to positive student outcomes.
2. Members are aware of their team membership, roles, and responsibilities.
3. Team interactions are regulated by shared norms.
4. Team members are interdependent.
5. Team members have unique skills and perspectives.

Another way of conceptualizing effective teams is an expansion of these characteristics summarized in Putting Ideas into Practice.

Clearly Articulated Goal of Effective Service Delivery Having a mutual goal is an essential element of every team definition, regardless of professional discipline. In education and related services, that goal typically focuses on some type of service delivery. That is, whether the team's specific purpose is to study and plan a child's program or to deliver specific programs or interventions directly, service delivery is key. From this perspective, teams include those groups (often comprised of some members who will not be working with a student) that make decisions about a student's eligibility for services, as well as co-teaching teams or teacher–parent teams working to implement home and school behavior intervention programs. Maintaining the team's focus on the delivery of services is an important team function (Runhaar, ten Brinke, Kuijpers, Wesselink, & Mulder, 2014; Snell & Janney, 2005). This is particularly true when disagreements occur or when team members are distracted from the central task. Research has produced convincing evidence that teams that develop and pursue clearly articulated goals have greater success than those without such goals (Bang et al., 2010).

Awareness of Team Membership, Roles, and Responsibilities Individuals cannot be part of a team unless they perceive themselves to be so. Extending this notion, team members also must be perceived by others as forming a team—a situation that clearly existed in the case study presented at the beginning of this chapter. Although this characteristic

PUTTING IDEAS INTO PRACTICE
A Checklist for Effective Teamwork

Researchers and theorists have described many characteristics of successful and efficient teams (e.g., Bang, Fuglesang, Ovesen, & Eilertsen, 2010; Berckemeyer, 2013; Johnson & Johnson, 2013). Consider the teams in which you participate. To what extent is each of the following characteristics descriptive of your teams? What are examples of each concept? What specific actions might you take to help your team reach these important benchmarks?

- Team members are committed to their work.
- The team understands its purpose and establishes clear goals.
- Team members differentiate their roles and responsibilities.
- The team works to ensure regular information sharing using appropriate communication skills.
- Members recognize that teamwork requires effort and recognize when they are being productive and should proceed versus when they are not being productive and should reconsider their work.
- Members value each other's unique expertise, experiences, perspectives, and ideas.
- The team uses a wide variety of interaction processes and strategies depending on the issue that it is addressing and its context.
- Team members can examine differences in their opinions openly and use those differences as a tool in their discussions. That is, differences are seen as valued parts of teaming.
- Team members are comfortable in assuming differing roles that help the team accomplish its work; for example, they may function as leader, follower, consensus builder, or information seeker. They may occasionally take on each other's roles.
- Members recognize the team's limits within the context of the school or agency.

of teams may seem almost too fundamental to mention, it is an issue in many schools. For example, a group of professionals in diverse roles is assigned to a staff development team to help colleagues become more proficient at implementing inclusive practices. The group functions effectively in its initial planning meetings, but then two members express surprise that they are supposed to coordinate their efforts and participate with others in order to function as a clearly delineated work group that provides ongoing staff development. The two members thought they were included initially only to give advice and share their expertise. Their actions (or lack thereof) reflect this confusion. Thus, just knowing that someone is a team member and that others are, too, is a critical first step of teaming.

Membership for teams involved in making program decisions and delivering services to students is not as straightforward as it may at first appear. Changes and lack of clarity regarding membership sometimes make this a complex matter. For example, the role of a paraprofessional may be extremely important to a team, and that individual may be regarded as a member of a specific team. Yet schedule conflicts and time-limited work schedules may make it impossible for the paraprofessional to participate as an active and full team member, especially in meetings and decision making that occur outside of the paraprofessional's scheduled work hours. In such situations, the paraprofessional may not be able to function as a team member despite best intentions. Similarly, a school psychologist who serves several schools may not be able to attend some decision-making meetings and, thus, may not act as a fully integrated team member. Another particular challenge—transient membership—occurs as the caseloads or school assignments of professionals change or as students are transferred to new programs or classes. For example, when a speech/language therapist leaves a school district mid-year, his or her caseload has to be assigned to others. As a result, the speech/language therapist on the special education team for all those students suddenly is a different person. This has ramifications not only for decision making for the students; the relationships among team members also shifts as they adjust to the new member. The dynamic nature of school teams requires members to take special care in monitoring team membership and clarifying changes to it (Downing, 2008; Leader-Janssen, Swain, Delkamiller, & Ritzman, 2012).

Regulation of Interactions by Shared Norms A team is an organized system of individuals whose behavior is regulated by a common set of norms or values (Johnson & Johnson, 2013; Rice, Davidson, Dannenhoffer, & Gay, 2007). For example, teams may have both formal as well as unspoken but clear expectations for members about arriving on time, using lay language when parents are present, articulating and resolving conflict among members, and so on. In addition, regular and direct interaction among team members is central to the concept of a team (Killumets, D'Innocenzo, Maynard, & Mathieu, 2015; Sargeant, Loney, & Murphy, 2008). Shared norms regarding how interactions occur, what acceptable team member behavior is, and the way team business is conducted facilitate effective team functioning (Harris & Sherblom, 2011; Levi, 2014).

When teams are first established, they need to devote considerable time to establishing these norms. This is sometimes a deliberate effort that results in written ground rules. More often, though, this process is less formal, even though it also may be quite deliberate. In these cases, team members establish and learn norms through their successful and unsuccessful interactions with one another. When team membership changes frequently, an already noted characteristic of many school teams, challenges may be encountered in maintaining team norms (Downing, 2008). In fact, as team membership changes, team norms likewise may change, and all members may need to review and recommit to them.

Interdependence of Team Members Members of teams are highly interdependent because their organizational roles are functionally interrelated (Harris & Sherblom, 2011; Johnson & Johnson, 2013). That is, an event that affects one member is likely to affect the rest of the team, and conversely team actions will affect each individual member. For example, if one team member is suddenly called into a conference that conflicts with a team meeting, the remaining members may not be able to make important decisions because of that person's absence. Interdependence extends to the delivery of services as well (Mellin et al., 2010). Consider a situation in which a team develops an integrated service plan that calls for one person to supply a communication device and teach a student to use it. A second team member is to design class discussions in which the student can use the communication device to develop better language skills. If the first person is unable to secure the needed device, it will be most difficult for the second team member to proceed with the planned language instruction. The effectiveness of one team member has direct impact on the effectiveness of another, and perhaps on that of the entire team.

Unique Skills and Perspectives of Team Members Most discussions of teams in the context of educational service delivery emphasize the unique and diverse skills and abilities of team members as essential. For example, the entire premise of an IEP team is that each of the professionals participating—special education and general education teachers, administrators, related services personnel, and parents—brings unique and valuable perspectives that enhance planning (Weaver, Rosen, Salas, Baum, & King, 2010). A similar perspective is offered for teams that exist to support preschool children with disabilities (Hunt, Soto, Maier, Liborion, & Bae, 2004). Of particular importance is the viewpoint brought to a team by parents, a perspective that is essential for effective team outcomes (Herman et al., 2014; Olivos, Gallagher, & Aguilar, 2010). Regardless of the purpose or size of a team, the unique skills, expertise, or perspectives of team members create a rich context for creating effective programs and services.

Developmental Stages for Teams

Professionals generally agree that teams progress through developmental stages in their formation and operation (Johnson & Johnson, 2013; Levi, 2014). Teams have life cycles that progress from infancy to maturity regardless of their purposes or the tasks they must perform. Stages in the development of a team were described some time ago by Tuckman (1965) as forming, storming, norming, and performing. The notion of adjourning was later added (Tuckman & Jensen, 1977). The characteristics of teams at each of these stages are summarized in Figure 6.1.

> **Learn More About**
> These teachers' words as well as nonverbal signals convey that they are part of a tight-knit and effective special education team.

FIGURE 6.1 **The life cycle of teams.**

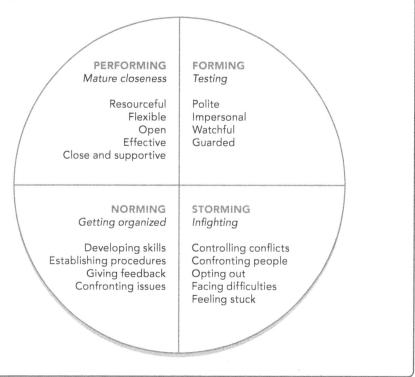

More than four decades ago, Tuckman (1965) identified four stages that teams go through as members learn about each other and learn to work together to accomplish their goals—forming, storming, norming, and performing—with the following summary of how teams might function during each of these stages. Most professionals who have studied teams agree that teams are most effective when members spend time discussing their function, member roles, and their procedures rather than addressing only the work at hand.

Source: Richardson, J. (2005). Originally in Bruce W. Tuckman, "Developmental sequence in small groups," *Psychological Bulletin, 63* (1965): 384–399. Copyright American Psychological Association. Reprinted with permission.

Understanding the stages through which teams progress can help you appreciate how teams operate. When a team initially comes together, its members typically do not fully understand their task, and they are not clear about how they will relate to each other and to the team leader, if there is one. During the initial stage, forming, members tend to want clear directions from others, and they are polite in their efforts to learn about each other and their purpose for becoming a team. They work to create social and task-oriented structures that will guide their interactions. The storming stage demonstrates that a group can become a team by resolving issues of leadership, procedures, and purpose. During the storming stage, members are more comfortable with one another and communicate freely—they recognize that creating consensus on an issue is often difficult and can lead instead to conflict. They may challenge the team's leadership and disagree with one another as they vie for power and strive to gain a shared understanding of their task and how to approach it. Having weathered the storm, reconciled differences, and agreed on a course of action, a team enters the norming stage. It is at this stage that members begin to build trust as they redefine and establish roles, relationships, and procedures for accomplishing their work and handling conflicts. Norming is necessary for teams to establish their patterns of functioning that have to do with record keeping, seating arrangements, communication patterns, procedures, and so on. What is most important at this stage is that a team culture develops and gives the team its unique identity. The performing stage occurs when a team's development levels off and the team can focus its primary efforts on

Learn More About The stages of teaming are further clarified in this video clip that outlines the Tuckman model.
(https://www.youtube.com/watch?v=MNgzjYb02JM)

accomplishing its goals. Finally, a team progresses to adjourning when its tasks are complete. For many special services teams, this latter stage may occur only when a school year ends or a student leaves the school.

The developmental stages detail the stages that naturally occur during team development. With the knowledge of these stages, team members can take steps to improve their capacity to function in a manner that enhances the contributions of individual members and the effectiveness of the team. Team members may take actions to manage their relationships during team development. Some suggestions for doing so are presented in Putting Ideas into Practice.

PUTTING IDEAS INTO PRACTICE

Managing Relationships During the Stages of Team Development

The developmental stages of teams describe what groups do when left to their own devices as they organize themselves. Kozlowski, Gully, Nason, and Smith (1999) have advanced a theory that suggests individuals should work at fitting into the team and understanding their role in its mission. By doing this, a socialization process evolves, and individuals develop interpersonal knowledge of their teammates, a team orientation, and a normative structure. Next, they develop task knowledge, mastery, and self-regulation. At that point, their roles become routine, and they can focus their energies on the team and its continuous improvement. Four suggestions for relationship management are useful to keep in mind.

Become the Model for Valuing the Other Point of View

Analyze your own personal strengths, and tell your team how you think these bring value to the group. Also, acknowledge that you realize that each person's greatest weakness is the reverse side of his or her greatest strength. Get the group members to talk about how they depend on people with whom they work to have strengths that complement each other's strengths, as well as compensate for corresponding weaknesses. Encourage the team members to identify the work styles of each co-worker.

Talk Frequently About the Organizational Value of Different Points of View

If examples are raised often enough, team members will begin to notice that they actually do depend on and benefit from each other's differences. For example, if you comment on how you appreciate a colleague's explanation of the recent shift in standards and the impact this has on curriculum pacing, noting that the information helps you in designing the specialized instruction some students need, you are clearly recognizing the importance of diverse domains of expertise. In time, the members of a truly effective group will begin to celebrate differences.

Never Discuss a Process Problem Unless All of the People Involved Are Present

Involving all of the team members in developing the solution to an organizational or team problem is time consuming, but it is actually quite efficient. If people discuss a problem when a significant member is not in the room, the language often becomes harsh and judgmental. Only part of the story emerges, and it is nearly impossible to predict the effectiveness or consequences of a solution developed in the absence of everyone who will be affected by it. Trying to develop solutions in this way leads to many false "starts" and may require repeated interactions to try to adjust the course. These false starts waste both time and goodwill and can be avoided by ensuring that all members are involved in problem solving. A simple problem of this sort might be a teammate who typically arrives late at team meetings and expects others to repeat information that he or she has missed. Clearly, a discussion of this issue is best held with all team members present and contributing. It could be that the tardiness is unavoidable and the meeting should be started 15 minutes later than currently scheduled.

When All Team Members Are Present, Be Sure to Communicate Effectively

It is important to convene all members and encourage them to work together to be sure the description of the problem is objective and all of the contributing factors are addressed at the same time. Team members are more likely to leave the meeting with a shared understanding of what needs to be done and the likely consequences of the proposed solution. Ideally, each stakeholder will also leave with a sense that, together, the team can solve this and other problems.

It takes time, but within months team members will find that the time spent managing their working relationships has had a very big payoff. While the leader or even the full team focused attention on how people work together, the team has also been working with more efficiency and effectiveness.

Other suggestions for helping team development can be derived from research conducted by Sargeant et al. (2008). These researchers examined the development of interprofessional teams of health-care providers and identified five major characteristics of successful teams: Team members (1) understand and respect each other's roles; (2) appreciate that teamwork requires commitment and effort; (3) have expertise in their assigned roles; (4) possess the ability to provide specialized services to an individual; and (5) communicate information about that service to others. Central to all of these characteristics is that the participants in the study identified communication as "the big thing." This emphasis on communication stressed two specific conditions. First, team members need to be available to other members; and second, they must have the ability to communicate appropriately. Specific communication skills identified were listening to others and also expressing one's own perspective respectfully and assertively, if necessary. Ms. Liberatore, in the opening case, did not demonstrate this communication skill. She listened to her colleagues and to Nathan's parents, but instead of sharing her perspective, she remained silent. Thus, she did not contribute to the group's effectiveness; by not raising her concerns about Nathan's transition to middle school, she did not serve Nathan as well as she might have.

Rationale for and Benefits of Teams

The primary rationale for a team approach to decision making and service delivery lies in its efficiency and potential for high-quality outcomes. If you accept the premise that educating students with special needs requires the participation of professionals with diverse and specialized skills, the challenge of coordinating the information and intervention efforts of the individual members of the group becomes clear. Having all professionals meet to plan and discuss implementation of programs is far more efficient than any kind of individual reporting could be. Moreover, the process of group communication might lead to decisions and changes in perspectives that would not be possible in one-to-one communication. Implementing a coordinated and coherent program is more efficient and, happily, more effective when all professionals involved are in communication with each other.

Parthasarathy (2006) indicated that by working alone in the current system, individual contributors can improve system performance 5 to 15 percent of the time. A team approach may well be needed to achieve the other 85 to 95 percent of the needed improvements, as they require changing the system itself—a task that cannot be accomplished by an individual acting in isolation.

Given that teams are an application of collaboration, all the benefits and outcomes to be realized through collaboration (see Chapter 1) are also possible through teamwork (e.g., Correa et al., 2005; Howard, Williams, & Lepper, 2010; Villa, Thousand, & Nevin, 2008). Specifically, all the emergent characteristics of collaboration could become outcomes of effective teaming. Team members can be expected to develop a high level of interpersonal trust and, thus, more respect for one another. As trust grows, so, too, does the sense of community among team members.

Drawbacks of Teams

Reviewing the stages of team development, organizing a team meeting in your school, or having had unsuccessful group experiences in school or in other parts of your life might lead you to recognize that, while powerful and responsible for significant outcomes, teams are not always the best approach. Team approaches are time consuming, and time is a very precious commodity in schools and other service settings. In addition to not having enough time, team members might not have the common time available as a result of their complex and varied schedules.

The following questions are useful in deciding whether to use a team approach:

1. Is a single discipline or person sufficient to resolve a problem, or is the problem so complex as to require individuals with different expertise?
2. Are there experts available with the needed knowledge and skills to help develop a solution to the complex problem?

3. Are those who will be most affected by the decision be part of the team so that they can buy into the solution and thus facilitate implementation?
4. Are the physical requirements of the task such that team implementation is required?
5. Is the problem or the focus of the solution so large as to require change in an entire process rather than just one element?
6. Is the issue so broad or new that several minds are needed?

Despite the challenges and identified drawbacks to using team approaches, the potential for positive results is too great to ignore. The enumeration of challenges is given primarily to help you identify those hopefully limited areas in which teaming may not be the best option.

Disciplinary Relationships on Teams

One approach to classifying teams and their work is based on the relationships that exist among the professionals who are members. Specifically, the composition of student-centered teams, the type that most often exists for students with exceptionalities, varies according to the team's purposes and the student's needs. Team members may be direct service providers or support staff; students sometimes also may be team members (Barnard-Brak & Lechtenberger, 2010; Walter & Petr, 2011). Direct service providers are parents and staff members who work directly with students on a regular basis. Support staff generally are professionals who provide indirect services, on a periodic basis, such as teacher consultation, technical assistance, or staff development. They may work directly with children or their families, but this is usually on a restricted or limited basis (e.g., to demonstrate how to best use an assistive technology device with a student in the general education classroom). Support staff members may include psychologists, occupational therapists, augmentative communication specialists, or other professionals whose services are not required on an intensive basis. Note, though, that whether a particular professional is a direct service provider or support depends on student assessed needs and goals.

Just noting the range of professional who may be on a team is not sufficient for understanding the team, however. The nature of the working relationships among team members of different disciplines is just as important. Three models have evolved over the years that occur along a continuum from little to extensive collaboration. These are multidisciplinary, interdisciplinary, and transdisciplinary teams. The order in which these approaches developed in the field parallels their order on a collaboration continuum, as you can see by reviewing the summary in Putting Ideas into Practice.

Multidisciplinary Teams

Although teams formed to address individual students have a long history in special education and related fields, the passage of P.L. 94-142 in 1975 established as a federal requirement that multidisciplinary teams—including school professionals, parents, and sometimes the student—implement evaluation and placement procedures for youth with disabilities. With this mandate and its reiteration in the IDEA, multidisciplinary assessment and group decision making regarding classification, placement, and the development of an IEP became formal elements of special education procedures. The term *multidisciplinary* was applied to such teams to convey that a number of perspectives and disciplines were represented when decisions about students with disabilities are to be made.

The rationale for multidisciplinary special education teams is that a group decision provides safeguards against bias or individual errors in judgment and ensures greater adherence to the law's due process requirements. Research in behavioral sciences supports this use of teams to improve decision-making effectiveness and quality (Choi & Pak, 2007; Mueller, 2009b). Benefits include the following:

- A group offers a greater amount and wider range of knowledge and experience
- A greater number of possible approaches to resolve a problem exists within a group

PUTTING IDEAS INTO PRACTICE

Three Models of Team Interaction

Team models may be distinguished by the nature of the working relationships among professionals from different disciplines—a notion that applies in the medical, science, communications, entertainment, and many other fields as well as in education. As you review the following summary, think about how the goals, procedures, and outcomes for each type of team might differ. When might each team model be most appropriate in your work?

Component	Multidisciplinary	Interdisciplinary	Transdisciplinary
Philosophy of team interaction	Members acknowledge importance of contributions from several disciplines; services remain independent.	Members share responsibility for services among disciplines; individuals are primarily responsible for specific disciplines.	Members commit to teach, learn, and work across disciplines in planning and providing integrated services.
Role of the family	Families typically meet with team members separately by discipline.	Families may meet with the team; individual team members report by discipline.	Families are members of the team and determine their own team roles.
Lines of communication	Members exchange information about independent work; they may not see themselves as part of a team.	Teams meet regularly for case conferences and consultations.	Teams meet regularly for information sharing, learning across disciplines, consultation, and team building.
Assessment process	Members conduct assessments by discipline and in separate environments.	Members conduct assessments by discipline and share results.	Members participate in collaborative assessment, observing and recording across disciplines.
Service plan development	Members develop separate plans for intervention within their discipline.	Goals are developed by discipline and shared with the team to form a single service plan.	Staff and family members develop a plan together based on family concerns, resources, and priorities.
Service plan implementation	Members implement their plans separately by discipline.	Members implement the parts of the plan for which their discipline is responsible; coordinated services are an expectation.	Members share responsibility and accountability for how the plan is implemented by the team.

- Participation in decision making increases acceptance of the decision and "buy in" needed for implementation
- Problem solving in a group involves greater communication and understanding of the decision

Multidisciplinary teams that make decisions about eligibility and programs may well enjoy these benefits, but such teams operate under some limitations as well. The professionals from different disciplines who make up the team maintain independence from one another as they perform their related duties. Representatives of each discipline contribute unique information and perspectives, but their efforts are not deliberately coordinated or integrated. For example, the general education teacher may gather assessment data related to language, but the speech/language therapist may complete an assessment for this purpose. Similarly, members of multidisciplinary teams provide specialized and discrete services directly to students: Students "go to speech" and also receive language instruction in the special education

Learn More About
This team clearly is multidisciplinary, with each member separately providing detailed information about the student from his or her professional perspective.

classroom or general education classroom. In this model, the professionals function independently, work toward their individual treatment/educational goals, and do not consistently share or coordinate information. They communicate simply to exchange information about their independent work. This model might best be viewed as a patchwork quilt in which different—sometimes contrasting—pieces (of information) are placed together, but not necessarily with a blended, unified result. As this description illustrates, true collaboration in a multidisciplinary team model often is minimal, if it occurs at all. One still-common example is when the team decides that a student's placement is the general education classroom and the special education teacher delivers services there, but at the same time the occupational therapist and counselor—without coordination of their individual intervention plans—pull the same student out of the classroom to deliver those services.

Interdisciplinary Teams

Unlike the multidisciplinary teams, interdisciplinary teams coordinate the interventions they deliver to students. In fact, coordination of information and services is the primary goal shared by members of interdisciplinary teams (Havnes, 2009; Shapiro & Sayers, 2003). In this model, as in the multidisciplinary model, professionals from different disciplines perform specialized assessments and services independent of each other. However, they jointly develop goals for the student and communicate more regularly than do members of multidisciplinary teams. Their ongoing sharing of information is instrumental in their efforts to develop and work toward their collective intervention goals and shared education plan. By doing this, they are more likely to develop and pursue interventions that support and complement one another. This helps to ensure that the services they provide students are not duplicated and that gaps do not occur. The coordination of services is such a central feature of interdisciplinary models that a specific role for managing such a team (sometimes called a service coordinator) may be established (Cook, Klein, & Chen, 2012; Howard et al., 2010).

Interdisciplinary teaming to provide special education services is relatively common. For example, the speech/language therapist, working on a goal related to articulation, may ask the general and special education teacher for vocabulary words being learned so that they can be integrated into the speech/language therapy sessions. A counselor, special educator, and transition specialist focus their efforts across different contexts to work on the goal for a student with autism of appropriately initiating interactions with peers and adults.

Transdisciplinary Teams

Transdisciplinary approaches to teaming are the most recent to have evolved in special education and related services, and they also are the most collaborative of all the team models. In these teams, professionals perform their related tasks interactively and, through a process known as role release, individual team members may share or blend their roles at least in part. One or two team members may be responsible for delivering all interventions to a student, while other team members remain available to assist and advise the primary interventionists through consultation, training, and feedback (Howard et al., 2010). Members with different disciplinary expertise share their skills and engage in mutual training and staff development in order to make this possible.

Early intervention and preschool programs for young children often are implemented by transdisciplinary teams (Cook et al., 2012). This is considered to be a holistic approach in which primary interventionists implement strategies common to their own disciplines as well as some that are derived from other disciplines. For example, a preschool teacher may implement specific language development interventions designed and modeled by the speech/language specialist. After receiving some training and technical assistance from the physical therapist, the teacher may also implement certain positioning routines. It is not uncommon for the teacher, who is a generalist in this situation, to feel insecure about his or her skills in the specialized language and physical therapy areas. The in-depth knowledge of the specialists is essential for designing interventions and assisting primary interventionists to implement them. However, the generalist orientation of the teacher may actually be best suited to providing services for the whole child in a way that embeds them throughout the course of the child's instruction instead of only during occasional, time-limited sessions.

The true integration of services and their delivery by a teacher has clear benefits, but it has challenges as well. Teacher understanding of specific techniques and approaches and recognition of typical or serious problems during implementation can be difficult. Such challenges may be mitigated by appropriate supervision and support of the teacher by the interventionists from other disciplines. A matter that should remain in the forefront of your thinking, however, is the appropriate extent and limitations of your professional preparation and role. The Council for Exceptional Children (CEC) articulates the standards of practice for the profession, and a tenet of Professional and Ethical Practice is that "special educators practice within their professional knowledge and skills and seek appropriate external support and consultation whenever needed" (CEC, 2012). In concert with this principle, special educators on transdisciplinary teams should be particularly vigilant in monitoring their practice to ensure that the interventions are appropriate to their level and area of professional preparation. In monitoring and managing your role, collaboration with other specialists on the team is critical.

Clearly the role relationships among members from different disciplines varies across multidisciplinary, interdisciplinary, and transdisciplinary teams. Yet there are some elements that are seen in successful teams regardless of the model they represent. Specifically, research has demonstrated that certain factors facilitate while others impede team success. These factors are summarized in A Basis in Research.

A BASIS IN RESEARCH

Successful Teamwork: Facilitators and Barriers

Many descriptions of effective teams and successful teamwork have been published, often derived from qualitative studies using team members' reports of satisfaction with the process. However, research has been lacking on the factors that promote collaboration resulting in successful outcomes and on the factors that act as barriers to such collaboration and its resulting outcomes. Choi and Pak (2007) conducted an extensive review of the literature on teams composed of members representing multiple disciplines working in healthcare fields. In examining the relationship between team processes and outcomes, they identified teamwork factors that promote successful outcomes and those that act as barriers to successful outcomes.

Facilitators of team success include:

- Good selection of members with diverse areas of expertise
- Members with willingness to participate and to assume different roles
- Members with maturity, flexibility, and personal commitment
- Physical proximity of team members
- Institutional support, changes in the workplace, and incentives
- Clarity of common goal and shared vision
- Effective communication, including the use of constructive comments among members
- The Internet and e-mail as supporting platforms

Barriers to team success include:

- Narrow range in areas of expertise among members
- Poor structure and ground rules for team functioning
- Lack of predetermined measures to evaluate success of outcomes
- Lack of guidelines for determining how successes are recognized
- Insufficient time or resources for implementing the task
- Institutional constraints and unequal power/influence among members
- Conflicts among members lacking skills to resolve them
- Lack of, or ineffective, communication

What are the implications of this information for the professional teams on which you are or will be a member?

Student-Centered Teams

Although the disciplinary relationship among team members is often used to characterize teams related to special services, a second dimension on which teams can vary is their purpose or function. The teams that we address in this text are those that exist on behalf of students, or student-centered teams, and they are the focus of this discussion. In this section, we consider three types of student-centered teams that differ in their primary purpose. The first we refer to as *instructional teams*, as they focus on delivery of instruction or other interventions, and they are found in both general and special education. The second type, *student-centered problem-solving teams*, also focuses on students and addresses their educational needs, but these typically exist within general education. The third type, *special education teams*, makes decisions about eligibility for, and delivery of, special education and related services. These teams differ from the others in their purpose, their basis in law, and their accountability. All three types of student-centered teams are common in schools, and you are likely to have a role in more than one of these.

As you consider these variations in teams, consider, too, the ideas presented in E-Partnerships and how they can enhance the sharing of information and ideas among team members.

Instructional Teams

A number of team structures exist to plan and deliver education and related services to students. You may be familiar with examples such as teaching teams in middle school, grade-level teams in elementary school, and co-teaching teams at any level. These teams focus largely on planning for, implementing, and evaluating the ongoing, often daily, delivery of educational services to one or more students. They are used in general education classrooms regardless of whether the class includes students with disabilities. These team approaches have all been found to facilitate the inclusion of students with disabilities; and co-teaching, as defined here, is most frequently associated with this goal (Friend & Barron, 2015).

Co-Teaching Teams In special education, co-teaching is an increasingly common service delivery arrangement in which special education teachers and general education teachers share planning and classroom instructional responsibilities in inclusive settings (Friend, 2014). In this type of team, general education and special education teachers engage in team planning and in jointly delivering instruction for a class period or segment of time to a diverse group of students.

For example, Ms. Garcia and Ms. Crichton co-teach in seventh-grade language arts. Their class of 28 students includes 7 students with disabilities. The two teachers ensure that the general curriculum is delivered to all the students, but they also ensure that the seven targeted students receive the specially designed instruction that will enable them to reach their IEP goals. Their intent is that the students with disabilities will accelerate their rate of learning but that other students likewise will benefit from the teachers' shared expertise.

Co-teaching is a common but complex example of instructional teaming. It is such an integral part of the roles of teachers in today's schools that it is explored in depth in Chapter 7.

Middle School Teams In many middle schools, interdisciplinary teams of teachers, each with an area of expertise in a core academic area, instruct the same group of students (Berkemeyer, 2013). They typically do not teach in the same classroom, but they likely have consistent expectations related to discipline, use the same organization procedures (e.g., all student homework from each teacher is written in a single student planner), and

E-PARTNERSHIPS

Teaming in the Cloud

Given the number of responsibilities educators have and the limited time available for meetings, teams increasingly rely on options for completing their work electronically. Such options have many advantages: They eliminate the often disorganized mailbox clutter that occurs when e-mail messages are flying among team members, they permit professionals to contribute to the team within the constraints of their own schedules, and they create a record of the work that the team is addressing. Here are three options that are especially helpful for today's teams, options that also are often used in business and other professions:

Google Tools (https://www.google.com/edu/products/productivity-tools/)

Google is ubiquitous, and many school districts are adopting its suites of tools for administrators, teachers, and students. For teams, these Google tools can be especially helpful:

- *Google Docs.* You may already use this Google tool. In Docs you can create a document, share it with others and invite their input, work with other team members on a document in real time, and chat with them as you collaborate. Docs also automatically saves all changes made to the document, decreasing the likelihood of losing important information.
- *Google Sheets.* Sheets is Google's spreadsheet, a tool team members often need. Sheets can be used to list student cases underway, track progress on them, and prepare reports on team productivity.
- *Google Forms.* Forms can be utilized if you need to contact parents for information, poll staff members not on the team to get their opinions related to decisions being considered, or create a template for ensuring that all necessary information is available related to each student. As with other Google tools, team members can collaborate to use Forms.

Trello (trello.com)

Trello is designed specifically to assist teams to manage their work, and it is considered a valuable, free collaboration tool. Some of its features include:

- Each project is captured on a "board." For example, if your team is charged with reviewing grade level or course assessment data, this could be a board. Similarly, on a response to intervention (RTI) team, each student receiving intervention could have a board.
- Within the board, team members add a "card." Cards could include ideas that are being considered, a to-do list, a summary of work in progress, and final outcomes.
- Members are invited to the collaboration, and they can all contribute. There is no limit to the number of individuals on the team.
- Items can be moved from card to card as needed (e.g., from the to-do card to the completed card) so progress is easily tracked and record keeping is efficient.
- Members can post comments within Trello, thus eliminating the need to exchange e-mail.

Other Team Collaboration Options

Many other team collaboration tools are available, and generally they are free or inexpensive. These include Moxtra (moxtra.com), Basecamp (basecamp.com), and Zoho (zoho.com). One way to learn about and become comfortable using such tools is to try them out, perhaps as a class exercise or to complete a group project for a course.

---

jointly plan interdisciplinary units (e.g., a unit on personal health and fitness that incorporates language arts, math, science, and social studies).

This team model produces a wide range of benefits when there is strong team leadership, adequate planning time, and a commitment to the interdisciplinary team concept demonstrated through team members' willingness to use planning time for team participation. Specifically, middle school teaching teams can increase the effectiveness of instruction, provide teachers with a much needed support system, help ensure that students' problems are recognized and solved, and improve students' work and attitudes. For example, if one teacher notes that James is experiencing behavior problems in his or her class, he or she would ask team members if they are noticing the same problem. If so, they

> **Learn More About**
> How does this twist on a well-known fable apply to working with colleagues and parents in school settings?
> (https://www.youtube.com/watch?v=xevQ2yTyK9Y)

would work together to identify the problem, plan and implement a solution, and determine its effectiveness. If other teachers have not noticed the behavior issue, team members would help the teacher identify what might be triggering the behavior and could offer suggestions of strategies they use with James to address behavior.

Grade-Level Teams   A grade-level team structure is very similar to that of the middle school teaching team, even though it has not received wide attention in the professional literature. Grade-level teams (common in elementary schools) or departmental teams (common in high schools) are constructed around members with highly similar interests and expertise (i.e., the grade level or subject matter they teach). The nature of the decisions these groups make may focus on curriculum, division of labor for instructional preparation, schedule, budget, or other matters of group interest or concern. If a special educator can regularly attend such meetings to facilitate discussions about student needs, these teams can serve a function similar to that of pre-referral teams.

On an elementary grade level team, for example, the topic is the upcoming unit on using evidence from informational text. One teacher may be assigned the lead role; he or she focuses the discussion and ensures that all elements of the standard are being addressed. Other team members may have the responsibility for finding a web site to support the unit of instruction and for finding materials with differentiated reading levels so that all students can reach the standard, even if they cannot read at grade level. On a high school department team, the department chair may lead a discussion about the common formative assessments that are now required. Various department members volunteer to lead the development of these unit tests, working with partners to draft the assessments, receiving feedback from colleagues, completing the revisions, and disseminating the final products.

Student-Centered Problem-Solving Teams

A second type of student-centered team exists to address issues that occur related to specific students. These student-centered problem-solving teams generally are building- or site-based and are intended to assist teachers in accommodating students with behavioral or learning difficulties (but not disabilities) in their general education classrooms. Historically, these teams were created to augment the formal referral and evaluation processes in special education. The first models, generally known as pre-referral teams or pre-referral intervention teams, were meant to provide pre-referral screening for special education services and immediate support for teachers trying to develop appropriate in-class interventions. These teams are briefly described in the next section. Over the past several years, the focus for such teams has shifted to preventive problem solving, collegial support for responding to challenging student academic and behavior needs, and opportunities for professionals to problem solve about students—even if they do not have IEPs (Lhospital & Gregory, 2009; Papalia-Berardi & Hall, 2007; Phillippo & Stone, 2006; Young & Gaughan, 2010). The most well-known contemporary model is RTI, and that model outlined subsequently to the historical models.

Traditional Student Problem-Solving Teams   Two well-known traditional student problem-solving team models—teacher assistance teams and intervention assistance teams—illustrate the logic, philosophy, and practices reflected in early approaches to supporting students and their teachers through teaming. Although each of these models could be found in a "pure" form in some schools, from the beginning the models were implemented in very diverse and idiosyncratic ways as educators modified and adjusted them to accommodate the specific ecology of their schools and their own perspectives. As you read about these early team options, you will no doubt identify adjustments you believe would be necessary for them to be effective in your setting.

Teacher assistance teams (TATs) served as one of the earliest examples of a pre-referral intervention assistance model. Originally developed by Chalfant, Pysh, and Moultrie (1979), this teacher support system or peer problem-solving group consists of three elected teachers and the referring teacher. Parents are invited to become members and, when appropriate, specialists also are included; the latter, however, are not regular members. The team provides teachers with the support needed to accommodate students with learning and behavior disorders in their classrooms. The referring teacher defines the concern regarding the student, designs alternative interventions jointly with other TAT members, and then selects a preferred intervention. The TAT functions on the assumption that general education teachers have the knowledge and skill individually or jointly to resolve a great number of the challenges they encounter in teaching students with learning and behavior problems, clearly reflecting a belief in the superiority of group decision making. This model continues to have strong proponents and is appreciated by teachers who derive support from the process (e.g., Papalia-Berardi & Hall, 2007), but it is no longer widely implemented.

Another traditional student-centered problem-solving team is the *intervention assistance team* (IAT). This team is premised on the belief that solving problems about students experiencing behavioral and learning problems should enlist all of the resources available at a school, including those of special education and related services staff members (Ortiz, Wilkinson, Robertson-Courtney, & Kushner, 2006; Rafoth & Foriska, 2006). The IAT model uses procedures similar to those of the TAT: The classroom teacher refers a student, team members gather additional information, and they all meet to consider the information as they engage in a team problem-solving process. The primary difference between IATs and TATs is that the IAT approach goes beyond general education teachers and includes a special education teacher and often other specialists, such as a speech/language therapist, counselor, school psychologist, and social worker. Notably, these teams have been found to be effective in meeting student needs and providing support to teachers, but success is not guaranteed

One of the newer type of teams in schools, RTI teams strive to address student learning problems as soon as they are recognized with the goal of preventing, if possible, the need for referral for special education services.

(e.g., McNamara, Rasheed, & Delamatre, 2008; Papalia-Berardi & Hall, 2007). IATs are still in place in some locales, but RTI, described next, is far more common.

Response to Intervention (RTI) Teams The 2004 reauthorization of Individuals with Disabilities Education Act (IDEA) explicitly permits the use of information about students' response to the instruction they are provided to be used in the identification of students with learning disabilities. Statutory permission to use RTI was originally intended to decrease the dependence on the ability–achievement discrepancy in identification (Maki, Floyd, & Roberson, 2015). In practice, RTI has become widespread as a means of focusing attention on student instructional challenges at their first appearance with the goal of providing students with intensive instruction to avoid, if at all possible, the need for special education (Sugai & Horner, 2009; Vujnovic et al., 2014). It is noteworthy that RTI models are as diverse and idiosyncratic as the older pre-referral approaches they usually replaced (Hoover & Love, 2011).

The two most commonly promoted approaches to RTI are (a) the problem-solving approach (Ikeda et al., 2007) and (b) the standard protocol (Fuchs, Fuchs, & Vaughn, 2008). In Chapter 5, the standard protocol approach was described as technical problem solving and compared to general interpersonal problem solving. That comparison pointed to the greater breadth allowed by interpersonal problem solving, but it was not intended to suggest that the standard protocol approach lacks usefulness. Several features of the standard protocol approach have been summarized by Hoover and Love (2011) and characterize key principles of RTI.

Figure 6.2 contrasts traditional student-centered pre-referral problem solving with standard protocol RTI, noting the strengths of the more contemporary model. But what about the second common form of RTI, problem solving? Because the use of the term *problem solving* may be confusing, the more specific term *RTI problem solving* is preferred. RTI problem solving incorporates many of the main elements of RTI, including an emphasis on monitoring the student's response to research-based instruction and intervention. Further, it often closely follows the general steps of group problem solving and can be considered a specific application of the group problem-solving process.

In all variations of RTI, collaboration and teamwork are critical (Nellis, Sickman, Newman, & Harman, 2014). This is true when RTI is based in a school leadership team

FIGURE 6.2 **Comparison of elements in the RTI model and pre-referral problem-solving approaches.**

Element	RTI Model	Pre-Referral Approaches
Screening	School-wide screening used in academics as often as three times annually	No school-wide screening implemented in academics or behavior
Student identification	Universal screening is conducted to identify students early who are struggling in school	Students identified as having recognizable struggles become the subjects of pre-referral interventions
Core instruction	Core instruction in general education must be research based	General education instruction may not be research based
Tiers of instruction	Three tiers of instruction are provided: core, supplemental, and intensive	Two types of instruction are typically offered: pre-referral and special education (intensive)
Assessment decision	Focus is on the quality of instruction and student response to it	Focus is on disorders in the student

A BASIS IN RESEARCH
General Education Teachers and Pre-Referral Teaming

Pre-referral teams play a crucial role in addressing concerns of general education teachers regarding student academic achievement and behavior, and the effectiveness of these teams may have a profound influence on the effectiveness of special education referral procedures. Slonski-Fowler and Truscott (2004) examined the perceptions of 12 experienced elementary teachers (kindergarten through grade 4) as they brought a total of 27 students to the pre-referral intervention teams in their two suburban elementary schools. In this ethnographic study, the authors used interviews, observations at team meetings, and classroom observations, examining these data sets for patterns and themes. Eight of the teachers were strongly negative about the team process, and the researchers found three consistent themes among the teachers' perceptions that led to a withdrawal from the process:

1. Teachers sometimes perceived that their input was devalued or ignored by the team.
2. The intervention strategies suggested by team members tended to be limited and lacked clarity, and teachers believed it was just an exercise in documentation in preparation for referral for special education.
3. Teams demonstrated little accountability for strategy implementation or outcomes.

While acknowledging the limitations of this type of study—for example, lack of generalizability—Slonski-Fowler and Truscott concluded that many of the problems they found were related to collaboration: valuing team members' (i.e., general education teachers') input, effective communication among team members, and shared responsibility for the implementation of ideas and a sense of accountability for outcomes. What other collaboration factors do you think might have influenced these teams' functioning?

---

that guides the assessment and analysis of student progress data (Sugai & Horner, 2009), when professionals are integrating Tier 1 and Tier 2 instruction to improve all students' academic outcomes (Hoover & Love, 2011), when a team meets to address specific student problems (Ikeda et al., 2007), or when members are planning implementation with administrators (Mahdavi & Beebe-Frankenberger, 2009). Like other types of teamwork, the contributions by diverse professionals and the collective insights they achieve are instrumental in designing interventions effective in accelerating student learning.

In summary, student-centered teams are now strongly grounded in general education and are effective only to the extent that general education teachers perceive their value and seek from them support and ideas for addressing student concerns. When teachers perceive these teams negatively or when biases exist in their functioning, serious problems may occur. General educators' perceptions of such teams are addressed in A Basis in Research.

> **Learn More About**
> As a member of a special education team, one of your responsibilities is to review with parents the progress their children have made and to collaborate with them on plans for the future.

Special Education Teams

Special education teams, the third type of student-centered team considered in this chapter, exist to make decisions about a student's eligibility for special education and the nature of the services to be provided (Rothstein & Johnson, 2010; Yell 2012). Following appropriate systematic interventions and assessments, the team is convened for the purpose of determining a student's eligibility for special education and related services and, if appropriate, developing an IEP. The team also has responsibility for planning, monitoring, and evaluating the provision of the special services (Lentz, 2012). This type of team is often referred to as "the IEP team." The specific composition, structure, and procedures of such a team vary across states, but the team must operate in a manner consistent with the requirements put forth in IDEA and highlighted in Putting Ideas into Practice. Members of these teams usually include a parent, a representative of the school district who is knowledgeable about special and general education services, a general education teacher, a special education teacher, a psychologist, and other specialists whose expertise may be needed to evaluate the student and plan programs to meet his or her unique needs. Whenever appropriate, the student about whom the decisions are being made also should be included. These teams gather and review information about referred students and determine whether additional assessment is needed. If an assessment is carried out, the team reviews the results and determines (1) whether the student has a disability that interferes with his or her ability to progress in the general curriculum; (2) whether the student requires special education and related services; (3) what goals and, in some cases, objectives should be set to address the student's unique needs; and (4) which setting is most appropriate for the student's education. If problems arise in implementing the student's program, the team reconvenes to consider strategies for resolving them.

Another serious barrier to effective special education teams may stem from the fact that they are mandatory. This characteristic has led to a narrow definition of the team's purpose and functioning, preventing such teams from appropriately clarifying and expanding their influence. Without a clearly understood foundation, some teams lack the grounding on which to build a more cohesive structure. The result is that many multidisciplinary teams serve mostly as gatekeepers of special education rather than as workgroups that provide optimal instructional program designs and support for all of the students they consider.

Special education teams reconvene annually to review the student's progress and make adjustments in the individualized program, although not all members of the

PUTTING IDEAS INTO PRACTICE

IDEA Guidelines for IEP Team Composition

IDEA (P.L. 108-446) provides guidelines—outlined below—for the composition of multidisciplinary teams. However, a provision that had not been part of earlier versions of this law outlines conditions under which certain team members may be excused from the team meeting. Considering the definition of a team and the characteristics presented thus far, what do you think the impact of excusing a team member might be?

Team Membership

The term *individualized education program team* or *IEP team* means a group of individuals composed of—

i. the parents of a child with a disability;
ii. not less than one regular education teacher of such child (if the child is, or may be, participating in the regular education environment);
iii. not less than one special education teacher, or where appropriate, not less than one special education provider of such child;
iv. a representative of the local educational agency who—
   a. is qualified to provide, or supervise the provision of specially designed instruction to meet the unique needs of children with disabilities;
   b. is knowledgeable about the general education curriculum; and
   c. is knowledgeable about the availability of resources of the local educational agency;
v. an individual who can interpret the instructional implications of evaluation results, who may be a member of the team described in clauses (ii) through (vi);
vi. at the discretion of the parent or the agency, other individuals who have knowledge or special expertise regarding the child, including related services personnel as appropriate; and
vii. whenever appropriate, the child with a disability.

Team Meeting Attendance

i. Attendance not necessary—A member of the IEP team shall not be required to attend an IEP meeting, in whole or in part, if the parent of a child with a disability and the local educational agency agree that the attendance of such member is not necessary because the member's area of the curriculum or related services is not being modified or discussed in the meeting.
ii. Excusal—A member of the IEP team may be excused from attending an IEP meeting, in whole or in part, when the meeting involves a modification to or discussion of the member's area of the curriculum or related services, if—
   a. the parent and the local educational agency consent to the excusal; and
   b. the member submits, in writing to the parent and the IEP team, input into the development of the IEP prior to the meeting.

original team that assessed the student to determine whether special education was needed are required to be part of these interactions. The team meeting you read about at the beginning of this chapter represented the work of this type of team. In that case, Ms. Liberatore and probably others were uncomfortable with the team's decision, and so they established a follow-up date for another team meeting to consider Nathan's progress in his new placement.

The rationale for special education teams, including the presumed superiority of decisions made by these teams, was discussed earlier in this chapter. However, even though multidisciplinary special education teams were envisioned as having the potential to enhance school-based services to students with disabilities, early research demonstrated many problems with such teams. For example, research conducted shortly after the passage of P.L. 94-142 revealed that team functioning was adversely affected by (1) use of nonsystematic approaches to collecting and analyzing diagnostic information, (2) minimal participation by parents or general educators on the teams, (3) use of an unclear decision-making/planning process, (4) lack of interdisciplinary collaboration and trust, (5) territoriality, (6) ambiguous role definition and accountability, and (7) lack of experience and training for professionals to work together (Fenton, Yoshida, Maxwell, & Kaufman, 1979; Kaiser & Woodman, 1985; Pfeiffer, 1981).

As the field recognized the shortcomings of the multidisciplinary team concept, various proposals for improving team functioning were advanced. Among the problems most frequently addressed was the lack of preparation in effective collaboration and team participation skills (Havnes, 2009; Mueller, 2009b). Now, some (but not all) professional preparation programs require that all educators demonstrate these skills (Allday, Neilsen-Gatti, & Hudson, 2013).

In the earlier discussion of team characteristics and in the previous considerations about team effectiveness, the importance of stable membership and regular interactions among team members is apparent. How does a team develop shared norms, shared service delivery goals, and a sense of interdependence among members if the membership varies and if meetings are infrequent? This is a critical issue for IEP teams. Some members may participate in several IEP teams, but the general educator, parents, and student certainly change. It is also likely that other members may change based on the students under discussion. The instability of membership and infrequency of meetings challenge the concept of the IEP team as a true team as defined in this chapter.

As you think about student-centered teams, remember that any given team may be classified simultaneously along both the disciplinary or functional dimensions. For example, a service delivery team may be multidisciplinary, interdisciplinary, or transdisciplinary in its approach. A special education decision-making team or a problem-solving team may be similarly classified. As you work as a professional educator, you may find that these two dimensions of teams are assumed and seldom discussed. However, if you understand the differences in team functioning related to these dimensions, you can be a more effective team member, tailoring your contributions based on your understanding.

Effectiveness of Teams

The effectiveness of a team can be evaluated in terms of whether it reaches its stated goal because, as noted earlier, the team's purpose for existence is to achieve this outcome. That is, teams are only effective when they are able to demonstrate that they have improved services and outcomes for students at risk, those with disabilities, and those with other special needs.

Another criterion for judging team effectiveness is output, meeting or exceeding the organization's standards of quality and quantity (Johnson & Johnson, 2013). In schools, team output should meet the standards of education and the expectations of administrators, parents, colleagues, and others (e.g., community members). Output might be the number of interventions that prevent unnecessary referrals to special education, the number of students on whose behalf problem solving occurs, or the number of students for whom in-class, evidence-based intervention is successful.

However, most teams' effectiveness is also judged on other factors that may not readily be measured. That is, the ultimate effectiveness of a team often depends on (1) the level of effort team members devote to the team's task, (2) the level of knowledge and skills within the team, and (3) the strategies the team uses to accomplish its work (Gülcan, 2014; Qiu et al., 2009). Further, these factors are affected by the design of the task, the composition of the team, and the appropriateness of the strategies used by the team. Additional criteria for judging team effectiveness are derived from the studies of multidisciplinary teams mentioned earlier and included in the characteristics of effective teams described next.

The Team's Goals Are Clear

The goals of an effective team are clearly understood by all team members. Mutual goals represent the team's primary purposes, but each activity the team pursues to achieve its purposes will also have goals. Members of effective teams clearly understand both the central goals and the activity or process goals, and their actions as a team reflect this understanding.

Members' Needs Are Met

In effective teams, the personal needs of team members are satisfied more than frustrated by the group experience. The interpersonal needs of being included, respected, and valued can be met through active participation in a team. Conversely, teams in schools are not likely to be effective in achieving their goals if the team prevents individuals from meeting these interpersonal needs or attaining their individual professional goals. Satisfying members' needs, however, does not mean that individuals always "get their way." When members' needs differ, resistance and conflict may occur. These topics are addressed in Chapter 9.

> **Learn More About**
> After you watch the many examples of teams shown in this video, think about the teams of which you are a member. How do the characteristics of effective teams apply to them?
> (https://www.youtube.com/watch?v=FJVS__j_lio)

Like boaters, unless team members row in the same direction by understanding their shared goal, progress is unlikely.

Members Have Individual Accountability

Team members should clearly understand their roles as well as those of other members. Earlier, we identified role interdependence as a defining characteristic of teams because work teams are constructed with members who have complementary and interconnected parts to play, such as data gathering, recording, or record keeping. Each member has responsibility for something the group needs in order to function. The structure of an effective team provides for individual accountability that increases the tendency of team members to devote adequate effort to meeting their team responsibilities.

Group Processes Maintain the Team

The group processes used in effective teams serve to increase, or at least maintain, the team's capacity to work collaboratively on future endeavors. Specifically, these group processes ensure that leadership and participation are distributed throughout the team. Leadership skills, such as initiating discussion, setting standards, encouraging, summarizing, and gaining consensus, can be used by different members of the team. A team that wants to make maximum use of the diverse experience, expertise, and information of its members distributes leadership roles. Team members recognize that leadership is necessarily a shared responsibility and assume that role when necessary to support the functioning of the group.

Team Members Have Leadership Skills

A considerable literature documents the need for effective team leadership (e.g., Gustavson & Liff, 2014; Johnson & Johnson, 2013). Most teaming experts agree that all team members need to have leadership skills, even when they are not assuming the formal role of team leader. Leadership skills are those that help the group function effectively and progress toward its goals. From that perspective, it should be clear that a group member other than the designated leader may take an active role in facilitating the team's progress. By offering a summary of positions stated by others, asking clarifying questions, or simply helping to ensure that all team members have the opportunity to participate in discussion and decision making, a team member demonstrates leadership and helps the team progress.

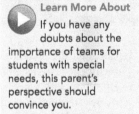

Learn More About
If you have any doubts about the importance of teams for students with special needs, this parent's perspective should convince you.

(https://www.youtube.com/watch?v=3_cLnIuASXM)

Collaboration and Teams

The first part of this chapter examined variations in school teams, distinguishing among many models for teaming based on a continuum of collaboration among members from different disciplines or perspectives. You learned that multidisciplinary teams have the least collaboration, interdisciplinary teams function with more, and transdisciplinary teams have the most collaboration of the three models. Collaboration is not limited to these team structures; it can be applied broadly to all types of teams.

The distinctions between the elements of a collaborative style and those of a team structure are not always completely clear, nor do they necessarily need to be. This is partly because the defining characteristics of a team are those that define the relationship among team members, just as the defining characteristics of collaboration are those that define the relationship among participants in any collaborative activity. Moreover, the defining characteristics of a team are very similar to those of collaboration because it is the elements of collaboration that distinguish a team from a loosely constructed work group or committee.

Overall, effective teams are characterized by strong collaborative relationships among members (e.g., Ash & D'Auria, 2013; White, Vanc, & Stafford, 2010). Team members share parity, a common goal, responsibility for decision making, and accountability for outcomes. Teams have common norms and shared beliefs and values, and team members trust one another. Collaboration's emergent characteristic of interdependence is a critical defining trait of a team. The relationship between teams and collaboration is simple: An effective team is a collaborative work group (Bang et al., 2010; Beebe & Masterson, 2015). However, when some members dominate interactions or insist on pursuing only their own agenda, or when members defer to someone perceived as having the greatest power, a group referred to as a "team" is not functioning in a collaborative way, regardless of its label.

SUMMARY

- An educational team composed of interdependent individuals with unique skills and perspectives who interact directly to achieve their mutual goal has defining characteristics that include a shared goal of effective service delivery, awareness of team membership, shared norms, interdependence, and members with diverse skills and perspectives. Teams progress through stages as they mature, including being polite and seeking direction and purpose (forming); establishing leadership and purpose (storming); creating roles and procedures (norming); and effectively completing the tasks needed to meet team goals (performing).

- Teaming in schools is often described by the working relationship among people from different disciplines, including multidisciplinary, interdisciplinary, and transdisciplinary models.
- Three types of student-centered teams include (1) instructional teams that focus on the delivery of instruction or other interventions; (2) student-centered problem-solving teams; and (3) special education teams that make decisions about student referral, assessment, and eligibility for special education and related services.
- Features of effective teams include clear goals, individual accountability, shared responsibility, functional group processes, and leadership.

BACK TO THE CASE

1. Consider the qualities of effective teams and team members' responsibilities. How could an advocate attending with parents affect—positively or negatively—the outcomes of a team meeting? What are your responsibilities as an educator for responding to concerns raised by an advocate at a team meeting?
2. Team members are likely to have different points of view. To what extent should all school professionals agree before a meeting with parents about the recommendations they will make? Defend your point of view.
3. At the conclusion of the case, Ms. Liberatore wonders if another team would have handled the issue of Nathan's team meeting differently. What do you think could have been said by team members that might have led Ms. Liberatore to be more satisfied with the outcome?

COLLABORATIVE ACTIVITIES

1. List the teams of which you are a member. To what extent does each of these teams demonstrate the characteristics of teams described in this chapter? What is the relationship between the team's characteristics and its effectiveness in achieving its purpose?
2. Identify a team experience that you have had or observed that was not as successful as you would have liked it to be. Using the characteristics of collaboration presented in Chapter 1 and the issues raised in this chapter, analyze the situation and describe how factors related to collaboration may have contributed to the problems.
3. Think about the differences among multidisciplinary, interdisciplinary, and transdisciplinary teams. How might each type of team be the most effective in schools? Create the profile of a student with a disability or other special needs with your classmates, or find an already prepared case study. What might each type of team accomplish on behalf of this student? How would these teams be similar to each other? Different from each other?
4. Recall a team meeting you recently attended. Prepare a description of member roles, and then outline behaviors that were helpful to the team's functioning and those that were not. What formal

and informal roles did you observe team members assuming? If you were providing feedback to team members, what would be the three most important points you would make?
5. Imagine holding a team meeting with five of your colleagues, one of whom is not a particularly good listener or "team player." What ground rules would you want to establish to make the meeting productive? What steps would you take in advance to maximize the potential for success in this meeting?

CHECK YOUR UNDERSTANDING

Click here to gauge your understanding of this chapter's essential concepts.

7 Co-Teaching

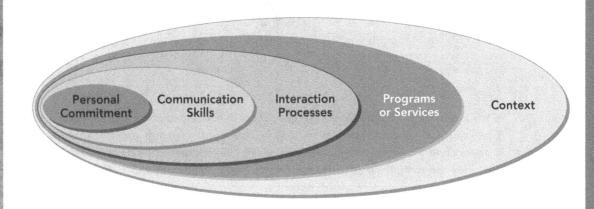

CONNECTIONS

In Chapter 6 you learned that teams represent a collaborative practice enhanced when professionals use effective interpersonal communication skills (Chapters 2, 3, and 4) and problem solving (Chapter 5). In Chapter 7, we add another example of collaboration in action—co-teaching. Co-teaching is a widely adopted means for providing special education instruction for students with disabilities, but you will learn that it has other applications as well. Generally, it is a unique blending of professional expertise in which a general educator and a special educator or another specialist jointly instruct pupils in a single general education classroom. Co-teaching's growth can be attributed to the continued federal and state governmental expectation that educators will reduce the gap in achievement between students with disabilities and their typical peers. A logical result of this pressure, one consistent with the Individuals with Disabilities Education Act (IDEA) mandate of education in the least restrictive environment (LRE), is that all students must have access to the general curriculum, and co-teaching is a way they can both have that access and receive special education. In this chapter, you will learn about the essential elements of co-teaching as well as ideas to make your co-teaching practice effective and efficient.

LEARNING OUTCOMES

After reading this chapter you will be able to:

1. Define co-teaching and distinguish it from related concepts (e.g., inclusion, team teaching).
2. Articulate a rationale for using co-teaching to effectively educate diverse groups of learners.
3. Identify six approaches for implementing co-teaching, describe examples and variations of each, and indicate when each might be instructionally appropriate.
4. Examine the relationship between co-teaching and collaboration, applying your knowledge and skills to consider common co-teaching professional dilemmas and strategies for resolving them.
5. Discuss common administrative and logistical issues that can foster or constrain co-teaching.
6. Analyze the co-teaching challenge of shared planning time and apply realistic solutions for addressing it.

A CASE FOR COLLABORATION

A Co-Teaching Quandary

Ms. Shea, the principal at Jefferson Middle School, is concerned about Rita Smithson and George Ruiz, two early career educators assigned to co-teach this year. Although they began slowly and seemed to have differing views related to the effective teaching approaches and classroom discipline, Ms. Shea thought that they had formed a productive partnership and worked out a way to make their instruction more intensive and responsive to student needs. Recently, though, Ms. Smithson reported that Mr. Ruiz will not let her take an active role during instruction, justifying this position by saying that he, as the math expert, needs to lead lessons. She said that she feels like a classroom assistant, and she is worried that's what students think, too. Mr. Ruiz, in a separate conversation, expressed frustration that Ms. Smithson does not understand the math curriculum well enough to lead instruction, noting that he sometimes has to correct errors she makes that confuse students. He also thinks she too quickly makes excuses for students and does not hold them to a high enough standard. Ms. Shea overheard him tell a colleague that co-teaching is like having a student teacher.

Co-teaching has become an important service option at Jefferson Middle School and recent data strongly support its positive impact on the achievement of diverse learners, and so Ms. Shea is determined to address this situation. She has scheduled a meeting with both teachers for tomorrow. She believes they have all the skills to make their co-teaching successful, if they can just work on their relationship in the classroom. As she plans for the meeting, she is thinking about how to go about discussing this sensitive topic with them.

Introduction

Co-teaching has intuitive appeal. It makes tremendous sense to partner general education teachers with special educators or other specialists in order to create instructional options that can effectively meet diverse student needs. Further, co-teaching has the potential to accomplish that positive result while at the same time avoiding several critical problems that accompany pullout or separate setting service models, including instruction by teachers who may not have academic background in some subject areas, the stigma of going to a special education or another special class, fragmentation of educational services delivered in multiple settings, and academic and social isolation (e.g., Basso & McCoy, 2009; Friend, 2014).

In many instances, co-teaching is living up to its promise and is tremendously successful, improving student outcomes and resulting in strongly positive professional and parent perceptions. However, as noted in A Case for Collaboration highlighting Ms. Smithson and Mr. Ruiz, co-teaching—like many other aspects of collaborative practice—can be complicated. The purposes of this chapter are to outline critical concepts related to co-teaching, demonstrate exemplary co-teaching practice, and explore its logistics and complexities. The goal is to explore the potential of co-teaching while at the same time acknowledging the very real factors that may constrain its implementation.

Co-Teaching Concepts

As co-teaching has become a popular service delivery model, its use has encompassed students with a variety of needs. In some locales, co-teaching is an option only for students with mild or moderate disabilities (e.g., Pearl, Dieker, & Kirkpatrick, 2012). In others, it is a means of supporting students with significant disabilities as well (Causton-Theoharis & Theoharis, 2008). In addition, co-teaching is part of response to intervention (RTI), sometimes used as a Tier 1 or Tier 2 intervention for reading or mathematics (e.g., Conderman &

Hedin, 2012). It is being implemented to support English learners (e.g., Honigsfeld & Dove, 2012a), and to provide speech/language therapy (Cirrin et al., 2010) and other related services. In many schools, co-teaching also occurs in settings outside a general education classroom. For example, an English as a Second Language (ESL) teacher and a special educator might partner in a separate special education classroom. Similarly, a speech/language therapist or occupational therapist may co-teach with a special educator in a self-contained setting.

One other application of the concept of co-teaching concerns field experiences for teacher candidates (Anderson & Stillman, 2013; Bacharach, Heck, & Dahlberg, 2010). This arrangement, although not meeting all the components of co-teaching described in this chapter (Friend, Embury, & Clark, 2015), reflects contemporary efforts to make student teaching a much more collaborative experience than ever before. This type of apprenticeship experience is described in Putting Ideas into Practice.

Co-Teaching Definition

Across all applications of co-teaching, similarities exist. And although co-teaching has been defined in various ways and with various levels of precision (e.g., Brinkmann & Twiford, 2012; Conderman, 2011b; Rivera, McMahon, & Keys, 2014), analysis of the similarities and review of various definitions leads us to offer the following as the technical meaning of this term: *Co-teaching* is a service delivery option for providing specialized services to

PUTTING IDEAS INTO PRACTICE

Co-Teaching Versus Student Teaching

Many teacher educators have realized that traditional approaches to student teaching, in which a candidate first observes a master teacher and then gradually takes over instruction until responsible—alone—for all aspects of that professional's role, is in many ways outdated. Given the importance of collaboration in today's schools, it is not surprising that the same notion is being applied to student teaching or internship experiences. In some locales, this more collaborative approach has been labeled *co-teaching*, even though a more accurate term for it might be *apprentice teaching* (Friend et al., 2015). Even though the two experiences might have some similarities, here are three key differences between co-teaching and apprentice teaching:

1. **Purpose.** In apprentice teaching, the goal is for the teacher candidate to apply their knowledge and skills over a specified period of time to a particular subject or class so that they can complete requirements for their teaching credential. In co-teaching, the purpose is to ensure that the diverse needs of students are met while simultaneously providing access to the general curriculum.
2. **Areas of expertise.** In apprentice teaching, the candidate and master teacher have comparable areas of expertise. That is, both may be elementary teachers, both may have a university major in math, or both may have specialist preparation. In co-teaching, an explicit defining characteristic is that the participants have differing but complementary areas of expertise.
3. **Power.** In apprentice teaching, even when the candidate and master teacher have a strong and positive professional relationship in which power is not overtly a concern, the latter professional clearly has more power. That individual can direct the candidate to change practices, can assign to the candidate particular responsibilities, and may write a summative evaluation of the candidate's performance. Although power can be an issue in co-teaching, the relationship between two professionals with equivalent licensure provides the groundwork for parity in a way that is not possible in the apprentice model.

Collaboration as a significant element of becoming a teacher is a positive addition to professional preparation. It is essential, though, that the distinctions between apprentice teaching and co-teaching be kept in mind so that all participants—candidates, master teachers, and university supervisors—understand the appropriate use of each one.

Learn More About
This video clip includes early career middle school co-teachers teaching in their shared classroom and sharing their partnership story.

(https://www.youtube.com/watch?v=8ple6CZX6PM)

students with disabilities or other special needs while they remain in their general education classes. Co-teaching occurs when two or more professionals with distinctly different areas of expertise jointly deliver core or supplemental instruction to a diverse, blended group of students, primarily in a single physical space (Friend, 2014).

Characteristics of Co-Teaching

Teacher teams have used various structures for joint instructional efforts for more than six decades at elementary, middle school, and high school levels (e.g., Crespin, 1971; Lange, Huff, Silverman, & Wallace, 2012; Trump, 1966; Warwick, 1971). Most of those teams, however, consisted of two general education teachers who pooled their class groups and their instructional efforts in a model generally called *team teaching*. Only more recently has the use of teacher partnerships been seen as a mechanism for providing services to students with special needs by partnering teachers with different types of expertise (Bauwens, Hourcade, & Friend, 1989; Fenty, McDuffie-Landrum, & Fisher, 2012; McClure & Cahnmann-Taylor, 2010). In fact, the amount of research on co-teaching, although gradually increasing, is still relatively meager, a topic discussed in A Basis in Research.

A BASIS IN RESEARCH

Co-Teaching: Promise Versus Evidence

Hundreds of articles have been written about co-teaching, and many of them describe programs, offer suggestions for improving instruction, or relate anecdotes about co-teachers' positive or negative experiences (e.g., Brown, Horwerter, & Morgan, 2013; McClure & Cahnmann-Taylor, 2010; Nierengarten, 2013; Ploessl, Rock, Schoenfeld, & Blanks, 2010). Although this literature is valuable and shows the promise of co-teaching, also essential is evidence demonstrating the impact of co-teaching on student outcomes. Although still too scarce, studies demonstrating this impact can be identified:

- Hang and Rabren (2009) studied 45 co-teachers and 58 students with disabilities. All participants were new to co-teaching at the time of the investigation. The researchers gathered data through surveys, classroom observations, and a review of relevant records. They found that students with disabilities in co-taught classes significantly increased in achievement on standardized tests from the year prior to co-teaching and that these students' achievement was not significantly different from the overall achievement of all students in their grade level.
- Walsh (2012) summarized data from Maryland school districts gathered over a 20-year span of co-teaching implementation. Co-teaching was undertaken as a means of ensuring access to the general curriculum. He reported that students with disabilities who received their services through co-teaching demonstrated an accelerated rate of achievement on state-mandated reading and math tests, illustrating co-teaching's effectiveness using six years of data from one school district that was especially successful in improving outcomes for these students.
- Dessemontet and Bless (2013) studied the impact of students with intellectual disabilities being educated in the primary grades with their peers without disabilities on the achievement of those peers, including those who struggled to achieve, those who were average, and those who were high achievers. The students with disabilities spent at least 70 percent of the day in general education and their services included co-teaching. These authors report no negative impact of inclusive practices on the educational outcomes of any of the other student groups.
- Pardini (2006) reported one of the only studies of the impact of co-teaching on English learners. After implementing co-teaching as an alternative to traditional separate services for many of these students, the gap between the reading and math achievement of these students and their English-speaking peers was significantly reduced.

Co-teaching is challenging to study because it can be so greatly affected by teachers' characteristics, the professional relationship, the characteristics of the students, and the quality of instruction in the co-taught class. Research on co-teaching is likely to continue to evolve as a result of the growing trend to educate students with diverse needs in general education settings. What type of data could you collect in your own classroom to evaluate both the practices and the outcomes of co-teaching?

An appropriate starting point for mastering co-teaching practice is understanding its defining characteristics. It is these key traits that underscore co-teaching's uniqueness as a collaborative service delivery alternative.

Two or More Professionals with Different Primary Areas of Expertise Co-teaching involves at least two appropriately credentialed professionals—two teachers (e.g., a general education teacher and a special education teacher who may be highly qualified only in special education or in special education as well as in the academic content area); a teacher and a related services professional (e.g., a teacher and a speech/language therapist, or a teacher and an occupational therapist); or a teacher and another specialist (e.g., a teacher and a literacy coach or media specialist, or a teacher and an ESL teacher). The importance of this characteristic comes first from the notion that co-teachers are peers—they have equivalent credentials and employment status and thus can truly be partners in their instructional endeavors on behalf of students. Second, it emphasizes that co-teaching is powerful because the professionals bring significantly different types of expertise to their practice.

Notice that this co-teaching element excludes paraeducators. Generally, paraeducators and other adults who might work in general education classrooms (e.g., volunteers, interns) should provide support rather than co-teaching. They typically have not had the professional preparation to co-teach, and the instructional partnership of co-teaching is not an appropriate role expectation for them (Giangreco, Suter, & Hurley, 2013). Even if a paraeducator has a teaching license, this individual is not employed to carry out the responsibilities of a teacher and usually has a job description to that effect (Ashbaker & Morgan, 2012b). To underscore the differences in roles, classrooms in which paraeducators are delivering services sometimes are called *supported* or *assisted classrooms*, not *co-taught classrooms*. This distinction helps everyone involved to remember that, although paraprofessionals are valuable classroom personnel, they should not be asked to function in the same way as staff employed in positions requiring professional licensure or certification; it also clarifies for general education teachers the nature of the services being provided. Of course, saying paraeducators generally should not co-teach does not in any way imply they do not have significant classroom responsibilities. They still work with individual students and groups, but under the direction of teachers or other specialists to reinforce or supplement core instruction, not to routinely introduce it. Appropriate roles and responsibilities for paraprofessionals are discussed in detail in Chapter 10.

Joint Delivery of Instruction In schools across the country, we have found a disturbing number of educators who call their arrangement "co-teaching" simply because it involves two educators in a classroom at the same time. In some situations, the general education teacher conducts lessons as though alone in the classroom. That teacher may even express gratitude for having in the classroom "an extra set of hands." The second teacher, usually a special educator but sometimes another specialist, has the de facto role of instructional assistant for students with disabilities and possibly for other students who struggle to learn. This individual hovers at the fringes of the class until the instruction is delivered and then helps those who need it, monitors and addresses student behavior problems, or pulls individual students or a small group aside to deliver instruction completely separate from that being provided to the rest of the class. This type of situation is described in this chapter's opening case study.

Although such arrangements may occur occasionally in co-taught classes, particularly if a student (or students) in the class has significant disabilities, if these practices are routine, the arrangement—which quickly becomes frustrating for both teachers, as Ms. Smithson and Mr. Ruiz demonstrated—should not be referred to as co-teaching. Instead, this situation is a woeful and inappropriate underuse of a qualified professional. It is a practice likely to stigmatize students at least as much as pullout strategies and to possibly demean special services providers. It is also a circumstance in which any benefits derived from appropriate separate instruction are diminished by the increased noise and activity in the classroom. These considerations give rise to questions about why professionals consistently would use this arrangement for any length of time. A variation of this situation occurs when the educators decide to split teaching duties, each professional teaching on alternate days or possibly alternate weeks. Although not as obviously negative as the first example, it still represents a misunderstanding of co-teaching. To achieve positive outcomes in co-taught classes, both educators should be actively and simultaneously engaged in the teaching of each lesson.

Additionally, each professional in co-taught classes has an important contribution to make in coordinating and delivering core instruction (Eisenman, Pleet, Wandry, & McGinley, 2011; Morehead & Grillo, 2013). This does not mean that they always work with students in large groups, but it does mean that they share decision making about instruction and ensure that both have appropriate teaching roles (Pancsofar & Petroff, 2013). Specifically, the two professionals plan and use unique and high-involvement instructional strategies to engage all students in ways that are not possible when only one teacher is present (Friend, Burrello, & Burrello, 2009). In doing so, they also integrate specially designed instruction or other specialized strategies into the general education teaching/learning environment. The standard curriculum provides the instructional framework for the class, yet that curriculum is differentiated as necessary to foster student success enhanced through the use of specialized instructional strategies for the students who need them, and sometimes modified for students with the most significant needs (U.S. Department of Education, 2005). Keep in mind the expectation that two qualified teachers or other professionals should arrange instruction to enhance learning options for all students. For example, all students should have more opportunities to participate during lessons, and thus instructional intensity is increased and learning enhanced. However, more is required. Specifically, students with disabilities should also receive as part of their instruction the specially designed instruction that is necessary in order for them to accomplish their individualized education program (IEP) goals; students in other programs (e.g., ESL) likewise should receive the specialized instruction to which they are entitled.

Diverse Group of Students   Co-teachers provide instruction to a diverse group of students that includes those with disabilities and other special needs as well as other learners so identified (Seglem & VanZant, 2010). In fact, this dimension is one of the major advantages of co-teaching. Teachers sometimes initially express uncertainty at the thought of teaching classes with students with disabilities or those learning English, but as they implement highly effective instructional interventions through their partnerships, they learn to value the arrangement. Co-teaching allows professionals to respond effectively to the varied needs of their students, lowers the teacher–student ratio, and multiplies the expertise that can be directed to those needs. It is true that the inclusion of one or several students with an array of learning challenges can be daunting, but the addition of another teacher who brings an entire repertoire of instructional ideas creates an exciting array of new opportunities for meeting those students' needs.

Co-teachers need to ensure that the diversity in the classroom does not inadvertently result in an inappropriate seating arrangement. For example, some co-teachers try to seat students with special needs together, presumably so that they can more easily be helped with schoolwork. Other teachers seat students with disabilities or other special needs on the periphery of the classroom so that when they are receiving assistance other students are not distracted. Although both these strategies are well intentioned, they may have the result of socially isolating students, often the very students who are most likely to need encouragement and instruction in social skills.

Shared Classroom Space   Co-teaching is premised on the partners instructing in a single physical space or classroom. This characteristic of co-teaching is important as a contrast to earlier variations of teaching teams that commonly planned together, grouped students, and then taught them in separate classrooms (Geen, 1985; Trump, 1966).

Co-teaching is based on blending the general educator's academic content knowledge with the strategy and learning process knowledge of the special educator or specialist.

Although one teacher may occasionally take a small, heterogeneous group of students to a separate location for a specific instructional purpose and for a limited time period (e.g., to the media center where the computers are located so students can complete web-based research), co-teaching generally should be considered an instructional approach that occurs in a single physical environment. This definitional element helps to distinguish co-teaching from the practice of regrouping students for different kinds of pullout programs. It also points out that the teacher relationship issues, illustrated at the beginning of this chapter and discussed in a later section, are far more significant when a physical location is shared than when teachers deliver instruction in separate locations. Finally, working in a shared classroom ensures that teachers eliminate potential problems related to the teacher qualifications (e.g., in a middle or high school when a special educator may not have credentials in the co-taught content area) and avoid violations of IEPs (i.e., pulling students out of the classroom when IEPs indicate services should occur in general education).

Learn More About
As you watch this veteran special educator discuss his co-teaching experiences, think about the responsibilities he assigns to professionals for making co-teaching a success.

Does co-teaching sound like an exciting but somewhat challenging service option for students with disabilities and other special needs? In Putting Ideas into Practice, you'll find some suggestions for getting a new co-teaching program off to a good start.

APPLY YOUR KNOWLEDGE 7.1

Rationale for Co-Teaching

Understanding the rationale for co-teaching provides a foundation on which professionals can ground the definition and consider co-teaching designs and structures for implementation in their schools. Co-teaching is first and foremost a means to deliver services to particular students (Friend, 2014; Friend, Cook, Hurley-Chamberlain, & Shamberger, 2010). Thus, the driving force for creating co-teaching programs between general education teachers and special educators, related services personnel, ESL teachers, or other specialists is ensuring high-quality education for students who have disabilities or other unique

PUTTING IDEAS INTO PRACTICE
Beginning Co-Teaching on a Positive Note

Have you thought about what the first few days of co-teaching might be like? You can help ensure a successful start to co-teaching by addressing these topics:

1. Begin co-teaching on the first day of school in most cases. This practice establishes that co-teaching is an integral element of instruction, not an activity tacked on after the first few weeks of school have been completed. For students with disabilities, it also ensures required services are provided in a timely manner.
2. Prepare in detail for the first day of co-teaching: For example, imagine you and your co-teaching colleague are beginning a lesson. How will you introduce yourselves to students? If you ensure that both teachers speak approximately the same amount of time, perhaps each introducing the other teacher, you will communicate to students that you are instructional partners.
3. If you co-teach in middle school or high school, think about how you will explain co-teaching to your students. Many teachers base this discussion on the specialized skills teachers bring to the class—content expertise versus specialized strategies. If you teach in elementary school, such explanations are seldom needed because either students do not question the presence of a second teacher, or they accept a simple explanation that the class will "sometimes have two teachers."
4. Use detailed planning, even scripting, for the early days of co-teaching to help to establish parity while you and your co-teacher become accustomed to each other and shared teaching.
5. Plan to meet, at least for a few minutes, after the end of the first week of co-teaching. This interaction should give each teacher a chance to raise concerns or questions, to resolve differences before they become serious issues, and to celebrate their shared teaching.
6. Develop the habit of using "we" language—"our students," "our classroom," "the lessons we planned." Even more than the other strategies listed, the words used will convey to both adults and students the belief that co-teaching is truly about partnership and parity in the instructional process.

needs; and co-teaching should result in direct instructional and social benefits for these students (Brusca-Vega, Brown, & Yasutake, 2011; Friend, 2014; Hang & Rabren, 2009; McClure & Cahnmann-Taylor, 2010). For example, students who are academically gifted may have more opportunities in a co-taught class to complete alternative assignments and participate in enrichment activities. Average students should receive more adult attention in co-taught classrooms and benefit from more teacher-led, small-group activities. Students at risk for learning failure but who do not qualify for special programs often receive the instructional boost they need to make better academic progress.

A second part of the rationale for co-teaching concerns curricular access and instruction (e.g., Walsh, 2012). We have stressed that the goal of co-teaching is to bring intense and individualized instruction to students in a general education setting while working as much as possible within the framework of the curriculum used there. As such, co-teaching should lead to a less fragmented and more contextualized education for students with disabilities and other special needs as well as to greater instructional intensity and engaged time. For example, in elementary schools, co-teaching may eliminate for some students the need to leave their classrooms, often during crucial instruction, to go to a special education setting for developmental or remedial work or to a speech/language therapy session. In middle schools and high schools, co-teaching enables students to learn curricular content from teachers who are specialists in those subjects while at the same time receiving the individualized support they need (Hunt, 2010; Rance-Roney, 2009). Of course, an overriding consideration in co-teaching is that the students with special needs who are to participate in the co-taught classroom should be those whose unique educational needs can be met through the general education curriculum with appropriate specially designed instruction, accommodations, modifications, and other supports.

In addition to instructional benefits for diverse groups of students, co-teaching may have other positive effects. For example, in elementary schools it often reduces the stigma associated with students leaving their general education classrooms and going to a separate place to receive special or remedial services. In secondary settings, it increases the opportunities students have to take electives and consider themselves truly part of their class groups, because they may not have class periods allocated for special education or other remedial or specialized services. Teachers can also use co-teaching as a vehicle for creating opportunities for positive social interactions between students with disabilities or other special needs and their typical peers.

Finally, co-teachers often report that this approach to education provides them with a sense of collegial support (Graziano & Navarrete, 2012; Sileo, 2011). Co-teachers are not expected to master all of each other's expertise, but they learn from each other in ways that enhance their own skills. For example, consider these observations from an algebra classroom: A special educator noted that she had to work very hard to master the concepts for the course, but that her partner was always ready to answer her questions. The general educator commented that he had learned that even a high school algebra class benefited when students used manipulatives and accessed learning visually, auditorily, and kinesthetically. Co-teachers also receive emotional support from someone with whom they share both classroom successes and challenges. Notice how this approach to thinking about co-teaching could help Ms. Smithson and Mr. Ruiz, introduced at the beginning of the chapter.

> **Learn More About**
> Watch this video in which high school co-teachers discuss their shared instruction and the benefits to students of each educator's contribution.
> (https://www.youtube.com/watch?v=TUvVGyR_k3o)

Co-Teaching Approaches

The instructional potential of co-teaching makes it imperative that those involved collaborate effectively in designing and delivering instruction and interventions that will best meet the unique learning needs of the students. Co-teachers consider a large number of factors when deciding how to structure and deliver their instruction. They make decisions about what should occur during co-teaching based on student needs, the physical characteristics of the classroom, demands of the curriculum and the requirement to use evidence-based practices, teachers' comfort level and skills for teaching and co-teaching, and the amount of time available for co-teaching and planning lessons. Working within these elements, they design many creative strategies that bring out the best in students and teachers. The following six co-teaching approaches depicted in Figure 7.1—(1) one teaching, one observing; (2) station teaching; (3) parallel teaching; (4) alternative teaching; (5) teaming; and (6) one teaching, one assisting—represent a core set of options used most frequently (Friend, 2014). To keep co-teaching relationships and instructional arrangements fresh and effective, teachers should consider trying several of the approaches, periodically changing their co-teaching methods, and experimenting with variations on the basic information provided here.

One Teaching, One Observing

Co-teachers often find that they have options unavailable to other teachers for carefully and formally observing their students in order to gain a sophisticated understanding of their academic, behavioral, and social functioning. When one professional teaches while the other observes, the first has primary responsibility for designing and delivering specific instruction to the entire group, whether that is a large-group lesson, individual assignments that the teacher is monitoring, cooperative groups, or any other teaching/learning arrangement. The second professional has the goal of systematically collecting data related to a single student, a small group of students, or the entire class for behaviors the professionals have previously agreed should be noted. For example, as students work in cooperative groups in third-grade math, Ms. Jackson circulates among the students to be sure they understand their tasks while Ms. Phelps uses a data chart to analyze whether three students who are English learners are initiating conversation during the

FIGURE 7.1 Co-teaching approaches.

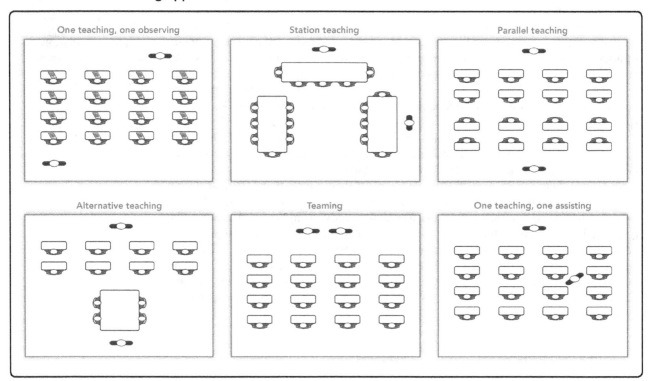

activity, responding to others who ask them questions, or remaining passive. In the same classroom, Joshua, a student with autism, has as a goal making eye contact with peers and adults when interacting with them. This behavior is also being charted. Similarly, in the English class that Mr. St. James and Mrs. Goud co-teach, several students seem to be having difficulty getting started on individual assignments. The teachers agree to observe Michael, José, James, and Sarah to find out whether the problem is comprehension (the students do not begin the task and are looking around to see what others are doing) or a matter of delay (by the time the students find their pens and get headings on their papers, they forget the instructions and ask to have them repeated). In sixth-grade social studies, Ms. Rodriguez and Ms. Wilson decide to observe students to determine who attempts to participate in class discussion by raising his or her hand.

The one teaching, one observing approach requires little joint planning and, if arranged appropriately, provides opportunities for both educators. For example, special services professionals can focus attention on a student with significant needs to learn how to better provide support that is important for that student's success. General educators can scan the student group to learn more about the students' responses to instruction and possibly to gauge whether the behavior of a student perceived as having a problem really is different from that of other students, or just, for some reason, more noticed by the teachers. Early in the school year, both teachers can use this approach to deepen their shared understanding of students while learning about each other's teaching styles. As the year progresses, observational data can be used as the basis for forming student instructional groups.

The one teaching, one observing approach can have a serious drawback, however. If it is used indiscriminately or exclusively, it can result in one professional, most typically the special education teacher or specialist, being relegated to the role of assistant. For this approach to be beneficial, the educators periodically should exchange roles. This strategy has two positive effects: First, it ensures that general education teachers have the opportunity to step back from the intensity of being the classroom manager to focus completely on what is occurring with students. Second, it clarifies for students that their class is led by two teachers with equivalent responsibility and authority.

To make observations most valuable, co-teachers should jointly decide on specific students (as noted, individual, small group, or whole class) and specific behaviors to analyze. For example, a pair of co-teachers may agree that they have serious concerns about Gary, a student who does not seem to be making much progress in reading and who seems to be expressing his frustration by refusing to work and occasionally distracting other students, taking their papers or pencils or calling them names. They decide to observe him at least three times each week across two weeks to tally what he does when given independent work. By completing these observations, the co-teachers can be better prepared for a meeting they have scheduled with the RTI team.

In addition to making decisions about whom to observe and for what purpose, co-teachers should also use a systematic method for recording their observations, whether they do so on class lists, seating charts, or more formal behavioral data forms. Whenever they can, they should take advantage of options for electronic data collection. They should also be sure that both professionals have a copy of the information gathered. When co-teachers meet, they then can discuss their observations and make instructional decisions based on what they have learned.

Learn More About
You can download and print this annotated list of several data collection tools that co-teachers have found useful for making decisions about grouping students, monitoring their learning, and addressing behavior concerns.

Station Teaching

Station teaching actively involves both educators in instruction, and it enables them to make a clear division of labor during co-teaching. The co-teachers divide the instructional content, and each takes responsibility for planning and teaching part of it. In a classroom where station teaching is used, students move from one station to another according to a predetermined schedule. A third station may be used for students to complete independent work assignments, to participate in peer tutoring, or to work under supervision if a student teacher, paraeducator, or another adult is available in the classroom. For example, in a third-grade classroom, one group of students is reviewing the concept of cause and effect with one of the teachers. Another group is working with the other teacher on comprehension activities related to a story read the previous day. In the third group, students are working with partners to edit their writing assignments. During the 50-minute period of time for this instruction, each student participates in each of the groups. In a high school civics class during an 85-minute block, one teacher works with students using the textbook to review the structure of American government; the second teacher discusses with students issues in an upcoming local election; and in the third group, students work independently on web reports on their state's representatives and senators.

Although station teaching requires that the teachers share responsibility for planning sufficiently to divide the instructional content, it has the advantage that each professional has separate responsibility for delivering instruction. And so this technique can be effective even when teachers have significantly different teaching styles or do not know each other well. In addition, students generally benefit from the lower teacher–pupil ratio, and teachers have more opportunity to embed specially designed instruction (e.g., a writing strategy) for targeted students as they instruct these small groups. Further, because in this approach each teacher instructs all of the students, albeit in different groups, the equal status of both the students and the teachers can be maximized so parity is clearly established.

To get the greatest benefit from station teaching, co-teachers may need to think carefully about how to divide instruction so that the order in which the curriculum is presented does not affect students' understanding. Material that is sequential cannot be presented using this approach. For example, in a social studies class, it would not work to have students in one group reading the chapter, students in a second group discussing the information, and students in a third group answering questions from the text: The group expected to write answers first, before reading or discussion, certainly would be at a disadvantage! In contrast, in a math class students participate in stations to review measures of central tendency; they work with their teachers on mean and median, and they complete an independent activity related to mode. The order in which students participate in each segment of instruction does not matter. Educators also need to estimate the amount of time required at each station; if one station takes much longer to complete than another, problems may arise.

Two common problems in using station teaching concern the amount of noise and movement that may occur during instruction. Some teachers may be bothered by having two teachers talking at the same time, particularly if one of the educators has a loud or distinctive voice. Co-teachers may also worry that having students move around the room seems disruptive. To effectively address such concerns, co-teachers can take several actions. If a student tends to have attention problems, that student might best be seated next to the teacher. With elementary and middle school students, co-teachers can make available sound-muffling headphones for students to use in the independent group when an individual assignment is given, or they can provide appropriate music for some students to listen to using their own earbuds. They can also provide desk carrels to help reduce visual distractions. Rearranging the classroom slightly—for example, by having the teachers back to back—may also help reduce the distracting sound of both teachers' voices.

If transitions are time consuming, instead of having students move from station to station, perhaps the teachers could move. Alternatively, the teachers could reward students for moving efficiently from station to station; experienced co-teachers report that transitions can be kept to approximately 30 seconds. Co-teachers also may also want to develop a set of signals to monitor time. For example, they might agree to use a timer to signal the end of a station. Of course, teachers also should ask for feedback from their teaching partners and periodically discuss topics such as these as part of their ongoing monitoring of their co-taught instruction.

Parallel Teaching

The first purpose of parallel teaching is to lower the teacher–student ratio. In this type of co-teaching, the teachers jointly plan the instruction, but each delivers it to a heterogeneous group comprised of half of the students in the class. The teachers do not exchange groups as in station teaching. This approach requires both that the teachers coordinate their efforts so that all students receive essentially the same instruction and that grouping decisions are based on maintaining diversity within each group. For example, in Mr. Harris and Ms. Brisky's history class, students are preparing for a unit exam. Mr. Harris has half of the students, including two students with learning disabilities and three English learners. Ms. Brisky has the other half of the group, which includes a student with autism and four students who are English learners. The teachers are discussing key concepts that they have decided students are unclear on and helping students go through a study guide. Simultaneously, Mr. Harris is reviewing with the students with learning disabilities a keyword strategy they have learned earlier in this unit to facilitate their memory of key battles of the Civil War. Their intent was to arrange the students so that each one had several opportunities to participate in discussion and to ask questions, so that the students receiving specialized instruction had the opportunity to review the strategy.

This type of parallel teaching often is appropriate for drill-and-practice activities, test reviews, topics needing an extended student discussion, or projects needing close teacher supervision. It enables all students to participate more in instructional conversations and gives especially shy students or those still learning English a smaller audience. However, parallel teaching can even be used for more creative teaching activities: Each co-teacher might take a particular point of view in presenting a topic or issue, orient students to that viewpoint, and then bring the students together later for large-group discussion. For example, as part of the history class, the co-teachers address current events. One time, Mr. Harris took the position that the United States was making a mistake in its actions regarding international trade and discussed this with half the students. Ms. Brisky adopted the opposite point of view with her group. When the students came together for large-group follow-up, the teachers were able to integrate information about understanding facts and opinions, the influence of the media on people's beliefs, and other related topics, as well as debate the issue at hand.

Learn More About
Watch portions of this video to see examples of the co-teaching approaches as implemented by general education and ESL teachers.
(http://www.youtube.com/watch?v=XNqMsMspbec&list=LLsZBWMSg3PXu3TKFbkriHdg&feature=mh_lolz)

In another type of example, parallel teaching facilitates tiering of instruction; that is, teaching all students the same core concepts, but differentiating practice. This strategy is common when co-teaching is part of response to intervention or when students' reading levels or knowledge of the content is exceptionally diverse. For example, co-teachers of a language arts class review similes and metaphors, and all students participate. However, the teachers then divide the students into two groups to read passages and identify similes and metaphors, with one group having more difficult reading material than the other.

Note that this approach cannot be used for initial core instruction unless both professionals can accurately teach the material and are comfortable doing so. Although seldom a serious concern in the primary grades, this can be a significant matter in intermediate grades and secondary schools, and it is a topic co-teachers should directly discuss. In terms of pragmatic issues, noise and activity levels may need to be monitored, as in station teaching. Also, as in station teaching, teachers need to pace instruction similarly.

To implement parallel teaching, teachers should begin by checking that they are both prepared to teach the assigned content. Especially in new co-teaching partnerships, co-teachers might want to use outlines, guiding questions, or notes to foster teaching consistency. Remember that if one group of students has significantly different instruction from the other, it will be difficult to make judgments about student mastery. Students also may complain that the disparity leads to unfairness during assessments. To address the issues of noise and distraction, elementary and middle school teachers may find that it works well to have the two student groups on the floor in opposite corners of the classroom, with desks or tables used as a sight and sound barrier. Noise and distraction are not as likely to be significant issues in secondary classrooms using this approach, but if they are, co-teachers might arrange the class to group students on opposite sides of the room, and they should consider sitting while teaching instead of standing in order to reduce how much their voices carry.

Learn More About
Would you like to review some lessons plans co-teachers have implemented? You can find examples on the web site Co-Teaching Connection.

Alternative Teaching

In nearly every classroom, co-teachers sometimes decide to select a small group of students to receive instruction that is different from that in which the large group is participating. For example, some students with learning and behavior disabilities require specially designed instruction in the form of pre-teaching, a strategy for organizing the rather complex material to be introduced. Other students who benefit from pre-teaching might include those with ADHD, those who need reassurance about their knowledge or skills, those learning English, and those for whom repetition is beneficial. Re-teaching instructional content is appropriate for students who did not understand concepts taught or for students who missed instruction because of absence. Sometimes an alternative group is useful for conducting a skills assessment. One additional example concerns enrichment: Students who already have mastered concepts being taught might work in a small group to extend their learning. Thus, in alternative teaching, one teacher works with a small group of students while the other instructs the large group in some content or activity that the small group can afford to miss.

Alternative teaching is a strategy for providing highly intensive instruction within the general education classroom. Further, this approach can also be used to ensure that all students in a class receive opportunities to interact with a teacher in a small group. If one or two students have serious behavior disorders that cause classroom disruptions, sometimes having them work in a small group—one that includes positive class models—can help them and possibly alleviate classroom disturbances.

The greatest risk in alternative teaching is that students with disabilities or other special needs may be stigmatized by being grouped repeatedly for pre-teaching or re-teaching even if other students are rotated through the small instructional group. A variation of this approach, in which one teacher is located at a table and announces that students seeking assistance may come to the table, can also cause problems. Particularly with older groups, the student most likely to come to work with the teacher is the one who is capable of doing the task but who craves adult attention or seeks reassurance. The student who possibly would not join the teacher is the student with a disability or who struggles academically who clearly needs assistance but is embarrassed to seek it in front of peers.

When co-teachers use alternative teaching, they first should be sure that each teacher sometimes takes responsibility for the small group. For example, sometimes re-teaching is best accomplished by the general education teacher, not the special educator or specialist. In addition, co-teachers might keep a record of which students were assigned to which small groups so that they ensure all students participate and no student is stigmatized. Of course, group composition and group membership should be fluid, with both factors varying depending on student need and planned small-group activity. One additional strategy is to adapt this approach: With most of the class working on a reading or writing assignment, both teachers can work with small groups on editing their reports; thus creating two alternative groups and eventually, but perhaps for varying lengths of time, call all students into the alternative groups.

Teaming

In teaming, both teachers are responsible for a lesson. They share the instruction of all students, whether that occurs in a large group, in monitoring students working independently, or in facilitating groups of students working on shared projects. For example, the teachers may lead a discussion by trading ideas with each other, or they may take on the roles of characters in a story as they act out a scene. One co-teacher may explain while the other demonstrates a concept or lab procedure; one may speak while the other models note-taking on a Smartboard, and so on. Both teachers may circulate around the room as students work on dioramas that illustrate a piece of poetry, asking questions to stimulate student discussion or to check comprehension. Teachers may role-play, debate, simulate conflict, and model appropriate question asking or summarizing.

Co-teachers who team frequently report that it results in a synergy that enhances student participation and invigorates the professionals, sometimes even prompting teachers to try innovative techniques and activities that they would not have tried teaching alone. They discuss how well it works when the teachers "click" and are able to have instructional conversations with each other and students. Some co-teachers consider teaming the most rewarding approach. This co-teaching approach also clearly communicates to students that both educators truly have equal status.

However, of the six co-teaching approaches, teaming requires the greatest level of mutual trust and commitment. If professionals are not comfortable working together in a classroom, attempting to team may communicate that discomfort to students. Teaming also requires that co-teachers mesh their teaching styles. If co-teachers are significantly different in their use of humor, their pacing, or their instructional format, the flow of the teaming often is not successful. Teachers may use different styles, but they should take care to complement each other.

Novice co-teachers should not feel obligated to attempt teaming. Although some do and are successful, for many this approach is too fluid and relies too much on teacher compatibility and flexibility for use in a new relationship. Similarly, if a special educator or specialist is co-teaching with a teacher who seems uncomfortable with a shared classroom, perhaps experiencing some of the situations described in Putting Ideas into Practice, this approach is probably not one to emphasize, at least at the outset. When teaming is implemented, co-teachers should check frequently to ensure that both are satisfied with their use of it and that it is having the impact of enhancing student learning.

One Teaching, One Assisting

A final and relatively simple approach for co-teaching is to have one teacher teaching while the other supports the instructional process. That is, one teacher maintains the primary role for managing the classroom and leading instruction while the other walks around the

PUTTING IDEAS INTO PRACTICE

Co-Teaching Dilemmas

Both novice and experienced co-teachers often have questions about the best ways to deal with dilemmas that occur during co-teaching. Here are a few common concerns and ideas for addressing them.

- My co-teacher is responsible for students with emotional disabilities. He is frequently called away from our co-teaching to deal with a student problem. What should we do?

In some schools, general education teachers genuinely believe that they cannot address student issues and that the special educator is the only one equipped to respond to students with emotional disabilities. Although it is prudent to call for the special educator if a student is having a crisis, it is sometimes helpful to talk with participating teachers about what constitutes a crisis and to explicitly outline how noncrisis problems should be handled (e.g., ignoring, asking for administrator help). Of course, administrators should also provide assistance in resolving this dilemma.

- When I enter the classroom as a specialist to co-teach, the general education teacher seems to think it is to release her for an extra preparation period. What should I do?

If a teacher repeatedly leaves the room or withdraws from instruction (e.g., grades papers) during co-teaching, the specialist should approach that person with words such as these: "I'm concerned that I've miscommunicated what co-teaching is about. It's very important for both of us to be here, actively working with students, for it to be successful." If this does not resolve the issue, the specialist should then enlist the assistance of a supervisor or administrator to settle the matter.

- The specialist with whom I work is most comfortable sitting at the back of the room, occasionally asking a question when he thinks students don't understand a concept or working with individual students on his roster. So, I do all the teaching. I also do all the planning, all the grading of assignments, and I'm the one accountable for testing outcomes. What should specialists do in a co-taught class? What are their responsibilities?

The best way to avoid this co-teaching problem is to discuss roles and responsibilities with your co-teacher—preferably before co-teaching ever begins. If expectations have been clarified before co-teaching is initiated, this issue is less likely to occur. Also, if co-teachers use the six approaches outlined in this chapter, along with the many variations of them, both teachers can and should have an active role in instruction. For some special educators and specialists, this response reflects discomfort with the curriculum content; for others, it may signal uncertainty about the co-teacher's receptivity to classroom partnerships. Although straightforward conversation may help, it may also be necessary to enlist the assistance of an administrator in clarifying classroom expectations, with that professional perhaps observing and giving feedback to co-teachers.

---

room to assist students who need redirection or who have questions about their schoolwork. For example, as Ms. Ramirez explains to students the process for substituting variables in systems of equations, Mr. Siler monitors all the students to be sure that they are correctly completing the examples on their papers. The teachers' goal is to be sure that all students, including those who have disabilities or other special needs, are accurately solving the problems and to address any student confusion as soon as it is detected.

This approach to co-teaching requires little joint planning, and so it makes co-teaching possible even when shared planning time is scarce. It also gives a role to professionals in situations in which they may not feel qualified to lead instruction (e.g., a special education teacher with an elementary education background and a K–12 special education license co-teaching in a high school geometry class for the first time).

However, one teaching, one assisting is also fraught with problems and should be used only occasionally. First, it becomes the sole or primary co-teaching approach in too many classrooms, particularly when planning time is scarce. The general education teacher usually takes the lead role, and the other educator becomes an "assistant." Unfortunately, this arrangement is a common one, particularly in secondary classrooms (Scruggs, Mastropieri, & McDuffie, 2007; Solis, Vaughn, Swanson, & McCulley, 2012). Not only does it deny an active teaching role to the special educator or specialist, but it also undermines that person's credibility, especially with older students. Second, a classroom in which one teacher continuously moves around the room during large-group instruction can be distracting to students. When professionals are walking around they can be a visual distraction, and when they whisper to individual students they may be an auditory distraction. In addition, when one teacher whispers to an individual student while the other teacher continues instruction, it is likely that the student will miss critical information and thus be confused or have gaps in learning. Finally, this co-teaching approach includes the risk of encouraging students to become dependent learners. When one teacher is always available to help on student demand, students who crave adult attention but who should be capable of doing assigned work may develop a habit of saying "I can't" in order to get extra attention and assistance. Co-teachers need to be very alert to this possibility. If they have students needing adult attention, they should give it—but not at the cost of a student's independent learning skills.

Educators can take advantage of the positive aspects of the one teaching, one assisting approach and avoid the negative aspects by limiting their use of it and ensuring that when it is used, each teacher leads instruction and each teacher takes the role of assisting. Further, co-teachers should use this approach only when it will not distract students from their learning and when no other co-teaching approach seems appropriate for the instructional situation (Friend, 2014).

APPLY YOUR KNOWLEDGE 7.2

Understanding these six basic approaches for arranging teachers and students in a shared classroom is just a beginning. As you experiment with co-teaching and share ideas with classmates or colleagues, you will find that many variations of each approach exist and that approaches can be combined to even better address student needs. For example, co-teachers might blend parallel and station teaching. They divide the class in half with each person responsible for the same instruction. But then each teacher divides her half of the class into two groups, spending half of the available instructional time with each while the other half completes an activity with a peer partner. In another example, if a paraeducator is assigned to a classroom along with a special educator, co-teachers might decide to arrange four stations, directing the paraeducator to reread the current literature with students at the fourth station. In a classroom with co-teachers and a student teacher, parallel teaching could occur with three groups instead of the usual two.

Most important, the co-teaching approaches demonstrate the importance of collaboration in co-teaching. In the next section, pragmatic and conceptual issues related to the professional relationships in co-teaching are presented to increase your readiness to implement this service delivery option.

Co-Teaching and Collaboration

We have identified co-teaching as a specific service delivery option that is based on collaboration. As you can see, however, co-teaching is not a synonym for collaboration. Like teaming, co-teaching is an activity that teachers may choose to engage in using a collaborative style of interaction. Some would argue that collaboration is more critical to co-teaching than to applications such as teaming because it involves an ongoing and intensive relationship between two or more professionals engaged in the essence of their responsibilities—teaching. We believe that co-teaching is optimized when a strong collaborative relationship exists; but we recognize that co-teaching can also exist, although in a significantly limited form, with nominal collaboration. In short, we agree with veteran co-teachers who tell us that in ideal situations, "Co-teaching is like a professional marriage."

Understanding the Co-Teaching Relationship

The most sophisticated types of co-teaching and the collaboration they require are not for everyone. The type of co-teaching and the level of collaboration in the relationship depend on the situation (e.g., Fenty et al., 2012). But they also depend on both the personal characteristics of the co-teachers and their skills in communication and collaboration (Conderman, 2011b; Van Hover, Hicks, & Sayeski, 2012), as well as the quality of the preservice preparation or professional development they received prior to co-teaching (e.g., Nichols, Dowdy, & Nichols, 2010).

Many aspects of co-teaching can be challenging—sometimes even threatening—to potential participants. This collaborative structure requires a willingness to change teaching styles and preferences, to work closely with another adult, to share responsibility, and to rely on another individual in order to perform tasks previously done alone. All of these factors can cause stress for teachers. Yet, what causes some teachers stress can be a source of excitement and motivation for others (Gürür & Uzuner, 2010; Ploessl et al., 2010).

Specific skills and personal characteristics can be associated with successful co-teachers. The most essential self-reported requirement is flexibility (Van Hover et al., 2012). Commitment to co-teaching and to the co-teaching relationship also is needed (Rytivaara & Kershner, 2012; Tannock, 2009). In addition, professionals generally concur that strong interpersonal skills—particularly problem-solving and decision-making skills—are essential for co-teachers (Forbes & Billet, 2012; Friend, 2007).

Co-teaching often is referred to as a professional marriage. How is this an apt metaphor? In what ways might it be considered inaccurate?

Learn More About
In this video, two early career co-teachers discuss the development of their strong positive working relationship, which they refer to as a professional marriage.
(https://www.youtube.com/watch?v=_pnxst7dkLk)

Another consideration for co-teachers is their broader background and culture. Just as stereotypes or other misunderstandings can undermine teacher–student and teacher–parent/family interactions, they can also affect co-teachers (Friend et al., 2010; Rytivaara, 2012). For example, co-teachers may wish to learn a little about each other's own school experiences and how they affect their teaching styles and preferences. Similarly, co-teachers may find they need to discuss the basis for their beliefs about disabilities. Perhaps one teacher has a sibling with a disability and has been strongly affected by this experience. Perhaps the other teacher was raised in a culture in which disabilities are seen as a challenge given by God or as a punishment to parents for a wrongdoing. Such conversations lead co-teachers to a much deeper understanding of each other's perceptions of students, expectations for them, and instructional approaches. To enhance collaboration, co-teachers should reflect on their own characteristics, experiences, and expectations and express a willingness to share those reflections with their co-teaching partners. The checklist in Figure 7.2 can provide a start for this type of discussion.

Diversity can directly affect co-teachers' relationships in other ways as well. A veteran teacher from a culture in which young people are expected to defer to elders may be affronted by a novice educator's direct and uninvited suggestions for changes in instruction. A male teacher from a culture in which women should defer to men's judgment likewise may find co-teaching difficult if the assigned partner is a female teacher who does not defer as the male teacher expects. Other cultural differences, including those related to language, beliefs about discipline, and classroom management, may enrich a co-taught class; but they also can become sources of stress that need discussion so that the goal of better educating students can remain the focus of co-teaching.

FIGURE 7.2 Checking your readiness for co-teaching.

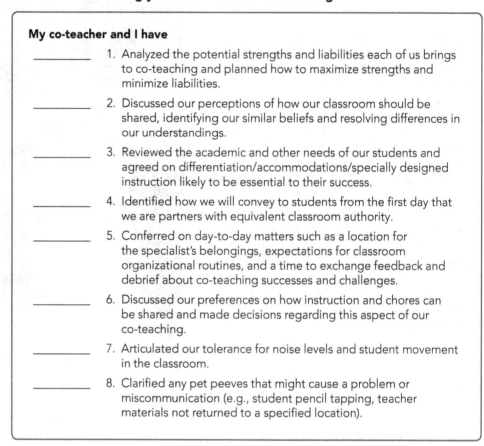

My co-teacher and I have

_____ 1. Analyzed the potential strengths and liabilities each of us brings to co-teaching and planned how to maximize strengths and minimize liabilities.

_____ 2. Discussed our perceptions of how our classroom should be shared, identifying our similar beliefs and resolving differences in our understandings.

_____ 3. Reviewed the academic and other needs of our students and agreed on differentiation/accommodations/specially designed instruction likely to be essential to their success.

_____ 4. Identified how we will convey to students from the first day that we are partners with equivalent classroom authority.

_____ 5. Conferred on day-to-day matters such as a location for the specialist's belongings, expectations for classroom organizational routines, and a time to exchange feedback and debrief about co-teaching successes and challenges.

_____ 6. Discussed our preferences on how instruction and chores can be shared and made decisions regarding this aspect of our co-teaching.

_____ 7. Articulated our tolerance for noise levels and student movement in the classroom.

_____ 8. Clarified any pet peeves that might cause a problem or miscommunication (e.g., student pencil tapping, teacher materials not returned to a specified location).

Finally, co-teachers should recognize that their relationship will evolve over time. At the beginning, both partners may be somewhat tentative, worried about miscommunicating or causing a problem in the classroom. As they implement co-teaching, they may experiment with co-teaching approaches and also find ways to blend their teaching styles and personalities. For example, with assistance from the principal, Ms. Shea, Ms. Smithson, and Mr. Ruiz can discuss their different perspectives and negotiate their classroom practices. Their second year of partnership thus should be quite different from the first because the teachers have addressed many of the important issues that arose when they began co-teaching. By a third year with the same partner (and often earlier), co-teachers typically have a solid foundation of understanding of their work and a high degree of trust with each other.

Maintaining Collaborative Relationships in Co-Teaching

Because effective co-teaching relies on teaching pairs having positive, collaborative working relationships, the skills discussed throughout this text, including those for effective communication (Chapter 2, Chapter 3, and Chapter 4) and the resolution of disagreements (Chapter 9), clearly are essential for co-teachers. In addition, though, numerous specific topics routinely require discussion by teaching partners. These topics are summarized on the following pages. What questions might you ask a co-teacher related to each of them in order to clarify your roles and strengthen your partnership?

Philosophy and Beliefs Understanding each other's general instructional beliefs, as well as those related to specific classroom matters, is essential to a strong co-teaching relationship. Examples of topics partners should explore include the following:

- The degree to which co-teachers agree on their expectations that all students learn the general curriculum
- Co-teachers' beliefs about the right of all students to experience success and how that occurs
- Teachers' roles in and responsibilities for student learning
- Alternative ways for students to demonstrate what they have learned (i.e., beyond traditional assignments or tests)
- Acceptable levels of noise and movement in the co-taught classroom
- Classroom practices each teacher finds particularly problematic (e.g., repeating directions, students calling out answers)

Parity Signals The nature of co-teaching requires that teaching partners have parity and recognize it. To that end, co-teachers find that determining in advance how they will ensure that students and others recognize their equal status helps them to build and maintain their relationship. Examples of parity signals include the following:

- Both teachers' names on the board or in the printed course schedule
- Both teachers' signatures on correspondence to parents
- Desk or storage space for both in the classroom
- An agreement on how to share responsibility for classroom management and teaching chores (e.g., writing objectives on the whiteboard, preparing materials for a science lab)
- Shared participation in teaching (e.g., approximately equal divided instructional talk, including a significant amount of simultaneous instruction)
- Shared responsibility for grading assignments and assigning report card grades

Co-teachers should spend a few minutes generating additional ideas about how they can communicate to students and parents, as well as remind each other, that co-teaching is about true partnership.

Classroom Routines Experienced teachers have preferred classroom routines. These include instructional routines (such as how students are expected to seek help and follow rules about formats for papers) and organizational routines (such as how students manage instructional materials and follow specific procedures at the beginning of the school day or a class period). Teachers rarely are aware of how many routines they have established. When co-teachers make this discovery, they face the task of agreeing to what routines they will employ in their shared classroom. It is not particularly important whose routines are adopted by the co-teachers, and in many instances the special educator or specialist defers to the preferences of the general educator, especially when co-teaching occurs only for a brief segment of time or single class period. However, both teachers should know what the routines are so that they can consistently communicate them to the students.

Discipline What each educator believes is acceptable behavior and what each views as appropriate responses to unacceptable student behavior should be discussed and, if necessary, negotiated early in the co-teaching relationship. One beginning discussion is to agree on the type of behavior management system to be used in the class: Is it based on students earning rewards? Or is it grounded in a series of increasingly negative consequences for behavior infractions? Because professionals tend to have stronger reactions to behavior transgressions than to academic difficulties, it is particularly important that co-teachers agree on how they will respond to students who violate classroom behavior expectations. For example, how critical is it to each teacher that students keep their heads up off their desks during instruction? May students wear hats in the classroom? Snack during instruction? In an elementary school, what are the consequences for saying something disrespectful to a peer or teacher? What is each co-teacher's perception of who should intervene when misbehavior occurs?

Feedback Knowing your own preferred way to receive feedback from a colleague is a significant first step in determining how you and a co-teacher will give each other feedback about your activities in a shared classroom. Some teachers prefer to hear their co-teachers' reaction to a co-taught lesson immediately after its completion. Others are more receptive if they have a break before debriefing. As important as *when* teachers give each other feedback is *how* they do so, a topic that was addressed in detail in Chapter 3. Note that an assumption is made regarding this topic—namely, that co-teachers need to review and discuss their shared efforts periodically in order to maintain their professional relationship. Feedback should include not only highlighting those aspects of instruction that are especially successful and satisfying but also planning alternatives to instructional dilemmas that occur.

Noise Teachers sometimes differ as significantly in their tolerance for classroom noise as they do in preferences for discipline strategies or classroom routines. Noise includes teacher talk as well as student-generated noise. Because three of the six co-teaching approaches have noise levels as potential drawbacks, co-teachers should reflect on and acknowledge their tolerance for noise and talk with one another about it. As part of their feedback, they may decide either to modify specific co-teaching approaches to reduce noise or to develop signals to indicate that noise is approaching an unacceptable level. Depending on students' needs, they may also need to monitor the impact of classroom noise on student attention.

Pet Peeves All teachers have a few items that are especially important to them in their professional activities or, more likely, that bother them a great deal. Pet peeves are specific triggers that could put relationships in jeopardy and negatively affect instruction. For some it may be interruptions during instruction; for others it may be the removal of supplies from their desks or failure to put materials away. Some co-teachers do not permit students to return to their lockers after they have come to class, and some are very particular in how assignments are graded. Pet peeves can be about student issues, classroom arrangements or materials, or professional preferences. The critical task for co-teachers is to identify their own and their co-teacher's pet peeves, discuss these openly, respect differences, and negotiate responses to them.

By carefully considering what co-teaching is and how it is enhanced through collaboration, co-teachers can select approaches that enable them to begin their partnership safely and nurture it until it encompasses a wide array of shared teaching activities that optimize student learning (Huber, 2005). By initially discussing and periodically reviewing topics that can influence co-teaching success, teachers can strengthen their professional relationship and identify and resolve challenges or disagreements before they threaten classroom practice and student outcomes.

Administrative Matters Related to Co-Teaching

This chapter has emphasized the key concepts related to co-teaching, the ways that co-teachers can arrange students and themselves to take full advantage of their differing expertise, and the types of topics and issues that co-teachers should discuss in order to build their partnerships. However, for co-teaching to be more than an interesting option that professionals use when they like each other and when their schedules permit, strong administrative support also must be present (Boscardin, Mainzer, & Kealy, 2011; Causton & Theoharis, 2013; Madigan & Schroth-Cavataio, 2011). If co-teaching is to be a feasible service delivery option, administrators should address issues such as the following:

- The need for shared co-teacher planning time
- Scheduling of teachers (e.g., the number of co-taught sections and the range of their assignments)
- Scheduling of students (e.g., classes with a heterogeneous mix of students rather than primarily students with learning and behavior challenges)
- A mechanism for problem solving when difficulties arise
- Communication of a standard in the school that any teacher might be asked to co-teach, not just the individuals who initially volunteered
- Resolution of personnel issues when one or both co-teachers are resistant or performing below expectations

Figure 7.3 outlines a number of other issues that administrators may need to address in order for co-teaching to be sustainable. Are there others that you would add to the list?

As a co-teacher, you may find that you have strong administrative support, or you may find that you are mostly left, with your colleagues, to figure out the intricacies of this service delivery option (e.g., Kamens, Susko, & Elliott, 2013). If you are in the former circumstance, you likely will know the specific goals for the program, you probably will receive professional development and be coached to refine your practices, and you will be expected to share your successes and address challenges that arise. If you are in the latter situation, you and your co-teacher may form a strong and effective partnership, but if challenges arise you may find that you are expected to find solutions without assistance. If you and your partner disagree about any aspect of shared teaching, you may need to draw on all the skills you have learned and will learn in this book so that you can find an acceptable solution.

Time for Planning

The most common concern among co-teachers is lack of common planning time (e.g., Murawski, 2012; Vannest & Hagan-Burke, 2010). However, before offering ideas for finding this precious time, here are some ideas to consider related to the amount of time co-teachers need and the effective use of any time that is available.

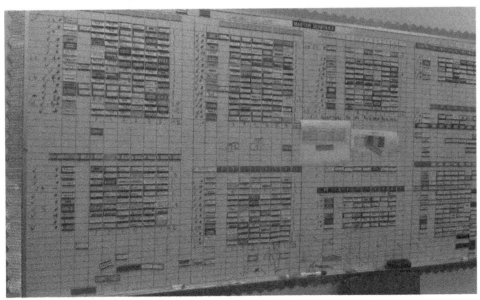

Administrators play a key role in supporting co-teachers by creating a feasible master schedule and arranging for common planning time.

FIGURE 7.3 **Practical issues in co-teaching.**

Issue	Impact
Caseloads/class sizes	When specialists have high caseloads, co-teaching becomes difficult because they may not be able to get to all classes where their students are learning, or they may have too many responsibilities that limit availability for co-teaching. When general education teachers have large class groups, it can be challenging to group students because of space issues and noise levels.
Distribution of students with special needs across classes/sections	If students with special needs are randomly placed in classes/sections, the special services provider may not be able to co-teach in all the classrooms where it is needed. If too many students with special needs are assigned to one class/section, the co-teachers may not be able to establish or maintain instructional momentum. Additionally, few student academic and behavior models may be available and student learning and behavior problems may result.
Co-teaching within the context of other service models	If some services (e.g., special education) are largely delivered through co-teaching while others (e.g., remedial reading, speech/language therapy) are largely delivered using pullout models, scheduling may be difficult, and general educators may become frustrated. School leaders should make decisions about service delivery models in the context of overall school improvement planning so that all services are coordinated and represent a single set of beliefs and priorities.
Teacher and specialist schedules	If specialists are asked to provide services in two or even more classes during any single instructional period, they are more likely to consult than co-teach, especially in secondary schools with traditional (as opposed to block) schedules. When general education teachers are asked to co-teach with more than one specialist (e.g., the special educator and the reading specialist), it can become burdensome to juggle the planning and multiple classroom partnerships.

First, time alone is seldom the problem in fostering co-teaching partnerships. Nearly all school professionals have a "relative yardstick" on the topic of time: No matter what their caseloads or other responsibilities, they find they need more time for collaboration. We hear nearly the same number of comments about time from special education teachers with caseloads of 8 students with high-incidence disabilities as from reading specialists with caseloads of 40 or more students; and we hear similar concerns from those with weekly shared planning time and those with virtually no shared planning time. Elementary teachers raise planning time issues as frequently as middle and high school teachers. This similarity is due partly to a perception of time and partly to the priorities educators give to their various tasks that influence the time available for collaboration.

Second, experienced co-teachers have raised a time issue specific to that endeavor but applicable to all collaborative work. When time is available, it needs to be used to its fullest advantage. Because many educators still spend much of the day working in isolation, when they have the opportunity to interact with another adult outside the presence of students, they sometimes want to chat about the day's events, vent concerns about school district and school issues, and socialize. Although such conversations serve a purpose, they need to be limited to ensure that time is available for collaboration. As you can easily understand, if chatting takes one-third of a planning session, it is difficult to justify a request for additional shared time.

Third, co-teachers should pay careful attention to the procedures they use for planning (Embury & Dinnesen, 2012; Howard & Potts, 2009). It is helpful to think of planning as a three-part process. The general education teacher does the first part prior to the meeting by thinking about and outlining upcoming curricular content and typical related instructional activities. The second part of the planning occurs with both the general education teacher and the special educator or specialist and should be based on data teachers have gathered. They jointly review the curricular material and decide how to arrange teachers and students in order to accomplish the learning goals. They also make judgments about topics or activities that are likely to be easily understood by students with special needs as well as those likely to be challenging. The special educator or specialist carries out the third part of the

E-PARTNERSHIPS

Electronic Planning for Co-Teachers

Co-teachers are finding that they need less face-to-face planning time when they take full advantage of electronic planning options that were not available just a few years ago. These include shared calendars and dedicated electronic teacher plan books.

Planning on a Shared Calendar

What type of electronic calendar do you use? Google (https://www.google.com/calendar)? Microsoft Outlook? These (and other) calendars have built-in features that facilitate co-teaching planning. First, one partner should create a calendar just for co-teaching (any user may have more than one calendar). That calendar is shared with his or her teaching partner. Then, the co-teaching time is entered as a daily appointment (e.g., Monday through Friday 9 a.m. until 10:30 a.m.). The general educator clicks on the daily appointment to open the description section and enters details of that day's lesson in the provided blank space. The programs also allow teachers to attach multiple files (e.g., presentation slides, rubrics, assignment sheets). If lessons are posted two or three days before they are scheduled, the special educator or specialist can then embed notes about specially designed instruction for particular students, prepare needed strategies or materials, make accommodations on attached files as needed, and so on.

Electronic Teacher Plan Books

Several electronic teacher plan books are available, and these have many features developed specifically to facilitate teacher planning. One example is Planbook (https://www.planbook.com/), available on a wide variety of devices and through all major operating systems, which offers a free trial version and an inexpensive version with full features. Planbook enables teachers to import into their lessons the standards they are addressing, it has options for bumping lessons to the next day in case plans are disrupted, and it allows users to transfer lesson plans from one school year to the next. Attachments can be added and the plans can be shared. As with calendars, co-teachers can post the general education lesson and specialists can add accommodations and specially designed instruction for identified students. Because this app was developed by teachers for teachers, it has many other features to streamline teachers' planning.

Shared calendars and electronic plan books are not the only options. Some teachers plan using a wiki (e.g., Google Groups), and others create a planning option for teachers embedded in a social learning platform such as Edmodo (Edmodo.com) or Schoology (schoology.com). The key for co-teachers is to explore electronic planning, stay abreast of this rapidly evolving domain, and take advantage of these options to streamline their shared work.

---

planning process after the joint meeting. This professional is responsible for preparing any significantly changed materials (e.g., simplified, shortened) or alternative materials that will be needed by students. This combination of shared planning and an appropriate division of the planning labor results in efficient and effective use of time, and it can also be applied to intervention assistance or RTI meetings, consultation, and other collaborative services.

Finally, the time required for planning for co-teaching decreases as professionals develop collaborative work relationships, learn specific interaction skills, and refine their time management skills. Eventually, shared planning can be met partly through the use of monthly, quarterly, or even summer meetings supplemented by brief planning meetings on an as-needed basis. And no matter how much common planning time co-teachers need and have, they should be sure to use electronic tools to stay in touch, a practice now common in most professions (e.g., Charles & Dickens, 2012) and detailed in E-Partnerships.

Options for Creating Shared Planning Time

The following three general ideas offer great promise for providing long-term solutions to creating planning time for co-teachers: using substitute teachers, arranging alternative types of class coverage, and employing instructional strategies that facilitate planning. These ideas also represent different points on a continuum of cost and need for administrative support. Additional planning time ideas are found in Putting Ideas into Practice.

Use of Substitutes One of the most common options for creating shared planning time is to employ substitute teachers to release professional staff members for collaboration. Many

PUTTING IDEAS INTO PRACTICE

Finding Common Planning Time

Although finding common planning time can be a significant barrier for co-teachers, here are several ways that principals and other administrators are creating such time:

- Teachers are scheduled for a shared lunch and preparation period. By scheduling these times back to back, teachers have a 90-minute block of common planning time, used once every other week for co-teaching planning.
- Teachers are paid once each month for two hours of planning outside the contract day. They are accountable for the time, submitting their common lesson plans.
- Co-teachers meet once or twice each month after school (sometimes with others from their school, sometimes with co-teaching colleagues from several schools). They are not paid for these sessions, but this planning time is applied toward required continuing professional development credit.
- On district professional development days, co-teachers are given a two-hour slot to use for planning.
- In an elementary school, students are dismissed 45 minutes early once each week so that all teachers can jointly plan, and some of this time is reserved for co-teachers. The instructional time lost that day is added to the other school days.
- In a high school, once each week the school day begins 45 minutes late, providing time for teacher planning, including planning for co-teaching. This option eliminates problems related to teachers' after-school obligations, including coaching and club or activity sponsorship.
- In an elementary school, grade-level teams are required to meet for 90 minutes each week to coordinate instruction. Specialists working at the grade level are released to attend at least 45 minutes of this time for co-teaching planning.
- In a large high school, a homeroom period has become part of the master schedule. During this 40-minute time period, students receive tutoring or enrichment. Although the school has 100 teachers, only 75 sections of homeroom exist. Teachers without assigned homeroom groups release other teachers on a regular rotation for co-teaching planning.

creative systems facilitate the maximum use of this type of resource. For example, in one district, a permanent substitute is employed and scheduled at each school one day every other week. If additional time is needed, a school administrator can request the time. In an elementary school in another district, a substitute is employed once each week. Specialists post a schedule of when they are available to meet with teachers. Teachers sign up to meet with the specialist with whom they work, and the substitute moves from class to class, releasing general education teachers as needed. In a high school, two substitutes are employed once a month. One substitute releases the special educator or specialist; the other releases general educators. Thus, in a single day these substitute teachers enable five or six sets of teaching partners to have planning time. Although funding for substitute teachers can be problematic, this is a relatively low-cost option for creating shared planning time.

Alternatives for Class Coverage If the challenges of finding funding for substitute teachers or recruiting qualified individuals for this type of role are insurmountable, you may still be able to arrange common planning time. You could suggest that one or more of the following ideas be tried:

- In some schools, principals and assistant principals cover classes to provide common planning time for co-teachers. Other licensed school staff members also could contribute a small amount of time for this purpose, including the counselor, school psychologist, literacy coach, media specialist, and others.
- In schools that employ paraeducators, co-teachers might be able to occasionally arrange for students to work on a project or assignment supervised by the paraeducator while the teachers confer in a quiet part of the classroom. This avoids the problem of inappropriately leaving a paraeducator with students during instruction and can create an opportunity for shared planning.

Learn More About
Learning how to collaboratively plan on a shared calendar is simple. This video will show you how to get started.
(http://www.youtube.com/watch?v=VAxsCOH-Z18)

- In a few schools, co-teachers cover for each other. That is, once per month one specialist misses co-teaching to cover the co-taught class of another specialist and his partner so that those teachers can plan. The following month the other specialist covers for the first pair of teachers. This type of strategy causes just a minor shift in services, but eliminates the need for external personnel.

Instructional Strategies That Facilitate Planning When release time is nonexistent, co-teachers can plan as part of instruction in a no-frills approach to creating time.

- In Ms. Mardell's English class, Ms. Lesson co-teaches four times each week. On these days, Ms. Mardell begins the class by explaining how each teacher will be working with students. This lets Ms. Lesson know how the class will operate and makes her feel more comfortable with co-teaching. It is not the same as having a shared planning time each week, but because Ms. Lesson co-teaches in four classrooms, that would not be possible anyway.
- Mr. Elliott uses a similar approach in his fourth-grade class. When Ms. Razmoski enters the room, he stops the instruction and asks students to review what they have covered so far. He then has the class explain what he had told them they would do when Ms. Razmoski arrived. This sound instructional practice—the mid-lesson review—helps students check their understanding and it also helps orient Ms. Razmoski.

When it comes to creating time for co-teaching planning, we endorse the idea that working together is a legitimate professional responsibility for educators. Equally important, though, is how time is used. You can find suggestions for the effective use of planning time in Putting Ideas into Practice.

PUTTING IDEAS INTO PRACTICE

Making the Most of Common Planning Time

Think about how late arrival, off-task conversations, interruptions from colleagues, and other distractions can reduce precious shared planning time. The following are tips for ensuring such time is used most effectively:

- Always have an agenda. The agenda reminds co-teachers of the many topics they need to discuss.
- Before the meeting, the general education teacher should prepare a brief overview of the curricular concepts to be addressed during the time the planning covers. For instance, what are the chapters, stories, concepts, and projects to be addressed? Reviewing this general plan is the first topic of the face-to-face meeting.
- Teachers next should review student data and briefly discuss the implications for addressing upcoming content, grouping students for instruction, and incorporating specially designed instruction. Which students are learning quickly? Which are struggling? What student behaviors are a source for concern?
- The specialist contributes the next component, summarizing information from IEPs or other individualized documents and raising options for incorporating specially designed instruction into upcoming lessons. Which vocabulary strategy would address the student's need to master the terms introduced in the upcoming unit? What method could be embedded into lessons to increase student reading fluency? Differentiation for all students may be part of this conversation, but the focus should be on meeting identified students' needs.
- The final topic the teachers should address, at least briefly, is their working relationship. Has anything occurred that troubles either teacher? What activities or strategies have been used that both teachers want to repeat? The goal is to celebrate their successes and resolve problems while they are minor.
- After the meeting, the special educator or specialist has the responsibility of preparing the specially designed instruction discussed during planning. What are the evidence-based writing strategies to use to enable the student to complete the research project? What techniques could be applied to improve student fluency in math computation? What approach could be used to teach students the social skills they need to work in problem-solving groups in the classroom?

This type of planning process maximizes the strengths of each teacher, provides an equitable division of labor, and focuses attention on both instruction and accommodation. Used consistently, it can help co-teachers be efficient and effective planners.

As you can see, common planning time is one co-teaching barrier that can be overcome. However, for this and other logistical matters, co-teachers usually rely on the leadership of their principals. Without a strong commitment from administrators, individual professionals are likely to have success, but co-teaching is not likely to be a widely implemented service option for students with special needs.

SUMMARY

- Co-teaching occurs when two or more professionals, each with a specific and complementary area of expertise, deliver substantive instruction to a diverse and blended group of students in a single classroom. They do this to address a wide range of diverse student needs, including specialized instruction, in general education settings.
- Successful co-teaching helps avoid the instructional fragmentation that can occur in more traditional services and the stigmatization that may occur when students leave classrooms; it also addresses the requirements that virtually all students access the same curriculum as their peers and that all students are taught core academic content by highly qualified teachers. It also can be effective in reducing the achievement gap between students with disabilities and their typical peers.
- Six basic co-teaching approaches are these: one teaching, one observing; station teaching; parallel teaching; alternative teaching; teaming; and one teaching, one assisting. Teachers select these based on student needs, their own preferences, curricular goals, and pragmatic issues such as space available and options for common planning.
- Although co-teaching and collaboration are not synonyms, the former is greatly enhanced with the latter. In fact, the most effective teaching partners carefully nurture their collaborative relationship by identifying potential issues and constructively discussing and resolving them.
- In order for co-teaching to become an integral part of the special education service delivery system, strong administrative support is needed, especially related to planning time, class composition, and scheduling.
- Co-teachers' most common concern relates to shared planning time, but with administrative support, creative use of resources, and determination, they can find ways to prepare instruction to meet their students' needs.

BACK TO THE CASE

1. If you were going to ask Ms. Smithson and Mr. Ruiz to review the defining characteristics of co-teaching, which do you think they should discuss in most depth? What is the basis for your answer?
2. In an effort to work on rebuilding the partnership, Ms. Smithson and Mr. Ruiz have been assigned to plan a week's worth of lessons using specific co-teaching approaches. Given their uncomfortable situation, which approaches do you recommend they implement? Why?
3. Based on class discussions and your knowledge of collaboration characteristics, communication skills, and problem solving, what do you think might be the fundamental problem the teachers are experiencing? What advice would you give to Ms. Shea for talking to the teachers about their co-teaching?

COLLABORATIVE ACTIVITIES

1. Discuss co-teaching with classmates whose schools use it as a service delivery option. How does their understanding of what co-teaching is, the students for whom it is a service delivery option (e.g., English language learners, students with disabilities, students receiving RTI interventions), the amount of co-teaching occurring, and the issues that are part of co-teaching compare with the information presented in this book? How might you reconcile any differences? Write a reflective essay on your own

perspectives of co-teaching as a role responsibility for your professional group (e.g., special education teacher, middle school math or science teacher, speech/language therapist).

2. With several classmates, prepare a chart that compares the group's views of one-teacher classrooms versus two-teacher classrooms on as many elements as you can identify. For example, in a one-teacher classroom lessons are taught from a single perspective; but in a two-teacher classroom teachers may share the same perspective, need to blend their perspectives, or decide to use differing perspectives as part of instruction. What does this exercise tell you about aspects of co-teaching that might come easily for you? That might pose a difficulty for you?

3. Suppose you are co-teaching and a problem related to your collaborative relationship arises. Either you are dissatisfied with how a discipline matter is being addressed, or your partner believes that your standards for students are too flexible. What skills would you need to air the issue and work to resolve it? How might the problem-solving process assist you in this situation? Role-play with a classmate how such an interaction might proceed.

4. If you are enrolled in a program that uses the term *co-teaching* to describe student teaching or an apprenticeship, complete an analysis of the similarities and differences between that experience and co-teaching as described in this chapter. What are the implications for you as a teacher candidate as well as for you as a teaching partner once you complete your professional preparation?

5. Planning time is the most commonly mentioned challenge to effective co-teaching. How much planning time do you think co-teachers should have? Why? What are the several strategies for getting the most out of any planning time that is arranged? What do you think co-teachers should do if they do not have any scheduled planning time?

CHECK YOUR UNDERSTANDING

Click here to gauge your understanding of this chapter's essential concepts.

8 Consultation, Coaching, and Mentoring

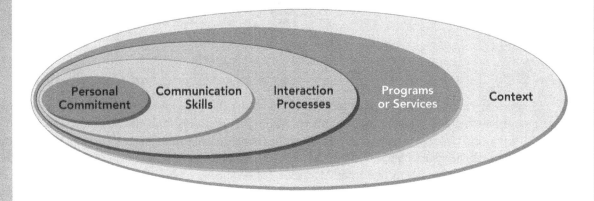

CONNECTIONS

Similar to Chapter 6 on teaming and Chapter 7 on co-teaching, Chapter 8 explores specific approaches to providing student support that emphasize collaboration. This chapter uses the introductory information about collaboration contained in Chapter 1 to examine the definition and characteristics of consultation, coaching, and mentoring; provide examples of each across a variety of school roles and contexts; and relate each of these approaches to collaboration. This chapter also provides additional opportunities to apply the problem-solving process that was outlined in Chapter 5, and it relies on the communication skills you learned in Chapters 2, 3, and 4. Finally, consultation, coaching, and mentoring are applications in which the skills for addressing difficult interactions, found in Chapter 9, sometimes may be needed.

LEARNING OUTCOMES

After reading this chapter you will be able to:

1. Define the term *consultation*, outline the characteristics of consulting in educational settings, explain a rationale for consultation's use in schools, and analyze when specific consultation models may be appropriately implemented to support students with special needs.
2. Define the term *coaching*, outline the characteristics of coaching in educational settings and explain a rationale for use, and analyze the appropriate use of coaching for improving student outcomes.
3. Define the term *mentoring*, outline the characteristics of mentoring in educational settings and explain a rationale for its use, and analyze the role of mentoring in the development of professional knowledge and skills.
4. Evaluate how consultation, coaching, and mentoring can be affected by the quality of the professional relationship, cultural differences, the need to preserve confidentiality, and practical matters such as time allocated for these indirect services.

A CASE FOR COLLABORATION

An Early Career Teacher's Experiences with Coaching and Consultation

Jessica Svoboda is a second-year teacher and knows she still has a lot to learn about effectively meeting her seventh-grade students' learning needs. As part of her professional development plan for this year, her principal directed that she participate in instructional coaching and, because her students include two with significant behavior problems, that she also work with the behavior specialist. The coach, Ms. Delacruz, met with her to discuss her teaching. She asked Ms. Svoboda how she wanted to refine her skills and how she would know that her skills had increased. She also asked Ms. Svoboda to be thinking about the relationship between particular teaching skills and the potential for improved student outcomes. As part of this process, Ms. Svoboda indicated that her greatest concern related to structuring her lessons, including transitioning from the previous day's work, and proceeding in a logical manner so that students could easily follow along. Ms. Delacruz then observed Ms. Svoboda's second-period class, taking extensive notes on the structure of the lesson. During Ms. Svoboda's preparation period, Ms. Delacruz met with her and shared the notes, helping her to analyze which parts of the lesson were clear and which could be improved. She offered to come to Ms. Svoboda's class the following week to model the beginning of a lesson.

Ms. Svoboda's interactions with the behavior specialist, Mr. Huber, are a bit different. He offers consultation to Ms. Svoboda concerning the students' behavior. For example, after Ms. Svoboda described her perception of the behaviors, he completed a classroom observation and discussed the data with her. Based on those data and the student needs they identified, Ms. Svoboda's classroom structures, and her receptivity to different types of behavior interventions, Mr. Huber worked with her to design a behavior plan for each student. He demonstrated how she could quickly gather data to see if the plans were working, and he met with her after two weeks to assess their implementation and effectiveness. When Ms. Svoboda shared that the plans were too complicated to follow consistently, he assisted her to adapt the plans, which made them more feasible and effective, leading to improved student behaviors and satisfaction for Ms. Svoboda that she created these positive changes.

Introduction

Teachers used to have few supports. Once they completed their professional preparation programs and obtained licensure, they were expected to have the knowledge and skills to address nearly any situation that arose in their classrooms. A principal or other supervisor might provide feedback as part of an evaluation process, but if teachers had questions or concerns, they mostly collaborated informally, asking colleagues for assistance.

Today it is different. When teachers face particularly complex situations or when their best efforts to meet student needs are not successful, they may request assistance from a consultant who problem solves with them to address the matter. As new knowledge and skills are expected of teachers, instructional coaching is often available as an integral component of professional development, as Ms. Svoboda, described in the introductory case study, learned. In addition, new teachers or those struggling in their jobs may be assigned a mentor to help guide their practice.

These supports—consultation, instructional coaching, and mentoring—are the focus of this chapter. All are implemented using elements of collaboration, and as a professional you may be either the recipient of such services or possibly the provider of them.

Consultation

Consultation has long been recognized as a way to provide support for students by working with teachers. For example, in the 1960s school psychologists acknowledged that they were too few in number to meet directly with all the students who should access their services; therefore, they began shifting their role responsibilities to consult with teachers, who then implemented in their classrooms the ideas that were generated during a structured problem-solving process (Tractman, 1961). Similarly, as the idea of mainstreaming grew in the late 1960s and early 1970s, special education teachers at times also assumed consulting roles (McKenzie, 1972). Their purpose was to provide assistance to general education teachers whose class groups included students with disabilities. They met with teachers to problem solve about needed classroom interventions and to troubleshoot with teachers when challenges arose, but they generally did not directly teach students.

With the emphasis in today's schools on curriculum access and accountability for all students' learning, consultation continues to be a service option used by school psychologists, reading and math specialists, ESL teachers, speech/language therapists, counselors, occupational therapists, early childhood educators, special education teachers, and other professionals (e.g., Butera & Martínez, 2014; Nellis, Sickman, Newman, & Harman, 2014; Newell, 2010; Wei, Wagner, Christiano, Shattuck, & Yu, 2014). For many of these professionals, consultation is just one role of several that they assume in providing support to students; for others, consultation is their primary job responsibility.

Because consultation has been used in schools for many decades, much has been written about it, and many definitions of the term have been offered. Some classic definitions have stressed that consultation is expertise offered by a counselor or psychologist to teachers to address student problems (Parker, 1975). Others have offered a more egalitarian view in which consultation occurs between any two professionals, one of whom has particular expertise to address the problem at hand (Caplan, 1970). More recent definitions have contributed the concepts that consultation is a voluntary and nonsupervisory interaction between individuals and that it is a specialized form of problem solving (Frank & Kratochwill, 2014; Rosenfield, 2013).

From our perspective, key elements of these definitions, as well as those proposed by many others (e.g., Brown, Pryzwansky, & Schulte, 2011; Dougherty, 2014; Kampwirth & Powers, 2015), contribute to a contemporary understanding of consultation. The definition of *consultation* can be summarized as follows:

> School consultation is a voluntary process in which one professional assists another to address a problem concerning a third party.

Notice that this definition implies that at any point in time, a professional could be providing consultation or receiving it. It further uses the broad phrase "third party" to clarify that school consultation often occurs regarding students, but that a principal, for example, might consult with an expert regarding a teacher. In this case, the third party would be the teacher.

Characteristics of Consultation

Of course, being familiar with a definition of consultation is only a beginning. In order to use consultation effectively, it is also important to know more about its nature. The characteristics of school consultation have been extensively described in the literature for school psychology, counseling psychology, special education, and other specialty areas in education (e.g., Dougherty, 2014; Kampwirth & Powers, 2015; Thornberg, 2014). Its most essential characteristics are discussed next.

Triadic and Indirect Relationship Although consultation in other disciplines (e.g., law, business, and medicine) may occur between two individuals and not relate immediately to a third party, in schools it typically is triadic, involving three parties and with an indirect relationship between the consultant and the client. The consultant (special services provider, specialist, or colleague) and the consultee (an individual teacher, special services provider, parent, administrator, or a group of professionals or parents) together design services that the consultee provides to the client (most often a student but, as noted above, could be a teacher or another individual). Generally, the client is not a direct participant in the interaction but is the beneficiary of the process. For example, a reading specialist who acts as a consultant might meet with a teacher to plan how the teacher could use a set of specific strategies to improve students' reading comprehension. Because the reading specialist does not interact with students, her relationship with them is indirect. Similarly, a consultant supporting students through the use of assistive technology might meet with a special education teacher, a general education teacher, the speech/language therapist, and a parent to discuss the types of devices that might enhance students' participation in the classroom and the software that could be used to help them acquire critical academic skills. With the exception of observing and possibly demonstrating how to use a new piece of equipment, the consultant's interactions are entirely with adults, yet they occur for the benefit of students.

Voluntariness A consultee may be puzzled or troubled by a situation and seek the assistance of a consultant, or a consultant may notice some difficulty and offer insight to a consultee for remedying a problem. In each case, both the consultant and the consultee have the prerogative of entering or terminating the relationship at any time. This characteristic of voluntariness establishes the principle that consultation cannot be a coerced process (Brown et al., 2011). Both professionals agree to participate, but they retain the option of withdrawing if they choose. For example, Mr. Caldwell, a middle school social studies teacher, might ask Ms. Goldstein, a school counselor, to meet with him because he has concerns about Craig's sudden immature behavior in class, a problem that he thinks might be related to Craig's parents' recent divorce and family upheaval. Ms. Goldstein agrees to meet to problem solve about the issue, she follows up two weeks later to see whether the strategies they planned were effective, and she raises the option of offering to Craig that he chat with her. Conversely, Ms. Goldstein might have heard about Craig's family situation and approached Mr. Caldwell and the rest of his team about it; the team might have welcomed the conversation she initiated, and felt relieved to discuss and address the problem. It is important to note, however, that the nature of consultation may change when the consultant rather than the consultee initiates the process; this form of consultation sometimes might feel to the consultee as though it is not truly voluntary.

Expert and Directional Relationship Most professionals who study consultation emphasize that consultants and consultees mutually influence each other and that consultants do not have authority over consultees. They also recommend that consultants be facilitative, empathic, and collegial. However, regardless of its democratic nature, the consulting relationship exists only because it is perceived that the consultee, not the consultant, has a work-related problem. Thus, the primary reason for the interaction is the consultee's perception of a problem that cannot be solved without another's expertise. In fact, it is difficult to imagine why consultees would participate in consultation unless they were relatively certain a consultant had expert knowledge and could provide insight on the matters they had been unable to improve themselves. In schools, even when both the consultant and the consultee have a significant interest in the student, the assumption for consultation is still that the general education teacher or whoever has primary daily teaching responsibility for the student (e.g., the special education teacher for a student who receives core instruction in a separate setting) is the direct beneficiary of consulting assistance.

Problem-Solving Process with Steps or Stages In Chapter 5, you learned that much collaboration in education centers on shared problem solving, and this point was illustrated in Chapter 6 as you learned about teaming. Consultation is yet another example of a specialized problem-solving process (Newell, 2010), one that gives particular attention to the beginning and end of the process. The number of steps in the consultation process varies according to the author outlining them, but they typically include the following:

- *Entry*, the physical and psychological beginning of a series of interactions and the establishment of trust and respect
- *Problem identification*, the establishment of a goal for the consultative interactions
- *Planning*, the decisions about how to reach the intended goal
- *Implementation*, the carrying out of the planned interventions
- *Evaluation*, the determination of intervention success
- *Exit*, the termination of the consulting relationship as related to the problem at hand

Some evidence suggests that consultants do not follow these steps in a rigid manner; the specific sequence followed depends on the situation (Erchul & Martens, 1997). Thus, knowing the precise steps or stages is not as critical as recognizing that consultation is a process comprised of such steps.

Learn More About
This video provides a brief description of the consulting process as implemented with parents, giving examples of what occurs at each step of the process.

(https://www.youtube.com/watch?v=CS5vJ3AmUzQ)

The process of consulting might look like this: A school psychologist meets with a middle school team to discuss Ernie, an eighth grader who is often absent, who is refusing to attempt assignments, and who is becoming disruptive in class. At that first meeting, the psychologist asks a few questions (e.g., In what areas does Ernie excel? How have Ernie's behaviors and patterns of learning changed since the beginning of the year?), but he mostly listens to the teachers discuss the problems they are encountering concerning Ernie. The group also jokes about its need for sweets to cope with stress and arranges for someone to stop at the local doughnut shop prior to the next session. At the second meeting, the psychologist and teachers more specifically identify the problems they will address, and they generate alternative solutions for them, weighing the pros and cons of each solution. Ernie's teachers agree to try several interventions for the next three weeks. After that time, the entire group meets (and another volunteer provides breakfast) to evaluate the effectiveness of the interventions. Some changes are made, and the psychologist clarifies that his role is essentially finished, but that he will check back with the group in approximately four weeks. The process, from entry to exit, has been carried out. If Ernie is receiving special education services through consultation, a series of problem-solving cycles would occur during the course of the school year. If the interventions for Ernie were not successful, the team might decide that he should be brought to the attention of the school's intervention team so that either a response to intervention (RTI) process could begin or the steps required for formal consideration of the need for possible special education could be undertaken.

Shared but Differentiated Responsibilities and Accountability Consultants and consultees do not share the same responsibility and accountability. If you are a consultant, your primary responsibility and areas of accountability are to ensure that the consulting process is appropriately followed and to offer specific and feasible assistance responsive to the consultee's needs. Because consultants do not control consultees' decisions about whether to accept and implement specific strategies, ultimately they cannot be accountable for the success or failure of the consultation outcomes if they have appropriately carried out their part of the process. On the other hand, if you are a consultee, you have the responsibility to participate in good faith in the consultation process and to seriously

Although consultation is most often a role for school psychologists or counselors, other professionals—including social workers, occupational and physical therapists, speech/language therapists, and teachers—also may have consulting responsibilities.

PUTTING IDEAS INTO PRACTICE

Fidelity of Implementation: A Key to Consultation Effectiveness

A unique aspect of consultation is that the consultant generally cannot control whether the consultee implements the planned intervention. This concept is called *fidelity of implementation*, or *treatment integrity*. It has two parts: (1) accuracy, that is, correctly implementing the agreed-upon intervention; and (2) consistency, that is, implementing the intervention across time as planned. Fidelity of implementation directly affects the effectiveness of consultation (McKenney, Waldron, & Conroy, 2013). For example, Wood, Umbreit, Liaupsin, and Gresham (2007) were able to document that an intervention designed specifically to address disruptive behaviors of a third grader (e.g., yelling, slamming his desk into classmates' desks) was effective when it was implemented with fidelity, but that the teacher sometimes neglected to accurately use the intervention. Without checking for fidelity of implementation, the consultant might have concluded that the overall intervention was not effective because the data on the student's behavior varied significantly. Here are ways that fidelity of implementation can be monitored:

- **Self-report.** You might list each part of the intervention you planned and then ask teachers to indicate on which days of the week each was implemented.
- **Permanent product.** If the intervention includes a concrete artifact (e.g., a data chart or student work), this information can help to establish fidelity.
- **Interview.** The consultant might discuss with the consultee the intervention and how it is being implemented. Skills for interviewing were addressed in detail in Chapter 4.
- **Observation.** Depending on the consultant's role, she may be able to observe the teacher using the intervention and judge treatment integrity on that basis, discussing the observation with the teacher.

How might fidelity of implementation issues affect you as a consultant? What might be the impact related to the programs and services discussed elsewhere in this chapter, including coaching and mentoring?

consider the assistance being offered. If you agree to use a strategy, you are responsible for doing so appropriately. This concept of *treatment integrity*, also referred to as *fidelity of implementation*—that is, the consistent implementation of strategies developed during the consultation process and carried out by a consultee—is essential (Frey, Sims, & Alvarez, 2013; Sanetti, Kratochwill, & Long, 2013), a point stressed in Putting Ideas into Practice. If consultees do not implement agreed-upon interventions, the effectiveness of consultation cannot be assessed. Finally, a consultee's accountability includes gathering data and making judgments about whether the problem has been resolved, or whether another intervention is needed and desired.

The characteristics of consultation can be identified whether the professional in the consulting role is a school psychologist, a counselor, a speech/language therapist, a reading or other subject-matter specialist, or a special education teacher. If you look back at the case that opened this chapter, which of the characteristics can you find examples of in Ms. Svoboda's work with Mr. Huber? How might the characteristics apply in a slightly different way to a reading specialist? To other professionals?

Rationale for and Benefits of Consultation

As with the other services discussed in this text, consultation is, first, a viable option for successfully educating students with disabilities or other special needs. Thus, when consultation is implemented, it should be designed to benefit such students. For example, some students with individualized education programs (IEPs) are entitled to supports, but they do not need the amount or intensity of service offered through co-teaching or instruction in a separate setting, or they need it in only certain domains (Eisenman, Pleet, Wandry, & McGinley, 2011). In such cases, consultation may be an appropriate service or part of a package of services. Consultation also might represent a transition strategy: If a student has made tremendous progress during elementary school, so much so that the student's eligibility for special services is marginal at best, the team might decide to send the student to middle school with consultative services instead of direct services. Consultation is provided as a means of helping the student move from elementary to middle school. In this case, it might also be a strategy for assisting the student and family to transition out of special education programs and services. A third example of the use of consultation relates to a different type of transition, that from an intensive services in a separate location (e.g., hospital or residential facility) back to school or even from school to school (e.g., Aronson & Perkins, 2013). For example, a transition specialist may meet with a student and her family (and other team members) to discuss opportunities for post-school education or employment; the student and family decide which options to pursue. Alternatively, a military family with a child with a disability may take advantage of consulting services established to facilitate the child's move from one school to another. Taking these various applications of consultation together, then, you can see that the overall rationale for consultation is that it comprises a low-intensity service that can be used to support students in a variety of ways.

Consultation, however, has many other benefits. For example, it can be a low-cost and efficient means by which students with special needs who do not have disabilities (e.g., at-risk learners, students in need because of a life event, such as a parent in the military being deployed overseas) can receive focused attention by professional staff. That is, a school psychologist may have time to arrange three meetings with a teacher who is concerned about a student, even though the psychologist could not justify working with that student directly over time. Similarly, Mr. Johns, an early career teacher, might seek help from the district literacy specialist for ideas on incorporating writing into his biology class.

In addition to providing a limited type of service to students at risk, consultation often plays a prevention role. If a general education teacher has a student with serious behavior issues, he or she can work with a psychologist to assist the student. As a team, they may be able to prevent the problems from becoming so serious that consideration for special education is needed (e.g., McKenney et al., 2013). Likewise, a speech/language therapist might assist a first-grade teacher in designing language development lessons to help several students, thus eliminating the need for them to be referred for formal services. Students who are entitled to special education or other services should receive them, but consultation can prevent some students from ever needing such high levels of support. One of the clearest uses of consultation as a preventive strategy can occur as part of RTI, the topic of Putting Ideas into Practice.

PUTTING IDEAS INTO PRACTICE

Response to Intervention Through Consultation

In some RTI models, consultation is central. For example, in an approach called *instructional consultation* (e.g., Berger et al., 2014), a team is charged with designing and evaluating the effectiveness of interventions for struggling students. However, the teacher is not a direct member of the team. Instead, this general procedure is followed:

- A teacher who is concerned about a student communicates with the team leader.
- The leader assigns one team member to meet with the teacher to learn more about the problem.
- If the informal conversation did not resolve the matter or result in specific ideas for the teacher to implement, the person who communicated with the teacher assumes the role of consultant to that teacher, taking the teacher's concerns to the team, participating with the team in understanding the concern and generating ideas for resolving it, transmitting those ideas to the teacher, monitoring their implementation, and evaluating their effectiveness.
- Other teachers with concerns about students are assigned to other team members, depending on the issue of concern and team members' expertise.

This model for implementing RTI provides a personalized liaison for the general education teacher, a relationship that exists for the duration of the process; and it distributes tasks among team members. It also eliminates the negative reactions that sometimes occur when teachers perceive other team approaches as a "them-against-me" arrangement. What other advantages might this approach have? Disadvantages?

Yet another benefit of consultation concerns professional development. When teachers seek assistance from consultants, one common incidental outcome is an increase in their knowledge and skills. For example, when Ms. Vogt asks Ms. Denton to observe DeWayne, a student with significant attention problems, and to work with her to help him be more successful in the classroom, Ms. Denton introduces strategies for active student participation. Thus, Ms. Vogt learns how to implement "One Say, All Say"—that is, having all students repeat the answer given by one student. This technique benefits DeWayne, but it also helps other students to focus attention and participate in lessons. This professional development aspect of consultation can be enhanced when consultants specifically point out to consultees how to apply the ideas generated for one student to other students and situations.

When the benefits of consultation are considered along with its rationale, you can view consultation as an alternative for meeting a wide variety of student needs and enhancing the strategies in consultees' repertoires by efficiently deploying the professional resources in a school. In today's schools, with students with IEPs in general education settings and many students who are at risk for failure commanding educators' attention, the value of consultation is clear. For example, recall the earlier discussion of Ernie and how the psychologist met with the middle school team. By doing this, all the teachers benefited from his expertise and were able to coordinate their intervention efforts. The psychologist's time investment was fairly limited, but the positive impact was significant.

Consultation Models

Knowing the definition and characteristics of consultation, along with the rationale for its being part of your school's services, sets the stage for the next level of specificity—exploring models through which consultation may be practiced. Although there is little variation in the general consultation process, the practice of consultation is based on theoretical perspectives that have led to the development of several distinct consultation models (Kampwirth & Powers, 2015; Ocasio, Alst, Koivunen, Huang, & Allegra, 2014; Sabatino, 2014). These models prescribe consultants' orientation and the assumptions that undergird their interactions with consultees. They also dictate the types of interventions consultants are likely to use. Two models that are particularly applicable to schools—behavioral consultation and clinical consultation—are explored in the following sections.

Behavioral Consultation Behavioral consultation is the most frequently used type of consultation in schools, employed by special education teachers, school psychologists, occupational therapists, autism specialists, and others (DiGennaro Reed & Jenkins, 2013). Behavioral consultants rely on several assumptions to guide their practice (Andersen et al., 2010). First, they themselves must have a thorough understanding of behavioral principles and practices and be able to apply them to their consultees. They also must ensure that consultees have either similar understanding or enough understanding of those principles to carry out behavioral interventions in a systematic way (e.g., Bear, 2013). Second, behavioral consultants presume that the consultee controls reinforcers that will be effective with the client or student. That is, teachers must have rewards or consequences that will affect student actions. Third, consultants using this model believe that data collection is not only important but also essential, and they stress data-based decision making (e.g., Dufrene, Lestremau, & Zoder-Martell, 2014). A Basis in Research presents an example of a study using behavioral consultation.

Procedure Of all the consultation models described in the professional literature, behavioral consultation has the most clearly defined steps or stages, which closely resemble both the general problem-solving process described in Chapter 5 as well as the consultation process outlined at the beginning of this chapter. These are the steps:

1. *Problem identification.* This step involves obtaining a description of the problem and determining how to gather information to confirm its existence and character.

A BASIS IN RESEARCH
Demonstrating the Effectiveness of Direct Behavioral Consultation

How effective is consultation? It depends on several key factors, including the knowledge and skill of the consultant, the receptivity of the consultee, consistency in implementation of the intervention, and the quality of the relationship established between participants. Here is an example of effective consultation having a positive impact on teacher behavior and student outcomes:

- Two teachers were the participants in this study, one with 25 years and one with 5 years of experience. Both teachers taught in alternative elementary classrooms (one with seven students, one with nine students) for students with significant behavior problems (disruptive behavior, dangerous behavior); most of the students had IEPs. The teachers had been identified as not consistently giving students specific verbal praise (e.g., John, you wrote four sentences for your paragraph; that's exactly what you were supposed to do. Great job!)

- First, in a 30-minute session that included the opportunity to ask questions, the teachers were taught about giving direct verbal praise, and they practiced this skill and received feedback on their use of it. Next, a consultant observed each teacher to determine how often they praised students and how often students displayed disruption behavior. In the next phase of the study, the consultant provided prompts to the teachers, that is, told them (using a receiver worn in the teacher's ear) exactly what to say to students exhibiting appropriate behavior. For one teacher, this intervention was sufficient. For the other teacher, the consultant also provided performance feedback, showing the teacher data about her use of verbal praise.

- The results of this study demonstrated that both teachers increased their use of verbal praise. At the same time, students' disruptive behavior declined significantly. The authors concluded the report of this study by commenting on the importance of consultation that includes direct instruction on targeted skills as a way to ensure that teachers implement interventions with accuracy and consistency.

2. *Problem analysis.* This step is closely related to the first. The consultant directs the consultee on how to gather detailed and objective information about the problem so that the gap between the current situation and an acceptable situation is identified and a strategy for addressing it can be devised.
3. *Intervention.* At this step, the consultant and the consultee plan a behavioral strategy to address the problem and positively affect the client, and they clarify each professional's responsibilities related to the intervention. For example, the teacher consultee might agree to provide a daily reward of 10 minutes of instructional computer time each day when the student has attempted all work without complaint during the class. The consultant might agree to write out the details of the agreement and to participate in introducing the plan to the student. During this step, the consultee carries out the plan with input as needed from the consultant.
4. *Evaluation.* Eventually, the final behavioral consultation step is reached. The consultant and the consultee use the data the consultee has been collecting to determine whether the strategy has had the desired impact. Based on what they find, they may choose to conclude the consultation, make changes in the strategy and continue, or begin again (Kampwirth & Powers, 2015).

Although the fundamental steps of behavioral consultation are very similar to the generic problem-solving steps that professionals carry out in team meetings, co-teaching planning, and informal interactions with colleagues, their uniqueness lies in their reliance on the principles of behaviorism—for example, describing problems in observable terms, using specific reinforcers applied to both the consultee and the client, using data to monitor progress, and employing a highly analytic approach to the entire process (Coffee & Kratochwill, 2013). Have you completed course work in behavior management? If so, you undoubtedly have learned the principles of behaviorism that would make it possible for you to offer this type of consultation assistance to general education teachers expressing concern about students with academic or social behavior problems.

Behavioral consultation sometimes occurs within special education as well. For example, if you teach a student with significant autism, you may work closely with an autism specialist or behavior specialist to find interventions that will help address student behaviors and social skills. Similarly, if you teach students with serious emotional disabilities, a consultant may assist you in designing therapeutic interventions. In what other types of situations—in special education or in general education—do you think behavior consultation would be most helpful?

Over the past several years, a new variation of behavioral consultation has emerged, and it represents a significant refinement of the model. In *conjoint behavioral consultation*, specialists, general education and special education teachers, and parents/families work closely together to design, implement, and evaluate interventions to improve student learning and behavior (Sheridan, Clarke, & Ransom, 2014). More than traditional behavioral consultation, this variation strongly emphasizes a collaborative approach and views all participants as contributors as well as recipients. With this emphasis, the key adults in a child's life can coordinate their efforts to assist the child. Research suggests that this model is perceived as being acceptable and effective by teachers and parents, and it is particularly valuable for increasing parent involvement in the child's education and building positive school–home relationships (e.g., Clarke, Sheridan, & Woods, 2014).

Clinical Consultation Clinical consultation is a diagnostic model that traditionally has been used by school and counseling psychologists, diagnosticians, speech/language specialists, and, to a lesser degree, by social workers, occupational and physical therapists, and special educators. In clinical consultation, the consultant is concerned with accurately identifying or diagnosing a client's problem and prescribing strategies for resolving it (Sabatino, 2014). Clinical consultants' first consideration is that the source of the problem generally is in the client, not the consultee. For example, if a teacher asked a behavior specialist for help in deciding how to respond to a student whose attention-getting behavior in the classroom was becoming a serious matter, the behavior specialist using a clinical model would assume that an intervention was needed for the student, not that the teacher's interactions with the student were rewarding the behavior. The consultant would try to help the classroom teacher see the problem clearly (perhaps the student's behavior was a means of avoiding difficult assignments) and to design a strategy to change the student's behavior (perhaps by giving the student only a small part of the assignment at one time). Only if this approach was not successful might the consultant look at the environment, the teacher's actions in the classroom, and so on.

In a clinical model, the consultant is not actually involved in the ongoing implementation of the intervention or the monitoring of it. The consultant presumes that the dilemma for the consultee is the identification of the specific problem rather than the implementation of strategies to resolve it. In the previous example, the behavior specialist would make suggestions about the intervention but would not stay involved in the situation unless the teacher asked for a follow-up.

Procedure The steps for clinical consultation are not as clearly prescribed as they are for behavioral consultation. Clinical consultants typically would meet with a consultee to learn about a student's apparent problem, and they would assess the specific problem. In this model, that assessment might include observing the student, interviewing the student, or even directly administering some type of diagnostic instrument. Clinical consultants would then analyze the problem the teacher reported by considering the diagnostic information they had gathered, including the student's strengths and needs. Next, they would suggest interventions for the consultee to try. Although clinical consultants would not implement the intervention, at a later date they might follow up to determine whether the outcome was successful.

Clinical consultation may be preferred when consultants have limited time in which to offer assistance to consultees or when a complex problem needs clarification that can be offered by an expert diagnostician. However, because this consultation model generally assumes that the problem exists primarily in the client, it is not particularly useful if the problem is one that involves not only the student but also the teacher, the environment, and other factors in combination. Also, this model is premised on the consultee having the professional skills to act on the consultant's recommendations. If the consultee does not understand the consultant's conceptualization of the problem, or does not have the skills to implement and monitor the intervention, the model has limited utility. How might this consultation model assist you whether you might be the consultant or the consultee? What are its strengths and drawbacks? If Mr. Huber followed a clinical consultation model in his work with Jessica Svoboda in the chapter-opening case, what might he do? What might Ms. Svoboda's responsibilities be?

Consultation Models in Practice

As you were reading about behavioral and clinical consultation, you might have wondered whether consultation actually occurs in the distinct steps and following the theoretical perspective outlined, or whether you should just take ideas from these models as well as others and blend them into your own style. As with many concepts and procedures related to your profession, the answer is probably to use both approaches, thinking about and understanding consultation models but adapting them to your own experiences and job setting.

That is, consultation is seldom as "pure" as the models described in the preceding sections. All consultants tend to put their own signatures on their work by incorporating their own personal styles, adapting procedures to fit contextual variables, and relating their consulting to their other role responsibilities, whether direct service to students, staff development, co-teaching, or others (e.g., Driver, 2013). This individualization of consultation models is certainly expected. The only caution to raise is that individualizing should not have the effect of altering the major assumptions and procedures of the model. If it does, it will undoubtedly compromise the likely effectiveness of the process.

Consultation and Collaboration

Relating collaboration and consultation can be traced to the early 1970s, particularly in the fields of school and counseling psychology (e.g., Kurpius & Brubaker, 1976; Pryzwansky, 1974). The viewpoint was expressed that consultative interactions were more likely to be successful if they were facilitative and supportive rather than prescriptive (e.g., Parker, 1975). By the end of the 1970s, it was clear that for psychologists and counselors in schools, a collaborative or facilitative approach to consultation was

Consultation, coaching, and mentoring often include reviewing student data as a strategy to evaluate the effectiveness of specific instructional practices.

generally recommended over other approaches. As special educators became more likely to assume consulting roles beginning at about the same time (e.g., Christie, McKenzie, & Burdett, 1972; Friend, 1988), their roles likewise evolved to be collaborative. This was not surprising, because many special educators in such roles were consulting with their general education teaching colleagues, and these professionals clearly believed that it was inappropriate for special education teachers to "fix" the practices of general education teachers through consultation. Further, because most special educators at this time worked exclusively in separate settings, they did not necessarily have a good understanding of the expectations and appropriate strategies for a general education setting. Instead, relationships based on parity and the other characteristics of collaboration evolved as most beneficial and satisfactory to all participants (Evans, 1980; Friend, 1984; Idol, Nevin, & Paolucci-Whitcomb, 2000).

It should be noted that today—with the continuing pressure for access to the general curriculum and the resulting increased enrollment of students with disabilities or other special needs in general education classrooms as well as the increasing use of RTI and other procedures designed to prevent the need for special education—the concept of collaboration and the notion of consultation often are framed as a discussion of voluntariness. In some instances, a special services provider as well as a general education teacher or another specialist has responsibility for a student's education. This situation increases the likelihood that the general education teacher will initiate some consultation but that the special educator or other specialist may initiate even more. For example, if a student with autism is included in an intermediate classroom, an inclusion facilitator might request a weekly meeting to determine the student's progress and design interventions. The teacher may benefit from these meetings but at the same time may feel unwanted pressure to participate in them, particularly during busy times of the school year. The teacher may not believe that the meetings are truly voluntary and may become resistant to the entire consultation process.

Learn More About
Still clarifying terminology and concepts? Here is a brief discussion of how to distinguish among collaboration, consultation, and communication.
(https://www.youtube.com/watch?v=JzjLjPTrE0Y)

Despite these historical and contemporary issues related to collaboration in consultation, by using our definitions the distinction between these two terms can be clearly articulated so that professionals who consult as well as those who are consultees can base their interactions on an understanding of each term. Because collaboration is a style or an approach to interaction, it can be attached to the consultation process, just as it can be attached to problem solving, teaming activities, and co-teaching. Moreover, a consultant may choose to use a collaborative approach at some consultation stages and not others, just as the consultant may choose to use it with some consultees and not with others.

However, ascribing collaboration to the consultation process does not make it a unique model (Dougherty, 2014) in the sense of the models presented earlier. *Any* model of consultation can be implemented collaboratively. For example, behavioral consultation has clear, theoretically based principles that prescribe its practice. Whether or not behavioral consultation is carried out collaboratively is an issue that is distinct from the model itself. Behavioral consultation can be conducted collaboratively within a relationship characterized by parity, mutual goals, shared decision making, and all the additional characteristics of collaboration. However, behavioral consultation also may be conducted by someone who, using a directive style, retains much of the decision-making responsibility, prescribes interventions, and offers expert advice and explanations to consultees. This same analogy could be made for clinical consultation: It could be implemented by a consultant who may or may not emphasize the use of a collaborative style of interaction.

Here is an example illustrating the varying styles of consulting relationships. Consider a consultation situation in which you and your colleague, Ms. Goodall, have been working together collaboratively for several weeks to design and evaluate a systematic reward system for use with Henry, a student in her class. Increasing district demands, the inclusion of many students with disabilities, and concerns about upcoming high-stakes achievement testing have created significant and competing demands for

Ms. Goodall. Henry, the student whom you share, is no longer responding satisfactorily to your jointly planned intervention and has begun to display again his problematic and disruptive behaviors. You and Ms. Goodall both recognize that you have a problem that must be addressed; but Ms. Goodall does not currently have the emotional, physical, or logistical resources to participate in any significant way in a collaborative problem-solving effort. Consequently, you may need to solve this pressing problem independently (e.g., by making an immediate adjustment in the implementation of the intervention with Henry). Alternatively, depending on the situation and your assessment of it, you may decide that neither a directive nor a collaborative approach is appropriate. If Henry's lack of progress appears to be only temporary and Ms. Goodall's stress seems to be the most salient issue, you may determine that a nondirective, supportive, or empathic style is most appropriate.

If you develop an understanding of how collaboration and consultation can be distinguished from one another and how they work in tandem, it will guide you in your own consulting interactions and help you communicate clearly with your colleagues and others. This is particularly important because much of what has been written about consultation has been written for school and counseling psychologists who provide this service, not for teachers or other specialists who could do the same. This situation is compounded by the fact that teachers and other specialists sometimes are assigned consultation responsibilities without attention being given to the knowledge and skills (i.e., consulting skills) they may need in order to effectively share their expertise (e.g., Allday, Neilsen-Gatti, & Hudson, 2013; McCall, McHatton, & Shealey, 2014).

APPLY YOUR KNOWLEDGE 8.1

Coaching

A second indirect service option that you may receive or be asked to deliver is *instructional coaching* (Gallucci, Van Lare, Yoon, & Boatright, 2010; Polly, Mraz, & Algozzine, 2013). Coaching evolved because of dissatisfaction with traditional approaches to professional development. That is, until the 1980s much professional development consisted of stand-alone workshops, often scattered throughout a school year and lacking a central theme or any follow-up to ensure that what was presented led to implementation in the classroom and improved outcomes for students (Joyce & Showers, 2002). The original instructional coaching model (e.g., Joyce & Showers, 1980) emphasized teacher peers meeting with each other to study the theory underlying the strategies they were learning to use, peer observation in classrooms, discussion of concerns related to using the strategies, and collegial support for everyone's implementation efforts. The goal was to create learning communities as a means of deepening teachers' knowledge and skills and ensuring a sense of support for them.

Based on the evolution of coaching, it generally can be defined as follows:

> Instructional coaching refers to a differentiated process in which an education professional with advanced knowledge and skills uses various strategies for job-embedded professional development and other support to increase the capacity of their colleagues so that they can produce expected student outcomes.

For example, with the agreement of staff members, your school leadership committee has decided to implement positive behavior supports (PBS) to encourage appropriate student behavior and reduce acting-out behavior. Everyone in the school participates in initial professional development that addresses strategies for use in the classroom and other areas of the school (e.g., hallways, multipurpose room). Emphasis is placed on positive discipline strategies and increasingly intensive levels of intervention for students exhibiting behavior problems. Such professional development is a

> **Learn More About**
> Coaches in schools have many important roles and responsibilities as summarized in this lighthearted video.
> (https://www.youtube.com/watch?v=32a5pR3CUEc)

strong foundation for implementing PBS, but it is unlikely by itself to lead to school-wide implementation with fidelity. More is needed, and so a PBS coach provided by the district visits your school approximately every two weeks throughout the school year, meeting with groups of teachers at their request, answering questions about PBS, observing in classrooms, modeling the use of positive behavior strategies for teachers who want to see the ideas "in action," providing feedback on procedures in place and those still needed, problem solving about topics of concern, and so on. As you might conclude, the likelihood of truly establishing the PBS system in the school is greatly enhanced through the coaching effort. Further, it is clear that such coaching is a highly collaborative service, one based on partnership between the coach and those coached (Knight, 2011).

Rationale for and Benefits of Coaching

Contemporary instructional coaching has different areas of emphasis, but it is premised on the notion that teachers are more likely to remember and use with fidelity instructional techniques if they perceive they are learning them in a partnership and if they have opportunities to reflect on, question, and refine their practices (Marsh, 2012). Instructional coaching is implemented to meet several needs in schools. First, it is a means to provide job-embedded professional development to teach educators skills, strategies, or techniques that will improve achievement outcomes for students (Brown, Reumann-Moore, Hugh, Christman, & Riffer, 2009; Knight, 2007). In addition, coaching is a vehicle for implementing school reform initiatives, such as an emphasis on data-driven decision making as a basis for designing and evaluating instruction (Marsh, McCombs, & Martorell, 2010). Finally, coaching sometimes is offered as a general support for teachers that is intended to assist them in whatever area of teaching they request (e.g., Rock et al., 2013).

Depending on the grade level in which you work and your locale, you may find that instructional coaching is identified by several different names (Denton & Hasbrouck, 2009). In elementary schools, a reading coach or a math coach may be available, but in secondary schools there may be a literacy coach. Similarly, you may learn that you will work with an academic coach or a reform coach. In other school districts the role is called *instructional facilitator*. And, as with consultation, you may find that you are the recipient of coaching or that you are expected to function in the role of instructional coach. If you receive coaching, you should prepare so that you receive maximum benefit from it; this is the topic of Putting Ideas into Practice. And whether you are a coaching recipient or provider, you will find that a single specific coaching process generally has not been widely accepted, but that various coaching models, addressed in the next section, have been identified.

Coaching Models

As with consultation, a number of coaching models have been developed. These models vary based on the purpose of the coaching approach, the role of the coach, and the types of activities or procedures employed (Denton & Hasbrouck, 2009). Two common models are technical coaching and reform coaching.

Technical Coaching Technical coaching has as its primary purposes introducing teachers to research-based practices, supporting them as they learn these practices, and facilitating problem solving as they encounter challenges in using the new practices. The most common example of this type of coaching across elementary, middle, and even high school levels is literacy coaching (Marsh, McCombs, & Martorell, 2012). In this approach, teachers with advanced professional preparation in the area of reading are charged with facilitating teachers' use of evidence-based strategies to improve reading outcomes or to incorporate reading strategies into other core content subjects.

PUTTING IDEAS INTO PRACTICE

Being a Consumer of Consultation, Coaching, or Mentoring

Although you may or may not provide consultation, coaching, or mentoring, you are very likely to be a recipient of one or more of these indirect services. Here are some ideas to help ensure you and your students get the most out of the experience:

- **Be proactive.** Prior to beginning consultation, coaching, or mentoring, think about the goals you have for the process. Outline those goals and share these with your collaboration partner.
- **Be prepared.** Depending on the situation, you may need to have your lesson plans, samples of student work, grades, records of correspondence with parents, data charts, or other materials. These items should be at your fingertips.
- **Be participative.** Consultation, coaching, and mentoring all rely on your active participation. As you offer information and insights, ask questions, and contribute to problem solving, you both increase the quality of the process and communicate to your collaboration partner that you are committed to making the process a success.
- **Be open.** You are likely to receive feedback during your interactions. It is essential that you learn to accept feedback without becoming defensive. Remember that the goal is to help you to improve outcomes for students, and without change on your part that goal is unlikely to be achieved.
- **Be persistent.** Consultation, coaching, and mentoring all are processes that occur over time. As you participate, you probably will be asked to try out a strategy, read materials, contact others, or gather data. Your good-faith efforts to carry out whatever tasks or activities you and your partner have agreed are necessary will help you move toward the goal.
- **Be reflective.** The more that you are willing to critically think about your practice, your teaching techniques, your interactions with students, and other areas related to the consultation, coaching, or mentoring in which you participate, the more effective the process will be. Your ability to recognize ways to change and grow as a professional can be a point of great pride for you, and it can establish a foundation for you to someday be in the role of consultant, coach, or mentor.

A study by Vanderburg and Stevens (2010) represents an example of this coaching approach. In this initiative, teachers in kindergarten through fifth grade received support from literacy coaches who had been trained in specific reading strategies and who themselves worked with a regional coach. The literacy coaches held twice-monthly seminars with teachers. The goal of these sessions was to introduce new reading strategies and to facilitate discussion about those strategies, but the exact content of the sessions was left to the discretion of the coaches and teachers. In addition, the coaches spent four days per week in teachers' classrooms, modeling the reading strategies and observing the teachers as they implemented the strategies. Interviews with the participating teachers revealed that they credited their coaches with motivating them to try new instructional practices, helping them to base their instruction on information from the professional literature, and creating more student-centered learning opportunities. Technical coaching is the type of coaching that Jessica Svoboda, whom you met at the beginning of this chapter, is receiving. What do you see as positive aspects of this type of coaching? What concerns might you have about such coaching?

As you might imagine, technical coaching is used across grade levels and subject areas. A new twist in this type of coaching is the use of technology that allows real-time coaching, even if the coach is in a different location than the teacher. This is called *virtual coaching*, the topic of E-Partnerships.

Reform Coaching If you work in a school where students are failing to reach the increasingly rigorous academic standards established through legislation and policy, you may work with a reform coach (Marsh et al., 2010). For example, at Crispus Attucks High School, only 23 percent of ninth graders are considered proficient in English and only 17 percent in algebra. These sobering data have led to a new principal being assigned to the

E-PARTNERSHIPS

Virtual Coaching

Although the consultation and coaching strategies mentioned in this chapter focus, for the most part, on face-to-face interactions, that is not the only option. In fact, technology is creating new opportunities for electronic collaboration. One example is called virtual bug-in-ear (VBIE) (Elford, Carter, & Aronin, 2013; Rock et al., 2013). Here is how this coaching option works:

- In the classroom, there is a webcam connected to a computer, pointed to capture the instruction. Skype or a similar Internet-based service is used for transmitting video and voice communication.
- The teacher wears a Bluetooth headset wirelessly synchronized with the computer equipment.
- The consultant or coach is located anywhere that another computer with Skype and an Internet connection are available. This could be a school district administrative office, a regional center, or a university setting.
- At prearranged times and following the principles of giving effective feedback, the consultant or coach and teacher connect via Skype. The consultant or coach observes the teacher, providing supportive feedback in real time as a lesson occurs. If desired, a recording of the classroom observation can be made and archived for later use.
- After the lesson, at a time convenient for both individuals, a follow-up session is held to discuss the observation and set goals for future practice.

One advantage of VBIE is that the professional assisting the teacher is unobtrusive because of being off site instead of in the classroom. In addition, the feedback is not only in real time but also private, thus enabling teachers to change practices on the spot without embarrassing them in front of students (e.g., Israel, Carnahan, Snyder, & Williamson, 2013).

What advantages might this type of coaching have for you? What concerns would you have about it?

---

school, and attention is now focused on improving outcomes in these two subject areas. Mr. Hamilton, the reform coach, has several key responsibilities. First, he is responsible for working with teachers to develop common formative assessments. That is, he ensures that all English 9 teachers and all Algebra I teachers participate in developing the instructional assessments given every four weeks in their subject areas. He also analyzes the data they

Instructional coaches often work with teachers one-to-one, but they may also meet with groups of professionals who are implementing new programs or practices.

gather, meets with teachers to help them understand what the data say about their instruction, and assists them to use the data inform next steps for their teaching. In addition, Mr. Hamilton observes in classrooms and makes general suggestions about lesson clarity and pacing, student engagement, and classroom management. He is responsible for meeting on a regular basis with Ms. Cochrane, the principal, keeping her apprised of this work. One role that Mr. Hamilton specifically does not assume is that of evaluator. His role is to be supportive, and teacher evaluation is completed by Ms. Cochrane and an assistant principal.

> **Learn More About**
> This video gives you a real-world glimpse into the work of early career educators and their instructional coaches.
> (https://www.youtube.com/watch?v=l5GkiBkXrxg)

Notice that reform coaching has a broad-based goal of raising student outcomes. This type of coaching is likely to involve many groups of teachers, and the focus usually is on helping these groups improve their practices. The coach may carry out responsibilities that are similar to those of a technical coach, but this professional has additional responsibilities. The coach in this model often has duties that are administrative and typically serves as a liaison between teachers and principals and district administrators.

Coaching in Practice

Coaching and consultation share a number of similarities. First, coaching, like consultation, is rarely implemented in a pure form. Instead, models provide guidelines for effective practices, but individual situations, district policies, and local culture typically shape implementation. In addition, coaches engage in shared problem solving based on the identified needs of the partner, much like a consultant. Directionality is also present, especially in programs in which individuals are employed with coaching as the primary responsibility. Coaches are likely to employ behavioral techniques, reinforcing teachers for their efforts to improve teaching practices. In addition, the teacher being coached has the responsibility of deciding to seek input and implement recommended ideas, whereas the coach has the responsibility of observing the desired teaching behavior and basing suggestions on the teacher's preferences and skills. And finally, as is true in consultative relationships, trust and clear communication are essential (e.g., Polly et al., 2013; Teemant, Wink, & Tyra, 2011).

One aspect of coaching is somewhat different from consulting. Generally, coaching is premised on collaboration. Although discussions occasionally emerge about coaching that is not voluntary, as is the case with Ms. Svoboda at the beginning of this chapter, the assumption is still that the coach and the recipient of coaching form a partnership and generally meet the criteria for collaboration. Coaches may share expertise in order to improve teacher practices, but teachers make the choice to incorporate this expertise into their classroom instruction.

APPLY YOUR KNOWLEDGE 8.3

Mentoring

Many novice teachers—estimates range from one-third to one-half—leave the profession within five years (Keigher, 2010; Sass, Flores, Claeys, & Pérez, 2012), and one key reason they depart is a perceived lack of support (e.g., Goldring, Taie, & Riddles, 2014). As a means of addressing this problem, as well as offering a leadership opportunity for experienced teachers, many general and special educators are asked to serve as mentors to preservice and novice educators (Ingersoll & Strong, 2011; Trautwein & Ammerman, 2010). In general, mentoring is defined as follows:

> Mentoring is personal guidance and support, usually provided by experienced educators, delivered to first-year or early career teachers for the purpose of inducting them into the profession and improving their retention in the field.

Think about Ms. Morehead. As a first-year special educator, she is feeling somewhat overwhelmed with all her responsibilities, which include co-teaching with two general educators, teaching her own classes, preparing student IEPs, and completing other duties such as monitoring students in the hallways and serving on the school improvement committee representing all the new teachers in her school. Of immediate concern are upcoming parent conferences. Ms. Morehead feels like she barely knows her way around school or her students' names and is not sure she is ready to confidently meet their parents and explain students' programs and services. However, when she raises her concerns with her mentor, veteran special educator Mr. Post, he helps put her at ease. He asks her what information she needs, assists her to plan for the conferences and to prepare information to share, and explains the school's procedures for the conferences (i.e., how much time should be allocated for each conference, how to manage conferences for students in co-taught classes, what to do if a parent asks a question she does not know how to answer). Although still a bit uncertain, Ms. Morehead feels much better prepared for these important parent interactions because of the support Mr. Post provided. In other meetings, as well as through electronic communication, Mr. Post continues to answer Ms. Morehead's questions, be a supportive listener as she reflects on the effectiveness of her lessons, and ask her critical questions intended to assist her to understand and respond appropriately to her students' diverse needs.

Mentoring has these characteristics similar to those of consultation:

- The goal of mentoring is to provide needed expertise to the novice through a strong and constructive professional relationship.
- The relationship is supportive and collaborative rather than evaluative. Teacher evaluation is the responsibility of the principal or another supervisor.
- Although having a mentor is often a requirement for new teachers, depending on school district policy (Mullen, 2011), it is most effective when both mentors and mentees embrace and actively participate in the partnership.
- The mentor's responsibilities are to provide expertise by responding to the novice's questions, offering suggestions to address problems, and advising when problems arise.
- The novice teacher's responsibilities are to raise topics of concern, seriously consider and act on mentor ideas, and integrate new knowledge and skills into teaching and learning practices.
- Although the direct beneficiary of mentoring is the novice, the intent is to help early career educators become experts so that they are better able to address student needs (e.g., Achinstein & Davis, 2014).

> **Learn More About**
> These teachers and mentors are part of a structure program to support new teachers. Their perspectives highlight the value of mentoring programs.
> (https://www.youtube.com/watch?v=tVoyzliq7Ro)

Mentoring typically is part of teacher induction, that is, an entire array of activities, professional development, and supervision for beginning teachers (Gut, Beam, Henning, Cochran, & Knight, 2014). An induction program, for example, might include six days of required professional development on student assessment, classroom management, and cultural responsiveness. In the same program, new teachers might be observed at least four times by an administrator or instructional coach and might be expected to participate in several small-group sessions that combine discussion of instructional issues with opportunities to socialize with teacher peers. An additional part of this induction program would be the assignment of a mentor, who is expected to contact the new teacher at least once per month and often does so far more often than that.

Mentoring programs generally have these four components (Waterman & He, 2011):

- Mentors are matched to the novice teachers with whom they work based on subject area or grade level
- Mentors are prepared through ongoing professional development activities to be effective in their roles
- Administrative structures support mentoring, including release time for mentors and mentees; stipends for educators functioning as mentors; and the development of school structures that foster collaboration, for example, professional learning communities
- An expectation is set for frequent contact between mentors and mentees, although novice teachers generally report opposing mandatory meetings

The Impact of Mentoring

The idea of mentoring for new teachers is intuitively appealing (Alhija, & Fresko, 2014). If you are preparing to be a teacher, you might find it comforting to know that someone would be there to answer your questions and assist you to navigate through the beginning stage of your career. If you are an experienced educator, the opportunity to serve as a mentor might be attractive and a means to demonstrate your leadership skills (Zuspan, 2013). However, research on the impact of mentoring includes mixed results. For example, the National Center for Education Evaluation and Regional Assistance (2009) found that a formal, structured mentoring program did not significantly change new teachers' practices, did not positively affect student achievement, and did not increase teacher retention. But other reports suggest that well-designed programs can help new teachers to learn effective teaching strategies and create positive school change (Caqtapano & Huisman, 2013; Hallam, Chou, Hite, & Hite, 2012). Others (e.g., Ingersoll & Strong, 2011; Waterman & He, 2011) have found mixed results from mentoring. These differences may be due in part to the fact that mentoring programs vary tremendously in terms of their requirements and procedures, and they may also reflect the fact that clear standards for effective mentoring have not been established. If you were to participate in mentoring—as either a provider or a recipient—what components would make it an effective program for you?

Learn More About
Even early career educators sometimes serve as mentors. This checklist can help you decide if mentoring is a role you would like to try.

Whether you function as a mentor or are assigned a mentor as you begin your career, keep in mind that mentoring is highly collaborative. Mentors typically base their input on the needs expressed by the mentee, and a critical component of mentors' success is the sense of parity and trust they establish in the partnership. If you review the characteristics of collaboration as presented in Chapter 1, you will find that they apply directly to the notion of mentoring, even when mentoring is a required district program for all new teachers.

As you think about mentoring and its potential impact, you should also be aware that technology is beginning to play a role in such programs. E-Partnerships describes how mentors can provide real-time support even without being present in the classroom.

E-PARTNERSHIPS

Electronic Mentoring

When professionals think about mentoring, they typically envision face-to-face meetings. But what if an appropriate mentor works in another school? What if the distance between schools makes it difficult for face-to-face interactions? One solution is electronic mentoring, either in groups or in a one-to-one format (Hunt, Powell, Little, & Mike, 2013). Gareis and Nussbaum-Beach (2007, pp. 236–237) have studied electronic mentoring and offer the following insights.

Content (topics mentors and mentees discussed)
- Planning for instruction
- Instructional delivery
- Assessment of learning
- Classroom management
- Professionalism

Function (types of supports mentors offered)
- Support/confirmation
- Guided advice
- Modeling
- Seeking clarification/direct questioning
- Prompting reflection
- Professional growth

What might be the opportunities or dilemmas of electronic mentoring as opposed to mentoring that occurs in person? How could the advantages of this approach be maximized and the disadvantages minimized?

APPLY YOUR KNOWLEDGE 8.3

Issues Related to Indirect Services

As professionals in the field of education expand their collaborative activities, a number of issues are increasingly critical. For the indirect services of consultation, instructional coaching, and mentoring, these include the following areas of concern as well as those included in Figure 8.1.

Understanding of the Professional Relationships

Consultation, coaching, and mentoring are effective only if both parties are active participants. The providers of such services must strive to avoid being seen as academic and behavioral magicians; recipients must contribute significant information about their classrooms and students for consultants, coaches, and mentors to offer meaningful assistance. A dilemma occurs in some schools, however. Some providers feel pressure to have solutions ready to dispense to recipients. In others, teachers expect consultants, coaches, or mentors to have answers and are disappointed when such on-the-spot advice does not improve the problem or concern at hand. The challenge for schools as they implement indirect services is to educate all participants about their roles in the processes and to discourage professionals from making inaccurate assumptions about others' roles and responsibilities. For example, consultants should resist the urge to offer advice without an adequate understanding of the classroom environment and teacher expectations. Teachers must reciprocate with patience, recognizing that high-quality results are only likely with considerable effort. It is in this type of mutual understanding of the possibilities and constraints of consultation, coaching, and mentoring that skills for collaboration might be most necessary for all participants.

Time Allocation for Professional Collaboration

The topic of time was raised in Chapter 7, regarding co-teaching, but it is an important factor for indirect services as well. For all educators, both those that provide consultation,

FIGURE 8.1 **Unresolved issues in the delivery of indirect services.**

> Although consultation, coaching, and mentoring are increasingly part of school practices, a number of issues related to these indirect services remain to be addressed. In addition to those described elsewhere in this chapter, here are several that could affect their future use:
>
> - The lack of data comparing specific models or approaches to indirect services in order to determine those that are most effective and those that are most well received by professionals
> - The lack of data on whether the perceived status of the professional delivering indirect services affects the outcomes of the progress (i.e., whether a school psychologist consulting with a teacher leads to better student outcomes than a special education teacher consulting with that same teacher)
> - The need for information on whether indirect services can be as effective as direct services (e.g., co-teaching) for improving student outcomes
> - Appropriate strategies for proceeding when the recipient of indirect services declines to participate or participates minimally even if directed to do so
> - Strategies for bridging cultural differences among participants in indirect services
> - Differences in consulting strategies when parents, rather than professionals, are the consultees
> - Administrative and school culture factors that may influence the outcomes of indirect services

coaching, or mentoring as well as those who participate in these services, problems often arise regarding the time available to collaborate (e.g., Vannest & Hagan-Burke, 2010). Understandably, time for working directly with students typically is arranged first, and too often indirect services become an informal, sometimes unstructured, and occasionally unsystematic add-on to professional schedules. Educators participating in consultation, coaching, or mentoring should have time allocated in their schedules for these important activities. If these services are seen as a luxury instead of as a necessity, the demands of direct instruction, testing, report preparation, and meetings may preclude their meaningful use.

Cultural Differences

Over the past several years, increased attention has been paid to issues that arise when professionals interacting with each other are from different cultures, or when professionals are from different cultures than the families with whom they work (Curry, 2013; Nathans & Revelle, 2013; Palawat & May, 2012). Concerns relate to language differences, views about status and power, and the subtle communication issues that may arise. They also pertain to professionals' appreciation of how their own culture may influence their practice (Lopez, 2013). For example, a coach whose own culture highly values students being formal in their interactions with teachers may perceive informality as disrespect and a signal of poor classroom management. In general, consultants, coaches, and mentors should ensure that they acquire and use appropriate cultural competence in the development of interpersonal relationships, in their awareness of their collaborative partners' receptivity to various interaction processes and communication styles, and in the appropriateness of various strategies and interventions suggested.

Confidentiality

When consultants, coaches, and mentors build trusting relationships with teachers and problem solve with them, information that should be held in confidence will likely be shared. For example, a teacher might mention that she is so frustrated with the acting-out behavior of a student that she finds herself negatively responding to nearly everything he does. This honest admission must not be shared with other colleagues. And although that might seem obvious, in the rush of completing many professional responsibilities and with the pressure that now comes with working in schools, professionals in consulting, coaching, or mentoring roles sometimes need to be reminded that they are obligated to keep confidences, even relatively small ones, in order to preserve the benefits of these services and to convey respect for their colleagues. Ultimately, confidentiality is an ethical issue, one that merits serious and continued attention in schools.

When considered as a whole, indirect services have an important niche in the array of services that ultimately help students to achieve. However, for them to be effective, the service providers must select an approach carefully, monitor the impact of their suggestions on their recipients and students, and constantly evaluate the quality of their practice. Some professionals, such as psychologists or those for whom indirect services are their sole or primary job responsibility, may find their roles comfortable and clear. For others, such as special education teachers and other professionals for whom indirect services are a new or secondary job responsibility, the skills for effective practice may have to be mindfully nurtured.

SUMMARY

- Consultation is a voluntary problem-solving process in which one professional assists another to address a problem concerning a third party, typically a student. It is also an expert and directional relationship involving shared but differentiated responsibilities for decisions and accountability for outcomes and is based on theoretical models (e.g., behavioral and clinical).
- Instructional coaching is a voluntary, collaborative, and ongoing process, based on principles of effective professional development, in which a highly skilled professional works with teachers in order to increase their capacity to improve student achievement. It is school-based, job-embedded, and teacher-directed, and it may be implemented as a means of providing specific new skills (i.e., technical coaching) or as part of school improvement efforts (i.e., reform coaching).
- Mentoring is a collaborative strategy to support new teachers as they enter the field, help them learn important skills, and to increase the likelihood they will stay in the field. Its effectiveness relies on skilled mentors matched to mentees, administrative support, and frequent mentor–mentee interactions.
- A number of issues exist regarding the indirect services described in this chapter, including participants' understanding of consultation, coaching, and mentoring and their roles and responsibilities in them; time allocation for these services; participants' awareness of and responses to their cultural differences; and confidentiality.

BACK TO THE CASE

1. Think about Jessica Svoboda's work with her instructional coach. What do you think are Ms. Svoboda's responsibilities for maximizing the benefit of this professional relationship? If you were in Ms. Svoboda's situation, what would be your questions and concerns about working with the coach?
2. Place yourself in the role of Ms. Delacruz, Ms. Svoboda's instructional coach. Why do you think she asked the types of questions described in the case study? What other questions might she pose? What do you see as the most essential skills that instructional coaches should have? How much teaching experience do you think a teacher needs before being asked to serve as a coach?
3. Ms. Svoboda is also working with a behavior specialist. What is different in terms of her relationship with Mr. Huber as compared to Ms. Delacruz? Based on your answers, create a set of distinctions between coaching and consultation and identify situations for which each might be more appropriate.
4. What would you do if you disagreed with the recommendations made by a behavior consultant? What might happen if you expressed your disagreement? How could you make such a potentially difficult interaction constructive in terms of identifying how best to meet student needs? Be sure to embed relevant information from earlier chapters in your answer.

COLLABORATIVE ACTIVITIES

1. Consultation often is recommended as an approach for working with parents and families. What might be the role of a teacher in providing this type of service? For what types of situations or student problems might a teacher serve in this consulting capacity? What are the opportunities and risks of this application of consultation? What strategies could you utilize in your consulting work with parents and families to ensure that your status as an education professional and your possible cultural differences would not limit your effectiveness?
2. If you were to be the recipient of instructional coaching—either technical or reform—what would be included on your list of dos and don'ts for your coach? Provide a rationale for each item you include, and then compare your list with those of your classmates.
3. If you are an experienced educator, recall your first year of teaching. What were your concerns and questions? Did you have a mentor? How did this experience help or interfere with your induction into teaching; or, if you did not have a mentor, how could it have helped or interfered? If you are a preservice educator, what types of supports do you think would help you the most as you begin your

teaching career? What concerns do you have about working with a mentor?
4. Think about your current or planned teaching assignment or professional role. For each of the issues related to indirect services (i.e., understanding roles, time, diversity, confidentiality), analyze how it might arise and propose actions you could take to address it. With classmates, discuss the relative importance of each issue as it relates to your current or likely professional position.
5. What similarities and differences do you find among consultation, coaching, mentoring, and interpersonal problem solving? Try to capture your thinking in a graphic organizer such as a Venn diagram or a chart.

CHECK YOUR UNDERSTANDING

Click here to gauge your understanding of this chapter's essential concepts.

9 Difficult Interactions

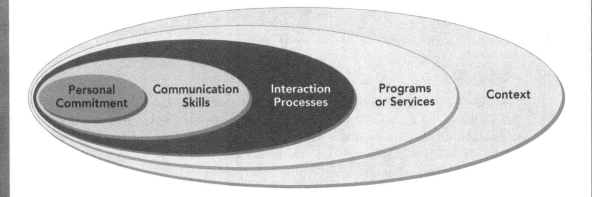

CONNECTIONS

As you have studied the topics addressed thus far in this textbook, you have learned the specific skills for effective communication (Chapters 2, 3, and 4) as well as the key process—group problem solving—in which that communication occurs (Chapter 5). You have also studied programs and services often found in collaborative schools, including teams, co-teaching, consultation, coaching, and mentoring (Chapters 6, 7, and 8). In this chapter, you have the opportunity to integrate your knowledge and skills for implementing collaborative practices because this chapter—about difficult interactions—explores the situations in which you most need those skills. When you find yourself interacting with a frustrated parent or a dissatisfied colleague who does not seem to share your priorities for working with students, you have a critical opportunity to demonstrate your expertise as a collaborator.

LEARNING OUTCOMES

After reading this chapter you will be able to:

1. Explain conflict as it occurs in educational settings, including four major causes, five typical professional conflict response styles, and principles of negotiation as a strategy for addressing it.
2. Outline resistance as it occurs in schools, including its causes and indicators as well as persuasion strategies useful for responding to it.
3. Apply knowledge and skills related to collaboration, communication, and problem solving to develop strategies for addressing conflict and resistance in situations you may encounter in your professional role.

A CASE FOR COLLABORATION

Sometimes No One Is Happy

Kelley Gardner is sitting in a staff meeting wishing she was anyplace else. It seems that all the concerns about the school's planned revision to their response to intervention (RTI) model, mandated by the school district, are surfacing at one time, and the atmosphere at the meeting is contentious to say the least. As she sits quietly hoping her principal, Ms. Bartkiewicz, will change the tone of the session, she hears these comments from her colleagues:

- "I thought we already had a pretty good process in place to address student needs. I don't really see how this is an improvement—it's just change for the sake of change."
- "Did I understand that we have to collect even more data than before? We already have so much data that we don't have time to figure out what it means. Who has time to gather more data? Why should we do that? Are we going to get extra assistants who will be trained to collect data? I bet the answer is 'no.'"
- "We already have enough going on, Ms. Bartkiewicz—with the new standards, the move of the program for students with autism to our school, and the changes in teacher evaluation. Now you've volunteered our school for this. Are you going to take away something else we have to do?"
- "This sounds like a way to keep us from referring students who need special education. I'm sure, given some of our parents, that they are going to object."
- "I know what the law says, and this may be encouraged, but it is not required. What's the point of adding more to our plates? I also wonder whether anyone has checked to see if this has been proven to be effective."
- "These interventions that have to be implemented—who's responsible for that? I hope it's the special education teachers. There is no one else to do them; it's not fair asking teachers to take time away from other students for this."

Ms. Gardner decides that many of her colleagues have not understood what RTI is about. As the meeting continues, she silently applauds as Ms. Bartkiewicz calmly listens to everyone's questions and promises to address them all. She does not indicate that the concerns inferred in the questions will delay implementing RTI. But Ms. Gardner wonders if Ms. Bartkiewicz realizes that many of the most serious questions and concerns have not been voiced to the group; they have been whispered among the teachers. The meeting adjourns, but a residual sense of dissension and dissatisfaction is apparent to everyone.

Introduction

Have you ever experienced a situation similar to the one described in A Case for Collaboration? Although few interactions with others at school have this air of tension, you should be prepared for those that do because those are the interactions that will require you to use all the collaboration skills you have been learning. Here are a few examples of situations that may be difficult or awkward to address:

- You call the technology coordinator to ask for a copy of a new program to be put on your computer. The coordinator explains that you are welcome to have a copy, but that the district's policy is that you must first attend a one-hour after-school workshop on its use. You reply that you are very adept at using the computer, have used the trial version of the software on your personal computer, and undoubtedly can figure out how to operate the full software package without having to take the workshop. The technology coordinator is sympathetic but says that the program will be installed only after you attend the after-school session. You're very busy, and this requirement seems like a waste of your time.

- The parents of a student refuse to give permission for an assessment, despite the student's persistent failing grades and the apparent failure of a series of increasingly intensive instructional interventions being implemented by teachers, teaching assistants, and specialists. You are a member of the team that agrees the student should be considered for possible eligibility for special education services, but the parents are adamant that the problem lies with staff members who are not effectively teaching their child.
- You have a bilingual teaching assistant who serves as an interpreter for several of your students. Your impression is that she is coddling the students, helping them too much, sometimes doing their work for them, and suggesting to them that they should listen to her rather than to you. When you raised the topic with her, she cried, accused you of being biased against her, and promised to do better. She then complained to the assistant principal, and you have been asked to explain yourself. The problem is compounded by the fact that the paraeducator's brother-in-law is a member of the school board, which has led you to be concerned about the security of your job if the situation is not amicably resolved.
- You arrange a twice-monthly series of meetings with your co-teacher to plan, wishing for more but grateful for these opportunities. The first meeting goes well, but at the last minute before the next meeting the other teacher cancels. Over the next four scheduled meetings, she cancels two, shows up for just a moment at one to explain that she has other work she must get completed, and spends the next meeting complaining about students and colleagues, blaming the principal for how students have been assigned to co-taught classes and for the limited amount of planning time arranged for co-teachers. You privately conclude that students would do a lot better if this scheduled time were used wisely and instructional planning focused on meeting diverse student needs. You wonder how to make the meetings, at least those that occur, more constructive.

Some incidents such as these are relatively trivial and mostly annoying, and you may be able to easily resolve them (e.g., by attending the workshop on the software). Others concern the fundamental decisions made about students' educational needs (e.g., planning for co-teaching). The first two scenarios as well as the one that opened this chapter are examples of conflict. The latter two are examples of resistance. In this chapter, you will learn more about both types of difficult interactions and how to respond to them. Conflict and resistance are natural occurrences in collaboration, but depending on your response to them, they can either enhance your work or impede it.

Understanding Conflict

Conflict has been defined by numerous individuals (e.g., Polsky & Gerschel, 2010; Wilmot & Hocker, 2014), and their definitions have tended to vary based on the theoretical perspective of the author. For example, some view conflict as a situation that occurs when one party perceives that his or her status is no longer equitable to that of another party; that is, it is viewed as a matter of perceived power inequity within a relationship (e.g., Coleman, Kugler, Mitchinson, Chung, & Musallam, 2010; Sadri, 2013). Others see it as the result of attributions that some individuals assign to others, as when teachers consider parents "too demanding" or when school staff members perceive some of their colleagues as "inflexible." For our discussion, we provide this definition of conflict:

> Conflict is a struggle that occurs when individuals, interdependent with others, perceive that those others are interfering with their goal attainment.

You can apply this definition to the scenario that opened the chapter. What might have been Ms. Gardner's goals? The goals of other teachers at the meeting? The principal, Ms. Bartkiewicz? What were the perceived types of interference?

Traditionally, school professionals have been uncomfortable directly addressing conflict; even most experienced educators can describe many instances of its occurrence.

In fact, Barsky (2007) notes that when compared to other professions (such as business, law, and psychology), education has neither evolved a systemic means of considering conflict as part of the work environment nor developed models for resolving it. This is especially surprising as considerable professional attention is given to conflict resolution for students (e.g., Ojanen, Smith-Schrandt, & Gesten, 2013).

In today's schools, with the emphasis on collaboration among educators, it is unlikely that conflict can be avoided, and understandings of conflict from a business perspective can be applied to school practices to explain why this is so (e.g., Tjosvold, Wong, & Wan, 2010). First, although in the past each individual in schools had clearly delineated tasks to accomplish and did these without relying to any great extent on others, now this isolation and delineation of individuals' tasks largely has changed. Increasingly, staff members are expected to work together, share data, create common assessments, and so on; they are therefore more likely to experience conflict just because they are in close proximity (Conderman, 2011a; Wilmot & Hocker, 2014). An example of this happens on teams: When professionals from several disciplines with different frames of reference are making decisions about student needs, they are likely to differ occasionally about desired outcomes (Behfar, Peterson, Mannix, & Trochin, 2008).

Second, the traditional value system of schools tended to downplay emotions and keep school somewhat impersonal. Emerging trends, however, support all workplaces—including schools—as being nurturing and psychologically safe environments (Bradley, Postlethwaite, Klotz, Hamdani, & Brown, 2012) that give voice to teachers' preferences and opinions and ensure they are valued (e.g., Bond, Tuckey, & Dollard, 2010). As more needs are expressed, conflict is likely to emerge, because meeting some individuals' needs can interfere with meeting the needs of others. For example, this may occur as professionals request smaller caseloads or lighter teaching or service assignments in order to implement innovative programs or to assume alternative responsibilities. Such requests imply that others should have larger class sizes or more responsibilities, or that more personnel should be hired, and both are likely to be problematic options.

A third reason conflict is increasingly common in schools is that leadership approaches have changed (e.g., Curry, 2014). In traditional schools, principals were considered effective when they were strongly directive in school decision making. Now, however, participatory management approaches are preferred (Grenda & Hackmann, 2014). The resulting increased staff involvement in decision making also increases opportunities for conflicts. For example, when school professionals are meeting to discuss the district's proposed pay-for-performance system, through which teacher bonuses will be tied to student achievement, conflict may occur. Similarly, when a grade-level team is deciding how to address curriculum goals and the administrative expectation is for a consistent approach to instruction across team members, disagreements are to be expected.

Because you are likely to experience at least some conflict in your professional role, you should also understand how it can be beneficial (e.g., Bradley et al., 2012). By itself, conflict is neither good nor bad (Dignath, Kiesel, & Eder, 2014). You determine whether it will have positive or negative outcomes. Consider these potentially positive results from conflict:

1. Decisions made after addressing a conflict often are of high quality because of the intense effort invested in discussing perspectives and generating alternatives.
2. Professionals implementing decisions emerging from conflict are likely to have a strong sense of ownership for the decisions and for the commitment to carry them out.
3. Conflict typically causes professionals to sharpen their thinking about their points of view so that they can clearly communicate them. The result is a more carefully reasoned discussion, which may include a wider range of ideas and options.
4. Often, professionals who successfully manage conflict develop more open, trusting relationships with one another because of this positive experience. This facilitates their subsequent interactions.
5. Practice in effectively communicating during conflict can make it easier to address future conflict situations.

Notice that we are not saying that interactions with conflict are simple or enjoyable; in fact, they are complex and often stressful (Avgar, Lee, & Chung, 2014; Hayashi, 2011). But conflict does not have to be viewed as exclusively negative. If you look at it as an opportunity it will be one. Expanding your understanding of why conflict occurs and how it can be managed will help you view it this way.

Causes of Conflict

Think about your school or a school with which you are familiar. What types of conflicts have occurred there? Who has been involved in these conflicts? When you review these professional conflicts, you might identify different reasons why they occurred. We categorize these as related to interests, rights, and power (Masters & Albright, 2002; Wilmot & Hocker, 2014).

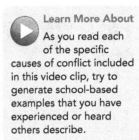

Learn More About
As you read each of the specific causes of conflict included in this video clip, try to generate school-based examples that you have experienced or heard others describe.

(https://www.youtube.com/watch?v=q5zdRpsnFUc)

Conflict Between Individuals with Different Goals One major cause of conflict occurs when two individuals want different outcomes but must settle for the same outcome. For example, in a suburban school district, team members and parents disagree about the mission of a proposed program to increase opportunities for students with moderate disabilities to access the general education setting. Some school professionals believe that few students will be able to be integrated because they cannot meet academic and social expectations and that this is not even an appropriate goal (e.g., Anastasiou, & Kauffman, 2011), especially given the current mandates and resulting pressures on teachers to ensure that students reach rigorous achievement standards. Others believe that the program's primary goal should be whatever is necessary in order to make access possible for all students for most of each school day (e.g., Obiakor, Harris, Mutua, Rotatori, & Algozzine, 2012). Some parents are not in favor of any change in their children's programs and services; they prefer the current service delivery system with the traditional opportunities for interacting with peers at lunch and during art, music, and physical education. Others want their children with typical peers all day.

Each of the groups in this example wants a different outcome concerning the inclusive program; they have different goals. However, when a decision is made about the program, all the groups must abide by those guidelines. Although students may spend varying amounts of the day in general education settings, where staff is deployed and how schedules are developed will rely on the mission statement adopted. A common example of conflict between individuals with different goals includes disagreements between parents and school professionals about whether a student should participate in the school's gifted program. Another example concerns the roles for specialists when they co-teach in general education classes: Are they there to teach all students as appropriate or to provide support just for those with disabilities, language differences, reading difficulties, or other special needs? A third example of conflicting goals often occurs in the field of special education, the topic of A Basis in Research. What additional examples of conflicts occurring for this reason have you observed in your professional role?

Conflict Between Individuals with the Same Goals A second major cause of conflict occurs when professionals all have the same goal, but not all of them can access it (e.g., Rispens, Greer, & Jehn, 2007). The master school schedule offers an example of this cause of conflict. In a local high school, the master schedule is created by first blocking in the academic courses; then the vocational and special subjects; and finally the remedial, co-taught, bilingual, and separate special education classes. However, with more diverse students enrolled in core academic classes, educators encounter problems arranging services. They request that the scheduling of separate special education classes, co-taught classes, and remedial classes occur immediately after the academic classes and before others. The special subject teachers argue that far more students are affected by art, music, and physical education classes and that those classes should have a higher priority. The teachers of the honors and advanced placement classes ask that other classes be arranged so that students who take courses at the local university in the afternoons are not penalized.

A BASIS IN RESEARCH

Conflict in Special Education: Advocates and Due Process

No matter your role in schools, you may hear about or experience controversy that occurs in special education. You may attend an individualized education program (IEP) meeting at which an advocate insists on certain services that school professionals do not think are appropriate, and conflict may be the result. You may also find that the parents of a student with a disability with whom you work have filed a complaint with the appropriate state office concerning their child's education, and you are required to contribute information and/or testify at a due process hearing. Such situations can be very stressful.

Advocates

Nespor and Hicks (2010) interviewed parents of children with significant disabilities, administrators, and special education consultants. They found that advocates played several key roles for families, including these:

- Translating between parents' hopes for their child and the technical and mandated procedures of special education
- Leveling the balance of power during meetings and in discussions of types and amounts of services
- Creating "paper trails" related to special education procedures, agreements, and IEP issues
- Prompting parents to write letters and otherwise contact school professionals, as necessary
- Fostering systemic change; that is, change that would positively affect students with disabilities in addition to the child for whom they are advocating

This study presented a constructive and problem-solving viewpoint of the work of advocates. What might be the perspectives of school psychologists, special education directors, principals, and teachers? How could you use strategies from this chapter in an interaction with an advocate?

Due Process

Zirkel and Scala (2010) provided important information related to the number and locations of due process hearings. They reported the following:

- Nationwide, there were 2,033 adjudicated hearings across the states and the District of Columbia.
- The jurisdictions with the highest numbers of adjudicated hearings were the District of Columbia ($N = 880$), New York ($N = 550$), California ($N = 119$), New Jersey ($N = 89$), and Pennsylvania ($N = 84$). These represented 85 percent of all hearings.
- Comparing these data to previously gathered data, the number of hearings across the country has decreased significantly over the past several years (N = approximately 2,800 hearings in 2005).

These data should give you a sense of the likelihood that you may be involved in or affected by a due process hearing (i.e., there are far more hearings in certain locations on the East Coast and West Coast, and far fewer in the middle of the country). More importantly, the data indicated that resolutions increasingly are found prior to the action of convening a formal due process hearing.

In this example, the various parties have the same goal: receiving priority treatment in the scheduling process. However, when one group is given priority, the others cannot have it. One group is likely to be dissatisfied with the resolution of this conflict. You have probably witnessed or participated in many similar conflicts, such as when only two individuals can go to a professional conference and several more requested to attend, when a position in a preferred school opened and several individuals requested a transfer, and so on. Scarce resources often result in competing goal conflicts (Martinez, 2004).

Conflict About Power In some cases, conflict is not about goals at all. Instead, it may be about each person's perceived sense of power (Coleman et al., 2010; Halevy, Cohen, Chou, Katz, & Panter, 2014). If a principal, for instance, mandates that certain professionals are to be members of the school's RTI team, conflict may result. It is not a matter of whether the educators want to participate or want to assist students—it is the fact that they were told to accept this responsibility instead of being given a choice. Another example sometimes occurs in co-teaching. One teacher may contradict the other during instruction or change the directions given, and these difficult interactions may result in conflict. A careful analysis shows, though, that a common reason for these issues is one teacher's perception of needing to establish power and status in the classroom. What are other examples of conflicts about power that occur in schools?

Conflict Within Individuals One additional cause of conflict is an internal discrepancy that you perceive within your own goals. We mention this cause of conflict for completeness: Intrapersonal conflict does not necessarily affect others, but it can pose a very serious job stressor for professionals (Keranen & Prudencio, 2014). For example, suppose you are responsible for a group of students, and their diverse needs seem too numerous to meet. You can easily identify ways that you could differentiate instruction and otherwise support all the students, but you simply cannot implement all your ideas. You are in conflict with yourself about which strategies to implement, which students to focus your efforts on, and whether you are favoring some students over others, an ethical dilemma. Similarly, a specialist might encounter intrapersonal conflict in scheduling services for a student: More services might lead to an improved outcome, but this could also take services away from other students. Internal causes of conflict such as these are extremely common in schools where professional roles are changing and where expectations for student achievement are increasing rapidly.

Intrapersonal conflict may cause unclear communication, which negatively affects professional interactions. When you discuss a situation such as those just described, you may say one thing but imply another. You may also argue for one perspective one day, but support a different approach the next day. That is, your interpersonal conflict may lead you to communicate contradictory perceptions or preferences.

The Influence of Organizational Variables

Understanding the causes of conflict provides a framework for identifying and managing it. However, other factors interact with these causes to affect the frequency and intensity of conflicts in your school setting. One factor particularly important for school professionals concerns organizational variables.

School Administration and Organization The conflict you encounter is influenced significantly by the organization and administration of your school (Hahn Tapper, 2013; Shipps & White, 2009; Zirkel, 2012). For example, your principal's leadership style affects conflict. If the principal tends to use a hands-off style, you and your colleagues may find yourselves in conflict with one another for scarce resources. Without leadership to set guidelines on the distribution of resources, you may disagree with their allocation and compete with one another for them.

Another cause of conflict in schools is lack of clarity in procedures (Isenhart & Spangle, 2000). For example, some professionals believe that permission to attend a staff development conference is to be given by the principal. Others know that the director of curriculum is responsible for paying the registration fees, and so they believe that the director must give permission. Various staff members contact one of these two individuals. In the confusion, more people initially receive approval to attend than funds exist to support their attendance. Some professionals express anger when they are later told that they cannot attend, and they question how attendees were selected.

Communication Patterns Another critical organizational variable that affects conflict is the pattern of communication among the individuals in various parts of the organization (Keim, Landis, Pierce, & Earnest, 2014; Polsky & Gerschel, 2010). Many different types of dysfunctional communication can create conflict situations. One type occurs when similar information is not available to all individuals. For example, the school psychologists and social workers are informed that the procedures for RTI are changing, but the teachers do not receive this notice. At a subsequent meeting, the teachers challenge the change in procedures initiated by the school psychologists and question whether the change is mandatory or optional. Because the communication was dysfunctional, a conflict was caused.

Another dysfunctional communication pattern that affects the likelihood of conflict occurs when information is conveyed differently by the individuals who communicate with the same staff members. Specialists experience this when they attend a meeting with all the other members of their discipline and learn a new piece of information about data collection expectations. A week later, they attend a meeting for all school personnel, and a different set of instructions is given about the same topic. Shortly after these meetings, several staff members experience conflict about the expectations. Their differences are attributable to the conflicting information they received about the change.

Conflict Response Styles

The next component in learning to understand and respond to conflict concerns the style you are likely to use when participating in a conflict interaction. Figure 9.1 visually represents common conflict response styles, and the E-Partnerships feature provides you with additional resources for learning about responding to conflict. Notice that the styles vary along two dimensions: the importance of the relationship and the importance of the outcome. Avoidance has the least amount of both characteristics; consensus built through collaboration has the greatest amount of each concern; and compromise has roughly equal, moderate amounts of both types of concern (Wilmot & Hocker, 2014). You can assess your style using the Conflict Management Style Survey included in the appendix at the end of this chapter.

Most people have a preferred style for responding to conflict (Baillien, Bollen, Euwema, & De Witte, 2014; Tatum & Eberlin, 2006). As each style is explained on the following pages, keep in mind that no style is entirely positive or negative. Depending on the situations in which a style is used, it has both merits and drawbacks. Remember, too, that your response to conflict may depend partly on the specific situation in which the conflict occurs. For example, you may respond somewhat differently to conflict in a personal relationship than to conflict in a professional setting.

FIGURE 9.1 Styles for resolving conflict.

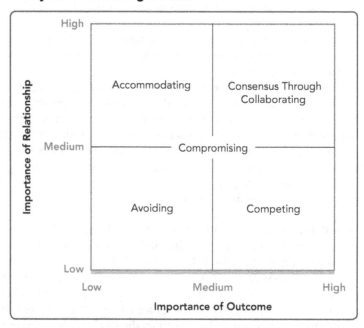

Source: Adapted by permission of the publisher from *The Complete Guide to Conflict Resolution in the Workplace* by Marick F. Masters and Robert R. Albright. © 2002 Marick F. Masters, AMACOM Books, American Management Association, New York, NY. All rights reserved. http://www.amanet.org

E-PARTNERSHIPS

Skills for Difficult Interactions

You can find many Internet sites that provide valuable information for understanding conflict and resistance and that can help you to refine your skills for responding to difficult situations. Here are examples of resources you might want to access.

MindTools: Communication Skills
(http://www.mindtools.com/page8.html?)

Mind Tools is a web site with the purpose of providing knowledge and skills that contribute to successful careers. Clicking on the category called *difficult interactions* will take you to a set of brief but practical articles on topics such as dealing with unreasonable people, handling criticism, and addressing conflict.

Conflict Resolution Network
(http://www.crnhq.org/content.aspx?file=66138|37479i)

The Conflict Resolution Network (CRN) is dedicated to creating a conflict-resolving community across all types of professional and personal situations. On this page of the CRN web site, you can find practical information on 12 specific skills related to conflict resolution, skills applicable across many situations, both professional and personal. Topics addressed include the following:

- Thinking about conflict from a win–win perspective
- Learning to be appropriately assertive
- Managing your emotions during interactions involving conflict
- Seeking options to resolve conflict

Video Series About Difficult Interactions
(www.youtube.com/watch?v=NgnAY_eXYbI)

In this four-part PBS program that has been posted on YouTube (the other clips will be visible on the same page as this video), psychologist Dr. Bill Crawford discusses interactions with difficult people. The video clips explore sources of conflict and strategies for constructively and satisfactorily responding during such challenging interactions.

The Advocacy Institute
(http://www.advocacyinstitute.org/resources/Preparing.for.SpEd.Mediation.Resolution.Sessions.pdf)

The Advocacy Institute, dedicated to improving the lives of individuals with disabilities, provides this guide to special education mediation. The guide, written primarily for parents and families, includes definitions of all the terms associated with special education dispute resolution, a clear explanation of the procedures followed, and suggestions for constructively participating in the process.

Competitive Style Some individuals address conflict using a competitive style, which is sometimes associated with the use of power or force, as people who use it might attempt to overpower others. Their goal tends to be winning, regardless of the potential negative repercussions of their strategy.

A competitive conflict management style might be desirable when ethical issues are at stake or when you are certain that you are right, and that your perspective on the issue at hand is critical to student success (e.g., Rios, DeMarree, & Statzer, 2014). Occasionally, you may use this style when a decision must be made for which group input is sought but for which you alone have responsibility. The disadvantages of this style relate to its inappropriate use: If you frequently compete during conflict, others may stop interacting with you in a meaningful way. Too much use of a competitive style can seriously damage collaborative relationships. Also, few issues in schools have an absolute "right" solution; most are a matter of interpretation. If you often compete because you are certain you are right, you may be perceived by others as rigid and directive.

Avoidance Style Individuals who prefer avoidance usually try to ignore the discrepancy between their own goals and those of others. They deal with conflict by turning away from it (e.g., Guerrero & Gross, 2014). If you have ever participated in a meeting in which an issue needed to be brought to the surface but everyone appeared to have tacitly agreed not to discuss it, you were experiencing avoidance. Notice that in this situation the conflict is not being resolved and may continue to trouble the group.

In particular circumstances, avoidance is advisable. If a conflict is extremely serious and emotion laden, temporary avoidance may enable the individuals involved to think about their positions and participate more constructively. Similarly, if there is not enough time to adequately address a conflict or if the issue is relatively inconsequential, avoidance may be the preferred strategy. However, using avoidance may create difficulties in your collaborative relationships. For example, if you and a colleague disagree on a teaching technique or the amount of support needed by an English learner participating in a general education class, avoiding discussion of the topic can exacerbate the conflict. Avoidance is a seductive strategy because it gives the appearance that all is well; its hidden danger is that a situation may become more difficult or awkward because of inaction.

Accommodative Style Individuals who use an accommodative style set aside their own needs in order to ensure that others' needs are met. Their characteristic response to conflict is to give in (e.g., Saeed, Almas, Anis-ul-Haq, & Niazi, 2014). Occasionally, special educators and other specialists use this style because they believe it may help to initiate or preserve positive relationships with colleagues, particularly in highly collaborative situations such as co-teaching.

An accommodative style can be beneficial when the issue is relatively unimportant or when you cannot alter the situation. Accommodating has a distinct advantage in that it brings conflict to a quick close, enabling you to turn your attention to other matters. The drawbacks of accommodating include the risk of feeling as though others are taking advantage of you, the potential that the issue is one for which you have the best answer and yet you do not insist that it be selected, and the possible devaluing of your ideas when you quickly accommodate on an important matter. Generally, accommodating can be especially appropriate for professionals who need to overcome the tendency to try to win every disagreement; it is often inappropriate for those who feel powerless in their professional relationships.

Compromising Style Many school professionals use a compromising style in responding to conflict. They give up some of their ideas related to an issue and insist that others do the same. They keep some of their ideas and go along with some of the ideas others have proposed. The result typically is an outcome that may not exactly meet everyone's needs but is acceptable to all.

Because compromising is a style whose strength is expedience, it is often appropriate when limited time is available to manage a conflict. It is also useful when the issue at hand is not especially problematic and when two competitive individuals have a conflict (e.g., Mesko, Lang, Czibor, Szijjarto, & Bereczkei, 2014). Although compromise seems to be an ideal style because it implies that part of each individual's goal is achieved, it has drawbacks, too. For example, sometimes typically competitive professionals who decide to compromise feel that they have partly "lost" and so may be somewhat dissatisfied. As a result, additional conflict may occur later. The compromised resolution of an issue can be a bit like the agreement reached for a seaside vacation planned by two friends, one of whom wanted to go to the East Coast while the other wanted to go to the West Coast: They ended up in Kansas, and neither person was truly happy.

Consensus Through Collaboration Style Although some level of collaboration is required for most conflict resolution, it is particularly important when the goal is to reach consensus. Consensus generally is the most satisfying approach to resolving conflict (Evans, 2012). Use of a consensual style requires commitment to the defining elements of collaboration we described as a foundation to this text, as well as to the emergent characteristics of collaboration. It often includes developing a completely new alternative to resolve the conflict situation. For example, a collaborative response to the vacation example might be for the friends to decide that the vacation was not the issue at all. Because both were looking for a relaxing experience near water, they could decide to spend a week in a lakeside retreat only 50 miles from their hometown. Unlike compromise, which means taking some of each person's ideas and rejecting some of each person's ideas, consensus is premised on creating options that all participants completely endorse. When consensus is achieved, each participant fully embraces the resolution.

Although consensus has many positive aspects, in conflict situations it cannot always be achieved: It is time consuming, it requires that certain defining elements be in place, and it can be undertaken only as professionals learn about and come to trust one another. Thus, achieving consensus through collaboration is sometimes not even an option for addressing conflict. In such cases, a much more likely and still appropriate option is compromise.

By learning to monitor the style you use to respond to conflict in your professional interactions, you will grow in your knowledge about how you handle such situations. Further, by knowing what causes conflict, understanding conflict response styles, and learning specific strategies such as those described next and in A Basis in Research, you will be more successful in managing difficult interactions.

APPLY YOUR KNOWLEDGE 9.1

Resolving Conflict Through Negotiation

Negotiation is a conflict management technique that has a long history of success in business settings (Marcus, Dorn, & McNulty, 2012; Pruitt, 2011) that can also help you resolve school conflict. Negotiation can be used in many types of conflict. Here are examples of conflicts in school settings that could be addressed through negotiation:

- The number of planning sessions a pair of co-teachers will get for the school year (between principals and co-teachers)
- Who will take responsibility for which parts of the shared planning tasks on the grade-level or department team (among teachers)
- The dates the counselor will come to the class to work with students on a unit on friendship (teacher and specialist)
- The type of communication system that will be implemented among the English as a Second Language (ESL) teacher, the general educator, and the parent (teachers and parent)
- The amount of service that will adequately address a student's assessed needs for special education and related services (teachers, parents, administrator)

A BASIS IN RESEARCH

Constructive Conflict and Psychological Safety

Whenever you work in a group, including on teams, conflict may occur. But the type of conflict and the context in which it occurs can either help teams become more productive or interfere with their work. Bradley et al., (2012) studied conflict on teams with a large sample of undergraduate students. These teams ($N = 117$) completed team-building activities to establish interpersonal relationships and then were assigned specific tasks to complete. After the teaming experience, the participants completed three instruments designed to rate the level of conflict experienced on the team related to the assigned tasks, the level of psychological safety on the team, and the quality of the team's performance. Some of the findings included the following:

- Team performance ratings were correlated with participants' ratings of psychological safety on the team. That is, when ratings of psychological safety were lower, team members' ratings of their team's performance were lower. This suggests that a constructive environment, rather than one laced with fear of verbal attacks, is likely to lead to better outcomes.
- When psychological safety was rated as high, higher task conflict was positively correlated with ratings of team performance. That is, if team members felt psychologically safe, more conflict led them to perceive that their team had performed at a higher level. This suggests that conflict can be perceived as helpful for stimulating productive discussions and creating new options.

The authors of this study concluded that team members should work diligently to make all members feel safe as a means of improving team functioning. How could you apply these interesting findings about conflict on teams to the teams on which you might serve as an educator?

Notice that negotiation sometimes occurs on small, day-to-day matters, and sometimes it occurs on significant issues. The strategies for negotiation across all types of conflicts are the same.

The key to successful negotiation, whether it is formal or informal, is to keep in mind that the object of the interaction is not for one person to win while the other loses. In their extensive work on this topic, Ury and his colleagues (Fisher, Ury, & Patton, 1997; Ury, 1991; Ury, Brett, & Goldberg, 2005) have derived the following principles, employed in many professions, for successful negotiation:

1. Focus on issues, not people, whenever you experience conflict. Instead of saying, "You don't understand how changing the intervention will affect the entire class," you might say, "The strategy we're discussing now could cause problems. I think it might negatively affect classroom routine." The former makes the disagreement an adversarial situation based on people; the latter acknowledges disagreement but anchors it on the proposed intervention instead of on the person who proposed it.

2. To the greatest extent possible, keep the conflict focused on issues that have the potential to be agreed on. This reminds you as well as the others that you have a common ground from which to work to manage the conflict. For example, it is often more constructive to suggest a specific remedial intervention for a student than to discuss a colleague's disagreement that the student can be successful in the teacher's class. The former can be addressed; in most cases, the latter cannot.

3. Reduce the emotional component of the conflict. If the issue in conflict has raised strong emotional responses, you may find that it is not possible to proceed and temporary avoidance is needed. However, you can sometimes defuse emotions by responding positively to others' negative comments, by not responding to comments that might cause you to become angry, and by acknowledging others' feelings (Jordan & Troth, 2004; Scott, 2008).

4. We would be remiss if we did not include a final strategy: the option for you to adapt to the issue or, if possible, to exit the situation. At some point, it becomes self-defeating to continue to try to address a conflict if the other person does not view the matter as an issue or if you cannot influence the conflict situation. Resolving the matter within yourself so that you no longer fret about it may be extraordinarily difficult, especially if you feel strongly about it. However, "letting go" may also be the most viable option. If that is not possible and the issue is critical, you may choose to leave the situation or even the school setting. For example, a student with a moderate cognitive disability is moving to first grade. The first-year special education teacher believes strongly that the child should spend most of the day with peers without disabilities. The first-grade teachers are adamant that they do not know how to meet the child's needs. The principal does not want to anger the first-grade teachers, and so she is tending to agree with their point of view unless the district is willing to provide a one-to-one assistant for the student. The parent is not strongly advocating for any arrangement but does like the idea of the assistant. In spite of repeated efforts using superb communication skills and in light of so many factors constraining placement in a typical classroom, including the fact that no assistant will be assigned, the special educator might decide that she should simply keep quiet about her beliefs. If this pattern of making decisions about children were common, she might decide that she would prefer to work in another school or another district. Sometimes the decision to keep quiet or leave relates to a combination of factors, including the importance of the conflict, the school culture, and a person's status (e.g., nontenured). Many professionals find options related to accepting or leaving a situation extraordinarily difficult because of their commitment to their students and profession, but a discussion of conflict resolution would not be complete without mentioning this choice as an alternative.

Consider how each of the ideas just outlined can be applied to each of difficult interaction examples outlined in this chapter section If you use these principles for effective negotiation and think of negotiation as specialized problem solving, you can use steps such

---

Learn More About

As you watch this video clip on negotiation, think about how you could put into practice in a school setting the suggestions it offers. How could these ideas make you more effective as you collaborate with your colleagues?

(https://www.youtube.com/watch?v=1FeM6kp9Q80)

PUTTING IDEAS INTO PRACTICE

Effective Negotiation

In addition to understanding the principles on which successful negotiation is based, you can use the following steps to guide your negotiation to a positive conclusion:

- *Understand your own motivation and that of others.* What are the motivations of those involved in the conflict? Is the basis of the conflict a value difference? Is it an issue of limited resources and the stress caused by the situation? Is it a matter of differing opinions about interventions?
- *Clarify the issues.* If you and the other person(s) involved in a conflict do not have a mutual understanding of the issues, you are unlikely to resolve them.
- *Set your expectations.* This requires examining your ideal solution to the conflict and then tempering it with your understanding of motivations as well as other factors influencing the situation. This step is called *goal setting*.
- *Discuss each issue involved in the conflict.* Sometimes it is tempting to have a general discussion in which all the issues related to the conflict are raised. The result can be unclear communication and, sometimes, additional conflict.
- *Make and respond to offers.* This is the part of negotiation that includes give-and-take among participants. Remember that if you will not consider other options, you are not negotiating in good faith.
- *Monitor for ethics and integrity.* Negotiation in conflict situations can be successful only if you work in good faith. If you withhold information or manipulate others' words, you may worsen the situation instead of improving it. At the same time, you should be aware of the ethical issues involved in serving the needs of students with disabilities. Your goal for concluding a negotiation should be to enable everyone to "save face," while at the same time resolving the dilemma in a professional manner.

as those in Putting Ideas into Practice to respond to conflict positively and constructively. For additional practice, you might consider using the case that opened this chapter as a basis for discussing how such conflicts might be addressed by school professionals.

Resolving Conflict Through Mediation

You probably have experienced formal negotiation if you have been involved in the discussion of teacher contracts through your local professional association. Perhaps you have informally negotiated with colleagues concerning team planning time, the clarification of roles in a co-taught class, or the arrangement of a single classroom shared among you and two other reading specialists. However, what should you do if negotiation fails to resolve the conflict? What strategies remain when you cannot simply retreat from the situation and are not satisfied with the current situation? A specialized form of negotiation—mediation—is a process in which a third party, who is neutral in regard to the issue at hand, guides the individuals in conflict through a voluntary discussion with the goal of settling the dispute (Coke, 2014; Pruitt, 2011). Like negotiation, mediation is used in many disciplines, including education (e.g., Bernardin, Richey, & Castro, 2011; Charkoudian, 2010; Eigen & Litwin, 2014; Otis, 2011).

Consider the situation previously mentioned about the appropriate role for each professional in a co-taught class. The general education teacher is not comfortable with another adult contributing during large-group instruction and prefers that you remain seated and quiet during such times. You maintain that you are highly qualified and experienced and that, with less large-group instruction and more use of small groups, you can actively participate in instruction and better provide a range of supports and services to students in the classroom. At an impasse, perhaps you ask your assistant principal or your school's literacy coach to meet with both of you to discuss possible solutions. Alternatively, perhaps your school district employs a nonsupervisory staff member who has the responsibility of fostering collaboration and ensuring that students with special needs receive an appropriate education. This individual also might serve in the role of mediator.

School professionals turn potentially adversarial situations into constructive ones when they use negotiation or mediation.

You could be involved in mediation in a more formal context. As you know, the Individuals with Disabilities Education Act (IDEA) includes the provision that mediation must be offered to parents who are in conflict with schools concerning their children's special education (Burke & Goldman, 2014). Further, it establishes an informal resolution session as part of the due process procedure (Mueller, 2009a), and this session can function as a type of informal mediation. Although mediation may not be a successful strategy when the disputed issues concern a legal interpretation of the law or personnel changes, it has several advantages over due process hearings (Heitin, 2013). For example, mediation is considered a much less formal approach, which may prevent an adversarial climate from developing (Brubaker, Noble, Fincher, Park, & Press, 2014). Further, it is focused on the future, emphasizes clear and direct communication, keeps control of the process in the hands of the parties directly involved, and is far less expensive than a due process hearing. Of course, if parents do not wish to engage in informal or formal mediation—including a resolution session—or if school professionals have a negative disposition toward the conflict situation and the potential of mediation, it is not the preferred option (Mueller & Carranza, 2011).

Many sources of information exist regarding how to successfully mediate during conflict. Some of the most helpful suggestions include the following (McCorkle & Reese, 2015; Mercer & Davis, 2011):

> **Learn More About**
>
> Mediation can be an important and constructive alternative to due process hearings in special education. This video explains the basics of the mediation process.
>
> (https://www.youtube.com/watch?v=E56LXt1QsxU)

1. In any type of mediation, preparation is essential. Whether this involves understanding the context in which a conflict is occurring, the perspectives of participants, or the impact of the outcome on each individual, an effective mediator has a solid basis of understanding from the very start.
2. Mediation begins with an orientation—that is, an explanation to all participants of the ground rules. Often, mediators emphasize the importance of clear communication, the priority given to making the situation feel "safe" to everyone, and the optimistic intent to resolve the conflict. A focus on establishing a positive climate of collaboration is particularly helpful.
3. Early in mediation, each party explains his or her perspective, and the specific issues that comprise the conflict are articulated. The rationale for this process is that each person has a unique perspective regarding the conflict and that sharing perspectives sometimes helps to generate solutions.
4. The most critical step of mediation occurs when needs and interests are explored; each party looks for areas of *shared* needs and interests that might be elements of resolution. If this stage of mediation is not successful, the process is likely to flounder.
5. Once interests are identified, the strategies of negotiation and problem solving are used. An effective mediator will at this point subtly remind participants of the costs of failing to reach an agreement.
6. When some type of agreement is reached, it should be clearly articulated, either in writing or through an oral, point-by-point summary completed during the meeting. This helps prevent miscommunication and the potential for new conflict.
7. Finally, it is often beneficial in mediation for a follow-up meeting to be scheduled so that progress can be reviewed, the current situation assessed, and feedback obtained from the involved parties.

If you think about your roles and responsibilities in schools, you may have numerous opportunities to function informally as a mediator. You might first think of taking this role in assisting students to resolve disagreements. However, you might also serve as a mediator in a conflict among members of a grade-level or department team. You could mediate when parents of a student have a conflict with another teacher or specialist. Finally, you can use the thinking of mediation in your own interactions with your colleagues and the parents and families of the students with whom you work (e.g., Hedeen, Moses, & Peter, 2011).

Conflict and Diversity

A discussion about conflict would not be complete without mentioning diversity. If you review the information contained throughout this section, you should realize that a key underlying principle for successfully resolving conflict is to analyze it and base your response on that analysis. As part of this process, you should consider culture (Murayama, Ryan, Shimizu, Kurebayashi, & Miura, 2015). That is, you should look beyond race, nationality, or ethnicity to understand more clearly the beliefs, perceptions, and preferences that each person in a conflict holds. Even more so than in day-to-day interactions, when you participate in a difficult interaction with professionals, paraeducators, parents, or others from a background different from your own, it is essential first that you recognize your own point of view and how it is influenced by your culture—your need to preserve harmony, your comfort level with confrontation, the nonverbal cues that you most respond to, your need for formality or informality, and so on (Nan, 2011). Then you can juxtapose your culture against the cultures of others in order to deliberately communicate and use procedures likely to lead to resolution (Irvine, 2012). Specific suggestions for doing this are included in Putting Ideas into Practice.

PUTTING IDEAS INTO PRACTICE

Addressing Difficult Interactions in Diverse Groups

Throughout your professional preparation and practice, you have learned and remained aware of cultural differences in child-rearing practices, importance placed on education, perspectives on time, and many other factors. It is just as important to understand that individuals from various cultures may respond differently when disagreements occur (Loode, 2011; Sadri, 2013). Here are a few suggestions to consider when faced with such situations.

- Most conflict resolution experts advise using strategies that rely heavily on talk. However, in some cases, alternatives such as these may be better:
  - Suggest a few moments of silence for participants to think about their needs.
  - Create options for using visual presentations of the points of view being expressed.
  - Identify a shared emotion a bit removed from the situation at hand to help diffuse the tension and open options for a constructive resolution (Von Glinow, Shapiro, & Brett, 2004).

- The sense of urgency for resolution of a conflict may vary by culture (Brew & Cairns, 2004). If you sense that others are feeling pressured to resolve a dispute before they are ready, you might suggest adjourning the meeting and reconvening it at a point in the near future.

- Across many cultures, a perceived threat to "face"—that is, a person's social image—can become a significant roadblock to discussion and resolution (Kemp, 2009). The implication is that all ideas shared when an interaction is difficult should be thought of in terms of how others will perceive them. For example, some family members may sense they lose face if they follow "orders" from school professionals on how to address their child's behavior.

APPLY YOUR KNOWLEDGE 9.2

Understanding Resistance

Resistance has been a topic of concern in many fields, including business and the helping professions as well as education (e.g., Burke, 2011; Choi & Ruona, 2011; García-Cabrera & García-Barba Hernández, 2014; Murray, 2007). It most typically occurs as a response to an interpersonal change or an organizational change that has a personal impact. One apt characterization of resistance defines it as the ability to *not get what is not wanted from the environment*. The use of two negatives in this definition is critical: Resistance occurs only in response to a perceived impending change. If no change exists, resistance vanishes.

The use of negatives in the definition, however, should not lead you to conclude that resistance itself is undesirable. In fact, the opposite is true. Resistance is a defense mechanism that prevents individuals from undertaking change that is too risky for their sense of safety. In addition, resistance sometimes leads to an appropriate decision not to participate in an activity or change. The concern in professional relationships arises when resistance becomes a barrier to effective interactions and needed innovation (Stanleigh, 2013). Think about the issues that contribute to resistance in the following two examples:

> The school improvement committee is meeting to finalize all staff members' assignments for the upcoming school year. The group reviewing the school's positive behavior support system is established as is the data team. Now the team responsible for creating three professional learning communities on the topics of inclusion, students with autism, and students who are English language learners must be identified.
>
> Mr. Powers, the principal, says to Ms. Bennett, the counselor, "I'd like you to lead this work because the topics all relate to struggling learners. Ms. Nelson, Mr. Jordan, and Ms. Hartman are my recommendations for the other committee members." Ms. Bennett conveys nonverbally her dissatisfaction with this assignment, and Mr. Powers observes, "You don't seem comfortable with this assignment. I thought it would be exactly what you'd prefer."
>
> Ms. Bennett replies, "Last year I worked on a committee with Ms. Nelson and Mr. Jordan. I don't know how to say this politely, but I ended up doing all the work. They always had reasons to decline helping to get things finished. I'd rather work with other people."

> Shortly before the holidays, Ms. Hill, the school psychologist, is meeting with Mr. Neal, the fifth-grade teacher, about a behavioral contract for Reggie, a student with behavior disorders who is inattentive and has been swearing at the teacher and other students. As Ms. Hill explains the contract as a possible intervention, Mr. Neal comments, "You know, I don't mind having Reggie in my class. But I don't know about this contract idea. It's not fair to the other kids to give Reggie special treatment. I predict I'll get parent phone calls about this." After more discussion, Mr. Neal reluctantly agrees to try the intervention.
>
> A week later, Ms. Hill stops by Mr. Neal's classroom to check on Reggie. "How's the contract working for Reggie?"
>
> "Well …"
>
> "What's going on?"
>
> "Actually," says Mr. Neal, "I tried it for two days and it just wasn't fitting into my classroom routine. Besides, Reggie probably didn't like being singled out. We need to change it, but for now, with the holidays coming, I just don't have the time to attend to this. Let's talk after the beginning of the year."

In the first example, the resistance to working with colleagues who in the past did not do their share of the work is fairly straightforward: The counselor appears to be concerned about her actual experience working with the other teachers. She is protecting herself from anticipated uneven work distribution. In the second example, the resistance is more difficult to discern clearly, but it is still related to protection: Mr. Neal's response might be interpreted as meaning that he is concerned with his psychological safety. Perhaps he is unfamiliar with the contracting approach Ms. Hill proposed, and he does not want to let her know this. Perhaps he is overwhelmed by the pressures of his job (which might include a new math curriculum, an overcrowded room, or several students with extraordinary needs), and he simply cannot manage one more demand. The knowledge you have gained about individuals' perspectives can help you to consider a wide range of meanings in these and similar situations.

Given the amount and pace of change currently taking place in schools, it is not surprising to find that resistance is common. And when you reflect on the changes occurring in the education of students with special needs, you should conclude that resistance is likely among specialists as well as between specialists and other staff. The fact that many school changes result in increased adult–adult interactions only compounds the issue because such interactions increase the likelihood that each individual's resistance will be known and will affect others.

Causes of Resistance

Although many causes of resistance have been described in the professional literature (e.g., Kampwirth & Powers, 2015; van Dijk & van Dick, 2009), they can be summarized as addressing just one critical concept: Resistance is an emotional response based on a rational or irrational fear or concern related to whatever change is proposed or occurring. These fears may pertain to (1) the by change itself; (2) the impact of the change on the resistant person; (3) other persons initiating, participating in, or affected by the change; and (4) homeostasis.

Concerns About the Proposed Change   One common source of resistance is professionals' and parents' perceptions of the anticipated outcomes associated with a change. For example, parents of typical learners as well as parents of students with special needs may be resistant to their children participating in a co-taught class; they may believe that the risks to their children's education outweigh the potential gains.

Another example of fear related to the change itself may be the philosophy or value system associated with the change (Barsky, 2008; Danışman, 2010). If you are an ESL teacher who believes strongly in the value of instruction offered in a separate classroom, then the plan to have you work with students primarily in general education classes may cause you to be resistant. Alternatively, if you are a speech/language therapist and believe that integrative therapy should be the standard in your field, you are likely to be resistant to a plan in which you will provide primarily articulation therapy in a separate clinical setting. For general education teachers, this type of resistance may arise when considering the use of an instructional approach (e.g., new , problem-based math curriculum) that they perceive will dilute or interfere with their instructional effectiveness. In each example, resistance is attached to a belief system that is associated with a specific change. This form of resistance is especially likely to occur when change is not clearly explained.

Concerns About the Personal Impact of the Change   Fear about the personal impact of change is the category into which most professional resistance falls (Jackson, 2010). It generally includes the following issues:

1. Some individuals faced with changing their professional functioning are afraid of failing. They may anticipate that they do not have the skills to participate in the change, and they may perceive that they cannot acquire them.
2. Some professionals fear the frustration that may occur while learning new skills and practices. Whenever changes are undertaken in activities, programs, or services, professionals require time to adjust their practices. However, because time is a luxury that simply cannot be afforded in many schools, they often are expected to assimilate change rapidly and to immediately function effectively, sometimes beyond the point of reasonable expectations.

> **Learn More About**
> How could you apply the helpful tips in this video on change and resistance to situations you may encounter as a school professional? Which ideas seem most powerful? Which might apply to you when you are confronted with a change and are resistant to it?
>
> (https://www.youtube.com/watch?v=T_y1qV8eTrI)

"So basically you are looking for books on changing everyone except yourself"

3. Personal fear about change also relates to losing autonomy. Many school professionals are accustomed to completing their job responsibilities with little input from others. When a change is proposed, particularly one that appears to threaten this autonomy, fear sometimes results. Resistance is an expected outcome.

Concerns About Others Involved in the Change The third category of concerns that may lead to resistance focuses on other individuals involved. First, concern may be directed at the person initiating the change (Oreg & Sverdlik, 2011). Have you ever decided before hearing about a new strategy, service, or program that you probably did not want to participate just because you had a negative perception of the person whose idea it was? Perhaps you did not respect that individual, experienced a great deal of miscommunication with the person, or had discrepant personal styles. It should be noted that this is another example of resistance that, in some cases, has a strongly rational basis; in others, it is emotional.

The second major type of concern included in this category is the threat of change in your relationships with others. If you participate in a change, it may affect how other staff members view you and your status with them. For example, a newly hired English teacher at the high school is asked by the curriculum director to lead the school's professional learning community (PLC) on teacher leadership. Other teachers are opposed to the PLC idea, and they have openly expressed reluctance to participating in it. If you were the English teacher, how would you respond? One approach would be to develop the program alone, hoping to positively influence colleagues in the process. Another would be to let the other teachers know about the responsibility you have and then to collaborate with them to avoid meeting it. Even if this were inappropriate, the latter option might appeal to the English teacher if she felt excluded by the other teachers and had concerns about how they would respond if the PLC were developed. This type of situation clearly has many alternative solutions. The point here is that the relationship issue may supersede others and lead to resistance (e.g., Battilana & Casciaro, 2013).

Homeostasis The tendency of some individuals and systems to prefer sameness to change is referred to as *homeostasis*. Some individuals, once they become accustomed to a particular way of carrying out responsibilities, working with students, and otherwise fulfilling their professional obligations, may struggle to consider alternative ways to do those tasks. The degree to which homeostasis plays a part in resistance varies greatly from person to person and with the nature of the change that is at issue.

Organizations also seek to maintain some level of homeostasis and in doing so may encourage resistance (Zins & Illback, 2008). In some school settings, it is considered the norm to resist any change, regardless of its source. We have worked in school settings in which the professionals quickly stated that their schools were difficult places to initiate new programs because staff members simply did not like change. Although this situation relates to individual homeostasis, it is distinguished from it because of its pervasiveness in the school's culture. Several staff members in the school may be risk takers or change agents, but their individual characteristics may have been overshadowed by the norm.

Homeostasis may result from another dilemma referred to as *change fatigue* (Beaudan, 2006). That is, in schools where change has been constant, professionals may become very reluctant to participate. A fairly complex example illustrates this concept: An urban high school has had three principals in the past four years. In addition, the school district has changed the high-stakes testing requirements twice during that time. There has been relatively high staff turnover, and no special educator or ESL teacher at the school has more than three years of teaching experience. The school attempted to place more students with special needs in general education settings about four years ago but encountered serious problems related to teacher acceptance, scheduling, parent concerns, and student behavior. When the new principal announces at a meeting for all staff members that her top priority is to improve general education access, teachers roll their eyes and look at each other skeptically. Their reaction, without even hearing about the proposal, is negative. Given the situation, however, it is understandable—they have difficulty comprehending how they can manage yet one more change, one that does not seem feasible.

Indicators of Resistance

Resistance often is indicated through subtle behaviors and can be difficult to clearly recognize. Most behaviors that signal resistance have alternative, legitimate interpretations, but when examined closely, they actually function as a means of avoiding change. Thus, in order to address resistance, you should have a clear picture of how resistance is likely to be manifested. The most common ways include the following:

- Refusing to participate
- Supporting a change with words but not actions
- Displacing responsibility
- Deferring change to a future time
- Relying on past practice.

Each of these signals of resistance is presented with examples in Figure 9.2.

In considering signals of resistance, it is particularly important to look for patterns of behavior. Anyone can encounter a crisis that leads to the cancellation of a meeting. However, repeated cancellations may indicate resistance. Similarly, anyone can have a straightforward reason for delaying a change. However, repeated excuses may indicate resistance. Your role in working with others is to distinguish between legitimate problems and resistance and to base your actions on such distinctions.

Assessing Whether to Address Resistance

The next consideration when you perceive resistance is to decide whether it should be addressed. Your deliberations should examine the following:

- The appropriateness of the resistance
- Whether addressing it is warranted
- Others' commitment to change

Determine Whether Resistance Is an Appropriate Response The concept that resistance is sometimes appropriate has already been mentioned (Ford & Ford, 2010), and overall you may have noticed that this chapter on resistance does not necessarily focus on making it go away. Instead, as you approach resistant interactions, you should first consider the situation from the other individual's point of view, drawing on your understanding of perspective as introduced in Chapter 2. If the change will place too great a burden on the person resisting, that response may be a positive reaction and should not be addressed. In general, if you remember that addressing resistance should have as a goal respecting it, exploring it, and potentially (but not invariably) responding to it, you will be more effective in your professional relationships. Although our examples tend to make others the resistant parties, also keep in mind a point made at the beginning of this chapter: We all resist—including you (and us)—given the right circumstances.

FIGURE 9.2   Indicators of resistance.

Indicator	Explanation
Refusing to participate	Response to change is "No, thank you." Examples: - "I figure this is just a fad. By next year it'll be gone. I'd rather not waste my time on this." - "I just can't deal with doing that right now. I have too many other responsibilities." - "I don't want to get involved with this issue. Please ask someone else."
Supporting without substance	Response to change is "bobble head" head-nodding without meaning. Examples: - "Yeah—that's great." - "Okay—I see." - "That makes sense—uh-huh."
Displacing responsibility	Response to change is claiming others will not permit it. Examples: - "The other parents are going to complain." - "I understand that the state has said this is not legal." - "The principal doesn't allow it."
Deferring to a future time	Response to change is putting it off. Examples: - [in September] "Everything is so hectic with the start of the year. Let's give it a little time and then try it." - [in November] "The holidays are almost here and you know how disrupted the schedule gets."
Relying on past practice	Response to change is to call on tradition as a reason to retain the status quo. Examples: - "We've always done it this way." - "If it's not broken, don't fix it." - "This way has always been good enough for us." - "We can't just rush into this type of intervention. It's too different from what we're used to."

Assess Whether Addressing Resistance Is Warranted Another consideration when deciding whether to respond to a resistant situation is the appropriateness of attempting to address it (Hernandez, 2013). The same questions presented in Chapter 5 for deciding whether to problem solve are applicable for resistance. In some instances, the best response to resistance, even if it is not rational, may be no response at all. For example, if a colleague is planning to leave her job at the end of the year, your efforts to address her resistance to a new learning strategy may not be worth the effort. The same could be said for those who are transferring to other schools or retiring. Other situations that may not warrant addressing resistance are those in which administrative support is lacking or contextual variables (such as a lack of resources) make the proposed strategy or intervention unrealistic.

Consider the Extent of Others' Commitment to Change Understanding the likelihood that others will change can assist you in gauging your own commitment to change. Individuals are more likely to participate in a change if they feel they have a moderate or low level of positive or negative feeling about the nature of the change (Battilana & Casciaro, 2013; Harvey, 2010). They are less likely to change if they have strong negative feelings about it. The implication is that change is less likely to be successful if offered when emotions are intense. A more constructive alternative would be to wait, if possible, until feelings are less intense.

Persuasion as a Strategy for Responding to Resistance

One critical strategy for addressing resistant situations is persuasion. Persuasion is your ability to convince another person to agree to your perception or plan regarding an issue or idea (Simons & Jones, 2011). For example, you may be faced with the task of convincing a resistant colleague that a different way to teach equations in remedial algebra has an evidence base and will foster student learning. Similarly, you may attempt to convince a parent that the educational services proposed by the team are in the best interests of the child.

Persuasion Approaches Approaches for persuading are heavily influenced by theories that describe how individuals respond when faced with an idea or activity to which they are resistant (e.g., Barden & Tormala, 2014). For example, in a *behavioral approach* to persuasion, the goal is to provide positive reinforcement to resistant individuals in order to convince them to change. This would occur if a teacher were offered a preferred classroom assignment in return for participating in a pilot co-teaching project. Another example would be recruiting new co-teachers by arranging for them to attend professional development on this topic with their teaching partners.

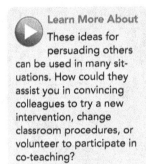

Learn More About
These ideas for persuading others can be used in many situations. How could they assist you in convincing colleagues to try a new intervention, change classroom procedures, or volunteer to participate in co-teaching?
(https://www.youtube.com/watch?v=ap-jifFP4Z0)

A second theoretical orientation to persuasion is a *consistency approach*, which is based on the notion that individuals are more likely to change if they have a sense of cognitive dissonance (Festinger, 1957). For example, by suggesting to Ms. Boesche that she has already been successful with a student very much like the one she is currently expressing resistance about having in her class, you might plant a seed that eventually prompts her to be more accepting of the new student.

A *perceptual approach* is also considered a means for persuading others. Individuals applying this model recognize that people have a certain tolerance for change. If the proposed change is somewhat close to an activity a person is already comfortable doing, that person is more likely to accept the new activity than if it is perceived as radically different. For example, in discussing a new school initiative related to mentoring, a principal might explain that teachers in the school are already informally implementing many of the strategies that the mentoring program formalizes and that the initiative is simply an extension of the work they are already doing.

Finally, a *functional approach* to persuasion suggests that the process of convincing someone to change must take into account adult learning characteristics. For example, if Ms. Schwartz complained that she dislikes the way students are constantly leaving the room to receive special education, ESL, speech/language, and remedial reading services, you might suggest that she would prefer to have students stay in the room. This could acknowledge her desire for control over student movement and the sense of classroom community as well as create an opportunity to discuss integrated in-class instruction.

Persuasion Strategies The knowledge base on theoretical approaches to persuasion leads to a number of suggestions for you to use in encouraging colleagues and others to change. Consider how the following ideas might apply to the resistance demonstrated by the teachers in the case presented at the beginning of this chapter:

1. *Seek ways to provide incentives.* Incentives could include a trade-off or reduction of workloads, assistance with classroom chores, provision of special materials, or opportunities to participate in professional development activities. If you think of any situation in which you need to persuade others, you probably can identify incentives that could be offered to positively affect the outcome.

How could you use the principles of persuasion used in advertising to assist you in your professional interactions with colleagues and parents?

2. *Relate the proposed change issue to a positive image.* To many teachers, the word *change* is a negative stimulus; they immediately associate it with anxiety, stress, more work, and more meetings. One strategy for persuading others is to relate the change to a reduction of anxiety, work, and meetings while also associating it with improved student achievement and personal and professional satisfaction and acclaim. Obviously, this strategy is effective only to the extent that a workload reduction and student improvement can, in fact, be accomplished. The complement to this is to avoid saying anything negative about the change; such messages tend to be remembered and gain strength with time (Kumkale & Albarracin, 2004). However tempting it is to complain, these comments make change even more difficult.

3. *Provide opportunities for others to become familiar with the change through observation.* If a professional observes others successfully carrying out a change, he or she may sense it is feasible after all. For some educators, this could include visiting neighboring school districts where similar activities or services are offered. For others, it may be just an observation period in a nearby colleague's classroom or therapeutic setting. The information about peer coaching presented in Chapter 8 may be useful in thinking about how observations could be arranged.

4. *Create discrepancies that can be brought to the attention of resistant individuals.* Imagine a history teacher who fears that a student with a disability will require too much of the teacher's attention. One strategy would be to arrange an informal meeting between the history teacher and another subject-area teacher who has worked with the student and who can share the positive experiences the student had in a general education class. Knowing about the student's success creates a discrepancy and makes resistance less likely.

5. *Link the proposed change with the resolution of the discrepancy.* Persuasion involves more than simply creating dissonance; it also involves efforts to influence how the dissonance will be resolved. In the example just presented, the dissonance exists because of the history teacher's belief that the student cannot be successful and the other teacher's perspective that the student can be successful. To influence the history teacher to resolve the dissonance by agreeing the student could succeed, you might comment on the teacher's ability to work with other difficult students, the fact that he or she would be on the "cutting edge" for the district integration program and in compliance with emerging policy, and the satisfaction experienced by working with the student.

6. *Relate the change to others' knowledge and experience.* Keeping both the nature and the description of the proposed change within a framework of familiarity for others is a basic strategy of persuasion. A simple illustration of this point concerns the use of technical vocabulary. If you have a strong background in behavioral approaches, you might tend to speak to others about a school-wide positive behavior support (PBS) system using psychological terms such as *reinforcers*, *extinction*, and *punishers*. If you change your language so that your terminology sounds more familiar to your colleagues—*rewards*, *ignoring*, and *consequences*—you may find that less resistance occurs.

7. *Propose changes within the value system of others.* This strategy is a powerful extension of the preceding strategy. Proponents of change should examine participants' value systems and tailor ideas to stay within those parameters.
8. *Gain public commitment.* One strategy for ensuring that a proposed change falls within individuals' tolerance levels is to obtain their overt commitment to the change. Once they have made such a commitment, they are more likely to try to expand their own levels of tolerance for the change. Public commitment significantly raises the probability of implementation.
9. *Involve others early in the planning stages.* Whether you are discussing a single intervention, a change for a classroom, a program change, or change that could affect an entire grade level, team, department, or school, the change will be more readily accomplished if you include others in planning. Doing so enables you to be more responsive to others' needs. Change thus becomes less threatening, and the potential for resistance is decreased. This is especially true regarding those who are most resistant; their participation may mitigate their resistance.
10. *Be sensitive to adult learning preferences.* Certain conditions may make change for adults easier. In fact, knowledge about adult learning is important when planning for change. Examples of adult learning preferences include incorporating ideas based on the life experiences of participants, using novelty to introduce an idea, and engaging participants in meaningful activities related to accomplishing the change. Although none of these techniques seems strongly persuasive, each has the potential to add enough appeal to the proposed change to make it attractive to the individuals affected by it.
11. *Clarify ownership of the task or activity.* Whenever people are working together toward a goal, they should specify how ownership will be assigned. If change is the issue, the more individuals feel like they have contributed to designing and implementing the change, the more likely it is they will participate in it.
12. *Obtain and use feedback from participants.* Feedback is one type of information that participants can contribute to change. The obligation of professionals fostering change is to use this information in a meaningful way. For example, suppose you were part of the team that was developing the RTI process introduced in the case at the beginning of this chapter. Before implementing the process, you and your teammates might want to share an outline of the process, with a timeline, to obtain others' reaction to it. You might also provide information about the interventions being planned for Tiers 1, 2, and 3 and seek input from colleagues about the alignment with core instructional programs. Such discussions are valuable in designing an RTI approach likely to be perceived as feasible. Simply announcing a completed plan would be counterproductive, that is, explaining the procedures to be followed and interventions to be used, without inviting input from teachers and others, is unlikely to lead to success.

Putting the Pieces Together

At the opening of this chapter, you were alerted to the fact that difficult interactions provide opportunities to learn and apply the skills that have been presented in earlier chapters in this text. Whether conflict or resistance emerges as part of teams, consultation, or co-teaching, or whether either occurs in interactions with paraeducators or family members, the topics addressed in chapters that follow, your knowledge of problem-solving strategies and communication skills are the tools that enable you to address such situations confidently (Putnam, 2010). Examples of applying your knowledge and skills are provided in Putting Ideas into Practice.

PUTTING IDEAS INTO PRACTICE

Using Communication Skills During Difficult Interactions

When you face a situation that includes conflict or resistance, you have the opportunity to use the communication skills you have learned to good advantage. Consider this example: A behavior specialist and a teacher have been working to implement a self-monitoring strategy for Alex, a student who is experiencing ongoing behavior problems. He is to keep an index card taped to his desk, and when he begins a requested task without making a comment out loud in class, he is to make a check on the card. In the discussion, it becomes clear that the teacher is not encouraging Alex to use the strategy and sometimes seems to be going back to a pattern of confronting Alex about call-outs. At the same time, it is apparent that the teacher thinks the strategy is too time consuming, perhaps stigmatizing, and not particularly effective in a class with several students who need frequent special attention. He comments that Alex will not follow directions or accept guidance.

How might each of the following aspects of positive communication help these professionals to have a constructive conversation that leads to a better outcome for the student?

Perspective (Chapter 2)

- When the teacher says, "I've been really careful about using the strategy and it's not working," what might the teacher mean? What response might the behavior specialist make? How might you determine whether the teacher's comment is a signal of resistance?

Feedback and Indirect Question (Chapters 3 and 4)

- The specialist points out to the teacher, "During the period when I had stopped by your class to observe Alex using the strategy, I noticed that you asked him not to call out four times. I did not notice you direct him to the index card. I wonder whether there is something about using the index card strategy that doesn't fit into your classroom routine." Why might this be an appropriate question? What is another effective way the specialist could communicate this information to the teacher?

Presupposition (Chapter 4)

- The specialist asks the teacher, "In the two weeks that we've been trying this strategy in your class, what about it has been most effective?" (After a reply) "How does using the strategy break down?" What purpose is served by these questions? What might be the next step in a problem-solving process concerning this matter?

Open Question (Chapter 4)

- The specialist asks the teacher, "What do you think we should do to make this strategy—or some other one that will accomplish the same purpose—more effective for Alex and more workable for you?" What responses might the teacher make? Make a list of these. What next question should the specialist ask? How would the next question vary based on the response given by the teacher?

What other communication skills might help these professionals to have a productive meeting? To create an opportunity to practice your skills, design a role-play to demonstrate the use of the skills mentioned here as well as others you identify.

SUMMARY

- Conflict, an expectation when collaboration is a norm, is any situation in which people perceive that others are interfering with their ability to meet their goals, as occurs when (a) two individuals want different outcomes but must settle for the same one, (b) when they want the same outcome but it cannot be available to both, (c) when there is a difference in perceptions of personal power, or (d) when one individual internally experiences conflicting reactions to a situation. Most individuals have a preferred style for responding to conflict—either competitive, avoidance, accommodative, compromising, or consensus through collaboration—which may be part of negotiation or persuasion, two constructive conflict resolution strategies.

- Resistance is the ability to avoid what is not wanted from the environment. It can be a rational response based on previous experiences, but most often it is an emotional response to change based on a variety of professional fears related to the change. Resistance may be demonstrated with many indicators, including refusal to participate, support without substance, displacement of responsibility, deferral to a future time, and reliance on past experience. Persuasion—using behavioral, consistency, perceptual, and functional approaches—offers many techniques for addressing resistance.

BACK TO THE CASE

1. Think about the comments made by the teachers in the chapter-opening case study. What elements of conflict and resistance can you identify among them?
2. If you were a novice (and untenured) teacher member at this school, what would you do if a more experienced colleague made one of these comments to you? How could you respond in order to avoid participating in a negative way but preserving your collegial relationship?
3. If you were advising Kelley Gardner's principal, what could she do regarding the implementation of the RTI program? Using the specific strategies outlined in the chapter, what could she do to reduce conflict and resistance?
4. If you were asked to present at the next faculty meeting regarding RTI and its implementation at your school, what points would you stress, given the apparent mixed reaction to its use by your colleagues? How would you engage them in a constructive conversation about its value?

COLLABORATIVE ACTIVITIES

1. Many schools and school districts are continuing to make progress toward becoming more inclusive, and these efforts include implementing co-teaching and using indirect services such as consultation. As you think about the concerns that often are raised in regard to inclusive practices, consider how they might lead to conflict. Categorize the conflicts that might arise using the four-part analysis of causes of conflict presented in this chapter. What conclusions does this activity lead you to regarding your school's efforts related to inclusive practices?
2. The following are some examples of conflict that might occur in schools. Using your knowledge of principles of collaboration, communication skills, and strategies for responding to conflict, role-play how each situation could be addressed.

    - As a high school science teacher, your analysis indicates that you have most of the students with language, learning, and behavior problems; you are concerned about the impact of so many struggling learners on your test scores, especially since the evaluation of your teaching skills will be based partly on these students' year-end achievement level.
    - You are discussing grading with a colleague. He notes that he understands the need to make changes in the term paper assignment for some students, but he does not think they should be able to earn an A when such changes are made. He states that it is not fair to the other students.
    - A parent has asked for a meeting with you. At the meeting, she accuses you of unfairly picking on her son. She is referring to her son's interpretation of your reaction to his classroom misbehavior. However, the parent is not interested in hearing your perspective on what occurred.

3. Think about negotiation and mediation. Create a Venn diagram of how they are alike and how they are different. In what situation do you think each might be most effective? Why do you think mediation and informal dispute resolution are part of special education due process procedures?
4. Why is it more common to find resistance among school professionals than conflict? What symptoms of resistance do you find are most common in schools? What are examples of each symptom? On what topics are *you* resistant to change?
5. Think about the topics addressed in this chapter. Write a critical analysis of how effective communication and problem-solving skills affect conflict, resistance, negotiation, and persuasion. Then apply your thinking to teaming, co-teaching, and consultation. What types of conflicts or resistance might occur in each of these service delivery models? How might negotiation and persuasion be effectively used for each?

 CHECK YOUR UNDERSTANDING

Click here to gauge your understanding of this chapter's essential concepts.

Appendix 9.1 Conflict Management Style Survey

This Conflict Management Style Survey has been designed to help you become more aware of your characteristic approach, or style, in responding to conflict. In completing this survey, you are invited to respond by making choices that correspond with your typical behavior or attitudes in conflict situations.

Date _____

Instructions: Choose a single frame of reference for answering all 15 items; in this case, use work-related conflicts.

Allocate 10 points among the four alternative answers given for each of the 15 items below based on how you assess you would be most likely to respond.

Example: When the people I work with become involved in a personal conflict, I usually:

Intervene to settle the dispute.	Call a meeting to talk over the problem.	Offer to help if I can.	Ignore the problem.
3	6	1	0

Be certain that your answers add up to 10 points.

1. When someone *I care about* is actively hostile toward me (i.e., yelling, threatening, abusive, etc.), I tend to:

Column 1	Column 2	Column 3	Column 4
Respond in a hostile manner.	Try to persuade the person to give up his or her actively hostile behavior.	Stay and listen as long as possible.	Walk away.

2. When someone *who is relatively unimportant to me* is actively hostile toward me (i.e., yelling, threatening, abusive, etc.), I tend to:

Respond in a hostile manner.	Try to persuade the person to give up his or her actively hostile behavior.	Stay and listen as long as possible.	Walk away.

3. When I observe people in conflicts in which anger, threats, hostility, and strong opinions are present, I tend to:

Become involved and take a position.	Attempt to mediate.	Observe to see what happens.	Leave as quickly as possible.

4. When I perceive another person as meeting his or her needs at my expense, I am apt to:

Work to do anything I can to change that person.	Rely on persuasion and "facts" when attempting to have that person change.	Work hard at changing how I relate to that person.	Accept the situation as it is.

5. When involved in an interpersonal dispute, my general pattern is to:

Draw the other person into seeing the problem as I do.	Examine the issues between us as logically as possible.	Look hard for a workable compromise.	Let time take its course and let the problem work itself out.

6. The quality that I value the most in dealing with conflict would be:

Emotional strength and security.	Intelligence.	Love and openness.	Patience.

7. Following a serious altercation with someone *I care for deeply*, I:

Strongly desire to go back and settle things my way.	Want to go back and work it out—whatever give-and-take is necessary.	Worry about it a lot but not plan to initiate further contact.	Let it lie and not plan to initiate further contact.

8. When I see a serious conflict developing between two people *I care about*, I tend to:

Express my disappointment that this had to happen.	Attempt to persuade them to resolve their differences.	Watch to see what develops.	Leave the scene.

9. When I see a serious conflict developing between two people *who are relatively unimportant to me*, I tend to:

Express my disappointment that this had to happen.	Attempt to persuade them to resolve their differences.	Watch to see what develops.	Leave the scene.

10. The feedback that I receive from most people about how I behave when faced with conflict and opposition indicates that I:

Try hard to get my way.	Try to work out differences cooperatively.	Am easy going and take a soft or conciliatory position.	Usually avoid the conflict.

11. When communicating with someone with whom I am having a serious conflict, I:

Try to overpower the other person with my speech.	Talk a little bit more than I listen.	Am an active listener (feeding back words and feelings).	Am a passive listener (agreeing and apologizing).

12. When involved in an unpleasant conflict, I:

Use humor with the other party.	Make an occasional quip or joke about the situation or the relationship.	Relate humor only to myself.	Suppress all attempts at humor.

13. When someone does something that irritates me (e.g., smokes in a nonsmoking area or crowds into line in front of me), my tendency in communicating with the offending person is to:

Insist that the person look me in the eye.	Look the person directly in the eye and maintain eye contact.	Maintain intermittent eye contact.	Avoid looking directly at the person.

14. (Same situation as #13)

Stand close and make physical contact.	Use my hands and body to illustrate my point.	Stand close to the person without touching him or her.	Stand back and keep my hands to myself.

15. (Same situation as #13)

Use strong, direct language and tell the person to stop.	Try to persuade the person to stop.	Talk gently and tell the person what my feelings are.	Say and do nothing.

Scoring Instructions

Step	Action
1	Add your scores vertically, resulting in 4 column totals. Fill in the column totals in the chart below.
2	Total your scores for columns 1 and 2 and fill in the total for Score A. Total your scores for columns 3 and 4 and fill in the total for Score B.
3	Darken in the bar graph to reflect your totals for each column.

Total Column 1	Total Column 2	Total Column 3	Total Column 4
Score A		Score B	

Bar Graph of Total Scores for Each Column

	Column 1	Column 2	Column 3	Column 4
150				
125				
100				
75				
50				
25				
0				

Interpretation

Column	Description
1	**Aggressive/Confrontive (Competing)**
	High scores indicate a tendency toward "taking the bull by the horns" and a strong need to control situations and people. Those who use this style are often directive and judgmental.
	The opposite of accommodating: One uses whatever seems appropriate to win one's own position.
2	**Assertive/Persuasive (Collaborating)**
	High scores indicate a tendency to stand up for oneself without being pushy, a proactive approach to conflict, and a willingness to collaborate. People who use this style depend heavily on their verbal skills.
	The opposite of avoiding: One works with the other person to find a solution that both fully satisfies one's own concerns and those of the other.
3	**Observant/Introspective (Accommodating)**
	High scores indicate a tendency to observe others and examine oneself analytically in response to conflict situations as well as a need to adopt counseling and listening modes of behavior. Those who use this style are likely to be cooperative, even conciliatory.
	One seeks to satisfy the other person's concerns at the expense of one's own.
4	**Avoiding/Reactive (Avoiding)**
	High scores indicate a tendency toward passivity or withdrawal in conflict situations and a need to avoid confrontation. Those who use this style are usually accepting and patient, often suppressing their strong feelings.
	A person neglects his or her own concerns as well as those of the other person by not raising or addressing the conflict issue.
	Compromising (Intermediate in Cooperativeness and Assertiveness)
	One seeks an expedient middle-ground position that provides partial satisfaction for both parties.

Score	Description
A	If significantly higher than Score B (25 points or more), may indicate a tendency toward aggressive/assertive conflict management.
B	If significantly higher than Score A (25 points or more), may indicate a more conciliatory approach.

Source: Conflict-Management Style Survey. Pfeiffer and Company Instrumentation Software (PCIS): Using Instruments in Human Resources Development (HRD). Reprinted with permission from John Wiley & Sons, Inc.

10 Paraeducators

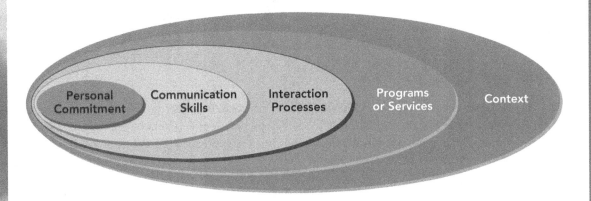

CONNECTIONS

In Chapters 7, 8, and 9, you learned about services that rely heavily on collaboration among school professionals. However, other school staff members are also part of the team and contribute to the success of students' education. This chapter addresses the roles and responsibilities of paraprofessionals, or paraeducators—staff members who often spend a significant amount of time working with students with disabilities or other special needs. In this chapter, you will explore paraeducators' participation in the educational process—in general education and special education classrooms and other settings—and the nature of your working relationship and interactions with them. You will also learn about several considerations for collaborating with paraeducators, factors that are somewhat different from those involved in your collaboration with other teachers, administrators, specialists, and related services professionals.

LEARNING OUTCOMES

After reading this chapter you will be able to:

1. Describe the characteristics of paraprofessionals employed in special education and other educational programs and analyze how their place in schools has grown and changed over the past several decades.
2. Explain instructional and noninstructional responsibilities of paraeducators, and clarify activities that should and should not be assigned to paraeducators.
3. Evaluate potential ethical dilemmas that may occur related to paraprofessionals, including those related to their responsibilities, those related to their supervision, and those related to their relationships with students and family members.
4. Apply to your teaching situation strategies for effectively working with paraeducators as you assist them in understanding the scope of their responsibilities, provide them with professional development, plan with them, maintain clear communication with them, and supervise their work with students.
5. Describe how collaboration pertains to the interactions between paraeducators and professionals.

A CASE FOR COLLABORATION

Help or Hindrance?

Barely four weeks into the school year, Emily Reynolds is concerned. She has a number of students with special needs in her class: four students who have learning or behavioral disabilities and five who are English learners. An additional student has a section 504 plan based on his diagnosis as having ADHD, and he is also an English learner. But the diversity of her students is not the issue; instead, it is the paraeducator assigned to work with her. Viviana Barnett has worked at this school for 22 years and has two grandchildren who attend here. On the first day of school, she informed Ms. Reynolds that she could explain all the procedures, including when the students with disabilities should leave the classroom to receive special instruction. Ms. Barnett cares deeply about all the students, perhaps a bit too deeply. She is eager to work with them and they clearly respond well to her. She also provides Spanish language support, but Ms. Reynolds is concerned that Ms. Barnett helps students when they are capable of working independently, both those with special needs as well as others. She tends to hover around certain students and explains that she does so because she knows they need help. She has also, on at least three occasions, explained to Ms. Reynolds that what she asked her to do with students was not needed or not appropriate. Ms. Reynolds wants to have a strong partnership with Ms. Barnett, but right now she is seeing emerging tension and possible conflict.

Introduction

Whether you are a novice or an experienced teacher, you may find that not only do you need to interact effectively with other teachers, administrators, specialists, other special services providers, as well as parents and families, but you are also assigned to work with one or more paraeducators. Consider these situations:

- As a resource teacher in a local high school, your caseload has crept up from the locally allowed 25 students to 32. Given student numbers and types of needs, administrators have decided that it is not necessary to employ another special education teacher, but they have notified you that they are seeking a paraeducator to assist you with your workload.
- In your job as a kindergarten teacher, you learn that the four kindergarten teachers share a paraeducator. It is up to the teachers to decide how to divide the paraeducator's time among them and what tasks she will complete.
- You work in an elementary school in a large, urban district. Your district has contracted with a private company to provide a paraeducator to support one of your students who has extraordinary needs related to behavior. You have many questions about your role in providing information to this person, directing his work, and communicating about student progress and needs.
- In your highly inclusive high school, you are responsible as the special educator for guiding the work of three paraeducators who are assigned to work one-to-one with students with significant needs in general education and special education classrooms. You also share a fourth paraeducator with the another special education teacher.

Learn More About
This brief video introduces you to a committed and enthusiastic paraeducator who in a few words captures the essence of this role.
(https://www.youtube.com/watch?v=jpKUUL2hZxw)

Have you encountered a situation similar to any of these? Do you know teachers who have? Collectively, these scenarios illustrate that paraeducators can be a tremendous benefit to students and professionals, can be helpful yet somewhat problematic, or can be needed but time consuming to supervise. In all instances, the use of paraeducators is a dimension of the adult–adult interactions in schools that has grown in importance and that requires careful consideration by the professionals responsible for working with them and directing their activities on a day-to-day basis (Wasburn-Moses, Chun, & Kaldenberg, 2013).

Understanding Paraeducators

Paraeducators are individuals who provide direct or indirect instructional and other services to students and who are supervised by licensed professionals who are responsible for student outcomes (Shyman, 2010). They also may be known as paraprofessionals, instructional assistants, classroom assistants, therapy assistants, transition trainers, teacher aides, or teacher assistants. Paraeducators may provide interventions in response to intervention (RTI) programs, or they may work in remedial reading or math, English as a Second Language (ESL), and special education programs. They may also serve—especially in large elementary schools—in a more general capacity to assist teachers in their classrooms, particularly in primary grade classrooms or when class sizes are large. They also may have responsibilities for supervising students during noninstructional activities such as lunch and recess, and they may complete clerical chores. Most paraeducators are women who have lived in their communities for a long time (e.g., Carter, O'Rourke, Sisco, & Pelsue, 2009), and some of them may be the parent or grandparent of a child in the school, as is true for Viviana Barnett, introduced at the beginning of this chapter. Although various types of paraeducators are mentioned in the following sections, the emphasis in this chapter is on paraeducators who are employed for the purpose of assisting in the delivery of services, across a variety of settings, to students who have disabilities.

Learn More About
Paraeducators work in a wide variety of school settings with carrying out many types of tasks in order to enhance students' education, information succinctly illustrated in this video.
(https://www.youtube.com/watch?v=--wWvccbf7M)

Paraeducator Qualifications

The matter of paraeducator qualifications used to be straightforward: States and local school districts simply decided on the education and skills expected of these school personnel—whether a high school diploma, some type of specialized training, or a certain number of college credits. Now, though, the expectations for paraeducator credentials are more likely to be carefully prescribed. The qualifications required of paraeducators still can vary widely, but federal law has established some parameters. Paraeducators who work in schools that receive Title I funds (i.e., schools whose students have high levels of poverty) must have appropriate preparation for their roles—an associate's degree or the equivalent, or training such that they can pass a test demonstrating their skills for assisting in the areas of reading, writing, math, and school readiness. In such schools, this requirement applies to paraeducators who work with students with disabilities as well as to other instructional paraprofessionals. In some school districts, these requirements are being applied to all paraprofessionals who provide instruction, regardless of the specific schools in which they work. Across all school districts, the most common employment criterion is holding a high school diploma (National Center for Education Statistics, 2007). Although some paraeducators have much more education and a few may even have teaching credentials, this minimal educational expectation should alert professionals that they may need to provide significant guidance to paraeducators, avoiding assumptions that these individuals will know what is expected of them and how they should work with students (Fisher & Pleasants, 2012; Giles, 2010).

Note that the standards just discussed may not have to be met by paraeducators who do not have classroom instructional responsibilities. Examples of staff members in these roles include paraprofessionals whose jobs consist of increasing parent involvement in schools, providing personal care to students, acting as translators, working in the cafeteria or on a bus, or serving as a clerical assistant. As you might expect, though, many paraeducators have both instructional and noninstructional responsibilities, and these individuals are required to meet the higher standard of qualifications.

The Individuals with Disabilities Education Act (IDEA) provides a small amount of additional information about paraeducator qualifications. It specifies that these individuals must be "appropriately trained" (20 U.S.C. §1412 (a)(14)(B)(iii)). That is, paraeducators must have the knowledge and skills necessary to appropriately work with students with disabilities, for example, learning how to safely lift a student, communicate clearly with a student, use technology or equipment that is required for the student, or respond appropriately to a student's behaviors.

One additional facet of paraeducator qualifications should be mentioned. You may find that the paraeducator with whom you work is in the process of becoming a teacher (e.g., Burbank, Bates, & Schrum, 2009). Some paraeducators make this decision because they find that they enjoy their work with children; others have become paraeducators because they see the role as a means of entering the teaching profession once they complete their studies. In some districts, especially those with high rates of poverty or high numbers of students from diverse cultures, paraeducators who live in the community are encouraged to prepare as teachers because of the tremendous value they bring in terms of their understanding of students and their cultures. What is important to keep in mind is that paraeducators becoming teachers are acquiring the knowledge and skills that you have; they may request to have additional responsibilities as they progress through their preparation or to apply what they are learning in their studies to classroom practice. In many ways, teachers can serve as informal mentors for these paraeducators.

Paraeducators support students and teachers in many roles, including reinforcing instruction, helping address behavior problems, providing personal assistance, and assisting students to access the general curriculum.

Paraeducators as Key Personnel in Today's Schools

The importance of working effectively with paraeducators can perhaps best be illustrated by examining their prevalence in schools. The most recent estimate of the number of paraeducators working in all capacities in public schools is approximately 1.2 million (U.S. Department of Labor, 2014). Of those, approximately 411,756 are employed to provide support for students with disabilities ages 3 through 21 (U.S. Department of Education, 2014). When you realize that there are 405,832 special education teachers nationwide for this group of students (U.S. Department of Education, 2014), you can see that paraeducators are very likely to be involved in these students' education, either to instruct them or to provide other supports (Rutherford, 2011). In fact, in many schools, more paraeducator time (full-time equivalencies, or FTEs) are allocated for special education than special education teacher time.

The number of paraeducators in schools is likely to increase. In fact, the U.S. Department of Labor (2014) indicates that 110,000 paraeducator jobs will become available between 2012 and 2022, a growth rate of approximately 9 percent. These data imply that it is very likely that you will work in a school in which paraeducators are key members of the staff and that you will be expected, in some capacity, to direct their activities with students.

The increasing number of paraeducators in schools is not particularly surprising. The rising emphasis on early childhood programs has undoubtedly contributed (Jones, Ratcliff, Sheehan, & Hunt, 2012), as has the growth in programs to assist students in transitioning from school to work or community settings and the growing number of students and their families for whom English is not their first language (Stacey, Harvey, & Richards, 2013; Vadasy, Nelson, & Sanders, 2013). The expectation that all students will reach higher academic standards also contributes to this trend (e.g., Carter, O'Rourke, et al., 2009), especially when paraeducators are employed to provide supplemental remedial instruction in RTI programs. In some instances, often related to services for students with disabilities, paraeducators are employed to supplement the services of teachers as an understandable but sometimes questionable means of saving money; that is, the cost of employing a paraeducator is significantly less than the cost of employing an additional special education teacher (U.S. Department of Labor, 2014).

In some parts of the country, the trend toward inclusive practices also is an influence on the number of paraeducators being employed (Giangreco, Suter, & Doyle, 2010). When students with complex special needs are assigned to general education classrooms, their teachers report that paraeducator support is not only helpful but essential (Fisher & Pleasants, 2012; Giangreco et al., 2010). However, even for students with mild needs who typically are distributed among many classrooms in inclusive schools, paraeducators have become critical in supplementing the services of special educators who cannot themselves provide adequate services to every student every day (Suter & Giangreco, 2009).

Paraeducator Roles and Responsibilities

Historically, paraeducators were expected to assume largely clerical duties (French, 1999). They graded papers, took attendance, and collected lunch money, acting mostly to free teachers from routine tasks so the teachers could spend more time instructing their students. Now, however, most paraeducators are expected to spend the majority of their time working with individual students or small groups of students. Generally, today's paraeducators work in one of three ways: First, some paraeducators provide general support to teachers and classrooms, either because of the number of students in a class, the need for language support, or the implementation of supplemental instructional programs, for example, in the area of reading (e.g., Vadasy & Sanders, 2008). These paraeducators may work with students with disabilities, but they are not employed specifically for that purpose.

Second, some paraeducators are assigned as one-to-one assistants for students whose disabilities present extraordinary needs. These individuals typically spend most of the day with the particular student, whether in a general education or a special education classroom (e.g., Cameron, Cook, & Tankersley, 2012); they sometimes are referred to as one-to-one paraeducators. Students who may need such intensive support may include those with autism, those with significant intellectual disabilities, and those with complex physical needs (Martin & Alborz, 2014; Rossetti & Goessling, 2010). For example, Robert, a paraeducator, may be responsible for meeting Josh, a student with multiple disabilities, when he arrives at school on the bus; he ensures that Josh is transported, as needed, to any location in the school. Robert also makes sure that Josh has his school supplies and changes Josh's diaper when needed. Josh participates in a general education art class, and Robert is responsible for getting Josh's art supplies and helping him to use them, attaching charcoal pencils and paintbrushes to the special adapted holder that Josh uses. Robert also accompanies Josh when he goes to his vocational exploratory class each afternoon—job experiences designed to help Josh decide on the type of work he would like to do after he graduates from high school.

Third, some paraeducators support special education programs but are not assigned to specific students (Giangreco, Suter, & Hurley, 2013), as is true for Ms. Barnett whom you met at the beginning of this chapter. For example, Joseph is a paraeducator in a high school program for students with learning disabilities. His daily schedule includes a wide array of tasks. He works in general education classes for two periods, carrying out instructional supports as directed by the general education teacher and touching base with two students who need assistance keeping their materials organized. In an additional class, U.S. History, he is assigned to take notes for a student who cannot do this himself. Joseph also spends two periods in the school's assessment center where he reads tests to students needing such service. In elementary schools, paraeducators providing general support on behalf of students with disabilities may be assigned to a single grade level, or they may work across several grade levels, based on the needs of students.

Learn More About Cynthia Eborall is a special education paraeducator who students trust. As a result she is highly successful in assisting them to reach their goals.

(https://www.youtube.com/watch?v=wXVaUAg7I_M)

Although you might assume that the specific roles and responsibilities for paraeducators would be found in their job descriptions, you may find that most descriptions focus on the number of hours the individual is to work, qualifications for the job, and general expectations about working in schools (U.S. Department of Education, n.d.). Some school districts, particularly large ones, have clear and detailed job descriptions and may even distinguish among types of paraeducators (e.g., those providing supplemental instruction in reading or math, those addressing student behavior, those providing personal care, those assisting with instruction for students with disabilities), but in many cases, you will not have specific guidelines to help you assign tasks to a paraeducator. Generally, paraeducator responsibilities can be divided into those that directly relate to instruction and those that are noninstructional (Causton-Theoharis, 2009).

Instructional Responsibilities

Whether working with an individual student or to support teachers and programs so that any number of students can be successful, the most common tasks for today's paraprofessionals relate to instruction (e.g., Bingham, Hall-Kenyon, & Culatta, 2010; Webster, Blatchford, & Russell, 2013), especially for students with disabilities. These tasks may include delivery of instruction, but they may also involve preparation for or follow-up to instruction.

Instructional Delivery The number of examples of instructional delivery appropriate for paraeducators is almost infinite (e.g., Lane, Carter, & Sisco, 2012; O'Keeffe, Slocum, & Magnusson, 2013; Robinson, 2011). Here are some examples of paraeducator instructional activities:

- Provide a specific intervention for fourth- and fifth-grade students who read below grade level; a teacher taught the paraeducator how to correctly carry out the intervention.

- Review instructions given earlier to ensure student understanding.
- Lead some students through the steps for completing an in-class assignment, monitoring to be sure that they complete each step correctly before introducing the next.
- Read tests to students.
- Help students find appropriate resources for an assigned project or paper.
- Assist students in keeping books, materials, and papers organized.
- Facilitate student friendship by arranging a group of students with and without disabilities to work together on an assigned task.
- As other students work on multiplication, support a student with a significant disability to identify numbers 1 through 5 or otherwise help to implement an aligned curriculum for the student.
- Observe student behavior, recording it as explained and giving the student rewards as directed by the teacher.

This list of potential paraeducator instructional activities demonstrates the value that paraeducators bring to classrooms. However, it also illustrates the importance of teachers' roles in deciding which tasks are appropriate for paraeducators to do and in directing their work, a key topic addressed later in this chapter.

Other Instructional Responsibilities Like delivery-of-instruction responsibilities, the preparation and follow-up activities of paraeducators vary greatly. They may prepare flash cards for students, use a computer program to create a picture-based version of a story to be read, scan print material so that the student can "read" it using a computer, and adjust classroom materials (e.g., shorten, make larger, rearrange; Lewis & McKenzie, 2010). They may also prepare materials to facilitate students' participation in school activities, including writing social stories for students with autism. After instruction, the paraeducator might grade student work based on an answer key or rubric provided by the teacher, record information about student performance on particular tasks, and prepare routine correspondence for parents about a student's activities that day.

One issue should be raised regarding the instructional responsibilities of paraeducators. Despite all the anecdotal information about the instructional assistance paraeducators provide to students, studies clearly establishing that student achievement improves as a result of interventions by paraeducators remain limited (Giangreco et al., 2010). A few isolated studies indicate that when paraeducators receive specific training to carry out interventions, students with whom they work benefit (e.g., O'Keeffe et al., 2013; Therrien, Kirk, & Woods-Groves, 2012), particularly young children (French, 2003). In general, though, current practices on the instructional tasks paraeducators complete, the amount of time they spend in inclusive general education classes, the intensity of their contacts with students, and the impact of their preparation for their responsibilities are based largely on intuition and experience not data-based knowledge. This situation should remind you of the importance of gathering your own data about paraeducators' work so that you can create your own knowledge base on the most effective use of their services for the students for whom you are responsible.

Learn More About Lisa Stringer, a paraeducator, takes great satisfaction in working with students who struggle the most and realizes that sometimes students can relate to her in a way that is different from the way they relate to a teacher.
(https://www.youtube.com/watch?v=k9EyiVhv0I8)

Noninstructional Responsibilities

Even though instruction often is a paraeducator's primary responsibility, many paraeducators also have noninstructional duties (Carter, O'Rourke, et al., 2009; Doyle, 2002). These responsibilities, often assigned to paraeducators who work with students with disabilities, may involve support for students, clerical work, or other activities that serve students in an indirect way.

Support for Students Some students can receive instruction in public schools only because paraeducators provide for their personal care. This may involve feeding a student, moving the student from place to place, carrying out procedures such as catheterization, changing diapers, or assisting a student in using the toilet. Paraeducators who carry out these types of responsibilities often develop close relationships with their students, and they may even babysit for students on weekends and during holidays. Mary Ellen, for example, works as a one-to-one assistant for Lisa, an elementary student with autism. Mary Ellen is very knowledgeable concerning Lisa's personality and special needs, especially what to do if Lisa becomes upset because of a change in routine. Mary Ellen usually leaves school with Lisa on Wednesday afternoons, spending two or three hours with her at Lisa's home so that Lisa's mom can complete errands. If a paraeducator has this type of responsibility, usually clear plans need to be in place in case the paraeducator is absent.

Many paraeducators assist educators in student supervision. Some accompany students to class, recess, lunch, or assemblies to provide behavior support (e.g., Orsati & Causton-Theoharis, 2013; Simpson & Mundschenk, 2012). Others assist in getting students safely off buses and into the school building. Yet others are assigned a limited amount of lunchroom supervision, time-out monitoring, or playground duty. If a student is unable to self-ambulate, or if a student has serious behavior problems likely to be demonstrated during unstructured time such as during passing periods between classes, a paraeducator may accompany such a student from class to class for safety and efficiency.

Clerical Responsibilities Both general and special education include a significant amount of paperwork. Paraeducators sometimes assist in getting this work completed. They may enter into the electronic record-keeping system students' scores on a recent assessment, update progress notes regarding student learning, or enter data on a behavior intervention plan. They also may assist in the day-to-day clerical work of teachers, duplicating instructional worksheets, gathering money for field trips, or laminating materials that will be used several times. In addition, they may draft general correspondence being sent to all parents (e.g., about upcoming conferences) and assist in obtaining information from or relaying information to outside agencies.

It may be tempting to assign a paraeducator many clerical responsibilities in order to free teacher time to work with students. However, you should keep in mind that paraeducators, like teachers, have student instruction and support as a primary responsibility. In particular, unless specific to their assignments, they should not be asked to assist in the school office for extended time periods, to cover responsibilities for clerical assistants who are absent, or to carry out clerical chores during the time that they have been assigned to work with students. When paraeducators are expected to complete such work, it detracts from the services students should be receiving.

Other Noninstructional Responsibilities Paraeducators may have other responsibilities that facilitate student success and support the educational process. For example, in schools where a significant number of students or family members are not native English speakers, some paraeducators provide translation. Whether assisting a special education or a general education teacher during a routine phone call, communicating with parents who come to school to meet with professionals, or clarifying technical terms during any interaction, translation may be an essential paraeducator responsibility. An indirect benefit may result as well: Family members may be more comfortable when a paraeducator who shares their culture and language is present, and better communication often results. Other positive results of paraeducators bringing their culture to their responsibilities—both instructional and noninstructional—are addressed in A Basis in Research.

Paraeducators also can function as members of the instructional team (Hamilton-Jones & Moore, 2013). When they work with students on a daily basis, they may have valuable insights about student learning or behavior that can help shape decisions being made. Similarly, they may notice small problems students are encountering that professionals have missed (Gerlach, 2015). Of course, this responsibility requires their attendance at meetings to discuss students—sometimes a problem

A BASIS IN RESEARCH
Paraeducators Supporting Students from Diverse Backgrounds

For all students from minority cultures, but especially for students with special needs, learning is assisted when students can interact with adults who understand their language, culture, and communities. Studies of paraeducators who share the cultural background of the students with whom they work suggest these important benefits (e.g., Abbate-Vaughn, 2007; Monzó & Rueda, 2000; Theoharis & O'Toole, 2011):

1. *Using motherhood as a basis for interacting with students.* Paraeducators sometimes find that their own experiences as mothers within their cultures guide the expectations they set and ways of interacting with students.
2. *Demonstrating cariño.* Paraeducators may use cultural terms of endearment, touch, and softened facial expressions, particularly when correcting student behavior or academic work.
3. *Using a relaxed instructional style.* The paraeducators may allow students to chat with peers while they work and to speak spontaneously during instruction. The relaxed style enables paraeducators to learn about students' lives outside school.
4. *Accepting students' styles.* Paraeducators may respond to student misbehaviors in a way congruent with their cultural background. They may be more likely to talk with students about behaviors than to remove privileges.
5. *Incorporating student language and knowledge into instruction.* Paraeducators may use both English and their first language to facilitate instruction. For example, they may use the first language to direct students about getting out materials or following other directions while using English for the discussion of the vocabulary. They may also relate concepts being taught in school to students' homes and communities, thus fostering student understanding and participation.
6. *Employing wait time.* Paraeducators may wait longer for student responses than would typically be expected. This often relates to understanding the language-processing problems of students for whom English is a second language.
7. *Sharing experiences.* Noninstructional interactions between paraeducators and students often occur in the student's native language. Paraeducators indicate this approach helps them to connect to the students.

These findings offer important insights into informal contributions that paraeducators can make in the instructional process. For example, if the teacher is from a culture different from that of students, a paraeducator may help to serve as a cultural liaison between student and professional, especially when that individual is a member of the community. Likewise, because professionals often are balancing the needs of many students and a wide range of setting factors, the paraeducators may be more able than the professionals to build a relationship with a reticent student.

if those meetings typically are held after school hours, time outside most paraeducators' contracted workday.

APPLY YOUR KNOWLEDGE 10.1

Ethical Considerations

Because the use of paraeducators is not clearly articulated in federal law and their roles continue to evolve in this era of higher student achievement standards, you may find that some of the roles we have described are common for paraeducators in your locale, but others are unusual or specifically prohibited. In addition, any of several ethical issues may arise concerning their work. Your responsibility is to make decisions concerning paraeducator assignments, keeping in mind local policies as well as factors such as those that follow.

Paraeducators Supplement Rather than Supplant Instruction

Although paraeducators provide valuable instructional support to students, it is clear that they are to supplement instruction that is delivered by professionals; they may not supplant it (Carter, O'Rourke, et al., 2009; Darrow, 2010). This fact affects accountability: Even if a paraeducator delivers a specific intervention or service to a student, the professional staff member—that is, the person who gave the directions to the paraeducator—is ultimately accountable for the outcome of that intervention or service. For example, in Mr. Baker and Ms. Wright's co-taught classroom, three days each week Ms. Scott, the paraeducator, is also present. The three educators usually establish stations for these lessons. Mr. Baker and Ms. Wright provide instruction on specific skills while Ms. Scott either reviews skills taught earlier or rereads a story or set of poems the students are studying. This arrangement is appropriate: The professionals are delivering the initial instruction, and the paraeducator supplements it through review. In another example, Mr. Wiley is a paraeducator in a self-contained class for high school students with significant disabilities. He works with students individually on verbal or technology-assisted communication following plans prepared by Ms. Reid, the special educator.

Paraeducators themselves have raised issues related to instruction. They report that they feel a strong sense of ownership of and commitment to their work with the students to whom they are assigned, but that they sometimes are asked to take responsibility for making instructional decisions they do not feel qualified to make (Glazzard, 2011; Martin & Alborz, 2014). For example, Downing, Ryndak, and Clark (2000) interviewed paraeducators working with students with severe disabilities. The paraeducators reported that they were primarily responsible for making curricular modifications and other decisions that could have a significant impact on students' education—decisions that they believed should have been made by the teachers.

Others have added a sobering sociocultural perspective on this issue of paraeducators' work. They note that in too many situations paraeducators may become *de facto* teachers, especially for students with significant disabilities (e.g., Cook, Cameron, & Tankersley, 2007; Suter & Giangreco, 2009). In fact, some professionals are concerned that paraeducators' attention to students may interfere with some teachers' sense of responsibility for providing instruction (Giangreco et al., 2010). They raise questions about the potential negative impact on the general education teachers' and typical learners' perceptions when the group of staff members generally considered least powerful in schools provides most services for the students who are likely perceived as least powerful (i.e., those with disabilities).

A discussion of ethics and paraeducators' instructional roles also raises questions about co-teaching. Although some professionals refer to paraeducators as co-teachers (e.g., Nevin, Villa, & Thousand, 2009), this implies that teachers and paraeducators have instructional parity, and clearly this is not the case. If you review the co-teaching approaches in Chapter 7, you can see that teachers and paraeducators can use some of them appropriately—but with clear understanding that the teacher makes the decisions about the paraeducator's appropriate assignment. For example, students could be assigned to three groups with the teacher providing new instruction while the paraeducator reviews vocabulary and students work on a project. Likewise, a paraeducator could work to reread a chapter with a small group of students while the teacher worked with other students on a writing assignment. In both cases, the structures are those used in co-teaching, but the paraeducator is providing appropriate instructional support, not new instruction. This is different from the partnerships of co-teaching as discussed in Chapter 7.

An unpleasant but realistic sidebar to this discussion of the ethical responsibilities for paraeducators concerns the unfortunate administrative rationale for employing them. In a few locales, paraeducators are seen as an inexpensive alternative to hiring professional

In addition to other responsibilities, paraeducators sometimes serve as a language and cultural liaison between families and professionals.

staff, particularly if the intent is to get "an extra set of hands" into classrooms with struggling learners or those with disabilities. This approach reflects a gross underestimation of professional staff members' contributions, and it is a highly questionable means of delivering student services.

Ultimately, a few matters related to what paraeducators instructionally should *not* do are clear and include the following:

- Write individualized education plan (IEP) goals and/or objectives for students with disabilities.
- Interpret data gathered in order to plan appropriate educational goals for students or to plan instruction.
- Make decisions about what instructional, behavioral, or other interventions or programs are needed by students.
- Decide that particular programs or interventions are no longer needed by students and stop providing them.
- Design and deliver initial core instruction without teacher supervision.
- Make other critical decisions concerning student education or safety.

Ultimately, paraeducators should not bear sole responsibility for any part of a student's education. Rather, they should assist professionals in related tasks and carry out their work with ongoing and high-quality professional involvement. Can you think of any additional issues related to instruction that should be added to this list?

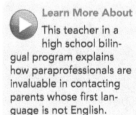

Learn More About This teacher in a high school bilingual program explains how paraprofessionals are invaluable in contacting parents whose first language is not English.
(https://www.youtube.com/watch?v=Zq3C0VCOmJk&list=PLoU659hwTdDYlei0mmgsyHWriBMXBohLY)

Paraeducators Complete Only Routine Parent Communication

Another ethical issue that can arise in the work of paraeducators relates to communication with families. Concerning what topics and under which circumstances should paraeducators communicate with parents? This seemingly simple matter can become complex. Many special educators ask paraeducators to record in a notebook two or three highlights of the day for students with significant disabilities who cannot communicate what they have experienced at school. Other teachers may request that paraeducators call parents to alert them that a form needing parent signature or an announcement of an upcoming school event is being sent home. However, if a discussion is needed about a behavior problem a student is experiencing or a concern related to a student's education, the teacher should be responsible for this communication. Complexity may arise when a paraeducator knows family members well. In such cases, a paraeducator may inadvertently or deliberately share information beyond the scope of what is appropriate. For example, Terry Jeppesen, a paraeducator, told Tony's mother that Tony had had a terrible day at school. Tony's mother called the teacher, who was surprised at the mother's concern. The teacher's perception was that Tony's behavior was the result of a changed schedule because of a special program and not a cause for alarm. The paraeducator's comments caused a miscommunication and could have had more serious consequences.

Paraeducators Balance the Need for Support with the Goal of Independence

Learn More About

As demonstrated in this video, paraeducators are instrumental in fostering student confidence and independence.

(https://www.youtube.com/watch?v=jMwaruBi3M4)

One other issue can arise related to paraeducators and their work. When a team decides that part of a student's instruction can be provided by a paraeducator, parents and families are entitled to understand the qualifications of the individual delivering services and the scope of that person's responsibilities. Often, professionals and parents alike are faced with an ethical dilemma: How much support from a paraeducator is optimal (e.g., Giangreco, Broer, & Suter, 2011)? Is more always better? What is the rationale that should be employed for deciding on the right blend of professional and paraeducator services?

Paraeducators report that they believe they are crucial for helping students succeed, and educators generally report that paraeducators are highly valuable staff members (e.g., Giangreco et al., 2010; Glazzard, 2011), even though scant research exists to support these perceptions (e.g., McGrath, Johns, & Mathur, 2010). Sometimes, however, these laudable characteristics can lead to a dilemma. Particularly for those paraeducators assigned to a specific student with a disability in an inclusive setting, a risk exists that by remaining in close physical proximity to the student, negative outcomes can occur (Giangreco, 2013; Harris, 2011). Among these are losing opportunities for the student to have typical social interactions with other students, inadvertently encouraging dependent instead of independent student behaviors, and unintentionally communicating to the general education teacher that he or she is not the primary teacher of the student (Giangreco, Doyle, & Suter, 2012). In addition, some concern also exists that assistants in close proximity may place students at greater risk for sexual abuse because the students do not learn appropriate social distance (Giangreco, Edelman, Luiselli, & MacFarland, 1997).

Generally, paraeducators should be taught that the goal of their work with an individual student with a disability is to gradually move away from directly and intrusively interacting with that student except as absolutely needed (e.g., helping the student move from place to place). Although no one would want to deprive a student of needed supports, what also is important is that the student learn to interact with classmates in a natural way, to seek assistance from them without adult intervention, and to experience school in a way that adult mediation cannot replicate (Toelken & Miltenberger, 2012; Young & Bittel, 2011). If you are a special education teacher or a general education teacher, you may find it necessary to guide paraeducators in this responsibility, helping them to find the best balance between providing individual assistance and nurturing independence (Whitburn, 2013).

APPLY YOUR KNOWLEDGE 10.2

Working with Paraeducators

Thus far, this chapter has addressed the scope of a paraeducator's roles and responsibilities. The essential complement to that discussion is one about your roles and responsibilities as a professional working with paraeducators (Carnahan, Williamson, Clarke, & Sorenson, 2009; Stephens & Woodbury, 2011). You may find that you need to be competent and feel confident to address these five areas: teaching paraeducators to perform expected duties, planning with paraeducators, effectively assigning specific responsibilities to paraeducators, communicating with paraeducators, and supervising these personnel. You may also learn that you have to think carefully about the subject of delegating responsibilities to paraeducators, which is the topic of Putting Ideas into Practice.

Teaching Paraeducators About Their Roles and Responsibilities

Although federal law clearly states that paraeducators should be prepared for the responsibilities they have in their jobs, the way in which this is accomplished varies by state and school district (Giles, 2010). Some school districts offer general staff development to paraeducators through workshops or videotapes in order to prepare them to succeed on the required assessment of their skills. In other locales, completion of a community college program or a specific number of college credits is a condition of employment. However, the initial general preparation that paraeducators receive seldom can provide enough preparation for the specific roles and responsibilities they assume. This more specific training often is the responsibility of professional staff (Martin & Alborz, 2014). That

Learn More About
In classrooms serving students with complex needs, a variety of paraeducators often carry out specific tasks working as team members with professionals—teachers and others—in the program.
(https://www.youtube.com/watch?v=INnGHazHT60)

PUTTING IDEAS INTO PRACTICE
Delegating Responsibilities to Paraeducators

Delegating responsibility, that is, making decisions about what a teacher should do and what a paraeducator should do, can be difficult. Some special education teachers, general education teachers, and other specialists (e.g., speech/language therapists) struggle with the notion of directing the work of paraeducators by assigning tasks to them and holding them accountable for completing those tasks. Here are a few of the reasons why professionals say delegating is challenging (French, 2003).

- I am a perfectionist and the paraeducator is unlikely to complete the task in the way that I want it done.
- To do this activity, the paraeducator should be trained and there is no time for training in the schedule. Someone besides me should be responsible for training paraeducators.
- I like to do this activity, even though it might be more appropriately completed by the paraeducator.
- I am not confident about the quality of the work that the paraeducator does.
- I can do it faster myself.
- When I direct the paraeducator to do a task, I feel bossy and I'm worried that the paraeducator won't like me.
- Paraeducators are paid too little to expect them to do many of the tasks that need attention.

How do you think each of these issues should be addressed, especially those that consider paraeducator skills and training?

Here are some reasons why delegation is so important.

- Delegation makes the most of all the time available to provide services to students—that of both paraeducators and professionals.
- Delegation provides clear direction to paraeducators, eliminating confusion and responsibilities.
- Delegation creates teams in which everyone feels a sense of commitment.
- Delegation challenges paraeducators to learn new skills and stretch their expertise.
- Delegation empowers paraeducators, communicating to them that you trust and respect them.
- Delegation means that you don't have to do everything yourself, permitting you to better manage all your responsibilities.

is, professionals need to provide student-specific and context-based information in order for paraeducators to do their jobs effectively. The sample needs assessment in Figure 10.1 illustrates this need for specific training for paraeducators across academic, behavior, and general areas. A similar list could be generated for additional domains in which paraeducators might have responsibility, including understanding of unique student characteristics, personal care, use of assistive technology, and others.

FIGURE 10.1 **Paraeducator needs assessment.**

5—highly proficient/knowledgeable
3—somewhat proficient/knowledgeable
1—not at all proficient/knowledgeable

Paraeducator Self-Rating	Domains of Responsibility	Teacher Rating
	Knowledge of core academic content	
5 4 3 2 1	Reading	5 4 3 2 1
5 4 3 2 1	Language Arts	5 4 3 2 1
5 4 3 2 1	Math	5 4 3 2 1
5 4 3 2 1	Science	5 4 3 2 1
5 4 3 2 1	Social Studies	5 4 3 2 1
	Knowledge of strategies to teach core academic content	
5 4 3 2 1	Reading	5 4 3 2 1
5 4 3 2 1	Language Arts	5 4 3 2 1
5 4 3 2 1	Math	5 4 3 2 1
5 4 3 2 1	Science	5 4 3 2 1
5 4 3 2 1	Social Studies	5 4 3 2 1
	Knowledge of strategies to respond to student behavior	
5 4 3 2 1	Gathering and recording student behavior data	5 4 3 2 1
5 4 3 2 1	Principles of behavior modification, including rewards	5 4 3 2 1
5 4 3 2 1	Appropriately explaining rules, procedures, and routines to students	5 4 3 2 1
5 4 3 2 1	Using natural consequences to respond to student behavior	5 4 3 2 1
5 4 3 2 1	Motivating students	5 4 3 2 1
	Knowledge of communication strategies	
5 4 3 2 1	With teachers and/or supervisor	5 4 3 2 1
5 4 3 2 1	With students	5 4 3 2 1
5 4 3 2 1	With parents	5 4 3 2 1
	Knowledge of other strategies	
5 4 3 2 1	Organizing and managing assigned work	5 4 3 2 1
5 4 3 2 1	Managing time	5 4 3 2 1
5 4 3 2 1	Following directions	5 4 3 2 1
5 4 3 2 1	Dealing with work stress	5 4 3 2 1
5 4 3 2 1	Managing differences with staff and/or students	5 4 3 2 1
5 4 3 2 1	Using computers and other technology	5 4 3 2 1
5 4 3 2 1	Using office equipment	5 4 3 2 1

You should discuss with your administrator and other colleagues how paraeducators in your school receive this focused preparation. If no planned program is available, you might wish to look for a detailed needs assessment or create one tailored to the responsibilities you understand paraeducators in your school/classroom should have, perhaps collaborating with colleagues to create a year-long plan for staff development for all the paraeducators in your school. As you work on this project, you should take into consideration the practical matter of finding brief periods of time during the school day during which this activity can occur. Exploring the use of online resources, such as those listed in E-Partnerships, can greatly facilitate this effort.

What is not acceptable, even for novice educators, is to presume that helping paraeducators to develop needed skills should be someone else's responsibility. Although it is helpful if staff development is available through other means, paraeducators work at the direction of teachers or other professional staff, and so these individuals ultimately have the responsibility for ensuring that work can be completed efficiently and effectively (Ashbaker & Morgan, 2012a). This often means teaching paraeducators how to carry out assigned tasks as well as directing them on matters related to parent communication, appropriate language for interacting with students, strategies for speaking with others about students with disabilities, and all the other topics that might need attention.

E-PARTNERSHIPS

Paraeducators on the Web

Many electronic resources are available to increase your knowledge about working with paraeducators and to enhance paraeducators' skills. The following web sites contain a wealth of information. Be sure to check your school or district's web site as well.

Connecticut Paraeducator Information and Resources
(www.sde.ct.gov/sde/cwp/view.asp?a=2618&q=321752)

The Connecticut State Department of Education offers this web site to assist paraprofessionals, teachers, and administrators in ensuring that students receive optimum benefit from paraeducators. The site includes links to valuable information, including an instrument for assessing paraeducator job performance, strategies for communicating with paraeducators, and guidelines for paraeducator communication with parents.

National Resource Center for Paraeducators
(www.nrcpara.org)

On this organization's website you will find a wealth of information about paraeducators, their responsibilities, and best practices for their use in public schools. The site includes links to many other useful items, including a state-by-state list of relevant resources. Many state paraeducator handbooks can be accessed and these include a variety of useful tools, including checklists, suggestions for supervision, and strategies for ensuring strong professional–paraeducator relationships.

NEA: Paraeducator Roles and Responsibilities
(http://www.nea.org/home/20783.htm)

The National Education Association (NEA) has a web page dedicated to paraeducators. It includes a downloadable handbook as well as other free resources. An interesting feature on this site is the list of more than 30 possible titles for paraeducators.

www.paracenter.org/PARACenter

The Paraprofessional Resource and Research Center (PAR^{2}A Center) at the University of Colorado at Denver has many types of information related to the roles, responsibilities, preparation, supervision, and employment of paraeducators. Its mission is to contribute research related to paraeducators so that they are most effectively used to support students. One recent article addresses the collaboration between parents and paraeducators in inclusive classrooms.

www.uvm.edu/~cdci/prlc

The Paraeducator Resource and Learning Center (PRLC) might assist you in helping a paraeducator understand his or her responsibilities. It includes six educational modules for paraeducators about topics such as working as a member of a team, families and cultural sensitivity, and inclusive education. The modules are free and could be a powerful component of paraeducator professional development.

Planning with Paraeducators

Clearly, paraeducators are supposed to work under the direction of a teacher or other professional. This implies that a need exists for professionals and paraeducators to meet so that plans can be discussed, dilemmas raised and resolved, and student progress monitored. However, the limited data available suggest that such interactions are the exception rather than the rule.

Not surprisingly, the biggest reported obstacle to professional–paraeducator planning is time to meet (Fisher & Pleasants, 2012). For example, in many school districts paraeducators have the same work hours as the school day for students, and so they are not available before or after school hours. Similarly, paraeducators typically are not paid on teacher workdays when students are not present or for preparation days prior to the start of the school year. Without administrative commitment to professional–paraeducator planning, no simple solution to this problem exists. However, you can use some of the suggestions in Chapter 7 on finding time for collaboration to create opportunities for shared planning. In addition, you can be sure that the schedule you create for paraeducators working with you includes at least one planning period per week.

Assigning Responsibilities to Paraeducators

Perhaps the most important responsibility you have related to paraeducators is assigning particular tasks or responsibilities to them. Although the range of these responsibilities is almost endless, keep in mind the following points:

- If you are a special educator working in an inclusive school, consider assigning paraeducators to work in general education classrooms where student needs are minimal and teacher support is not warranted. Examples might be science or social studies classes or lessons in which students use many manipulatives.
- If the need for a second adult in a general education classroom pertains to a student who has a behavior intervention plan, consider training a paraeducator on the plan and assigning her to that classroom. Keep in mind, though, that if a student's behavior is unpredictable and problems are occurring with the plan, a teacher's presence may be necessary.
- In some classrooms, teachers need someone to help them implement the instruction that they have designed. This can be particularly true in early elementary grades. If paraeducator assistance is assigned, the teacher should identify review and supplemental tasks the paraprofessional can complete under the teacher's direction.
- When paraeducators have received specific training to deliver remedial reading or math instruction, they may be assigned to this responsibility for part or all of the day (Granger & Greek, 2005). For example, as schools implement RTI procedures, paraeducators may play a key role in assisting in the delivery of Tier 2 instruction (e.g., Lushen, Kim, & Reid, 2012). You should check local policies regarding the use of paraeducators for such instruction.
- In some inclusive schools, paraeducators are assigned based on schedules rather than specific student and classroom needs. Although the difficulty of scheduling is clear, keep in mind that schedules alone should not dictate how paraeducators are assigned.
- If paraeducators are working in special education classrooms, they often review specific skills with students while the special educator provides initial instruction with other students. This model is common in both resource classes as well as self-contained classes. The caution about paraeducators not offering ongoing initial instruction holds in the special education setting as well as in the general education setting. Initial instruction should be delivered by teachers or, when it is appropriate, with the direct supervision of teachers.
- Another common assignment for paraeducators working with students with significant needs is accompanying one or several students to related arts classes such as

> **Learn More About**
> Students with significant needs in high school often form special bonds with their paraprofessionals. When they leave school for post-school opportunities, both paraprofessionals and students miss each other.
>
> (https://www.youtube.com/watch?v=mdW_iPx3Oqw)

Paraeducators and teachers often collaborate in planning and delivering instruction, but teachers ultimately are responsible for directing paraeducators' work.

art, music, physical education, or computer lab (e.g., Darrow, 2010). In such cases, any specialized tasks the paraeducator must perform should be clarified and unique issues (e.g., those related to safety) should be addressed directly.

Remember that the examples just noted are intended to give you a sense of the types of assignments paraeducators may have and your role in maximizing the positive impact of paraeducators on student achievement, but there are many other possibilities. In addition, it is imperative that you monitor paraeducators' work to ensure that their time is well used on behalf of students and that their interactions with other professionals are appropriate.

Communicating with Paraeducators

Even if you have regularly scheduled planning periods with paraeducators, you will still need to use effective and efficient communication strategies to keep in touch with them and to monitor their work and student progress. The communication skills you learned in Chapters 2, 3, and 4 are essential, as they are for all your professional interactions, but several other strategies can also be used. These are briefly described in Putting Ideas into Practice.

Communication entails more than interactions about instruction and student concerns, however. One initial form of communication is the paraeducator's job description. This is the instrument through which you can discuss with paraeducators key job expectations. You might want to check about the availability of a job description because, as noted earlier, not all school districts have them, and some that do have not updated them in many years. You also should provide the following:

- Orientation at the beginning of the school year for paraeducators, including basic school policies and procedures about everything from parking to mailboxes to dress codes
- Information on topics about which confusion or misunderstanding could occur, including cell phone use, scheduled breaks or lunch times, and acceptable reasons for not being in an assigned classroom when specified

PUTTING IDEAS INTO PRACTICE
Communicating with Your Paraeducator When There Is No Time to Meet

In most schools, professionals and paraeducators have little, if any, time to formally meet, and they must become creative to maintain effective communication. Here are a few informal strategies for communicating about student academic and behavior programs with your paraeducator.

- Create for each of you a planning agenda that is laminated and can be used repeatedly. For example, the agenda might include sections for instructional issues, assistive technology matters, student behaviors, and/or team concerns. You and your paraeducator note items as you become aware of them, using a water-based marker. When you do have a few minutes to interact, you have a ready agenda to ensure your time is used wisely. After the meeting, agendas can be wiped clean and used again.
- Use a clipboard agenda. Hang or place a clipboard with a pad of paper in a location easily accessible to the paraeducator, general education teacher, and/or special educator, but away from students (e.g., a teacher mailbox, in a teacher's desk drawer, behind a teacher's desk). Anyone lists agenda items on the paper, and when the meeting occurs copies of the list are distributed and form the agenda.
- Make maximum use of electronic options for planning and organizing. A schedule for a paraeducator could be created in a spreadsheet so that it can be revised easily. Activities for specific students can be communicated through a shared calendar or using a tool such as Google Docs. Information can also be shared using other in-the-cloud options such as Evernote, OneNote, or Dropbox.
- E-mail communication can also help professionals keep in touch with paraeducators. If you establish a routine—say, spending 5 minutes each morning or afternoon providing e-mailed directions to your assistant—you can be certain that you are documenting the assigned work. If the paraeducator also e-mails with notes about implementing the directions, a detailed record exists and communication is assured. Although text messages can be helpful for urgent updates or simple reminders, the drawbacks (e.g., no record kept of possible critical communication, potential to be disruptive during instruction, possible use conflict with school policies) often make it impractical.
- If the paraeducator uses teacher's manuals or other materials in his or her work with students, you can use self-stick removable notes to provide directions and comments. Select one color to use for this purpose, and attach the note on the page where input is needed. The paraeducator could reply with notes in another color. Although this strategy is not shared planning, it can be an efficient and direct means of communication.

- Daily schedule (although this often changes several times at the beginning of the school year)
- The communication system to be used between the paraeducator and you, including the way planning will occur and steps to take if the paraeducator is uncomfortable with an assignment or assigned activity with a student or is concerned about the paraeducator–teacher partnership.
- Your expectations for paraeducator interactions with students and other school staff
- Information about the school's philosophy (e.g., inclusive, problem-based learning)
- Steps to take if a problem arises either with a student or with a staff member

The more information that you formally communicate to paraeducators, the less they will have to learn incidentally and the less likely it is that miscommunication will occur.

Supervising Paraeducators

It has been implied throughout this chapter, but at this point it needs to be stated directly: Special education teachers, general education teachers, and other professionals have the responsibility of supervising paraeducators and the work they do with students

(Ashbaker & Morgan, 2012a). This is usually not a formal responsibility; in most school districts, principals are assigned the task of formally supervising and evaluating paraeducators. However, even when this is the case, in providing feedback to paraeducators those administrators rely heavily on input from the day-to-day supervision experiences of professionals.

What have you learned in your other course work about supervising paraeducators? Paraeducators report that teachers are not proficient in guiding their work (Jones et al., 2012). Further, teachers sometimes indicate that they are reluctant to think of themselves as supervisors or to function in that capacity; they believe that it interferes with their working relationship with paraeducators (French, 1998). Whether you share these perceptions or not, in today's schools educators should assume that they will have supervisory responsibilities such as the following related to paraeducators:

- Monitoring whether paraeducators are carrying out the specific tasks that have been assigned to them
- Providing feedback to paraeducators on their work with students, pointing out strategies or techniques they are using appropriately, and redirecting them when the strategies they are using are not effective or are detrimental to the student
- Modeling effective ways to interact with students and instructional techniques to use with them
- Problem solving with paraeducators when disagreements arise about paraeducator roles in the general education or special education settings
- Confirming that paraeducators adhere to school policies
- Ensuring that paraeducators follow a code of ethics, particularly on matters such as confidentiality (Fleury, 2000)
- Supporting paraeducators by answering their questions regarding students, classroom practices, instructional strategies, legal issues, and other related topics
- Arranging for some type of public acknowledgment of the work that paraeducators do (e.g., holding an appreciation day, having students make cards, conveying positive parent comments)
- Keeping appropriate records to document paraeducator activities and feedback provided
- Bringing to the attention of administrators or other supervisors chronic issues related to paraeducators that have not been resolved through discussion and redirection

The Matter of Conflict One aspect of supervision that may be inevitable is conflict. Although you might think that conflict with paraeducators is rare, you should be prepared for the occasional situation in which it occurs. One common example concerns veteran paraeducators working with novice educators (McGrath et al., 2010). The paraeducator may inappropriately try to decide how the classroom may be run, how students should complete their work, or what information should be shared with parents. For example, think about the case study at the beginning of this chapter. Ms. Reynolds has the responsibility to direct Ms. Barnett's work, but Ms. Barnett seems to perceive that she knows what students should do and should inform Ms. Reynolds about school policies and practices. What types of conflict could this raise? Note that the strategies you learned in Chapter 9 for addressing conflict sometimes are a critical element of your work with paraeducators.

Instances of conflict require that you use all the skills that you learn throughout this book. Your paraeducator may truly have valuable insights to share about students and their programs and progress, but you ultimately are accountable for students' education. Your goals should be to listen carefully to paraeducator input, consider it in your own planning and problem solving, and make decisions based on that input as well as your own knowledge and skills. Additional suggestions for interacting with a paraprofessional when a disagreement has occurred are included in the Putting Ideas into Practice.

PUTTING IDEAS INTO PRACTICE

At Odds... When Professionals and Paraeducators Disagree

In most instances, teachers and paraeducators establish strong, positive working relationships, always keeping in mind their shared goal of effectively educating the students for whom they are responsible. However, it would be naive to think that problems do not sometimes occur. Here are a few examples:

- The paraeducator feels her schedule is unrealistic, placing her in too many general education classrooms and creating an expectation that she work with too many students with disabilities on too many different tasks. She complains to the principal.
- The paraeducator admits that he does not like one of the students with whom he is supposed to work. He avoids this student as much as possible.
- The paraeducator loves her job and loves the children, but the teacher perceives that she helps students too much and unintentionally encourages them to give up or avoid challenging assignments (e.g., she comments that the work is too difficult and either answers for the student or gives the student permission to not complete it).

As the teacher (or other professional) who ultimately is accountable for student outcomes, it is your responsibility to directly address situations such as these. The communication ideas presented throughout this book should be the basis for your responses, but here are a few specific suggestions:

- When an issue comes to your attention, prioritize making time to meet with the paraeducator to discuss it. Difficult conversations should not be attempted in the five minutes between classes or as students are returning from lunch or recess.
- Listen first. Use all your listening skills in order to gain a deep understanding of the paraeducator's perspective on the topic. Be sure to paraphrase frequently.
- As appropriate, ask the paraeducator if he has ideas for resolving the situation. Be sure to phrase this inquiry in a way that does not imply you will definitely act on these ideas. For example, you might say, "You've probably thought about what to do about this situation. As I think about how to proceed, I'd appreciate having your input."
- If the situation is complex, defer decisions. It might be important for you to obtain additional information, observe the paraeducator working in the general education classroom, or think about creative solutions for the issue. It is far better to make a decision after reflection than to feel pressured to immediately respond.
- Remember that you should direct the paraeducator's actions. If you decide, for example, that the paraeducator is offering too much assistance to a student, you should clearly state what you expect as an alternative: "When Antonio asks you to help him, say this to him: 'You try to complete the first two problems on your own. I'll come back to check on how you're doing in two minutes.'" The goal is for you to be clear about your expectations.
- Express confidence that the matter can be resolved. Phrases such as "I'm sure we can find a solution" or "I appreciate your hard work on behalf of students and am confident we can make this work" set a constructive tone.
- Keep in mind that if the disagreement concerns your actions, you should be willing to consider that your expectations or behaviors are inappropriate. The paraeducator may have a reasonable concern that requires change on your part.

Disagreements may lead to interpersonal discomfort, but with careful timing and application of your knowledge and skills for interacting with others you can successfully respond to such situations.

Of course, unless you are the formally identified supervisor for paraeducators, if significant issues arise related to paraeducator performance you should alert the appropriate administrator so that more formal procedures can be implemented if conflict occurs and persists. It is also important to keep in mind that addressing small conflicts is far easier than avoiding a problem that has the potential to become more serious.

APPLY YOUR KNOWLEDGE 10.3

Paraeducators and Collaboration

Perhaps you have been wondering whether all the information in this chapter is supposed to give a particular message about collaboration and working with paraeducators. The primary intent is to articulate the fact that your relationship with paraeducators is perhaps at this time the least understood and most complex of all the professional relationships you will have in your job.

Is it possible to collaborate with a paraeducator? Of course! Remember that collaboration is a style, and you may use the style when interacting with a paraeducator just as you use it with other professionals and parents/families. What is less clear, however, is the extent to which collaboration with paraeducators is appropriate, how boundaries should be established related to collegiality in the relationship, and how special education professionals can balance their preference for collaborative interactions with paraeducators with their responsibility to supervise them (Gilrane, Russell, & Roberts, 2008).

This is an area in which clear guidelines simply do not exist and the available data are worrisome. In some cases, teachers want to treat paraeducators just like other teachers, to ask them to take over a class, to be peers. Even some administrative literature suggests that this is acceptable practice (Daniels & McBride, 2001). At the same time, most paraeducators do not have professional credentials, they do not have a professional array of responsibilities in their job descriptions, and they do not make a professional salary. Taken together, these factors suggest that in some interactions all the conditions for collaboration can be met, but in others they cannot (Giangreco et al., 2010; Jones, 2012). Putting Ideas into Practice offers additional information for reflecting on the topic of collaboration with paraeducators.

PUTTING IDEAS INTO PRACTICE

Collaborating with Paraeducators

In some circumstances, professionals and paraeducators can and should collaborate. However, professionals must keep in mind that in other situations their accountability for decisions made should lead to an invitation for paraeducator input but not necessarily collaboration. Unfortunately, there is no single clear set of guidelines related to teacher–paraeducator collaboration, and your professional judgment must be used. Here are a few examples of collaboration opportunities. How do the characteristics of collaboration outlined in Chapter 1 apply? Why might each of these situations be appropriate for collaboration?

- A student who uses a wheelchair or who is otherwise accompanied from class to class because of other special needs (e.g., behavior problems, inability to find each classroom) is arriving late at least twice each week. An alternative arrangement needs to be made for these transitions.
- The mother of a student with a disability who does not speak English has communicated to the paraeducator (who speaks the parent's language) that she plans to care for her child at home even after high school and wants professionals to lower their expectations for him.
- Despite best efforts, the amount of time it is taking in the special education classroom to transition from activity to activity is too high. During a recent observation, the assistant principal commented that too much instructional time is being lost. The teacher and paraeducator are working to improve transitions.
- A one-to-one paraprofessional who spends the day with a student in general education is concerned that neither the general education teachers nor other students interact frequently with the student. The special educator, general educator, and paraeducator are brainstorming ways to improve this situation.

As you apply the characteristics of collaboration to these scenarios, what do you see as the difference between these situations and those in which collaboration might not be an appropriate option?

SUMMARY

- Paraeducators are individuals who work under the direction of a teacher in supporting the education of students, often specifically those with disabilities, and are employed in most school districts. Depending on federal policy as well as state and local norms, their preparation for their positions can vary greatly, from a high school diploma to a college degree. You are likely to be responsible for working with and guiding the activities of paraeducators.
- Although paraeducators in the past often focused on clerical tasks, now they typically spend the majority of their time completing direct and indirect instructional responsibilities, such as reviewing concepts taught, practicing skills, and supporting appropriate behavior. They also complete noninstructional responsibilities such as personal care, assistance moving from place to place (for students with significant disabilities), and supervision of lunch or recess.
- Ethical dilemmas sometimes occur in working with paraeducators. These may pertain to the appropriate scope of their instructional responsibilities, their communication with students and families, and their role in fostering student independence rather than dependence.
- Professionals have a specific set of duties for ensuring they can work effectively with paraeducators. These include teaching paraeducators about their responsibilities, including providing professional development as needed, arranging a time to plan with them, creating their specific assignments in general and special education settings, clearly communicating with them, and appropriately supervising their work.
- Collaboration between professionals and paraeducators is recommended, but it must be tempered with an understanding of the difference in status between the individuals participating and the context in which the interactions occur.

BACK TO THE CASE

1. Take the role of Emily Reynolds, the general educator. Using the information in this chapter as well as skills learned in earlier chapters, how would you communicate with Ms. Barnett about your concerns? What would you do if, after you began to speak with her, she became angry? She became sullen? She started crying and explaining that she was only trying to do her job?
2. Next, take on the role of the special education teacher responsible for the students in Ms. Reynolds's class. Create a role-play in which one person plays Viviana Barnett, one plays Emily Reynolds, and one plays the special educator. The purpose of the meeting is to address Ms. Reynolds's concerns. How could you begin this meeting with a positive tone? What skills are most important for addressing Ms. Reynolds's concerns related to Ms. Barnett?
3. How would you go about clarifying for Ms. Barnett what her appropriate responsibilities are in Emily's classroom? Under what circumstances do you think it would be necessary to involve a principal or other administrator to address the situation?

COLLABORATIVE ACTIVITIES

1. Suppose you accept a position to be a special education teacher in an inclusive middle school. Your students with mild to moderate learning and behavior disabilities are on two teams, but you are assigned a teaching assistant to ensure that all students receive appropriate services. What factors would you consider in deciding how to assign tasks to your paraeducator? How would you ensure that you retained appropriate accountability for the progress of students served primarily by the paraeducator?
2. Although most paraeducators are wonderful, committed individuals who truly make a significant contribution to student success, problems can also occur. How would you respond to the following situations?
   - The paraeducator, who is supposed to be in your classroom all morning, seems to disappear frequently for 15 to 20 minutes at a time.
   - The paraeducator, who is nearly finished with a teaching credential, comments about today's

lesson: "I don't think this information is appropriate for Joe. It's too difficult. I'll just pull him to the side and do something different. I hope you're okay with that."
- In your opinion, the paraeducator seems to be doing too much to assist several students; and you believe the students should have more responsibility for beginning and completing assignments independently, turning them in, and behaving appropriately.

3. If you were asked to provide a one-hour staff development session to school staff members on the roles and responsibilities of paraeducators, what topics would you prioritize? How would you address the topic of collaboration between professionals and paraeducators? What topics do you think would be of particular interest to general education teachers? Special education teachers? Other professionals?

4. Imagine that it is the first day of school, and you have just met the newly hired paraeducator who is to assist you. What would you do to ensure that the paraeducator feels comfortable in his new job and school? That you and the paraeducator develop a strong and positive working relationship right from the beginning? That the paraeducator understands the scope of his responsibilities? Compare your responses to those of your classmates so that you can develop your own master checklist for getting started.

5. Many educators note that paraeducators have valuable information about students, but that they often are not provided with planning time with teachers and are not usually included in meetings and interactions with parents. What should be the role of the paraeducator on a teaching team? What would you say to convince your administrator to make time available for paraeducators to participate in these collaborative opportunities? How could you use electronic planning strategies presented in this chapter and Chapter 7 to facilitate planning with a paraprofessional?

CHECK YOUR UNDERSTANDING

Click here to gauge your understanding of this chapter's essential concepts.

11 Families

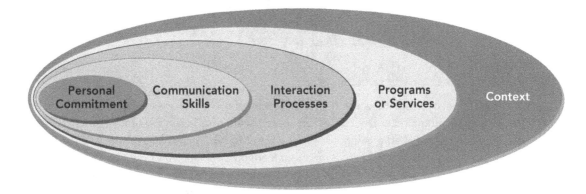

CONNECTIONS

You have learned many concepts and skills important to collaboration and discussed partnerships with other professionals and with paraeducators. In this chapter, the special considerations related to understanding and working with families are presented. The information is grounded in family systems theory, but it also takes into account the life cycles of families. The discussion incorporates attention to the crucial influence of culture on your interactions with family members and also addresses other factors that may shape your work with them. Finally, the role you play in fostering strong and meaningful family participation in their children's education is clarified, including strategies for supporting and collaborating with parents and other family members. Ultimately, this chapter forms an opportunity to integrate most of the information you have explored throughout Chapters 1–9.

LEARNING OUTCOMES

After reading this chapter you will be able to:

1. Describe the historical and current roles of parents and families in the education of children and youth with disabilities, including the principles of family systems theory.
2. Analyze special considerations and challenges for families of children with disabilities at each of the four life stages of families.
3. Outline professional roles and responsibilities for interacting with families, taking into consideration culture and cultural responsiveness as well as other influencing factors.
4. Identify strategies for promoting family participation in educational decision making.

A CASE FOR COLLABORATION

How Much Is Enough?

Returning from overseas duty with the military, Mr. Johnson, William's father, has rejoined his family. He is a devoted father and is very concerned about his fifth-grade son's recently identified learning disability. Mr. Johnson has had a one-hour meeting with Ms. Albright, William's special education teacher, for each of the last three Mondays to learn more about learning disabilities and what he can do to help William at home. He has read all of the print materials given to him, and he has been reading extensively about learning disabilities, relying heavily on resources from the Internet. Not surprisingly, he has found some relevant and solid information, but he has also found several unsubstantiated "studies" with results that suggest using highly questionable strategies at home and school to "cure" William's learning disability. Mr. Johnson indicates to Ms. Albright that he would like to start meeting twice a week to discuss treatments. Despite her commitment to working with parents, she is unable to schedule this much time for him because she has 20 annual reviews and several eligibility meetings to schedule and complete in the next few weeks, along with all her other professional responsibilities.

Ms. Albright understands her responsibility to parents and wants to collaborate with families on behalf of their children. Mr. Johnson is a caring and involved parent who is somewhat anxious about his son's school performance. He has not yet found work since he returned from the service and so he has extra time to devote to William. His interest in his son is commendable, but his anxiety is exacerbated by the wide range of information and myths he is discovering on the Internet. Ms. Albright can help him make better judgments about the material he is reading and give him more instructive information to read. However, she does not have the time to meet with him as often as he would like, even if more meetings could help him to understand and accept William's disability.

Introduction

You are likely to have a different working relationship with each of the families with which you interact. Your relationships are likely to depend on the needs of the student; the interests, resources, and needs of the families; and the extent of your skills, resources, and attitude (e.g., Dykens, 2015). Consider these situations:

- Susan's parents are both professionals working in high-pressure jobs. They did not attend Back-to-School Night and never come in for routine parent–teacher conferences. When you call one of them, you usually receive a return call from a secretary or the nanny offering to convey your message to the parent. However, Susan's father just called to demand a meeting and threatened to file for a due process hearing. He told you that Susan is not receiving the services to which she is entitled and that you clearly are not doing your job. He hung up before you could ask for more information; you have no idea what has prompted this sudden outburst.
- Drew's mother has scheduled two conferences with you and has canceled both of them. She typically cancels meetings at the last minute because another child is ill, her car breaks down, or she is unable to get away from work. She calls you apologetically and wants to discuss matters on the phone rather than come to school. Yesterday she did attend Drew's annual review meeting, but with her were her infant and a neighbor's preschool child, whose presence was disruptive to the meeting.

Every school professional can relate to a range of relationships with parents. In the introductory case, Mr. Johnson's investment in William's progress is requiring more time than his teacher can give and may not be helpful to William. Susan's parents seem unwilling to commit to participating in their daughter's program until they perceive a problem, and then her father adopted an accusatory manner. You have little information about their relationship with Susan. Drew's mother is committed to Drew; but the other children, her work, and related demands for her time make it exceptionally difficult for her to attend meetings at school. Nevertheless, she wants to know how he is doing and what she can do to support him at home.

Collaboration is a worthy goal and is something to aim for with all families, although the intensity of your collaboration will vary based on the needs of the family. When you consider the range of situations faced by families, you will realize that you need to adjust your expectations to match the capacity of an individual family to engage in different levels of collaboration. For some families, active participation in school activities is not an appropriate goal. If you are only going to talk with Susan's nanny or her mother's secretary, it may not be possible for you to engage the family in school activities or for you and the parents to have sufficient interaction for collaboration to occur. Some parents may have so many obligations and demands that active collaboration is difficult. For others, such as Drew's mother, who have difficult schedules and competing demands but are able to maintain contact by telephone or e-mail or who can arrange early morning or early evening meetings, active collaboration is appropriate and recommended. You may find that, with work, this could be the case with Susan's parents, too. Collaboration with Mr. Johnson is appropriate, but the restrictions on your schedule simply will not permit it at the level he wishes. In this case, you will have to communicate your situation to him, maintain the level of collaboration you can, and refer him to another professional, such as the school counselor, or to an information and referral resource.

Despite the strength of your collaboration, your primary responsibilities in working with families are to understand the family needs and to facilitate family participation in decision making about the education of the family member with a disability. These responsibilities—understanding and facilitating participation—are discussed in the following section. In addition, throughout this chapter the emphasis is on providing supportive, family-centered services. This goal is more easily attained when you blend your knowledge of students with disabilities or other special needs, your knowledge and skills for collaborating, and your understanding of families (West & Pirtle, 2014).

> **Learn More About**
> As noted in this video clip, meetings about students with disabilities can be intimidating for parents, and all educators have a role to play in making meetings meaningful for them.

Understanding Families

In Chapter 1, you learned that a number of provisions in the Individuals with Disabilities Education Act (IDEA) provide for parental representation and participation in developing and implementing educational programs for their children. For example, IDEA mandates that parents must be part of the team that makes eligibility, placement, and services decisions; that parents must be regularly informed of their child's progress; that parents must be given copies of evaluation reports and have a right to ask for reviews of individualized education programs (IEPs); and that states must offer no-cost mediation to parents to resolve disputes. Part C of the law mandates family-based early intervention services that may include parent education, support, and counseling as delineated in the individualized family service plan (IFSP). Parent training and information centers (PTIs) in each state and territory are also required by law to provide assistance so that parents and families can participate meaningfully in meeting the needs of their family member with a disability. With each reauthorization of IDEA since it was originally passed in 1975, the role of parents and families in their family member's education has become increasingly more significant (Meyer, 2012; White, 2014; Yell, 2012). The professional literature has also called for increased collaboration between families and schools (Olivos, Gallagher, & Aguilar, 2010; Rodriguez, Blatz, & Elbaum, 2014).

Professionals must understand families and their perspectives in order to know what supports they need as well as when and how to engage them in collaboration (Anderson, Howland, & McCoach, 2015). Although each family is unique and it is necessary to learn about them individually, some special considerations apply when you seek to understand

> Learn More About Trust and ongoing communication can be instrumental in encouraging parent participation in the education of their children with disabilities.

any family. In Chapter 2, you considered prerequisites to effective interactions that involve your self-awareness and your ability to understand others. These concepts—frame of reference, cultural self-awareness, and selective perception—accompanied by nonverbal communication, listening, and responding skills are important foundations for understanding others, including families. The application of your knowledge and skills must be carefully situated in the context of a family systems framework that offers insights into functions and tasks of families at various life stages.

A brief examination of the evolution of families and their relationships with educators is an appropriate starting point. Professionals have long focused on the parental roles and functions in the care and education of children with disabilities. Turnbull and Turnbull (2001) described parents' major roles over the years, including the cause of their child's disability, organization members, service developers, recipients of professionals' decisions, teachers, political advocates, and educational decision makers. They added an eighth role—families as collaborators—as having emerged in the 1990s, and stressed that the emphasis on families signals a recognition that all family members, not just parents, are important to the care and education of children.

The shift in emphasis from parents to families occurred following the period from 1981 to 1989, when cultural diversity in the United States was expanded by the almost 6 million Asian, African, European, and Latin American people who became U.S. citizens. Entwisle (1994) observed that increased cultural diversity and economic and social pressures led to considerable structural diversity among these families and expanded concepts of what constitutes family.

Family has been defined in many ways. Traditionally, the narrow, nuclear view of mother, father, and children has been normative, sometimes expanded to include others who live in the home. Yet children of single-parent families, stepfamilies, extended families, families with same-sex parents, families with grandparents acting as parents, and families with adopted or foster children are all represented in today's schools. People from some ethnic groups view the concept of family quite narrowly, whereas others conceive of families in a much broader way and include grandparents, aunts, uncles, and even neighbors or community elders. One definition of family that is consistent with contemporary thinking is the following:

> two or more people who regard themselves as a family and who perform some of the functions that families typically perform. These people may or may not be related by blood or marriage and may or may not usually live together. (Turnbull, Turnbull, Erwin, Soodak, & Shogren, 2015, p. 6)

It is essential that you define family in the broadest manner and accept the definition used by the parents and caregivers with whom you interact. For instance, if a mother suggests that her sister or aunt will be attending a parent conference in her place, it would be appropriate to accept that decision while continuing to encourage the mother's participation. Of course, legal matters such as accessing confidential information or taking a child from school require written permission from the child's parent or legal guardian. Your responsibility is to balance these two elements as part of each student's education—perception of family and legal status.

Family Systems Theory

Although the importance of systems theory has been recognized in related fields since the 1960s (Lambie, 2008), only over the past three decades has it become a major influence in how professionals view and respond to families of children with disabilities. In systems theory, the family is seen as a complex and interactive social system in which all members' needs and experiences affect the others. Murray Bowen (1978), the "father" of family systems theory, theorized eight interlocking concepts that characterize families: As one element is affected, so, too, are the others. Turnbull et al. (2015) use Satir's (1972) metaphor of a mobile to describe these interactions within the family system: The pieces of a mobile can be grouped and balanced by lengthening or shortening strings, but the repositioning of one piece causes a reaction or imbalance that affects the others. So it is with families.

The opening case illustrates this point: The return of William's father from active duty caused the metaphoric mobile to lose its balance. The balance was even further disturbed because Mr. Johnson was not able to find employment, and so he was spending an extraordinary amount of time focused on William. This constituted a significant departure from the last few months when he was absent and William had some independence in getting his homework completed and managing his household chores. Such an imbalance is likely to manifest in William's school behaviors and the teacher needs to be sensitive to it.

As you learn more about families, keep in mind that each is a whole made up of parts that seek balance. Systems theory and its principles, described next, can help professionals to better understand a student's behavior, strengths, and challenges.

> **Learn More About** Parents' understanding of their rights related to their children with special needs may affect their perceptions of their child and influence their participation during IEP and other meetings.

Principle 1: No individual can be understood without recognizing how he or she fits within the entire family This principle is central in systems theory. It is not just that each family member is a part of the whole. What is important is understanding how the members interact with one another and how their individual and collective histories have developed. Specifically, you should be alert to recognizing how each family member affects and is affected by the others and their situations. For example, when a parent loses a job the financial assets of the family change. Depending on the reason for and the length of the unemployment period, the parent's attitudes, affect, and behavior may also change and have significant impact on the other family members. A teacher or counselor might view a behavioral or academic change in a student differently if he knew that the student's only parent had been laid off from his or her job, was unable to find work for several weeks, and was beginning to look for an alternative place to live. Thus, noting the nature of a student's academic or behavioral change is not adequate for understanding the family or how these changes affect the family members. Similarly, understanding a child's disability is not sufficient to provide you with understanding of the family. Nor is understanding the child's sibling a sufficient condition for understanding the family. The family consists of many parts, and professionals need to know all of the parts and understand their influence on the child if they are to understand the child.

Principle 2: Families need rules for structure and for change Rules for structure guide the family and its behavior in day-to-day events. For example, a single working mother with two children may have a clear work schedule, specific household chores for the children or babysitter, a routine with a sister for sharing transportation to events, and arrangements with a neighbor or friend to share child-care responsibilities. If a mother's work schedule changes, or if she becomes unemployed and needs to seek a new job, many or all of the rules and arrangements must be renegotiated. If she is not able to readily renegotiate these matters, tensions are likely to build and affect her as well as the other members of the family. Children might seem disoriented at school, be tired from sleep missed due to schedule changes, and even display anxiety or other emotional changes if they sense and respond to these feelings from their parent.

Principle 3: Family interaction with the school, community, extended family, and friends is essential to the life of the family For families to be healthy and function well, members must have their external social and affiliation needs met. That is, although a family exists to meet the needs of its members, it is unlikely to be able independently to meet that goal for each family member. Real benefits accrue through relations with persons outside of the nuclear family, and family members require such interactions. Children need peer relationships and adults want to interact with other adults. The importance of parents interacting with and deriving support from other parents is discussed later in this chapter. Here, the point is that families that isolate themselves are likely to become lonely, possibly hostile, and often dysfunctional; and they may then view their child in a less-than-positive way.

Psychology has provided new insights into the value of social networking for the child and other members of the family. People who have others they can trust and rely on are healthier, happier, and more productive (Meadan, Halle, & Ebata, 2010; Minnes, Perry, &

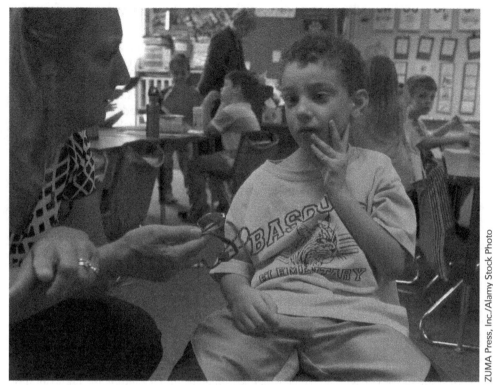

When parents have difficulty understanding the disabilities of their children and their accompanying limitations and assets, professionals should provide opportunities for them to observe their children's performance and learn strategies to facilitate their academic, behavioral, social, and emotional growth.

> **Learn More About**
> This video clip provides a brief summary of the overall goals of family systems theory. How does this information pertain directly to your work with families?
>
> (https://www.youtube.com/watch?v=Lu5rLJYJSSs)

Weiss, 2015). These positive interactions and the associated emotions provide individuals with stronger interpersonal relationships. Participation in mutually supportive networks results in increased skill at asking for help, appreciation of the help received, recognition of and response to others' needs, and a general sense of feeling happier (Adler, Rodman, & Cropley, 2012).

APPLY YOUR KNOWLEDGE 11.1

Family Life Cycles

Family systems theory is a foundation for your work with parents and other family members, but it is not enough. Much like human development, this theory views the family as undergoing a series of developmental tasks that vary along several life stages. Nichols (1996) described the family cycle as "being concerned with the developmental tasks of the family itself as it deals with the needs of the adult members and the developmental needs of the offspring" (p. 57). Family life stages help describe how families change over time. Generally, each family experiences these predictable phases of development and they represent changes the family undergoes (Lambie, 2008). As a family progresses from one stage to the next, family members' responsibilities shift, and the family is said to undergo transition. Transitions are the periods between stages when family members are readjusting their roles and interactions in order to meet the next set of expectations and tasks. These transitions usually are shorter in duration than are the stages, but they are characterized by confusion and often by increased stress. By attending and being sensitive to the life stages of the families with which you collaborate, and by assisting them in taking appropriate steps to support their child with a disability you can be especially effective in your collaboration with them.

As children grow older and transition from early intervention, to early childhood programs, to elementary school, to secondary school, and so on, the presumption of family-centered services diminishes (Dempsey & Keen, 2008; Dunst, 2002). This is particularly disappointing when one considers the dynamics of family systems. Families with members with disabilities at all phases of their life cycle face complexities that others do not and that likely require the expertise and support of professionals and others with similar experiences to achieve successful outcomes. Providing the extra support families need during transitions to new or different services that are likely to be less family centered is an important professional responsibility and one that families need across all life stages.

Many theorists have proposed family life stages and advanced models that typically delineate from four to over 20 stages. In Putting Ideas into Practice, we summarize the typical functions and tasks advanced by several of those theorists (e.g., Carter & McGoldrick, 2005; Lambie, 2008; McGoldrick, Carter, & Garcia-Preto, 2011) and place them within a four-stage framework developed by Turnbull et al. (2015). Each stage includes special issues for families of children with disabilities and the basis for actions professionals can take to support family members and their children.

Birth and Early Childhood

The focus for parents whose children's disabilities were identified at birth or during early childhood is understanding the disability and working through feelings about the diagnosis. Adjusting to a typically developing child is an important task for families, and a child with a disability can make the task infinitely more complex (Tiba, Johnson, & Vadineanu, 2012).

PUTTING IDEAS INTO PRACTICE

Tasks and Functions at Four Family Life Stages

This brief description of tasks and functions families face at different stages can help you to anticipate the experiences and needs of your students' families and how to respond to them.

Birth and Early Childhood

With the introduction of a child through birth or adoption, the primary family functions become nurturing and caring for the infant or young child and providing culturally appropriate behavioral limits. Tasks are to realign family relationships as well as relationships with friends and extended families to accommodate the presence of the young child and the duties of parenthood.

Childhood

The primary themes for families with children in their elementary school years are affiliation and allowing others to be brought within the family boundaries. The family functions are demonstrating sensitivity to the child's developmental needs and enjoying the child's experiences. In Western cultures, families typically encourage the child's independence, but this is not the case in all cultures. Tasks to be accomplished are linking with a peer network and establishing family responsibilities and sibling roles.

Adolescence

This stage is characterized by themes of decentralization and the relaxing of boundaries. Parents' essential functions are to accept the efforts their child makes to "distance" them and to provide the adolescent with support needed to establish his or her identity, a matter especially important for young people with disabilities. The tasks that parents face include managing the adolescent's increasing independence, refocusing on their own careers and marriage, and developing more flexible roles.

Adulthood

Adulthood is characterized by themes of detachment, dissolving ties, and letting go. Family functions focus on supporting and facilitating independence while encouraging the young adult to accept more responsibility. Some families need to turn their attention to arrangements for providing care for their adult child with a disability as the parents age and can no longer serve that function.

> **Learn More About**
> Learning that a young child has a disability can be life altering for some families, but the services accessed and support offered by professionals can support family members as they adjust their understanding and expectations.
>
> (https://www.youtube.com/watch?v=KHiuMpNKVpY)

A primary task for families at this stage is receiving and accepting their child's disability diagnosis. Kübler-Ross (1969) proposed a grief cycle model to describe the stages a person goes through when dealing with the death of a loved one. Some authors use this model to describe the stages that many parents experience as they learn about and grow to accept their child's disability. Not all parents go through the same process, and the stages may not be sequential or of equal duration; but in this model the stages generally include shock and denial, guilt and anger, shame and depression, and acceptance. Little empirical evidence has been offered for this process in families of children with disabilities, and yet the model is frequently referenced in professional literature. Because you are likely to encounter this model elsewhere, it warrants brief consideration.

A word about the grief cycle is required here. Remember that grief is a stage in a *cycle*, not a static state or a simple linear set of steps, and the end result is acceptance of the child's disability and commitment to making the adjustments necessary for the child and family to live productive lives. Some families may stay focused on the grief and may struggle to make the adjustments needed to help their children grow into emotionally healthy individuals (e.g., Griffith, Hastings, Petalas, & Lloyd, 2015). Sensitive professionals who make extra efforts to support the families may inadvertently encourage them to remain in the grief stage or in another stage that prevents them from constructively addressing their child's education. The challenge for professionals is to respond with empathy as families transition through the various stages but to continually foster their progress to the next stages.

Traditional interventions or supports that were thought to be helpful to families as they came to terms with their child's disability included patience, listening with acceptance, and providing resource and referral information (Cook, Tessier, & Klein, 1992). More contemporary family systems approaches also advocate "re-storying," that is, assisting families to move away from a "problem" orientation in order to construct a new story that allows them to focus on their ability to work actively to realize new possibilities for their child (Ivey, Ivey, Zalaquett, & Quirk, 2016; Petrina, Carter, & Stephenson, 2015). Professionals should provide a supportive and accepting environment for families and acknowledge their feelings while also helping them to re-story and begin to see their family life in a new way (Blacher, Begum, Marcoulides, & Baker, 2013). Professionals should also facilitate family awareness of support groups or parent-to-parent groups. As families accept their child's disabilities, needs, and strengths, they also typically need assistance in setting realistic goals for the child.

A second major task for the family of a young child with disabilities is accessing and participating in early intervention or early childhood services. The system into which a child and family enter is largely determined by the child's age. Based on Part C of IDEA, children with disabilities from birth through two years of age are eligible for early intervention services. Although culturally and linguistically diverse families tend to be somewhat less satisfied than others, more than two-thirds of the families in a U.S. Department of Education study perceived that early intervention programs had a significant impact on the developmental gains of their children (Bailey, Hebbler, Scarborough, Spiker, & Malik, 2004). At age three, children and their families face a significant transition as they exit early intervention and enter preschool programs established under the provisions of IDEA Part B. This is more than a transition to a new service. It generally involves movement from one coordinating agency to another (e.g., from the state's health and human services department to its department of education). Further, with this transition come different regulations, rights, and services. Researchers have found that although both early intervention and preschool services are family centered and collaborative, the emphasis is somewhat less so at the preschool level than it was during early intervention services (Dunst, 2002). Professionals need to be sensitive to this and work toward increasing the support they provide families as they transition from one service to another and from one agency to another. In Chapter 12, we consider the dynamics of interagency services and transitions, but it is important to develop awareness of the challenges in the current context.

Childhood

The typical functions and tasks required of the childhood stage are more complex for the family of a child who is identified with a disability than is true for other families. For children with disabilities who are not diagnosed at birth, the most common period for diagnosis is during the elementary school years. Regardless of when the diagnosis occurs, the family is likely to experience the grief cycle or some variation of it. Major activities for families of elementary school-age children are clarifying family goals for the child, deciding on appropriate services, and deciding on placement in self-contained, resource, general education, or other classroom options. Many issues associated with making decisions about educational placement for a child weigh heavily on families during this stage. Brief references to these concerns are seen in Putting Ideas into Practice. Parents may have opinions, and certainly they have had advice from friends and other professionals, but they are likely to feel ill equipped to make decisions about this critically important subject. Many parents are reluctant to challenge or disagree with educators for cultural reasons or for fear that their disagreement may result in bias against their child.

Families particularly value professionals who are accessible, available, and supportive to them at this stage. Parents appreciate professionals who are willing to assume responsibilities that may seem to be beyond the strict scope of their positions (Nelson, Summers, & Turnbull, 2004; Turnbull & Turnbull, 2015). They also value professionals who support them by listening with empathy to their concerns and sharing objective information in response to their questions (e.g., Hardin, Blanchard, Kemmery, Appenzeller, & Parker, 2014). Often, it is also helpful to assist families in connecting with other families who may provide information or take them to visit different programs that may contribute to their understanding and decision making. Additional tasks that families with elementary school-age children face include handling the reactions of the child's peer groups and siblings to his or her disability (Tudor & Lerner, 2015; Webster & Carter, 2013). At this life cycle stage, in which affiliation is a primary theme, potential ostracism by peers is especially worrisome (Rowley et al., 2012). Professionals can help the child and his or her family to understand the disability and find

PUTTING IDEAS INTO PRACTICE

Some Parental Concerns About Inclusion

Many families have understandable concerns about the impact of inclusion on themselves and their family members with a disability. They may believe that inclusion benefits everyone and society in general. Or they may fear that inclusion is a means of saving money by "dumping" children with disabilities into general education classrooms or other settings with typically developing peers but without necessary supports. Parents may have little information about the characteristics and benefits of services provided in separate versus general education settings. The questions that follow are among those for which parents seek answers.

- Will my child be safe in the proposed setting?
- What are the benefits of services in general education versus those in a separate setting?
- In which setting or combination of settings can my child's IFSP or IEP goals best be met?
- In which setting or combination of settings will his academic skills most develop?
- Will placement in a general education classroom negatively affect the time and attention available for my child?
- In the proposed setting(s), will my child receive the specially designed instruction he needs?
- How will matters related to behavior management be addressed in the proposed setting(s)?
- What will the teachers expect of me?
- In which setting or combination of settings will my child's potential best be developed? Will my child receive the most appropriate services?
- How does inclusiveness exist across settings? If my child is in a separate setting, what would be considered inclusive for him? If my child is in a general education setting, how is inclusiveness made a reality rather than a theory?

appropriate and effective ways to talk with others about it. Affiliation is also a theme for other family members. This is a good time to encourage families to join support groups if they have not already done so. Information about such groups is presented later in this chapter. Parents who are engaged in parent support groups or receive other sorts of social support report the highest levels of enjoyment in parenting a child with a disability (Turnbull et al., 2015).

Adolescence

> **Learn More About**
> What do you think that parent "comfort" would be when interacting with professionals about a child with a disability who is in high school?

Adolescence is a tumultuous time. It is a period during which young people experience rapid growth, hormonal changes, a newfound sexuality, and typically a need to challenge authority. Rebellion in one form or another is to be expected. Surely you are familiar with this. Perhaps you work or live with adolescents, or you may remember some challenges you posed for your own parents during that period of your life. Few people would disagree that being an adolescent or having one in your home or classroom can be daunting.

Dwairy and Achoui (2010) suggest that adolescence is more influenced by cultural context than any other life cycle stage. European Americans typically view adulthood as beginning at age 18, whereas various ethnic or religious groups believe that adulthood commences earlier. As an example, consider the Jewish bar and bat mitzvahs. In these rituals, 13-year-old adolescents become adult members of their organizations. Other, less familiar, examples exist in other world religions and in different ethnic and cultural groups in which adolescents are perceived to be adults. Professionals are well advised to learn about the traditions and beliefs of a family toward adolescents and their roles and to respect those traditions in their interactions with the family.

Some challenging issues arise for adolescents with disabilities. One of the tasks of adolescence is to develop a sense of self or personal identity. According to Bowen (1978), this is the most critical of the tasks of this stage. All adolescents begin to compare themselves with others during this stage, and they start to develop a sense of their own strengths and weaknesses. The presence of autism, a learning disability, a physical impairment, a behavior disorder, or any other disability may negatively influence the adolescent's self-esteem and identity. Typical adolescent resistance to authority may exhibit itself for adolescents with disabilities as noncompliance with medical treatments, such as refusal to monitor blood sugar or take insulin by an adolescent with diabetes or refusal to take prescribed medication by an adolescent with seizure disorder. The struggle between dependence and independence that characterizes many adolescent relationships is intensified for families of adolescents with disabilities. While developing independence is a primary task at this stage, very real physical, cognitive, and emotional needs often make the struggle more complex for adolescents with disabilities and their families (Cheak-Zamora, Teti, & First, 2015).

Families have a profound impact on their adolescents with disabilities. Riley, De Anda and Blackaller (2007) summarized research demonstrating that social and family support played significant roles in adolescents' adjustment. In their research, they identified family variables to which successful adults with disabilities attributed their success and adjustment. Specifically, they found the most salient factors to be family support and the family's perception of the adolescent's abilities and potential. The individuals studied were articulate in describing the impact of family views of their abilities and talents throughout their childhood and especially during their adolescence. They even identified specific family members and their positive contributions. These findings have implications for professionals: In addition to communicating your own belief in the capacity and potential of the adolescent with disabilities, you may need to help families see the strengths and talents of their children and encourage them to express those positive perceptions to the adolescent.

Several educational issues gain significance as families and professionals collaborate in designing programs and activities for adolescents with disabilities. This is the stage at which planning for vocational development and eventual careers as appropriate, community participation and the importance of social networks, and post-school transition become particularly critical (Carter, Brock, & Trainor, 2014). This topic is addressed in Chapter 12, but its relationship to this family life stage should be mentioned briefly here. As the adolescent is assessing her strengths and needs and developing a personal identity, consideration should be given to goals and vocational options. For example: How limiting is the student's disability? What are her individual assets and needs? What dreams and expectations for the future do she and her family have? The family and school professionals should collaborate to help the student set appropriate and realistic goals consistent with her potential and interests. But keep in mind the student's struggle for autonomy and independence at this stage. The range and number of options should not be reduced prematurely, and efforts should be made to enhance the student's self-determination skills (Carter et al., 2013; Snell & Brown, 2011).

Other plans are also critical at this stage. For example, the adolescent becomes more involved in the decision making at her annual review and IEP meetings in preparation for assuming, at age 18, the role that has heretofore been held by the parents. This is a move toward independence that may require the professional to provide support and guidance to the adolescent as well as to the other family members.

Adolescents' changes associated with puberty and sexual development create a need for sexuality education (Travers, Tincani, Whitby, & Boutot, 2014). Sexuality curriculum should include general development, sexually transmitted diseases, birth control, responsibility, same- and opposite-sex relationships, avoidance of sexual abuse, and marriage and family relationships and responsibilities (Hatton & Tector, 2010; Mahoney & Poling, 2011). Turnbull et al. (2015) stress that sexuality issues may also present educational needs for families. They note that parents often are unaware of their adolescent's sexual needs and interests. This suggests that professionals may also need to assist families to develop a better understanding of the sexuality issues commencing in adolescence.

> **Learn More About**
> This brief video clip addresses the anxiety a parent may experience when interacting with professionals about her child with a disability; it serves as a good reminder of parents' reliance on clear communication with school professionals.

Adulthood

Adulthood is the final stage for families that is directly applicable to educators. Many of the issues of adulthood are discussed, and strategies for addressing them are identified in Chapter 12. Here, the essential message concerns the significant educational and life decisions that occur at this stage (e.g., Bindels-de Hens, van Staa, van Vliet, Ewals, & Hilberink, 2013). Together, families and professionals must identify and access appropriate services to prepare these young adults for postsecondary educational and employment options. Depending on their goals, abilities, and limitations, students might need assistance selecting and preparing for postsecondary education, vocational training, or supported employment. Some individuals also may need to access supported living arrangements.

A special concern becomes prominent at this point: What will happen to the individual with a disability when aging parents are no longer able to provide care for or guidance to the individual? Who will care for this person? How will he or she fare as an adult without parents? This is generally a more significant concern for families of individuals with significant disabilities who will always need some type of care and support, but it is a real concern for many parents. The tasks in this family life stage include renegotiating relationships among parents and other family members; redefining roles with adult children; realigning relationships to include the adult child's housemate, assistant, spouse, and/or in-laws; and dealing with the death of family members.

When you keep the family life cycle stages in mind as you interact with students and their parents and other family members, you are likely to demonstrate respect for the family unit and understanding of the stresses members are facing. Your demonstration of understanding and use of the suggestions such as those included in Putting Ideas into Practice will help you to build a strong and productive partnership with them.

PUTTING IDEAS INTO PRACTICE

Enhancing Successful Transitions

Are you wondering what you can do in your professional role to assist families in making successful transitions as their children grow and reach new developmental milestones? Here are some suggestions for these age-related transitions.

From Early Intervention to Early Childhood

- Suggest that parents begin preparing for the separation of preschool children by periodically leaving the child with others.
- Encourage parents to gather information and visit preschools in the community.
- Encourage participation in Parent to Parent programs. (Veteran parents are matched in one-to-one relationships with parents who are just beginning the transition process.) Familiarize parents with possible school (elementary and secondary) programs, career options, or adult programs so they have an idea of future opportunities.

From Early Childhood to Early School Age

- Provide parents with an overview of curricular options.
- Ensure that IEP meetings provide an empowering context for family collaboration.
- Encourage participation in Parent to Parent matches, workshops, or family support groups to discuss transitions with others.

From Early School Age to Adolescence

- Assist families and adolescents to identify community leisure-time activities.
- Incorporate into the IEP skills that will be needed in future career and vocational programs.
- Visit or become familiar with a variety of career and living options.
- Develop a mentor relationship with an adult with a similar exceptionality and an individual who has a career that matches the student's strengths and preferences.

From Adolescence to Adulthood

- Provide preferred information to families about guardianship, estate planning, wills, and trusts.
- Assist family members in transferring responsibilities to the individual with an exceptionality, other family members, or service providers as appropriate.
- Assist the young adult and family members with career or vocational choices.
- Address the issues and responsibilities of marriage and family for the young adult.

Source: Adapted from *Families, Professionals, and Exceptionality: Positive Outcomes Through Partnerships and Trust*, (p. 90), by A. Turnbull, H. R. Turnbull, E. J. Erwin, L. C. Soodak, and K. A. Shogren, 2015, Upper Saddle River, NJ: Pearson Education, Inc. Copyright 2015 by Pearson Education, Inc. Reprinted and electronically reproduced with permission.

Factors Affecting Professionals' Interactions with Families

Understanding family systems theory and the life cycle of families forms a beginning to effective interactions with parents and other family members, but these understandings are insufficient. To meaningfully collaborate with them you should also review and expand your knowledge of how cultural factors may affect your relationships with families and how family functioning and interactions with you may be affected by the nature of a child's disability.

Cultural Influences

The United States is one of the world's most culturally, ethnically, and linguistically diverse nations, and few professionals practice in school environments in which families of diverse cultures are not represented. The vast majority of professionals interact with families from many different backgrounds and must be culturally competent (Aceves, 2014) and able to offer culturally sensitive and relevant services (He, 2013). Throughout this book, you have learned about cultural patterns and the impact these may have on various collaborative activities, from problem solving, teaming, and co-teaching, to home–school communication patterns and conflict resolution. We bring attention to this topic one last time as a reminder to you of the importance of becoming culturally competent in order to be successful in your collaborative endeavors.

Three points offered by Lynch (2011a) are particularly relevant for a discussion of culture and working with families:

- Culture is dynamic—always changing and evolving; it is not static. What individuals remember from a culture in which they were raised is probably not the way the culture is practiced in the same place today.
- Culture, language, ethnicity, and race are powerful influences on an individual's values, beliefs, and behaviors, but they are not the sole influences. One's socioeconomic status, education, socialization, and life experiences greatly influence one's identity and frame of reference. These, in turn, influence how a family functions.
- No cultural, ethnic, linguistic, or racial group is homogeneous. Great diversity exists in the attitudes, values, beliefs, and behaviors within groups of people who share a common culture.

Understanding the culture of a student's family is fundamental to understanding and effectively serving the student because a family's culture contributes significantly to its structure, values, and beliefs—all critical influences on the student. But how do you go about gaining such knowledge and developing intercultural competence? As you know from learning about frame of reference and perspective in Chapter 2, the first step is gaining cultural self-awareness. The second step in the journey toward cultural competence is learning specific information about other cultures (Lynch, 2011b). This learning can be achieved through reading, travel, and interactions with representatives of specific cultural groups. Although many useful resources are available for this purpose, the most enjoyable learning may come from direct interaction and experience. Learning firsthand about the art, music, dance, foods, values, and traditions of a culture different from your own is an exciting and stimulating experience. Learning the language of another cultural group can also be a very powerful tool in learning about that culture because many traditions and values are conveyed through language. Although interesting and useful, language learning is not always feasible, and it is not necessary to learn another language for one to become culturally competent.

Developing a culture-generic awareness is the step that follows understanding your own and others' cultures. Many values are shared across cultures and variations in values exist within cultural groups (Al Khateeb, Al Hadidi, & Al Khatib, 2014; Rothstein-Fisch, Trumbull, & Garcia, 2009). This recognition can help you understand that although some values may be more characteristic of one cultural group than another, no culture is monolithic. For example, much is currently written about African American, Asian American, and Mexican American families. These terms do not give you an accurate picture of a specific family because they do not take into account the geographic area in which the family lives nor family members' religious preferences, lifestyles, or economic status. Cultural variations are best viewed as continuous, rather than dichotomous, perspectives (Lynch, 2011b). This implies that you should recognize that individuals' and family members' positions along the continuum are not static. They may vary at any given time based on such factors as age, education, life experiences, vocation, and socioeconomic status. Moreover, to even better understand the culture of your students and their families, you should to consider their perspectives along several different dimensions as illustrated in Putting Ideas into Practice.

PUTTING IDEAS INTO PRACTICE

Cultural Continua

Rather than contrasting lists of values and beliefs to understand cultural differences, Lynch (2011b) proposes that educators acknowledge that certain value sets are common across all cultures and are best understood if each is viewed as a continuum.

Family Constellation Continuum

Some families are large and have extended kinship networks that are intimately involved with nearly every aspect of the family's daily life. Others are smaller units with responsibility for all decisions and activities, and they operate independently of an extended family.

Interdependence/Independence Continuum

Interdependence is the primary value in some families and cultures. Contributions to the whole are more highly valued than expressing one's individuality, which could be seen as selfish and rejecting of the family. For other families, individuality—the expression of one's uniqueness—is the greatest value.

Nurturance/Independence Continuum

Although most people nurture young children, the behaviors viewed to be nurturing vary significantly from one individual or group to another. What one group sees as nurturing, another group may see as coddling or overindulgent.

Time Continuum

On one end of the continuum, the amount of time needed for a task or interaction is given to it. At the other end, the task or interaction is given only the amount of time that has been scheduled for it.

Tradition/Technology Continuum

From one perspective, respect for age, tradition, and ritual provides a solid base for contemporary life. The divergent perspective is one that places greater value on the future, innovation, technology, and youth.

Ownership Continuum

This reflects a range of perspectives on possessions, from the notion that things are individually owned to the perspective that they are shared broadly.

Rights and Responsibilities Continuum

The concept of equality is the fundamental concern. In some groups, equal and non-differentiated roles are ascribed to both men and women. In others, women are the caretakers and men are the providers and intermediaries between the family and the community.

Harmony/Control Continuum

Some groups primarily value living in harmony and synchrony with their environments; others believe it is more important to control their environments and the events in their lives.

One additional step that is critical toward achieving cultural competence is the acquisition of specific information about cultural practices relative to children, child rearing, health, disability, and help seeking (Johnson, Radesky, & Zuckerman, 2013; Long, Kao, Plante, Seifer, & Lobato, 2015). The views that family members hold toward disability and their beliefs about its causes are likely to affect how they respond to the child's disability and to the interventions that are recommended. You should also expect that families will differ notably in their preferred levels of involvement and collaboration with professionals based on their values regarding help seeking and self-sufficiency as well as privacy.

The increasing diversity in the U.S. population has an impact on the use of collaborative strategies for educating students with disabilities (Cramer & Bennett, 2015). At the same time that you work to base your collaboration on understanding your colleagues or your students and their families as individuals, you also need to be aware that culture influences individuals' interactions in many ways that can positively or negatively influence collaborative activities (Banks, 2008). For example, the directness of your conversations and the topics they address might be influenced by cultural expectations. Some cultural groups turn to their extended families in times of need and may be reluctant to share information with school professionals. This could be viewed by school professionals as resistance.

Another example is based on individuals' perceptions of themselves in relation to the rest of society. If colleagues or family members see themselves primarily as part of a disenfranchised group, they may interact in a way that conveys powerlessness, thus undermining the essential collaborative characteristic of parity. Conversely, in possibly attempting to overcome their sense of not having control, the same individuals may interact so assertively that others feel powerless. Professionals may experience this in interactions with a family member who begins by making many accusatory statements and extraordinary demands. This can occur because of the family member's sense of powerlessness.

A final consideration about collaboration involving ethnically or culturally diverse groups concerns understanding, respecting, and valuing. Every individual who participates in a collaborative activity should begin with the understanding that the only culture one understands is one's own. That is a relatively simple statement to make, but a challenging notion to translate into practice. However, if taken to heart, this critical awareness can lead all involved to strive for better understanding and more patience if miscommunication does occur.

The contexts in which you, as a professional educator, are likely to experience the greatest diversity are in interacting with families and in communities where students live. Many of the challenges or dilemmas you encounter as you collaborate in multicultural settings will reflect your frame of reference and the cultural perspectives you hold and how they differ from those held by the people with whom you interact. Although we encourage you to develop awareness and knowledge of the cultures of families with which you work and the community in which your school is located, it is not necessary for you to know everything about a particular culture in order to provide culturally sensitive and responsive services. If professionals value and are respectful of differences, open to learning, and committed to self-examination and change, they can develop culturally responsive and productive relationships with diverse families.

Several authors have made timeless suggestions for providing culturally responsive services (Harry, 2008; Olivos, 2009) and family-centered programs (Allen, 2007; Dempsey & Keen, 2008; Knopf & Swick, 2007). These are several of the most valuable:

1. Focus on the family as the unit of attention.
2. Enhance your self-awareness.
3. Respect the uniqueness of each family system.
4. Develop a personalized, informal helping relationship.
5. Organize assistance and support in ways requested by the family.
6. Learn about other cultures and how they view disability.
7. Gather and provide information in culturally responsive ways.
8. Seek to focus on family strengths and holistic family needs.
9. Give families complete and accurate information in a supportive manner.
10. Create alliances with community leaders and their representatives and allies.
11. Develop a shared vision.
12. Provide families with choices of services that meet their needs.
13. Ensure accessibility of services with minimal disruption to the family.
14. Obtain family evaluation of the process followed and the results.

Most of all, be a self-reflective student of culture. By seeking information from families, learning about their communities, encouraging them to teach you about their priorities, and recognizing your own potential biases, you will transcend potential cultural barriers to collaboration with family members.

Factors Related to Having a Child with a Disability

The next component of a framework for understanding families and working effectively with them concerns basic functions of families and how they may be affected by having a family member with a disability. For some families, the impact is minimal; in others, however, it can be significant and permeate every aspect of the family's existence.

> **Learn More About**
> As you watch this segment about Billy, identify ways that the family might have been affected by his special needs, and discuss your responses with classmates.
> (https://www.youtube.com/watch?v=a0NAptuWZz4)

Families perform a number of functions that benefit their members. For example, successful families emphasize the importance of sharing affection with one another through the exchange of physical or verbal affection. In addition, their interactions assist each member to establish a self-identity and sense of worth or self-esteem. They also transmit cultural and personal spiritual beliefs across generations. Next, families perform an economic function; they must earn income to provide for their basic needs. Families also function to meet the day-to-day physical and health needs of their members. Social activity and affiliations as well as leisure and recreational activities are important functions for the health of individuals and their families.

Consider what the impact of a moderate disability might be on all the functions just described. First, some families report that there is greater affection in their families as a result of having a child with a disability (Poller & Fabe, 2009), but some families, when first learning of their child's disability, may have difficulty feeling or expressing affection. And although the affection is likely to develop later, that initial response may cause a disruption in the bonding process between parents and child. The family may have a difficult time helping the child with a disability to develop a positive self-identity. In fact, cultural and peer relations may also intervene, and the self-esteem of the parent or siblings may also be affected. Families also must earn and decide how to spend income. They report that they spend more money on a child with a disability, especially if he or she has health care needs or requires special equipment or clothing. Moreover, providing for the other daily care needs such as transportation, medical procedures, or behavior management is often so demanding that parents may not perform as well at work as they would otherwise; they potentially may lose economic or career opportunities. The same physical and emotional demands that sometimes lead to lost career opportunities may also interfere with family members' recreation and leisure activities.

We do not wish to imply that having a child with a disability is an overwhelming burden. In fact, in spite of the challenges, many families believe that a child with a disability strengthens their families and increases the enjoyment they get from seeing their child succeed. Research on the positive contributions of having a child with a disability consistently finds that the child is a catalyst for increased spirituality of family members (Stainton & Besser, 1998; Zhang, 2012). Nevertheless, a child with a disability generally requires more of a family's physical, emotional, temporal, and fiscal resources than do other children.

Factors Related to Life Conditions

The life conditions of some families may pose challenges for them and make school participation and collaborative family–professional interactions difficult. Consider some of the following situations identified by Howard, Williams, and Lepper (2010) and how they affect a family's ability to participate in school activities and meetings.

- Single parents often have less income, increased need for respite care, resource and time management challenges, and possibly transportation difficulties, which conflict with work and family responsibilities.

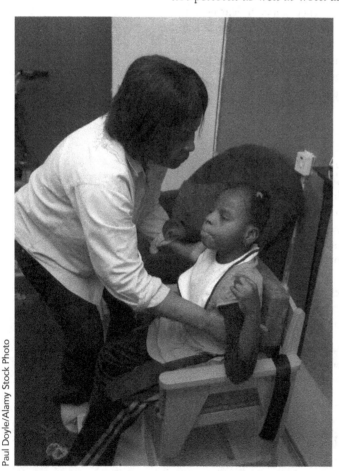

Children with disabilities, regardless of their specific family situation, rely on the quality of the partnerships you form with their parents to ensure they reach their potential.

- Nontraditional families that rely on the broad view of families—that includes such variations as extended family, same-sex parents, and foster families—may bring to the surface some prejudice or judgmental responses from service providers.
- Child-care needs may strain families with lack of resources for child care for infants, toddlers, and young children with disabilities.
- Poverty may result in lack of transportation to and from services, limited phone services, or as in the case of homeless families, the lack of a permanent address.

Two additional barriers to family participation in children's educational programs have been identified (Dunst & Dempsey, 2007; Kochhar-Bryant, 2008; Lo, 2012). First, many parents of children with disabilities lack the knowledge and skills needed to contribute substantially to the education of their children. For example, parents of students with special needs may have limiting disabilities themselves. Similarly, they may lack the knowledge of programs and service options that are being discussed.

A second barrier is attitudinal, such as lack of confidence or assertiveness that prevents parents from actively contributing to the educational programs of their children. When such barriers are present, professionals strive to help family members feel valued and comfortable participating in their child's education program at whatever level possible. Given the range of parental abilities and preferences for involvement in interactions with school professionals, it is appropriate to ask to what extent collaboration is a reasonable expectation with particular parents. Knowing how to foster effective communication with and provide support to parents is important whether or not collaboration is the goal.

Educators need to be mindful of the many demands on families and consider them when they assess family strengths and set expectations for their work with families. Throughout this chapter and in most textbooks for teachers, you will read about the importance of parent participation and collaboration. We concur. But you also should recognize the very real demands on families as well as the challenges to family–professional interaction and gauge your expectations accordingly.

Family Participation in Decision Making

Your role as a professional is to provide families with information they need to support their family member with a disability and to be effective participants in educational decision making. This includes communicating effectively, providing information about disabilities and educational concerns, and reporting evaluation results and student progress. In Chapters 2, 3, and 4, you learned the concepts and basic communication skills needed for effectively sharing information with families. You should practice those skills and employ them as you provide families with information.

Providing Information to Families

Families should have readily understood information about their child's educational needs, available services, resources, and procedural information about their rights and responsibilities if they are to participate effectively in their child's education. Their information needs are different at different life stages, as discussed earlier. Those needs and how educators respond to them influence the feelings families have about special education services.

A Basis in Research summarizes a study of parent satisfaction with special education services and points to several variables that influence how families view the information and services they and their children receive. Awareness of these influences should help you to recognize and respond appropriately to the needs of families.

When family members learn of their child's disability, they seek to understand the nature and consequences of the disability. They may need to learn about medical treatments or other related services as well as other physical matters. When the child enters school, they will require information about various programs and options. As the child matures, they will access information about social, emotional, physical, and cognitive development. Families should have clear and accurate information in these areas in order to adjust their expectations and goals for their child. Realistic expectations are central to setting appropriate educational goals.

In addition to information about the child's disability and its characteristics, families require procedural information regarding due process, placement, parent rights and responsibilities, and other legal provisions that affect their child (Lo, 2012). They further rely on you providing details about educational and related services that may be appropriate for their child. In early years, the decisions may be focused on whether the toddler or young child receives services in a center or in a home-based program. During elementary and middle school years, choices of specific instructional approaches or different

A BASIS IN RESEARCH

Family Involvement in and Satisfaction with Special Education Processes

How do families perceive special education? Hernandez, Harry, and Newman (2009) conducted a large-scale study of 1,417 parents (72 percent response rate) regarding their involvement in and satisfaction with services for their children receiving special education in Los Angeles Unified School District (LAUSD). These researchers identified five characteristics that influence the nature of the family–school relationship. As they note, the findings may seem intuitive, but a large-scale study such as this serves a purpose in verifying such perceptions. It also uncovers and raises some unanticipated questions and need for further study. Key findings from the study include these:

- *Socioeconomic status (SES)*, specifically income, has the most pronounced effect on family engagement. The most difficulties with the special education system were experienced by families with the lowest incomes (i.e., less than $25,000 annually). The lowest income families had lower attendance at IEP meetings, were less likely to report that they received information guides or information about their rights, and were more likely to report that their children received sufficient services even though often the services were fewer than indicated in the IEP.
- *Race/ethnicity and primary language* influence family–school relations. However, because the categories often overlap, it is often difficult to discern the relative importance of each. In this study, race/ethnicity had a greater impact than primary language. Latino parents reported the least awareness of available resources and their rights related to IDEA, although they also were the most likely to indicate that their children were receiving enough services. Primary language, though difficult to isolate from race and ethnicity, was also found to have an impact. English-speaking parents more often reported awareness of special education rights and resources, receipt of district information regarding rights and procedures, and ability to secure services for their children. They also were the most likely to indicate that their children were not getting enough service.
- *Student's age/grade level*, as described elsewhere in this chapter, was found to be a significant factor. Greater involvement in special education processes and programs was reported by parents of preschool and elementary school children than parents of secondary school children. They also tended to have more positive evaluations of the services than did parents of older students.
- *Nature and severity of disability* was one of the strongest differentiating variables. Parents of children with low-incidence disabilities were more likely to have received district information and attended IEP meetings. Yet these same parents tended to report less satisfaction with the amount of services or ease in accessing services.

inclusionary practices become more focal. By adolescence, families should obtain information about postsecondary employment and education options so that they can begin planning for the next phase in their children's lives.

Professionals have additional responsibilities for providing families with the results of diagnostic evaluations. This can be a highly sensitive matter, and you are advised to take care in communicating evaluation results to parents, especially when first communicating about the possible presence of a disability. However, it remains a potentially emotional issue throughout the child's educational career. Thomas, Correa, and Morsink (2001) offer the following suggestions for providing details about evaluation data to family members:

- Provide feedback in a private, safe, and comfortable environment.
- Keep the number of professionals to a minimum.
- Begin by asking parents their feelings about the child's strengths as well as weaknesses.
- Provide evaluation results in a jargon-free manner, using examples of test items and behavioral observations throughout.
- Provide parents with results from a variety of assessment activities, including standardized tests, criterion-referenced tests, direct behavioral observations, play-based or community-based assessment, and judgment-based approaches.
- Be sensitive to viewing the child as an individual and a "whole" child when reporting various evaluation results.
- Allow the parent time to digest the results before educational planning begins.
- Be sensitive to linguistically different families and the use of interpreters with the possibility of information being conveyed incompletely or in a confusing manner.
- Prepare for the meeting with the other team members, clarifying any possible conflicts in the evaluation information before the meeting so as to be as clear as possible when communicating with family members.
- Use conflict resolution strategies to manage possible conflicts with families.

Language Matters Professionals must recognize the information needs just outlined, answer questions, and provide clear, useful information and referrals when needed. One additional communication strategy should be mentioned: Whenever possible, communication with families should be in a language in which they are fluent and preferably in their primary language. The written forms and materials used to communicate or plan programs, announcements from school, and fact sheets for information resources should all be translated into the family's primary language. Many of the web site resources in this chapter offer materials in languages other than English or provide links to appropriate related resources. If a family uses a language other than that of the professionals, interpreters generally should be used. However, sometimes they may not be needed, particularly for informal communication, if the family or professional has some proficiency in the primary language. In informal communication with limited-English-proficient families, it may be sufficient to speak slowly and clearly and provide the family with written information.

A number of matters should be considered when selecting and using an interpreter. One of the most important recommendations is that you avoid using the student or a sibling as the interpreter. This is an inappropriate role for either youngster, and it removes him or her from the appropriate role of participant. You should also be sensitive to confidentiality issues. Although professional interpreters have a code of ethics that honors confidentiality, parents may not fully understand this and may be uncomfortable sharing sensitive information. In these cases, you should explain the interpreter's role and responsibility to maintain confidentiality. The following list offered by Tribe (2007) and others summarizes several additional recommendations for the use of interpreters:

- Encourage the family to choose a preferred interpreter.
- Have interpreters introduce their role to you and to the family in their language.
- Provide the interpreter with a glossary or list of key terms in advance.
- Discuss the agenda of the meeting and source of any documents.
- Schedule extra time; the meeting is likely to take longer than when an interpreter is not needed.

> **Learn More About**
> Communication occurs in informal as well as formal ways, as illustrated by these special educators' discussion of their home-school communication systems.

- Provide a break every 30 minutes.
- Pause frequently to allow the interpreter to communicate all the information to family members.
- Be aware of nonverbal communication.
- Recognize that anything you say may be interpreted.
- Encourage the interpreter to be a cultural broker and to advise you if you communicate with the family in a culturally inappropriate manner.
- Avoid idiomatic words, slang, and metaphors that are difficult to translate.
- As much as possible, avoid complex sentences and technical vocabulary.
- Speak clearly and at a moderate pace directly to the family member, not to the interpreter.
- Be sure your eye contact is mainly with the family.

To apply these ideas, the following is the Aguilar family's experience as they explored program offerings for their son.

This was the third site that Mr. and Mrs. Aguilar had visited as they sought a program for their son. Guillermo had a language disability, and they wanted to find an educational program that would provide him with appropriate language models. The principal greeted them with a wide smile. Mr. Aguilar nodded and smiled slightly, and Mrs. Aguilar praised the lobby decor. As the principal walked them to the meeting room, they passed one of the classrooms where the children played happily with age-appropriate toys. What stood out to the Aguilars was that the children were not talking with one another or with the adults. Mr. and Mrs. Aguilar and the principal entered the meeting room where five program support personnel were waiting at a large oval-shaped table. As the Aguilars joined the group, everyone introduced themselves, and the principal addressed Mr. Aguilar slowly in English, "I'm so sorry that we were not able to get an interpreter today. I hope you will understand what is going to be said." Mr. and Mrs. Aguilar exchanged glances and their faces became flushed. Mrs. Aguilar replied quietly, "We will understand." The meeting commenced with an explanation of the benefits of their school and the type of services that would be provided in English. All comments were addressed to Mrs. Aguilar, who asked some questions while her husband remained stoic. At the end of the exchange, the principal commented that he was certain that Guillermo would benefit from their excellent program, stood up, and extended his hand. Mr. Aguilar ignored the gesture and stood up as well. He looked at each member present and in perfect English said, "Based on your accounts, we feel that this is not the setting we are seeking for our son. And to address the comment you made at the beginning, no translation was needed." They walked out, leaving the room in silence.

This is an example of poor preparation and poor interpersonal skills on the part of the principal. He seemed to be following a district guideline about securing interpreters for families whose home language may not be English. But he did so blindly with no apparent interest in, knowledge about, or regard for the family. Failure to provide an interpreter conveys lack of concern for the family. But assuming any parent with an ethnic surname requires an interpreter also conveys stereotyping of the family. Common sense and deliberate effort to determine the family's need should take precedence over standard procedures.

Communication Structures Language consideration and communication skills learned in earlier chapters will be useful in your interactions with families, but planning the appropriate structure and mechanism for addressing family information needs can be almost as important (Vesely, Ewaida, & Anderson, 2014). For example, it is worth your time to consider which information needs of families might best be met through one-way information reporting, informal conferences, structured meetings, parent education or workshop sessions, or parent-to-parent groups.

One-way information sharing is often useful to keep the school and home aware of the child's experiences and performance in both settings. Typically, families and professionals use notes, progress reports, or school–home journals to share information about school assignments, schedule changes, homework, and behavior. With advances in technology, some schools have established web sites for posting school and classroom information, and more families have and are comfortable with e-mail. Some apps enable teachers to communicate directly and live with parents, sharing gathered data throughout the school day. Voice mail offers another asynchronous method of communication. One-way communication is often necessary for efficient information sharing, but two-way structures such as those discussed next are essential for effective communication and productive relationships with families.

Informal meetings are often spontaneous and may be more relaxed than meetings planned in advance. These meetings are sometimes characterized as informal "chats" or "visits." They may take place at school, in a parking lot, or during an accidental meeting in the community. Informal or casual meetings can be useful for sharing general information, clarifying a point of concern, and generally (and perhaps most importantly) building rapport. Such conversations can help to prepare participants for effective interactions in subsequent formal meetings. Another advantage of the casual conference or meeting is that it not only allows the educator to assess the child's interests and abilities but also affords opportunities to learn about the family's culture and how it is transmitted to family members.

Structured meetings or purposeful conferences are events scheduled to discuss a particular topic or agenda. Meetings with an agenda focused on one student and one family are discussed in the following section. The focus here is on structured or purposeful meetings that involve members from several families, such as parent information workshops or family support groups.

Several topics have been identified in the previous discussions that represent typical information needs of families at various stages. Most or all families need overview information about disability and appropriate interventions as their child is identified and as the child transitions from one stage to another. Workshops represent an efficient way of providing such information to many families simultaneously. This strategy frequently is used in preschool programs and in high school during the preparation for a student's transition to vocational and employment services. School professionals often offer these workshops or information seminars, but such training activities are also available from parent training and information centers as well as from other community and nonprofit groups.

Parent or family support groups are another type of purposeful meeting. Similar to informational groups, these usually are organized around some common element or family

Professionals working with families from diverse cultures have an obligation to increase their cultural competence in order to foster clear communication and positive outcomes for students.

need such as groups with early childhood interests, groups for families of students with the same disability, or groups composed of persons with the same roles, such as fathers or siblings. Various structures exist for support groups as well. Some are groups of family members with a professional leader or facilitator, others are led by family members themselves, and still others provide one-to-one support. Research conducted by the Beach Center on Disability (1999) documented the effectiveness of one-to-one support in a program titled Parent to Parent Support. This program, which matches parents with other parent support providers, was used in five states and was rated by nearly 400 parents. The findings indicated that the program increases parents' acceptance of their situation and their coping strategies, and it also helps parents to make progress on the need or problem that was their reason for participating. Fifty-five percent of the respondents reported that they were satisfied with the companionship they derived from the program, and 18 percent reported that they received meaningful information services through it. Additional studies have also identified the benefits of parent-to-parent groups (Todd et al., 2010). Parent to Parent programs exist in 29 states. Similar efforts to support siblings are conducted through the national Sibling Support Project. Many additional support groups can be identified through local and regional informational and referral services.

Numerous valuable resources for families and education professionals can be found on the Internet and several of them are included in E-Partnerships. Having access to resources such as these would have been useful in responding to Mr. Johnson in the opening case. These are resources that families can use independent of the service providers, and it is often helpful for teachers to have such a list as a guide for families. Many of these resources have an option for communication through discussion boards or similar mechanisms, and so they also function as a purposeful means of support.

E-PARTNERSHIPS

Families on the Web

Many resources for families of individuals with disabilities and for the professionals who work with them may be accessed on the Internet. The web sites listed here include a wide array of information designed specifically for parents and other family members, and most provide links to other valuable sites.

Beach Center on Disability (www.beachcenter.org)

This web site provides research briefs and fact sheets on topics of interest to families (and professionals). The information briefs are particularly useful for addressing the needs of families for educational, vocational, or adult living decisions. Additional resources include information and first-person stories that support families, their children with disabilities, and professionals.

The Fathers Network (FN) (www.fathersnetwork.org)

FN provides resources and support to men who have children with special needs through the development of national and statewide databases of fathers from diverse ethnic, racial, and geographic backgrounds; establishment of father support and mentoring programs; and provision of varied educational and technical assistance services.

The HEATH Resource Center (www.heath.gwu.edu)

HEATH provides online, web-based resources on postsecondary education for individuals with disabilities. HEATH addresses available educational disability support services policies, procedures, and adaptations as well as information on accessing college or university campuses, career-technical schools, and other postsecondary training entities. It also summarizes information on financial assistance, scholarships, and materials that help students with disabilities transition into college, university, career-technical schools, or other postsecondary programs.

Kids Together, Inc. (www.kidstogether.org)

This web site is intended to foster inclusiveness for all people with a focus on reaching families, professionals, educators, advocates, self-advocates, and the community. The various postings on the site include many topics of interest to families and professionals.

Center for Parent Information and Resources (CPIR) (http://www.parentcenterhub.org)

CPIR is a repository for a wealth of information for parents of children with disabilities. Its mission is to gather on a single web site resources from other parent support organizations so that they are readily accessible. Included on the site are legacy NICHCY materials; visitors to the site may also search for information by topic. Many items are available in both English and Spanish.

OSEP Ideas That Work (www.osepideasthatwork.org)

This web site is designed to provide quick access to information from research to practice initiatives funded by the U.S. Office of Special Education Programs (OSEP) that address the provisions of IDEA and No Child Left Behind (NCLB). This site includes resources, links, and other important information resulting from OSEP's efforts to translate research to practice, including parent-specific materials.

Parent Advocacy Coalition for Educational Rights (PACER) (www.pacer.org)

PACER's mission is to expand opportunities and enhance the quality of life of children and young adults with disabilities and their families based on the concept of parents helping parents. PACER provides assistance to individual families, workshops, materials for parents and professionals, and leadership in securing a free and appropriate public education for all children. Material is available in English, Hmong, Somali, and Spanish.

Parents Helping Parents (http://www.php.com/)

This comprehensive resource and information center is run for and by parents. The web site provides useful links to information about support groups for family members and information resources for families and professionals. A call-in number for parents experiencing extraordinary stress is also included.

Sibling Support Project (www.siblingsupport.org)

The Sibling Support Project exists to address the needs of the brothers and sisters of children with disabilities. This is accomplished by training local service providers to create community-based peer support programs for young siblings; hosting workshops, listservs, and web sites for young and adult siblings; and increasing parents' and providers' awareness of siblings' unique, lifelong, and ever-changing concerns through workshops, web sites, and written materials. Siblings can link to other siblings through the web site.

Social Security Benefits for Children with Disabilities (www.ssa.gov/pubs/10026.html)

This electronic booklet, updated in 2015, is for the parents, caregivers, or representatives of children under age 18 who have disabilities that might make them eligible for Supplemental Security Income (SSI) payments. It is also for adults who became disabled in childhood and who might be entitled to Social Security Disability Insurance (SSDI) benefits.

Assisting Families to Participate in Student-Centered Meetings

We noted earlier that one of your primary responsibilities in working with families is to facilitate their effective participation in educational decision making, a sometimes difficult goal. Most of your interactions with families probably focus on understanding, planning for, and making decisions about their family member with a disability. Many of those interactions occur in meetings that are structured to focus on the child and family and discuss matters such as student progress, behavior, school–home communication, or evaluation results. These meetings are often parent conferences, IEP meetings, or annual review meetings.

Many examples exist of the failure on the part of school professionals to ensure that family participation occurs. In some settings, for example, students' IEPs are written prior to conferring with families, with the excuse that it takes too much time to discuss everything and write goals and, possibly, objectives at a meeting. Sometimes this approach is used in order to have a draft document as an efficient starting point for a full discussion in which all participants will contribute to writing new material or modifying the draft. School professionals using this strategy risk communicating that they know what the student needs better than the family does. In the worst case of this practice, someone at the meeting says to the parent, after all the prewritten information has been reviewed, "Do you have anything you would like to add or change?" At best, such a comment severely limits participation for most family members; at worst, it completely excludes them from their child's educational planning process. When using draft material, it is crucial to explain that it is truly a draft that all participants may elaborate or modify. It is equally important to then structure the interaction so that family members share their ideas, concerns, and goals.

A second, more indirect, example of limiting family participation also needs to be considered. School professionals may touch base to identify and resolve potential conflicts about the student's educational plan before meeting with a family. This can be perceived as creating a united front exclusive of family participation, and it can create an adversarial climate in the interaction (Stein & Sharkey, 2015). What is even more unfortunate is that this effort could unintentionally indicate that controversy and alternative perspectives are not part of decision making when families are involved. Professionals should structure preplanning activities in ways that promote efficiency while still ensuring meaningful and honest family participation.

Your obligation is to carefully reflect on how the formal and informal procedures for working with families in schools might constrain family participation, especially in interactions at IEP and other group meetings. If you can foster participation and collaboration, your interactions with families are more likely to be in the best interest of students (e.g., Cobb, 2014).

To supplement related material in previous chapters, here are a few straightforward ideas for fostering family participation:

1. In group meetings, create a welcoming and supportive environment. You can accomplish this in several ways. For example, prepare parents for meetings by sending home in advance a summary of the topics to be addressed and a list of possible questions they might want to ask. Suggest that they bring to school examples of their child's work that they would like to discuss, information about their child's friends and responsibilities at home, and other information that parents have (and school professionals do not) that can contribute to an understanding of the child. At the meeting, have professionals stay in the vicinity of the meeting room, chatting informally until the parent arrives, and have all participants be seated at the same time, rather than having parents enter a room where everyone else has already been seated. A variation is to be sure that the professional the parents know best accompanies and sits next to them.

2. At meetings, have a file folder with samples of the student's work, copies of forms being discussed, and blank paper and pen for the parents. The reason for this is simple: If you think about most meetings, all the school professionals arrive with folders, binders, reports, schedules, plan books, and a plethora of other paperwork. Many parents arrive carrying nothing and thus are at a subtle but immediate disadvantage. Unobtrusively providing materials at least helps reduce this inequity.

3. Structure meetings so that parents have opportunities to provide input throughout. It is still too common in interactions with families for the professionals to share their information or make their requests and only afterward to seek family input. For example, at IEP meetings, each professional often shares the results of his or her assessment, suggests goals, and then asks family members whether the goals are acceptable. An alternative strategy is to discuss issues related to students by domains. To do this, first address the student's academic strengths and needs, soliciting input from any team members who have pertinent information including family members. Then address social and emotional areas, using the same procedure, and so on through the domains that need to be addressed. This approach to a meeting can help ensure that a dialogue occurs rather than a series of report readings followed by an expectation for parental approval.

4. Maximize opportunities for families to make informed decisions. Have a variety of choices for parents and students to make (e.g., alternatives for elective classes, communication or self-help priorities, or social skill training options), and actively engage them in decision making. To the extent possible, make sure they understand the choices and how they will affect the student's program and future opportunities. When you are considering new program options for a student, such as a community-based instructional component or involvement in an after-school recreational program, ensure that family members are well informed about them. You can do this by arranging for them to tour a new setting, observe a program, or meet with other family members who are involved in the alternative setting. If they are unable to adjust their schedules for such meetings or observations, prepare written and visual materials to inform them in as much detail as possible about the alternatives. Photographs or videotapes are most useful for these purposes. Family members are more likely to invest in joint decision making and collaborate with you to set realistic goals and make future plans for their children when they have adequate information.

SUMMARY

- Parent participation has long been a key feature of education for individuals with disabilities, and it is guaranteed in IDEA. Over the years, the emphasis has moved from parent to family participation, and a broad definition of family has become accepted. Understanding families is based in family systems theory and its key principles.
- Families generally have four life stages—birth and early childhood, childhood, adolescence, and adulthood—each with its own priority tasks. Understanding these stages can help professionals to understand the priorities family members may have for their children.
- Many factors influence families' interactions with school professionals. Two that are especially significant are (a) the family's culture and the professionals' responsiveness to it, and (b) the family's response to having a child with a disability.
- Professional responsibilities for effective family interactions and collaboration include: understanding families and their needs as well as facilitating family participation in making decisions about the educational program for the family member with a disability, using strategies such as creating a welcoming environment, soliciting and using information from families, and ensuring that families have the knowledge and resources integral to making informed decisions.

BACK TO THE CASE

1. Think about how family systems theory is illustrated in Mr. Johnson's interactions with Ms. Albright. What hypotheses could you make regarding Mr. Johnson's family situation? In what ways might family systems theory help you to better understand him? How might it guide questions you ask him, suggestions you make to him, and information you provide to him?
2. Consider Mr. Johnson's behavior. His situation illustrates the point that families progress through different life stages at different rates and often in a different sequence of stages. Describe the family life stage you think Mr. Johnson is experiencing and describe the dynamics.
3. How would you respond if Mr. Johnson became upset when you indicated that you could not meet with him twice each week? Using skills you have learned throughout this book, map out a strategy for interacting with him, including your goal and specific types of statements and questions you would probably use in communicating with him.

COLLABORATIVE ACTIVITIES

1. Conduct an informational interview with the family members of a student with a disability. Ask them about their experiences related to the eligibility, placement, and IEP processes, as well as their experiences working with school professionals. What have been the positive elements of their experiences? What have been the negative elements? What suggestions would they make for improving collaboration between home and school?
2. Create an information packet to give to family members prior to or during IEP meetings. Include in the packet a clarification of educational jargon; information about their rights; an explanation of the IEP process; contact information for school personnel; and any additional information about expectations in your program such as a homework schedule, material about maintaining notebooks or study schedules, and more.
3. Review culture-specific information resources provided on the web sites suggested in this chapter and in Chapter 1. Consider the cultural groups represented among the students with whom you work. Identify what school-based or classroom-based practices you could institute that would make your environment more culturally responsive for students and families.
4. Think of a recent meeting with a family of a child with a disability. Did you include more than one family member in the discussion or meeting? Even if only one parent attended the meeting, what explicit actions did you take to ensure that the roles and concerns of other family members were considered? What are specific actions you could take at the next meeting to include other family members and/or to address their information needs and concerns?

 CHECK YOUR UNDERSTANDING

Click here to gauge your understanding of this chapter's essential concepts.

12 Special Considerations

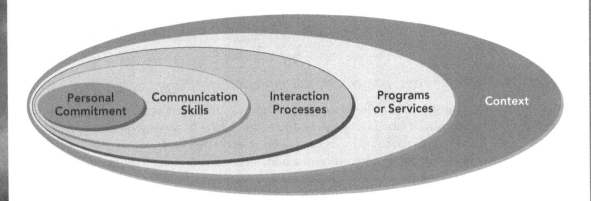

CONNECTIONS

Your study of collaboration is nearly complete. You have analyzed what collaboration is (Chapter 1) and have practiced the communication skills that foster collaboration in educational settings (Chapters 2, 3, and 4). You have learned about the steps for completing key interaction processes such as problem solving (Chapter 5) as well as the most common collaborative school applications (Chapters 6, 7, and 8). You have practiced strategies for addressing difficult situations (Chapter 9); you have also considered your work with paraeducators (Chapter 10), and families (Chapter 11). But collaboration has facets that have not yet been directly addressed. The topics included in this chapter—interagency and community collaboration, collaboration with individuals in particular professional roles, systemic matters related to collaboration, and ethical issues that may arise in collaboration—are relevant across all the other chapters of this book and thus merit focused attention.

LEARNING OUTCOMES

After reading this chapter you will be able to:

1. Identify unique challenges that may occur for school professionals in community and interagency collaboration, including those that may occur as part of students' transitions across programs and services, and analyze and apply to your current or future position strategies for overcoming these challenges.
2. Assess how professional roles and responsibilities may affect the nature of school collaboration.
3. Examine factors that make school-based collaboration a complex endeavor, including systemic barriers such as scheduling and service coordination.
4. Analyze the current practice of education collaboration as a basis for considering its future, including issues related to professional ethics.

A CASE FOR COLLABORATION

Sometimes It's Ideal…and Sometimes Not

School has been in session for more than a month, and Rosalee Decker and Jonathan Ehrsam, both first-year teachers at Northwest Regional High School, have become good friends. However, they have agreed that they do not feel like they have all the facets of their jobs under control. As a special educator, Ms. Decker is assigned to teach one section of a study skills class for ninth-grade students and one section of Algebra I for ninth-grade students who struggle most to understand math. She also co-teaches two sections of Algebra I and one section of Geometry. With Mr. Myers in Algebra I, everything is great, and student test scores are demonstrating the effectiveness of their partnership. With Ms. Pierce in Geometry, the situation is not as positive, and Ms. Decker feels like a glorified paraprofessional. Mr. Ehrsam's assignments are likewise mixed. He is teaching three sections of World History, and two of those sections are co-taught, one with a special educator and one with an English as a Second Language (ESL) teacher. He is finding that trying to juggle their preferences and teaching approaches with his own emerging style is quite stressful; he didn't learn in his teacher preparation program that he would be expected to co-teach. And he feels uncomfortable saying too much because the other teachers are both veterans. Mr. Ehrsam was also assigned to serve on the school's response to intervention (RTI) committee, but he is still unsure of his role and uncertain about how he can discuss struggling students when he is just learning about the realities of being a teacher. Ms. Decker and Mr. Ehrsam wish they had been partnered for co-teaching. Though their areas of expertise are different, they think they would be a fabulous team. They are tempted to discuss this idea with their assistant principal, but they are worried that their idea will be perceived as more about them than about student achievement.

Introduction

As you have read this book, we hope you have recognized that collaboration is a multidimensional endeavor, in terms of both the subtleties that can make it effective or ineffective and the number of school activities and applications that benefit from it. Because of this, it is often impossible to attend to all the significant factors that can influence collaborative practice, particularly in the typically frenetic daily lives of school professionals, as Ms. Decker and Mr. Ehrsam, the teachers in the introductory case study, are finding out.

This chapter is intended to help you integrate what you have learned about collaboration—conceptually and technically—by highlighting four topics that require a clear and sophisticated understanding of it. The first topic involves the collaboration that occurs largely outside the immediate school context, that is, with community programs and agencies serving students with disabilities in domains other than education. The second topic comprises the nuances of collaborating with people in particular roles, that is, administrators, general educators, specialists, and even students. The third topic pertains to the complexities of collaboration, including the challenges of scheduling and the coordination of services. The final topic concerns the current status and likely future of education collaboration, including several ethical issues professionals should be prepared to resolve.

The rationale for devoting a chapter to these topics is to highlight them, providing an opportunity for you to reflect on how the knowledge and skills you have learned in studying this book are applicable across whatever situations you encounter and whatever career path you follow. It is also intended to focus your attention on the intricacy of collaboration, to leave you excited about the potential of collaboration for improving outcomes for students but sensitive to its sometimes fragile and evolving nature. As you read this chapter, you might find it helpful to refer back to chapters you have already completed, applying what you learned in them to the types of situations described in these pages.

Community and Interagency Collaboration

Much of your day-to-day collaboration will involve those in your school, whether with the teacher down the hall or in the same department or grade level, special educators or ESL teachers, or the media specialist. However, collaboration at least occasionally extends beyond the confines of the school. Depending on your specific role and your school's structure and culture, you may at sometimes participate in interagency and/or community collaboration. That is, you may be expected to partner, for example, with professionals who may lead a community recreation program or with a representative from a social services agency providing support to the student's family.

The Council for Exceptional Children (CEC), the standard bearer for the special education profession, has established policy regarding inclusive communities and the professional's relationship to them, strongly endorsing collaborative efforts:

> Inclusive schools must be located in inclusive communities; therefore, CEC invites all educators, other professionals, and family members to work together to create early intervention, educational, and vocational programs and experiences that are collegial, inclusive, and responsive to the diversity of children, youth, and young adults. Policy makers at the highest levels of state/provincial and local government, as well as school administration, also must support inclusion in the educational reforms they espouse.... As important, there must be interagency agreements and collaboration with local governments and business to help prepare students to assume a constructive role in an inclusive community (Council for Exceptional Children, 2011, p. H-13).

This statement emphasizes that school professionals alone cannot ensure their students' lifelong success. However, negotiating partnerships with individuals in community and other agencies can be an even more complex endeavor than collaboration with school colleagues.

Community Outreach

One effort professionals make to improve their schools is to connect with the community (e.g., Aceves, 2014). It is widely recognized that schools that enjoy community and family involvement have more positive outcomes with students than do schools that do not build these bridges (Sanders, 2014). And although most schools have some type of occasional community outreach, few schools have a specific plan for engaging families or community organizations or agencies. Often outreach is dependent upon a particular teacher or a group of school personnel. For example, Sara Hunt is a special educator concerned about student reading performance and committed to encouraging parents to read to their children every day. She has created a web site with resources to facilitate parents reading to children, and she has arranged for the school's library to be open once per month in the evening to encourage parents to help their children select books to read at home. By providing information and support to parents and community members, outreach programs encourage community members to collaboratively engage in important school and community issues (e.g., Ordonez-Jasis & Myck-Wayne, 2012).

A second type of outreach occurs when school professionals seek community members' support of school-based activities such as volunteering in classrooms, helping with school activities, advocating for a school's needs, and trying to influence local decision making and resource allocation (e.g., Rodriguez, Blatz, & Elbaum, 2014). Other efforts include providing opportunities for community members to participate in field trips and other community events, hosting community events at the school, and partnering with community organizations for translation and interpreting services (Resto & Alston, 2006). An example of this type of outreach is Diane, a middle school reading specialist who organized a program to have members of a local service group serve as tutors for students struggling to read.

> **Learn More About**
> The Schoolwide Integrated Framework for Transformation (SWIFT) project emphasizes how partnerships with families and community members have reciprocal benefits and lead to improved outcomes for students including those with special needs.
> (https://www.youtube.com/watch?v=AzvngdbG0g4)

A third type of outreach is based on the notion that the expertise that exists in a community is an extremely valuable but often overlooked resource for schools. Bringing community expertise into the classroom is a significant means of demonstrating your commitment to and respect for the community in which your students live. Your collaboration with community members can help make classroom learning more authentic for students. Some useful guidelines to consider as you work to establish these collaborations and ensure that they benefit your students are presented in Putting Ideas into Practice.

School–Community Partnerships

Learn More About
As you watch this video about strategies for creating community partnerships, pay particular attention to the range of opportunities described. They may exist in your community as well.

(https://www.youtube.com/watch?v=Lc_8Qjl2GPU)

When school professionals can move beyond outreach and develop a collective sense of purpose and a long-range plan for building school–community partnerships, they are likely to be able to establish truly collaborative relationships. Considerable evidence indicates that engaging families and community members in such partnerships with schools can improve low-performing schools, help to close achievement gaps, and greatly improve the school–community relationship (e.g., Shippen, Patterson, Green, & Smitherman, 2012; Talley & Travis, 2014). That is, when family members regularly engage with teachers and school staff, both elementary and secondary students adjust better to classroom activities and to their teachers. This results in improved student performance, academically, socially, and behaviorally (Crosby, Rasinski, Padak, & Yildirim, 2015).

A number of groups have studied the elements that constitute effective partnerships. For example, the National Education Association (NEA) studied key partnerships in 16 communities and identified 10 primary approaches that it deemed critical for the success of such collaboration (NEA, 2011). These central strategies are summarized in Putting Ideas into Practice.

PUTTING IDEAS INTO PRACTICE

Getting the Most from the Pros

The knowledge and experiential base of members of your school community are valuable resources and are generally valued by students. Here are tips for finding those resources.

- Make a resource booklet in which you collect information about the skills and expertise of parents and acquaintances.
- When searching for someone with experience in a particular field, take advantage of e-mail—you will get some great contacts when parents and colleagues forward your messages.
- Find out which local universities or colleges have a service learning office. Use those offices to get connected with people who will give their time in exchange for college credit.

Once you've found a community member who can come to your classroom to share his or her expertise, be sure to do the following.

- Inform the guest what the goal of their visit to the class will be. For example, when inviting a restaurant owner, you might write, "Our class is starting its own school coffee shop. Will you come to our class to share advice on supplies and budgets?"
- Meet in advance to address the specific needs of your students. Make sure that the presenter is comfortable with children in the grade level you teach.
- Let the expert see any work that has already been done on the project. Be open to feedback about the lesson or project.
- Give students information about the presentation ahead of time so that they can get the most from these interactions.
- Remind the class to make the guest feel welcome.
- After the visit, help the class write and send a thank-you note.
- Give the expert credit for his or her involvement with the project, including acknowledgments on written materials.

Source: Adapted from "What Kids Learn from Experts," by C. Dobbertin, 2010, *Educational Leadership*, 68(1), p. 66. Copyright 2010 by ASCD.

PUTTING IDEAS INTO PRACTICE

Ten Key Strategies for Effective Partnerships

In a partnership study in 16 communities, the NEA identified 10 major strategies and approaches that define the direction of efforts to foster school–community–family collaborations that promote student learning. These strategies focus on reaching out to, engaging, and listening to the community; building alliances linked to student learning with community partners; addressing cultural differences; and engaging students with the community.

1. *Agreeing on core values.* Taking time at the beginning to think deeply and reflect about what participants believe, and why they think the efforts will work.
2. *Listening to the community.* Identifying priorities and developing an action plan in a collaborative way that creates community consensus around what needs to happen and in what sequence.
3. *Using data to set priorities and focus strategies.* Looking closely at current achievement trends and addressing areas of weakness in students' knowledge and skills.
4. *Providing relevant, on-site professional development.* Basing professional development on data and conversations among stakeholders in a way that builds both educator–educator and educator–parent collaborations.
5. *Building collaborations with community partners.* Pulling in strategic partners and developing community buy-in—with colleges, social service agencies, community groups, faith-based organizations, local leaders, public officials, and businesses—to improve student learning and other outcomes.
6. *Using targeted outreach to focus on high-needs communities, schools, and students.* Identifying groups that need special attention, learning about their concerns and needs, and responding in culturally appropriate ways.
7. *Building one-to-one relationships between families and educators that are linked to learning.* Taking time to have conversations and reach agreement on how best to collaborate in order to improve student achievement.
8. *Setting, communicating, and supporting high and rigorous expectations.* Making it clear that success is the norm by creating pathways to college, especially for students at risk and those at the margins, and providing students with support to succeed.
9. *Addressing cultural differences.* Offering support for teachers and education support professionals to bridge barriers of culture, class, and language.
10. *Connecting students to the community.* Making learning hands-on and relevant to students' lives while also showing that students and schools serve the community.

How could you apply these ideas to your teaching situation and your efforts to link with families and your students' community?

Source: Adapted from *National Standards for Family–School Partnerships: An Implementation Guide*, National Parent Teacher Association, 2009, Washington, DC: National Congress of Parents and Teachers. Copyright 2009 by National Congress of Parents and Teachers.

Community Liaisons

When schools are committed to establishing and nurturing community relationships, they often employ a community liaison to serve as a link between the community and school. A case study conducted by the National Network of Partnership Schools (2008) identified three primary roles played by community liaisons that helped minimize the influence of class and cultural differences on school–community–home relations. The liaisons offered the following:

- *Direct service and support to families considered to be at risk.* The most common service was helping families to navigate the school system.
- *Support for teacher outreach.* The liaisons acted as cultural interpreters and "boundary crossers," and they modeled outreach strategies for the teachers.
- *Support for school-based partnership teams.* These personnel helped team members to plan and conduct school-wide activities for the families and the community.

By fulfilling these roles and the various tasks and services associated with them, community liaisons can be valuable assets to the community–school endeavors, including after-school programs.

After-School Programs One of the most common community-based program is an after-school program. The number of after-school programs has grown in recent years as the concept has received increasing attention, due in part to the 21st Century Community Learning Centers Program. Evaluation studies of after-school programs have produced equivocal results. Some studies have shown that after-school programs reduce undesirable behaviors (e.g., Tierney, Grossman, & Resch, 1995); others have shown no effect on behavior (Baker & Witt, 1996); and still others have found negative behaviors increase (Massachusetts 2020 and Boston Public Schools, 2004). Similar contradictions are found in the studies of academic performance of students in after-school programs (Kidron & Lindsay, 2014). In recent studies of successful after-school programs, two features stood out: These programs enjoyed both tightly knit partnerships between the after-school programs and the students' schools and communities and, surprisingly, a focus on high-quality arts, enrichment, and recreation rather than academic subjects (David, 2011).

Interagency Contexts

Although schools provide education and make contributions to the community, they cannot offer all of the services required by children and families, especially those with disabilities and other special needs. In fact, ensuring the educational development of children sometimes requires collaboration with other public and private agencies. Collaboration—with its emphasis on shared expertise, decision making, and responsibility—is a more promising response to the complexity of the educational challenges of today's schools than an individual's solitary response would be, and that includes partnerships that extend beyond the school. For example, consider a family whose child is receiving services from two or more agencies, perhaps the school, the mental health system, and child protective services. Each agency probably has its own set of unique eligibility criteria, intake procedures, and different vocabulary or terminology for similar services or situations. Having professionals to help the family navigate the different systems and resources increases the likelihood that the child and family will be able to access needed services (Porter, Bromer, & Moodie, 2011). Kochhar-Bryant (2008) refers to this as *system coordination*, that is, ensuring that services are integrated instead of fragmented.

Through viable interagency collaboration using combined expertise, services provided by different systems can be maximized, problems in services minimized, and costs reduced. The effectiveness of that collaboration depends in part on the ability of school professionals to convey the educational mission to the representatives of other agencies and to accurately assess and respond to the roles of the other agencies (Kochhar-Bryant, 2008; Minke & Vickers, 2015).

Collaboration is a challenging endeavor when professionals from within the same organization work together. It can be an even more ambitious goal when it involves interacting with individuals from one or sometimes several additional agencies (Chamberlain & Plucker, 2008; Watson & Kabler, 2012). Despite the difficulty, however, interagency collaboration plays an important role in the education of students with disabilities. Examples of interagency collaboration you may experience include working with staff members from a residential or hospital setting to transition a student back into a public school environment; participating on a team that includes professionals from mental health, juvenile justice, public school, and family services to create wraparound options for students for whom no traditional educational approach has been successful; or just working with a private practitioner who is counseling or teaching a student you also serve.

A number of issues can arise as part of interagency collaboration. First, the decision to collaborate may be reached by one set of professionals although the implementation of a collaborative effort is the responsibility of a different set of individuals. For example, the director of a private preschool and a special education director of a local district may reach an agreement to collaborate in serving students with disabilities in a preschool setting. However, neither the teachers nor the itinerant staff of the preschool have participated in the decision. Some staff members may support the decision and work together enthusiastically, but others may misunderstand the purpose of the decision or disagree with it entirely and undermine it through their actions. Clearly, communication and planning among the staff members within an agency is as important as communication and planning among agencies' administrators who agree to the collaboration.

A second issue that may arise in this type of collaboration concerns the blending of agencies with very different missions (Dougherty, 2014). Additionally, the policies and rules that guide each agency may vary considerably. Teachers in public schools routinely hold meetings with parents and others after the official school day has ended; the clinical staff from a hospital setting often work in a culture in which staff members come to the hospital very early for rounds but leave as soon as their workday has ended. There might also be disconnects in how the different agencies encourage a student's compliance with a new program. Professionals from the juvenile justice system may be accustomed to enforcing decisions reached by requesting a court order; professionals from public schools and family services more frequently rely on negotiating instructional arrangements and enforcing them by offering encouragement, providing incentives, and staying in close contact. The two approaches are strikingly different, just as their approaches to problem solving and decision making are likely to be.

Generally, most challenges that you will face in interagency collaboration derive from the differences in organizational cultures that reflect often stark differences in the orientation toward learning, "helping," treatment, disability, and systems operations. However, this type of collaboration has tremendous potential. You are likely to experience both the power and the frustration of interagency collaboration as schools and other settings become increasingly more connected. Your skillful use of the knowledge and techniques you have refined as you have studied this book are valuable tools for participating with noneducation professionals in creating positive outcomes for students.

Early Intervention and Preschool Programs

Collaboration is now central to all of education, but it has been a defining feature of programs that meet the needs of young children with disabilities almost since the inception of that field. Perhaps the best illustration of collaboration at the core of early intervention and preschool services is found in the Individuals with Disabilities Education Act (IDEA) rules and regulations that specify who participates on the team to develop the individualized family service plan (IFSP). In addition to the professionals serving the child, the team includes the parents, other family members the parents request, an advocate if requested, the service coordinator who has been working with the family or who has been assigned responsibility by a public agency, professionals who have assessed the child, and professionals who are likely to provide services to the child. Together, they design a plan to meet the needs of the child and his or her family.

Collaboration in early childhood education simultaneously exists at the professional or personal level and at the interagency or systems level. At the personal level, professionals and parents make joint decisions as they collaboratively plan, implement, and evaluate programs for young children with disabilities (Yang, Hossain, & Sitharthan, 2013). At the systems level, agencies strive for collaboration as they jointly work to provide coordinated and comprehensive programs for children and their families (Ordonez-Jasis & Myck-Wayne, 2012). Both levels of collaboration are needed to provide appropriate and well-designed services.

Services for young children and their families can be classified as belonging to one of three models: center based, home based, or a combination of the two. In all three approaches, cooperation and collaboration are integral. For example, center-based services require collaboration because the teacher must work as a member of a team that consists of staff members with expertise in several related disciplines (West-Olatunji,

> **Learn More About**
> The transition from early intervention to preschool programs can be highly stressful for parents, as Christine explains. Which collaboration skills might be especially important when interacting with her or other parents going through the transition process?
>
> (https://www.youtube.com/watch?v=t9QaCYVN7xM)

Behar-Horenstein, & Rant, 2008). Typically, the team includes speech/language specialists, medical personnel, special education and early childhood teachers, occupational therapists, adaptive physical education teachers, physical therapists, and social workers. These professionals and family members develop a comprehensive program likely to involve a number of service providers from different disciplines. Collaboration with parents and collaboration among professionals are central elements in this model (Bruder & Dunst, 2015).

In home-based services, professionals work with parents and other family members who become the child's primary teachers. The professional typically goes into the home once or more each week and teaches the parents and other family members to implement the appropriate interventions, monitor the child's progress, and evaluate outcomes. This has the advantage of teaching the child skills in the natural environment and making skill transfer unnecessary. It may also be more convenient for single-parent homes and for mothers working outside the home. Being able to interact effectively with parents and have them work as partners with the professionals is possibly the most central element in this approach (Cross, Traub, Hunter-Pishgahi, & Shelton, 2004).

Combination services are exactly what the name implies—a combination of home- and center-based services. The children go to a center once or more weekly, and the professionals also visit their homes and work with their families on a scheduled basis. These multifaceted programs require that teachers have extraordinary flexibility and sophisticated collaboration skills.

From this discussion and your understanding of parental participation as discussed in Chapter 11, you can see that collaboration in early childhood is essential but quite complex. Your role is to recognize the factors of collaboration that are especially important in these situations and to use your communication and interaction process skills to foster appropriate interactions, while at the same time using your knowledge of frame of reference to understand the challenges that may be faced.

Vocational and Community-Based Services

Transition specialists, vocational educators, vocational rehabilitation counselors, secondary teachers, and related personnel in public schools as well as adult service providers spend considerable time placing students with disabilities in school and community sites for prevocational and vocational services (Karpur, Brewer, & Golden, 2014). Planning, placing, training, and supporting students as they develop functional skills and prepare for adult living and employment are key responsibilities for these educators and related service professionals (e.g., Lee & Carter, 2012). Increasingly, these specialists are collaborating to plan for and support a student's community-based educational program and transition to post-school employment. There is value to having students involved in all the decisions made about their school programs; their role as team members was discussed in Chapter 6. In the case of transition planning, however, IDEA mandates that students be actively involved in their own program planning; therefore, they need to acquire the knowledge and skills to collaborate in the process (Griffin, Taylor, Urbano, & Hodapp, 2014; Kaehne & Beyer, 2014).

Prevocational and Vocational Services IDEA requires formal transition planning for students with disabilities beginning at age 16, and in some states this process may begin at an even earlier age. The importance of these IDEA provisions cannot be overstated. Significant evidence indicates the need for effective preparation for postsecondary educational, community, employment, and recreational involvement in order to achieve positive outcomes (Sabornie & deBettencourt, 2009; Test, Smith, & Carter, 2014), but the appropriate implementation of this provision is uneven and still evolving in many school districts. For the most part, prevocational skills such as following directions, timeliness, completion of assignments, and appropriate group behaviors can be addressed in the school curriculum as can career awareness and exploration activities. However, advanced prevocational skills generally are best acquired through community-based instructional programs.

Collaborating with community members in community-based learning activities shows respect and appreciation for the community and provides support for student learning.

Many of the concerns and complexities already noted for school–community collaboration are directly applicable to the transition process for students completing high school. Therefore, clear communication and collaboration among professionals, parents, and the student during goal setting, program planning, and implementation are especially critical (Smith & Anderson, 2014). Successful collaboration in this context is predicated on the articulation of shared goals and expectations and a commitment to honor individual values, needs, and beliefs. As students grow older and approach the end of their public school education, they must learn about post-school options, including jobs—how to get, perform, and keep them. They also need to learn how to use public facilities and services, prepare for safe and healthy adult living, and develop leisure and recreational skills. For many students, most notably those with moderate and severe disabilities, this requires community-based instruction.

Appropriate community-based instruction, like appropriate special education, is individualized. It is dependent on student needs and reflects the student's age, abilities and limitations, goals, and the community context (Cheney, 2012). In deciding on the amount of community-based instruction for a student, teams need to determine the appropriate balance of learning skills for successful community living and attending classes with students who do not have disabilities (P. Noonan, 2014). These decisions are also influenced by opportunities available through general education, and as schools expand integrated recreational activities and service learning programs, students' opportunities for meaningful community experiences also increase. However, in many cases, special education teams still must find the most appropriate blend of integrated and potentially isolated settings.

When community-based options are selected, secondary teachers, transition specialists, and often related service providers must collaborate to design and provide appropriate learning experiences (Hughes, Carter, & Wehman, 2012). The teacher and others on the transition team need to plan and conduct career education and community-based instruction, which entails locating placements as well as organizing and directing vocational training in local employment sites. At the same time, the team must continue to offer school programs that foster independence. Depending on student goals

> **Learn More About**
> This description of high school to postsecondary transition services includes many examples of the importance of collaboration. Try to identify at least five examples, whether involving colleagues, family members, vocational personnel, or other professionals.
>
> (https://www.youtube.com/watch?v=sdA92E4ggzk)

and preparation, interagency agreements or cooperative activities may also need to be established (Sabornie & deBettencourt, 2009). A number of challenges face these professionals, and they center largely on communication, coordination of services, and the delineation of responsibilities.

Many of the communication challenges for professionals engaged in community-based settings are similar to those associated with interagency collaboration. For example, the school schedule does not necessarily coordinate with the schedule for community activities. The immediate implication of this is a challenge for the professionals in arranging real-time communication with team members through meetings or phone calls. Community-based professionals often work with clients and agencies after school hours when teachers and other school personnel are most available for meetings or phone conferences. They are likely to have an irregular work schedule that may also include supporting clients at night or on weekends. In these cases, the team members have an added responsibility to develop communication strategies to share information regularly without face-to-face interactions. Popular options are using cell phones with scheduled conference times and asynchronous use of e-mail, text messages, or voice mail. For meaningful collaboration, however, periodically scheduling face-to-face meetings is a priority, especially when problem solving or decision making is needed.

Additional challenges to communication occur as a result of the number and diversity of individuals from the community who are involved in the placement and supervision of students. In developing job sites and other community options and then placing a student, the community-based specialist may meet with employers, human resources personnel, and the student's potential co-workers as well as observe the work setting to assess the requisite skills and abilities and to prepare the setting for the student's participation. The logistics of arranging these communications are often daunting, and they are made even more complex by the challenge of understanding the differing cultures, vocabularies, and values of the various professionals and community settings (e.g., Meadows, Davies, & Beamish, 2014). The community-based specialist, knowledgeable about both school and community cultures and expectations, becomes the critical player in facilitating effective communication and understanding among these professionals, the student, and the student's family. The team turns to the community-based specialist to ensure that clear and accurate information about the community-based program is being shared with all team members, including the student and family.

Closely related to communication and coordination is the matter of specifying functions and responsibilities for the professionals involved. Clearly described professional roles and responsibilities can facilitate effective communication by identifying the individuals with responsibility and accountability for distinct programmatic functions. For example, how will the student's progress in meeting transition goals be documented? Who is responsible for gathering these data? What types of records should all the individuals working with the student keep to log their time? How should this information be used? Delineation and clear communication of responsibilities and processes for these and similar functions are likely to facilitate your collaborative efforts with community-based professionals and agencies.

Transition Services Although state and federal rehabilitation programs have long helped achieve employment for individuals with disabilities, the collaboration of education agencies and rehabilitation services has been limited (Fleming, Del Valle, Kim, & Leahy, 2013). Just as the responsibility of schools for transition planning is made clear in IDEA, recent amendments to legislation governing the federal Rehabilitation Services Administration (RSA) include mandates that should lead to greater collaboration with schools in the area of transition. In fact, the individualized written rehabilitation program (IWRP), an option available to many (but not all) students with disabilities, has many of the same elements and provisions of the individualized education program (IEP) and is developed under a similar process. Since the 1992 Amendments to the Rehabilitation Act, RSA has used the same definition of transition services used in IDEA, and both vocational rehabilitation counselors and school professionals must agree on a coordinated set of activities that comprise an appropriate transition plan for an eligible student. These and many additional provisions require collaboration between the schools and rehabilitation agencies. This is yet another example of collaboration as part of transition, but it is not easily achieved as it is influenced by differences between IDEA and the Rehabilitation Act requirements relative to eligibility for services, assessment techniques and standards, diagnostic criteria, and availability of services. If this is a topic of particular interest to you, one option for finding out more and staying abreast of the most current information is to set up a rich site summary (RSS) feed, a resource explained in E-Partnerships.

Among the immediate concerns for collaborating with vocational rehabilitation colleagues are the need for professionals from both agencies to understand the different contexts in which they operate, the similarities and variations in their governing legislation, and the different professional orientations they bring to their work. In addition to learning definitional, assessment, and eligibility issues, they must understand the transition processes and resources of each agency. Based on this understanding, professionals can develop a shared language and understanding of the opportunities and constraints of both systems.

As is the case with IDEA, the Rehabilitation Act emphasizes collaboration with families and participation of individuals with disabilities. For this reason, school personnel have a responsibility to educate and prepare students and their families for effective participation as partners in the process as they implement transition plans for students. Several suggestions for facilitating collaboration with vocational rehabilitation counselors are offered in Putting Ideas into Practice.

E-PARTNERSHIPS

RSS: Sorting Through the Avalanche of Internet Information

Have you ever felt just a bit overwhelmed by the sheer quantity of information available on the Internet? You decide to look for information about school teams, type that term into a search engine, and it returns with 53,400,000 hits. You know that certain web sites usually include relevant and high-quality information, but you just don't have the time to keep checking them to see what is being uploaded.

A solution to such information overload is to set up and use RSS, or rich site summary (Richardson, 2009). Many weblogs and other web sites now are including in their content a feed that makes it possible for you to "subscribe" to content. As a result, when content you decide you want is published, it is sent to you. In the school team example above, you would identify sites that tend to have team information you want to keep up on, add them to your list of desired feeds, and then as team content is published, it is collected for you using aggregator software designed for that purpose. You then check your aggregator whenever you like, and just the information you want to learn about is available to you.

Interested? The easiest way to get started is to set up your aggregator using a no-cost option. One popular option is NewsBlur (https://newsblur.com). This aggregator lets you identify topics you want to follow, but it also permits you to link to original text or a feed. In addition, it has features to assist you in identifying new feeds and in filtering content. And so, follow your interests: Early career teachers? Co-teaching in high schools? Interventions for students who are English learners? You choose from feeds that look relevant and add them to your list.

The potential of this technology for collaboration is enormous. Not only can you track particular topics, but you can also receive feeds from other educators who share interests similar to yours. As you receive information, you can organize it and then share it with others by following additional simple instructions on the aggregator web site.

If you would like to learn more about RSS and how you can use it to enhance your collaboration, try these web sites:

- **What is RSS? RSS Explained (www.whatisrss.com)**
- **RSS in Plain English (www.youtube.com/watch?v=0klgLsSxGsU)**

PUTTING IDEAS INTO PRACTICE

Enhancing Collaboration with Vocational Rehabilitation Counselors

The collaboration that occurs as students prepare to transition from school to adult services can be particularly complex. These suggestions can enhance the effectiveness of such a process.

- Invite vocational rehabilitation counselors to make presentations for educators, parents, and students on eligibility and service provision requirements.
- Encourage vocational rehabilitation counselors to become involved with students early. The age at which a student becomes eligible for services varies by state, but school personnel should invite vocational rehabilitation counselors to visit classrooms, interact with students and parents, and become involved in cases at the earliest opportunity.
- Learn about appropriate transition activities for the age levels and needs of the students you teach. Infuse transition activities into subject matter classes and school programs.
- Invite the vocational rehabilitation counselor to speak in classes with a focus on transition to postsecondary options including educational and employment opportunities.
- Discuss specific disabilities and legal rights guaranteed by IDEA, Section 504 of the Rehabilitation Act, and the Americans with Disabilities Act with students and parents. They need to be able to describe the student's abilities and weaknesses and discuss service options if they are to be co-equal partners in decision-making processes.
- Prepare students to participate in vocational rehabilitation processes by teaching them to use self-advocacy strategies and equipping them with personal portfolios that include reports of their medical status, academic achievement, work history, career interest inventories, IEPs (including transition planning), and other relevant information.

APPLY YOUR KNOWLEDGE 12.1

Collaboration Influenced by Roles and Responsibilities

Although the ideas and skills detailed in this book relate to all your collaborative efforts, their application varies somewhat depending on the roles of those with whom you collaborate (e.g., Brennan, 2015; Talley & Travis, 2014; Youngs, Jones, & Low, 2011). As you learn about some of the factors that might influence your interactions with administrators, specialists such as literacy coaches and speech/language therapists, general education teachers, and even students, keep in mind that the information is not intended to form a prescription for your actions. Rather, it should assist you in understanding why you need to make subtle changes in how you respond to different individuals in order to effectively collaborate.

Working with Administrators

Administrators face unique challenges when they are participants in the collaborative efforts at their schools because they have dual roles. They are colleagues and peers in collaboration, but they are also supervisors responsible for evaluating job performance and making personnel decisions (Chenoweth, 2015; Louis & Wahlstrom, 2011). Keeping these two roles separate can be challenging.

Is It Collaborative or Not? Sometimes school professionals find it difficult to nurture a collaborative relationship with their administrator because the administrator does not clearly indicate whether the decision making at hand is intended to be collaborative. Consider the meeting Ms. Fox called to discuss the next steps for Julio, a student with emotional disabilities, who during lunch had knocked over a table displaying school shirts for sale. The special education and general education teachers, counselor, psychologist, and Ms. Fox spent almost an hour discussing Julio's needs and the lack of follow-through at home on recommendations. They considered various options—in-school suspension, a supervised lunch arrangement, and behavior contracts, among others. Both teachers

Administrators sometimes participate in interactions that are collaborative, but at other times they are appropriately directive or supervisory.

supported the supervision option. Toward the end of the meeting, Ms. Fox said, "Thank you for all your input. I have decided that Julio has to be suspended from school—an out-of-school suspension—because of this incident. Nothing you have said has made me change my mind. I'll proceed with the necessary arrangements, contact the district office because Julio receives special education, and call the parents." Needless to say, the professionals who had attended the meeting felt their time had been wasted. Ms. Fox had not communicated to the others that she wanted to hear what they had to say, but that she alone would be making the decision about what would happen with Julio.

When teachers and other professionals work with school administrators, it is important to clearly specify whether the shared interaction is intended to be collaborative, whether participants are functioning in an advisory (but not a decision-making) capacity, or whether they are really just being informed about a decision that has already been made. All of these options are sometimes appropriate. That is, principals do need information and sometimes seek advice, even when they have to make decisions based on additional factors unknown by others. They also sometimes inform staff about decisions that have already been reached, and sometimes they collaborate (Berebitsky, Goddard, & Carlisle, 2014; Cosner, 2011). Your responsibility is to recognize the place and impact of each type of situation and gauge your communication accordingly. To do this, you might have to ask directly whether an interaction is collaborative or advisory, or you might need to ask your administrator to clarify the purpose of a meeting in which you are to participate. Taking these steps can be essential for effective collaboration. In fact, we are sometimes surprised when professionals are frustrated about not having their input used by an administrator, even though the administrator had clearly stated that the input would be considered but not necessarily used as the primary factor in decision making.

Overreliance on Administrative Authority Another dilemma that sometimes arises when administrators are participants in collaboration—especially at team meetings, RTI meetings, IEP meetings, or conferences attended by several individuals—is inappropriate reliance by professionals on administrative authority (Cobb, 2015). For example, consider this team meeting:

> Ms. Payne, the literacy coach, is insistent that students who are English language learners (ELLs) receive ESL services and so should not be accessing the services of the reading specialist. She says that is a duplication of service and takes away support from other students who need it. The speech/language therapist tries to disagree, as does Mr. Reisen, the ESL teacher. However,

> **Learn More About**
> This middle school principal clearly articulates his role that involve both making decisions that are his responsibility and not matters for others' input as well as collaborating with staff. What are examples you notice?
>
> (https://www.youtube.com/watch?v=ZVPV_ObZ5UU)

Ms. Payne raises her voice and repeats her point of view until the others stop trying to change her mind; Ms. Smythe, a general educator, supports her view. As a result, the team decides that ELLs will receive reading support only from the ESL teacher and not the reading teachers. The principal remains silent during the interaction, explaining later that he thought the group had to reach its own decision. Following the meeting, though, the other team members complain to the principal that Ms. Payne had exerted too much influence over the decision and that the result will be duplication of services and a lack of coordination.

This is an example of a team abdicating responsibility for a group decision and hoping that the administrator would use his authority to "control" the situation—even though this matter would have been handled more appropriately through collaborative decision making.

Administrator Knowledge and Support An additional issue related to administrators and collaboration concerns administrators' understanding of topics related to it. For more than two decades, administrators have been moving toward greater use of collaborative models (Barth, 1991; Smith & Scott, 1990). It would be difficult to find a contemporary leadership text, article, or conference that does not emphasize collaboration as a key element in school success (e.g., Causton & Theoharis, 2014; Weathers, 2011). This includes general understanding of the importance of collaboration, the role of the administrator in fostering a school climate supportive of collaboration, and enough knowledge about collaborative activities to help make them a reality (e.g., Fullan, 2010; Robbins & Alvy 2014). However, professionals across the country often note that although administrators may be accomplished collaborative leaders in some areas, too many of them do not have adequate specific knowledge regarding collaborative approaches for educating students with disabilities or other special needs, or they do not actively address the collaborative practices needed to support all students.

Perhaps the clearest example of this issue occurs in schools that are beginning co-teaching programs as part of their service delivery system for ESL, gifted, or special education services. It is essential that principals understand the program philosophy and design, and they also need to know that co-teaching involves far more than specialists popping into classrooms to support students with special needs. Principals must recognize the importance of fostering a sense of partnership between teaching pairs, arranging shared planning time, scheduling with students' needs in mind, and avoiding assigning too many students with special needs to classrooms just because co-teaching is available there. In establishing goals and structures for collaborative efforts, teachers rely on their principals to ensure the feasibility and desirability of potential activities.

Recognizing that collaboration with its related activities is only one of many items competing for an administrator's attention, one strategy you can use to facilitate your interactions with your administrator is to help provide as much relevant information as you can. Some strategies for providing such information are given in Putting Ideas into Practice.

Working with Specialists

Although this book is intended to address a wide range of professionals, collaboration with specialists who are not teachers often presents several unique issues. These issues may directly and profoundly influence these professionals' interactions (Howard, Williams, & Lepper, 2010) with general education and special education teachers, administrators, family members, and others. Specialists include related services personnel—psychologists, social workers, speech/language therapists, counselors, occupational and physical therapists, adaptive physical educators, nurses, itinerant specialists (e.g., orientation and mobility specialists or inclusion facilitators)—and also others, such as media specialists or librarians, literacy or math coaches, and technology specialists. Each of these groups is important: Most students with special needs could not reach their potential without the direct or indirect services of several of these professionals. In addition, these professionals have the knowledge and talents to help you fulfill your responsibilities far better than you could independently accomplish them. When beginning careers in schools, many of our students tell us how helpful these professionals are and how reassuring it is to know that "We are not in this alone."

Yet, your colleagues in these disciplines do face unique challenges. These have to do with professional preparation and orientation, the limited amount of time that they may

PUTTING IDEAS INTO PRACTICE
Strategies for Developing Administrative Support

Principals have many responsibilities that demand their attention. Here are some strategies to help your principal learn about and develop a commitment to collaboration.

- Ask your administrator to participate in initial planning for any collaborative initiative in the school, including planning for communicating about the program to colleagues, parents, and students.
- Discuss with your principal the elements of collaboration you have included or wish to include in your program. Decide with your principal what support and resources you can expect for the program.
- Invite your principal or assistant principal to visit another school with you to observe a particularly good program emphasizing collaboration.
- Share journal articles on pertinent topics. You might have a goal to provide at least one article or clipping each month.
- Alert your administrator to professional development activities related to collaboration. Request permission to attend with a general education teacher, and ask your principal or assistant principal to accompany you.
- Share with your principal materials about collaboration received at professional conferences. You might even suggest that particularly relevant ones be distributed to the entire staff for discussion at a faculty, team, or department meeting.
- As you find web sites with information that could foster collaboration at your school, share those sites with your principal and others.
- Take a few moments on a regular basis to chat about the opportunities and challenges of your collaborative activities. This type of face-to-face interaction is sometimes more effective than written communication. Further, it can provide your administrator with enough information that he or she can make better decisions and be more supportive of your collaborative efforts.
- Maintain an ongoing log or list of topics relative to your collaborative efforts that you wish to discuss with your administrator. Determine the priority of each topic, and discuss one or two at each meeting.
- Invite your principal to join you in making presentations about your school's collaborative work to colleagues in other schools or districts and at professional conferences.

be available to spend at a single school or with a particular teacher, and other role-specific constraints they may experience (Raver & Childress, 2015).

Professional Orientation Some specialists, particularly related services professionals, do not have teaching credentials, nor may they have experience in working with large groups of students in a classroom environment. Further, some of them have professional preparation that is primarily clinical or medical in its focus. They may have had considerable experience with adults and limited course work or internship experience with school-age children or in education settings. Other specialists, such as technology experts, may have come to a school setting from a business environment. The result is that some specialists have orientations significantly different from those of general education, ESL, or special education teachers and other staff members.

During collaborative activities, the difference in preparation and orientation can lead to misunderstandings and miscommunication and sometimes to conflict and resistance. For example, an occupational therapist may propose working with a student on grasping and other fine motor skills in a pullout model. The general education teacher may argue that grasping and related skills can be addressed through writing, cutting, eating, playing with clay, and an entire array of other school activities and do not need to be taught through isolated tasks. Although the occupational therapist might see the value in those practice activities, she maintains that only an occupational therapist can really provide the instruction and that this needs to occur in a separate location. In another example, some speech/language therapists assert that most of their services should be delivered in small, quiet settings away from other students. In contrast, many teachers (and many speech/language therapists, it should be stressed) note that the classroom, home, and community are the best locations for students to learn most speech and language skills.

Time on Site A second dilemma for collaboration with specialists as well as itinerant teachers is their typical limited time at a single school site. This factor alone suggests that collaboration can be difficult and sometimes simply is not possible. These professionals frequently comment that they never quite know what is happening at any of their schools because they are never there long enough to become part of the school community. This leads to innumerable problems. For example, sometimes they arrive at a school to provide services only to find that all the students are at a special assembly. Or they are available to meet with a team only on Thursday mornings, and if the team meets at another time, they cannot be present and miss the discussion. Even when they do attend meetings, they may be late because they have to drive from another location and may be delayed. Conversely, school-based professionals sometimes express frustration with such personnel because of their scarce presence at the school, their rigid scheduling requirements, and their occasional tardiness (e.g., late to a meeting because of a crisis at another school). For example, a novice teacher may find that when something happens in the classroom and she needs advice, her instructional coach is not available until the beginning of the following week, too late for meaningful assistance.

Competing Professional Obligations A third set of issues for specialists, also related to time, concerns their other professional obligations. Many individuals in these professional groups have extremely large caseloads or several school assignments and, as a result, have extraordinary numbers of meetings and conferences to attend. Some may also be obligated to preserve a significant amount of time in their schedules for completing assessments, writing reports, and attending discipline-specific meetings. Some of these professionals may be assigned to help with other school programs and have extensive responsibilities for working with families and community agencies. In addition to creating scheduling difficulties, such responsibilities can fragment the attention of these professionals and limit the depth of their involvement in any particular school-based activity.

These and related factors often limit the extent to which specialists are able and willing to undertake collaborative endeavors. It may be necessary for these professionals and special and general education teachers to prioritize situations in which active participation on the part of the specialist is needed. The personnel in a single school also should stay aware of the constraints under which these professionals work and take that into account in scheduling meetings and professional development activities. Finally, if you hear dissatisfaction from other colleagues about these professionals, you might want to find out the nature and extent of the issues and either participate in resolving them or assist others in understanding the challenges involved.

Working with Other Teachers

Administrators and specialists are not the only ones with roles and responsibilities that may facilitate or constrain collaboration. Even teachers working with one another may find that they have to be aware of and respond to issues related to their professional duties, the topic of A Basis in Research.

Role-Specific Pressures Teachers sometimes experience challenges to collaboration when it is perceived as possibly in conflict with other professional responsibilities. For example, general education teachers sometimes are very concerned about how the scores of students with special needs may reflect—too often, poorly—on their teaching performance. This concern is understandable: In some school districts, teacher pay or bonuses are directly related to student achievement, and students with disabilities or other special needs often (although not always) struggle to achieve. This factor may make some general education teachers reluctant to share control in a co-taught class; they may note that their names are on the class rosters and achievement results, and so their preferences and priorities should dominate in the classroom (Friend, 2014).

Pressure related to student achievement may also prompt some teachers to dismiss as ineffective interventions developed collaboratively on an RTI team. They may urge referral

A BASIS IN RESEARCH

Roles and Responsibilities of Novice General and Special Educators

Educators new to their profession often struggle to understand and balance their many roles and responsibilities. Youngs et al. (2011) studied the differences in role expectations for beginning elementary general and special education teachers, and they also looked at how the novices addressed those expectations.

The researchers surveyed and then interviewed four teachers in a midsize midwestern school district in which 40 percent of the students were eligible for free or reduced cost lunches. The teachers were also queried about mentoring, collegial support, administrative support, and professional development opportunities.

Among many interesting findings, Youngs and his colleagues found the following:

- Although the curriculum for the general education teachers was clearly articulated and could easily be followed, the special educators were expected to either create supplemental curriculum or make significant changes to existing curriculum, and little guidance was provided for this work.
- The general educators had assigned class groups. The special education teachers had caseloads, but they were consistently asked to provide assistance to students in addition to those for whom they were formally responsible.
- The general educators, of course, taught in their assigned classrooms. The special educators split their time between teaching in their special education classrooms and working with general education teachers in their classrooms.
- The special educators had to establish ongoing relationships with many more professionals than their general education colleagues, and they were less likely to have an on-site mentor to support them. As a result, principal support was especially critical for them.

This study demonstrates that the early experiences of school professionals are not identical. If you are a novice educator, what factors might affect your early career? What types of supports would be helpful to you? If you're an experienced educator, how might you provide support to novice educators?

---

for special education assessment, anticipating that a determination of eligibility will reduce their accountability for student outcomes. They likewise may resist co-teaching with an ESL teacher because they would rather transfer responsibility for ELLs' achievement outcomes to those professionals.

Special educators and ESL teachers, too, may raise concerns about their roles and responsibilities as they relate to collaboration, not because they do not care or do not wish for collaborative practice, but because of the context in which they sometimes work. For example, ESL teachers sometimes report that they have so many students at so many levels of language learning that they do not believe they can attend meetings and consult with general education teachers, much less deliver services through co-teaching. Special education teachers may raise similar concerns. In addition, the latter group may experience role stress because of the expectation that they participate in delivering RTI services. That is, some special educators are assigned to provide Tier 2 and Tier 3 interventions as well as to meet the IEP goals and objectives of the students on their caseloads; feeling overwhelmed, they may withdraw from many collaborative interactions. As is the case for general educators, the pressures on ESL and special educators and the resulting difficulties created for collaboration are understandable and must be respected and addressed.

Learn More About
Collaborating with specialists sometimes involves resolving differences in points of view. What advice would you give to the teacher depicted in this video? (https://www.youtube.com/watch?v=xJXRU15fytc)

Control and Ownership One additional area of concern for teachers working together relates to their perception of control and ownership for groups of students. Many examples of this potential source of concern can be identified. In some cases, general education teachers say "my class," and the result may be that the other teacher or specialist is relegated to the role of helper. Similarly, "my class" may refer to the physical location, and other professionals receive the message that furniture is not to be moved or that materials are not for joint use. In some schools, general educators are given a choice of whether they work with students with special needs, especially through co-teaching, and so they may conclude that this should always be their choice rather than a responsibility integral to being a teacher.

Similar issues communicated by special education and ESL teachers may likewise constrain collaboration. For example, at a meeting to discuss the schedule for the following school year, Ms. Bryan repeatedly referred to the students on her special education caseload as "my kids," and before the meeting was over other teachers were referring to that group of students as "your kids." Instead of using the language of "our kids," which can foster collaboration, students had been divided based on their special needs. In another example, Ms. Guerra is on her school's committee to shift some ESL services to general education classrooms. For every option explored, she had an explanation of why it would be best for ESL services to continue to be offered in a separate setting.

It is important to realize that many professionals do not experience these constraints on collaboration related to roles and responsibilities. Sadly, though, they are still common enough that they must be acknowledged. When viewed as a whole, professionals should come to an understanding that they not only share their commitment to student success but also share the stress of a variety of pressures related to their roles and responsibilities. When dilemmas occur, such as the co-teaching problems Ms. Decker is experiencing and the uncertainty Mr. Ehrsam is feeling, working together for resolution can produce far better results than working alone.

Student–Professional Collaboration

One additional type of collaboration related to roles and responsibilities merits attention: the opportunity for student–professional collaboration. Although such partnerships seldom meet all the criteria for collaboration, they are an important consideration. In fact, research suggests that the most skilled teachers keep teacher–student collaboration in mind as a key understanding as they instruct (e.g., Rodriguez & Solis, 2013).

One example of an opportunity for teacher–student collaboration can be found in social learning platforms such as Edmodo. For students with disabilities, the most critical application often is participation in IEP meetings. To provide a context, professionals in the field of special education have for many years studied how to increase self-determination for students with disabilities, that is, to teach them how to make choices representing their own interests so that they can reach goals they have set (Bohanon, Castillo, & Afton, 2015; Wehmeyer et al., 2011). Self-determination becomes especially important as students reach age 16, the point in their school careers at which federal law mandates that planning commence for their post-school lives (e.g., employment, technical school, university). One key element of self-determination, then, can be student participation in their transition IEP meetings, but such participation may begin even during the elementary school years (Wagner, Newman, Cameto, Javitz, & Valdes, 2012).

For example, in the third grade, Melissa, a student with a learning disability, attended her IEP meeting. Her role was to introduce herself and to talk about what she liked about school, what she could do well at school, and what she found difficult. Her teachers helped to prepare her for her role in the meeting. As she entered middle school, Melissa's participation increased. She learned what the agenda for the meeting would be and she helped to facilitate the meeting. Her additional role was to discuss her goals for the next school year, to share some samples of work that she thought best showcased her strengths, and to participate in a discussion of the types of classroom supports that would help her succeed (e.g., permission to ask other students for help with difficult words, use of an iPad). In high school, Melissa became an even more central participant in the IEP meeting. She outlined her postgraduation goals (attend the local community college for two years, and then transfer to the local university to pursue a degree in management information systems). She also shared how she was beginning to prepare to reach her goals, and she discussed with teachers and others at the meeting what she thought she would need in terms of accommodations so that she could graduate on time and be prepared to achieve her career aspirations.

Learn More About
Although adult, rather than student, collaboration has been the focus of this book, contemporary educators also focus on teaching their students to work effectively with others.
(https://www.youtube.com/watch?v=0WdTS9u0h10)

Although not all students may be able to play a role this active, research strongly supports the benefit of participation. For example, Barnard-Brak and Lechtenberger (2010) analyzed a national education database of students with disabilities. They found that a strong positive relationship existed between student participation in IEP meetings and academic achievement. That is, IEP participation does not just provide students with a sense of controlling their own lives; it seems to be associated with stronger student outcomes.

Whatever your professional role, you should recognize the importance of this type of student–professional collaboration and help ensure that it occurs. Your responsibilities may involve speaking with parents about this type of student participation, coaching students to participate in IEP meetings, asking students clear questions during the meeting to facilitate their participation, and informally discussing with students their goals and progress toward achieving them.

Systemic Barriers to Collaboration

As noted in Chapter 1, schools are not particularly well designed to foster collaboration. This is true in terms of physical space, which often is inflexible and offers few locations for professionals to pursue shared work. It also includes the structures and systemic practices that may offer scant opportunities for collaboration, whether in elementary, middle, or high school.

Scheduling for Collaboration

Although the topic of scheduling time for collaborative planning was addressed in Chapter 7 as it relates to co-teaching, additional issues related to this logistic can be significant in schools that have a collaborative culture (Honigsfeld & Dove, 2010b; Murawski, 2012). Finding feasible scheduling options and creating services that complement rather than compete with other programs (e.g., reading or math remedial programs, enrichment programs, ESL services, special education, transition services that involve agencies outside of the school) often require setting aside assumptions about how students receive these services and what professional responsibilities should be related to delivering them (e.g., Barnard-Brak & Lechtenberger, 2010; Osgood, Foster, & Courtney, 2010). It also requires taking into account the hectic schedules of professionals such as Ms. Decker and Mr. Ehrsam, from the chapter-opening case.

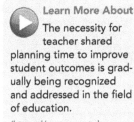

Learn More About
The necessity for teacher shared planning time to improve student outcomes is gradually being recognized and addressed in the field of education.
(https://www.youtube.com/watch?v=n06wCt8KK6E)

Although scheduling is an administrative matter, when professionals understand the issues related to it from a variety of perspectives, they can assist principals and other administrators in finding the best solutions for teachers and other professionals leading to maximum benefit for students. These are several scheduling issues for special educators and ESL specialists as well as those for general educators.

Scheduling Issues for Special Education and ESL Teachers When school professionals increase collaborative practices, a range of scheduling issues may arise. Two common examples illustrate the complexity of scheduling: (1) arranging co-teaching schedules on a daily or less-than-daily basis, and (2) creating flexibility in the specialist's daily schedule in order to accommodate all the required responsibilities.

Daily or Periodic Scheduling of Services One critical scheduling matter concerns co-teaching. Many special education and ESL teachers plan for co-teaching to be a daily service delivery option, but then they encounter difficulties meeting all the competing demands for their time. The schedule created by the special education staff of one middle school illustrates the dilemmas daily services can pose: The special education teachers had managed to ensure that co-teaching was occurring in each classroom as needed based on students' IEPs, and they also were managing to offer a small number of sections of a study skills class as well as just a single section each of core academic English and math for several students with intellectual and behavior disabilities. To make the schedule work, it was decided co-teaching would occur for only half of the 46-minute class period. Not surprisingly, both the special education teachers and the general education teachers sensed that students were not getting effective individualized instruction.

ESL teachers encounter similar difficulties (Peercy & Martin-Beltran, 2012). They may decide that they can split their time almost equally between co-teaching and instructing students in a separate setting, but when several students transfer to the school late in the fall, the teachers may find that the only way to carve out time for these students is to reduce the amount of co-teaching. This can be especially likely to happen when co-teaching is considered a luxury for the ESL program rather than an essential component for fostering student success.

When resources and staff are readily available, daily co-teaching permits both teachers to have a higher sense of ownership in the co-taught class and assists in maintaining the continuity of instruction. Other options can be viable, however. For example, in the middle school just described, the program was modified so that co-teaching occurred only in English and math classes but for an entire class period. Thus, teachers reduced the number of classrooms in which they co-taught daily. For the ESL teacher, co-teaching was prioritized in two classes with a high number of English learners who required the presence of the ESL teacher to succeed. In a high school, a special education teacher addressed the problem in this way: With support from his principal, he identified two fourth-period classes in which co-teaching was appropriate, and then he co-taught in each class twice each week, with the fifth day left open for flexible scheduling. Keeping less-than-daily co-teaching as a program option is one specific strategy for reaching more students and increasing service intensity. It can be particularly viable at the secondary level. Of course, the extent to which this can occur depends on the nature and extent of students' needs and the requirements for services.

Schedule Flexibility A second scheduling issue for special education and ESL teachers concerns retaining some flexibility in the daily schedule. Many educators have every minute of each day tightly scheduled, and when an emergency meeting is called, a new student requires attention, or an assessment has to be completed some service is canceled, often to the understanding but annoyance of general education and other specialist colleagues. ESL and special educators should keep a bit of flexibility, so that if they have to cancel a service, another option might be available so that students receive the services to which they are entitled. For example, in some elementary schools, these educators schedule their lunch and preparation periods back to back so that they can flip-flop them as the need to meet with colleagues arises. Yet others keep two blocks of time (for a total of 45 minutes to one hour, or two class periods) reserved each week for flexible use. The time is used for student observation, additional consultation, team meetings, accommodations of instructional materials, or makeup sessions if a regularly scheduled in-class service has to be canceled during the week.

Many appropriate strategies exist for creating a professional schedule that both meets the needs of students and promotes professional collaboration. One sample teaching schedule is shown in Figure 12.1. Yet, it must also be acknowledged that in schools that value collaboration as a strategy for meeting diverse student needs, professional schedules typically are periodically revised to reflect shifting priorities especially during the first few months of the school year.

Scheduling Issues for General Education Teachers General education teachers also contend with scheduling issues in collaborative schools. Two that are common are (1) being scheduled to work with several different specialists; and (2) being assigned to so many collaborative activities that it seems other responsibilities are neglected.

Scheduled with Multiple Specialists Many general educators are strongly supportive of collaborative service models for students with special needs, but they occasionally are asked to work with so many different professionals that they grow concerned.

FIGURE 12.1 **Sample teaching schedule for Edward, a Grades 3-5 special educator.**

Time	Mon	Tues	Wed	Thurs	Fri
8:00–8:30		Hall duty	Bus duty		
8:30–9:00	Reading skills pullout (groups change monthly)	Reading skills pullout (groups change monthly)	Reading skills pullout (groups change monthly)	Reading skills pullout (groups change monthly)	Reading skills pullout (groups change monthly)
9:00–9:45	Literacy (co-taught with Granger—4th)	Literacy (co-taught with Johnson—3rd)	Literacy (co-taught with Granger—4th)	Literacy (co-taught with Granger—4th)	Literacy pullout (4th, flexible)
9:45–10:30	Literacy (co-taught with Holt—5th)	Literacy (co-taught with Holt—5th)	Literacy (co-taught with Holt—5th)	Literacy (co-taught with Holt—5th)	Literacy pullout (5th, flexible)
10:30–11:15	Literacy (co-taught with Brownstein—3rd)	Literacy (co-taught with Brownstein—3rd)	Literacy (co-taught with Brownstein—3rd)	Literacy (co-taught with Brownstein—3rd)	Literacy pullout (5th, flexible)
11:15–12:15	Math (co-taught with Fairchild—5th)	Math (co-taught with Fairchild—5th)	Math (co-taught with Fairchild—5th)	Math (co-taught with Fairchild—5th)	Math (co-taught with Fairchild—5th)
12:15–1:15	Lunch/planning	Lunch/special education team meeting	Lunch/planning	Lunch/planning	Lunch/planning
1:15–2:00	Math (co-taught with Scott—3rd)	Math (co-taught with Scott—3rd)	Math (co-taught with Scott—3rd)	Math pullout (as needed)	Planning for co-teaching (rotated among teachers)
2:00–2:45	Math (co-taught with Tucker—4th)	Math (co-taught with Tucker—4th)	Math (co-taught with Tucker—4th)	Math (co-taught with Tucker—4th)	Math (co-taught with Tucker—4th)
2:45–3:15	Planning	Planning	Duty	Duty	Planning

For example, in an elementary school Mr. Lambert co-teaches with Ms. Suarez, the ESL teacher. However, he also co-teaches with Mr. Lord, the special educator. Twice each week, Ms. Collins joins him to deliver in-class speech/language therapy. He also is scheduled to co-teach for a two-week period with Ms. Raymond, the media specialist. Although he is trying to keep up with all the different expectations of the specialists and knows everyone is focused on improving student outcomes, he sometimes thinks that too many different professionals are entering the classroom.

A comparable dilemma sometimes occurs in high school co-teaching. Mr. Russell teaches five sections of Algebra I. Because of scheduling, though, in the three co-taught sections he has three different teaching partners. He wonders why the schedule couldn't have been developed so that he worked with the same special educator for each class period. The notion of coordinating schedules so that situations such as these do not occur is addressed more fully later in this section as part of whole-school scheduling issues.

Many Scheduled Collaborative Activities In some schools, the challenge is not a lack of collaboration. Instead, it is that many collaborative activities are scheduled and mandatory, and teachers sometimes believe that their other necessary work is neglected. For example, at Carter Middle School, students have an early release each Wednesday, and the one-and-a-half-hour period is for teacher collaboration. However, on the first Wednesday of each month, collaboration is defined as a school staff meeting. On the second Wednesday, the time is for job-alike meetings (e.g., all the math teachers meet, all the specialists meet). The third Wednesday is for professional learning communities (PLCs) based on books teachers are reading about various instructional practices. The fourth Wednesday is for individual planning, but co-teachers are supposed to use this block of time for their collaboration. When teachers work with several partners, they are responsible for meeting with all their colleagues in this single time block.

As you might suspect, general education teachers who work in this type of environment may strongly support collaboration, but they are likely to be frustrated because of the many demands on their time. They appropriately point out that collaboration should be a priority but that they should have a voice in allocating the time designated for it.

School Scheduling Issues Yet another type of scheduling problem concerns the overall schedule on which the school operates. Although informal collaboration often occurs in spite of a difficult school schedule, if collaboration is a valued professional activity and an expectation for teachers and other staff members, the school schedule might need to be modified to make it feasible (Nierengarten, 2013).

One common scheduling matter in elementary schools concerns the time of day when language arts is taught. Most collaborative specialized services (e.g., special education, ESL, speech/language therapy) are most easily delivered through co-teaching during language arts instruction; but all the general education teachers may be teaching language arts at the same time, thus making it impossible to deliver services in a timely manner in every classroom where they are needed. However, if the schedule for teaching language arts is staggered across teachers or grade levels, in-class services are far more likely to be a feasible option. Alternatively, in some schools, grade-level teachers plan to offer core academics at the same time so that the specialists can move among classrooms, or students can move across classrooms so as to be grouped for skills-based instruction.

Another scheduling matter for some elementary schools concerns art, music, physical education, media, and technology classes. In some districts, principals are working with central office administrators to arrange these classes simultaneously at one grade level. This creates an opportunity for team planning, and it allows for specialists to meet with grade-level teams. In very large schools—for example, those with 8 to 12 sections in a single grade level—this scheduling strategy can at least allow for half the grade level to be released at one time.

In high school, scheduling issues often concern the number of priorities that must be considered. Courses that have single sections (e.g., an advanced language course), courses that serve students across grade levels (e.g., chorus, band), and the need to distribute core courses throughout the day may make it difficult to schedule common planning time or give consideration to co-teachers' schedules. One solution for this problem, especially for special educators and in schools with several ESL teachers, is to assign specialists to specific departments. In addition to solving a scheduling problem, doing this has the advantage of ensuring that any general education teacher needs to contact only one person regarding a student concern, rather than try to figure out who the responsible specialist happens to be.

A final school scheduling issue relates to block scheduling versus traditional class periods (e.g., Gill, 2011; Zelkowski, 2010). Although the merits of longer or shorter instructional periods on student achievement continue to be debated, this aspect of scheduling also affects collaboration. For example, if co-teaching is a service delivery option, should specialists stay in one class for the entire 90 minutes of a block? Or would their time be better spent divided between two classes? Would the answer be different depending on the specialist (e.g., special educator, literacy coach, ESL teacher), the subject being taught, the type of block (i.e., classes that meet every day for a single semester versus classes that meet every other day for the entire school year), or the specific characteristics of the students? Questions such as these should be carefully considered, and in many cases, more than a single solution should be implemented. For example, in ninth-grade English, it might be valuable for the two teachers to work together for the entire block; in twelfth-grade government, this intensity of service may not be justified. How might these factors affect the co-teaching of Ms. Decker and Mr. Ehrsam, introduced in the case study at the beginning of this chapter?

Coordinating Services for Collaboration

In many cases, arranging a schedule that encourages collaboration is not sufficient. As hinted at earlier in this section, another dimension of scheduling also important to consider concerns its impact on the schedules of other service providers in a school and the programs and services they are operating (Friend, 2014). This matter of service coordination becomes especially important in elementary and middle schools in which most individualized services for students are delivered in the general education classroom. Consider this list of individuals who could be going into a classroom to work with general education teachers and students:

- Special education teachers (could be more than one, depending on school size, student needs, and service delivery patterns)
- Speech/language therapists
- Instructional coaches
- Counselors
- Social workers
- Psychologists
- Paraeducators (special education or from other programs)
- Title I math or reading teachers or specialists with similar roles
- Paid tutors
- Parent volunteers
- Interns or student teachers
- Members of Future Teachers of America
- ESL teachers

Imagine yourself as a teacher with several of these individuals assigned to your class. One teacher we know found herself in this exact situation. After a particularly grueling day, she told her principal to get everyone out, that she wanted just her classroom and her students by herself. She had had too much of a good thing.

Professionals delivering in-class services may need to assist each other in meeting student needs and carefully coordinate their efforts with the priorities and schedules of general education teachers. For example, if a speech/language therapist is co-teaching in a first-grade classroom and one student in the class has a learning disability, the therapist may be able to meet that student's needs (although this would not be considered special education services) instead of the special educator going into the classroom. This also eliminates the need for the first-grade teacher to manage co-teaching with two professionals. Similarly, if a literacy coach or ESL teacher is spending an hour each day in a fourth-grade class, this specialist may be able to address the instructional needs of students with disabilities who need reading instruction (although, again, this would not be considered special education service). In other words, care must be taken to prevent individual classrooms from being overrun by many service providers coming and going or otherwise disrupting instruction. This is especially true if the classroom already has a paraeducator assigned to it because of either large class size or identified student needs. At the same time, high-quality services often can be delivered and personnel resources used more efficiently if the professionals are flexible in their approaches and in their willingness to share their responsibilities for service delivery with each other as appropriate. Of course, these ideas are applicable only if the needs of students with disabilities or those needing other specialized services are being met and if local and state policies permit such sharing.

One other coordination issue should be raised. In some schools, collaboration is a priority, but its implementation relates to only certain programs but not others. Most commonly, special education services may be delivered in general education classrooms, but other service providers pull students out. The result can be fragmentation of instruction. Two teachers may be in the room teaching math, but four students leave during that time for ESL services. As they return, another three depart to work with the teacher for students who are gifted. The message to keep in mind is this: As more collaborative service models emerge, particularly in elementary schools, they have the potential to reach many students or to disrupt their education. Finding the best ways to coordinate services is a task that truly is worth the collaborative time it consumes.

Ethics in Collaborative Practice

As an educator you will face many ethical issues concerning your students, your interactions with families, the decisions made in your school district, and the views and actions of your colleagues (e.g., MacDonald, 2011; Summey & Lashley, 2014). However, even though the National Education Association, the Council for Exceptional Children, the American Speech-Language-Hearing Association, the National Association of School Psychologists, the American School Counselor Association, and other professional organizations have codes of ethics and standards of practice, in schools the topic too often is ignored.

When collaboration is added to the other ethical issues professionals face and given its likely continued importance and expansion in education, it becomes critical to recognize potential ethical dilemmas and to consider how you will address them. Three of several possible ethical issues are confidentiality, feasibility, and accountability.

Common Ethical Issues

One of the most frequent and basic ethical considerations in collaborative practice concerns *confidentiality* (e.g., Williams & Wehrman, 2010). Educators have been cautioned for many years about preserving confidentiality related to student and family information, but collaboration brings an entirely new dimension to this ethical matter. For example, suppose that two teachers are co-teaching, and the general education teacher shares his favorite teaching idea with the special educator. The latter individual sees that the idea has tremendous potential in several classrooms and enthusiastically but naively shares it with several other teachers. The second teacher is startled when the teacher confronts her about giving away "trade secrets." This example of a breach of confidentiality is not so much about teaching or learning as it is about developing and maintaining trusting relationships with colleagues.

Professional collaboration sometimes leads to ethical dilemmas, and educators should be proactive in clarifying their own ethical standards.

A second ethical dilemma concerns *feasibility*. We work in many schools in which professionals express belief in the power of collaboration yet have virtually no time or other supports for collaborative practice. Whether a collaborative effort involves a grade-level or department team planning interventions for struggling students or English learners, a transdisciplinary team preparing for the inclusion of a student with multiple disabilities, or a school leadership team responsible for implementing reforms to improve student achievement, if time does not exist to meet, the effort is unlikely to be successful. Logically, if the program design, no matter how popular, is not feasible or does not have the support necessary to meet the needs of students, it may be unethical to create assumptions about positive outcomes of working collaboratively until feasibility issues are addressed.

A third ethical dilemma can occur regarding *accountability*, and this topic is receiving increased attention as models of differentiated compensation based on student achievement evolve (Dieterle, Guarino, Reckase, & Wooldridge, 2015; McCaffrey et al., 2011). These questions arise: Who is accountable for ensuring that students with special needs are held to the highest expectations and that their unique learning needs are addressed? And how should accountability for these students' achievement be divided among general educators, special educators, ESL teachers, and other specialists?

Other ethical issues related to accountability exist as well. All ethical standards in school and child welfare fields include responsibilities to students or clients as central elements. In addition, special educators are responsible for ensuring that the needs of students receiving special education and related services are met. Together, these ethical guidelines assign responsibility to the professionals for promoting the total development of each student/client, including academic, vocational, personal, and social development (Schmidt, 2003). In collaboration, disagreement may occur concerning the nature of a student's needs and the strategies necessary to address them (Chenoweth, 2015). A general education teacher may perceive a student as needing services in a separate setting, whereas an ESL teacher believes the language-rich general education setting will foster a student's language learning. In another example, a speech/language therapist may see that a language-based program in an inclusive setting would best address a student's needs, but the special educator may identify the priority as offering the student a highly structured, small-group environment such as that found in a special education classroom. What other ethical dilemmas related to accountability might occur?

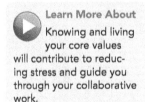

Learn More About
Knowing and living your core values will contribute to reducing stress and guide you through your collaborative work.

(https://www.youtube.com/watch?v=cjsbsnF_UUQ)

Finally, the ethical standards in special education and related fields require that a professional work collaboratively with other professionals in the school and the community and promote qualities of fairness, cooperation, respect, and objectivity. In the case of special education, the standards of the Council for Exceptional Children (2003) require that special educators "work cooperatively with and encourage other professionals to improve the provision of special education and related services to persons with exceptionalities" (p. 3).

Responding to Ethical Issues

Professionals need to reflect on and clarify their own ethical standards regarding students with disabilities and their own related professional behaviors. By doing this before entering into collaborative interactions and continuing during those interactions, you can recognize practices that you might not be comfortable with but can live with versus those that you cannot justify. By continuing the conversation about ethics as it relates to collaboration, you can balance your commitment to collaboration with your responsibilities to meet the needs of the students you serve. Shapiro and Stefkovich (2005) offer a framework for ethical reasoning that can help your thinking about the real-life ethical dilemmas you face, a framework that is especially relevant for the field of special education. It includes the following elements:

- *The ethic of justice*. This component relates to the legislative, policy, and legal basis for decision making. It is probably the clearest part of the ethical framework: You have the responsibility to ensure that in all situations the requirements of IDEA or other pertinent federal laws as well as state and local policy concerning students with disabilities, students who are English learners, or other students with special needs, are followed. However, this component also goes beyond the law. It implies that professionals must make sure that individuals who may not perceive themselves as having power (e.g., parents whose first language is not English) are respected and heard.

- *The ethic of critique.* This component of the ethical framework concerns the inequities that may exist in the entire system of specialized services and your responsibility for responding to such inequities. Perhaps the clearest example in this area concerns the disproportionate representation of African American males and English learners in special education (Albrecht, Skiba, Losen, Chung, & Middelberg, 2012; Bruce & Venkatesh, 2014). How might conversations among team members increase the likelihood that some students will be identified, possibly inappropriately, as having disabilities (Knotek, 2003)?
- *The ethic of care.* This component of the ethical framework concerns the outcomes of the decision making in which you participate. That is, when faced with a complex situation, you should ask yourself, "What is the likely impact of this decision for this student and her family, both now and for the future? Am I certain that the decision being made will truly help this student and his family or does it have the potential to hurt them?"
- *The ethic of the profession.* This final component of an ethical framework relates to the broad ethical standards—those that are formal and those that are informal—of one's profession. For example, in your interactions with colleagues and community members, an informal ethical standard exists that you not tolerate insensitive or derogatory remarks about individuals with disabilities or other special needs (e.g., a friend who refers to someone's actions as "retarded," a colleague who makes a disparaging racial remark). At the most general level, professional educators should use as the basis for their day-to-day work an understanding that all students are capable of learning and that diversity should be celebrated; they should communicate this belief as they work with others.

Ethical issues will always exist regarding students with special needs. As collaboration increasingly defines the roles and responsibilities of professional educators, these ethical issues are likely to become more frequent and sometimes more complex because the views of all participants must be considered. Your knowledge and skills for interacting effectively with others can provide you with the tools you will need to confidently face these perplexing situations.

Final Thoughts About Professional Collaboration

When the first edition of this textbook was published nearly 25 years ago, education collaboration was still more of a concept than a practice . Although there was a history of informal collaboration among special education professionals (e.g., teachers in separate schools working together, mental health professionals working with special educators), most authors were still writing about the physical and psychological isolation of educators (e.g., Little, 1982; Sarason, 1982), especially related to their professional roles and responsibilities. A few professionals, such as school psychologists, employed consultation to support teachers in their work with students (e.g., Brown, Przywansky, & Schulte, 1987), but most such applications were based on an expert model; that is, the consultant's responsibility being to provide guidance to the teacher.

So much has changed since then. Educators have moved from communicating via notes left in mailboxes or slow, unreliable, and simplistic e-mail systems to utilizing the highly interactive and collaborative-friendly tools of Web 2.0. Professional development has changed from periodic workshops, often unrelated to each other and sometimes with a purpose unclear to participants, to professional learning communities and other job-embedded options that rely on high-quality teacher collaboration. Administrators discuss the importance of distributed leadership (e.g., Heck & Hallinger, 2010) and establish teams to address school reform (Zrike & Connolly, 2015). Teachers seek advice from colleagues in their schools and across the region, country, and world using electronic collaboration, described in E-Partnerships, to find more effective ways to reach their diverse learners. Further, professionals across disciplines work together, when in classrooms through co-teaching or in various types of teams, to ensure that the highest standards are in place for all students and that all students have the opportunity to achieve those standards. University faculty members are stressing collaboration as an essential skill in professional preparation programs (Hoaglund, Birkenfeld, & Box, 2014), and both professional standards and emerging new-generation teacher evaluation systems stress the importance of collaborative work (e.g., Killion, 2011).

Taken together, the current attention to collaboration, the ways that it is being embedded in professional preparation and practice, its growing importance in the day-to-day operation of schools, and its increasingly demonstrable benefit for students and educators (e.g., Huberman, Navo, & Parrish, 2012; Silverman, Hazelwood, & Cronin, 2009) suggest that collaboration will continue to grow in importance for school professionals. This statement is bolstered by a review of collaboration's significance in the larger context, across business, social services, economics, medicine, and other professions. As noted in Chapter 1, collaboration has become a foundational element in twenty-first-century society, and so as schools reflect the larger society collaboration will become even more integral to their effectiveness.

E-PARTNERSHIPS

Collaboration 2.0? Twitter!

You probably use Twitter to stay in touch with classmates and friends, but are you tapping into its power for professionals? A quick look and you will find out that educators from around the world are sharing ideas, encouraging each other, and identifying valuable classroom resources. Twitter has even been praised as one of the best places for twenty-first-century teacher collaboration. Here are a few Twitter hashtags you might find helpful:

- #coteachat
  This account includes commentary by many well-known co-teaching experts.
- #elemchat
  A recent discussion concerned strategies for integrating technology throughout the curriculum.
- #spedchat
  Participants had a recent discussion pinpointing and addressing reading difficulties.
- #collaboration
  This conversation focuses on business applications of collaboration, but it includes information valuable for education (e.g., a discussion of negative aspects of collaboration).
- #esl
  Professionals teaching students whose first language is not English share many ideas for improving fluency and pronunciation. They also relate stories about their students.

Of course, these are just a few of thousands and thousands of conversations to follow and participate in by tweeting. If you just want to keep up with what is happening in your field, you can do that, too. For example, @usedgov is the Twitter page for the U.S. Department of Education. Concerned about issues in your state? Most states have an educator's chat—type a hashtag, your state's two-letter abbreviation, and *edchat* (e.g., #iledchat). Interested in your professional organization? It's probably on Twitter, too, such as @CECMembership, the Twitter page of CEC.

That is not to say that the path will be straight or smooth. It is likely in many locales that the infrastructure needed for education collaboration—adequate staffing, feasible schedules, common planning time, appropriate professional development—will be challenging to create and maintain. Likewise, building understanding among parents, school board members, and the community of the importance of such infrastructures in education is likely to be problematic. At the same time, although many professional preparation programs embrace the concept of collaboration, the large majority do not demonstrate its importance by offering courses co-taught by faculty members from different departments or courses about collaboration that are required for all education-related majors. The result is that some professionals will still enter the field inadequately prepared for their collaborative responsibilities, much like Jonathan Ehrsam from the chapter-opening case.

The future of collaboration is likely to be a combination of optimism and excitement tempered by the realization of the complexities of building and sustaining a high-quality practice. A positive point is that you have learned a great deal about collaboration; thus you can be a contributing voice in fostering professional collaboration. Doing so will be both rewarding and challenging.

SUMMARY

- The context in which you work with others to benefit students affects all dimensions of your collaboration. Specific issues arise when you work with individuals who are not pre-K–12 educators, but are members of the community, personnel from different agencies, or professionals involved in students' significant transitions across services (i.e., from early intervention to school programs and from school programs to post-school options).
- Professional roles and responsibilities help to shape the nature of school collaboration. When teachers work with administrators, specialists such as speech/language therapists, other teachers, or even students, they should take into account how the requirements of each individual's role may contribute to or detract from collaboration.
- Systemic matters likewise may profoundly influence collaboration in schools. Issues such as scheduling problems for special education and ESL teachers, for general education teachers, and for the school as a whole, as well as challenges in coordinating services, can be barriers to collaboration that must be overcome.
- Collaboration will continue to be central in the work of schools and is likely to increase and become more complex, even as its specific character evolves. Educators should know and follow fundamental ethical principles in their collaborative efforts.

BACK TO THE CASE

1. In the geometry class, Rosalee Decker feels like a paraeducator. What is her responsibility for addressing this with her teaching partner? What is the role of her principal or assistant principal? What should she do if the problem continues?
2. Mr. Ehrsam did not learn about co-teaching in his teacher preparation program and is now struggling to partner with two different specialists. How might co-teaching with an ESL teacher be similar to and different from co-teaching with a special educator? What are two pieces of advice you would give to Mr. Ehrsam as a new teacher to make the partnerships successful?
3. Think about Ms. Decker and Mr. Ehrsam and their wish that they could work together. Do you think this is a reasonable wish? What might be the advantages and disadvantages? How would their working together possibly affect their roles and responsibilities? What ethical issues might arise? Justify your responses.

COLLABORATIVE ACTIVITIES

1. Reflect on the professional role you are in or will be in. What type of community outreach or community partnership activity might enhance your students' education? What role could you play in building or sustaining that program? Who else would need to be involved? How could you go about enlisting those individuals' support?

2. Student participation in the IEP process is important at the elementary school level and essential at the secondary school level. Regardless of your professional assignment, what specific actions could you take to ensure that students have a meaningful role in their IEP meetings? How would you involve students' families in fostering student participation? Other team members?

3. Make a chart of the roles of individuals who typically participate in collaboration in your setting, whether that is your school, your field placement, or an activity on campus. For each, list the factors that foster their participation and those that constrain it. What does your analysis suggest about the potential for expanding collaboration in your setting?

4. Think about the school level at which you plan to work or currently work. What are the most pressing issues related to service coordination? If you were asked to chair a committee to address these issues, what priorities would you set? How would you try to resolve the issues (e.g., reading is taught across all elementary grade levels at the same time, the only time for middle school team planning occurs when the ESL teacher must have a group of students in a separate setting, special educators are working directly and through consultation with three or four teachers in different subject areas)? What concerns do you anticipate being expressed by other teachers? How would you address the concerns?

5. What are the ethical issues that you are most concerned about facing in your job? With classmates, discuss what guidance is offered by the elements of the ethical framework presented in this chapter. For each dilemma you discuss, propose at least three actions that a professional educator could take to address it.

 CHECK YOUR UNDERSTANDING

Click here to gauge your understanding of this chapter's essential concepts.

REFERENCES

Chapter 1

Anderson-Butcher, D., Lawson, H. A., Iachini, A., Flaspohler, P., Bean, J., & Wade-Mdivanian, R. (2010). Emergent evidence in support of a community collaboration model for school improvement. *Children & Schools, 32*, 160–171.

Ash, P. B., & D'Auria, J. (2013). Blueprint for a learning system: Create one larger, more flexible team that encourages collaboration in all directions. *Journal of Staff Development, 34*(3), 42–46.

Bangou, F., & Austin, T. (2011). Revisiting collaborative boundaries—Pioneering change in perspectives and relations of power. *Journal of Urban Learning, Teaching, and Research, 7*, 41–48.

Barth, R. S. (2006). Improving relationships within the schoolhouse. *Educational Leadership, 63*(6), 8–13.

Bennis, W., & Biederman, P. W. (1997). *Organizing genius: The secrets of creative collaboration.* Reading, MA: Addison-Wesley.

Bradley, R., Danielson, L., & Doolittle, J. (2007). Responsiveness to intervention: 1997–2007. *Teaching Exceptional Children, 39*(5), 8–12.

Brown-Chidsey, R., & Steege, M. W. (2010). *Response to intervention: Principles and strategies for effective practice* (2nd ed.). New York: Guilford Press.

Butera, G., & Martinez, R. S. (2014). Multidisciplinary collaboration to support struggling readers: Special issue introduction. *Journal of Educational and Psychological Consultation, 24*, 75–80.

Canter, L., Voytecki, K., Zambone, A., & Jones, J. (2011). School librarians: The forgotten partners. *Teaching Exceptional Children, 43*(3), 14–20.

Caron, E. A., & McLaughlin, M. J. (2002). Indicators of beacons of excellence schools: What do they tell us about collaborative practices? *Journal of Educational and Psychological Consultation, 13*, 285–313.

Carter, N., Prater, M., Jackson, A., & Marchant, M. (2009). Educators' perceptions of collaborative planning processes for students with disabilities. *Preventing School Failure, 54*, 60–70.

City, E. (2013, April). Leadership in challenging times. *Educational Leadership, 70*(7), 10–14.

Conoley, J., & Conoley, C. (2010). Why does collaboration work? Linking positive psychology and collaboration. *Journal of Educational and Psychological Consultation, 20*, 75–82.

Cook, L., & Friend, M. (2010). The state of the art of collaboration on behalf of students with disabilities: Introduction to the special issue. *Journal of Educational and Psychological Consultation, 20*, 1–8.

D'Agostino, C. (2013). Collaboration as an essential school social work skill. *Children & Schools, 35*, 248–251.

Dever, R., & Lash, M. J. (2013). Using common planning time to foster professional learning. *Middle School Journal, 45*(1), 12–17.

Dibble, R., & Gibson, C. (2013). Collaboration for the common good: An examination of challenges and adjustment processes in multicultural collaborations. *Journal of Organizational Behavior, 34*, 764–790.

DuFour, R., & Mattos, M. (2013). How do principals really improve schools? *Educational Leadership, 70*(7), 34–40.

Dulaney, S. K. (2013). A middle school's response-to-intervention journey: Building systematic processes of facilitation, collaboration, and implementation. *NASSP Bulletin, 97*(1), 53–77.

Ertesvåg, S. K. (2014). Teachers' collaborative activity in school-wide interventions. *Social Psychology of Education.* doi:10.1007/s11218-014-9262-x

Eslinger, J. C. (2014). Navigating between a rock and a hard place: Lessons from an urban school teacher. *Education and Urban Society, 46*, 209–233.

Fidelman, M. (2013, November 11). IBM: These are the top 7 social trends that will emerge in 2014. *Forbes Magazine.* Retrieved from http://www.forbes.com/sites/markfidelman/2013/11/18/ibm-these-are-the-top-7-social-trends-that-will-emerge-in-2014/

Frenkel, K. A. (2014, November). Mobile collaboration: Barriers and opportunities. *CIO Insight, 2*, 2.

Friend, M., & Barron, T. (2015). School to school collaboration. In J. D. Wright (Ed.), *International encyclopedia of the social and behavioral sciences* (2nd ed., vol. 21, pp. 112–118). Oxford, England: Elsevier.

Friend, M., Cook, L., Hurley-Chamberlain, D., & Shamberger, C. (2010). Co-teaching: An illustration of the complexity of collaboration in special education. *Journal of Educational and Psychological Consultation, 20*, 9–27.

Fullerton, A., Ruben, B. J., McBride, S., & Bert, S. (2011). Development and design of a merged secondary and special education teacher preparation program. *Teacher Education Quarterly, 38*(2), 27–44.

Fulton, J., & Myers, B. (2014). Your children, my children. Why not our children?: Dilemmas in early childhood teacher education. *Childhood Education, 90*(1), 3–10.

Garland, A. F., & Brookman-Frazee, L. (2015). Therapists and researchers: Advancing collaboration. *Psychotherapy Research, 25*(1), 95–107.

Geller, J. D., Doykos, B., Craven, K., Bess, K. D., & Nation, M. (2014). Engaging residents in community change: The critical role of trust in the development of a promise neighborhood. *Teachers College Record, 116*, 955–991.

Gobillot, E. (2011). *Leadershift: Reinventing leadership for the age of mass collaboration.* London: Kogan Page.

Goman, C. K. (2014). Collaborative leadership. *Leadership Excellence, 31*(4), 35.

Goold, M., & Barber, F. (2014). *Collaboration strategy: How to get what you want from employees, suppliers and business partners.* New York, NY: Bloomsbury Information Ltd.

Harlacher, J. E., & Siler, C. E. (2011). Factors related to successful RTI implementation. *Communique, 39*(6), 20–22.

Harvard Business Review. (2013). *HBR's 10 must reads on collaboration.* Cambridge, MA: Harvard Business Publishing.

Henning, N. (2013). We make the road by walking together: New teachers and the collaborative and context-specific appropriation of shared social justice-oriented practices and concepts. *Teaching and Teacher Education, 36,* 121–131.

Henry, L. A., Castek, J., O'Byrne, W. I., & Zawilinski, L. (2012). Using peer collaboration to support online reading, writing, and communication: An empowerment model for struggling readers. *Reading & Writing Quarterly, 28,* 279–306.

Honigsfeld, A., & Dove, M. G. (Eds.). (2012b). *Co-teaching and other collaborative practices in the EFL/ESL classroom.* Charlotte, NC: Information Age Publishing.

Hord, S. M. (2009). Professional learning communities. *Journal of Staff Development, 30*(1), 40–43.

Huberman, M., Navo, M., & Parrish, T. (2012). Effective practices in high performing districts serving students in special education. *Journal of Special Education Leadership, 25*(2), 59–71.

Johannessen, A., & Steihaug, S. (2014). The significance of professional roles in collaboration on patients' transitions from hospital to home via an intermediate unit. *Scandinavian Journal of Caring Sciences, 28,* 364–372.

Kampwirth, T. J., & Powers, K. M. (2015). *Collaborative consultation in the schools: Effective practices for students with learning and behavior problems* (5th ed.). E-book version. Upper Saddle River, NJ: Pearson.

Katz, J., & Sugden, R. (2013). The three-block model of universal design for learning implementation in a high school. *Canadian Journal of Educational Administration and Policy, 141.* Retrieved from http://files.eric.ed.gov/fulltext/EJ1008728.pdf

Knox, J. A., & Anfara, V. J. (2013). Understanding job satisfaction and its relationship to student academic performance. *Middle School Journal, 44*(3), 58–64.

Kuehner-Hebert, K. (2014, October). Teaching collaboration at MasterCard: Priceless. *Chief Learning Officer.* Retrieved from http://www.clomedia.com/articles/5898-teaching-collaboration-at-mastercard-priceless

Lalvani, P. (2013). Privilege, compromise, or social justice: Teachers' conceptualizations of inclusive education. *Disability & Society, 28*(1), 14–27.

Lopez, A. E. (2013). Collaborative mentorship: A mentoring approach to support and sustain teachers for equity and diversity. *Mentoring & Tutoring: Partnership in Learning, 21,* 292–311.

Ludlow, B. (2011). Collaboration. *Teaching Exceptional Children, 43*(3), 4.

Mangin, M., & Stoelinga, S. R. (2010). The future of instructional teacher leader roles. *Educational Forum, 74*(1), 49–62.

Martinez, M. (2010). Does group IQ trump individual IQ? *Phi Delta Kappan, 92*(1), 72–73.

McCoach, D. B., Goldstein, J., Behuniak, P., Reis, S. M., Black, A. C., Sullivan, E. E., & Rambo, K. (2010). Examining the unexpected: Outlier analyses of factors affecting student achievement. *Journal of Advanced Academics, 21,* 426–468.

McComb, S., & Simpson, V. (2014). The concept of shared mental models in healthcare collaboration. *Journal of Advanced Nursing, 70,* 1479–1488.

McKenzie, H. S. (1972). Special education and consulting teachers. In F. Clark, D. Evans, & L. Hammerlynk (Eds.), *Implementing behavioral programs for schools and clinics.* Champaign, IL: Research Press.

Miller, G. E., Arthur-Stanley, A., & Lines, C. (2012). Family-school collaboration services: Beliefs into action. *Communique, 40*(5), 1.

Murawski, W. W. (2012). Ten tips for using co-planning time more efficiently. *Teaching Exceptional Children, 44*(4), 8–15.

Nappi, J. S. (2014). The teacher leader: Improving schools by building social capital through shared leadership. *Delta Kappa Gamma Bulletin, 80*(4), 29–34.

National Association of Secondary School Principals. (2013). Clarke Central High School: One student at a time. *Principal Leadership, 13*(9), 26–31.

Nellis, L. M., Sickman, L. S., Newman, D. S., & Harman, D. R. (2014). Schoolwide collaboration to prevent and address reading difficulties: Opportunities for school psychologists and speech-language pathologists. *Journal of Educational & Psychological Consultation, 24,* 110–127.

Noonan, J. (2014). In here, out there: Professional learning and the process of school improvement. *Harvard Educational Review, 84,* 145–161.

Officer, S. H., Grim, J., Medina, M. A., Bringle, R. G., & Foreman, A. (2013). Strengthening community schools through university partnerships. *Peabody Journal of Education, 88,* 564–577.

Olivos, E. M. (2009). Collaboration with Latino families: A critical perspective of home–school interactions. *Intervention in School and Clinic, 45,* 109–115.

Pugach, M. C., Johnson, L. J., Drame, E. R., & Williamson, P. (2012). *Collaborative practitioners, collaborative schools* (3rd ed.). Denver, CO: Love Publishing.

Raven, B. H. (2008). The bases of power and the power/interaction model of interpersonal influence. *Analyses of Social Issues and Public Policy, 8*(1), 1–22.

Ray, J. A. (2005). Family-friendly teachers: Tips for working with diverse families. *Kappa Delta Pi Record, 41,* 72–76.

Reardon, C. (2011, July/August). A decade of *Social Work Today*—10 trends that transformed social work. *Social Work Today, 11*(4), 10.

Richardson, J. (2011). The ultimate practitioner. *Phi Delta Kappan, 93,* 27–32.

Savina, E., Simon, J., & Lester, M. (2014). School reintegration following psychiatric hospitalization: An ecological perspective. *Child & Youth Care Forum, 43,* 729–746.

Silverman, S. K., Hazelwood, C., & Cronin, P. (2009). *Universal education: Principles and practices for advancing achievement of students with disabilities,* 1–8. Retrieved September 29, 2011 from http://ohioleadership.org/up_doc/Universal_Ed_Report_2009-08.pdf

Solomon, J. (2009). The Boston teacher residency: District-based teacher education. *Journal of Teacher Education, 60,* 478–488.

Sparks, D. (2013). Strong teams, strong schools: Teacher-to-teacher collaboration creates synergy that benefits students. *Journal of Staff Development, 34*(2), 28–30.

Stearns, E., Banerjee, N., Mickelson, R., & Moller, S. (2014). Collective pedagogical teacher culture, teacher–student ethno-racial mismatch, and teacher job satisfaction. *Social Science Research, 45,* 56–72.

Stichler, J. F. (2014). Interprofessional practice: Magic at the intersection. *Health Environments Research & Design Journal (HERD), 7*(3), 9–12.

Sun, M., Penuel, W. R., Frank, K. A., Gallagher, H., & Youngs, P. (2013). Shaping professional development to promote the diffusion of instructional expertise among teachers. *Educational Evaluation and Policy Analysis, 35,* 344–369.

Taylor, M. J., Hallam, P. R., Charlton, C. T., & Wall, D. (2014). Formative assessment of collaborative teams (FACT): Development of a grade-level instructional team checklist. *NASSP Bulletin, 98*(1), 26–52.

Tharp, R., & Wetzel, R. (1969). *Behavior modification in the natural environment.* New York: Academic Press.

Thew, M. D. (2014). Partnerships, collaboration and fidelity in the provision of special education programs and services. *Journal of Special Education Leadership, 27*(1), 46–47.

U.S. Department of Education, Office of Planning, Evaluation and Policy Development. (2010). *ESEA Blueprint for Reform.* Washington, DC: Author.

Vuorinen, T., Sandberg, A., Sheridan, S., & Williams, P. (2014). Preschool teachers' views on competence in the context of home and preschool collaboration. *Early Child Development and Care, 184,* 149–159.

Walsh, J. M. (2012). Co-teaching as a school system strategy for continuous improvement. *Preventing School Failure, 56*(1), 29–36.

Watson, G. D., & Bellon-Harn, M. L. (2014). Speech-language pathologist and general educator collaboration: A model for tier 2 service delivery. *Intervention in School and Clinic, 49,* 237–243.

Weiss, S. L., & Friesen, A. (2014). Capitalizing on curriculum-based measurement for reading: Collaboration within a response to instruction framework. *Journal of Educational and Psychological Consultation, 24,* 96–109.

Williams, S. S., & Williams, J. W. (2014). Workplace wisdom: What educators can learn from the business world. *Journal of Staff Development, 35*(3), 10–14.

Ylimaki, R. M., & Brunner, C. C. (2011). Power and collaboration-consensus/conflict in curriculum leadership: Status quo or change? *American Educational Research Journal, 48,* 1258–1285.

Chapter 2

Adler, R. B., & Elmhorst, J. (2013). *Communicating at work: Principles and practices for business and the professions* (11th ed.). New York, NY: McGraw-Hill.

Adler, R. B., & Proctor, R. F. (2011). *Looking out, looking in* (13th ed.). Boston: Wadsworth.

Adler, R. B., Rodman, G., & du Pré, A. (2014). *Understanding human communication* (12th ed.). New York, NY: Oxford University Press.

Adler, R. B., Rosenfeld, L. B., & Proctor, R. F. (2015). *Interplay: The process of interpersonal communication* (13th ed.). New York, NY: Oxford University Press.

Beebe, S. A., & Masterson, J. T. (2015). *Communicating in small groups: Principles and practices* (11th ed.). Upper Saddle River, NJ: Pearson Higher Education.

Beebe, S. A., Beebe, S. J., & Redmond, M. V. (2014). *Interpersonal communication: Relating to others* (7th ed.). Upper Saddle River, NJ: Pearson.

Brantley, C., & Miller, M. (2008). *Effective communication for colleges* (11th ed.). Mason, OH: Thomson South-Western.

Cooper, K. S. (2014). Eliciting engagement in the high school classroom: A mixed-methods examination of teaching practices. *American Educational Research Journal, 51,* 363–402.

Council of Chief State School Officers. (2011, April). *Interstate Teacher Assessment and Support Consortium (InTASC) model core teaching standards: A resource for state dialogue.* Washington, DC: Author.

DeVito, J. A. (2013). *The interpersonal communication book* (13th ed.). Upper Saddle River, NJ: Pearson.

DeVito, J. A. (2015). *Human communication: The basic course* (13th ed.). Upper Saddle River, NJ: Pearson.

Floyd, K. (2014). Interpersonal communication's peculiar identity crisis. *Communication Studies, 65,* 429–431.

Goodman, G. (1978). *SASHA tape user's manual.* Unpublished manuscript, Department of Psychology, University of California, Los Angeles.

Goodman, G. (1984). SASHA tapes: Expanding options for help-intended communication. In D. Larson (Ed.), *Teaching psychological skills: Models for giving psychology away* (pp. 271–286). Monterey, CA: Brooks/Cole.

Hammond, J., & Morrison, J. (1996). *The stuff Americans are made of.* New York: Macmillan.

Harris, T. E., & Sherblom, J. C. (2011). *Small group and team communication* (5th ed.). Boston: Allyn & Bacon.

Hofstede, G. (1997). *Cultures and organizations: Software of the mind.* New York: McGraw-Hill.

Horvath, C. W. (1995). Biological origins of communicator style. *Communication Quarterly, 43,* 394–407.

Kim, J., Seo, M., Yu, H., & Neuendorf, K. (2014). Cultural differences in preference for entertainment messages that induce mixed responses of joy and sorrow. *Human Communication Research, 40,* 530–552.

Knapp, M. L., & Vangelisti, A. L. (2014). *Interpersonal communication and human relationships* (7th ed.). Upper Saddle River, NJ: Pearson.

Ladd, G. W., Kochenderfer-Ladd, B., Visconti, K. J., Ettekal, I., Sechler, C. M., & Cortes, K. I. (2014). Grade-school children's social collaborative skills: Links with partner preference and achievement. *American Educational Research Journal, 51,* 152–183.

Le Fevre, D. M., & Robinson, V. J. (2015). The interpersonal challenges of instructional leadership: Principals' effectiveness in conversations about performance issues. *Educational Administration Quarterly, 51*(1), 58–95.

Lustig, M. W., & Koester, J. (2013). *Intercultural competence: Interpersonal communication across cultures* (7th ed.). Upper Saddle River, NJ: Pearson.

Lynch, E. W. (2011b). Developing cross-cultural competence. In E. W. Lynch & M. J. Hanson (Eds.), *Developing cross-cultural competence: A guide for working with children and their families* (4th ed., pp. 41–77). Baltimore: Paul H. Brookes.

Martin, J. N., & Nakayama, T. K. (2015). Reconsidering intercultural (communication) competence in the workplace: A dialectical approach. *Language & Intercultural Communication, 15*(1), 13–28.

McCroskey, J. C., & Beatty, M. J. (2000). The communibiological perspective: Implications for communication in instruction. *Communication Education, 49,* 1–6.

McKay, M., Davis, M., & Fanning, P. (2009). *Messages: The communication skills book* (3rd ed.). Oakland, CA: New Harbinger.

Rothstein-Fisch, C., Trumbull, E., & Garcia, S. G. (2009). Making the implicit explicit: Supporting teachers to bridge cultures. *Early Childhood Research Quarterly, 24,* 474–486.

Samovar, L. A., Porter, R. E., McDaniel, E. R., & Roy, C. S. (2013). *Communication between cultures* (8th ed.). Boston, MA: Wadsworth.

Spitzberg, B. H. (2000). What is good communication? *Journal of the Association for Communication Administration, 29,* 103–119.

Steinfatt, T. M. (2009). Definitions of communication. In S. W. Littlejohn & K. A. Foss (Eds.), *Encyclopedia of communication theory*. Thousand Oaks, CA: Sage.

Trenholm, S. (2014). *Thinking through communication: An introduction to the study of human communication* (7th ed.). Upper Saddle River, NJ: Pearson.

Trumbull, E., & Rothstein-Fisch, C. (2008). Cultures in harmony. *Educational Leadership, 66*(1), 63–66.

Tuleja, E. A. (2014). Developing cultural intelligence for global leadership through mindfulness. *Journal of Teaching in International Business, 25*(1), 5–24.

van Hoorn, A. (2015). Individualist–collectivist culture and trust radius: A multilevel approach. *Journal of Cross-Cultural Psychology, 46*(2), 269–276.

Ventura, M., Salanova, M., & Llorens, S. (2015). Professional self-efficacy as a predictor of burnout and engagement: The role of challenge and hindrance demands. *Journal of Psychology: Interdisciplinary and Applied, 149,* 277–302.

Watkins, R., & Eatman, J. (2001). An introduction to cross-cultural communication. In *Cross-cultural considerations in early childhood special education* (Technical Report #14: Chapter 2 [Electronic version]). Champaign-Urbana, IL: Culturally and Linguistically Appropriate Services [CLAS] for Early Childhood Research Institute.

Watzlawick, P., & Beavin, J. (1967). Some formal aspects of communication. *American Behavioral Scientist, 10*(8), 4–8.

Wood, J. T. (2013). *Interpersonal communication: Everyday encounters* (7th ed.). Boston, MA: Wadsworth.

Chapter 3

Adler, R. B., Rodman, G., & du Pré, A. (2014). *Understanding human communication* (12th ed.). New York, NY: Oxford University Press.

Balconi, M., & Pagani, S. (2015). Social hierarchies and emotions: Cortical prefrontal activity, facial feedback (EMG), and cognitive performance in a dynamic interaction. *Social Neuroscience, 10,* 166–178.

Bawany, S. (2014). Leadership communication. *Leadership Excellence, 31*(9), 31.

Beebe, S. A., Beebe, S. J., & Redmond, M. V. (2014). *Interpersonal communication: Relating to others* (7th ed.). Upper Saddle River, NJ: Pearson.

Beukeboom, C. (2008). When words feel right: How affective expressions of listeners change a speaker's language use. *European Journal of Social Psychology, 39*(5), 747–756.

Boyd, S. D. (2001). The human side of teaching: Effective listening. *Techniques: Connecting Education and Careers, 76*(7), 60–62.

Buck, R., & Miller, M. (2015). Beyond facial expression: Spatial distance as a factor in the communication of discrete emotions. In A. Kostić & D. Chadee (Eds.), *The social psychology of nonverbal communication* (pp. 173–197). New York, NY: Palgrave Macmillan.

Bulach, C. R. (2003). The impact of human relations training on levels of openness and trust. *Research for Educational Reform, 8*(4), 43–57.

Burgoon, J. K., Proudfoot, J. G., Schuetzler, R., & Wilson, D. (2014). Patterns of nonverbal behavior associated with truth and deception: Illustrations from three experiments. *Journal of Nonverbal Behavior, 38,* 325–354.

Claeys, A., & Cauberghe, V. (2014). Keeping control: The importance of nonverbal expressions of power by organizational spokespersons in times of crisis. *Journal of Communication, 64,* 1160–1180.

DeVito, J. A. (2013). *The interpersonal communication book* (13th ed.). Upper Saddle River, NJ: Pearson.

Egan, G. (2014). *The skilled helper* (10th ed.). Belmont, CA: Brookes/Cole, Cengage Learning.

Elkins, A. C., & Derrick, D. C. (2013). The sound of trust: Voice as a measurement of trust during interactions with Embodied Conversational Agents. *Group Decision and Negotiation, 22,* 897–913.

Gamble, T. K., & Gamble, M. (2013). *Communication works* (10th ed.). New York, NY: McGraw-Hill.

Goodman, G. (1978). *SASHA tape user's manual*. Unpublished manuscript, Department of Psychology, University of California, Los Angeles.

Goulston, M. (2010). *Just listen: Discover the secret to getting through to absolutely anyone*. New York: American Management Association.

Hall, E. T. (1966). *The hidden dimension*. Garden City, NY: Doubleday.

Houmanfar, R. (2013). Performance feedback: From component analysis to application. *Journal of Organizational Behavior Management, 33,* 85–88.

Hybels, S., & Weaver, R. (2012). *Communicating effectively* (10th ed.). New York: McGraw-Hill.

Ivey, A. E., & Ivey, M. B. (2014). *Intentional interviewing and counseling: Facilitating client development in a multicultural society* (7th ed.). Belmont, CA: Brooks/Cole, Cengage Learning.

Ivey, A. E., Ivey, M. B., Zalaquett, C. P., & Quirk, K. (2016). *Essentials of intentional interviewing: Counseling in a multicultural world* (3rd ed.). Belmont, CA: Brooks/Cole, Cengage Learning.

Johnson, D. W. (2013). *Reaching out: Interpersonal effectiveness and self-actualization* (11th ed.). Upper Saddle River, NJ: Pearson.

Jones, J. M. (2010). What do you know about cultural styles? *Communique, 38*(7), 1, 20.

Kang, S., Tversky, B., & Black, J. B. (2015). Coordinating gesture, word, and diagram: Explanations for experts and novices. *Spatial Cognition and Computation, 15,* 1–26.

Koppensteiner, M., Stephan, P., & Jäschke, J. M. (2015). From body motion to cheers: Speakers' body movements as predictors of applause. *Personality and Individual Differences, 74,* 182–185.

Kostić, A., & Chadee, D. (2015). Emotional recognition, fear, and nonverbal behavior. In A. Kostić & D. Chadee (Eds.), *The social psychology of nonverbal communication* (pp. 134–150). New York, NY: Palgrave Macmillan.

Kuntze, J., Molen, H. T., & Born, M. P. (2009). Increasing counseling communication skills after basic and advanced microskills training. *The British Journal of Educational Psychology, 79,* 175–188.

Lynch, E. W. (2011a). Conceptual framework: From culture shock to cultural learning. In E. W. Lynch & M. J. Hanson (Eds.), *Developing cross-cultural competence: A guide for working with children and their families* (4th ed., pp. 20–40). Baltimore: Paul H. Brookes.

Mancillas, A. (2005, October). Empathic invalidations. *Counseling Today,* pp. 9, 19.

Mara, M., & Appel, M. (2015). Effects of lateral head tilt on user perceptions of humanoid and android robots. *Computers in Human Behavior, 44,* 326–334.

McNaughton, D., Hamlin, D., McCarthy, J., Head-Reeves, D., & Schreiner, M. (2007). Learning to listen: Teaching an active listening strategy to preservice education professionals. *Topics in Early Childhood Special Education, 27*(4), 223–231.

Mehu, M., & van der Maaten, L. (2014). Multimodal integration of dynamic audio–visual cues in the communication of agreement and disagreement. *Journal of Nonverbal Behavior, 38,* 569–597.

Pozzato, L. R. (2010). Interpreting nonverbal communication for use in detecting deception. *Forensic Examiner, 19,* 86–97.

Public Broadcasting System. (2005). *Martha Graham:About the dancer. American Masters Series.* Retrieved October 1, 2011, from www.pbs.org/wnet/americanmasters/episodes/martha-graham/about-the-dancer/497

Rogers, C. R. (1951). *Client-centered therapy: Its current practice, implications, and theory.* Boston: Houghton Mifflin.

Ruben, M. A., Hall, J. A., & Mast, M. S. (2015). Smiling in a job interview: When less is more. *Journal of Social Psychology, 155,* 107–126.

Ryan, E. B., Giles, H., & Sebastian, R. J. (1982). An integrative perspective for the study of attitudes toward language variation. In E. B. Ryan & H. Giles (Eds.), *Attitudes toward language variation: Social and applied contexts.* London: Arnold.

Seeley, K. (2005). The listening cure: Listening for culture in intercultural psychological treatments. *Psychoanalytic Review, 92*(3), 431–452.

Spunt, R. P. (2013). Mirroring, mentalizing, and the social neuroscience of listening. *International Journal of Listening, 27,* 61–72.

Stains, R. J. (2012). Reflection for connection: Deepening dialogue through reflective processes. *Conflict Resolution Quarterly, 30,* 33–51.

Stukenbrock, A. (2014). Pointing to an 'empty' space: Deixis am Phantasma in face-to-face interaction. *Journal of Pragmatics, 74,* 70–93.

Trenholm, S. (2014). *Thinking through communication: An introduction to the study of human communication* (7th ed.). Upper Saddle River, NJ: Pearson.

Wood, J. T. (2013). *Interpersonal communication: Everyday encounters* (7th ed.). Boston, MA: Wadsworth.

Chapter 4

Adler, R. B., & Elmhorst, J. (2013). *Communicating at work: Principles and practices for business and the professions* (11th ed.). New York, NY: McGraw-Hill.

Adler, R. B., Rosenfeld, L. B., & Proctor, R. F. (2015). *Interplay: The process of interpersonal communication* (13th ed.). New York, NY: Oxford University Press.

Beebe, S. A., Beebe, S. J., & Redmond, M. V. (2014). *Interpersonal communication: Relating to others* (7th ed.). Upper Saddle River, NJ: Pearson.

Brammer, L. M., & MacDonald, G. (2003). *The helping relationship: Process and skills* (8th ed.). Boston: Allyn & Bacon.

Brantley, C., & Miller, M. (2008). *Effective communication for colleges* (11th ed.). Mason, OH: Thomson South-Western.

Brinkley, R. C. (1989). Getting the most from client interviews. *Performance and Instruction, 28*(4), 5–8.

Cavanagh, M., Bower, M., Moloney, R., & Sweller, N. (2014). The effect over time of a video-based reflection system on preservice teachers' oral presentations. *Australian Journal of Teacher Education, 39*(6), 1–16.

Corey, G. (2013). *Theory and practice of counseling and psychotherapy* (9th ed.). Belmont, CA: Brooks/Cole, Cengage Learning.

Daniels, T., & Ivey, A. (2006). *Microcounseling* (3rd ed.). Springfield, IL: Thomas.

DeVito, J. A. (2013). *The interpersonal communication book* (13th ed.). Upper Saddle River, NJ: Pearson.

Dixon, J. (2013). Effective strategies for communication? Student views of a communication skills course eleven years on. *British Journal of Social Work, 43,* 1190–1205.

Gamble, T. K., & Gamble, M. (2013). *Communication works* (10th ed.). New York, NY: McGraw-Hill.

Hackett, D., & Martin, C. L. (1993). *Facilitation skills for team leaders.* Boston: Thomson.

Hargie, O., Saunders, C., & Dickson, D. (1994). *Social skills in interpersonal communication* (3rd ed.). New York: Routledge.

Heritage, M., & Heritage, J. (2013). Teacher questioning: The epicenter of instruction and assessment. *Applied Measurement in Education, 26,* 176–190.

Ivey, A. E., & Ivey, M. B. (2014). *Intentional interviewing and counseling: Facilitating client development in a multicultural society* (7th ed.). Belmont, CA: Brooks/Cole, Cengage Learning.

Ivey, A. E., Ivey, M. B., Zalaquett, C. P., & Quirk, K. (2016). *Essentials of intentional interviewing: Counseling in a multicultural world* (3rd ed.). Belmont, CA: Brooks/Cole, Cengage Learning.

Jacobs E., Masson, R., & Harvill, R. (2009). *Group counseling: Strategies and skills* (6th ed.). Belmont, CA: Thompson Higher Education.

Johnson, D. W. (2013). *Reaching out: Interpersonal effectiveness and self-actualization* (11th ed.). Upper Saddle River, NJ: Pearson.

Johnson, D. W., & Johnson, F. P. (2013). *Joining together: Group theory and group skills* (11th ed.). Upper Saddle River, NJ: Pearson Higher Education.

Johnson, S. D., & Roellke, C. F. (1999). Secondary teachers' and undergraduate education faculty members' perceptions of teaching-effectiveness criteria: A national survey [Electronic version]. *Communication Education, 48*, 127–138.

Knapp, M. L., & Vangelisti, A. L. (2014). *Interpersonal communication and human relationships* (7th ed.). Upper Saddle River, NJ: Pearson.

Liao, H. (2006). Toward an epistemology of participatory communication: A feminist perspective. *Howard Journal of Communications, 17*(2), 101–118.

Littauer, H., Sexton, H., & Wolf, R. (2005). Qualities clients wish for in their therapists. *Scandinavian Journal of Caring Sciences, 19*(1), 28–31.

McKay, M., Davis, M., & Fanning, P. (2009). *Messages: The communication skills book* (3rd ed.). Oakland, CA: New Harbinger.

McKenzie, F. (2014). *Interviewing for the helping professions: A relationship approach*. Chicago, IL: Lyceum.

Moore, J. K. (2014). The reflective observer model. *Conflict Resolution Quarterly, 31*, 403–419

National School Public Relations Association. (2011). *Communication survey: Results and analysis*. Rockville, MD: Author. Retrieved from www.nspra.org/2011capsurvey

Patterson, K., Grenny, J., McMillan, R., & Switzler, A. (2002). *Crucial conversations: Tools for talking when stakes are high* (2nd ed.). New York, NY: McGraw-Hill.

Powell, M. B., Hughes-Scholes, C. H., & Sharman, S. J. (2012). Skill in interviewing reduces confirmation bias. *Journal of Investigative Psychology and Offender Profiling, 9*, 126–134.

Richardson, J. V. (2002). *Open versus closed-ended questions*. Retrieved from http://polaris.gseis.ucla.edu/jrichardson/dis220/openclosed.htm

Roulston, K. (2014). Interactional problems in research interviews. *Qualitative Research, 14*, 277–293.

Schein, E. H. (2013). *Humble inquiry: The gentle art of asking instead of telling*. San Francisco, CA: Berrett-Koehler.

Sternberg, K., Lamb, M., Hershkowitz, I., Esplio, P., Redlich, A., & Sunshine, N. (1996). The relationship between investigative utterance types and informativeness of child witnesses. *Journal of Applied Developmental Psychology, 17*, 439–451.

Stewart, C., & Cash, W. (2014). *Interviewing: Principles and practices* (14th ed.). New York, NY: McGraw-Hill Higher Education.

Turnbull, A. P., Turnbull, H. R., Erwin, E., Soodak, L., & Shogren, K. A. (2015). *Families, professionals, and exceptionality: Positive outcomes through partnerships and trust* (7th ed.). Upper Saddle River, NJ: Pearson Higher Education.

Wolf, R. (1979). *Strategies for conducting naturalistic evaluation in socio-educational settings: The naturalistic interview*. Kalamazoo, MI: Occasional Series, Evaluation Center, Western Michigan University.

Chapter 5

Anderson, E. S., & Lennox, A. (2009). The Leicester model of interprofessional education: Developing, delivering and learning from student voices for 10 years. *Journal of Interprofessional Care, 23*, 557–573.

Aramovich, N. P. (2014). The effect of stereotype threat on group versus individual performance. *Small Group Research, 45*, 176–197.

Aramovich, N. P., & Larson, J. R. (2013). Strategic demonstration of problem solutions by groups: The effects of member preferences, confidence, and learning goals. *Organizational Behavior & Human Decision Processes, 122*, 36–52.

Arslan, E. (2010). Analysis of communication skill and interpersonal problem solving in preschool trainees. *Social Behavior and Personality: An International Journal, 38*, 523–530.

Artiles, A. J., Kozleski, E. B., Trent, S. C., Osher, D., & Ortiz, A. (2010). Justifying and explaining disproportionality, 1968–2008: A critique of underlying views of culture. *Exceptional Children, 76*, 279–299.

Bal, A., Sullivan, A. L., & Harper, J. (2014). A situated analysis of special education disproportionality for systemic transformation in an urban school district. *Remedial and Special Education, 35*, 3–14.

Brightman, H. J. (2002). *Group problem solving: An improved managerial approach*. East Lansing: Michigan State University Press.

Carey, R., & Jasgur, R. (2014). Forget the process—What's the problem? *Mortgage Banking, 74*(12), 76–80.

Carmeli, A., Sheaffer, Z., Binyamin, G., Reiter-Palmon, R., & Shimoni T. (2014). Transformational leadership and creative problem-solving: The mediating role of psychological safety and reflexivity. *Journal of Creative Behavior, 48*, 115–135.

Castellano, S. (2013). (Brain)storm chasers. *T+D, 67*(11), 16.

Castledine, G. (2010). Team nursing: Finding the ideal. *British Journal of Nursing (BJN), 19*(13), 869.

Cheatham, G. A., & Jimenez-Silva, M. (2012). Partnering with Latino families during kindergarten transition: Lessons learned from a parent-teacher conference. *Childhood Education, 88*, 177–184.

Chiu, M. M. (2000). Effects of status on solutions, leadership, and evaluations during group problem solving [Electronic version]. *Sociology of Education, 73*, 175–195.

Cho, H., & Kingston, N. (2013). Why IEP teams assign low performers with mild disabilities to the alternate assessment based on alternate achievement standards. *The Journal of Special Education, 47*, 162–174.

Clark, M., & Flynn, P. (2011). Rational thinking in school-based practice. *Language, Speech, and Hearing Services in Schools, 42*, 73–76.

Emelo, R. (2014). Facilitating social learning. *Training Journal, 21*(1), 31–34.

Engelmann, T., Kolodziej, R., & Hesse, F. W. (2014). Preventing undesirable effects of mutual trust and the development of skepticism in virtual groups by applying the knowledge and information awareness approach. *International Journal of Computer-Supported Collaborative Learning, 9*, 211–235.

Fiore, S. M., Wiltshire, T. J., Oglesby, J. M., O'Keefe, W. S., & Salas, E. (2014). Complex collaborative problem-solving processes in mission control. *Aviation, Space, and Environmental Medicine, 85*(4), 456–461.

Gobble, M. M. (2014a). Beyond brainstorming. *Research Technology Management, 57*(2), 60–62.

Gobble, M. M. (2014b). The persistence of brainstorming. *Research Technology Management, 57*(1), 64–66.

Honig, B., Lampel, J., & Drori, I. (2014). Organizational ingenuity: Concept, processes and strategies. *Organization Studies, 35*, 465–482.

Janssen, J., & Bodemer, D. (2013). Coordinated computer-supported collaborative learning: Awareness and awareness tools. *Educational Psychologist, 48*(1), 40–55.

Kampwirth, T. J., & Powers, K. M. (2015). *Collaborative consultation in the schools: Effective practices for students with learning and behavior problems* (5th ed.). E-book version. Upper Saddle River, NJ: Pearson.

Kaye, D. 2013. *Why innovation by brainstorming doesn't work* [Web log post]. Retrieved from http://www.fastcompany.com/3006322/why-innovation-brainstormingdoesnt-work

Knotek, S. (2003). Bias in problem solving and the social process of student study teams: A qualitative investigation. *Journal of Special Education, 37,* 2–14.

Laughlin, P. R. (2011). *Group problem solving.* Princeton, NJ: Princeton University Press.

Liu, S. (2014). Catching FIRE. *Quality Progress, 47*(5), 18–24.

Lopez-Fresno, P., & Savolainen, T. (2014). Working meetings: A tool for building or destroying trust in knowledge creation and sharing. *Electronic Journal of Knowledge Management, 12,* 137–143.

Lyons, R., Lum, H., Fiore, S. M., Salas, E., Warner, N., & Letsky, M. P. (2012). Considering the influence of task complexity on macrocognitive team processes. In E. Salas, S. M. Fiore, & M. P. Letsky (Eds.), *Theories of team cognition: Cross-disciplinary perspectives* (pp. 271–288). New York, NY: Routledge/Taylor & Francis Group.

Martinez, M. (2010/2011). Indiana example of collaboration and innovation. *Phi Delta Kappan, 92*(4), 74–75.

McMillan, S., Kelly, F., Sav, A., Kendall, E., King, M., Whitty, J., & Wheeler, A. (2014). Using the nominal group technique: How to analyse across multiple groups. *Health Services and Outcomes Research Methodology, 14,* 92–108.

Michinov, N. (2012). Is electronic brainstorming or brainwriting the best way to improve creative performance in groups? An overlooked comparison of two idea-generation techniques. *Journal of Applied Social Psychology, 42,* E222–E243.

Monroe, T. (2014). Creative problem solving in a fast-paced, guidance-rich environment. *Defense AT&L, 43*(4), 20–23.

Nardon, L., Steers, R. M., & Sanchez-Runde, C. J. (2011). Seeking common ground: Strategies for enhancing multicultural communication. *Organizational Dynamics, 40,* 85–95.

Newell, M. (2010). The implementation of problem-solving consultation: An analysis of problem conceptualization in a multiracial context. *Journal of Educational and Psychological Consultation, 20,* 83–105.

Newman, D. S., Salmon, D., Cavanaugh, K., & Schneider, M. F. (2014). The consulting role in a response-to-intervention context: An exploratory study of instructional consultation. *Journal of Applied School Psychology, 30,* 278–304.

Paulus, P. B., Kohn, N. W., & Arditti, L. E. (2011). Effects of quantity and quality instructions on brainstorming. *Journal of Creative Behavior, 45*(1), 38–46.

Ray, D. K., & Romano, N. J. (2013). Creative problem solving in GSS groups: Do creative styles matter? *Group Decision and Negotiation, 22,* 1129–1157.

Rijnbout, J. S., & McKimmie, B. M. (2014). Deviance in organizational decision making: Using unanimous decision rules to promote the positive effects and alleviate the negative effects of deviance. *Journal of Applied Social Psychology, 44,* 455–463.

Shelly, R. K., & Shelly, A. C. (2009). Speech content and the emergence of inequality in task groups. *Journal of Social Issues, 65,* 307–333.

Sio, U., & Ormerod, T. (2015). Incubation and cueing effects in problem-solving: Set aside the difficult problems but focus on the easy ones. *Thinking & Reasoning, 21,* 113–129.

Sullivan, A. L. (2011). Disproportionality in special education identification and placement of English language learners. *Exceptional Children, 77,* 317–334.

Tidikis, V., & Ash, I. K. (2013). Working in dyads and alone: Examining process variables in solving insight problems. *Creativity Research Journal, 25,* 189–198.

Trouche, E., Sander, E., & Mercier, H. (2014). Arguments, more than confidence, explain the good performance of reasoning groups. *Journal of Experimental Psychology, 143,* 1958–1971.

VanGundy, A. B. (2005). *101 activities for teaching creativity and problem solving.* San Francisco: Pfeiffer.

Weiss, S. L., & Friesen, A. (2014). Capitalizing on curriculum-based measurement for reading: Collaboration within a response to instruction framework. *Journal of Educational and Psychological Consultation, 24,* 96–109.

Wheelan, S. A. (2009). Group size, group development, and group productivity. *Small Group Research 40,* 247–267.

Chapter 6

Allday, R. A., Neilsen-Gatti, S., & Hudson, T. M. (2013). Preparation for inclusion in teacher education pre-service curricula. *Teacher Education and Special Education, 36,* 298–311.

Armer, B., & Thomas, B. K. (1978). Attitudes towards interdisciplinary collaboration in pupil personnel service teams. *Journal of School Psychology, 16,* 168–177.

Ash, P. B., & D'Auria, J. (2013). Blueprint for a learning system: Create one larger, more flexible team that encourages collaboration in all directions. *Journal of Staff Development, 34*(3), 42–46.

Bang, H., Fuglesang, S. L., Ovesen, M. R., & Eilertsen, D. E. (2010). Effectiveness in top management group meetings: The role of goal clarity, focused communication, and learning behavior. *Scandinavian Journal of Psychology, 51,* 253–261.

Barnard-Brak, L., & Lechtenberger, D. (2010). Student IEP participation and academic achievement across time. *Remedial and Special Education, 31,* 343–349.

Beebe, S. A., & Masterson, J. T. (2015). *Communicating in small groups: Principles and practices* (11th ed.). Upper Saddle River, NJ: Pearson Higher Education.

Berckemeyer, J. (2013). *Taming of the team: How great teams work together.* Chicago, IL: World Book.

Brandel, J., & Loeb, D. F. (2011). Program intensity and service delivery models in the schools: SLP survey results. *Language, Speech, and Hearing Services in Schools, 42*(4), 461–490.

Chalfant, J. C., Pysh, M. V., & Moultrie, R. (1979). Teacher assistance teams: A model for within building problem solving. *Learning Disability Quarterly, 2,* 85–96.

Choi, B. C. K., & Pak, A. W. P. (2007). Multidisciplinarity, interdisciplinarity, and transdisciplinarity in health research, services, education and policy: 2. Promoters, barriers, and strategies of enhancement. *Clinical and Investigative Medicine, 30,* E224–E232.

Cook, R. E., Klein, M. D., & Chen, D. (2012). *Adapting early childhood curricula for children with special needs* (8th ed.). Upper Saddle River, NJ: Pearson Education.

Correa, V. I., Jones, H. A., Thomas, C. C., & Morsink, C. V. (2005). *Interactive teaming: Enhancing programs for students with special needs* (4th ed.). Upper Saddle River, NJ: Merrill/Pearson Education.

Council for Exceptional Children. (2012). *CEC ethical principles for special education professionals.* Retrieved August 6, 2015, from https://www.cec.sped.org/Standards/Ethical-Principles-and-Practice-Standards

Downing, J. E. (2008). *Including students with severe and multiple disabilities in typical classrooms: Practical strategies for teachers* (3rd ed.). Baltimore: Paul H. Brookes.

DuBois, M., Koch, J., Hanlon, J., Nyatuga, B., & Kerr, N. (2015). Leadership styles of effective project managers: Techniques and traits to lead high performance teams. *Journal of Economic Development, Management, IT, Finance & Marketing, 7*(1), 30–46.

Elliott, S. N., & Sheridan, S. M. (1992). Consultation and teaming: Problem-solving among educators, parents, and support personnel. *Elementary School Journal, 92,* 315–338.

Ephross, P. H., & Vassil, T. V. (2005). *Groups that work: Structure and process* (2nd ed.). New York: Columbia University Press.

Fenton, K. S., Yoshida, R. K., Maxwell, J. P., & Kaufman, M. T. (1979). Recognition of team goals: An essential step toward rational decision-making. *Exceptional Children, 45,* 638–644.

Friend, M. (2014). *Co-Teach! Building and sustaining effective classroom partnerships in inclusive schools* (2nd ed.). Greensboro, NC: Marilyn Friend, Inc.

Friend, M., & Barron, T. (2015). School to school collaboration. In J. D. Wright (Ed.), *International encyclopedia of the social and behavioral sciences* (2nd ed., vol. 21, pp. 112–118). Oxford, England: Elsevier.

Fuchs, D., Fuchs, L. S., & Vaughn, S. (2008). *Response to intervention: A framework for reading educators.* Newark, DE: International Reading Association.

Gallivan-Fenlon, A. (1994). Integrated transdisciplinary teams. *Teaching Exceptional Children, 26*(3), 16–20.

Galloway, S. (2015). A model to bridge the gap from compliance to excellence. *Occupational Health & Safety, 84*(4), 62.

Gülcan, M. G. (2014). Comparison of teachers' understanding of team work according to various variables. *Educational Research and Reviews, 9*(2), 59–66.

Gustavson, P., & Liff, S. (2014). *A team of leaders: Empowering every member to take ownership, demonstrate initiative, and deliver results.* New York, NY: American Management Association.

Harris, T. E., & Sherblom, J. C. (2011). *Small group and team communication* (5th ed.). Boston: Allyn & Bacon.

Havnes, A. (2009). Talk, planning and decision-making in interdisciplinary teacher teams: A case study. *Teachers and Teaching, 15*(1), 155–176.

Herman, K. C., Reinke, W. M., Bradshaw, C. P., Lochman, J. E., Borden, L., & Darney, D. (2014). Increasing parental engagement in school-based interventions using team engagement and motivation methods. In M. D. Weist, N. A. Lever, C. P. Bradshaw, & J. Sarno Owens (Eds.), *Handbook of school mental health: Research, training, practice, and policy* (2nd ed., pp. 223–236). New York, NY: Springer Science + Business Media.

Hoover, J. J., & Love, E. (2011). Supporting school-based response to intervention: A practitioner's model. *Teaching Exceptional Children, 43*(3), 40–48.

Howard, V. F., Williams, B. F., & Lepper, C. (2010). *Very young children with special needs: A foundation for educators, families, and service providers* (4th ed.). Upper Saddle River, NJ: Pearson Education.

Hunt, P., Soto, G., Maier, J., Liborion, N., & Bae, S. (2004). Collaborative teaming to support preschoolers with severe disabilities who are placed in general education early childhood programs [Electronic version]. *Topics in Early Childhood Special Education, 24,* 123–142.

Ikeda, M. J., Rahn-Blakeslee, A., Niebling, B. C., Gustafson, J. K., Allison, R., & Stumme, J. (2007). The Heartland Area Education Agency 11 problem-solving approach: An overview and lessons learned. In S. R. Jimerson, M. K. Burns, & A. M. VanDerHeyden (Eds.), *Handbook of response to intervention* (pp. 255–268). New York: Springer.

Jehn, K. A., & Techakesari, P. (2014). High reliability teams: New directions for disaster management and conflict. *International Journal of Conflict Management (Emerald), 25,* 407–430.

Johnson, D. W., & Johnson, F. P. (2013). *Joining together: Group theory and group skills* (11th ed.). Upper Saddle River, NJ: Pearson Higher Education.

Kaiser, S. M., & Woodman, R. W. (1985). Multidisciplinary teams and group decision-making techniques: Possible solutions to decision-making problems. *School Psychology Review, 14,* 457–470.

Kaufman, R. C., & Ring, M. (2011). Pathways to leadership and professional development: Inspiring novice special educators. *Teaching Exceptional Children, 43*(5), 52–60.

Killumets, E., D'Innocenzo, L., Maynard, M. T., & Mathieu, J. E. (2015). A multilevel examination of the impact of team interpersonal processes. *Small Group Research, 46,* 227–259.

Kozlowski, D. V. (2008). Content and viewpoint discrimination: Malleable terms beget malleable doctrine. *Communication Law and Policy, 13*(2), 131–181.

Kozlowski, S. W. J., Gully, S. M., Nason, E. R., & Smith, E. M. (1999). Developing adaptive teams: A theory of compilation and performance across levels and time. In D. R. Ilgen & E. D. Pulakos (Eds.), *The changing nature of work performance: Implications for staffing, personnel actions, and development* (pp. 240–292). San Francisco: Jossey-Bass.

Leader-Janssen, E., Swain, K. D., Delkamiller, J., & Ritzman, M. J. (2012). Collaborative relationships for general education teachers working with students with disabilities. *Journal of Instructional Psychology, 39,* 112–118.

Lentz, K. (2012). *Transformational leadership in special education: Leading the IEP team.* Lanham, MD: Rowman & Littlefield Education.

Levi, D. J. (2014). *Group dynamics for teams*. Thousand Oaks, CA: Sage.

Lhospital, A. S., & Gregory, A. (2009). Changes in teacher stress through participation in pre-referral intervention teams. *Psychology in the Schools, 46,* 1098–1112.

Lustig, M. W., & Koester, J. (2013). *Intercultural competence: Interpersonal communication across cultures* (7th ed.). Upper Saddle River, NJ: Pearson.

Mahdavi, J. N., & Beebe-Frankenberger, M. E. (2009). Pioneering RtI systems that work: Social validity, collaboration, and context. *Teaching Exceptional Children, 42*(2), 64–72.

Maki, K. E., Floyd, R. G., & Roberson, T. (2015). State learning disability eligibility criteria: A comprehensive review. *School Psychology Quarterly*. Advance online publication. doi:10.1037/spq0000109

Marks, M. (2006). The science of team effectiveness. *Psychological Sciences in the Public Interest, 7,* i.

McIntosh, K., Predy, L. K., Upreti, G., Hume, A. E., Turri, M. G., & Mathews, S. (2014). Perceptions of contextual features related to implementation and sustainability of school-wide positive behavior support. *Journal of Positive Behavior Interventions, 16,* 31–43.

McNamara, K., Rasheed, H., & Delamatre, J. (2008). A statewide study of school-based intervention teams: Characteristics, member perceptions, and outcomes. *Journal of Educational and Psychological Consultation, 18,* 5–30.

Mellin, E. A., Bronstein, L., Anderson-Butcher, D., Amorose, A. J., Ball, A., & Green, J. (2010). Measuring interprofessional team collaboration in expanded school mental health: Model refinement and scale development. *Journal of Interprofessional Care, 24*(5), 514–523.

Menninger, W. C. (1950). Mental health in our schools. *Educational Leadership, 7,* 520.

Mueller, T. G. (2009b). IEP facilitation: A promising approach to resolving conflicts between families and schools. *Teaching Exceptional Children, 41*(3), 60–67.

Nellis, L. M., Sickman, L. S., Newman, D. S., & Harman, D. R. (2014). Schoolwide collaboration to prevent and address reading difficulties: Opportunities for school psychologists and speech-language pathologists. *Journal of Educational & Psychological Consultation, 24,* 110–127.

Olivos, E. M., Gallagher, R. J., & Aguilar, J. (2010). Fostering collaboration with culturally and linguistically diverse families of children with moderate to severe disabilities. *Journal of Educational and Psychological Consultation, 20,* 28–40.

Orelove, F., & Sobsey, D. (1987). *Educating children with multiple disabilities: A transdisciplinary approach*. Baltimore: Paul H. Brookes.

Ortiz, A. A., Wilkinson, C. Y., Robertson-Courtney, P., & Kushner, M. I. (2006). Considerations in implementing intervention assistance teams to support English language learners. *Remedial and Special Education, 27*(1), 53–63.

Papalia-Beradi, A., & Hall, T. E. (2007). Teacher assistance team social validity: A perspective from general education teachers. *Education and Treatment of Children, 30*(2), 89–110.

Parthasarathy, R. (2006, Winter). Team up to fail or fail to team up? *Journal for Quality and Participation, 29*(4), 34–37.

Pfeiffer, S. I. (1981). The school based interprofessional team: Recurring problems and some possible solutions. *Journal of School Psychology, 18,* 388–394.

Phillippo, K., & Stone, S. (2006). School-based collaborative teams: An exploratory study of tasks and activities. *Children & Schools, 28*(4), 229–235.

Polsky, L. (2015). Crucibles of change. *Leadership Excellence, 32*(4), 39–40.

Qiu, T., Qualls, W., Bohlmann, J., & Rupp, D. E. (2009). The effect of interactional fairness on the performance of cross-functional product development teams: A multilevel mediated model. *Journal of Product Innovation Management, 26*(2), 173–187.

Rafoth, M. A., & Foriska, T. (2006). Administrator participation in promoting effective problem-solving teams. *Remedial and Special Education, 27,* 130–135.

Rhodes, V., Stevens, D., & Hemmings, A. (2011). Creating positive culture in a new urban high school. *High School Journal, 94*(3), 82–94.

Rice, D. J., Davidson, B. D., Dannenhoffer, J. F., & Gay, G. K. (2007). Improving the effectiveness of virtual teams by adapting team processes. *Computer Supported Cooperative Work: The Journal of Collaborative Computing, 16*(6), 567–594.

Rothstein, L., & Johnson, S. F. (2010). *Special education law* (4th ed.). Thousand Oaks, CA: Sage.

Runhaar, P., ten Brinke, D., Kuijpers, M., Wesselink, R., & Mulder, M. (2014). Exploring the links between interdependence, team learning and a shared understanding among team members: The case of teachers facing an educational innovation. *Human Resource Development International, 17,* 67–87.

Sargeant, J., Loney, E., & Murphy, G. (2008). Effective interprofessional teams: "Contact is not enough" to build a team. *Journal of Continuing Education in the Health Professions, 28,* 228–234.

Sawchuk, S. (2011, April 20). Teacher-led corps helps turn around schools. *Education Week, 30*(28), 1–17.

Schwanenberger, M., & Ahearn, C. (2013). Teacher perceptions of the impact of the data team process on core instructional practices. *International Journal of Educational Leadership Preparation, 8,* 146–162.

Shapiro, D. R., & Sayers, L. K. (2003). Who does what on the interdisciplinary team regarding physical education for students with disabilities? *Teaching Exceptional Children, 36*(6), 32–38.

Silverman, K., Hong, S., & Trepanier-Street, M. (2010). Collaboration of teacher education and child disability health care: Transdisciplinary approach to inclusive practice for early childhood pre-service teachers. *Early Childhood Education Journal, 37,* 461–468.

Slonski-Fowler, K. E., & Truscott, S. D. (2004). General education teachers' perceptions of the prereferral intervention team process. *Journal of Educational and Psychological Consultation, 15,* 1–39.

Snell, M. E., & Janney, R. (2005). *Collaborative teaming* (2nd ed.). Baltimore: Paul H. Brookes.

Sugai, G., & Horner, R. H. (2009). Response to intervention and school-wide positive behavior supports: Integration of multi-tiered systems approaches. *Exceptionality, 17,* 233–237.

Taylor, M. J., Hallam, P. R., Charlton, C. T., & Wall, D. (2014). Formative assessment of collaborative teams (FACT): Development of a grade-level instructional team checklist. *NASSP Bulletin, 98*(1), 26–52.

Torres-Rodriguez, L., Beyard, K., & Goldstein, M. B. (2010). Critical elements of student assistance programs: A qualitative study. *Children & Schools, 32*(2), 93–102.

Tuckman, B. W. (1965). Developmental sequence in small groups. *Psychological Bulletin, 63*, 384–399.

Tuckman, B. W., & Jensen, M. A. (1977). Stages of small group development revisited. *Group and Organizational Studies, 2*, 419–427.

Villa, R. A., Thousand, J. S., & Nevin, A. I. (2008). *A guide to co-teaching: Practical tips for facilitating student learning* (2nd ed.). Thousand Oaks, CA: Corwin.

Vujnovic, R. K., Fabiano, G. A., Morris, K. L., Norman, K., Hallmark, C., & Hartley, C. (2014). Examining school psychologists' and teachers' application of approaches within a response to intervention framework. *Exceptionality, 22*, 129–140.

Walker, J. S., & Schutte, K. (2005). Quality and individualization in wraparound team planning. *Journal of Child and Family Studies, 14*, 251–267.

Walter, U. M., & Petr, C. G. (2011). Best practices in wraparound: A multidimensional view of the evidence. *Social Work, 56*(1), 73–80.

Weaver, S. J., Rosen, M. A., Salas, E., Baum, K. D., & King, H. B. (2010). Integrating the science of team training: Guidelines for continuing education. *Journal of Continuing Education in the Health Professions, 30*(4), 208–220.

White, C., Vanc, A., & Stafford, G. (2010). Internal communication, information satisfaction, and sense of community: The effect of personal influence. *Journal of Public Relations Research, 22*(1), 65–84.

Yell, M. L. (2012). *The law and special education* (3rd ed.). Upper Saddle River, NJ: Pearson Education.

Young, H. L., & Gaughan, E. (2010). A multiple method longitudinal investigation of pre-referral intervention team functioning: Four years in rural schools. *Journal of Educational and Psychological Consultation, 20*(2), 106–138.

Chapter 7

Anderson, L. M., & Stillman, J. A. (2013). Student teaching's contribution to preservice teacher development: A review of research focused on the preparation of teachers for urban and high-needs contexts. *Review of Educational Research, 83*, 3–69.

Ashbaker, B. Y., & Morgan, J. (2012b). *Paraprofessionals in the classroom: A survival guide* (2nd ed.). Upper Saddle River, NJ: Pearson.

Bacharach, N., Heck, T. W., & Dahlberg, K. (2010). Changing the face of student teaching through coteaching. *Action in Teacher Education, 32*, 3–14.

Basso, D., & McCoy, N. (2009). *The co-teaching manual: How general education teachers and specialists work together to educate students in an inclusive classroom* (4th ed.). Columbia, SC: Twins Publications.

Bauwens, J., Hourcade, J. J., & Friend, M. (1989). Cooperative teaching: A model for general and special education integration. *Remedial and Special Education, 10*(2), 17–22.

Boscardin, M. L., Mainzer, R., & Kealy, M. V. (2011). Commentary: A response to "Preparing special education administrators for inclusion in diverse, standards-based contexts," by Deborah L. Voltz and Loucrecia Collins. *Teacher Education and Special Education, 34*, 71–78.

Brinkmann, J., & Twiford, T. (2012). Voices from the field: Skill sets needed for effective collaboration and co-teaching. *International Journal of Educational Leadership Preparation, 7*, 1–13.

Brown, N., Howerter, C. S., & Morgan, J. (2013). Tools and strategies for making co-teaching work. *Intervention in School and Clinic, 49*, 84–91.

Brusca-Vega, R., Brown, K., & Yasutake, D. (2011). Science achievement of students in co-taught, inquiry-based classrooms. *Learning Disabilities: A Multidisciplinary Journal, 17*(1), 23–31.

Causton, J., & Theoharis, G. (2013). Inclusive schooling: Are we there yet? *School Administrator, 70*(2), 19–25.

Causton-Theoharis, J., & Theoharis, G. (2008). Creating inclusive schools for all students. *School Administrator, 65*(8), 24–25.

Charles, K. J., & Dickens, V. (2012). Closing the communication gap: Web 2.0 tools for enhanced planning and collaboration. *Teaching Exceptional Children, 45*(2), 24–32.

Cirrin, F. M., Schooling, T. L., Nelson, N. W., Diehl, S. F., Flynn, P. F., Staskowski, M., ... Adamczyk, D. F. (2010). Evidence-based systematic review: Effects of different service delivery models on communication outcomes for elementary school-age children. *Language, Speech, and Hearing Services in Schools, 41*, 233–264.

Conderman, G. (2011b). Middle school co-teaching: Effective practices and student reflections. *Middle School Journal, 42*(4), 24–31.

Conderman, G., & Hedin, L. (2012). Purposeful assessment practices for co-teachers. *Teaching Exceptional Children, 44*(4), 18–27.

Crespin, B. J. (1971). Means of facilitating education sought. *Education, 92*(2), 36–37.

Dessenmontet, R. S., & Bless, G. (2013). The impact of including children with intellectual disability in general education classrooms on the academic achievement of their low-, average-, and high-achieving peers. *Journal of Intellectual & Developmental Disability, 38*, 23–30.

Eisenman, L. T., Pleet, A. M., Wandry, D., & McGinley, V. (2011). Voices of special education teachers in an inclusive high school: Redefining responsibilities. *Remedial and Special Education, 32*, 91–104.

Embury, D. C., & Dinnesen, M. S. (2012). Planning for co-teaching in inclusive classrooms using structured collaborative planning. *Kentucky Journal of Excellence in College Teaching and Learning, 10*(31), 36–52.

Fenty, N. S., McDuffie-Landrum, K., & Fisher, G. (2012). Using collaboration, co-teaching, and question answer relationships to enhance content area literacy. *Teaching Exceptional Children, 44*(6), 28–37.

Forbes, L., & Billet, S. (2012). Successful co-teaching in the science classroom. *Science Scope, 36*(1), 61–64.

Friend, M. (2007). The co-teaching partnership. *Educational Leadership, 64*(5), 58–62.

Friend, M. (2014). *Co-Teach! Building and sustaining effective classroom partnerships in inclusive schools* (2nd ed.). Greensboro, NC: Marilyn Friend, Inc.

Friend, M., Burrello, L., & Burrello, J. (2009). *More power: Instruction in co-taught classes*. Bloomington, IN: Forum on Education, Indiana University.

Friend, M., Cook, L., Hurley-Chamberlain, D., & Shamberger, C. (2010). Co-teaching: An illustration of the complexity of collaboration in special education. *Journal of Educational and Psychological Consultation, 20*, 9–27.

Friend, M., Embury, D. C., & Clarke, L. (2015). Co-teaching and apprentice teaching: An analysis of similarities and differences. *Teacher Education and Special Education*.

Geen, A. G. (1985). Team teaching in the secondary schools of England and Wales. *Educational Review, 37*, 29–38.

Giangreco, M. F., Suter, J. C., & Hurley, S. M. (2013). Revisiting personnel utilization in inclusion-oriented schools. *Journal of Special Education, 47*, 121–132.

Graziano, K. J., & Navarrete, L. A. (2012). Co-teaching in a teacher education classroom: Collaboration, compromise, and creativity. *Issues in Teacher Education, 21*, 109–126.

Gürür, H., & Uzuner, Y. (2010). A phenomenological analysis of the views on co-teaching: Applications in the inclusion classroom. *Educational Sciences: Theory & Practice, 10*, 311–331.

Hang, Q., & Rabren, K. (2009). An examination of co-teaching: Perspectives and efficacy indicators. *Remedial and Special Education, 30*, 259–268.

Honigsfeld, A., & Dove, M. G. (2012a). Collaborative practices to support all students. *Principal Leadership, 12*(6), 40–44.

Howard, L., & Potts, E. A. (2009). Using co-planning time: Strategies for a successful co-teaching marriage. *Teaching Exceptional Children Plus, 5*(4). Retrieved from http://www.eric.ed.gov/contentdelivery/servlet/ERICServlet?accno=EJ967747

Huber, J. J. (2005). Collaborative units for addressing multiple grade levels. *Intervention in School and Clinic, 40*, 301–308.

Hunt, J. H. (2010). Master geometry while coteaching. *Mathematics Teaching in the Middle School, 16*, 154–161.

Kamens, M., Susko, J. P., & Elliott, J. S. (2013). Evaluation and supervision of co-teaching: A study of administrator practices in New Jersey. *NASSP Bulletin, 97*, 166–190.

Lange, C., Huff, K. L., Silverman, S., & Wallace, K. (2012). How to use the science of snow to engage middle school students in an interdisciplinary experience. *Science Activities: Classroom Projects and Curriculum Ideas, 49*(2), 37–43.

Madigan, J. C., & Schroth-Cavataio, G. (2011). Building collaborative partnerships. *Principal Leadership, 12*(3), 26–30.

McClure, G., & Cahnmann-Taylor, M. (2010). Pushing back against push-in: ESOL teacher resistance and the complexities of co-teaching. *TESOL Journal, 1*(1), 101–129.

Moorehead, T., & Grillo, K. (2013). Celebrating the reality of inclusive STEM education: Co-teaching in science and mathematics. *Teaching Exceptional Children, 45*(4), 50–57.

Murawski, W. W. (2012). Ten tips for using co-planning time more efficiently. *Teaching Exceptional Children, 44*(4), 8–15.

Nichols, J., Dowdy, A., & Nichols, C. (2010). Co-teaching: An educational promise for children with disabilities or a quick fix to meet the mandates of No Child Left Behind? *Education, 130*, 647–651.

Nierengarten, G. (2013). Supporting co-teaching teams in high schools: Twenty research-based practices. *American Secondary Education, 42*(1), 73–83.

Pancsofar, N., & Petroff, J. G. (2013). Professional development experiences in co-teaching: Associations with teacher confidence, interests, and attitudes. *Teacher Education and Special Education, 36*, 83–96.

Pardini, P. (2006). In one voice: Mainstream and ELL teachers work side-by-side in the classroom teaching language through content. *Journal of Staff Development, 27*(4), 20–25.

Pearl, C., Dieker, L., & Kirkpatrick, R. (2012). A five-year retrospective on the Arkansas Department of Education co-teaching project. *Professional Development in Education, 38*, 571–587.

Ploessl, D. M., Rock, M. L., Schoenfeld, N., & Blanks, B. (2010). On the same page: Practical techniques to enhance co-teaching interactions. *Intervention in School and Clinic, 45*, 158–168.

Rance-Roney, J. (2009). Best practices for adolescent ELLs. *Educational Leadership, 66*(7), 32–37.

Rivera, E. A., McMahon, S. D., & Keys, C. B. (2014). Collaborative teaching: School implementation and connections with outcomes among students with disabilities. *Journal of Prevention & Intervention in the Community, 42*(1), 72–85.

Rytivaara, A. (2012). "We don't question whether we can do this": Teacher identity in two co-teachers' narratives. *European Educational Research Journal, 11*, 302–313.

Rytivaara, A., & Kershner, R. (2012). Co-teaching as a context for teachers' professional learning and joint knowledge construction. *Teaching and Teacher Education, 28*, 999–1008.

Scruggs, T. E., Mastropieri, M. A., & McDuffie, K. A. (2007). Co-teaching in inclusive classrooms: A metasynthesis of qualitative research. *Exceptional Children, 73*, 392–416.

Seglem, R., & VanZant, M. (2010). Privileging students' voices: A co-teaching philosophy that evokes excellence in "all" learners. *English Journal, 100*(2), 41–47.

Sileo, J. M. (2011). Co-teaching: Getting to know your partner. *Teaching Exceptional Children, 43*(5), 32–38.

Solis, M., Vaughn, S., Swanson, E., & McCulley, L. (2012). Collaborative models of instruction: The empirical foundations of inclusion and co-teaching. *Psychology in the Schools, 49*, 498–510.

Tannock, M. T. (2009). Tangible and intangible elements of collaborative teaching. *Intervention in School and Clinic, 44*, 173–178.

Trump, J. L. (1966). Secondary education tomorrow: Four imperatives for improvement. *NASSP Bulletin, 50*(309), 87–95.

U.S. Department of Education. (2005). *Alternate achievement standards for students with the most significant cognitive disabilities: Non-regulatory guidance*. Retrieved February 16, 2012, from www.eric.ed.gov/PDFS/ED485842.pdf

Van Hover, S., Hicks, D., & Sayeski, K. (2012). A case study of co-teaching in an inclusive secondary high-stakes World History I classroom. *Theory & Research in Social Education, 40*, 260–291.

Vannest, K. J., & Hagan-Burke, S. (2010). Teacher time use in special education. *Remedial and Special Education, 31*, 126–142.

Walsh, J. M. (2012). Co-teaching as a school system strategy for continuous improvement. *Preventing School Failure, 56*(1), 29–36.

Warwick, D (1971). *Team teaching*. London: University of London.

Chapter 8

Achinstein, B., & Davis, E. (2014). The subject of mentoring: Towards a knowledge and practice base for content-focused mentoring of new teachers. *Mentoring & Tutoring: Partnership in Learning, 22,* 104–126.

Alhija, F. N. A., & Fresko, B. (2014). An exploration of the relationships between mentor recruitment, the implementation of mentoring, and mentors' attitudes. *Mentoring & Tutoring: Partnership in Learning, 22,* 162–180.

Allday, R. A., Neilsen-Gatti, S., & Hudson, T. M. (2013). Preparation for inclusion in teacher education pre-service curricula. *Teacher Education and Special Education, 36,* 298–311.

Andersen, M. N., Hofstadter, K. L., Kupzyk, S., Daly, E. I., Bleck, A. A., Collaro, A. L., … Blevins, C. A. (2010). A guiding framework for integrating the consultation process and behavior analytic practice in schools: The Treatment Validation Consultation model. *Journal of Behavior Assessment and Intervention in Children, 1*(1), 53–84.

Aronson, K. R., & Perkins, D. F. (2013). Challenges faced by military families: Perceptions of United States Marine Corps school liaisons. *Journal of Child and Family Studies, 22,* 516–525.

Bear, G. G. (2013). Teacher resistance to frequent rewards and praise: Lack of skill or a wise decision? *Journal of Educational & Psychological Consultation, 23,* 318–340.

Berger, J., Yiu, H. L., Nelson, D., Vaganek, M., Rosenfield, S., Gravois, T., … Hong, V. (2014). Teacher utilization of instructional consultation teams. *Journal of Educational & Psychological Consultation, 24,* 211–238.

Brown, D., Pryzwansky, W. B., & Schulte, A. C. (2011). *Psychological consultation and collaboration: Introduction to theory and practice* (7th ed.). Columbus, OH: Pearson/Merrill.

Brown, D., Reumann-Moore, R., Hugh, R., Christman, J., & Riffer, M. (2009, February). *Links to learning and sustainability: Year three report of the Pennsylvania High School Coaching Initiative* [Research for Action serial online]. (Eric Document Reproduction Service No. ED504284)

Butera, G., & Martinez, R. S. (2014). Multidisciplinary collaboration to support struggling readers: Special issue introduction. *Journal of Educational and Psychological Consultation, 24,* 75–80.

Caplan, G. (1970). *The theory and practice of mental health consultation.* New York: Basic Books.

Caqtapano, S., & Huisman, S. (2013). Leadership in hard-to-staff schools: Novice teachers as mentors. *Mentoring & Tutoring: Partnership in Learning, 21,* 258–271.

Christie, L. S., McKenzie, H. S., & Burdett, C. S. (1972). The consulting teacher approach to special education: Inservice training for regular classroom teachers. *Focus on Exceptional Children, 4,* 1–10.

Clarke, B. L., Sheridan, S. M., & Woods, K. E. (2014). Conjoint behavioral consultation: Implementing a tiered home-school partnership model to promote school readiness. *Journal of Prevention & Intervention in the Community, 42,* 300–314.

Coffee, G., & Kratochwill, T. R. (2013). Examining teacher use of praise taught during behavioral consultation: Implementation and generalization considerations. *Journal of Educational & Psychological Consultation, 23,* 1–35.

Curry, K. (2013). The silenced dialogue and pre-service teachers. *Multicultural Education, 20*(2), 27–32.

Denton, C. A., & Hasbrouck, J. (2009). A description of instructional coaching and its relationship to consultation. *Journal of Educational and Psychological Consultation, 19,* 150–175.

DiGennaro Reed, F. D., & Jenkins, S. R. (2013). Consultation in public school settings. In D. D. Reed, F. D. DiGennaro Reed, & J. K. Luiselli (Eds.), *Handbook of crisis intervention and developmental disabilities* (pp. 317–329). New York, NY: Springer Science + Business Media.

Dougherty, A. M. (2014). *Psychological consultation and collaboration in school and community settings* (6th ed.). Belmont, CA: Brooks/Cole.

Driver, M. K. (2013). Taking it all into account. *Principal Leadership, 13*(7), 42–45.

Dufrene, B. A., Lestremau, L., & Zoder-Martell, K. (2014). Direct behavioral consultation: Effects on teachers' praise and student disruptive behavior. *Psychology in the Schools, 51,* 567–580.

Eisenman, L. T., Pleet, A. M., Wandry, D., & McGinley, V. (2011). Voices of special education teachers in an inclusive high school: Redefining responsibilities. *Remedial and Special Education, 32,* 91–104.

Elford, M., Carter, R. J., & Aronin, S. (2013). Virtual reality check: Teachers use bug-in-ear coaching to practice feedback techniques with student avatars. *Journal of Staff Development, 34*(1), 40–43.

Erchul, W. P., & Martens, B. K. (1997). *School consultation: Conceptual and empirical bases of practice.* New York: Plenum.

Evans, S. B. (1980). The consultant role of the resource teacher. *Exceptional Children, 46,* 402–404.

Frank, J. L., & Kratochwill, T. R. (2014). School-based problem-solving consultation: Plotting a new course for evidence-based research and practice in consultation. In W. P. Erchul & S. M. Sheridan (Eds.), *Handbook of research in school consultation* (2nd ed., pp. 18–39). New York, NY: Routledge/Taylor & Francis Group.

Frey, A. J., Sims, K., & Alvarez, M. E. (2013). The promise of motivational interviewing for securing a niche in the RtI movement. *Children & Schools, 35,* 67–70.

Friend, M. (1984). Consultation skills for resource teachers. *Learning Disability Quarterly, 7,* 246–250.

Friend, M. (1988). Putting consultation into context: Historical and contemporary perspectives. *Remedial and Special Education, 9*(6), 7–13.

Gallucci, C., Van Lare, M., Yoon, I. H., & Boatright, B. (2010). Instructional coaching: Building theory about the role and organizational support for professional learning. *American Educational Research Journal, 47,* 919–963.

Gareis, C. R., & Nussbaum-Beach, S. (2007). Electronically mentoring to develop accomplished professional teachers. *Journal of Personnel Evaluation in Education, 20,* 227–246.

Goldring, R., Taie, S., and Riddles, M. (2014). *Teacher attrition and mobility: Results from the 2012–13 teacher follow-up survey* (NCES 2014-077). Washington, DC: U.S. Department of Education, National Center for Education Statistics. Retrieved from http://nces.ed.gov/pubsearch

Gut, D. M., Beam, P. C., Henning, J. E., Cochran, D. C., & Knight, R. T. (2014). Teachers' perceptions of their mentoring role in three different clinical settings: Student teaching, early field experiences, and entry year teaching. *Mentoring & Tutoring: Partnership in Learning, 22,* 240–263.

Hallam, P. R., Chou, P. N., Hite, J. M., & Hite, S. J. (2012). Two contrasting models for mentoring as they affect retention of beginning teachers. *NASSP Bulletin, 96,* 243–278.

Hunt, J. H., Powell, S., Little, M. E., & Mike, A. (2013). The effects of e-mentoring on beginning teacher competencies and perceptions. *Teacher Education and Special Education, 36,* 286–297.

Idol, L., Nevin, A., & Paolucci-Whitcomb, P. (2000). *Collaborative consultation* (3rd ed.). Austin, TX: Pro-Ed.

Ingersoll, R., & Strong, M. (2011). The impact of induction and mentoring programs for beginning teachers: A critical review of the research. *Review of Education Research, 81,* 201–233.

Israel, M., Carnahan, C. R., Snyder, K. K., & Williamson, P. (2013). Supporting new teachers of students with significant disabilities through virtual coaching: A proposed model. *Remedial and Special Education, 34,* 195–204.

Joyce, B., & Showers, B. (1980). Improving inservice training: The messages of research. *Educational Leadership, 37*(5), 379–385.

Joyce, B. R., & Showers, B. (2002). *Student achievement through staff development* (3rd ed.). Alexandria, VA: Association for Supervision and Curriculum Development.

Kampwirth, T. J., & Powers, K. M. (2015). *Collaborative consultation in the schools: Effective practices for students with learning and behavior problems* (5th ed.). E-book version. Upper Saddle River, NJ: Pearson.

Keigher, A. (2010). *Teacher attrition and mobility: Results from the 2008–09 teacher follow-up survey* (NCES 2010-353). Washington, DC: U.S. Department of Education, National Center for Education Statistics. Retrieved from http://nces.ed.gov/pubsearch

Knight, J. (2007). Five key points to building a coaching program. *Journal of Staff Development, 28*(1), 26–31.

Knight, J. (2011). What good coaches do. *Educational Leadership, 69*(2), 18–22.

Kurpius, D. J., & Brubaker, J. C. (1976). *Psycho-educational consultation: Definition, functions, preparation.* Bloomington: Indiana University.

Lopez, A. E. (2013). Collaborative mentorship: A mentoring approach to support and sustain teachers for equity and diversity. *Mentoring & Tutoring: Partnership in Learning, 21,* 292–311.

Marsh, J. A., McCombs, J. S., & Martorell, F. (2012). Reading coach quality: Findings from Florida middle schools. *Literacy Research and Instruction, 51*(1), 1–26.

Marsh, J. A., McCombs, J., & Martorell, F. (2010). How instructional coaches support data-driven decision making: Policy implementation and effects in Florida middle schools. *Educational Policy, 24,* 872–907.

McCall, Z., McHatton, P. A., & Shealey, M. W. (2014). Special education teacher candidate assessment: A review. *Teacher Education and Special Education, 37,* 51–70.

McKenney, E. W., Waldron, N., & Conroy, M. (2013). The effects of training and performance feedback during behavioral consultation on general education middle school teachers' integrity to functional analysis procedures. *Journal of Educational & Psychological Consultation, 23,* 63–85

McKenzie, H. S. (1972). Special education and consulting teachers. In F. Clark, D. Evans, & L. Hammerlynk (Eds.), *Implementing behavioral programs for schools and clinics.* Champaign, IL: Research Press.

Mullen, C. A. (2011). New teacher mentoring: A mandated direction of states. *Kappa Delta Pi Record, 47*(2), 63–67.

Nathans, L., & Revelle, C. (2013). An analysis of cultural diversity and recurring themes in preservice teachers' online discussions of Epstein's six types of parent involvement. *Teaching Education, 24,* 164–180.

National Center for Education Evaluation and Regional Assistance. (2009). *Comprehensive teacher induction* [NCEE evaluation brief 4069]. Author.

Nellis, L. M., Sickman, L. S., Newman, D. S., & Harman, D. R. (2014). Schoolwide collaboration to prevent and address reading difficulties: Opportunities for school psychologists and speech-language pathologists. *Journal of Educational & Psychological Consultation, 24,* 110–127.

Newell, M. (2010). The implementation of problem-solving consultation: An analysis of problem conceptualization in a multiracial context. *Journal of Educational and Psychological Consultation, 20,* 83–105.

Ocasio, K., Alst, D., Koivunen, J., Huang, C., & Allegra, C. (2014). Promoting preschool mental health: Results of a 3 year primary prevention strategy. *Journal of Child and Family Studies, 24,* 1800–1808.

Palawat, M., & May, M. E. (2012). The impact of cultural diversity on special education provision in the United States. *Journal of the International Association of Special Education, 13*(1), 58–63.

Parker, C. A. (Ed.). (1975). *Psychological consultation: Helping teachers meet special needs.* Minneapolis: University of Minnesota Leadership Training Institute.

Polly, D., Mraz, M., & Algozzine, R. (2013). Implications for developing and researching elementary school mathematics coaches. *School Science and Mathematics, 113,* 297–307.

Pryzwansky W. B. (1974). A reconsideration of the consultation model for delivery of school based psychological service. *American Journal of Orthopsychiatry, 44,* 579–583.

Rock, M. L., Schoenfeld, N., Zigmond, N., Gable, R. A., Gregg, M., Ploessl, D. M., & Salter, A. (2013). Can you Skype me now? Developing teachers' classroom management practices through virtual coaching. *Beyond Behavior, 22*(3), 15–23.

Rosenfield, S. (2013). Consultation in the schools—Are we there yet? *Consulting Psychology Journal: Practice and Research, 65,* 303–308.

Sabatino, C. A. (2014). *Consultation theory and practice: A handbook for school social workers.* New York, NY: Oxford University Press.

Sanetti, L. H., Kratochwill, T. R., & Long, A. J. (2013). Applying adult behavior change theory to support mediator-based intervention implementation. *School Psychology Quarterly, 28,* 47–62.

Sass, D. A., Flores, B. B., Claeys, L., & Pérez, B. (2012). Identifying personal and contextual factors that contribute to attrition rates for Texas public school teachers. *Education Policy Analysis Archives, 20*(15). Retrieved from http://epaa.asu.edu/ojs/article/view/967

Sheridan, S. M., Clarke, B. L., & Ransom, K. A. (2014). The past, present, and future of conjoint behavioral consultation research. In W. P. Erchul & S. M. Sheridan (Eds.), *Handbook of research in school consultation* (2nd ed., pp. 210–247). New York, NY: Routledge/Taylor & Francis Group.

Teemant, A., Wink, J., & Tyra, S. (2011). Effects of coaching on teacher use of sociocultural instructional practices. *Teaching and Teacher Education: An International Journal of Research and Studies, 27,* 683–693.

Thornberg, R. (2014). Consultation barriers between teachers and external consultants: A grounded theory of change resistance in school consultation. *Journal of Educational & Psychological Consultation, 24,* 183–210.

Tractman, G. M. (1961). New directions for school psychology. *Exceptional Children, 28,* 159–162.

Trautwein, B., & Ammerman, S. (2010). From pedagogy to practice: Mentoring and reciprocal peer coaching for preservice teachers. *Volta Review, 110,* 191–206.

Vanderburg, M., & Stephens, D. (2010). The impact of literacy coaches: What teachers value and how teachers change. *Elementary School Journal, 111,* 141–163.

Vannest, K. J., & Hagan-Burke, S. (2010). Teacher time use in special education. *Remedial and Special Education, 31,* 126–142.

Waterman, S., & He, Y. (2011). Effects of mentoring programs on new teacher retention: A literature review. *Mentoring & Tutoring: Partnership in Learning, 19,* 139–156.

Wei, X., Wagner, M., Christiano, E. A., Shattuck, P., & Yu, J. W. (2014). Special education services received by students with autism spectrum disorders from preschool through high school. *Journal of Special Education, 48,* 167–179.

Wood, B. K., Umbreit, C. J., Liaupsin, C. J., & Gresham, F. M. (2007). A treatment integrity analysis of function-based intervention. *Education and Treatment of Children, 30,* 105–120.

Zuspan, T. (2013). From teaching to coaching. *Teaching Children Mathematics, 20,* 154–161.

Chapter 9

Anastasiou, D., & Kauffman, J. M. (2011). A social constructionist approach to disability: Implications for special education. *Exceptional Children, 77,* 367–384.

Avgar, A., Lee, E. K., & Chung, W. (2014). Conflict in context: Perceptions of conflict, employee outcomes and the moderating role of discretion and social capital. *International Journal of Conflict Management, 25,* 276–303.

Baillien, E., Bollen, K., Euwema, M., & De Witte, H. (2014). Conflicts and conflict management styles as precursors of workplace bullying: A two-wave longitudinal study. *European Journal of Work and Organizational Psychology, 23,* 511–524.

Barden, J., & Tormala, Z. L. (2014). Elaboration and attitude strength: The new meta-cognitive perspective. *Social and Personality Psychology Compass, 8*(1), 17–29.

Barsky, A. (2008). A conflict resolution approach to teaching ethical decision making: Bridging conflicting values. *Journal of Jewish Communal Service, 83,* 164–169.

Barsky, A. E. (2007). *Conflict resolution for the helping professions* (2nd ed.). Boston: Cengage.

Battilana, J., & Casciaro, T. (2013). Overcoming resistance to organizational change: Strong ties and affective cooptation. *Management Science, 59,* 819–836.

Beaudan, E. (2006, January/February). Making change last: How to get beyond change fatigue. *Ivey Business Journal Online,* 1–7. Retrieved November 18, 2008, from www.ivey-businessjournal.com/view_article.asp?intArticle_ID=608

Behfar, K., Peterson, R. S., Mannix, E. A., & Trochin, W. M. K. (2008). The critical role of conflict resolution in teams: A closer look at the links between conflict type, conflict management strategies, and team outcomes. *Journal of Applied Psychology, 93,* 170–188.

Bernardin, H. J., Richey, B. E., & Castro, S. L. (2011). Mandatory and binding arbitration: Effects on employee attitudes and recruiting results. *Human Resource Management, 50,* 175–200.

Bond, S. A., Tuckey, M. R., & Dollard, M. F. (2010). Psychological safety climate, workplace bullying, and symptoms of posttraumatic stress. *Organization Development Journal, 28,* 38–56.

Bradley, B. H., Postlethwaite, B. E., Klotz, A. C., Hamdani, M. R., & Brown, K. G. (2012). Reaping the benefits of task conflict in teams: The critical role of team psychological safety climate. *Journal of Applied Psychology, 97,* 151–158.

Brew, F. P., & Cairns, D. R. (2004). Do culture or situational constraints determine choice of direct or indirect styles in intercultural workplace conflicts? [Electronic version] *International Journal of Intercultural Relations, 28,* 331–352.

Brubaker, D., Noble, C., Fincher, R., Park, S. K., & Press, S. (2014). Conflict resolution in the workplace: What will the future bring? *Conflict Resolution Quarterly, 31,* 357–386.

Burke, M. M., & Goldman, S. E. (2014). Identifying the associated factors of mediation and due process in families of students with autism spectrum disorder. *Journal of Autism and Developmental Disorders.* Advance online publication. doi:10.1007/s10803-014-2294-4

Burke, W. W. (2011). A perspective on the field of organization development and change: The Zeigamik effect. *Journal of Applied Behavioral Science, 47,* 143–167.

Charkoudian, L. (2010). Giving police and courts a break: The effect of community mediation on decreasing the use of police and court resources. *Conflict Resolution Quarterly, 28,* 141–155.

Choi, M., & Ruona, W. E. A. (2011). Individual readiness for organizational change and its implications for human resource and organization development. *Human Resource Development Review, 10*(1), 46–73.

Coke, T. (2014, June). Impartiality—the Holy Grail. *Training Journal,* 10–13. Retrieved from https://www.trainingjournal.com/articles/feature/impartiality-%E2%80%93-holy-grail

Coleman, P., Kugler, K., Mitchinson, A., Chung, C., & Musallam, N. (2010). The view from above and below: The effects of power and interdependence asymmetries on conflict dynamics and outcomes in organizations. *Negotiation and Conflict Management Research* [Serial online], *3,* 283–311.

Conderman, G. (2011a). Methods for addressing conflict in cotaught classrooms. *Intervention in School and Clinic, 46,* 221–229.

Curry, K. A. (2014). Team leadership: It's not for the faint of heart. *Journal of Cases in Educational Leadership, 17*(2), 20–40.

Danışman, A. (2010). Good intentions and failed implementations: Understanding culture-based resistance to organizational change. *European Journal of Work and Organizational Psychology, 19,* 200–220.

Dignath, D., Kiesel, A., & Eder, A. B. (2014). Flexible conflict management: Conflict avoidance and conflict adjustment in reactive cognitive control. *Journal of Experimental Psychology: Learning, Memory, and Cognition.* Advance online publication. http://dx.doi.org/10.1037/xlm0000089

Eigen, Z. J., & Litwin, A. S. (2014). Justice or just between us? Empirical evidence of the trade-off between procedural and interactional justice in workplace dispute resolution. *Industrial & Labor Relations Review, 67*, 171–201.

Evans, R. (2012). Getting to no: Building true collegiality in schools. *Independent School, 71*, 99–107.

Festinger, L. (1957). *A theory of cognitive dissonance.* Stanford, CA: Stanford University Press.

Fisher, R., Ury, W., & Patton, R. (1997). *Getting to yes: Negotiating agreement without giving in* (3rd ed.). Boston: Allyn & Bacon.

Ford, J. D., & Ford, L. W. (2010). Stop blaming resistance to change and start using it. *Organizational Dynamics, 38*(1), 24–36.

García-Cabrera, A. M., & García-Barba Hernández, F. (2014). Differentiating the three components of resistance to change: The moderating effect of organization-based self-esteem on the employee involvement-resistance relation. *Human Resource Development Quarterly, 25*, 441–469.

Grenda, J. P., & Hackmann, D. G. (2014). Advantages and challenges of distributing leadership in middle-level schools. *NASSP Bulletin, 98*, 53–74.

Guerrero, L. K., & Gross, M. A. (2014). Argumentativeness, avoidance, verbal aggressiveness, and verbal benevolence as predictors of partner perceptions of an individual's conflict style. *Negotiation and Conflict Management Research, 7*, 99–120.

Hahn Tapper, A. J. (2013). A pedagogy of social justice education: Social identity theory, intersectionality, and empowerment. *Conflict Resolution Quarterly, 30*, 411–445.

Halevy, N., Cohen, T. R., Chou, E. Y., Katz, J. J., & Panter, A. T. (2014). Mental models at work: Cognitive causes and consequences of conflict in organizations. *Personality and Social Psychology Bulletin, 40*, 92–110.

Harvey, T. R. (2010). *Resistance to change: A guide to harnessing its positive power.* Lanham, MD: Rowman & Littlefield.

Hayashi, S. K. (2011). *Conversations for change: 12 ways to say it right when it matters most.* New York: McGraw-Hill.

Hedeen, T., Moses, P., Peter, M. (2011). *Encouraging meaningful parent/educator collaboration: A review of recent literature.* Eugene, OR: Center for Appropriate Dispute Resolution in Special Education (CADRE). Retrieved from http://files.eric.ed.gov/fulltext/ED536983.pdf

Heitin, R. C. (2013). Advocating for children and their families within the school system: Reflections of a long-time special education advocate. *Odyssey: New Directions in Deaf Education, 14*, 44–47.

Hernandez, P. (2013, September). How to overcome resistance in the workplace. *Small Business Computing.* Retrieved from http://www.smallbusinesscomputing.com/tipsforsmallbusiness/how-to-overcome-resistance-in-the-workplace.html

Irvine, J. J. (2012). Complex relationships between multicultural education and special education: An African American perspective. *Journal of Teacher Education, 63*, 268–274.

Isenhart, M. W., & Spangle, M. (2000). *Collaborative approaches to resolving conflict.* Thousand Oaks, CA: Sage.

Jackson, D. D. (2010). The fear of change (1967). *Journal of Systemic Therapies, 29*(2), 69–73.

Jordan, P. J., & Troth, A. C. (2004). Managing emotions during team problem-solving: Emotional intelligence and conflict resolution [Electronic version]. *Human Performance, 17*, 195–218.

Kampwirth, T. J., & Powers, K. M. (2015). *Collaborative consultation in the schools: Effective practices for students with learning and behavior problems* (5th ed.). E-book version. Upper Saddle River, NJ: Pearson.

Keim, A. C., Landis, R. S., Pierce, C. A., & Earnest, D. R. (2014). Why do employees worry about their jobs? A meta-analytic review of predictors of job insecurity. *Journal of Occupational Health Psychology, 19*, 269–290.

Kemp, F. D. (2009). Saving Face. *Industrial Engineer: IE, 41*(5), 39–43.

Keranen, N., & Prudencio, F. E. (2014). Teacher collaboration praxis: Conflicts, borders, and ideologies from a micropolitical perspective. *PROFILE: Issues in Teachers' Professional Development, 16*(2), 37–47.

Kumkale, G. T., & Albarracin, D. (2004). The sleeper effect in persuasion: A meta-analytic review [Electronic version]. *Psychological Bulletin, 130*, 143–172.

Loode, S. (2011). Navigating the unchartered waters of cross-cultural conflict resolution education. *Conflict Resolution Quarterly, 29*, 65–84.

Marcus, L. J., Dorn, B. C., & McNulty, E. J. (2012). The walk in the woods: A step-by-step method for facilitating interest-based negotiation and conflict resolution. *Negotiation Journal, 28*, 337–349.

Martinez, M. C. (2004). *Teachers working together for school success.* Thousand Oaks, CA: Corwin.

Masters, M. F., & Albright, R. R. (2002). *The complete guide to conflict resolution in the workplace.* New York: American Management Association.

McCorkle, S., & Reese, M. J. (2015). *Mediation theory and practice* (2nd ed.). Thousand Oaks, CA: Sage.

Mercer, D., & Davis, J. M. (2011). *8 simple keys to building and growing a successful mediation or arbitration practice.* Playa del Rey, CA: Peace Talks Mediation Services.

Mesko, N., Lang, A., Czibor, A., Szijjarto, L., & Bereczkei, T. (2014). Compete and compomise: Machiavellianism and conflict resolution. *Electronic Journal of Business Ethics and Organization Studies, 19*(1), 14–18.

Mueller, T. G. (2009a). Alternative dispute resolution: A new agenda for special education policy. *Journal of Disability Policy Studies, 20*(1), 4–13.

Mueller, T. G., & Carranza, F. (2011). An examination of special education due process hearings. *Journal of Disability Policy Studies, 22*, 131–139.

Murayama, A., Ryan, C. S., Shimizu, H., Kurebayashi, K., & Miura, A. (2015). Cultural differences in perceptions of intragroup conflict and preferred conflict-management behavior: A scenario experiment. *Journal of Cross-Cultural Psychology, 46*, 88–100.

Murray, A. (2007). Overcoming resistance to change. *KM World, 16*(9), 24.

Nan, S. A. (2011). Consciousness in culture-based conflict and conflict resolution. *Conflict Resolution Quarterly, 28*, 239–262.

Nespor, J., & Hicks, D. (2010). Wizards and witches: Parent advocates and contention in special education in the USA. *Journal of Education Policy, 25,* 309–334.

Obiakor, F. E., Harris, M., Mutua, K., Rotatori, A., & Algozzine, B. (2012). Making inclusion work in general education classrooms. *Education & Treatment of Children, 35,* 477–490.

Ojanen, T., Smith-Schrandt, H. L., & Gesten, E. (2013). Associations among children's social goals, responses to peer conflict, and teacher-reported behavioral and academic adjustment at school. *Journal of Experimental Education, 81,* 68–83.

Oreg, S., & Sverdlik, N. (2011). Ambivalence toward imposed change: The conflict between dispositional resistance to change and the orientation toward the change agent. *Journal of Applied Psychology, 96*(2), 337–349.

Otis, M. R. (2011). Expanding collaborative divorce through the social sciences. *Family Court Review, 49,* 229–238.

Polsky, L., & Gerschel, A. (2010). *Perfect phrases for communicating change.* New York: McGraw-Hill.

Pruitt, D. G. (2011). Negotiation and mediation in intergroup conflict. In Bar-Tal, D. (Ed.), *Intergroup conflicts and their resolution: A social psychological perspective* (pp. 267–289). New York: Psychology Press.

Putnam, L. L. (2010). Communication as changing the negotiation game. *Journal of Applied Communication Research, 38,* 325–335.

Rios, K., DeMarree, K. G., & Statzer, J. (2014). Attitude certainty and conflict style: Divergent effects of correctness and clarity. *Personality and Social Psychology Bulletin, 40,* 819–830.

Rispens, S., Greer, L. L., & Jehn, K. A. (2007). It could be worse: A study on the alleviating roles of trust and connectedness in intragroup conflicts. *International Journal of Conflict Management, 18,* 325–344.

Sadri, G. (2013). Choosing conflict resolution by culture. *Industrial Management, 55*(5), 10–15.

Saeed, T., Almas, S., Anis-ul-Haq, M., & Niazi, G. (2014). Leadership styles: Relationship with conflict management styles. *International Journal of Conflict Management, 25,* 214–225.

Scott, G. (2008). Take emotion out of conflict resolution. *Training and Development, 62*(2), 84.

Shipps, D., & White, M. (2009). A new politics of the principalship? Accountability-driven change in New York City. *Peabody Journal of Education: Issues of Leadership, Policy, and Organizations, 84,* 350–373.

Simons, H. W., & Jones, J. G. (2011). *Persuasion in society* (2nd ed.). New York: Routledge/Taylor & Francis.

Stanleigh, M. (2013). Leading change. *Journal for Quality and Participation, 36*(2), 39–40.

Tatum, C. B., & Eberlin, R. J. (2006). Organizational justice and conflict management styles. *International Journal of Conflict Management, 17,* 66–81.

Tjosvold, D., Wong, A. S. H., & Wan, P. M. K. (2010). Conflict management for justice, innovation, and strategic advantage in organizational relationships. *Journal of Applied Social Psychology, 40,* 636–665.

Ury, W. (1991). *Getting past no: Negotiating your way from confrontation to cooperation.* New York: Bantam.

Ury, W. L., Brett, J. M., & Goldberg, S. B. (2005). Three approaches to resolving disputes: Interests, rights, and power. In M. H. Bazerman (Eds.), *Negotiation, decision making and conflict management, Vol 1* (pp. 239–260). Northampton, MA: Edward Elgar Publishing.

van Dijk, R., & van Dick, R. (2009). Navigating organizational change: Change leaders, employee resistance and work-based identities. *Journal of Change Management, 9,* 143–163.

Von Glinow, M. A., Shapiro, D. L., & Brett, J. M. (2004). Can we talk, and should we? Managing emotional conflict in multicultural teams [Electronic version]. *Academy of Management Review, 29,* 578–592.

Wilmot, W., & Hocker, J. (2014). *Interpersonal conflict* (9th ed.). New York, NY: McGraw-Hill.

Zins, J. E., & Illback, R. J. (2008). Consulting to facilitate planned organizational change in schools. *Journal of Educational and Psychological Consultation, 17,* 109–117.

Zirkel, P. A. (2012). A professional dilemma: Following the principle or the principal? *Communique, 40*(7), 10–11.

Zirkel, P. A., & Scala, G. (2010). Due process hearing systems under the IDEA: A state-by-state survey. *Journal of Disability Policy Studies, 21,* 3–8.

Chapter 10

Abbate-Vaughn, J. (2007). "Para aquí today, para afuera tomorrow": Uncertainty in urban bilingual paraprofessionals' work in the age of NCL. *Urban Review, 39*(5) 567–588.

Ashbaker, B., & Morgan, J. (2012a). Team players and team managers: Special educators working with paraeducators to support inclusive classrooms. *Creative Education, 3,* 322–327.

Bingham, G. A., Hall-Kenyon, K. M., & Culatta, B. (2010). Systematic and engaging early literacy: Examining the effects of paraeducator implemented early literacy instruction. *Communication Disorders Quarterly, 32,* 38–49.

Burbank, M. D., Bates, A. J., & Schrum, L. (2009). Expanding teacher preparation pathways for paraprofessionals: A recruiting seminar series. *Teacher Education Quarterly, 36,* 199–216.

Cameron, D. L., Cook, B. G., & Tankersley, M. (2012). An analysis of the different patterns of 1:1 interactions between educational professionals and their students with varying abilities in inclusive classrooms. *International Journal of Inclusive Education, 16,* 1335–1354.

Carnahan, C. R., Williamson, P., Clarke, L., & Sorensen, R. (2009). A systematic approach for supporting paraeducators in educational settings: A guide for teachers. *Teaching Exceptional Children, 41*(5), 34–43.

Carter, E., O'Rourke, L., Sisco, L. G., & Pelsue, D. (2009). Knowledge, responsibilities, and training needs of paraprofessionals in elementary and secondary schools. *Remedial and Special Education, 30,* 344–359.

Causton-Theoharis, J. (2009). *The paraprofessional's handbook for effective support in inclusive classrooms.* Baltimore, MD: Paul H. Brookes.

Cook, B. G., Cameron, D. L., & Tankersley, M. (2007). Inclusive teachers' attitudinal ratings of their students with disabilities. *Journal of Special Education, 40,* 230–238.

Daniels, V. I., & McBride, A. (2001). Paraeducators as critical team members: Redefining roles and responsibilities [Electronic version]. *NASSP Bulletin, 85*(623), 66–74.

Darrow, A. (2010). Working with paraprofessionals in the music classroom. *General Music Today, 23*(2), 35–37.

Downing, J. E., Ryndak, D. L., & Clark, D. (2000). Paraeducators in inclusive classrooms: Their own perceptions. *Remedial and Special Education, 21,* 171–181.

Doyle, M. B. (2002). *The paraprofessionals' guide to the inclusive classroom: Working as a team* (2nd ed.). Baltimore: Paul H. Brookes.

Fisher, M., & Pleasants, S. L. (2012). Roles, responsibilities, and concerns of paraeducators: Findings from a statewide survey. *Remedial and Special Education, 33,* 287–297.

Fleury, M. L. (2000). Confidentiality issues with substitutes and paraeducators. *Teaching Exceptional Children, 33*(1), 44–45.

French, N. K. (1998). Working together: Resource teachers and paraeducators. *Remedial and Special Education, 19,* 357–368.

French, N. K. (1999). Paraeducators and teachers: Shifting roles. *Teaching Exceptional Children, 32*(2), 69–73.

French, N. K. (2003). *Managing paraeducators in your school: How to hire, train, and supervise non-certified staff.* Thousand Oaks, CA: Corwin.

Gerlach, K. (2015). *Let's team up: A checklist for teachers, paraeducators & principals.* Port Chester, NY: Dude Publishing.

Giangreco, M. F. (2013). Teacher assistant supports in inclusive schools: Research, practices and alternatives. *Australasian Journal of Special Education, 37,* 93–106.

Giangreco, M. F., Broer, S. M., & Suter, J. C. (2011). Guidelines for selecting alternatives to overreliance on paraprofessionals: Field-testing in inclusion-oriented schools. *Remedial and Special Education, 32,* 22–38.

Giangreco, M. F., Doyle, M. B., & Suter, J. C. (2012). Constructively responding to requests for paraprofessionals: We keep asking the wrong questions. *Remedial and Special Education, 33,* 362–373.

Giangreco, M. F., Edelman, S. W., Luiselli, T. E., & MacFarland, S. Z. C. (1997). Helping or hovering? Effects of instructional assistant proximity on students with disabilities. *Exceptional Children, 64,* 7–18.

Giangreco, M. F., Suter, J. C., & Doyle, M. (2010). Paraprofessionals in inclusive schools: A review of recent research. *Journal of Educational and Psychological Consultation, 20,* 41–57.

Giangreco, M. F., Suter, J. C., & Hurley, S. M. (2013). Revisiting personnel utilization in inclusion-oriented schools. *Journal of Special Education, 47,* 121–132.

Giles, E. (2010). *Paraprofessionals' perceptions of training and efficacy: A phenomenological study.* Saarbrücken, Germany: Verlag Dr. Müller.

Gilrane, C., Russell, L., & Roberts, M. (2008). Building a community in which everyone teaches, learns, and reads: A case study. *Journal of Educational Research, 101,* 333–349.

Glazzard, J. (2011). Perceptions of the barriers to effective inclusion in one primary school: Voices of teachers and teaching assistants. *Support for Learning, 26*(2), 56–63.

Granger, J. D., & Greek, M. (2005). Struggling readers stretch their skills: Project maximizes use of paraprofessionals to teach reading. *Journal of Staff Development, 26*(3), 32–36.

Hamilton-Jones, B., & Moore, A. (2013). Ensuring high-quality inclusive practices: What co-teachers can do. *Kappa Delta Pi Record, 49,* 156–161.

Harris, B. A. (2011). Effects of the proximity of paraeducators on the interactions of Braille readers in inclusive settings. *Journal of Visual Impairment & Blindness, 105,* 467–478.

Jones, B. A. (2012). Fostering collaboration in inclusive settings: The special education students at a glance approach. *Intervention in School and Clinic, 47,* 297–306.

Jones, C. R., Ratcliff, N. J., Sheehan, H., & Hunt, G. H. (2012). An analysis of teachers' and paraeducators' roles and responsibilities with implications for professional development. *Early Childhood Education Journal, 40,* 19–24.

Lane, K. L., Carter, E. W., & Sisco, L. (2012). Paraprofessional involvement in self-determination instruction for students with high-incidence disabilities. *Exceptional Children, 78,* 237–251.

Lewis, S., & McKenzie, A. R. (2010). The competencies, roles, supervision, and training needs of paraeducators working with students with visual impairments in local and residential schools. *Journal of Visual Impairment & Blindness, 104,* 464–477.

Lushen, K., Kim, O., & Reid, R. (2012). Paraeducator-led strategy instruction for struggling writers. *Exceptionality, 20,* 250–265.

Martin, T., & Alborz, A. (2014). Supporting the education of pupils with profound intellectual and multiple disabilities: The views of teaching assistants regarding their own learning and development needs. *British Journal of Special Education, 41,* 309–327.

McGrath, M. Z., Johns, B. H., & Mathur, S. R. (2010). Empowered or overpowered? Strategies for working effectively with paraprofessionals. *Beyond Behavior, 19*(2), 2–6.

Monzó, L. D., & Rueda, R. S. (2000). *Examining Latino paraeducators: Interactions with Latino students.* Washington, DC: ERIC Clearinghouse on Language and Linguistics.

National Center for Education Statistics. (2007, June). *Issue brief: Description and employment criteria of instructional paraprofessionals.* Washington, DC: Author.

Nevin, A. I., Villa, R. A., & Thousand, J. S. (2009). *A guide to co-teaching with paraeducators: Practical tips for K–12 educators.* Thousand Oaks, CA: Corwin.

O'Keeffe, B. V., Slocum, T. A., & Magnusson, R. (2013). The effects of a fluency training package on paraprofessionals' presentation of a reading intervention. *Journal of Special Education, 47,* 14–27.

Orsati, F. T., & Causton-Theoharis, J. (2013). Challenging control: Inclusive teachers' and teaching assistants' discourse on students with challenging behaviour. *International Journal of Inclusive Education, 17,* 507–525.

Robinson, S. E. (2011). Teaching paraprofessionals of students with autism to implement pivotal response treatment in inclusive school settings using a brief video feedback training package. *Focus on Autism and Other Developmental Disabilities, 26,* 105–118.

Rossetti, Z. S., & Goessling, D. P. (2010). Paraeducators' roles in facilitating friendships between secondary students with and without autism spectrum disorders or developmental disabilities. *Teaching Exceptional Children, 42*(6), 64–70.

Rutherford, G. (2011). "Doing right by": Teacher aides, students with disabilities, and relational social justice. *Harvard Educational Review, 81,* 95–119.

Shyman, E. (2010). Identifying predictors of emotional exhaustion among special education paraeducators: A preliminary investigation. *Psychology in the Schools, 47,* 828–841.

Simpson, R., & Mundschenk, N. A. (2012). Inclusion and students with emotional and behavioral disorders. In J. Bakken, F. Obiakor, & A. Rotatori (Eds.), *Advances in Special Education Series: Vol. 22. Behavioral disorders: Current perspectives and issues* (pp. 1–22). Bingley, United Kingdom: Emerald Group Publishing.

Stacey, K., Harvey, S., & Richards, H. (2013). Teachers working with ESOL paraprofessionals in a secondary context: Examining supervision. *Teaching and Teacher Education, 36*(55–67).

Stephens, T. L., & Woodbury, C. (2011). Paraeducators. In C. G. Simpson, J. P. Bakken, C. G. Simpson, J. P. Bakken (Eds.), *Collaboration: A multidisciplinary approach to educating students with disabilities* (pp. 71–85). Waco, TX: Prufrock Press.

Suter, J. C., & Giangreco, M. F. (2009). Numbers that count: Exploring special education and paraprofessional service delivery in inclusion-oriented schools. *Journal of Special Education, 43,* 81–93.

Theoharis, G., & O'Toole, J. (2011). Leading inclusive ELL: Social justice leadership for English language learners. *Educational Administration Quarterly, 47,* 646–688.

Therrien, W. J., Kirk, J. F., & Woods-Groves, S. (2012). Comparison of a reading fluency intervention with and without passage repetition on reading achievement. *Remedial and Special Education, 33,* 309–319.

Toelken, S., & Miltenberger, R. G. (2012). Increasing independence among children diagnosed with autism using a brief embedded teaching strategy. *Behavioral Interventions, 27,* 93–104.

U.S. Department of Education. (2014). *36th annual report to Congress on the implementation of the Individuals with Disabilities Education Act.* Washington, DC: Office of Special Education and Rehabilitative Services, Office of Special Education Programs. Retrieved from http://www2.ed.gov/about/reports/annual/osep/2014/parts-b-c/36th-idea-arc.pdf

U.S. Department of Education. (n.d.). *Roles for education paraprofessionals in effective schools: An idea book.* Washington, DC: U.S. Department of Education, Planning and Evaluation Service.

U.S. Department of Labor. (2014). *Occupational outlook handbook: Teacher assistant.* Washington, DC: Bureau of Labor Statistics. Retrieved from http://www.bls.gov/ooh/education-training-and-library/teacher-assistants.htm

Vadasy, P. F., & Sanders, E. A. (2008). Benefits of repeated reading intervention for low-achieving fourth- and fifth-grade students. *Remedial and Special Education, 29,* 235–249.

Vadasy, P. F., Nelson, J. R., & Sanders, E. A. (2013). Longer term effects of a tier 2 kindergarten vocabulary intervention for English learners. *Remedial and Special Education, 34,* 91–101.

Wasburn-Moses, L., Chun, E., & Kaldenberg, E. (2013). Paraprofessional roles in an adolescent reading program: Lessons learned. *American Secondary Education, 41*(3), 34–49.

Webster, R., Blatchford, P., & Russell, A. (2013). Challenging and changing how schools use teaching assistants: Findings from the effective deployment of teaching assistants project. *School Leadership & Management, 33,* 78–96.

Whitburn, B. (2013). The dissection of paraprofessional support in inclusive education: "You're in mainstream with a chaperone." *Australasian Journal of Special Education, 37,* 147–161.

Young, N., & Bittel, P. (2011). Get in the conversation: Special-education efficiencies and paraprofessional staffing. *School Business Affairs, 77*(9), 18–20.

Chapter 11

Aceves, T. C. (2014). Supporting Latino families in special education through community agency-school partnerships. *Multicultural Education, 21*(3–4), 45–50.

Adler, R. B., Rodman, G., & Cropley, C. (2012). *Understanding human communication* (11th ed.). New York: Oxford University Press.

Al Khateeb, J. M., Al Hadidi, M. S., & Al Khatib, A. J. (2014). Addressing the unique needs of Arab American children with disabilities. *Journal of Child and Family Studies,* doi:10.1007/s10826-014-0046-x

Allen, S. F. (2007). Parents' perceptions of intervention practices in home visiting programs. *Infants & Young Children, 20,* 266–281.

Anderson, J. A., Howland, A. A., & McCoach, D. B. (2015). Parental characteristics and resiliency in identification rates for special education. *Preventing School Failure, 59,* 63–72.

Bailey, D. B., Hebbler, K., Scarborough, A., Spiker, D., & Malik, S. (2004). First experiences with early intervention: A national perspective. *Pediatrics, 113*(4), 887–896.

Banks, J. A. (2008). Diversity, group identity, and citizenship education in a global age. *Educational Researcher, 37,* 129–139.

Beach Center on Disability. (1999). *Effectiveness of parent to parent support* (Beach Center Research Brief). Lawrence, KS: University of Kansas.

Bindels-de Hens, K. B., van Staa, A., van Vliet, I., Ewals, F. M., & Hilberink, S. R. (2013). Transferring young people with profound intellectual and multiple disabilities from pediatric to adult medical care: Parents' experiences and recommendations. *Intellectual and Developmental Disabilities, 51,* 176–189.

Blacher, J., Begum, G. F., Marcoulides, G. A., & Baker, B. L. (2013). Longitudinal perspectives of child positive impact on families: Relationship to disability and culture. *American Journal on Intellectual and Developmental Disabilities, 118,* 141–155.

Bowen, M. (1978). *Family therapy in clinical practice.* New York: Jason Aronson.

Carter, E. A., & McGoldrick, M. (Eds.). (2005). *The expanded family life cycle: Individual, family, and social perspectives* (3rd ed.). Boston: Allyn & Bacon.

Carter, E. W., Brock, M. E., & Trainor, A. A. (2014). Transition assessment and planning for youth with severe intellectual and developmental disabilities. *Journal of Special Education, 47,* 245–255.

Carter, E. W., Lane, K. L., Cooney, M., Weir, K., Moss, C. K., & Machalicek, W. (2013). Self-determination among transition-age youth with autism or intellectual disability: Parent perspectives. *Research and Practice for Persons with Severe Disabilities, 38,* 129–138.

Cheak-Zamora, N. C., Teti, M., & First, J. (2015). 'Transitions are scary for our kids, and they're scary for us': Family member and youth perspectives on the challenges of transitioning to adulthood with autism. *Journal of Applied Research in Intellectual Disabilities.* doi:10.1111/jar.12150

Cobb, C. (2014). The three-legged stool of parental inclusion: The case of Hana. *British Journal of Special Education, 41*, 289–308.

Cook, R. E., Tessier, A., & Klein, M. D. (1992). *Adapting early childhood curricula for children with special needs.* Upper Saddle River, NJ: Merrill/Pearson Education.

Cramer, E. D., & Bennett, K. D. (2015). Implementing culturally responsive positive behavior interventions and supports in middle school classrooms. *Middle School Journal, 46*(3), 18–24.

Dempsey, I., & Keen, D. (2008). A review of processes and outcomes in family-centered services for children with a disability. *Topics in Early Childhood Special Education, 28*(1), 42–52.

Dunst, C. J. (2002). Family-centered practices: Birth through high school. *Journal of Special Education, 36*, 139–147.

Dunst, C. J., & Dempsey, I. (2007). Family–professional partnerships and parenting competence, confidence, and enjoyment. *International Journal of Disabilities, 54*(3), 305–315.

Dwairy, M., & Achoui, M. (2010). Adolescents–family connectedness: A first cross-cultural research on parenting and psychological adjustment of children. *Journal of Child and Family Studies, 19*, 8–15.

Dykens, E. M. (2015). Family adjustment and interventions in neurodevelopmental disorders. *Current Opinion in Psychiatry, 28*, 121–126.

Entwisle, D. R. (1994). Subcultural diversity in American families. In L. L'Abate (Ed.), *Handbook of developmental family psychology and psychopathology* (pp. 132–156). New York: Wiley.

Griffith, G. M., Hastings, R. P., Petalas, M. A., & Lloyd, T. J. (2015). Mothers' expressed emotion towards children with autism spectrum disorder and their siblings. *Journal of Intellectual Disability Research, 59*, 580–587.

Hardin, B. J., Blanchard, S. B., Kemmery, M. A., Appenzeller, M., & Parker, S. D. (2014). Family-centered practices and American Sign Language (ASL): Challenges and recommendations. *Exceptional Children, 81*, 107–123.

Harry, B. (2008). Collaboration with culturally and linguistically diverse families: Ideal versus reality. *Exceptional Children, 74*, 372–388.

Hatton, S., & Tector, A. (2010). Sexuality and relationship education for young people with autistic spectrum disorder: Curriculum change and staff support. *British Journal of Special Education, 37*(2), 69–76.

He, Y. (2013). Developing teachers' cultural competence: Application of appreciative inquiry in ESL teacher education. *Teacher Development, 17*(1), 55–71.

Hernandez, J. E., Harry, B., & Newman, L. (2009). Survey of family involvement in and satisfaction with the Los Angeles Unified School District special education processes. *Journal of Special Education Leadership, 21*(2), 84–93.

Howard, V. F., Williams, B. F., & Lepper, C. (2010). *Very young children with special needs: A foundation for educators, families, and service providers* (4th ed.). Upper Saddle River, NJ: Pearson Education.

Ivey, A. E., Ivey, M. B., Zalaquett, C. P., & Quirk, K. (2016). *Essentials of intentional interviewing: Counseling in a multicultural world* (3rd ed.). Belmont, CA: Brooks/Cole, Cengage Learning.

Johnson, L., Radesky, J., & Zuckerman, B. (2013). Cross-cultural parenting: Reflections on autonomy and interdependence. *Pediatrics, 131*, 631–633.

Knopf, H. T., & Swick, K. J. (2007). How parents feel about their child's teacher/school: Implications for early childhood professionals. *Early Childhood Education Journal, 34*, 291–296.

Kochhar-Bryant, C. A. (2008). *Collaboration and system coordination for students with special needs: From early childhood to the postsecondary years.* Upper Saddle River, NJ: Merrill/Pearson Education.

Kübler-Ross, E. (1969). *On death and dying.* New York: Macmillan.

Lambie, R. (2008). *Family systems within educational contexts: Understanding children who are at risk or have special needs* (3rd ed.). Denver, CO: Love.

Lo, L. (2012). Demystifying the IEP process for diverse parents of children with disabilities. *Teaching Exceptional Children, 44*(3), 14–20.

Long, K. A., Kao, B., Plante, W., Seifer, R., & Lobato, D. (2015). Cultural and child-related predictors of distress among Latina caregivers of children with intellectual disabilities. *American Journal on Intellectual and Developmental Disabilities, 120*, 145–165.

Lynch, E. W. (2011a). Conceptual framework: From culture shock to cultural learning. In E. W. Lynch & M. J. Hanson (Eds.), *Developing cross-cultural competence: A guide for working with children and their families* (4th ed., pp. 20–40). Baltimore: Paul H. Brookes.

Lynch, E. W. (2011b). Developing cross-cultural competence. In E. W. Lynch & M. J. Hanson (Eds.), *Developing cross-cultural competence: A guide for working with children and their families* (4th ed., pp. 41–77). Baltimore: Paul H. Brookes.

Mahoney, A., & Poling, A. (2011). Sexual abuse prevention for people with severe developmental disabilities. *Journal of Developmental and Physical Disabilities, 23*, 369–376.

McGoldrick, M., Carter, B., & Garcia-Preto, C. (2011). *The expanded family life cycle: Individual, family, and social perspectives* (4th ed.). Boston: Allyn & Bacon.

Meadan, H., Halle, J. W., & Ebata, A. T. (2010). Families with children who have autism spectrum disorders: Stress and support. *Exceptional Children, 77*(1), 7–36.

Meyer, L. H. (2012). Freedom, fairness, and justice: What now for severe disabilities?—A response to Turnbull. *Research and Practice for Persons with Severe Disabilities, 37*, 220–223.

Minnes, P., Perry, A., & Weiss, J. A. (2015). Predictors of distress and well-being in parents of young children with developmental delays and disabilities: The importance of parent perceptions. *Journal of Intellectual Disability Research, 59*, 551–560.

Nelson, L. G. L., Summers, J. A., & Turnbull, A. P. (2004). Boundaries in family–professional relationships: Implications for special education. *Remedial and Special Education, 25*, 153–165.

Nichols, W. C. (1996). *Treating people in families: An integrative framework.* New York: Guilford Press.

Olivos, E. M. (2009). Collaboration with Latino families: A critical perspective of home–school interactions. *Intervention in School and Clinic, 45,* 109–115.

Olivos, E. M., Gallagher, R. J., & Aguilar, J. (2010). Fostering collaboration with culturally and linguistically diverse families of children with moderate to severe disabilities. *Journal of Educational and Psychological Consultation, 20,* 28–40.

Petrina, N., Carter, M., & Stephenson, J. (2015). Parental perception of the importance of friendship and other outcome priorities in children with autism spectrum disorder. *European Journal of Special Needs Education, 30,* 61–74.

Poller, J. L., & Fabe, A. (2009). Legal and financial issues in a divorce when there is a "special needs" child. *American Journal of Family Law, 22,* 192–201.

Riley, D., Jr., De Anda, D., & Blackaller, C. A. (2007). The self-perceptions and interpersonal relationships of persons with significant physical disabilities: A qualitative pilot study. *Journal of Social Work in Disabilities and Rehabilitation, 6*(3), 1–31.

Rodriguez, R. J., Blatz, E. T., & Elbaum, B. (2014). Parents' views of schools' involvement efforts. *Exceptional Children, 81,* 79–95.

Rothstein-Fisch, C., Trumbull, E., & Garcia, S. G. (2009). Making the implicit explicit: Supporting teachers to bridge cultures. *Early Childhood Research Quarterly, 24,* 474–486.

Rowley, E., Chandler, S., Baird, G., Simonoff, E., Pickles, A., Loucas, T., & Charman, T. (2012). The experience of friendship, victimization and bullying in children with an autism spectrum disorder: Associations with child characteristics and school placement. *Research in Autism Spectrum Disorders, 6,* 1126–1134.

Satir, V. (1972). *Peoplemaking.* Palo Alto, CA: Science and Behavior.

Snell, M. E., & Brown, F. (2011). *Instruction of students with severe disabilities* (7th ed.). Upper Saddle River, NJ: Pearson Education.

Stainton, T., & Besser, H. (1998). The positive impact of children with an intellectual disability on the family. *Journal of Intellectual and Developmental Disability, 23*(1), 57–70.

Stein, R., & Sharkey, J. (2015). Your hands are (not) tied: School-based ethics when parents revoke special education consent. *Psychology in the Schools, 52,* 168–180.

Thomas, C. C., Correa, V. I., & Morsink, C. V. (2001). *Interactive teaming: Consultation and collaboration in special programs* (3rd ed.). Upper Saddle River, NJ: Prentice Hall.

Tiba, A., Johnson, C., & Vadineanu, A. (2012). Cognitive vulnerability and adjustment to having a child with a disability in parents of children with autistic spectrum disorder. *Journal of Cognitive and Behavioral Psychotherapies, 12,* 209–218.

Todd, S., Bromley, J., Ioannou, K., Harrison, J., Mellor, C., Taylor, E., & Crabtree, E. (2010). Using group-based parent training interventions with parents of children with disabilities: A description of process, content and outcomes in clinical practice. *Child and Adolescent Mental Health, 15*(3), 171–175.

Travers, J., Tincani, M., Whitby, P. S., & Boutot, E. A. (2014). Alignment of sexuality education with self-determination for people with significant disabilities: A review of research and future directions. *Education and Training in Autism and Developmental Disabilities, 49,* 232–247.

Tribe, R. (2007). Working with interpreters. *The Psychologist, 20*(3), 159–161.

Tudor, M. E., & Lerner, M. D. (2015). Intervention and support for siblings of youth with developmental disabilities: A systematic review. *Clinical Child and Family Psychology Review, 18,* 1–23.

Turnbull, A. P., & Turnbull, H. R. (2001). *Families, professionals, and exceptionality: Collaborating for empowerment* (4th ed.). Upper Saddle River, NJ: Merrill/Pearson Education.

Turnbull, A. P., Turnbull, H. R., Erwin, E., Soodak, L., & Shogren, K. A. (2015). *Families, professionals, and exceptionality: Positive outcomes through partnerships and trust* (7th ed.). Upper Saddle River, NJ: Pearson Higher Education.

Turnbull, R., & Turnbull, A. (2015). Looking backward and framing the future for parents' aspirations for their children with disabilities. *Remedial and Special Education, 36,* 52–57.

Vesely, C. K., Ewaida, M., & Anderson, E. A. (2014). Cultural competence of parenting education programs used by Latino families: A review. *Hispanic Journal of Behavioral Sciences, 36*(1), 27–47.

Webster, A. A., & Carter, M. (2013). Mutual liking, enjoyment, and shared interactions in the closest relationships between children with developmental disabilities and peers in inclusive school settings. *Journal of Developmental and Physical Disabilities, 25,* 373–393.

West, E. A., & Pirtle, J. M. (2014). Mothers' and fathers' perspectives on quality special educators and the attributes that influence effective inclusive practices. *Education and Training in Autism and Developmental Disabilities, 49,* 290–300.

White, S. E. (2014). Special education complaints filed by parents of students with autism spectrum disorders in the midwestern United States. *Focus on Autism and Other Developmental Disabilities, 29,* 80–87.

Yell, M. L. (2012). *The law and special education* (3rd ed.). Upper Saddle River, NJ: Pearson Education.

Zhang, K. (2012). Spirituality and early childhood special education: Exploring a "forgotten" dimension. *International Journal of Children's Spirituality, 17*(1), 39–49.

Chapter 12

Aceves, T. C. (2014). Supporting Latino families in special education through community agency-school partnerships. *Multicultural Education, 21*(3–4), 45–50.

Albrecht, S. F., Skiba, R. J., Losen, D. J., Chung, C., & Middelberg, L. (2012). Federal policy on disproportionality in special education: Is it moving us forward? *Journal of Disability Policy Studies, 23*(1), 14–25.

Baker, D., & Witt, P. (1996). Evaluation of the impact of two after-school programs. *Journal of Parks and Recreation Administration, 14,* 23–44.

Barnard-Brak, L., & Lechtenberger, D. (2010). Student IEP participation and academic achievement across time. *Remedial and Special Education, 31,* 343–349.

Barth, R. S. (1991). *Improving schools from within.* San Francisco: Jossey-Bass.

Berebitsky, D., Goddard, R. D., & Carlisle, J. F. (2014). An examination of teachers' perceptions of principal support for change and teachers' collaboration and communication around literacy instruction in Reading First schools. *Teachers College Record, 116*(4). Retrieved from file:///C:/Users/Marilyn%20Friend/Downloads/An%20Examination%20of%20Teachers%E2%80%99%20Perceptions%20of%20Principal%20Support%20for%20Change%20and%20Teachers%E2%80%99%20Collaboration%20and%20Communication%20Around%20Literacy%20Instruction%20in%20Reading%20First%20Schools.pdf

Bohanon, H., Castillo, J., & Afton, M. (2015). Embedding self-determination and futures planning within a schoolwide framework. *Intervention in School and Clinic, 50,* 203–209.

Brennan, D. D. (2015). Creating a climate for achievement. *Educational Leadership, 72*(5), 56–59.

Brown, D., Przywansky, W. B., & Schulte, A. C. (1987). *Psychological consultation: Introduction to theory and practice.* Boston: Allyn & Bacon.

Bruce, S. M., & Venkatesh, K. (2014). Special education disproportionality in the United States, Germany, Kenya, and India. *Disability & Society, 29,* 908–921.

Bruder, M. B., & Dunst, C. J. (2015). Parental judgments of early childhood intervention personnel practices: Applying a consumer science perspective. *Topics in Early Childhood Special Education, 34,* 200–210.

Causton, J., & Theoharis, G. (2014). *The principal's handbook for leading inclusive schools.* Baltimore, MD: Paul H. Brookes.

Chamberlin, M., & Plucker, J. (2008). P–16 education: Where are we going? Where have we been? *Phi Delta Kappan, 89,* 472–479.

Cheney, D. (2012). Transition tips for educators working with students with emotional and behavioral disabilities. *Intervention in School and Clinic, 48,* 22–29.

Chenoweth, K. (2015). How do we get there from here? *Educational Leadership, 72*(5), 16–20.

Cobb, C. (2015). Principals play many parts: A review of the research on school principals as special education leaders 2001–2011. *International Journal of Inclusive Education, 19,* 213–234.

Cosner, S. (2011). Teacher learning, instructional considerations and principal communication: Lessons from a longitudinal study of collaborative data use by teachers. *Educational Management Administration & Leadership, 39,* 568–589.

Council for Exceptional Children. (2003). *What every special educator must know: Ethics, standards, and guidelines for special education.* Arlington, VA: Author.

Council for Exceptional Children. (2011). Inclusive schools and community settings. *CEC Policy Manual, 2011* (p. H-13). Arlington, VA: Author.

Crosby, S. A., Rasinski, T., Padak, N., & Yildirim, K. (2015). A 3-year study of a school-based parental involvement program in early literacy. *Journal of Educational Research, 108,* 165–172.

Cross, A. F., Traub, E. K., Hunter-Pishgahi, L., & Shelton, G. (2004). Elements of successful inclusion for children with significant disabilities. *Topics in Early Childhood Special Education, 24*(3), 169–183.

David, J. L. (2011). After-school programs can pay off. *Educational Leadership, 68*(8), 84–85.

Dieterle, S., Guarino, C. M., Reckase, M. D., & Wooldridge, J. M. (2015). How do principals assign students to teachers? Finding evidence in administrative data and the implications for value added. *Journal of Policy Analysis and Management, 34*(1), 32–58.

Dobbertin, C. (2010). What kids learn from experts. *Educational Leadership, 68*(1), 64–67.

Dougherty, A. M. (2014). *Psychological consultation and collaboration in school and community settings* (6th ed.). Belmont, CA: Brooks/Cole.

Fleming, A. R., Del Valle, R., Kim, M., & Leahy, M. J. (2013). Best practice models of effective vocational rehabilitation service delivery in the public rehabilitation program: A review and synthesis of the empirical literature. *Rehabilitation Counseling Bulletin, 56,* 146–159.

Friend, M. (2014). *Co-Teach! Building and sustaining effective classroom partnerships in inclusive schools* (2nd ed.). Greensboro, NC: Marilyn Friend, Inc.

Fullan, M. (2010). The awesome power of the principal. *Principal, 89*(4), 10–12.

Gill, W. A. (2011). Middle school A/B block and traditional scheduling: An analysis of math and reading performance by race. *NASSP Bulletin, 95,* 281–301.

Griffin, M. M., Taylor, J. L., Urbano, R. C., & Hodapp, R. M. (2014). Involvement in transition planning meetings among high school students with autism spectrum disorders. *Journal of Special Education, 47*(4), 256–264.

Heck, R. H., & Hallinger, P. (2010). Testing a longitudinal model of distributed leadership effects on school improvement. *Leadership Quarterly, 21,* 867–885.

Hoaglund, A. E., Birkenfeld, K., & Box, J. A. (2014). Professional learning communities: Creating a foundation for collaboration skills in pre-service teachers. *Education, 134,* 521–528.

Honigsfeld, A., & Dove, M. G. (2010b). *Collaboration and co-teaching: Strategies for English learners.* Thousand Oaks, CA: Corwin.

Howard, V. F., Williams, B. F., & Lepper, C. (2010). *Very young children with special needs: A foundation for educators, families, and service providers* (4th ed.). Upper Saddle River, NJ: Pearson Education.

Huberman, M., Navo, M., & Parrish, T. (2012). Effective practices in high performing districts serving students in special education. *Journal of Special Education Leadership, 25*(2), 59–71.

Hughes, C., Carter, E., & Wehman, P. (2012). *The new transition handbook: Strategies high school teachers use that work!* Baltimore, MD: Paul H. Brookes.

Kaehne, A., & Beyer, S. (2014). Person-centred reviews as a mechanism for planning the post-school transition of young people with intellectual disability. *Journal of Intellectual Disability Research, 58*(7), 603–613.

Karpur, A., Brewer, D., & Golden, T. (2014). Critical program elements in transition to adulthood: Comparative analysis of New York State and the NLTS2. *Career Development and Transition for Exceptional Individuals, 37,* 119–130.

Kidron, Y., & Lindsay, J. (2014). Stated briefly: What does the research say about increased learning time and student outcomes? (REL 2015-061). Alexandria, VA: Regional Educational Laboratory Appalachia, CAN Corporation. (ERIC Document Reproduction No. ED547261) Retrieved from http://www.eric.ed.gov/contentdelivery/servlet/ERICServlet?accno=ED547261

Killion, J. (2011). A bold move forward: Consortium outlines new standards for teacher leaders. *Journal of Staff Development, 32*(3), 10–12.

Knotek, S. (2003). Bias in problem solving and the social process of student study teams: A qualitative investigation. *Journal of Special Education, 37,* 2–14.

Kochhar-Bryant, C. A. (2008). *Collaboration and system coordination for students with special needs: From early childhood to the postsecondary years.* Upper Saddle River, NJ: Merrill/Pearson Education.

Lee, G. K., & Carter, E. W. (2012). Preparing transition-age students with high-functioning autism spectrum disorders for meaningful work. *Psychology in the Schools, 49,* 988–1000.

Little, J. W. (1982). Norms of collegiality and experimentations: Workplace conditions of school success. *American Educational Research Journal, 19,* 325–340.

Louis, K., & Wahlstrom, K. (2011). Principals as cultural leaders. *Phi Delta Kappan, 92*(5), 52–56.

MacDonald, E. (2011). When nice won't suffice: Honest discourse is key to shifting school culture. *Journal of Staff Development, 32*(3), 45–47.

Massachusetts 2020 and Boston Public Schools. (2004). *The transition to success pilot project.* Boston: Massachusetts 2020.

McCaffrey, D. F., Pane, J. F., Springer, M. G., Burns, S. F., Haas, A., & Society for Research on Educational Effectiveness. (2011). *Team pay for performance: Experimental evidence from Round Rock's project on incentives in teaching* [Conference abstract]. Evanston, IL: Society for Research on Educational Effectiveness. (ERIC Document Reproduction Service No. ED518379)

Meadows, D., Davies, M., & Beamish, W. (2014). Teacher control over interagency collaboration: A roadblock for effective transitioning of youth with disabilities. *International Journal of Disability, Development and Education, 61,* 332–345.

Minke, K. M., & Vickers, H. S. (2015). Get families on board to navigate mental health issues. *Phi Delta Kappan, 96*(4), 22–28.

Murawski, W. W. (2012). Ten tips for using co-planning time more efficiently. *Teaching Exceptional Children, 44*(4), 8–15.

National Education Association. (2011). *Family–school–community partnerships 2.0: Collaborative strategies to advance student learning.* Washington, DC: Author.

National Network of Partnership Schools. (2008, Spring). Parent liaisons on action teams help bridge home and school. *Type 2 Research Brief,* 24. Retrieved from www.csos.jhu.edu/p2000/type2/issue24/researchbrief-24.htm

National Parent Teacher Association. (2009). *National standards for family–school partnerships: An implementation guide.* Washington, DC: National Congress of Parents and Teachers.

Nierengarten, G. (2013). Supporting co-teaching teams in high schools: Twenty research-based practices. *American Secondary Education, 42*(1), 73–83.

Noonan, P. (2014). *Transition teaming: 26 strategies for interagency collaboration.* Arlington, VA: Council for Exceptional Children.

Ordonez-Jasis, R., & Myck-Wayne, J. (2012). Community mapping in action: Uncovering resources and assets for young children and their families. *Young Exceptional Children, 15*(3), 31–45.

Osgood, D. W., Foster, E. M., & Courtney, M. E. (2010). Vulnerable populations and the transition to adulthood. *The Future of Children, 20,* 209–229.

Peercy, M., & Martin-Beltran, M. (2012). Envisioning collaboration: Including ESOL students and teachers in the mainstream classroom. *International Journal of Inclusive Education, 16,* 657–673.

Porter, T., Bromer, J., & Moodie, S. (2011). *Quality rating and improvement systems (QRIS) and family-sensitive caregiving in early care and education arrangements: Promising directions and challenges* (Issue brief OPRE 2011-11d). Washington, DC: Office of Planning, Research and Evaluation, Administration for Children and Families, U.S. Department of Health and Human Services.

Raver, S. A., & Childress, D. C. (2015). Collaboration and teamwork with families and professionals. In *Family-centered early intervention: Supporting infants and toddlers in natural environments* (pp. 31–52). Baltimore, MD: Paul H Brookes.

Resto & Alston. (2006). *Parent involvement at selected ready schools.* Washington, DC: Council of Chief State School Officers.

Richardson, W. (2009). *Blogs, wikis, podcasts, and other powerful Web tools for classrooms.* Thousand Oaks, CA: Corwin.

Robbins, P. M., & Alvy, H. B. (Eds.). (2014). *The principal's companion: Strategies to lead schools for student and teacher success.* Thousand Oaks, CA: Corwin.

Rodriguez, R. J., Blatz, E. T., & Elbaum, B. (2014). Parents' views of schools' involvement efforts. *Exceptional Children, 81,* 79–95.

Rodriguez, V., & Solis, S. L. (2013). Teachers' awareness of the learner–teacher interaction: Preliminary communication of a study investigating the teaching brain. *Mind, Brain, and Education, 7,* 161–169.

Sabornie, E. J., & deBettencourt, L. U. (2009). *Teaching students with mild and high-incidence disabilities at the secondary level* (3rd ed.). Upper Saddle River, NJ: Merrill/Pearson Education.

Sabornie, E. J., & deBettencourt, L. U. (2009). *Teaching students with mild and high-incidence disabilities at the secondary level* (3rd ed.). Upper Saddle River, NJ: Merrill/Pearson Education.

Sanders, M. G. (2014). Principal leadership for school, family, and community partnerships: The role of a systems approach to reform implementation. *American Journal of Education, 120,* 233–254.

Sarason, S. B. (1982). *The culture of the school and the problem of change* (2nd ed.). Boston: Allyn & Bacon.

Schmidt, J. J. (2003). *Counseling in schools: Essential services and comprehensive programs* (4th ed.). Boston, MA: Allyn & Bacon.

Shapiro, J. P., & Stefkovich, J. A. (2005). *Ethical leadership and decision making in education: Applying theoretical perspectives to complex dilemmas* (2nd ed.). Mahwah, NJ: Erlbaum.

Shippen, M. E., Patterson, D., Green, K. L., & Smitherman, T. (2012). Community and school practices to reduce delinquent behavior: Intervening on the school-to-prison pipeline. *Teacher Education and Special Education, 35,* 296–308.

Silverman, S. K., Hazelwood, C., & Cronin, P. (2009). *Universal education: Principles and practices for advancing achievement of students with disabilities,* 1–8. Retrieved September 29, 2011 from http://ohioleadership.org/up_doc/Universal_Ed_Report_2009-08.pdf

Smith, L. E., & Anderson, K. A. (2014). The roles and needs of families of adolescents with ASD. *Remedial and Special Education, 35*(2), 114–122.

Smith, S. C., & Scott, J. S. (1990). *The collaborative school: A work environment for effective instruction.* Eugene, OR: ERIC Clearinghouse on Educational Management, University of Oregon.

Summey, E., & Lashley, C. (2014). RtI at West Elementary: Supplement, supplant, or a little of each? *Journal of Cases in Educational Leadership, 17*(3), 12–20.

Talley, R. C., & Travis, S. S. (2014). *Multidisciplinary coordinated caregiving: Research, practice, policy.* New York, NY: Springer Science + Business Media.

Test, D. W., Smith, L. E., & Carter, E. W. (2014). Equipping youth with autism spectrum disorders for adulthood: Promoting rigor, relevance, and relationships. *Remedial and Special Education, 35*(2), 80–90.

Tierney, J., Grossman, J. B., & Resch, N. (1995). *Making a difference: An impact study of Big Brothers/Big Sisters.* Philadelphia: Public/Private Ventures.

Wagner, M., Newman, L., Cameto, R., Javitz, H., & Valdes, K. (2012). A national picture of parent and youth participation in IEP and transition planning meetings. *Journal of Disability Policy Studies, 23,* 140–155.

Watson, C., & Kabler, B. (2012). Improving educational outcomes for children in foster care. *Communique, 40*(5), 27–29.

Weathers, J. M. (2011). Teacher community in urban elementary schools: The role of leadership and bureaucratic accountability. *Education Policy Analysis Archives, 19*(3), 1–39.

Wehmeyer, M. L., Abery, B. H., Zhang, D., Heller, T., Hossain, W. A., Bacon, A.....Walker, H. M. (2011). Personal self-determination and moderating variables that impact efforts to promote self-determination. *Exceptionality, 19*(1), 19–30.

West-Olatunji, C., Behar-Horenstein, L., & Rant, J. (2008). Mediated lesson study, collaborative learning, and cultural competence among early childhood educators. *Journal of Research in Childhood Education, 23*(1), 96–108.

Williams, R. L., & Wehrman, J. D. (2010). Collaboration and confidentiality: Not a paradox but an understanding between principals and school counselors. *NASSP Bulletin, 94,* 107–119.

Yang, C., Hossain, S. Z., & Sitharthan, G. (2013). Collaborative practice in early childhood intervention from the perspectives of service providers. *Infants and Young Children, 26,* 57–73.

Youngs, P., Jones, N., & Low, M. (2011). How beginning special and general education elementary teachers negotiate role expectations and access professional resources. *Teachers College Record, 113,* 1506–1540.

Youngs, P., Jones, N., & Low, M. (2011). How beginning special and general education elementary teachers negotiate role expectations and access professional resources. *Teachers College Record, 113,* 1506–1540.

Zelkowski, J. (2010). Secondary mathematics: Four credits, block schedules, continuous enrollment? What maximizes college readiness? *Mathematics Educator, 20*(1), 8–21.

Zrike, S., & Connolly, C. (2015). Problem solvers: Teacher leader teams with content specialist to strengthen math instruction. *Journal of Staff Development, 36*(1), 20–22.

NAME INDEX

Abbate-Vaughn, J., 247
Abery, B. H., 306
Aceves, T. C., 275, 291
Achinstein, B., 202
Achoui, M., 272
Adamczyk, D. F., 159
Adler, R. B., 31, 32, 36, 43, 57, 60, 94, 98, 268
Afton, M., 306
Aguilar, J., 136, 265
Ahearn, C., 133
Al Hadidi, M. S., 275
Al Khateeb, J. M., 275
Al Khatib, A. J., 275
Albarracin, D., 230
Alborz, A., 244, 248, 251
Albrecht, S. F., 314
Albright, R. R., 213, 216
Algozzine, B., 213
Algozzine, R., 197, 201
Alhija, F. N. A., 203
Allday, R. A., 151, 197
Allegra, C., 192
Allen, S. F., 277
Allison, R., 148, 149
Almas, S., 218
Alst, D., 192
Alvarez, M. E., 190
Alvy, H. B., 302
Ammerman, S., 201
Amorose, A. J., 136
Anastasiou, D., 213
Andersen, M. N., 192
Anderson, E. A., 282
Anderson, E. S., 115
Anderson, J. A., 265
Anderson, K. A., 297
Anderson, L. M., 159
Anderson-Butcher, D., 4, 136
Anfara, V. J., 10
Anis-ul-Haq, M., 218
Appel, M., 55
Appenzeller, M., 271
Aramovich, N. P., 107, 127
Arditti, L. E., 117
Armer, B., 133
Aronin, S., 200
Aronson, K. R., 191

Arslan, E., 112, 115
Arthur-Stanley, A., 3
Artiles, A. J., 107
Ash, I. K., 104
Ash, P. B., 4, 153
Ashbaker, B., 253, 257
Ashbaker, B. Y., 161
Austin, T., 18
Avgar, A., 213
Bacharach, N., 159
Bacon, A., 306
Bae, S., 136
Bailey, D. B., 270
Baillien, E., 216
Baird, G., 271
Baker, B. L., 270
Baker, D., 294
Bal, A., 107
Balconi, M., 63
Ball, A., 136
Banerjee, N., 3
Bang, H., 134, 135, 153
Bangou, F., 18
Banks, J. A., 276
Barber, F., 11
Barden, J., 229
Barnard-Brak, L., 140, 307
Barron, T., 6, 144
Barsky, A., 225
Barsky, A. E., 212
Barth, R. S., 3, 302
Basso, D., 158
Bates, A. J., 242
Battilana, J., 226, 228
Baum, K. D., 136
Bauwens, J., 160
Bawany, S., 59
Beach Center on Disability, 284
Beam, P. C., 202
Beamish, W., 298
Bean, J., 4
Bear, G. G., 192
Beatty, M. J., 35
Beaudan, E., 227
Beavin, J., 33
Beebe, S. A., 27, 30, 34, 57, 94, 134, 153
Beebe, S. J., 34, 57, 94

Beebe-Frankenberger, M. E., 149
Begum, G. F., 270
Behar-Horenstein, L., 295–296
Behfar, K., 212
Behuniak, P., 3
Bellon-Harn, M. L., 13
Bennett, K. D., 276
Bennis, W., 12
Berckemeyer, J., 135
Berebitsky, D., 301
Bereczkei, T., 218
Berger, J., 191
Berckemeyer, J., 135
Bernardin, H. J., 221
Bert, S., 13
Bess, K. D., 14
Besser, H., 278
Beukeboom, C., 59
Beyard, K., 134
Beyer, S., 296
Biederman, P. W., 12
Billet, S., 173
Bindels-de Hens, K. B., 273
Bingham, G. A., 244
Binyamin, G., 127
Birkenfeld, K., 315
Bittel, P., 250
Blacher, J., 270
Black, A. C., 3
Black, J. B., 70
Blackaller, C. A., 272
Blanchard, S. B., 271
Blanks, B., 160, 173
Blatchford, P., 244
Blatz, E. T., 265, 291
Bleck, A. A., 192
Bless, G., 160
Blevins, C. A., 192
Boatright, B., 197
Bodemer, D., 110
Bohanon, H., 306
Bohlmann, J., 133, 152
Bollen, K., 216
Bond, S. A., 212
Borden, L., 136
Born, M. P., 62
Boscardin, M. L., 176
Boutot, E. A., 273
Bowen, M., 266, 272
Bower, M., 96
Box, J. A., 315

Boyd, S. D., 60
Bradley, B. H., 212, 219, 220
Bradley, R., 12
Bradshaw, C. P., 136
Brammer, L. M., 83
Brandel, J., 134
Brantley, C., 32, 41, 85
Brennan, D. D., 300
Brett, J. M., 220, 223
Brew, F. P., 223
Brewer, D., 296
Brightman, H. J., 112
Bringle, R. G., 13
Brinkley, R. C., 81
Brinkmann, J., 159
Brock, M. E., 273
Broer, S. M., 250
Bromer, J., 294
Bromley, J., 284
Bronstein, L., 136
Brookman-Frazee, L., 12
Brown, D., 187, 188, 198, 314
Brown, F., 273
Brown, K., 164
Brown, K. G., 212, 219, 220
Brown, N., 160
Brown-Chidsey, R., 13
Brubaker, D., 222
Brubaker, J. C., 195
Bruce, S. M., 314
Bruder, M. B., 296
Brunner, C. C., 18
Brusca-Vega, R., 164
Buck, R., 54, 56
Bulach, C. R., 62
Burbank, M. D., 242
Burdett, C. S., 196
Burgoon, J. K., 54
Burke, M. M., 222
Burke, W. W., 224
Burns, S. F., 313
Burrello, J., 162
Burrello, L., 162
Butera, G., 3, 187
Cahnmann-Taylor, M., 160, 164
Cairns, D. R., 223
Cameron, D. L., 244, 248
Cameto, R., 306
Canter, L., 13
Caplan, G., 187
Caqtapano, S., 203

Carey, R., 112
Carlisle, J. F., 301
Carmeli, A., 127
Carnahan, C. R., 200, 251
Caron, E. A., 9
Carranza, F., 222
Carter, E., 241, 243, 245, 248, 297
Carter, E. A., 269
Carter, E. W., 244, 273, 296
Carter, M., 270, 271
Carter, N., 20
Carter, R. J., 200
Carter, B., 269
Casciaro, T., 226, 228
Cash, W., 82
Castek, J., 14
Castellano, S., 117
Castillo, J., 306
Castledine, G., 105
Castro, S. L., 221
Cauberghe, V., 56
Causton, J., 176, 302
Causton-Theoharis, J., 158, 244, 246
Cavanagh, M., 96
Cavanaugh, K., 104
Chadee, D., 55
Chalfant, J. C., 147
Chamberlin, M., 294
Chandler, S., 271
Charkoudian, L., 221
Charles, K. J., 179
Charlton, C. T., 18, 132
Charman, T., 271
Cheak-Zamora, N. C., 272
Cheatham, G. A., 104
Chen, D., 142
Cheney, D., 297
Chenoweth, K., 300, 313
Childress, D. C., 303
Chiu, M. M., 105
Cho, H., 104
Choi, B. C. K., 140, 143
Choi, M., 224
Chou, E. Y., 214
Chou, P. N., 203
Christiano, E. A., 187
Christie, L. S., 196
Christman, J., 198
Chun, E., 241
Chung, C., 211, 214, 314
Chung, W., 213

Cirrin, F. M., 159
City, E., 10
Claeys, A., 56
Claeys, L., 201
Clark, D., 248
Clark, M., 104
Clarke, B. L., 194
Clarke, L., 159, 251
Cobb, C., 286, 301
Cochran, D. C., 202
Coffee, G., 194
Cohen, T. R., 214
Coke, T., 221
Coleman, P., 211, 214
Collaro, A. L., 192
Conderman, G., 158–159, 173, 212
Connolly, C., 315
Conoley, C., 10
Conoley, J., 10
Conroy, M., 190, 191
Cook, B. G., 244, 248
Cook, L., 6, 21, 163, 173
Cook, R. E., 142, 270
Cooney, M., 273
Cooper, K. S., 27
Corey, G., 83
Correa, V. I., 134, 139, 281
Cortes, K. I., 27
Cosner, S., 301
Council for Chief State School Officers, 27
Council for Exceptional Children, 143, 291, 313
Courtney, M. E., 307
Crabtree, E., 284
Cramer, E. D., 276
Craven, K., 14
Crespin, B. J., 160
Cronin, P., 315
Cropley, C., 268
Crosby, S. A., 292
Cross, A. F., 296
Culatta, B., 244
Curry, K., 205
Curry, K. A., 212
Czibor, A., 218
D'Agostino, C., 13
Dahlberg, K., 159
Daly, E. I., 192
Daniels, T., 84
Daniels, V. I., 259
Danielson, L., 12
Danışman, A., 225

Dannenhoffer, J. F., 136
Darney, D., 136
Darrow, A., 248, 255
D'Auria, J., 4, 153
David, J. L., 294
Davidson, B. D., 136
Davies, M., 298
Davis, E., 202
Davis, J. M., 222
Davis, M., 36, 94
De Anda, D., 272
De Witte, H., 216
deBettencourt, L. U., 296, 298
Del Valle, R., 298
Delamatre, J., 148
Delkamiller, J., 135
DeMarree, K. G., 217
Dempsey, I., 269, 277, 279
Denton, C. A., 198
Derrick, D. C., 54
Dessenmontet, R. S., 160
Dever, R., 17
DeVito, J. A., 31, 41, 59, 88, 93, 96
Dibble, R., 22
Dickens, V., 179
Dickson, D., 86
Diehl, S. F., 159
Dieker, L., 158
Dieterle, S., 313
DiGennaro Reed, F. D., 192
Dignath, D., 212
Dinnesen, M. S., 178
D'Innocenzo, L., 136
Dixon, J., 100
Dollard, M. F., 212
Doolittle, J., 12
Dorn, B. C., 219
Dougherty, A. M., 187, 196, 295
Dove, M. G., 4, 159, 307
Dowdy, A., 173
Downing, J. E., 135, 136, 248
Doykos, B., 14
Doyle, M., 243, 245, 248, 250, 259
Doyle, M. B., 245, 250
Drame, E. R., 5
Driver, M. K., 195
Drori, I., 117
du Pré, A., 36, 43, 57, 60
DuBois, M., 133
DuFour, R., 3, 5
Dufrene, B. A., 192

Dulaney, S. K., 3, 13
Dunst, C. J., 269, 270, 279, 296
Dwairy, M., 272
Dykens, E. M., 264
Earnest, D. R., 215
Eatman, J., 41
Ebata, A. T., 267
Eberlin, R. J., 216
Edelman, S. W., 250
Eder, A. B., 212
Egan, G., 54, 57
Eigen, Z. J., 221
Eilertsen, D. E., 134, 135, 153
Eisenman, L. T., 162, 190
Elbaum, B., 265, 291
Elford, M., 200
Elkins, A. C., 54
Elliott, J. S., 177
Elliott, S. N., 133
Elmhorst, J., 32, 36, 98
Embury, D. C., 159, 178
Emelo, R., 105
Engelmann, T., 110
Entwisle, D. R., 266
Ephross, P. H., 132
Erchul, W. P., 189
Ertesvåg, S. K., 5
Erwin, E., 96, 266
Erwin, E. J., 274
Eslinger, J. C., 3
Esplio, P., 84
Ettekal, I., 27
Euwema, M., 216
Evans, R., 218
Evans, S. B., 196
Ewaida, M., 282
Ewals, F. M., 273
Fabe, A., 278
Fabiano, G. A., 148
Fanning, P., 36, 94
Fenton, K. S., 151
Fenty, N. S., 160, 173
Festinger, L., 229
Fidelman, M., 11
Fincher, R., 222
Fiore, S. M., 105, 114
First, J., 272
Fisher, G., 160, 173
Fisher, M., 241, 243, 254
Flaspohler, P., 4
Fleming, A. R., 298

Fleury, M. L., 257
Flores, B. B., 201
Floyd, K., 27
Floyd, R. G., 148
Flynn, P., 104
Flynn, P. F., 159
Forbes, L., 173
Ford, J. D., 227
Ford, L. W., 227
Foreman, A., 13
Foriska, T., 147
Foster, E. M., 307
Frank, J. L., 187
Frank, K. A., 3
French, N. K., 243, 245, 251, 257
Frenkel, K. A., 11
Fresko, B., 203
Frey, A. J., 190
Friend, M., 6, 21, 144, 158, 159, 160, 162, 163, 164, 165, 172, 173, 196, 304, 311
Friesen, A., 3, 104
Fuchs, D., 148
Fuchs, L. S., 148
Fuglesang, S. L., 134, 135, 153
Fullan, M., 302
Fullerton, A., 13
Fulton, J., 15
Gable, R. A., 198, 200
Gallagher, H., 3
Gallagher, R. J., 136, 265
Gallivan-Fenlon, A., 133
Galloway, S., 133
Gallucci, C., 197
Gamble, M., 60, 81, 85, 88
Gamble, T. K., 60, 81, 85, 88
Garcia, S. G., 41, 275
García-Barba Hernández, F., 224
García-Cabrera, A. M., 224
Garcia-Preto, C., 269
Gareis, C. R., 203
Garland, A. F., 12
Gaughan, E., 146
Gay, G. K., 136
Geen, A. G., 162
Geller, J. D., 14
Gerlach, K., 246
Gerschel, A., 211, 215
Gesten, E., 212
Giangreco, M. F., 161, 243, 244, 245, 248, 250, 259
Gibson, C., 22
Giles, E., 241, 251

Giles, H., 68
Gill, W. A., 310
Gilrane, C., 259
Glazzard, J., 248, 250
Gobble, M. M., 117
Gobillot, E., 11
Goddard, R. D., 301
Goessling, D. P., 244
Goldberg, S. B., 220
Golden, T., 296
Goldman, S. E., 222
Goldring, R., 201
Goldstein, J., 3
Goldstein, M. B., 134
Goman, C. K., 12
Goodman, G., 47, 68
Goold, M., 11
Goulston, M., 57, 59
Granger, J. D., 254
Gravois, T., 191
Graziano, K. J., 165
Greek, M., 254
Green, J., 136
Green, K. L., 292
Greer, L. L., 213
Gregg, M., 198, 200
Gregory, A., 146
Grenda, J. P., 212
Grenny, J., 82
Gresham, F. M., 190
Griffin, M. M., 296
Griffith, G. M., 270
Grillo, K., 162
Grim, J., 13
Gross, M. A., 217
Grossman, J. B., 294
Guarino, C. M., 313
Guerrero, L. K., 217
Gülcan, M. G., 152
Gully, S. M., 138
Gürür, H., 173
Gustafson, J. K., 148, 149
Gustavson, P., 133, 153
Gut, D. M., 202
Haas, A., 313
Hackett, D., 83
Hackmann, D. G., 212
Hagan-Burke, S., 177, 205
Hahn Tapper, A. J., 215
Halevy, N., 214
Hall, E. T., 56

Hall, J. A., 63
Hall, T. E., 146, 147, 148
Hallam, P. R., 18, 132, 203
Halle, J. W., 267
Hallinger, P., 315
Hall-Kenyon, K. M., 244
Hallmark, C., 148
Hamdani, M. R., 212, 219, 220
Hamilton-Jones, B., 246
Hamlin, D., 62
Hammond, J., 40
Hang, Q., 160, 164
Hanlon, J., 133
Hardin, B. J., 271
Hargie, O., 86
Harlacher, J. E., 12
Harman, D. R., 12, 13, 148, 187
Harper, J., 107
Harris, B. A., 250
Harris, M., 213
Harris, T. E., 30, 136
Harrison, J., 284
Harry, B., 277, 280
Hartley, C., 148
Harvard Business Review, 11
Harvey, S., 243
Harvey, T. R., 228
Harvill, R., 98
Hasbrouck, J., 198
Hastings, R. P., 270
Hatton, S., 273
Havnes, A., 142, 151
Hayashi, S. K., 213
Hazelwood, C., 315
He, Y., 202, 203, 275
Head-Reeves, D., 62
Hebbler, K., 270
Heck, R. H., 315
Heck, T. W., 159
Hedeen, T., 223
Hedin, L., 158–159
Heitin, R. C., 222
Heller, T., 306
Hemmings, A., 132
Henning, J. E., 202
Henning, N., 3
Henry, L. A., 14
Heritage, J., 100
Heritage, M., 100
Herman, K. C., 136
Hernandez, J. E., 280

Hernandez, P., 228
Hershkowitz, I., 84
Hesse, F. W., 110
Hicks, D., 173, 214
Hilberink, S. R., 273
Hite, J. M., 203
Hite, S. J., 203
Hoaglund, A. E., 315
Hocker, J., 211, 212, 213, 216
Hodapp, R. M., 296
Hofstadter, K. L., 192
Hofstede, G., 41
Hong, S., 134
Hong, V., 191
Honig, B., 117
Honigsfeld, A., 4, 159, 307
Hoover, J. J., 148, 149
Hord, S. M., 10
Horner, R. H., 148, 149
Horvath, C. W., 35
Hossain, S. Z., 295
Hossain, W. A., 306
Houmanfar, R., 75
Hourcade, J. J., 160
Howard, L., 178
Howard, V. F., 139, 142, 278, 302
Howerter, C. S., 160
Howland, A. A., 265
Huang, C., 192
Huber, J. J., 176
Huberman, M., 5, 9, 16, 315
Hudson, T. M., 151, 197
Huff, K. L., 160
Hugh, R., 198
Hughes, C., 297
Hughes-Scholes, C. H., 82
Huisman, S., 203
Hume, A. E., 133
Hunt, G. H., 243, 257
Hunt, J. H., 164, 203
Hunt, P., 136
Hunter-Pishgahi, L., 296
Hurley, S. M., 161, 244
Hurley-Chamberlain, D., 6, 163, 173
Hybels, S., 52
Iachini, A., 4
Idol, L., 196
Ikeda, M. J., 148, 149
Illback, R. J., 226
Ingersoll, R., 201, 203
Ioannou, K., 284

NAME INDEX

Irvine, J. J., 223
Isenhart, M. W., 215
Israel, M., 200
Ivey, A., 84
Ivey, A. E., 59, 61, 62, 81, 84, 85, 86, 270
Ivey, M. B., 59, 61, 62, 81, 84, 85, 86, 270
Jackson, A., 20
Jackson, D. D., 226
Jacobs E., 98
Janney, R., 134
Janssen, J., 110
Jäschke, J. M., 55
Jasgur, R., 112
Javitz, H., 306
Jehn, K. A., 133, 213
Jenkins, S. R., 192
Jensen, M. A., 136
Jimenez-Silva, M., 104
Johannessen, A., 12
Johns, B. H., 250, 257
Johnson, C., 269
Johnson, D. W., 54, 83, 85, 94, 135, 136, 151, 153
Johnson, F. P., 85, 135, 136, 151, 153
Johnson, L., 276
Johnson, L. J., 5
Johnson, S. D., 96
Johnson, S. F., 149
Jones, B. A., 259
Jones, C. R., 243, 257
Jones, H. A., 134, 139
Jones, J., 13
Jones, J. G., 229
Jones, J. M., 55
Jones, N., 300, 305
Jordan, P. J., 220
Joyce, B., 197
Joyce, B. R., 197
Kabler, B., 294
Kaehne, A., 296
Kaiser, S. M., 151
Kaldenberg, E., 241
Kamens, M., 177
Kampwirth, T. J., 5, 112, 187, 192, 193, 225
Kang, S., 70
Kao, B., 276
Karpur, A., 296
Katz, J., 10
Katz, J. J., 214
Kauffman, J. M., 213
Kaufman, M. T., 151
Kaufman, R. C., 133

Kaye, D., 121
Kealy, M. V., 176
Keen, D., 269, 277
Keigher, A., 201
Keim, A. C., 215
Kelly, F., 119
Kemmery, M. A., 271
Kemp, F. D., 223
Kendall, E., 119
Keranen, N., 215
Kerr, N., 133
Kershner, R., 173
Keys, C. B., 159
Kidron, Y., 294
Kiesel, A., 212
Killion, J., 315
Killumets, E., 136
Kim, J., 41
Kim, M., 298
Kim, O., 254
King, H. B., 136
King, M., 119
Kingston, N., 104
Kirk, J. F., 245
Kirkpatrick, R., 158
Klein, M. D., 142, 270
Klotz, A. C., 212, 219, 220
Knapp, M. L., 34, 94
Knight, J., 198
Knight, R. T., 202
Knopf, H. T., 277
Knotek, S., 108, 314
Knox, J. A., 10
Koch, J., 133
Kochenderfer-Ladd, B., 27
Kochhar-Bryant, C. A., 279, 294
Koester, J., 27, 36, 39, 40, 132
Kohn, N. W., 117
Koivunen, J., 192
Kolodziej, R., 110
Koppensteiner, M., 55
Kostić, A., 55
Kozleski, E. B., 107
Kozlowski, D. V., 134
Kozlowski, S. W. J., 138
Kratochwill, T. R., 187, 190, 194
Kübler-Ross, E., 270
Kuehner-Hebert, K., 11
Kugler, K., 211, 214
Kuijpers, M., 134
Kumkale, G. T., 230

Kuntze, J., 62
Kupzyk, S., 192
Kurebayashi, K., 223
Kurpius, D. J., 195
Kushner, M. I., 147
Ladd, G. W., 27
Lalvani, P., 3
Lamb, M., 84
Lambie, R., 266, 268, 269
Lampel, J., 117
Landis, R. S., 215
Lane, K. L., 244, 273
Lang, A., 218
Lange, C., 160
Larson, J. R., 127
Lash, M. J., 17
Lashley, C., 312
Laughlin, P. R., 107, 112
Lawson, H. A., 4
Le Fevre, D. M., 44
Leader-Janssen, E., 135
Leahy, M. J., 298
Lechtenberger, D., 140, 307
Lee, E. K., 213
Lee, G. K., 296
Lennox, A., 115
Lentz, K., 149
Lepper, C., 139, 278, 302
Lerner, M. D., 271
Lester, M., 12
Lestremau, L., 192
Letsky, M. P., 114
Levi, D. J., 136
Lewis, S., 245
Lhospital, A. S., 146
Liao, H., 98
Liaupsin, C. J., 190
Liborion, N., 136
Liff, S., 133, 153
Lindsay, J., 294
Lines, C., 3
Littauer, H., 84
Little, J. W., 314
Little, M. E., 203
Litwin, A. S., 221
Liu, S., 117, 118
Llorens, S., 36
Lloyd, T. J., 270
Lo, L., 279, 280
Lobato, D., 276
Lochman, J. E., 136

Loeb, D. F., 134
Loney, E., 136, 139
Long, A. J., 190
Long, K. A., 276
Loode, S., 223
Lopez, A. E., 4, 205
Lopez-Fresno, P., 107
Losen, D. J., 314
Loucas, T., 271
Louis, K., 300
Love, E., 148, 149
Low, M., 300, 305
Ludlow, B., 14
Luiselli, T. E., 250
Lum, H., 114
Lushen, K., 254
Lustig, M. W., 27, 36, 39, 40, 132
Lynch, E. W., 41, 56, 275, 276
Lyons, R., 114
MacDonald, E., 312
MacDonald, G., 83
MacFarland, S. Z. C., 250
Machalicek, W., 273
Madigan, J. C., 176
Magnusson, R., 244, 245
Mahdavi, J. N., 149
Mahoney, A., 273
Maier, J., 136
Mainzer, R., 176
Maki, K. E., 148
Malik, S., 270
Mancillas, A., 67
Mangin, M., 14
Mannix, E. A., 212
Mara, M., 55
Marchant, M., 20
Marcoulides, G. A., 270
Marcus, L. J., 219
Marks, M., 133
Marsh, J. A., 198, 199
Martens, B. K., 189
Martin, C. L., 83
Martin, J. N., 43
Martin, T., 244, 248, 251
Martin-Beltran, M., 308
Martinez, M., 3, 107
Martinez, M. C., 214
Martinez, R. S., 3, 187
Martorell, F., 198, 199
Massachusetts 2020 and Boston Public Schools, 294
Masson, R., 98

Mast, M. S., 63
Masters, M. F., 213, 216
Masterson, J. T., 27, 30, 134, 153
Mastropieri, M. A., 171
Mathews, S., 133
Mathieu, J. E., 136
Mathur, S. R., 250, 257
Mattos, M., 3, 5
Maxwell, J. P., 151
May, M. E., 205
Maynard, M. T., 136
McBride, A., 259
McBride, S., 13
McCaffrey, D. F., 313
McCall, Z., 197
McCarthy, J., 62
McClure, G., 160, 164
McCoach, D. B., 3, 265
McComb, S., 12
McCombs, J., 198, 199
McCombs, J. S., 198
McCorkle, S., 222
McCoy, N., 158
McCroskey, J. C., 35
McCulley, L., 171
McDaniel, E. R., 43
McDuffie, K. A., 171
McDuffie-Landrum, K., 160, 173
McGinley, V., 162, 190
McGoldrick, M., 269
McGrath, M. Z., 250, 257
McHatton, P. A., 197
McIntosh, K., 133
McKay, M., 36, 94
McKenney, E. W., 190, 191
McKenzie, A. R., 245
McKenzie, F., 82
McKenzie, H. S., 15, 187, 196
McKimmie, B. M., 127
McLaughlin, M. J., 9
McMahon, S. D., 159
McMillan, R., 82
McMillan, S., 119
McNamara, K., 148
McNaughton, D., 62
McNulty, E. J., 219
Meadan, H., 267
Meadows, D., 298
Medina, M. A., 13
Mehu, M., 70
Mellin, E. A., 136

Mellor, C., 284
Menninger, W. C., 133
Mercer, D., 222
Mercier, H., 127
Mesko, N., 218
Meyer, L. H., 265
Michinov, N., 118
Mickelson, R., 3
Middelberg, L., 314
Mike, A., 203
Miller, G. E., 3
Miller, M., 32, 41, 54, 56, 85
Miltenberger, R. G., 250
Minke, K. M., 294
Minnes, P., 267–268
Mitchinson, A., 211, 214
Miura, A., 223
Molen, H. T., 62
Moller, S., 3
Moloney, R., 96
Monroe, T., 112
Monzó, L. D., 247
Moodie, S., 294
Moore, A., 246
Moore, J. K., 99
Moorehead, T., 162
Morgan, J., 160, 161, 253, 257
Morris, K. L., 148
Morrison, J., 40
Morsink, C. V., 134, 139, 281
Moses, P., 223
Moss, C. K., 273
Moultrie, R., 147
Mraz, M., 197, 201
Mueller, T. G., 140, 151, 222
Mulder, M., 134
Mullen, C. A., 202
Mundschenk, N. A., 246
Murawski, W. W., 20, 177, 307
Murayama, A., 223
Murphy, G., 136, 139
Murray, A., 224
Musallam, N., 211, 214
Mutua, K., 213
Myck-Wayne, J., 291, 295
Myers, B., 15
Nakayama, T. K., 43
Nan, S. A., 223
Nappi, J. S., 14
Nardon, L., 115
Nason, E. R., 138

Nathans, L., 205
Nation, M., 14
National Association of Secondary School Principals, 10
National Center for Education Evaluation and Regional Assistance, 203
National Center for Education Statistics, 241
National Education Association, 292
National Network of Partnership Schools, 293
National Parent Teacher Association, 293
National School Public Relations Association, 89
Navarrete, L. A., 165
Navo, M., 5, 9, 16, 315
Neilsen-Gatti, S., 151, 197
Nellis, L. M., 12, 13, 148, 187
Nelson, D., 191
Nelson, J. R., 243
Nelson, L. G. L., 271
Nelson, N. W., 159
Nespor, J., 214
Neuendorf, K., 41
Nevin, A., 196
Nevin, A. I., 139, 248
Newell, M., 108, 112, 187, 189
Newman, D. S., 12, 13, 104, 148, 187
Newman, L., 280, 306
Niazi, G., 218
Nichols, C., 173
Nichols, J., 173
Nichols, W. C., 268
Niebling, B. C., 148, 149
Nierengarten, G., 160, 310
Noble, C., 222
Noonan, J., 13
Noonan, P., 297
Norman, K., 148
Nussbaum-Beach, S., 203
Nyatuga, B., 133
Obiakor, F. E., 213
O'Byrne, W. I., 14
Ocasio, K., 192
Officer, S. H., 13
Oglesby, J. M., 105
Ojanen, T., 212
O'Keefe, W. S., 105
O'Keeffe, B. V., 244, 245
Olivos, E. M., 4, 136, 265, 277
Ordonez-Jasis, R., 291, 295
Oreg, S., 226
Orelove, F., 133
Ormerod, T., 105
O'Rourke, L., 241, 243, 245, 248

Orsati, F. T., 246
Ortiz, A., 107
Ortiz, A. A., 147
Osgood, D. W., 307
Osher, D., 107
Otis, M. R., 221
O'Toole, J., 247
Ovesen, M. R., 134, 135, 153
Padak, N., 292
Pagani, S., 63
Pak, A. W. P., 140, 143
Palawat, M., 205
Pancsofar, N., 162
Pane, J. F., 313
Panter, A. T., 214
Paolucci-Whitcomb, P., 196
Papalia-Beradi, A., 146, 147, 148
Pardini, P., 160
Park, S. K., 222
Parker, C. A., 187, 195
Parker, S. D., 271
Parrish, T., 5, 9, 16, 315
Parthasarathy, R., 139
Patterson, D., 292
Patterson, K., 82
Paulus, P. B., 117
Pearl, C., 158
Peercy, M., 308
Pelsue, D., 241, 243, 245, 248
Penuel, W. R., 3
Pérez, B., 201
Perkins, D. F., 191
Perry, A., 267–268
Petalas, M. A., 270
Peter, M., 223
Peterson, R. S., 212
Petr, C. G., 140
Petrina, N., 270
Petroff, J. G., 162
Pfeiffer, S. I., 151
Phillippo, K., 146
Pickles, A., 271
Pierce, C. A., 215
Pirtle, J. M., 265
Plante, W., 276
Pleasants, S. L., 241, 243, 254
Pleet, A. M., 162, 190
Ploessl, D. M., 160, 173, 198, 200
Plucker, J., 294
Poling, A., 273
Poller, J. L., 278

Polly, D., 197, 201
Polsky, L., 133, 211, 215
Porter, R. E., 43
Porter, T., 294
Postlethwaite, B. E., 212, 219, 220
Potts, E. A., 178
Powell, M. B., 82
Powell, S., 203
Powers, K. M., 5, 112, 187, 192, 193, 225
Pozzato, L. R., 54
Prater, M., 20
Predy, L. K., 133
Press, S., 222
Proctor, R. F., 31, 36, 94
Proudfoot, J. G., 54
Prudencio, F. E., 215
Pruitt, D. G., 219, 221
Pryzwansky, W. B., 187, 188, 195, 314
Public Broadcasting System, 55
Pugach, M. C., 5
Putnam, L. L., 231
Pysh, M. V., 147
Qiu, T., 133, 152
Qualls, W., 133, 152
Quirk, K., 61, 81, 86, 270
Rabren, K., 160, 164
Radesky, J., 276
Rafoth, M. A., 147
Rahn-Blakeslee, A., 148, 149
Rambo, K., 3
Rance-Roney, J., 164
Ransom, K. A., 194
Rant, J., 295–296
Rasheed, H., 148
Rasinski, T., 292
Ratcliff, N. J., 243, 257
Raven, B. H., 18
Raver, S. A., 303
Ray, D. K., 122
Ray, J. A., 4
Reardon, C., 11
Reckase, M. D., 313
Redlich, A., 84
Redmond, M. V., 34, 57, 94
Reese, M. J., 222
Reid, R., 254
Reinke, W. M., 136
Reis, S. M., 3
Reiter-Palmon, R., 127
Resch, N., 294
Resto & Alston, 291

Reumann-Moore, R., 198
Revelle, C., 205
Rhodes, V., 132
Rice, D. J., 136
Richards, H., 243
Richardson, J., 3, 137
Richardson, J. V., 84
Richardson, W., 299
Richey, B. E., 221
Riddles, M., 201
Riffer, M., 198
Rijnbout, J. S., 127
Riley, D., Jr., 272
Ring, M., 133
Rios, K., 217
Rispens, S., 213
Ritzman, M. J., 135
Rivera, E. A., 159
Robbins, P. M., 302
Roberson, T., 148
Roberts, M., 259
Robertson-Courtney, P., 147
Robinson, S. E., 244
Robinson, V. J., 44
Rock, M. L., 160, 173, 198, 200
Rodman, G., 36, 43, 57, 60, 268
Rodriguez, R. J., 265, 291
Rodriguez, V., 306
Roellke, C. F., 96
Rogers, C. R., 70
Romano, N. J., 122
Rosen, M. A., 136
Rosenfeld, L. B., 31, 94
Rosenfield, S., 187, 191
Rossetti, Z. S., 244
Rotatori, A., 213
Rothstein, L., 149
Rothstein-Fisch, C., 41, 275
Roulston, K., 94
Rowley, E., 271
Roy, C. S., 43
Ruben, B. J., 13
Ruben, M. A., 63
Rueda, R. S., 247
Runhaar, P., 134
Ruona, W. E. A., 224
Rupp, D. E., 133, 152
Russell, A., 244
Russell, L., 259
Rutherford, G., 243
Ryan, C. S., 223

Ryan, E. B., 68
Ryndak, D. L., 248
Rytivaara, A., 173
Sabatino, C. A., 192, 194
Sabornie, E. J., 296, 298
Sadri, G., 211, 223
Saeed, T., 218
Salanova, M., 36
Salas, E, 105
Salas, E., 114, 136
Salmon, D., 104
Salter, A., 198, 200
Samovar, L. A., 43
Sanchez-Runde, C. J., 115
Sandberg, A., 15
Sanders, E. A., 243
Sanders, M. G., 291
Sanetti, L. H., 190
Sarason, S. B., 314
Sargeant, J., 136, 139
Sass, D. A., 201
Satir, V., 266
Saunders, C., 86
Sav, A., 119
Savina, E., 12
Savolainen, T., 107
Sawchuk, S., 133
Sayers, L. K., 142
Sayeski, K., 173
Scala, G., 214
Scarborough, A., 270
Schein, E. H., 82
Schmidt, J. J., 313
Schneider, M. F., 104
Schoenfeld, N., 160, 173, 198, 200
Schooling, T. L., 159
Schreiner, M., 62
Schroth-Cavataio, G., 176
Schrum, L., 242
Schuetzler, R., 54
Schulte, A. C., 187, 188, 314
Schutte, K., 133
Schwanenberger, M., 133
Scott, G., 220
Scott, J. S., 302
Scruggs, T. E., 171
Sebastian, R. J., 68
Sechler, C. M., 27
Seeley, K., 59
Seglem, R., 162
Seifer, R., 276

Seo, M., 41
Sexton, H., 84
Shamberger, C., 6, 163, 173
Shapiro, D. L., 223
Shapiro, D. R., 142
Shapiro, J. P., 313
Sharkey, J., 286
Sharman, S. J., 82
Shattuck, P., 187
Sheaffer, Z., 127
Shealey, M. W., 197
Sheehan, H., 243, 257
Shelly, A. C., 115
Shelly, R. K., 115
Shelton, G., 296
Sherblom, J. C., 30, 136
Sheridan, S., 15
Sheridan, S. M., 133, 194
Shimizu, H., 223
Shimoni T., 127
Shippen, M. E., 292
Shipps, D., 215
Shogren, K. A., 96, 266, 274
Showers, B., 197
Shyman, E., 241
Sickman, L. S., 12, 13, 148, 187
Sileo, J. M., 165
Siler, C. E., 12
Silverman, K., 134
Silverman, S., 160
Silverman, S. K., 315
Simon, J., 12
Simonoff, E., 271
Simons, H. W., 229
Simpson, R., 246
Simpson, V., 12
Sims, K., 190
Sio, U., 105
Sisco, L., 244
Sisco, L. G., 241, 243, 245, 248
Sitharthan, G., 295
Skiba, R. J., 314
Slocum, T. A., 244, 245
Slonski-Fowler, K. E., 149
Smith, E. M., 138
Smith, L. E., 296, 297
Smith, S. C., 302
Smitherman, T., 292
Smith-Schrandt, H. L., 212
Snell, M. E., 134, 273
Snyder, K. K., 200

Sobsey, D., 133
Society for Research on Educational Effectiveness, 313
Solis, M., 171
Solis, S. L., 306
Solomon, J., 13
Soodak, L., 96, 266
Soodak, L. C., 274
Sorensen, R., 251
Soto, G., 136
Spangle, M., 215
Sparks, D., 3
Spiker, D., 270
Spitzberg, B. H., 43
Springer, M. G., 313
Spunt, R. P., 54, 57
Stacey, K., 243
Stafford, G., 153
Stains, R. J., 67
Stainton, T., 278
Stanleigh, M., 224
Staskowski, M., 159
Statzer, J., 217
Stearns, E., 3
Steege, M. W., 13
Steers, R. M., 115
Stefkovich, J. A., 313
Steihaug, S., 12
Stein, R., 286
Steinfatt, T. M., 31
Stephan, P., 55
Stephens, D., 199
Stephens, T. L., 251
Stephenson, J., 270
Sternberg, K., 84
Stevens, D., 132
Stewart, C., 82
Stichler, J. F., 12
Stillman, J. A., 159
Stoelinga, S. R., 14
Stone, S., 146
Strong, M., 201, 203
Stukenbrock, A., 54
Stumme, J., 148, 149
Sugai, G., 148, 149
Sugden, R., 10
Sullivan, A. L., 107
Sullivan, E. E., 3
Summers, J. A., 271
Summey, E., 312
Sun, M., 3
Sunshine, N., 84

Susko, J. P., 177
Suter, J. C., 161, 243, 244, 245, 248, 250, 259
Sverdlik, N., 226
Swain, K. D., 135
Swanson, E., 171
Sweller, N., 96
Swick, K. J., 277
Switzler, A., 82
Szijjarto, L., 218
Taie, S., 201
Talley, R. C., 292, 300
Tankersley, M., 244, 248
Tannock, M. T., 173
Tatum, C. B., 216
Taylor, E., 284
Taylor, J. L., 296
Taylor, M. J., 18, 132
Techakesari, P., 133
Tector, A., 273
Teemant, A., 201
ten Brinke, D., 134
Tessier, A., 270
Test, D. W., 296
Teti, M., 272
Tharp, R., 15
Theoharis, G., 158, 176, 247, 302
Therrien, W. J., 245
Thew, M. D., 3
Thomas, B. K., 133
Thomas, C. C., 134, 139, 281
Thornberg, R., 187
Thousand, J. S., 139, 248
Tiba, A., 269
Tidikis, V., 104
Tierney, J., 294
Tincani, M., 273
Tjosvold, D., 212
Todd, S., 284
Toelken, S., 250
Tormala, Z. L., 229
Torres-Rodriguez, L., 134
Tractman, G. M., 187
Trainor, A. A., 273
Traub, E. K., 296
Trautwein, B., 201
Travers, J., 273
Travis, S. S., 292, 300
Trenholm, S., 43, 67
Trent, S. C., 107
Trepanier-Street, M., 134
Tribe, R., 281

Trochin, W. M. K., 212
Troth, A. C., 220
Trouche, E.; Sander, E., 127
Trumbull, E., 41, 275
Trump, J. L., 160, 162
Truscott, S. D., 149
Tuckey, M. R., 212
Tuckman, B. W., 136, 137
Tudor, M. E., 271
Tuleja, E. A., 40
Turnbull, A., 99, 266, 269, 271, 272, 273, 274
Turnbull, A. P., 96, 266, 271
Turnbull, H. R., 96, 266, 274
Turnbull, R., 99, 266, 269, 271, 272, 273
Turri, M. G., 133
Tversky, B., 70
Twiford, T., 159
Tyra, S., 201
Umbreit, C. J., 190
Upreti, G., 133
Urbano, R. C., 296
Ury, W., 220
Ury, W. L., 220
U.S. Department of Education, 3, 162, 243, 244
U.S. Department of Labor, 243
Uzuner, Y., 173
Vadasy, P. F., 243
Vadineanu, A., 269
Vaganek, M., 191
Valdes, K., 306
van der Maaten, L., 70
van Dick, R., 225
van Dijk, R., 225
van Hoorn, A., 41
Van Hover, S., 173
Van Lare, M., 197
van Staa, A., 273
van Vliet, I., 273
Vanc, A., 153
Vanderburg, M., 199
Vangelisti, A. L., 34, 94
VanGundy, A. B., 117
Vannest, K. J., 177, 205
VanZant, M., 162
Vassil, T. V., 132
Vaughn, S., 148, 171
Venkatesh, K., 314
Ventura, M., 36
Vesely, C. K., 282
Vickers, H. S., 294

Villa, R. A., 139, 248
Visconti, K. J., 27
Von Glinow, M. A., 223
Voytecki, K., 13
Vujnovic, R. K., 148
Vuorinen, T., 15
Wade-Mdivanian, R., 4
Wagner, M., 187, 306
Wahlstrom, K., 300
Waldron, N., 190, 191
Walker, H. M., 306
Walker, J. S., 133
Wall, D., 18, 132
Wallace, K., 160
Walsh, J. M., 16, 160, 164
Walter, U. M., 140
Wan, P. M. K., 212
Wandry, D., 162, 190
Warner, N., 114
Warwick, D., 160
Wasburn-Moses, L., 241
Waterman, S., 202, 203
Watkins, R., 41
Watson, C., 294
Watson, G. D., 13
Watzlawick, P., 33
Weathers, J. M., 302
Weaver, R., 52
Weaver, S. J., 136
Webster, A. A., 271
Webster, R., 244
Wehman, P., 297
Wehmeyer, M. L., 306
Wehrman, J. D., 312
Wei, X., 187
Weir, K., 273
Weiss, J. A., 267–268
Weiss, S. L., 3, 104
Wesselink, R., 134
West, E. A., 265
West-Olatunji, C., 295–296
Wetzel, R., 15
Wheelan, S. A., 112
Wheeler, A., 119
Whitburn, B., 250
Whitby, P. S., 273
White, C., 153
White, M., 215
White, S. E., 265
Whitty, J., 119
Wilkinson, C. Y., 147

Williams, B. F., 139, 278, 302
Williams, J. W., 11
Williams, P., 15
Williams, R. L., 312
Williams, S. S., 11
Williamson, P., 5, 200, 251
Wilmot, W., 211, 212, 213, 216
Wilson, D., 54
Wiltshire, T. J., 105
Wink, J., 201
Witt, P., 294
Wolf, R., 84, 91
Wong, A. S. H., 212
Wood, B. K., 190
Wood, J. T., 30, 36, 57
Woodbury, C., 251
Woodman, R. W., 151
Woods, K. E., 194
Woods-Groves, S., 245
Wooldridge, J. M., 313
Yang, C., 295
Yasutake, D., 164
Yell, M. L., 149, 265

Yildirim, K., 292
Yiu, H. L., 191
Ylimaki, R. M., 18
Yoon, I. H., 197
Yoshida, R. K., 151
Young, H. L., 146
Young, N., 250
Youngs, P., 3, 300, 305
Yu, H., 41
Yu, J. W., 187
Zalaquett, C. P., 61, 81, 86, 270
Zambone, A., 13
Zawilinski, L., 14
Zelkowski, J., 310
Zhang, D., 306
Zhang, K., 278
Zigmond, N., 198, 200
Zins, J. E., 226
Zirkel, P. A., 214, 215
Zoder-Martell, K., 192
Zrike, S., 315
Zuckerman, B., 276
Zuspan, T., 203

SUBJECT INDEX

Accommodative style of conflict response, 216, 218
Accountability
  collaboration and, 313
  consultation and, 189–190
  individual, 153
  for outcomes, 9
  paraeducators and, 248
  teams and, 153
Acting-out behavior, 108
Adapted communication, 44
Administration/administrators
  collaboration and, 14, 300–302
  co-teaching and, 176–177
  support, developing, 303
Adolescence, 269, 272–273, 274
Adult learning preferences, 231
Adulthood, 269, 273, 274
Advice, 97–98
Advisory feedback, 72–73
Advisory statements, 93–94, 95
Advocacy Institute, 217
Advocates, 214
Affection, 278
Affiliation, 269, 271–272
African Americans, 56
After-school programs, 294
Age, parity and, 7
Agenda, 181, 256
All Things PLC, 17
Alternative teaching, 166, 169–170
Ambiguity, high tolerance for, 40, 41, 75
American School Counselor Association, 312
American Speech-Language-Hearing Association, 312
Americans with Disabilities Act, 300
Anglo-European Americans, 56
Apprentice teaching, 14, 159
Appropriate communication, 43
Asian Americans, 56
Assessment
  process of, 15
  RTI model vs. pre-referral approaches, 148, 149, 150
  in team models, 141
Assisted classrooms, 161
Attending, 60
Attending and selecting, 37
Autism, 272

Avoidance style of conflict resolution, 216, 217–218
Avoidance style of conflict response, 217–218

Basecamp, 145
Beach Center on Disability, 17, 284
Behavior intervention plan, 254
Behavioral approach to persuasion, 229
Behavioral consultation, 192–194, 196
Behaviors, and feedback, 73
Bias
  in group problem solving, 108
  managing perceptions, 38
Birth and early childhood, 269–270
Blended families, 4
Blended teacher preparation, 13
Block scheduling, 310
Body, of an interview, 81
Body language, 54–56
Body movement, 55
Brainstorming, 112, 117–118, 120, 123
Brainwriting, 118–119, 123

Care, ethic of, 314
Career development, 272–273
Cariño, 247
Caseload, 178
Categorization process, 36
CEC (Council for Exceptional Children), 19, 143, 291, 312, 313
Center for Parent Information and Resources (CPIR), 284–285
Center for School Improvement, 9
Center-based programs, 295–296
Chaining, 118, 123
Change. *See also* Resistance
  concerns about, 225
  concerns about others involved in, 226
  homeostasis, 226–227
  personal impact of, 226
  rules for in family systems theory, 267
Change fatigue, 227
Channel
  definition of, 28
  in linear communication, 27
  multiple, 31–32
  selection of, 32, 47
  in transactional communication, 30

Checking, 69
Checking for accuracy, 69, 73–74
Checklists
 for effective teamwork, 135
 for problem identification, 116
Child-care needs, 279
Childhood, 269, 271–272
Clarification, managing perceptions and, 38
Class coverage, planning time and, 179–181
Class sizes, 178
Classroom routines, co-teaching and, 175
Classroom space, shared, 162–163
Clerical responsibilities, 243, 246
Clinical consultation, 194–195, 196
Clipboard agenda, 256
Close, of an interview, 81
Closed questions, 68–69, 85–86, 92
Cloud, teams and, 145
Coaching
 being a consumer of, 199
 benefits of, 198
 collaboration and, 201
 indirect services, issues related to, 204–205
 introduction to, 197–198
 models of, 198–201
 rationale for, 198
 virtual, 200
Coercive power, 18
Cognitive dissonance, 229
Collaboration
 accountability and, 313
 across professions, 12
 challenges of, 16–21
 characteristics of, 6–9
 coaching and, 201
 community and interagency, 291–300
 components of, 21
 concepts, 4–11
 consultation and, 195–197
 coordinating services for, 311–312
 co-teaching and, 172–176
 definition of, 5–6
 diversity and, 276
 emergent characteristics of, 10–11
 ethics in, 312–314
 families and, 265
 final thoughts, 314–316
 framework for learning about, 21–22
 interagency context, 294–295
 introduction to, 3–4
 misunderstandings about, 5

online resources for, 17
 other teachers, working with, 304–306
 paraeducators and, 259
 roles and responsibilities, influence of, 300–307
 school collaboration, 12–16
 in a societal context, 11–16
 specialists and, 302–304, 308–309
 student-professional collaboration, 306–307
 systemic barriers to, 307–312
 teams and, 153
 time allocation for professional collaboration, 204–205
 tools for, 145
 Twitter, 315
Collaborative ethos, 53
Collectivist orientation, 40, 41–43, 75, 99
Collegiality, stress and, 20
Combination services, 295–296
Commands, 84–85, 98
Communication. *See also* Interpersonal communication
 in community-based settings, 298
 competence, 43–45
 conflict and, 215–216
 environment and noise in, 33, 47
 families, providing information to, 282–284
 feedback, 29–30, 72–75
 interactional view of, 28, 29–30
 lines of in team models, 141
 listening, 57–63
 nonverbal, 53–57
 with paraeducators, 255–256
 principles for effective verbal and nonverbal communication, 69–72
 responding, 63–69
 teaching, 62
 in teams, 138, 139, 141
 terms, 28
 through multiple channels, 31–32
 uncooperative communication, 97
 understanding, 26–30
 views of, 27–30
Communication competence, 35
Communication events, planning for and evaluating, 47
Communication skills
 as a component of collaboration, 21–22
 difficult interactions, 232
 practicing, 62
 teams and, 139

358 SUBJECT INDEX

Communicator, 28
Community, sense of, 10–11
Community and interagency collaboration
    community liaisons, 293–294
    community outreach, 291–292
    early intervention and preschool programs, 295–296
    interagency context, 294–295
    school-community partnerships, 292–293
    vocational and community-based services, 296–299
Community liaisons, 293–294
Community outreach, 291–292
Community-based services, 296–299
Competence, cultural, 275–277
Competent communication, 43–45
Competitive style of conflict response, 216, 217
Compromising style of conflict response, 216, 218
Concentration, listening and, 64
Concise feedback, 73
Conclusions, 38
Concrete and specific language, 115
Concreteness, 71–72
Confidentiality, 32, 58, 205, 312
Confirmation bias, 38
Conflict. *See also* Difficult interactions
    causes of, 213–215
    communication and, 215–216
    constructive conflict and psychological safety, 219
    cultural differences and, 223
    definition of, 211
    diversity and, 223
    individualized education programs (IEPs) and, 214
    introduction to, 211–213
    organizational variables, influence of, 215–216
    paraeducators and, 257–258
    power and, 214–215
    response styles, 216–219
    response styles survey, 234–237
    in special education, 214
Conflict resolution
    interaction process, 53
    through mediation, 15, 221–223, 265
    through negotiation, 219–221
Conflict Resolution Network (CRN), 217
Congruence, 70
Conjoint behavioral consultation, 194
Connecticut Paraeducator Information and Resources, 253
Consensus through collaboration style of conflict response, 216, 218–219
Consistency approach to persuasion, 229
Constructive conflict, 219

Consultation
    accountability and, 189–190
    being a consumer of, 199
    benefits of, 190–192
    characteristics of, 187–190
    collaboration and, 195–197
    definition of, 187
    direct behavioral consultation, demonstrating effectiveness of, 193
    fidelity of implementation, 190
    indirect services, issues related to, 204–205
    individualized education programs (IEPs) and, 190–191
    interviews and, 190
    introduction to, 186–187
    models of, 192–195
    problem solving and, 188–189
    rationale for, 190–192
    response to intervention through, 189, 191
    transitions and, 190–191
Consulting teaching, 14–15
Content dimension of interpersonal communication, 34–35
Content of spoken messages, 63, 64
Context
    as a component of collaboration, 21–22
    of problem solving, 113, 116–117
    of spoken messages, 63
Continuum, 92
Control, and collaboration, 305–306
Controversy, email and, 58
Convergent elements of problem identification, 114–115
Coordination of information and services, 142
Core instruction, 148
Corrective feedback, 75
Co-taught classrooms, 161
Co-teaching
    administrative matters, 176–177
    administrator knowledge and support, 302
    alternative teaching, 166, 169–170
    approaches, overview of, 166
    approaches to, 165–176
    beginning, 164
    characteristics of, 160–163
    collaboration and, 172–176
    concepts, 158–163
    coordinating services for collaboration, 311
    creating shared planning time, 179–182
    cultural differences and, 173
    definition of, 159–160
    dilemmas in, 171

discipline and, 175
diversity and, 162, 173
electronic planning, 179
expertise and, 160, 161
feedback and, 176
intellectual disabilities and, 160
introduction to, 158
maintaining collaborative relationships, 174–176
novice educators and, 170, 171
observation and, 165–167
one teaching, one assisting, 170–172
one teaching, one observing, 165–167
paraeducators and, 161, 248
parallel teaching, 166, 168–169
philosophy/beliefs and, 174–175
planning time, 177–182
practical issues in, 178
promise vs. evidence, 160
rationale for, 163–165
readiness for, 174
relationship, understanding, 173–174
response to intervention (RTI) and, 158, 169
scheduling issues, 177, 178, 307–308
station teaching, 166, 167–168
vs. student teaching, 159
teaming, 166, 170
Co-teaching teams, 144–145
Council for Exceptional Children (CEC), 19, 143, 291, 312, 313
Covert information, describing, 94–95
CPIR (Center for Parent Information and Resources), 284–285
Crawford, Bill, 217
Crispus Attucks High School, 199
Critique, ethic of, 314
CRN (Conflict Resolution Network), 217
Cultural competence, 275–277
Cultural context
  adolescence and, 272
  attending to in interviews, 99
  awareness of other cultural perspectives, 40–41
Cultural continua, 276
Cultural self-awareness, 40, 266
Cultural variations, 275
Culturally responsive services, 277
Culturally sensitive feedback, 75
Culture/cultural differences
  addressing, 293
  body language and, 55–56
  characteristics of, 275
  conflict and, 223
  co-teaching and, 173
  interactions with families, 274–277
  perspective and, 39–41
  professional collaboration and, 205
  stress and, 20
Culture-generic awareness, 275
Curricular access and instruction, 164

Daily schedule, 256
Data-based decision making, 192
Daydreaming, 61
Decentralization, 269
Decision making
  family participation in, 279–286
  interaction process, 53
  shared responsibility for, 8
Decoding, 28
Deferring, as an indicator of resistance, 228
Departmental teams, 146
Descriptive feedback, 72–73
Descriptive statements, 93–95, 96
Detachment, 269
Developmental stages of teams, 136–139
Difficult interactions. *See also* Conflict
  communication skills, 232
  conflict, understanding, 211–223
  in diverse groups, 223
  introduction to, 210–211
  resistance, 224–231
  skills for, 217
  summary of, 231
Direct behavioral consultation, 193
Direct commands, 98
Direct feedback, 74
Direct instruction in communication skills, 62
Direct questions, 68–69, 83–85, 86
Direct service providers, 140
Directional relationship, 188
Directionality, 201
Directness, in intercultural communication, 42
Disabilities, children with
  adolescence, 272–273
  birth and early childhood, 269–270
  childhood, 271–272
  families and, 277–278
  functions of family and, 278
  inclusion, 271
  joint delivery of instruction, 161–162
  nature and severity of, 280
  paraeducators and, 243–244, 245–246, 248–250

Disciplinary relationships, on teams, 140–144
Discipline, co-teaching and, 175
Discipline and behavior support plans, 15
Disconfirmation bias, 38
Discrepancies, 230
Dispute resolution, mediation and, 15, 221–223, 265. *See also* Conflict
Distracted communicator, 97
Distractions, and listening, 61, 62
Distribution of students, 178
Divergent elements of problem identification, 114–115
Diverse families, 4
Diversity
    conflict and, 223
    co-teaching and, 162, 173
    expansion of, 266
    families, interactions with, 274–277
    paraeducators and student support, 247
    parity and, 7
    problem solving and, 107–108
Downcast eyes, 55, 57
Dropbox, 256
Due process, 214, 222

Early childhood, 269–270
Early childhood programs, 15, 243, 274
Early intervention programs, 15, 143, 270, 274, 295–296
Edmodo, 179, 306
Education for All Handicapped Children Act, 133
Effective communication, 43
Effectiveness, of teams, 151–153
Elaborated responses, 85–86
Electronic communication, 89
Electronic mentoring, 203
Electronic planning, 179
Electronic teacher plan books, 179
Elementary schools, scheduling in, 310
E-mail
    asking questions via, 89
    communications with paraeducators, 256
    effective use of, 58
    nonverbal communication and, 57–58
Emotional component of conflict, 220
Emotional disabilities, 171
Empathic listening, 67
Encoding, 28
English as a Second Language (ESL) programs, 241, 307–308
English learners, 107, 159, 160
Enrichment, 169
Entry step in consultation, 189
Environment, 27, 28, 33, 47
ELL teachers, 305, 306, 307–308

Ethics
    in collaborative practice, 312–314
    in interpersonal communication, 43
    negotiation and, 221
    paraeducators and, 247–250, 257
    responding to ethical issue, 313–314
Evaluation
    in behavioral consultation, 189, 193
    of solutions, 121–122
Evaluative feedback, 72–73
Evaluative statements, 93–94, 95
Evernote, 256
Exemplar, 91–92
Exit step in consultation, 189
Expectations, 221, 293
Expert relationship, 188
Expertise
    apprentice teaching, 159
    from the community, 292
    co-teaching and, 160, 161
    in teams, 138
Explanations, 96–97
External distractions, 62
Eye contact, 55–56, 63, 64, 71
"Face," threats to, 223

Facebook, 89
Facial expressions, 55
Families
    barriers to family participation in education, 279
    children with disabilities in, 277–278
    collaboration and, 265
    cultural influences, 274–277
    decision making, participation in, 279–286
    definition of, 266
    individualized education programs (IEPs) and, 265, 285–286
    interactions with, factors in, 274–279
    introduction to, 264–265
    involvement with special education processes, 280
    life conditions, factors related to, 278–279
    life cycles, 268–274
    listening and, 266
    online resources, 284–285
    providing information to, 279–284
    role of in team models, 141
    sharing resources with, 8–9
    student-centered meetings, participation in, 285–286
    understanding, 265–268
Family boundaries, 269
Family constellation continuum, 276
Family interaction, 267–268

Family life cycles
    adolescence, 269, 272–273, 274
    adulthood, 269, 273, 274
    birth and early childhood, 269–270
    childhood, 269, 271–272
    transitions, 268–269, 274
Family systems theory, 266–268
Family-based early intervention services, 265
Family-centered programs, 277
Fathers Network (FN), 284
Faulty assumptions, 60
Feasibility, 122, 313
Feedback
    advisory, 72–73
    communication skills during difficult interactions, 232
    co-teaching and, 176
    definition of, 28
    guidelines for giving, 74–75
    immediacy of, 75
    imposed, 74
    indirect, 74
    in interactional communication, 29–30
    interpersonal, 72–74
    in linear communication, 29
    paraeducators and, 257
    in persuasion, 231
    verbal, 72–75
Feedback continuum, 71
Fidelity instructional techniques, 197–198
Fidelity of implementation, 190
Filtering messages, 61
Flexibility, 173
Flow of speech, 56, 57
FN (Fathers Network), 284
Focused inquiry
    introduction to, 87–88, 90
    prefatory statements, 91–92, 99
    presupposition, 90–91, 99, 232
Formal collaboration, 3
Forming stage of team development, 137
Foster families, 4
Frame of reference, 266
Functional approach to persuasion, 229
Functions, in family life stages, 269
Functions, of families, 278
Funnel approaches to sequencing questions, 92

Gender, parity and, 7
General education teachers, 39, 308–310
General feedback, 73
Generalities, 89
Gestures, 55

Gifted students, 164
Goal setting, 221
Goals
    of communication, 47
    conflict and, 213–214
    realistic and flexible, 20
    of teams, 152
Google apps, 110
Google Docs, 145, 256
Google Forms, 145
Google Sheets, 145
Google Tools, 145
Grade-level teams, 146
Graham, Martha, 55
Grief cycle model, 270, 271
Group problem solving. *See also* Problem solving
    bias in, 108
    decision to problem solve, 108–110
    diversity and, 107–108
    evaluating potential solutions, 121–122
    evaluating the outcome, 125–126
    generating potential solutions, 113, 117–121
    identifying the problem, 112–117, 126, 189, 192
    implementing the solution, 113, 122–124
    introduction to, 104–105
    model for, 113
    outlining tasks for potential solutions, 122
    practice, 123
    as a professional responsibility, 105–112
    putting the pieces together, 126–127
    reactive and proactive problem solving, 107
    response to intervention, 111–112
    responsibility chart, 124
    selecting the solution, 122
    situations calling for different approaches, 109
    steps in, 112–126
    virtual, 110
Group processes, and teams, 153
GROU.PS, 110
Growth, 53
Guiding statements, 96–98

Hall, Edward, 56
Harmony/control continuum, 276
Hashtags, 315
Hearing, 60
HEATH Resource Center, 284
High ambiguity tolerance, 40, 41, 75
High schools, scheduling in, 310
High-context cultures, 40, 41, 42, 75
High-context strategies, 99
Home-based programs, 295–296

Homeostasis, 226–227
Honesty, 53

IAT (Intervention assistance teams), 146–148
IDEA. *See* Individuals with Disabilities Education Act (IDEA)
IEP. *See* Individualized education programs (IEPs)
IEP teams, 15, 136, 149–150
IFSP (Individualized family service plan), 265, 295
Ill-defined problems, 106–107
Immediacy of feedback, 75
Implementation
  fidelity of, 190
  problem solving and, 189
  of service plan, 141
  of solutions, 113, 122–124
Implications. *See* Plus/Minus/Implications (PMI)
Imposed feedback, 74
Incentives, 229
Inclusion, 271
Incongruence, 70
Independence, 250, 272–273
Indirect feedback, 74
Indirect questions, 83–85, 86, 232
Indirect relationships, 187–188
Indirect services, 204–205. *See also* Coaching; Consultation; Mentoring
Indirectness, in intercultural communication, 42
Individual accountability, 153
Individual preference, in problem solving, 122
Individualist orientation, 40, 41–43, 75, 99
Individuality, 70–71
Individualization, of consultation models, 194
Individualized education program team. *See* IEP teams
Individualized education programs (IEPs)
  conflict and, 214
  consultation and, 190–191
  families and, 265
  family participation in, 285–286
  student-professional collaboration, 306–307
Individualized family service plan (IFSP), 265, 295
Individualized written rehabilitation program (IWRP), 298
Individuals, conflict within, 215
Individuals, in family systems theory, 267
Individuals with Disabilities Education Act (IDEA)
  early intervention and preschool programs, 270, 295
  expectations of collaboration, 15
  mediation, 222
  multidisciplinary teams, 140
  paraeducators qualifications, 242
  parental representation and participation, 265
  prevocational and vocational services, 296
  response to intervention, 148
  team approach, 133
  transition services, 298–299
  vocational rehabilitation, 300
Inferential statements, 94–95
Informal collaboration, 3
Informal meetings, 283
Information, flow of, 11
Information seeking
  focused inquiry, 87–92
  funnel approaches to sequencing questions, 92
  generalities, 89
  in nonthreatening ways, 88
  question format, 82–87
Information sharing, 96
Informational power, 18
Insincere questions, 69
Instruction
  core, 148
  curricular access and, 164
  joint delivery of, 161–162
  remedial, 254
  strategies that facilitate planning, 181–182
  tiers of, 148, 149, 169
Instructional coaching, 197–201
Instructional consultation, 191
Instructional delivery, paraeducators and, 244–245
Instructional facilitator, 198. *See also* Coaching
Instructional responsibilities, of paraeducators, 244–245
Instructional teams, 144–146
Insufficient time for communication, 61
Intellectual disabilities, co-teaching and, 160
Interaction, collaboration as a style of, 5–6
Interaction processes, 21–22, 53
Interaction skills, 53
Interactional view of communication, 28, 29–30
Interactive teaming, 134
Interagency context, collaboration in, 294–295
Intercultural competence, 53
Interdependence, and teams, 136
Interdependence/independence continuum, 276
Interdisciplinary teams, 141, 142
Internal distractions, 62
Internet, and collaboration, 17, 19
Interpersonal communication. *See also* Communication
  concepts, 31–33
  content dimension, 34–35
  definition of, 30–35
  ethics in, 43
  interpersonal competence, 35–48

introduction to, 26
openness in, 45–46, 62
principles of, 33–35
providing information, 93–98
suggestions for improvement, 45–48
understanding communication, 26–30
Interpersonal competence
competent communication and, 43–45
perception, 35–43
perspective, 35
professional perspective, 38–39
suggestions for improvement, 45–48
Interpersonal feedback, 72–74
Interpersonal skills, 173
Interpersonal style of collaboration, 10
Interpretation
of information, 37
language, 281–282
vs. reflection, 68
Interruptions, 47
Interruptions, and listening, 63
Intervention, 193
Intervention assistance teams (IAT), 146–148
Interviews
consultation and, 190
cultural context, 99
information seeking, 82–92
interaction process, 21–22, 53
introduction to, 80–82
monitor information-seeking interactions, 99
pauses, using effectively, 46–48, 88, 97, 98–99
suggestions for, 98–100
unexpected events/situations and, 100
Intimate distance, 56
Intrapersonal conflict, 215
Introduction, in interviews, 81
Introspection, 83
Intrusiveness, in problem-solving, 122
Inverted funnel approach, 92
Issues, focus on during conflict negotiation, 220
IWRP (Individualized written rehabilitation program), 298

Joint delivery of instruction, 161–162
Justice, ethic of, 313–314

Kids Together, Inc, 284

Labor needs, changes in, 11
Language, 247, 280, 281–282
Language arts, 310
Leadership skills, 153, 203, 215
Least restrictive environment, 15
Legitimate power, 18
Life conditions, 278–279
Life cycles. *See* Family life cycles
Linear view of communication, 27–29
Listening, 57
to the community, 293
distractions, 61, 62
empathic listening, 67
factors that interfere with, 60–61
families and, 266
paraeducators and conflict, 258
perception and, 64
as a process, 59–60
rationale for, 58–59
responding, 60
signaling on the telephone, 34
suggestions for improvement, 61–63, 64
Listening fidelity, 60
Listening goals, 61–62
Literacy coaching, 198–199
Los Angeles Unified School District (LAUSD), 280
Low ambiguity tolerance, 40, 41, 75
Low-context cultures, 40, 41, 42, 75

Mainstreaming, 187
Mean, 167
Meaning, creation of, 32–33
Meaning, in interpersonal communication, 32–33, 46
Median, 167
Mediation and dispute resolution, 15, 221–223, 265
Meeting attendance, 150
Members' needs, on teams, 152
Membership in teams, 134–135
Mentoring
being a consumer of, 199
electronic, 203
impact of, 203
indirect services, issues related to, 204–205
introduction to, 201–202
Message, 28
Message-to-noise ratio, 47
Microskills, 62
Middle school approaches, 13
Middle school teams, 145–146
Middle Web, 17
MindTools, 217
Minimal encouragers, 64
Minus. *See* Plus/Minus/Implications (PMI)

Missions, and interagency collaboration, 295
Mobile metaphor for family systems, 266
Mode, 167
Modeling, 257
Motherhood, as a basis for student interactions, 247
Motivation, 221
Moxtra, 145
Multidisciplinary teams, 140–142
Multigenerational families, 4
Multiple channels, 31–32
Multiple questions, 86–87
Mutual goals, 7–8

National Association of School Psychologists, 312
National Center for Education Evaluation and Regional Assistance, 203
National Education Association (NEA), 253, 292–293, 312
National Resource Center for Paraeducators, 253
NEA: Paraeducator Roles and Responsibilities, 253
Needs and interests, mediation and, 222
Needs assessment, for paraeducators, 252
Negative listeners, 59
Negotiation
   conflict resolution through, 219–221
   effectiveness of, 221
   ethics and, 221
   mediation and, 222
   in transactional communication, 36, 37
NewsBlur, 299
NGT (Nominal group technique), 119–121
Noise
   in communication, 27, 28, 33, 47
   co-teaching and, 176
   distraction and, 61
   in transactional communication, 30
Nominal group technique (NGT), 119–121
Noninstructional responsibilities, of paraeducators, 245–247
Nonthreatening ways of seeking information, 88
Nontraditional families, 279
Nonverbal attending behaviors, 53
Nonverbal communication
   families and, 266
   linear view, 27
   principles for, 69–72
   types of, 54–57
   value of, 53–54
Nonverbal contradictions, 54
Nonverbal cues, 64
Nonverbal reinforcements, 54

Nonverbal substitutions, 54
Norming stage of team development, 137
Norms, 136
Novice educators. *See also* Mentoring
   co-teaching and, 170, 171
   paraeducators and, 257
   roles and responsibilities, 305
Nurturance/independence continuum, 276

Observation, 165–167, 190, 230
Ohio Department of Education, 9
OneNote, 256
One-to-one assistants, 244
Online resources
   collaboration, 17
   for families, 284–285
   paraeducators and, 253
   RSS, 299
Open questions, 84, 85–86, 90, 92, 232
Openness, 53
   importance of, 95
   in interpersonal communication, 45–46, 62
   in successful listening, 64
Organization of information, 36, 37
Organizational variables, conflict and, 215–216
Orientation, 55, 222
OSEP Ideas That Work, 285
Ostracism, 271–272
Outcomes
   accountability for, 9
   evaluation of, 113, 124, 125–126
   importance of, 216
Output, and team effectiveness, 151–152
Overly expressive communicator, 97
Overly talkative communicator, 97
Overt information, describing, 93–94
Overtalk, 47
Ownership, and collaboration, 305–306
Ownership, clarification of, 231
Ownership continuum, 276

Pace of speech, 56, 57
Paraeducator Resource and Learning Center (PRLC), 253
Paraeducators
   accountability and, 248
   becoming teachers, 242
   class coverage, 180
   collaboration and, 15, 259
   communicating with, 255–256

conflict and, 257–258
co-teaching and, 161, 248
disabilities, children with and, 243–244, 245–246, 248–250
ethical considerations, 247–250, 257
feedback and, 257
introduction to, 240–241
as key personnel, 243
needs assessment, 252
novice educators and, 257
online resources, 253
planning with, 254
prevalence of in schools, 243
qualifications, 241–242
response to intervention (RTI) and, 241
roles and responsibilities, 243–247, 251–253, 254–255
special education and, 241, 244, 254
supervising, 256–258
support for students and, 245–246, 247
understanding, 241–243
working with, 251–258
Paralanguage, 56. *See also* Vocal cues
Parallel teaching, 166, 168–169
Paraphrasing, 53, 65–66
Paraprofessional Resource and Research Center (PAR²A Center), 253
Parent Advocacy Coalition for Educational Rights (PACER), 285
Parent communication, paraeducators and, 249–250
Parent training and information centers (PTIs), 265
Parental representation and participation and IDEA, 265
Parents Helping Parents, 285
Parity among participants, 7
Parity signals, 175
Partially defined problems, 106
Participation, refusing to as an indicator of resistance, 228
Participatory management, 212
Partnerships, strategies for, 293
Passive communicator, 97
Past practice, relying on, 228
Pauses, using effectively, 46–48, 88, 97, 98–99
PBS (Positive behavior supports), 197–198, 230
Peer collaboration, 14
Perception
  interpersonal competence, 35–43
  listening and, 64
  management of, 38
Perception checking, 69

Perceptual approach to persuasion, 229
Performing stage of team development, 137–138
Permanent product, 190
Personal commitment, 21–22
Personal distance, 56
Personal identity, 272–273
Personal impact of change, 226
Personal state, 38
Personal views, 38
Perspective
  communication skills during difficult interactions, 232
  culture and, 39–41
  interpersonal competence, 35
  of team members, 136
Perspective-taking skills, 44–45
Persuasion, 53, 229–231
Pet peeves, 176
Philosophy/beliefs
  change and, 231
  co-teaching and, 174–175
  resistance to change and, 225
  of team interactions, 141
Phrasing problems as questions, 112
Physical noise, 33
Physiological noise, 33
Pinterest, 17
Pitch, 56
Planbook, 179
Planning
  for co-teaching, 164
  electronic, 179
  with paraeducators, 254
  problem solving and, 189
  procedures for, 178–179
Planning agenda, 256
Planning stages, involving others in, 231
Planning time
  co-teaching and, 177–182
  making the most of, 181
  options for creating, 179–182
PLCs (Professional learning communities), 14, 225
Plus/Minus/Implications (PMI), 121–122
Points of view, valuing, 138
Positive behavior supports (PBS), 197–198, 230
Positive image, relating proposed changes to, 230
Positive listeners, 59
Positive reinforcement, 229
Posture, 55
Poverty, 108, 279

Power
    in apprentice teaching, 159
    as a challenge to collaboration, 18–19
    coercive, 18
    conflict and, 214–215
Power inequity, 211
Practicing communication skills, 62
Prefatory statements, 91–92, 99
Prejudgments, 62–63
Premature assumptions, 71
Preoccupied communicator, 97
Preparation, for mediation, 222
Pre-referral approaches, 148
Pre-referral intervention assistance model, 147
Pre-referral teaming, 146, 149
Preschool programs, 143, 270, 295–296
Presupposition, 90–91, 99, 232
Pre-teaching, 169
Prevention, consultation and, 191
Prevocational services, 296
Primary language, 280, 281–282
Principals, 300–301. *See also* Administrators, and collaboration
Priorities, establishment of, 20
PRLC (Paraeducator Resource and Learning Center), 253
Proactive problem solving, 107
Problem analysis, 193
Problem identification, 112–117, 126, 189, 192
Problem solving. *See also* Group problem solving
    consultation and, 188–189
    context of, 113, 116–117
    diversity and, 107–108
    interaction process, 21–22, 53
    mediation and, 222
Problems. *See also* Group problem solving
    adequate time for problem identification, 116
    characteristics of well-defined problems, 112–114
    confirming with multiple sources of information, 115–116
    discrepancy between current and desired situations, 112–114
    divergent and convergent elements, 114–115
    identification of, 112–117, 126, 189, 192
    monitoring context, 116–117
    precise description of, 115
    shared perception that the problem exists, 114
Problem-solving approach to RTI, 148
Problem-solving teams, 146–149
Profession, ethic of the, 314
Professional collaboration, 204–205
Professional development, 192, 293. *See also* Coaching
Professional learning communities (PLCs), 14, 225
Professional perspective, 38–39
Professional relationships, 204
Professional socialization, 17–18
Professional standards of practice, 52
Programs or services, as a component of collaboration, 21–22
Progress monitoring, 12–13
Prompting, 53, 64
Providing information
    covert information, 94–95
    descriptive statements, 93–95, 96
    guiding statements, 96–98
    overt information, 93–94
    tips for, 96
Pseudo-communicator, 97
Psychological noise, 33
Psychological safety, 219
PTIs (Parent training and information centers), 265
Public commitment, 231
Public distance, 56
Purposeful meetings, 283–284

Qualifications, for paraeducators, 241–242
Question formats, 82
    direct/indirect, 68–69, 83–85, 86, 232
    electronic, 89
    evidence-based information about, 84
    funnel approaches to sequencing, 92
    open/closed, 85–86
    single/multiple, 86–87
Question sequencing, 92
Questioning, 53, 68–69

Race/ethnicity, 280. *See also* Culture/cultural differences; Diversity
Reactive problem solving, 107
Rebellion, 272
Referent power, 18
Reflecting, 53, 66–68
Reflection, 83
Reform coaching, 199–201
Rehabilitation Act, 298–299, 300
Rehabilitation Services Administration (RSA), 298–299
Rehearsing response, 61
Reinforcers, 192
Relational dimension of interpersonal communication, 34–35
Relationship
    in co-teaching, 173–174
    importance of, 216

indirect, 187–188
    maintaining collaborative relationships in co-teaching, 174–176
    managing during team development, 138
    matching communication to, 48
    open vs. closed questions and, 86
    professional relationships, 204
    resistance to change and, 225
Relaxed instructional style, 247
Remedial instruction, 254
Remembering, in the listening process, 60
Research
    bias in group problem solving, 108
    collaboration and student achievement, 9
    on competent communication, 44
    conflict in special education, 214
    constructive conflict and psychological safety, 219
    on co-teaching, 160
    direct behavioral consultation, demonstrating effectiveness of, 193
    family involvement in and satisfaction with special education processes, 280–281
    on listening, 59
    paraeducators supporting students from diverse backgrounds, 247
    on questions, 84
    on successful teamwork, 143
Residency programs, 13
Resistance
    addressing, 227–229
    causes of, 225–227
    indicators of, 227, 228
    introduction to, 224–225
    persuasion strategy, 229–231
Resistance management, 53
Resource booklet, 292
Resources, sharing, 8–9. *See also* Online resources
Respect, 53
Responding, 63
    families and, 266
    in the listening process, 60
    paraphrasing, 53, 65–66
    prompting, 64
    questioning, 68–69
    reflecting, 53, 66–68
Responding skills, 53
Response rehearsing, 61
Response styles to conflict, 216–219, 234–237
Response to intervention (RIT) teams, 148–149
Response to intervention (RTI)
    consultation and, 189, 191
    co-teaching and, 158, 169
    group problem solving, 111–112
    paraeducators and, 241
    problem-solving approach to, 148
    school collaboration, 12–13
    student-centered problem-solving teams, 146
Responses, limiting the range of, 85
Responsibility, 53
    collaboration influenced by, 300–307
    consultation and, 189–190
    delegation of, 251
    displacing, 228
    of paraeducators, 243–247, 251–253, 254–255
    teams and, 134–135
"Re-storying," 270
Re-teaching, 169
Reward power, 18
Rich site summary, 299
Rights and responsibilities continuum, 276
Roles
    collaboration influenced by, 300–307
    of novice educators, 305
    of paraeducators, 243–247, 251–253, 254–255
    respect for, 138
    stress and, 20
    teams and, 134–135
Role-specific pressures, 304–305
RSA (Rehabilitation Services Administration), 298–299
RTI. *See* Response to intervention (RTI)
RTI problem solving, 148
Rules, in family systems theory, 267

Same-sex families, 4
Schedule flexibility, 308
Schedules, and co-teaching, 177, 178, 307–308
Scheduling for collaboration, 307–310
School collaboration
    examples of, 13–14
    response to intervention, 12–13
    special education collaboration, 14–16
School culture, as a challenge to collaboration, 16–17
School environments, and conflict, 212
School principals, competent communication and, 44
School reform initiatives, 198
School reform teams, 14
School scheduling issues, 310
School–community collaboration, 14
School-community partnerships, 292–293
Schoology, 179
School–university partnerships, 13
Screening, RTI model vs. pre-referral approaches, 148
Seeking information. *See* Information seeking

Selective perception, 266
Selective process, 36, 37
Self, sense of, 272
Self-awareness, 40, 108, 266, 277
Self-determination, 306
Self-disclosure, 94
Self-esteem, 278
Self-identity, 278
Self-monitoring, 44–45
Self-report, 190
Service delivery, 134
Service plan development and implementation, 141
SES (Socioeconomic status), 280
Sexuality education, 273
Shared calendars, 179
Shared norms, 136
Shared responsibility and decision making, 8
Sibling Support Project, 285
Silence, 46–48, 64
"Silence response," 47
Single parents, 278
Single questions, 86–87
Single-parent families, 4
Situations, and feedback, 73
Skills repertoire for interpersonal communication, 44
Smile, 59
Social development, and paraeducators, 250
Social distance, 56
Social learning platforms, 179, 306
Social media, 315
Social networking, 267–268, 273
Social Security Benefits for Children with Disabilities, 285
Socialization of isolation, 17–18
Societal context, collaboration in, 11–16
Socioeconomic status (SES), 280
Solicited feedback, 74
Solutions
  carrying out, 124
  evaluation of, 121–122
  generating potential solutions, 113, 117–121
  implementation of, 113, 122–124
  outlining tasks for, 122
  selection of, 122
Spatial relations, 55, 56–57
Special considerations
  collaboration influenced by roles and responsibilities, 300–307
  community and interagency collaboration, 291–300
  ethics in collaborative practice, 312–314
  introduction to, 290
  systemic barriers to collaboration, 307–312
Special education
  behavioral consultation, 194
  conflict in, 214
  family involvement in and satisfaction with, 280
  paraeducators and, 241, 244, 254
  scheduling issues, 307–308
Special education collaboration, 14–16
Special education teams, 144, 149–151
Special educators, 196, 305, 306, 307–308
Special service providers, 39
Specialists, and collaboration, 302–304, 308–309
Specific feedback, 73
Standard protocol and RTI, 148
Station teaching, 166, 167–168
Stereotypes, 36
Storming stage of team development, 137
Stress management, 20
Structure, rules for, 267
Structured meetings, 283–284
Student achievement, 9
Student identification, RTI model vs. pre-referral approaches, 148
Student supervision, 246
Student teaching, 159
Student-centered meetings, family participation in, 285–286
Student-centered teams
  disciplinary relationships, 140
  instructional teams, 144–146
  problem-solving teams, 144, 146–149
  special education teams, 149–151
Student-professional collaboration, 306–307
Substitutes, planning time and, 179–180
Supervision, of paraeducators, 256–258
Support, stress and, 20
Support for students, 245–246, 247, 250
Support staff, 140
Support without substance, 228
Supported classrooms, 161
System coordination, 294

Talking less, and listening, 62
Targeted outreach, 293
Task, matching communication to, 48
Tasks, in family life stages, 269
TATs (Teacher assistance teams), 146–147
Teach Thought, 17
Teacher assistance teams (TATs), 146–147
Teacher candidates, co-teaching and, 159
Teacher induction, 202
Teacher Lingo, 19
Teacher outreach, 293
Teacher plan books, electronic, 179
Teacher requirements, 15
Teacher-student ratio, 168

Team teaching, 160
Teaming, 166, 170
Teams
  accountability and, 153
  awareness of membership, roles, and responsibilities, 134–135
  benefits of, 139
  characteristics of, 134–136, 138
  cloud and, 145
  collaboration and, 153
  communication in, 138, 139, 141
  communication skills and, 139
  concepts, 133–140
  definition of, 133–134
  developmental stages, 136–139
  disciplinary relationships, 140–144
  drawbacks of, 139–140
  effectiveness of, 151–153
  expertise in, 138
  facilitators and barriers, 143
  IEP teams, 15, 136, 149–150
  importance of, 133
  instructional teams, 144–146
  introduction to, 132–133
  lifecycle of, 137
  membership in, 134–135
  models of team interaction, 141
  problem-solving teams, 146–149
  rationale for, 139
  responsibility and, 134–135
  special education teams, 144, 149–151
  student-centered, 144–151
Technical coaching, 198–199
Technical problem solving, 111
Technology, virtual group problem solving and, 110
Technology-mediated communication, 57
Telephone communications, 34
Tiers of instruction, 148, 149, 169
Time
  allocation of for professional collaboration, 204–205
  drawbacks of teams, 139
  insufficient for communication, 61
Time continuum, 276
Time problems, 123
Topic of conversation, and personal space, 57
Traditional interventions/supports, 270
Traditional student problem-solving teams, 146–148
Tradition/technology continuum, 276
Training, listening and, 61
Transactional view of communication, 28, 30, 31
Transdisciplinary teams, 141, 142–144
Transient membership, 135
Transitions, 15
  consultation and, 190–191
  from early intervention to preschool programs, 270
  in family life cycles, 268–269, 274
  in Individuals with Disabilities Education Act (IDEA), 298–299
  post-school, 273
Translation services, 246
Treatment integrity, 190
Trello, 145
Trends, societal, 11, 212
Triadic relationships, 187–188
Trust, 10, 62
Tumblr, 19
Turn-taking, in intercultural communication, 42
21st Century Community Learning Centers Program, 294
Twitter, 89, 315

Uncooperative communications, 97
Understanding, in the listening process, 60
Unilateral communication, 27, 29
Unique skills, and teams, 136

Values, 231, 275, 293. *See also* Philosophy/beliefs
VBIE (Virtual bug-in-ear), 200
Venn diagram, 33
Verbal feedback, 72–75
Verbal messages, 27
Verbal praise, 193
Verbal spacing, 47–48
Video Series About Difficult Interactions, 217
Virtual bug-in-ear (VBIE), 200
Virtual coaching, 200
Virtual group problem solving, 110
Vocal cues, 54–55, 56
Vocational development, 272–273
Vocational rehabilitation counselors, 300
Vocational services, 296–299
Voluntariness, 6–7, 188, 196

Wait time, 247
"Wait to fail" model, 12
"We" language, 164
Well-defined problems, 106
Well-identified problems, 112–114
Well-times feedback, 75
Wikis, 179
Work conditions, 20

Yammer, 110

Zoho, 145